THE ARCHAEOLOGY OF ANCIENT ISRAEL

Yale University Press

The Open University

New Haven and London

of Israel

THE ARCHAEOLOGY

OF

ANCIENT ISRAEL

Edited by Amnon Ben-Tor

Translated by R. Greenberg

The publication of this book has been made possible through the support of the Dorot
Foundation, the Jesselson Foundation, and the Laura Julia Foundation.
The Hebrew edition was published by The Open University of Israel.

Designed by James J. Johnson. Set in Stempel Garamond type by The Composing Room of
Michigan, Inc. Grand Rapids, Michigan. Printed in the United States of America.

Library of Congress Cataloging-in-Publication Data
Mavo la-arkhe ʻologyah shel Erets-Yiśra ʻel bi-teḵufat ha-Miḵra.
  English.
    The archaeology of ancient Israel / edited by Amnon Ben-Tor ;
  translated by R. Greenberg.
        p.   cm.
    Revised translation of: Mavo la-arkhe ʻologyah shel Erets-Yiśra ʻel
  bi-teḵufat ha-Miḵra.
    Includes bibliographical references and index.
    ISBN 0-300-05919-1 (pbk.)
    1. Palestine–Antiquities.   2. Excavations (Archaeology)–Palestine.   3. Bible. O.T.–
  Antiquities.   I. Ben-Tor, Amnon.   II. Title.
  DS111.A2M3513   1991
  933–dc20   91–9016

The paper in this book meets the guidelines for permanence and durability of the
Committee on Production Guidelines for Book Longevity of the Council on Library
Resources.

10 9 8 7 6 5 4

Contents

Illustrations

MAPS

Tables

Preface

This book is based on the introductory course entitled "The Archaeology of the Land of Israel in Biblical Times," offered by the Open University, Israel. While the textbook to this course was being prepared, it became evident that it would provide an up-to-date overview of the archaeology of the biblical periods. Previous attempts to provide such a synthesis include *The Archaeology of Palestine* (1949, 1954, 1956), by W. F. Albright, which reflects the state of research in the forties and fifties; *Archaeology in the Holy Land* (1965), by Kathleen Kenyon, updated to the early sixties; and Y. Aharoni's *The Archaeology of the Land of Israel* (1982), which includes advances made up to the late seventies. It seems, however, that the days have passed when a single scholar could presume to compass the wealth of material that has accumulated. To provide as complete a picture as possible, a team effort is required, and this book—which attempts to provide a synthesis of archaeological knowledge updated to the eighties—represents just such an effort.

This book also marks the one-hundredth anniversary of the first stratigraphic excavation in the Land of Israel, an excavation in 1890 that saw the beginning of scientific archaeological investigation in this country. During a century of exploration, hundreds of sites have been excavated and surveyed, yielding a multitude of finds relating to the history of the land from the very beginnings of human habitation to the modern period.

Public interest in the archaeology of the Land of Israel, the Land of the Bible, is enormous. It is hardly surprising that the first two excavations there, in the 1860s, took place in Jerusalem and Jericho, the very names of which conjure up the biblical figures of David, Solomon, Joshua, and their like. But what is the "Land of the Bible," and how are we to define the biblical period? Surely Syria, Lebanon, and Jordan, and to some extent Egypt and Iraq as well, are closely linked with biblical history and should be brought within our purview. And indeed, insofar as the developments in these countries have a direct bearing on events in the Land of Israel (and this varies from one period to another), they are included within the scope of this volume. However, the archaeological investigation of Syria, Lebanon, and Jordan—not to mention that of Egypt and Iraq—has reached the stage where each comprises an independent scientific discipline. Thus the Land of the Bible, for the purposes of this work, includes only the region that forms the focus of biblical history—the Land of Israel, from the Jordan River to the Mediterranean Sea and from the Galilee to the Negev.

As for the scope of the biblical period, it may indeed be claimed that the periods described at the start of this volume, the Neolithic, Chalcolithic, and Early Bronze ages, can hardly be considered biblical periods in the strict sense of the term. It was nonetheless deemed proper to include them in the discussion because it was in these periods that the foundations of the settlement pattern, the economy, and the sociopolitical setting of the land were established, providing the background for the central events of biblical history.

A group of scholars, experts in the study of various periods, were requested to prepare chapters summarizing the information concerning each period. Various aspects were to be covered—public and private architecture, everyday objects, industry and crafts, art, cult, trade relations, and the like—and each period was to be placed in its proper chronological setting. Not surprisingly, the discussion of the different periods is not made of one cloth, as each chapter reflects the personal bent of its author. Our editorial policy did not seek to change this state of affairs; on the contrary, it seemed preferable to expose the reader to a variety of approaches to the task of describing one of a sequence of periods in the history of the Land of Israel. It remained to the editor merely to smooth the transitions between the periods covered by different authors, that is, to ensure that no gaps were formed between the periods discussed, that references to course work were removed, and that a general uniformity in style, terminology, and place-names was maintained.

Had the original work, after the editorial changes described above, been translated as was, the English version would have been twice as long as the present volume. To attain a practical size, much condensation and reduction were required, in some cases leading to the elimination of entire subjects. For me, these reductions meant cutting the living flesh, but in every case it was ensured that the major issues would be fully presented. The material presented is up to date to the mid-eighties, when the original manuscript was completed.

In the task of preparing the manuscript I received the assistance of a great many people, who cannot all be named here. First and foremost I owe a debt of gratitude to the directors of the Open University and Yale University Press, who recognized the importance of the preparation of this English edition. To the presidents of the Open University, Prof. A. Ginzburg, succeeded by Prof. N. Levtzion, who exhibited enthusiasm from the start, provided valuable advice, and provided all possible assistance, both in manpower and in the funds needed to produce the manuscript; to J. Ferris, editor at Yale University Press, who accompanied the preparation of the English manuscript from its inception and who constantly egged me on and refused to compromise until everything came out just right; to Lorraine Atherton, who edited the manuscript, and to James Johnson and Lawrence Kenney at Yale University Press; to the authors of the various chapters, who read the English versions of their chapters and submitted, though not always willingly, to the changes and abridgments; to L. Vinitzky, my assistant, without whom work would have ground to a halt and no manuscript would have been completed; to the graphics department at the Open University, which produced the plans and drawings, making the innumerable alterations required; to R. Greenberg, who did much more than merely translate; to my friends and colleagues O. Lipschitz, N. Naaman, and Y. Shatzman, for their friendship, advice, and assistance, sorely needed along the long road leading from the preparation of the Hebrew manuscript to the completion of the English edition presented to the reader; to all these, and to many others not mentioned here—my heartfelt thanks.

Amnon Ben-Tor
Jerusalem, 1989

THE ARCHAEOLOGY OF ANCIENT ISRAEL

1

Introduction

AMNON BEN-TOR

People are the main interest of archaeology, and the objects they have
created are the means through which
archaeology seeks to learn about
them. It is therefore clear that the
beginning of archaeology—that is,
the earliest period with which it is
concerned—is the period of earliest
human existence. When humans
emerged is a matter of debate among
scholars, as is the definition of the
first species that can be called
human. It may therefore suffice to
use a relative date for the beginning
of archaeology, stating that it begins
when tool-using and—more important—tool-making humans first
emerge.

It is easier to define the end of
archaeology, that is, the end of that
past with which it is concerned:
when does an object cease to be of
interest to the archaeologist? The
matter is usually determined by law,
for in most countries—Israel among
them—there are laws designed to
protect movable and immovable antiquities, to regulate trade in antiquities, etc. The Israel antiquities law
(1978) defines an antiquity as "a
man-made relic created before the
year 1700 C.E." or "a relic made in
the year 1700 C.E. or later which is
of historical value and which the
Minister [of Education and Culture]

has declared an antiquity"; "zoo-
logical and botanical remains pre-
dating the year 1300 C.E." are also
considered antiquities. In other
words, in Israel, objects of archaeological value are those made by
man before the year 1700 C.E. As for
later objects, a special declaration of
the minister responsible for the im-
plementation of the antiquities law is
required. Faunal and floral remains
predating the year 1300 C.E. may
also be considered of archaeological
concern.

Both the upper and lower temporal limits of archaeology lie outside the scope of the present volume,
which begins with the Neolithic period, well after the emergence of
humans, and ends with the destruction of the First Temple, well before
the limit set in the antiquities law.
This interval lies between the true
prehistoric era on the one hand and
the Classical period on the other.
Indeed, neither the Neolithic period
nor the Chalcolithic period that followed it, nor even the Early Bronze
Age, saw the advent of literacy in
the Land of Israel; thus, the archaeology of these periods is, strictly
speaking, prehistoric. However, it
should be stressed that the processes
either originating in the Neolithic
period or greatly accelerated at this

1

time—such as agriculture, sedentarization, the rise in the carrying
capacity of the land, population
growth, the beginning of pottery
production and the like—all suggest
that the period be viewed as the first
chapter of a new story, wherein may
be observed the origins of processes
that were to mold the character of
the land in the following periods.
As for the ending of our survey at
the beginning of the sixth century
B.C.E., it can hardly be disputed that
the destruction of the First Temple
was an event of decisive historical
and cultural significance. Furthermore, this point marks a terminological division: earlier periods are
defined by terms drawn from the
realm of raw-material technologies
—Neolithic, Chalcolithic, Bronze,
and Iron (though there are some
who prefer the terms "Canaanite
period" and "Israelite period" over
the terms "Iron" and "Bronze"
ages). Starting in the sixth century,
however, the generally accepted archaeological terminology is drawn
from the realm of political history,
and the periods are termed Persian,
Hellenistic, Roman, Byzantine,
Arab (Islamic), and so on.

Table 1.1 is a chronological list-
ing of the periods covered in this
volume.

Turning to the spatial boundaries
of the archaeology of the Land of
Israel, we must define the geographical regions covered by this term.
Here we come upon an issue regarding which no scholarly consensus
has yet been achieved. Is the use of
the term "the Land of Israel" justified? Was the land called "Israel"
during the Neolithic period, some
ten thousand years ago, or even in
later historical periods such as the
Middle or Late Bronze Age (the
second millennium B.C.E.)? Or is
there, perhaps, a better alternative?
In his classic work, W. F. Albright
chose to use the term "Palestine"
(*The Archaeology of Palestine*),
though clearly that term is even less
justified, historically speaking, than
"the Land of Israel" (at least until
the Classical period). Others, such
as Kathleen Kenyon, have preferred
the term "Holy Land" (*Archaeology
in the Holy Land*), the term also
used in the encyclopaedia published
by the Israel Exploration Society,
*Encyclopaedia of Archaeological Ex-
cavations in the Holy Land;* but

since when has the Land of Israel in
fact been a holy land? That term
certainly does not apply to the period covered in the present volume. In
recent years, the term "Syria-Palestine" has achieved a degree of
popularity; it too is no solution: not
only is the term "Syria," like "Israel," historically inappropriate to the
period treated here, but from the
aspect of material culture (archaeology's primary interest), that which
prevailed in most of what is now
Syria differs in many senses from
that of the Land of Israel. Other
terms that have surfaced in scholarly
literature ("Canaan," "Southern Levant") suffer from similar drawbacks. In the absence of a generally
accepted term, the designations
"Palestine," "Land of Israel," or
"Canaan" are employed in the following chapters. Their use reflects
the preference of the individual
authors.

The difficulty in finding an accepted term to define the geographical unit under discussion is but a
reflection of the situation of the
country, which lacks, apart from the
sea on the west, clear natural and
cultural boundaries. When we come
to deal with the material culture of
the Land of Israel in a given period
(and this is, after all, the essence of
archaeology), what are the boundaries of that land? Those of the
Promised Land? The borders of the
British Mandate? The 1949 armistice
lines? And, as our chief concern lies
with material culture, do cultural
horizons necessarily adhere to political boundaries? At first glance, the
clearest natural boundary of the
Land of Israel, after the Mediterranean Sea, is its eastern boundary,
the Jordan River, which has in fact
served as a political boundary during
extended periods. But in practice, it
is often difficult to distinguish between the material cultures of the
Land of Israel and Transjordan, so
that this natural-political boundary

Table 1.1 Chronology of the Periods Covered in this Book.

Pre-Pottery Neolithic A	8300–7300
Pre-Pottery Neolithic B	7300–6000/5800
Pottery Neolithic	6000/5800–5000/4800
Early Chalcolithic	5000/4800–4200/4000
Middle–Late Chalcolithic	4200/4000–3200/3000
Early Bronze I	3200/3000–2950/2900
Early Bronze II	2950/2900–2700/2650
Early Bronze III	2700/2650–2350
Early Bronze IV	2350–2200
Intermediate Bronze (Middle Bronze I)	2200–2000
Middle Bronze IIa	2000–1750
Middle Bronze IIb	1750–1600/1550
Late Bronze I	1600/1550–1400
Late Bronze II	1400–1300
Late Bronze III	1300–1200/1150
Iron I	1200/1150–1000
Iron IIa	1000–800
Iron IIb	800–700
Iron IIIa	700–586
Iron IIIb	586–520

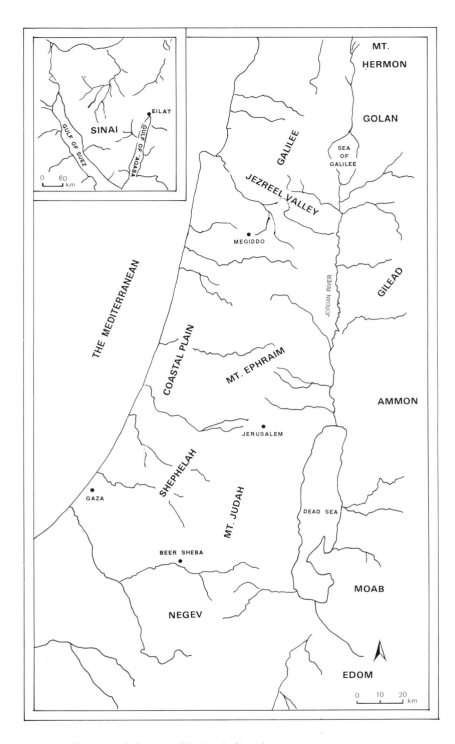

Map 1.1. The regional divisions of the Land of Israel

dan" would suit archaeological reality far better than "Syria-Palestine"). Turning southwards, we find the Sinai peninsula situated at the point of contact between the cultures of Egypt and the Land of Israel. This is a characteristic buffer zone, arid and sparsely populated, which has been an organic part neither of the Land of Israel nor of Egypt. Even in times when there was Egyptian control of the peninsula, it concentrated mainly on the important highway that traversed northern Sinai. Archaeologically, however, do the Sinai sites belong more to the Egyptian cultural sphere or to that of the Land of Israel? Or, perhaps, have they a distinctive character all their own? As it happens, all three possibilities are reflected in the archaeological record: there are periods when Sinai is more Egyptian, others when it is more Canaanite, and yet others when both Egyptian and Canaanite elements are present.

The northern border presents difficulties of a different kind. Unlike the south, this is not a thinly populated desert zone with a dominant political-cultural entity situated on its far side. A degree of ethnic and cultural affinity between the people living on either side of the imaginary northern border always existed. Archaeology has revealed periods when considerable cultural unity between the Land of Israel and what is today called Lebanon prevailed, in contrast to cultural dissimilarity between the two units on the one hand and the northeast (Syria) on the other. That, however, was not always the case, and other periods saw a greater degree of cultural resemblance between Syria and the Land of Israel.

As for those lands and cultures sharing no borders with the Land of Israel, the great cultural centers of the ancient Near East—Egypt, Mesopotamia, Asia Minor, Cyprus, Greece, and others—all influenced,

has virtually no archaeological significance. The degree of similarity generally varies from cultural identity to a close affinity, but never can we speak of two separate entities (in this respect, the term "Israel-Jorin one way or another, the material and spiritual culture of the Land of Israel. Their influence was communicated in different ways: population movements, commercial importation, or the like. It did not always emanate from the same centers, nor was it always of equal intensity, but it was nearly always present. We may take, for example, the cuneiform system of writing, which originated in the Mesopotamian cultural sphere. The cuneiform script and the Akkadian language served the Canaanite rulers in their political correspondence with their Egyptian overlords during the Late Bronze Age, for Akkadian was at that time the international language of diplomacy. The spread of writing and language facilitated the infiltration of Mesopotamian influence into other realms of spiritual life. Further examples of external influence include the pottery imports from Mycenae (Greece), which were imitated, after a time, by local potters; the import of copper ore for the production of tools and weapons from Cyprus and the North; the importation and imitation of art objects such as ivories and seals; and so on.

The Land of Israel always maintained contacts, of varying intensity, with neighboring cultures, either those directly bordering it or others that were part of the cultural assemblage of the ancient Near East. Hence, the geographical boundaries of the archaeology of the Land of Israel are not fixed: at times Sinai must be included, at others not; at times Lebanon must be included, at times not; and so on. The same goes for the degree of influence exerted by the Near Eastern cultures on that of the Land of Israel; at times the influence of one culture dominates, at times that of another. As a rule,

the Land of Israel will be the focus of study, but we will not be exempted from recognizing and taking account of the mutual influence between the cultures of the Land of Israel and those of neighboring lands, and at times we will be able to understand local events only by viewing them within a broader perspective.

One last point should be emphasized. What has been said in previous paragraphs implies a monolithic view of the culture of the Land of Israel. It should, therefore, be kept in mind that despite its small size, variations in the material culture of different regions—Israel and Judah, the Negev or the Coastal Plain—can be distinguished. Those regional variations too are not equally marked in each period. Sometimes the differences stand out, sometimes they are blurred and a greater degree of cultural unity is apparent.

Fig. 1.1. A group of Iron Age vessels from Tel Lachish

The Past Forty Years of Archaeological Activity

Three main avenues of inquiry have dominated archaeological activity in Israel since the 1950s and the establishment of the state of Israel, leading to an accelerated and unprecedented development in the archaeology of the land.

RENEWED EXCAVATIONS AT PREVIOUSLY EXCAVATED MOUNDS

This has been the domain chiefly of American expeditions, which have excavated at sites such as Shechem (1956–69) under the direction of G. E. Wright, Ta'anach (1963–68) under the direction of P. Lapp, and Ai (1964–72) under the direction of J. A. Callaway. Gezer was reexcavated from 1964 to 1973, under Wright, W. G. Dever, and J. Seger, and renewed excavations at Tell el-Hesi (1970–83) were led by D. G. Rose and L. E. Toombs.

The most important British excavation of these years was conducted at Jericho, in 1952–58, under the direction of Kathleen Kenyon. The importance of that excavation lies mainly in the Neolithic-period discoveries made there and in the crystallization, during the excavation, of the so-called Kenyon method of excavation.

The renewed excavations provided material of the greatest interest and contributed much to the clarification of the stratigraphic sequences in the mounds and to the correction of the mistakes of previous excavators.

NEW EXCAVATIONS

Among the important sites excavated during this period we may mention Tell el-Far'ah North, excavated from 1946 to 1960 by Père R. de Vaux, and the sites of the Chalcolithic Beersheba culture, excavated from 1951 to 1960 by J. Perrot.

Important prehistoric excavations include those of M. Stekelis at Sha'ar Ha-Golan from 1949 to 1952, at Kebara cave from 1951 to 1957, at Nahal Oren in 1954–60, and at 'Ubeidiya in 1960–66 (continued under the direction of O. Bar-Yosef and E. Tchernov from 1967 to 1974).

Of major importance are Y. Yadin's excavations at Hazor (the largest mound in Israel) in 1955–58

Fig. 1.2. Hebrew document from Judaean desert cave (height 4 centimeters)

and 1968, S. Yeivin's 1956–61 excavations at Tel Erani, the excavations at En Gedi in 1961–65 led by B. Mazar, the 1962–72 excavations at Ashdod directed by M. Dothan, Y. Aharoni's excavation of the Iron Age strata at Arad in 1962–67 and Ruth Amiran's ongoing excavations of the Early Bronze Age city at the same site (begun in 1962), T. Dothan's excavations at Deir el-Balah (1972–82), and A. Biran's excavations at Tel Dan (in progress since 1966). Since the reunification of Jerusalem in 1967, the excavations in various parts of that city have taken a prominent position in the Israeli archaeological scene. The three major excavations are those of B. Mazar to the south and west of the Temple Mount (1968–77), N. Avigad's excavations in the Jewish Quarter of the Old City (1969–83), and Y. Shiloh's excavations at the City of David from 1978 to 1985.

Two unusual archaeological enterprises were undertaken during this period in the Judaean desert, both under the leadership of Y. Yadin. The first was a survey of the Judaean desert caves. Initiated by Aharoni in the fifties, the survey achieved its greatest momentum in

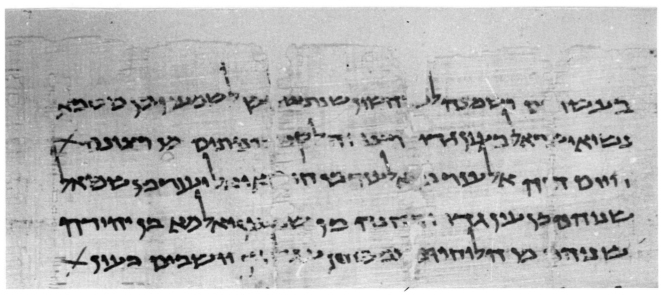

1960–61 under the direction of Yadin. Important finds include written remains dating to the Bar Kochba rebellion, discovered by Yadin's survey crew in the Cave of Letters in Nahal Hever, and the Chalcolithic hoard found in the Cave of the Treasure in Nahal Mishmar by P. Bar Adon.

The second major effort was the excavation of Masada, the most difficult and extensive archaeological campaign ever conducted in the Land of Israel. The investigation of Masada had begun in the fifties under the direction of S. Gutman, but the bulk of the excavation and restoration was performed by Yadin's expedition in 1963–65.

In addition to the sensational finds provided by those two expeditions, it should be noted that they are unique in the magnitude of the logistical difficulties faced by the organizers, in the backing offered them by government authorities (involving the Israel Defense Force in both organizational and excavation capacities), and in the establishment of a corps of volunteers, which bore the brunt of fieldwork. Many of the excavations undertaken since that time have been made possible by a similar use of volunteer labor.

The archaeological survey too was vigorously pursued. In areas surveyed more than once in earlier times, the existence of hundreds of previously unrecognized ancient sites was revealed, revolutionizing our understanding of the settlement pattern in different periods. Among the surveys we may mention the new Israel Survey conducted by the Society for the Survey of Israel, under the auspices of the Department of Antiquities. Within the framework of the Israel Survey, intensive surveys have been carried out in the central hill zones, particularly in the tribal territories of Ephraim and Mannasseh, by I. Finkelstein and A. Zertal; the hundreds of hitherto unknown sites revealed in the surveys have added a new dimension to our understanding of this region, enabling the formulation of new answers to questions that have occupied archaeologists for decades, such as the question of the character of the Israelite settlement during the Iron Age I. The survey of the Negev, undertaken in conjunction with the redeployment of the IDF following the peace treaty with Egypt, has also been of major importance.

Other surveys conducted since 1967 include the Golan Survey, headed by Claire Epstein and S. Gutman (the excavator in recent years of Gamla), and extensive surveys in the Sinai conducted largely by expeditions led by E. Oren, Y. Bet Arieh, and O. Bar-Yosef.

THE EMERGENCE OF SCHOOLS AND METHODS OF RESEARCH

This is the third area of archaeological activity that has seen intensified development over recent years. First and foremost, there has been a development and extension of research and educational activity.

Fig. 1.3. Aerial view of Tel Beersheba

In Israel, new archaeological departments have opened at the universities of Tel Aviv, Beersheba, and Haifa, augmenting the long extant department of the Hebrew University in Jerusalem.

Two major schools, Israeli and American, have evolved over this period. The latter, formed mainly in the wake of renewed excavations—chiefly by American scholars—at previously excavated sites, centers on figures such as Dever, Lapp, N. Glueck, Callaway, and Wright. The outstanding proponents of the Israeli school include scholars such as M. Avi-Yonah in the field of Jewish and Classical archaeology and Stekelis in the field of prehistory; in the realm of "biblical archaeology" (more on this phrase below) mention may be made of figures such as Aharoni, Yadin, and Amiran. A formative role in the development and practice of the Israeli method of excavation, which differs in many respects from that adopted by the Americans, may be attributed to the architect E. Dunayevsky. While noting the existence of these schools, it should be kept in mind that if within each school there is considerable agreement about how material should be recovered in the field—that is, excavation methods—there is no such agreement over the interpretation of the material recovered. Thus, for example, there are severe differences of opinion within the American school regarding the place the Bible should occupy in archaeological research, with scholars such as Dever and Wright taking opposing views. Similarly, with the Israeli school, a major difference of opinion emerged over the interpretation of archaeological data involving the period of the conquest and settlement of the Israelites, with Yadin and Aharoni dominating the opposing sides of the archaeological fence.

A significant development in Israeli archaeological research is the coming to the fore of a generation of archaeologists who received their archaeological education in the fifties and sixties at the Institute of Archaeology in the Hebrew University of Jerusalem, including D. Bahat (ancient Jerusalem), D. Barag (ancient glass), O. Bar-Yosef (Ha-Yonim cave), P. Beck (Aphek), A. Ben-Tor (Yoqne'am), R. Cohen (the Negev), A. Eitan (director of the Department of Antiquities), G. Foerster (ancient synagogues), R. Gophna (En Besor), Y. Israeli (chief curator of archaeology, Israel Museum), A. Kempinski (Masos), M. Kochavi (Aphek), A. Mazar (Batash), Y. Meshorer (numismatics), O. Negbi (Jerishe), A. Negev (Avdat), E. Netzer (Herodium), E. Oren (Sera'), A. Raban (marine archaeology), A. Ronen (Sefunim cave), Y. Shiloh (City of David), E. Stern (Dor), D. Ussishkin (Lachish), Y. Tsafrir (Rehovot in the Negev), and others. These scholars and their colleagues have been active not only in the field but in realms of theoretical research as well, including that of archaeological method.

This is the place to mention a direction of research that has occupied a central position in archaeology over the past two decades: New Archaeology. We will not here undertake a detailed definition of this research outlook. Suffice it to say that in recent years research methods and data-processing methods used in other fields—mainly the social sciences, such as sociology, social anthropology, statistics, and ecology—have had considerable influence on archaeology. The new approach to archaeology, advocating far-reaching changes both in excavation techniques and in data processing, brought on an incisive debate leading to a division between proponents and opponents. Looking back, it seems that the initial enthusiasm led to an extreme and over-

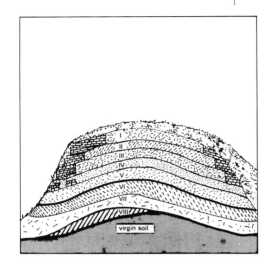

Fig. 1.4. Schematic diagram showing the structure of an archaeological mound

simplified approach; in recent years, as the debate has cooled, archaeologists have adopted to a greater or lesser extent some of the new approaches, means, and methods of research.

What Is Biblical Archaeology?

We cannot end this introductory survey without addressing the controversial issue of biblical archaeology. Were archaeologists alone involved in the debate, the matter could be overlooked, but that is not the case. The relation of the Bible to archaeology is a major ingredient in the interaction of the archaeologist and the lay public, and the clarification of this issue is therefore of central importance.

As is well known, the results of excavations at "biblical" sites (mounds in the Land of Israel or Syria occupied from some time in the second millennium to the mid first millennium) arouse much public interest in the western world and in Israel in particular. Because of the special position of the Bible in our culture, the intense interest, and at times fervent emotions, shown by the general public far exceed the attention usually accorded to sites in other lands or of different periods. This general interest in anything that appears to have a relation to the Bible leads to demands that are often archaeologically unacceptable.

The attitude of the public to the Bible is divided; at one end of the spectrum stand those who see the scriptures as the word of God. The Bible is thus a divine creation and must be accepted literally. At the other end stand those who consider the Bible a human creation that suffers from the limitations of all human creations. It must therefore be considered and judged according to the same standards generally applied to literary texts. Between the two extremes lie the points of view that attribute to the scriptures a greater or lesser measure of divine inspiration.

In any case, the broad consensus is that the Bible cannot be viewed in a monolithic manner; rather, it is made up of different literary genres such as prophecy, psalmody, wisdom literature, and historiography, originating in different periods and social backgrounds. The portions of biblical historiography of special interest to biblical archaeology are the patriarchal narratives, the story of the conquest and settlement of Israel, and the history of the Israelite kingdoms. It should in this context be emphasized that there is no objective history; written history always reflects the author's point of view and is intended to convey or promote a certain message. The fundamental message of biblical historiography is that all events reflect God's will and that anything that befalls the individual or the community can only be the result of the relations between Israel and God; thus, Sennacherib fails to conquer Jerusalem because Hezekiah prays to God, and God answers his prayers. It is the angel of God who smites the Assyrian camp and causes the siege to be lifted. One may well suppose that the version of this story told by the Assyrian annalist would be quite different.

Hence to the attitude of archaeologists to the biblical text. We may take as an example two radically different approaches, as expressed in the statements of intent of two research institutions founded over a century ago; the first, the Palestine Exploration Fund, was founded in Great Britain in 1865. The aim of the fund, in the words of its founders, was "the accurate and systematic investigation of the archaeology, topography, the geology and physical geography, the manners and customs of the Holy Land, for biblical illustration." In contrast, the Committee of the Palestine Exploration Society, founded in New York five years later, defined their aim as "the illustration and *defense* of the Bible" (emphasis added). "Modern scepticism," they added, "assails the Bible at the point of reality. . . . Hence whatever goes to verify Bible history as real . . . is a refutation of unbelief. . . . The Committee feels that they have in trust a sacred service for science and for religion."

The viewpoint here adopted by the founders of the American society is, in this author's opinion, the root of all evil as far as the discipline of biblical archaeology is concerned: terms such as "defense" and "verification" of the Bible, all in the service of religion (the founders of the P.E.F. stated that in no case was the fund to be administered as a religious institution), are completely out of place. Does religion need to be defended? Can biblical truths be proven? What has all this to do with religious belief? In any event, this approach was adopted by not a few scholars, and more important, it prescribed the level of public expectation from archaeological research.

In the thirties and forties a series of studies devoted to important texts discovered in excavations—chiefly those of Mari, Nuzi, and Ugarit—was published by archaeologists, biblicists, and historians. The texts cast light upon the life-style, laws, and customs current among the peoples of the ancient Near East, the Israelites among them. They thus served to illustrate the Bible, and that is how they were perceived by scholars, among whom Albright was the dominating figure (the concern of Albright and others with the texts and their relation to the Bible was, to a great extent, a reaction to the German school of biblical criticism, which at that time cast grave doubts on the antiquity of many biblical texts relating to the antiquity of the Israelites). Unfortunately, that was not appreciated by the public at large, which understood the writings of Albright and others to be a proof of the Bible. The title of a most popular book written during the period illustrates this point: *The Bible as History: Archaeology Confirms the Book of Books* (W. Keller, 1956).

It would be nigh impossible to estimate the amounts of money and human energy wasted in futile efforts such as the searches for Noah's Ark on Mt. Ararat, the tomb of Moses at Mount Nebo, Pharaoh's hordes in the Sea of Reeds, or the remains of Sodom and Gomorrah in the Dead Sea, all fueled by an irrational impulse to prove the historical authenticity of the biblical narrative. Surely the substance of a tale such as that of Sodom and Gomorrah lies in the punishment of the wicked, the reward of the righteous, and Abraham's negotiation with God to prevent the punishment of the just with the wicked; the Bible uses the tale of Sodom and Gomorrah to transmit this eternal message. Can it be in any way impaired should it transpire that Sodom and Gomorrah never existed but were invented as a parable, or even that Abraham himself is not a historical figure? Or, alternatively, would the message be clearer and of greater import if those cities were to be found and proof discovered of Abraham's physical existence?

This intense urge to prove the Bible cannot affect the pious believer. For such a person, the scriptures contain their own truth and need not be criticized or proven. This need is prevalent, in what must be construed as an irrational manner, among large segments of the secular public, which find it important that the archaeologists prove that all the events described in the Bible did indeed occur and that all the figures mentioned and the episodes described are entirely consistent with reality. There is in this demand a violation of archaeological integrity and an attempt to impose upon archaeology unattainable objectives—that is, the proof of faith. In recent years, it may be observed, we have been witness to another kind of imposition: attempts at political control over archaeological research. These attempts are no more legitimate and, like the attempts to make archaeology prove the Bible, should be roundly condemned.

It is therefore not a coincidence that a considerable proportion of the archaeologists active in the Land of Israel over the past one hundred years have come from the religious establishment. Many of them received a large part of their education at various theological seminaries, while their archaeological training was often deficient. This is particularly evident among American archaeologists; Dever has estimated that over 80 percent of the researchers affiliated with the American School of Oriental Research in Jerusalem since its foundation in 1900 came from within the religious establishment. He has also estimated

that the same proportions existed within archaeological expeditions such as those of Shechem, Gezer, and Ai. Among the German and French archaeologists there was also a considerable proportion of theologians, though not as high as among the Americans; the fact remains that the umbrella organization of French archaeologists in the Land of Israel is controlled by the Dominican Fathers and that of the Germans by the Evangelical Church. In contrast, not one major British or Israeli archaeological figure has been a member of the religious establishment.

This state of affairs has given biblical archaeology a reputation for amateurism in some archaeological circles. Modern scientific excavation is so complex that those who have not received adequate training (which is the case with most of those educated at theological seminaries) cannot conduct one properly. The most successful American excavation before World War I, the Harvard Samaria Expedition, was far ahead of its time in its fieldwork, recording, and publication, a precocity attributed to its sponsorship by an expressly secular institution. Thus, in recent years, the call has gone forth to sever archaeology from the Bible and to abandon the term "biblical archaeology." It is perhaps not surprising that this suggestion has originated in the United States, where the religious establishment was (and still is, to some extent) overly involved in archaeological research in the Land of Israel.

But that suggestion cannot be accepted. The two fields are naturally related and mutually enriching. It is as unreasonable as to demand that classical archaeology be separated from Homer and other writings of antiquity. Eliminate the Bible from the archaeology of the Land of Israel in the second and first

millennia b.c.e., and you have deprived it of its soul. The way to overcome the difficulties associated with biblical archaeology should be sought in the education of a public unaware of what constitutes a legitimate demand from archaeology, and in the mutual cooperation of biblicists, historians, and archaeologists, who are not always sufficiently informed about the disciplines of their colleagues. The public should be taught what archaeology can (and should) or cannot do, while biblical archaeologists should be guided by two seemingly opposed approaches: on the one hand, modern research demands that they specialize in restricted fields, and on the other, they must acquire at least a basic grounding in bordering fields of study, chiefly in biblical studies and in the history and languages of the ancient Near East.

Archaeologists differ in methods for recovery of material culture (excavation), in methods of data processing (excavation reports), and in the questions they address (interpretation). In accord with those approaches, they are sometimes classified as traditionalist, new, and the like. This kind of classification appears to us immaterial. What is of essence is the care, precision, and thoroughness with which archaeologists recover material and process data, their willingness and ability to cooperate with others—for it is no longer possible for one person to be conversant with so wide a range of fields—and their openness to new questions. It is essential that the archaeologist be aware that all the above are but means, whereas the object of all the human and monetary investment in archaeological enterprise is man himself.

2

The Neolithic Period

OFER BAR-YOSEF

The Neolithic period marks the beginning of a new chapter in human history. Preceded by two million years of the hunter-gatherer way of life—during which human evolution produced no major economic changes—it was in the Neolithic period that people first began to subsist from the cultivation of cereals and legumes, accompanied by domesticated sheep and goats, and not only from the gathering of seeds, fruits, and tubers found in the wild and from the hunting of game animals. There is little division of scholarly opinion regarding the finds of Neolithic excavations throughout the Near East; the debate revolves mainly around the causes of this socioeconomic development and the evaluation of the importance of the different phases of change. The significance of the change may be understood by reviewing the differences between two modes of subsistence: the earlier, preagricultural mode, of about 11,000 B.C.E., and the later mode, of about 6000 B.C.E. During this five-thousand-year interval (dated by carbon-14 analysis), Near Eastern society passed from small hunting bands, subsisting on the gathering of food and the hunting of available game (gazelle, ibex, fallow deer, red

deer, and others), to an agricultural society. In the fertile zones of the Levant there were established agricultural villages (ranging in size from 0.2 hectare to 12 hectares) that subsisted on cultivation of cereals and legumes, gathering wild seeds and fruits, animal husbandry, hunting, and a network of trade in obsidian (volcanic glass) and other products. The term "Neolithic period," as coined in Europe, indicates the existence of agricultural villages with polished stone axes, pottery, and remains of domesticated cereals and animals (sheep, goats, cattle, and dogs); these attributes characterize a later phase in the Levantine Neolithic.

In the twentieth century, attempts to explain the causes and circumstances behind this dramatic change in human history have given rise to two schools of interpretation. The first includes those who see environmental and other ecological changes as the principal force acting on human society. This approach may be termed environmental determinism. The second school sees the evolution of human culture as the expression of social interaction between humans or the differences in capabilities and social organization between societies. Those who take this approach do not ignore environmental conditions, but they see human society as the main locus of development, of which the material and spiritual culture form the outward expression.

The differences between these approaches may be clearly seen in the explanations they provide for fundamental questions related to the agricultural revolution: Why did the Neolithic revolution take place in the Near East ten thousand years ago and not in another time and place? Does the origin of those social and economic changes lie in new needs, in adaptation to changing conditions caused by changes in climate, or is it to be explained in terms of a series of innovations and improved technologies? Was the transition from one economic base to another gradual or sudden (a revolution), and did social organization change before the economic change or in its wake? What part does the human factor play in this process? Did population growth spur economic change, or did the changes in the size and health of the population come only after and because of the agricultural revolution?

THE OASIS THEORY (ENVIRONMENTAL DETERMINISM)

Gordon Childe was the leading proponent of the theory that climatic changes at the end of the glacial period were the principal factor in environmental changes. As the glaciers retreated, Mediterranean or even the temperate zones became desiccated, turning into deserts and forcing human groups to converge on the river valleys—the Nile, Euphrates, and Tigris—which functioned as oases. The closer interaction of humans, plants, and animals led people to a closer acquaintance with the growth cycle of plants and the reproductive cycle of animals, and the possibilities for their exploitation increased. People, originally plant cultivators, would become herders, husbanding both the fields and the flocks.

Childe's theory, presented in 1952 in his volume *New Light on the Most Ancient East,* could be tested in the field. For example, archaeological research could ascertain whether agriculture did indeed begin in the Nile valley, or whether there is any reflection in botanical, palynological, or faunal remains of a sharp change of climate in the Near East at the end of the glacial period.

THE THEORY OF THE NUCLEAR ZONE, OR NATURAL HABITATS

The first to test Childe's theory in the field was American archaeologist Robert Braidwood, of the Oriental Institute of the University of Chicago. Following in the footsteps of previous researchers who relied on botanical studies, Braidwood suggested that agriculture had emerged where cereals comprise an integral part of the annual grasses. The hilly flanks of the Zagros (Iraq) and Taurus (Turkey) mountains were thought to be the most suitable area to test the hypothesis. Braidwood invited the active cooperation of zoologists, geologists, and other scientists who could test Childe's basic theory in the field. The development of the carbon-14 dating method, invented by W. Libby during those years (1947 and on), enabled the actual dating of the changes observed in the archaeological assemblages.

Braidwood believed that the valleys descending from the Zagros, Taurus, and other ranges, 300 to 1500 meters above sea level, constituted the natural zone, or nuclear area, for the growth of wild grains and that agricultural villages were first established in these areas. He viewed the environmental factor as secondary. The technology of food gathering and processing developed during the Upper Paleolithic era permitted humans to exploit new food sources such as small mammals, fish, shellfish, and wild cereals. This abundance permitted the establishment of villages, which then became sedentary. Permanent settlement laid the foundation for experimentation in deliberate cultivation, first of plants, then of herd animals, in their natural habitats.

According to this view, the urge toward innovation was the result of the internal evolution of human society and not a result of external circumstances. This point of view has been adopted by the French prehistorians Jacques and Marie-Claire Cauvin. They have concentrated mainly on Syria, and in their excavations at Tell Mureybet in the Euphrates valley, they identified transitional phases between Epipaleolithic and Neolithic society. They believe that socioeconomic change was stimulated not by a dearth of food resources but rather by a continually abundant food supply that permitted choice.

THE DEMOGRAPHIC PRESSURE THEORY

In 1965 the Danish economist E. Boserap, in *The Conditions of Agricultural Growth,* linked rapid population growth with food production technology. Through observations in developing countries she came to the conclusion that demographic pressure brings about changes in methods of food production by constraint, not by free choice. The first to test the thesis were P. E. L. Smith and T. C. Young, who saw the climatic change occurring in the Zagros at the end of the Pleistocene as the factor favoring sedentism. Sedentary settlements led naturally to population increase, as the number of births among women in mobile groups is smaller than among sedentarists. The inhabitants then attempted grain cultivation, which could succeed where wild cereals grew. The increased food supply led to further population increase, which in turn required further improvements in food production and supply. In this manner, hoe agriculture was born, and irrigation developed. It should be emphasized that, as Smith and Young see it, population growth was a catalyst for the improvement of food-obtaining methods, the most basic of which is the intentional cultivation of plants.

Some scholars believed that the first agricultural villages were to be found outside those zones where wild cereals were plentiful. The outstanding examples for this are Tell Mureybet and Tell Abu Hureyra in the Euphrates valley, at least 150 kilometers from the nearest wild grain. This led to another interpretation linking demographic pressure and environmental changes of the terminal Pleistocene and early Holocene, published separately by L. Binford and K. Flannery. Changes in climate led to a change of the economic base, and instead of selective hunting or minimal gathering, Epipaleolithic groups began to systematically exploit a broad spectrum of food sources. This included the hunting of small mammals, fishing, and plant collecting (wild cereals, legumes). As such populations naturally adapt their size to the carrying capacity of the region, the shift to farming can be advantageous only in two situations: serious environmental change, or change of the demographic structure of an entire region.

At the end of the Pleistocene, sometime around the ninth millennium b.c.e., the climate changed as a result of the melting of the glaciers, reflected in a rise of temperatures and the spread of deserts. The demographic change was pre-

dictable, as some groups maintain a fixed size and others grow and are forced to expand beyond the fertile area and its abundant food sources to the desert margins. Such expansion could have been successful under good climatic conditions, but population pressure arose when the environment changed. Groups that had to leave the areas of permanent settlement, therefore, brought cereals into the desert margins and raised them there. The cultivation of plants outside their natural habitat constituted a selective factor, stimulating the emergence of domesticated wheat and barley. In this view, grain domestication occurred in the marginal areas, not within Braidwood's nuclear area.

NEW DIRECTIONS IN INTERPRETATION, OR THE SYNTHESIS OF THEORIES

This short survey of the different models has shown that most of the elements relevant to the explanation of the origin of agricultural settlement are presently in hand. They include environmental changes; behavior patterns and social organization of hunter-gatherers, supplied by a copious body of ethnographic literature; the distribution and unique features of each type of plant and animal; possibilities for social transitions and organizational changes; accessories, installations, and tools required for an agricultural society that were invented earlier, such as mortars. Without attempting to predict future directions of scientific advance, it appears that an accurate interpretation (that can be tested in the field) will have to take account of all these elements while clarifying their relative importance. Such an approach has been proposed by Charles Redman in *The Rise of Civilization*, published in 1978. The data accumulated thus

far in archaeological and bioarchaeological (relating to floral finds, palynological cores, and zooarchaeology) literature cannot answer every question raised within the framework of a multifaceted interpretation. Without further fieldwork, requiring a variety of means and years of laboratory analysis, it will be difficult to test the validity of alternative interpretations.

Dates and Terminology

Table 2.1 sums up the chronology and terminology used in the present chapter.

The period discussed here has so far been dated by carbon-14 dates alone. Only the sixth and fifth millennia b.c.e. are covered by the new calibration of these dates. To avoid confusion, all the dates mentioned below will be given as carbon-14 dates based on the uncalibrated Libby half-life of 5570 years. Dates noted as b.c.e. are based on the conventional subtraction of 1950 years from the b.p. date provided by the laboratory performing the analysis. Thus, when discussing the seventh millennium b.c.e., we refer to objects dated in the laboratories between 9000 and 8000 b.p., which is 7000–6000 b.c.e.

One example of the changes in terminology effected in the 1950s is the addition of the adjective "Pre-Pottery" to part of the Neolithic sequence. Kenyon, who coined the term, was well aware that the use of "Neolithic" in Europe implied the presence of pottery. In her excavations at Jericho she rediscovered the strata first excavated by J. Garstang in the 1930s; they had all the Neolithic attributes—houses, stone axes, arrowheads, cereal cultivation, domesticated sheep and goats—with the exception of pottery. She therefore termed the period Pre-Pottery Neolithic and, on the basis of the stratigraphy at Jericho, distinguished an earlier and later phase, termed Pre-Pottery Neolithic A (PPNA) and Pre-Pottery Neolithic B (PPNB). The following period, the Pottery Neolithic, was similarly subdivided by Kenyon into two phases, PNA and PNB.

A different approach to archaeological terminology is represented by the anthropological-historical, or sociocultural method. Scholars who take this approach try to define a social unit on the basis of the archaeological assemblages. The method may be explained as follows: A given society may be identified according to residues of material culture at different sites (representing the year-round activity of that society). Beyond the varying frequencies of tool forms, installations, structures, and so on, a uniform style will be evident. The stylistic details characterizing this society will be observed in high frequencies within a geographic region. The history of the social group occupying a given territory, or at least the extent of a phase of its history, may be reconstructed with the aid of radiometric dating. This method suited the expectations of archaeologists who adapted an ethnographic approach. The attempt to identify a social unit—a people or tribe—in the archaeological record persists to this day.

A concrete application of this method to the Neolithic period may be seen in the definition of the Sultanian culture. The term was coined by Joan Crowfoot-Payne on the basis of flint tools found at the site of Jericho (Tell el-Sultan). As the term "Jerichoan" had already been proposed as the specific appellation for Pottery Neolithic assemblages at Jericho, Crowfoot-Payne preferred "Sultanian" as a generic term for all the PPNA assemblages uncovered in the region. From now on, all sites with a high frequency of axes, sickle blades, el-Khiam arrowheads, awls, borers, and a wealth of retouched blades or blades showing signs of utilization on their tips were to be attributed to the Sultanian culture.

The economic basis of the sites was also found to be identical—the raising of cereals and pulse and the hunting of wild animals—whether they were in Transjordan, the Jordan valley, or the plains and hill country of the Land of Israel. In desert regions (the Negev, Sinai, and the Syro-Arabian desert) other cultures conceivably used similar tools (identical arrowheads) but their pattern of settlement and subsistence was different. The Sultanian culture was thus an agricultural culture situated in zones of Mediterranean and Irano-Turanian vegetation.

Emergence of Farmer-Hunter Societies

Under the prevailing trends of Neolithic research, two kinds of terms are used to define the period in question. The first, based on chronological criteria, names the period Pre-Pottery Neolithic A. The second, in the attempt to define cultures (life-style and customs), defines archaeological assemblages as Khiamian and Sultanian. The Khiamian, which some scholars prefer to include in the PPNA, is a hunter-gatherer culture. The term "Sultanian" indicates a culture of hunter-farmers. Whereas the different groups identified in the Epipaleolithic period have an identical or similar economic base, cultural definitions used in Neolithic research comprehend the distinctive economic aspect of each group. Thus, we find hunter-gatherer cultures of the desert areas coexisting with the Sultanian, a farmer-hunter culture.

ENVIRONMENTAL CONDITIONS

Environmental data may be gathered directly by such means as palynological sections, by geo-

Table 2.1 Chronology and Terminology of the Neolithic Period.

C-14 dates BCE	Period	Cultures and their geographic distribution	Principal sites
8300	Pre-Pottery Neolithic A	Khiamian and Sultanian (north of Beersheba valley in Mediterranean Zone) Desert Khiamian (Sinai)	Salibiya IX, Jericho, Netiv Ha-Gdud, Gilgal, Gesher, Abu-Madi I
7300	Pre-Pottery Neolithic B	Tahunian (in Mediterranean Zone)	Jericho, Beisamun, Yiftahel, 'Ain-Ghazal, Munhata, Abu Ghosh, Beidha, N. Hemar
		Desert cultures, Negev and Sinai	Wadi Tbeiq, Ujrat el-Mehed, N. 'Issaron
6000/5800	Pottery Neolithic	Yarmukian (Sha'ar Ha-Golan and Munhata phases) in Mediterranean Zone Coastal cultures Negev and Sinai (unnamed)	Sha'ar Ha-Golan, Munhata, 'Ain Soda, 'Ain Ghazal, Tel Aviv, Herzliya, Nizzanim, Givat Ha-Parsa, Qatif, N. 'Issaron, Kadesh Barnea 3
5000/4800	Early Chalcolithic	Wadi Rabah (north of Beersheba valley)	Wadi Rabah, Teluliot Batashi, Tell Qiri

morphological research, or indirectly, through study of temperature
changes in other parts of the world,
changes in sea level charted for the
Atlantic Ocean, and so on.

The warming trend begun in the
ninth millennium B.C.E. continued
into the eighth millennium as well,
though the great glaciers had not yet
entirely melted and the coastline still
lay west of its present location (in
tectonically stable areas, the ancient
coastline is currently submerged
about thirty meters below sea level).
The flora of the Land of Israel, then
as now, was Mediterranean and
Irano-Turanian, but it appears that
rainfall patterns were more regular
than they are today. Furthermore,
though the quantity of precipitation
may not have been great, its even
distribution through the winter (and
perhaps summer) months encour-
aged the establishment of farming.

The location of early Neolithic
sites such as Jericho or Netiv Ha-
Gdud on alluvial fans near the out-
lets of wadis from the hills provides
evidence for changes in the flow of
these watercourses over time. The
mound of Netiv Ha-Gdud is a particularly good example because it is
directly opposite the mouth of a
wadi. From the abandonment of the
settlement (about 7200 B.C.E.) until
the present, the entire western slope
of the mound (facing the mountain
scarp) has been buried under a thick
layer of alluvium.

The success of an agricultural
economy, based on deliberate cultivation of cereals and pulse, shows
that environmental conditions promoted the emergence of large social
units, both in the Land of Israel and
in other parts of the Near East.

SITE DISTRIBUTION

A prevalent error in the available
literature lies in the attempt to draw
conclusions regarding the distribution of sites in prehistoric periods.

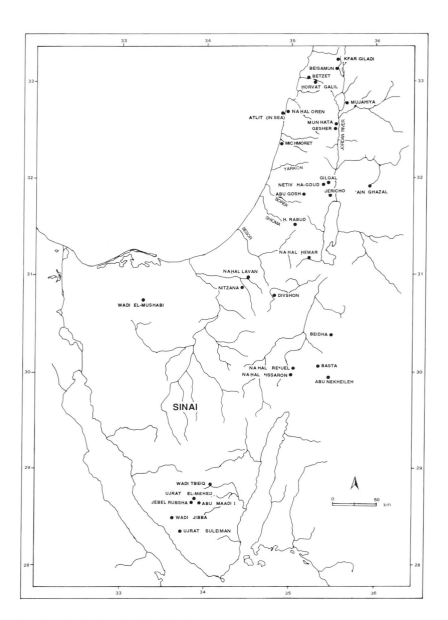

Map 2.1. Pre-Pottery Neolithic A-B sites

As Natufian sites are generally in
caves or areas not covered by alluvium, an impression is gained that
they are more numerous than sites
of later periods. In contrast, sites of
the Pre-Pottery Neolithic A in Israel
have not fared so well, and for many
years the only known sites of this
period were Jericho and Nahal Oren.
In recent years, the sites of Netiv
Ha-Gdud, Gilgal, and Gesher in the
Jordan valley and Hatula in the Ju-

daean hills have been discovered and
excavated. The evidence seems to
point to two possible explanations
for this phenomenon: one, that the
sites of this period formed the foundations for later villages and are thus
buried under the debris of mounds
such as Jericho; the other, that the
sites of this period are buried under
alluvial fans and terraces in Israel
and neighboring countries. The discovery in recent years of partly or
wholly buried Neolithic sites (such

as 'Ain Ghazal in Transjordan, Yiftahel and Beisamun in the Land of Israel) serves to show that distribution maps are as yet far from reflecting the reality of the Neolithic period.

The burial of important sites under alluvium could have occurred only because of a change in the economic structure of the settlement system. Although in more advanced periods there is no proof that plants were cultivated, the evidence so far published from the Jericho and Netiv Ha-Gdud excavations is sufficient to show the presence of an agricultural economy combining the cultivation of cereals and legumes. Alluvial fans or wadi terraces provided suitable locations for simple farming techniques, as they could easily be cleared of their natural vegetation. Yearly inundation assured the continued fertility of the soil, and the steady and well-distributed rainfall assured the success of the crops. This may explain why Neolithic agricultural villages were located in the lowlands.

A scatter of contemporary sites found in desert regions provides evidence for the continuance of hunting and food-gathering. Some of them may be considered seasonal encampments of agriculturalist hunting bands. Others, quite remote, which testify in their lithic assemblages to the continued existence of ancient flint knapping traditions, must have been connected with a different population group that carried on its desert subsistence strategies.

This dichotomy between the populations of the desert and the sown is more sharply outlined in the study of the following period (PPNB).

ARCHITECTURE

The domestic architecture of the period is known from excavations at Jericho (where building fragments

and only one complete house were cleared), Gilgal, Netiv Ha-Gdud, and Nahal Oren. The outline of the buildings ranges from circular to oval, with a diameter of 3–9 meters. The lower part of the structures was generally dug into the soil, and the wall foundations lined the excavated area. These foundations generally consist of stones or slabs reinforced with mortar, and occasionally of brick. In all cases the walls themselves were built of bricks or of mud applied to a framework of branches.

Well-preserved bricks from Jericho and Netiv Ha-Gdud resemble large loaves of bread—they have a plano-convex longitudinal and latitudinal cross-section. Their length is not fixed, ranging from 30 to 40 centimeters.

In and near the cleared structures, domestic installations have been found—hearths, stone slabs with cupmarks (usually one to four), and small storage installations (with a diameter and depth of 30–50 centimeters) usually made of stone slabs.

A range of thirteen structures has been excavated at Nahal Oren, covering 250 square meters. They range in area from 5 to 15 square meters (most being 7 to 10 square meters). A different picture has been obtained at Netiv Ha-Gdud, which may be assumed to represent the situation at the nearby site of Jericho, where similar building methods have been observed. The structures at the site may be divided into round and oval buildings. Preliminary excavation suggests that some were joined together, serving as rooms. The area of the small rooms ranges from 6 to 10 square meters and that of the larger ones from 20 to 30 square meters. While the small structures could have been roofed with a superstructure made of planks, branches, sticks, and hides, or with clay-covered mats, it would seem that the larger structures required

further support. Evidence for this has yet to be observed in the excavations, but it may be that internal wooden posts were set on stone slabs, which would be quite difficult to identify with certainty among the finds on the house floors.

The floors, as excavated in Jericho and Netiv Ha-Gdud, were plastered with clay or levigated mud. At times impressions of mats, laid upon the clay while it was still wet, have survived. Some of the floors were laid on a foundation of pebbles and stones, which prevented sinking and perhaps also helped keep the moisture out. At Nahal Oren the clay floors were not preserved, and the occupation levels were identified only by changes in soil color and the repeated presence of hearths accompanied by stone slabs with four cupmarks.

Though the relatively large size of the Neolithic sites bears testimony to the presence of at least a rudimentary level of social organization, direct evidence of joint communal effort is provided chiefly by the wall and tower of Jericho.

In Kenyon's 1952–58 excavations at Jericho, three major trenches were excavated. The western trench (Trench I) was the most important. A series of walls, or one wall reinforced several times, was discovered, and just inside it was a massive tower. Both wall and tower were built and abandoned within the Pre-Pottery Neolithic A period. Traces of this town wall—as Kenyon called it—were also discovered in the northern and southern trenches, but they consisted only of one or two foundation courses. The description of the Neolithic wall therefore centers on the finds of the western trench.

The first wall to be erected had a breadth of 1.8 meters at its base and 1.6 meters at the top and was preserved to a height of 3.65 meters. It was built of the fieldstones readily available around Jericho. A ditch 8 meters wide was excavated at the foot of the wall. As time wore on, the wall was repaired and reinforced several times, so that in its final stage it was 3.5 meters wide.

Inside the wall stood a tower 8.2 meters high. Its diameter was about 9 meters at the base and 7 meters at the top. It too was repaired during the PPNA, and an encasing wall was added linking it to the wall. Inside the tower was a staircase with twenty steps. The lower entrance to the staircase faced the settlement, and the stairs led to the roof of the tower.

This roof was somewhat damaged by erosive activity, which occurred after the PPNA. The tower too was built of fieldstones, and particular effort was invested in the staircase, especially in the cutting of the stone slabs that support its roof. No rooms were discovered inside the tower, and it is assumed that it was, in fact, solid. With time, debris collected around its base, and in one phase a structure was built in front of it, necessitating alterations in the entrance. Later, skeletons were laid in the staircase, indicating that it had gone out of use.

The continued accumulation of debris, of collapse, and of new structures finally reached the top of the tower, putting it out of use before the end of the period. The same fate overtook the wall. Layers of deposits (probably flood-borne) accumulated continuously outside the wall, until they began to overflow into the settlement; the wall was finally buried by the late PPNA. An erosive phase affecting the entire mound, dated roughly to 7300 B.C.E. (or somewhat later), had little effect on the wall and tower.

The presence of the wall and tower of Jericho led Kenyon to the conclusion that the site was a fortified town, and in consideration of its antiquity, Jericho earned the title "the oldest town in the world." Kenyon estimated the size of the site at 4 hectares and its population at 2000–3000 persons (the basis of her calculation was a survey of modern Arab villages). A revised estimate of the area of the mound indicates its size as only 2.5 hectares. Currently accepted population estimates, based on many years of research, mainly in Iran, range from 150 to 400 persons per hectare. Thus the revised population estimate of Jericho should be lowered to only 375 to 1000 inhabitants.

In addition, P. Dorrell has calculated that if Jericho was surrounded by a wall 600 meters long, 4 meters high, and 2 meters wide, only 1360 workdays of one builder (based on a rate of 3.3 cubic meters per day), or a week's work of 200 laborers, would have been required to construct it. Even if the wall had been 650 meters long (the maximum perimeter of 2.5 hectares), with the other dimensions the same as those estimated by Dorrell, only 1580 work days would have been required to build it. And even if the number

Fig. 2.1. Neolithic tower at Jericho

of men in Jericho were lower than estimated (one in four or five persons), such a wall could have been constructed at the rate estimated by 75 laborers, men and women, in 21 workdays. In short, though the communal effort should be valued as an important indicator of social development, it was not an enormous task requiring vast means (time and energy), considering the span of time under discussion.

As the wall and tower are, thus far, unique phenomena in the early Neolithic period, it may be questioned to what extent they were intended for defense against human adversaries. Who were the enemies of Jericho? Why wasn't the wall rebuilt after it ceased to function within the PPNA? Why have no traces been found of fortifications against a human enemy in any other site, including those of the following period? Why was the tower built inside the wall instead of as an exterior projection, as in all other known fortification systems, from the sixth millennium and on through the historical periods?

An alternative explanation for the function of the wall at Jericho is based on evidence from the site. In the northern trench, Kenyon found that the wall had been washed away by floods, which left a channel 15 meters wide. The source of the channel can be traced only to the ridge adjacent to Jericho, about half a kilometer away. The amount of runoff from this ridge is so small that it must be assumed that the channel is the result of a cloudburst or of extremely heavy rains.

As the site was erected on a moderate slope, descending from the western ridge to the valley floor, heavy water flow would have endangered the dwellings. The alluvial fans to the north and south of this ridge (Wadi Nu'eima and Wadi Dwek) come close to the site. It does not, however, appear that the current flood regime was characteristic of that period. In fact, the opposite may be true: the situation of Netiv Ha-Gdud in the mouth of a wadi indicates that the flow was comprised mainly of water and mud and not of large rocks and boulders. It may therefore be surmised that the wall was built to prevent the settlement from being submerged by water and mud.

This interpretation may be supported by viewing the settlement pattern in a broad perspective. The hunter-gatherer populations who continued to inhabit the Irano-Turanian and Saharo-Arabian vegetation zones (in the Negev, Sinai, and Syro-Arabian desert, and the margins of the Transjordanian plateau) were as yet untainted by intergroup rivalry, such as that which developed with the emergence of pastoral societies. The contrast between herders and farmers had not yet been born in the Pre-Pottery Neolithic A period. Agriculture, though allowing population growth and accumulation of food, had not yet become firmly established, and the inhabitants of Jericho resorted to the hunt to maintain their supply of animal fats and protein. In other words, the inhabitants of Jericho had no large groups of enemies, and there was therefore no need for fortifications of the type known from the sixth millennium and on. This explains why the wall was never rebuilt after it was buried under the debris: the mound of Jericho was by then high enough to afford protection for its houses from chance flooding.

A characteristic example of protection against erosion or flooding by mud or sand is provided by the finds of Diana Kirkbride's excavations at Beidha, near Petra in Transjordan. Though the site dates from the following period—the PPNB— it is, as a relatively large site, essentially similar to Jericho. Beidha, built on the banks of a wadi, had a protective wall 2 meters high built along the streambed. This terrace wall prevented the erosion of the natural sediments upon which the site was founded. In this case, there was no talk of a defense system, perhaps because of the early discovery of a stairway adjoining the outer face of the stone wall.

Finally, there remains the question of the function of the tower, which also went out of use before the end of the period. Its fine state of preservation seems to indicate, indirectly, that the staircase did not lead to an open platform but rather to a brick structure erected on top of the tower. Attached to the north side of the tower were deep, round structures accessible through apertures in their upper part. Kenyon interpreted these brick structures as water tanks, an odd conclusion in view of the proximity of a gushing spring, only a few dozen meters from the tower, which could have been included in the town wall's compass. Her suggestion that the structures served in the next phase of their existence as grain silos has not received support from the botanical finds, which were only randomly collected during the excavations. In any case, these structures again testify to the unique character of the tower, near which, in its first phase, no dwellings were constructed. It may therefore be surmised that the tower fulfilled some public-religious function.

BURIAL CUSTOMS

Many burials were cleared at Jericho (262 skeletons) and Netiv Ha-Gdud (about 25 skeletons), and a few more at the site of Nahal Oren. Common to all the burials is the practice of laying the bodies in a flexed or semiflexed position, in continuation of the ancient tradition attested in Natufian sites.

The principal innovation (which begins, apparently, in the Late Natufian) is the removal of the skull, usually without the lower jaw, from some of the adults buried at the site. A number of such skulls were found in secondary burials in structures or pits, the significance of which has not yet been sufficiently understood. Thus far, no plastered skulls, such as are characteristic of the following period, have been found, but the possibility of such finds in the future must not be discounted.

No grave goods were discovered in the vast majority of the burials, nor were there any headdresses and necklaces of the type frequently found in the Natufian burials. Isolated finds from some graves in Jericho include bone needles and points, which may have been used to fasten the clothes or cloth in which the dead were wrapped. Traces of matting were observed at Jericho, in both primary and secondary burials. The nature of the latter is not clear. Secondary burials of complete or fragmentary skeletons are known as early as the Natufian culture. The practice was continued in the Neolithic period. The need for sec-

ondary burials may be related to construction activity; skeletons discovered during the construction of a new building could have been moved to a different place within the settlement site. Many burials were found under floors, but it cannot be established in every case that the dead were indeed buried by the inhabitants under the floor of their house. The burials may have been originally in open areas between the houses, and only when a new house was built did they become, ex post facto, intramural burials. Only extremely careful excavation will enable the resolution of this question.

Anthropological study of the Jericho skeletons has shown that they belong to a local population termed proto-Mediterranean, closely related to the bearers of the Natufian culture. Another phenomenon observed at Jericho are the traces of partial skull deformation, inflicted during life. This indicates, at least in these cases, the practice of using head coverings (strips of cloth wrapped tightly around the head) among part of the Neolithic population. Evidence of the continuance of the custom has been found in skeletons of a later period from Byblos.

LITHIC ASSEMBLAGES

Two major phenomena characterize the flint tool industry of this period: in the agricultural areas, a distinct change in the knapping techniques of the primary elements (blades and flakes) and in the technique of tool preparation occurs, whereas in the desert regions, the Epipaleolithic tradition is carried on for several hundred years.

The change in techniques may be observed through the comparison of the Khiamian and Natufian assemblages. The first conspicuous difference is the significant drop in the number of microliths. Their proportion is reduced to about twenty percent of the entire flint tool industry, as opposed to about forty percent or more in the Natufian industry. This indicates a reduction in the production of bladelets, from which the microliths were fashioned, and a rise in the number of flint tools made of short blades.

The difference is even more conspicuous in the Sultanian culture. The Sultanian flint industry is presently known from the excavations of Jericho, Gilgal, and Netiv Ha-Gdud. Its basic components include blades,

Fig. 2.2. Pre-Pottery Neolithic flint tool assemblage: arrowheads (1–3), sickle blade (4), axe (5), chisel (6), and core (7)

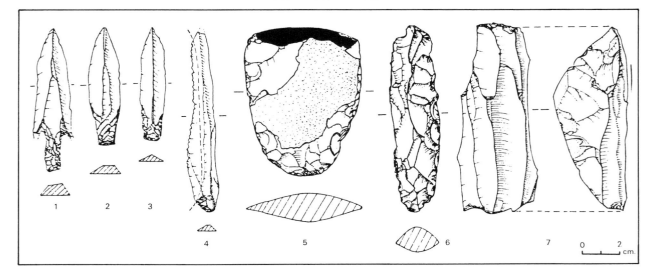

usually short, and a low frequency of bladelets. From the blades and bladelets, el-Khiam arrowheads, awls, and borers were fashioned. Medium and large blades were used to fashion sickle blades. One sickle-blade type had a back (the part inserted into the haft) formed by bifacial knapping (resembling the characteristic early Natufian Helwan retouch, only larger and broader). Traces of the asphalt used to affix the blade to the haft are sometimes present, and the cutting edge generally bears a sheen. This blade has been named the Beit Ta'amir knife, after the village near Bethlehem where it was first found.

Another important class of tools is that of the axe-adzes. These were shaped directly on flint chunks, by bifacial knapping, and take the form of an elongated oval. The pointed end was probably the one inserted in the haft. The broad end was formed by transversal blows, creating an efficient and useful cutting edge. These tools could be used both as axes or adzes. Their frequency in zones of Mediterranean and Irano-Turanian vegetation and preliminary results of microwear analyses show that they were used more for woodworking than for hoeing.

In conclusion, significant differences appear between the Natufian and Sultanian (PPNA) industries. Further changes are evidenced in site size and economic base. All these changes indicate that the beginning of agriculture took place in the arable areas (for example, the Jordan valley). The similarities between the two cultures, expressed in the round to oval house plans, show that the transition to agriculture did not have an immediate effect on the entire population of the Near East, but in a historical perspective, its effect was gradual.

ECONOMY

As noted, the Pre-Pottery Neolithic A saw a clear shift in the economic base of the societies inhabiting the arable zones. Instead of the limited exploitation of wild cereals, legumes, seeds, and fruits practiced in Natufian society, systematic cultivation of cereals and legumes was begun, alongside the continued gathering of wild plants. Hunting and fishing, which had made meat an important element in the Natufian diet, were pursued to a lesser extent in the PPNA.

The principal transformation occurred in the transition from food gathering and the exploitation of naturally occurring resources to plant cultivation. We must therefore, before detailing the archaeological record that allows us to draw a picture, if only fragmentary, of the emergence of agriculture, describe briefly the types of plants that were domesticated and their particular attributes.

CEREALS. Cereals are annual grasses that generally grow under oak cover or on the fringes of the Mediterranean forest. Wild barley, more resilient to cold and drought, may also be found on the desert margins. The nutritional value of cereals lies in their protein and carbohydrate content. Domestication effected few genetic changes in the cereals, but they were sufficient to do away with the main impediments to human use: the hard husks and the tendency of the ears to fall apart.

The cereals include barley, which is domesticated wild barley, and wheat, of which there are two types. The first is einkorn, which occurs in wild stands in southern Turkey and the Zagros flanks; the second is emmer wheat, found chiefly in the Land of Israel and Transjordan. Einkorn wheat was introduced quite early in the Land of Israel (PPNB)

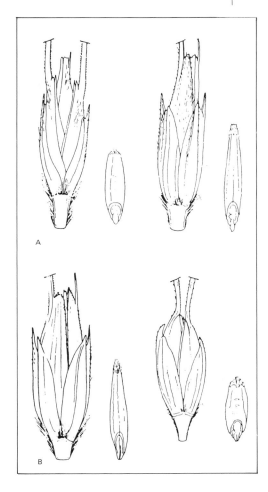

Fig. 2.3. Ears of wild einkorn and emmer wheat (A), and ears of domesticated einkorn and emmer wheat (B)

and was cultivated alongside domesticated emmer wheat.

The natural distribution of wild species is today influenced by two factors: the presence of cereal cultivation over the past ten thousand years and the considerable climatic change since the end of the Pleistocene. The distribution of the wild species cannot, therefore, be taken to indicate ancient centers of cereal domestication. Rather, direct archaeological evidence is required to identify them.

LEGUMES. Wild legumes have many advantages, which can explain why they became part of the human diet as early as the Palaeolithic period. Legumes ripen in March-April, about a month before the cereals. They do not all ripen at once, and edible pods may be found at the base of stalks still in flower. This means that one stand may be picked several times, so that its exploitation is increased. Legumes can be hand-picked, and after drying (if they are not eaten green), the pods open and the seeds can be easily collected and processed in various ways. The nutritional value of legumes is high, and they are especially rich in protein.

FRUIT TREES. There is little evidence for the domestication of fruit trees before the Chalcolithic period. It seems that only with the further progress of agriculture were trees domesticated as well, and the first orchards (whether vine, almond, or olive) cannot be identified in the archaeological record before 4000 B.C.E.

The archaeological evidence for the processes here briefly described is presently quite meager. At Netiv Ha-Gdud, Gilgal, and Jericho, domesticated barley and possibly wheat have been found. Similar discoveries have been made in the lower layers of the excavations at Tell Aswad (near Damascus), dated to the early eighth millennium B.C.E. Accompanying the cereals were lentils and peas, for as noted, legumes were probably among the first domesticated plants. The few botanical finds from pre-Neolithic sites do not include domesticated wheat or barley but rather legumes. It is therefore possible that legumes were domesticated before cereals.

The gathering of vegetable foods continued in the Neolithic period, particularly the gathering of wild barley and wild fruits—almonds, acorns, and figs. The picture is no doubt incomplete, as it is only in recent years that excavators have be-

come more meticulous, adopting special techniques for the retrieval of botanical remains.

The question of the proportion of vegetable food in the daily or yearly menu of the Neolithic inhabitants of these sites is a difficult one. Its difficulty lies not only in the scarcity of botanical remains but also in the interpretation of the faunal remains. Those found in Jericho allowed the generalized conclusion that the animals consumed by the inhabitants were wild, mainly gazelle, some boar, wild cattle, and fox. The presence of dogs in this period, with their predilection for gnawing bones, has resulted in the recovery of a small number of bones in the Jericho excavations, relative to the volume excavated. Furthermore, it is difficult to say—regarding the assemblage as a whole—whether the hunting activities were not performed in part by contemporary groups of hunter-gatherers living in the desert margins. At any rate, it may be stated with certainty that the first agriculturalists continued to hunt. The domestication of herd animals—sheep and goats—though occurring as early as the late eighth or early seventh millennium B.C.E., did not take place in the Levant but in the Zagros region (Iran). Only in the following period, the Pre-Pottery Neolithic B, do we find all the characteristic remains of the agricultural society as we know it today—cereals, legumes, sheep, and goats.

TRADE

Evidence for trade in this period is relatively slender. At Jericho, obsidian of central Anatolian provenance was discovered. Some greenstone beads, apparently from a source outside the Land of Israel, must have come by way of exchange. There is a clear hierarchy among the various excavated sites when the rel-

ative quantities of transported commodities are taken into account. Thus, Jericho is the richest site, followed by Netiv Ha-Gdud and Gilgal. Few seashells are in evidence at this time, with the exception of cowrie shells from the Red Sea. Because of its shape (oval, with a plano-convex cross-section and an aperture along the flat side bounded by two corrugated lips), it has been suggested that this shell represents the female sexual organ. It would thus reflect a facet of the development of the fertility cult, which is considered a characteristic of the Neolithic period.

ART

The art objects of the PPNA include only anthropomorphic figurines; animals are not represented at all. It should, however, be pointed out that in both the preceding Natufian culture and the following period, there are many more types of art objects; it is therefore likely that the finds are meager because of the limited extent of the excavations.

The figurines so far discovered are made of clay and chalk. The clay figurines from Jericho (both broken) depict, in one case, a woman's torso, of which the breasts have been preserved, and in the other part of the breast and neck of a figure whose sex is difficult to determine. At Netiv Ha-Gdud a seated female figurine with extended legs was found. The breasts and hips were fashioned in a naturalistic manner, while the face is shown in outline, with only the eyes marked. Two additional fragments of a similar figurine, in which only the outline of the eyes and part of the breast may be identified, probably represent the same seated female figure. Recently a standing female figurine wearing a string skirt was uncovered in Gilgal. European Palaeolithic figurines suggest that this dress was already known for generations and perhaps was mainly used in cultic activities.

A schematic female figure carved on a limestone pebble was discovered at Nahal Oren, and similar fragments have been found at el-Khiam terrace and at Tell Mureybet, on the Middle Euphrates. Another large stone figurine reminiscent of the female form (with a rounded and incised lower part, which appears to be in a crouching position), found on the slopes of the site of Gilgal, may be attributed to the period as well.

Establishment of Farmer-Pastoralist Villages

The archaeological data sets about this period are immeasurably greater than those accumulated for the previous period (PPNA) or the following one (the Pottery Neolithic). The reason is, quite simply, that a larger number of sites have been excavated, and the number of sites identified in surveys in various parts of the country, especially in the Negev and Sinai, is greater than in other periods. The proliferation of Pre-Pottery Neolithic B sites in arid zones is not surprising, as it has been established that the seventh millennium B.C.E. enjoyed ameliorated climatic conditions, expressed primarily in greater amounts of rainfall.

The archaeological record of this period provides a clear picture of what was going on in the different parts of the Near East. Excavations in Anatolia, Syria, and Jordan, as well as in northern and western Sinai, the western Negev, the Negev Highlands, the margins of the Aravah valley, and the northern regions of the Land of Israel, permit a regional-cultural reconstruction. Rapid modern development has made away with many sites, whether in the hills (near Bethlehem and Jerusalem) or the coastal plain. However, the many collections found in local and regional museums reveal the abundance, wealth, and distribution of the sites of this period.

In the last decade, detailed chronological information regarding the period has become available. A large number of sites, particularly in the south and in Sinai, have provided radiocarbon dates. An extensive report on the Jericho excavations has appeared, with tens of such dates. Concurrently, technotypological research describing the variations in tool forms has been carried out, particularly with regard to arrowheads formed on flint blades, and it seems that these variations have a fixed pattern. It has also been discovered that the Near East may be divided into a number of cultural zones in which differences in material culture and aspects of the economic and social structure may be observed. It is from this wealth of data that the picture presented in the following pages has been composed.

ENVIRONMENTAL CONDITIONS

Both direct and indirect data may contribute to the understanding of the extent of environmental change in this period. The palynological sequence obtained from the Hula valley and from the Ghab marshes in Syria indicates that the period was a moist one, during which the lakes expanded. For sites such as Tell Aswad and Tell Ghoraife, on the shores of the Hijana and 'Ataibeh lakes near Damascus, the annual inundation assured the success of the grain crops. Seasonal and even perennial lakes existed in parts of Arabia that are now arid in the extreme.

Another source of information are the deep-sea cores taken from the Mediterranean and Red Sea floors and dated radiometrically. They show that southern Sinai was watered by heavy rains, perhaps as a result of the penetration of the monsoon belt. Supporting evidence is provided by the discovery that heavy monsoon rains in Ethiopia increased the flow of the Nile, leading to a temporary reduction in the salinity of the Mediterranean Sea.

Geomorphological evidence attests to the continued accumulation of alluvium in the valleys. Sites such as Beisamun (in the Hula valley), Yiftahel (the lower Galilee), and Abu Gosh (in the Judaean hills) were buried under the alluvium. It is not improbable that deforestation and the burning of woodlands by humans sped up the erosive process.

SITE DISTRIBUTION

The sites of this period are scattered throughout all the regions of the Land of Israel, from the Galilee to the Negev, and from the Coastal Plain to the Jordan valley. A similar pattern of distribution is being revealed in Transjordan, and research in Sinai, though still in its infancy, points in the same direction.

The mere statement that sites are situated in all ecological zones does not mean that all were coexistent or that they all shared the same importance in terms of the size of the strata and the character of the remains. The creation of social stratification, as expressed in the variety of site sizes, began in the Pre-Pottery Neolithic A and received a further impetus in this period.

The largest sites so far discovered lie outside the Land of Israel. Abu Hureyra, on the Euphrates River in Syria, has an area of 12 hectares, similar to that of the site of 'Ain Ghazal near Amman. The largest sites in the Land of Israel are Beisamun (about 10 hectares) and Jericho and Yiftahel (2.5–4 hectares). Sites 0.2–0.5 hectares in size include Abu Gosh and Munhata, and sites such as El-Khiam Terrace, Nahal Oren, Kfar Giladi, and the sites of the Negev and Sinai occupy less than

1000 square meters (most range from 50 to 250 square meters). There seems to be a rather clear progression from north to south, paralleling the transition from areas of Mediterranean vegetation (of that time) to the steppe and desert zones.

A hierarchy of sites may also be found within the different regions of the Land of Israel. In the Hula valley, for example, there are large sites such as Beisamun alongside small ones such as Qat, En Ha-Shomer, Kfar Giladi, and others. A possible explanation may be that large central villages were formed, providing space not only for the largest number of people but also for the main economic and social activities. Within such a system of large and small villages, a simple system of government may emerge, characteristic of tribal chiefdoms.

The degree to which all the sites of the Mediterranean and Irano-Turanian zones were permanently inhabited is not easily determined. Though the crafts of building and making plaster floors testify to the investment of great effort, the possibility remains that for at least short periods, the inhabitants may have left what appear to be their permanent settlements to live in sites whose remains indicate transience. Such patterns of migration may appear when a part of the diet is obtained directly elsewhere and not by exchange. Winter migration with the flocks and the return to the permanent settlements during the harvest season is a phenomenon well attested to in later periods. The fact that sheep and goats were raised during this period requires that archaeologists investigate the possible existence of such a settlement pattern. Another pattern could have been based on the cultivation of cereals at a distance from the permanent sites, with a springtime or early summertime migration. This possibility too may be examined by searching excavations for corroborating evidence.

ARCHITECTURE

Most of the information on the types of houses and their manner of construction in or near the Land of Israel comes from the excavations of Beisamun, Munhata, Yiftahel, 'Ain Ghazal, Jericho, and Beidha. Farther north, in Anatolia or the Euphrates valley, there are many more remains, with entire domestic quarters cleared at some sites.

The architectural remains of the period are impressive, exhibiting a great investment of effort. Best known are the rectilinear houses, with their (usually) plastered floors. It appears that north of the Beer-sheba valley (and between Edom and the Damascus plateau), there extended the cultural sphere of permanent settlement sites with rectilinear houses. To the south (the Negev and Sinai) and east extended the world of hunter-gatherers, and perhaps early pastoralists, where the ancient building traditions survived and where houses and courtyards therefore preserved a circular or oval shape.

RECTILINEAR HOUSES. There is no doubt that the general trend of development in the Near East led from rounded structures, in the Epipaleolithic and early Neolithic, to square and rectilinear ones. This development characterizes those areas in which an agricultural economy became established, domesticated animals were added to the household (goats, sheep, and, later, cattle and pigs), and population increased. It has been proposed that the cause of this development lay in the need to add rooms for members of the extended family. Such additions are more easily constructed in rectilinear architecture and are more economical, in terms of space. Thus, in a relatively small area, space may be allotted to a large number of rooms.

PLANNING AND CONSTRUCTION OF THE HOUSES. In most houses wall foundations were built of fieldstones, and the superstructures of mudbrick or adobe. At Jericho, the bricks were usually loaf- or cigar-shaped and had rows of thumb impressions.

Another innovation accompanying the change in house plans was the plastering of the houses. The plaster was made by firing crushed limestone, pounding it, and mixing it with water and ash and sometimes with sand and gravel. The process of burning limestone required the gathering or simple quarrying of stone, the felling of trees, and the construction of kilns, activities that indicate group organization and some sort of social hierarchy. Clearly, the preparation of plaster floors required know-how and intensive effort. The introduction of this innovation, which often but not always replaced floors of beaten earth and perhaps indicated wealth, may have been intended to raise the level of hygiene in the settlement. A rise in the number of inhabitants at a site increases the frequency of infectious disease, such as dysentery. Such a problem never occurs among mobile hunter-gatherers, who simply move to another site when the first gets too dirty.

The lime-plaster floors discovered at Jericho, Yiftahel, Beisamun, Abu Gosh, 'Ain Ghazal, and elsewhere were sometimes colored red. The plaster often curves up the base of the walls, so that even when the walls themselves are not preserved, they can be located according to

Fig. 2.4. Pre-Pottery Neolithic B dwellings: Beidha (A), Beisamun (B), Yiftah'el (C), Nahal 'Issaron (D)

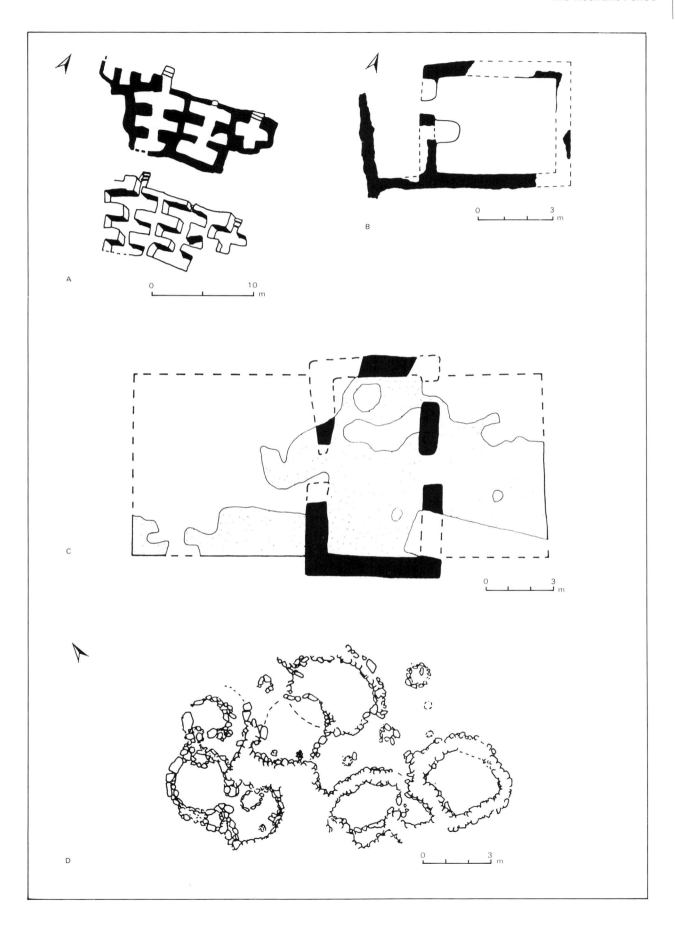

the floor edges. In most cases there were no finds abandoned on the floors (a recurring phenomenon at multilayered sites such as Bouqras), evidence that the houses were abandoned intentionally.

HOUSE PLANS. On the basis of the house remains found to date in the Land of Israel and in neighboring areas, the presence of several types of living quarters may be inferred. Thus, for example, some of the structures discovered at Jericho were longhouses composed of a series of rooms, with the entrances between them ranged along the long axis of the structure. Another example is the rectangular house at Beisamun, of which only the stone foundations remain. The discovery of two postholes for wood posts testifies to the roofing of the structure.

A different type of house was found recently at Yiftahel. It had two plastered and roofed courtyards flanking a rectangular broadroom with two entrances. In a corner of the room and in one of the courtyards there were found traces of plastered grain bins. At Beidha, so-called corridor houses were discovered. Two or three steps lead to an entrance and corridor sited on the long axis. Two cells flank the corridor on each side and a broadroom lies at the end of the building. All the cells (including the endmost) are of identical width (1–1.5 meters). The thickness of the walls permits us to assume that there was originally a second story. Finds on some of the cell floors led the excavator of the site, Diana Kirkbride, to conclude that they were used as workshops, for tanning leather, preparing bone tools, and other tasks. But it is also possible that the ground floor contained only storerooms, while domestic activities took place on the second floor.

These fragmentary descriptions

of dwellings testify to the lack of a site in which the preservation of buildings and the extent of excavation have been sufficient to provide a clearer picture of the internal organization of the Neolithic village. It is therefore not surprising that there is little information at hand about communal construction efforts or central structures. The terrace wall at Jericho may be taken as such a communal effort. It is two meters high, intended to permit the construction of houses both above and below it; at one time it was thought to be a defense wall. Another wall erected some distance away, to the west, as the settlement grew in size, also served as a terrace support wall. A similar construction was found at Beidha, where a terrace wall was cleared for a length of about fifty meters (its entire extent is unknown). A stairway near structures interpreted by the excavator as cultic leads down the face of the wall and outside the settlement.

Another building found within the settlement of Beidha, in the same stratum as the corridor houses, is a large structure with a central room (9 × 7 meters). The floor of the room is plastered, and a plastered hearth was built in its center. Near the hearth, not far from the entrance, was a stone table slab set in the floor. A band of red paint bordered the floor, decorated the hearth and stone table, and marked the place of a silo or underground storage pit. Along two of this building's walls was a broad corridor with two entrances. The corridor was also paved with plaster. The marked difference between this structure and the corridor buildings found nearby suggests an unusual but so far unknown function.

Cultic structures were identified at Jericho as well. First among them is the megaron (stratum VII) uncovered by Garstang. The outstanding feature of this structure is the

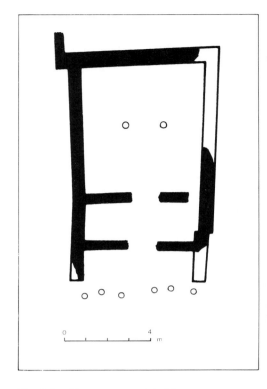

Fig. 2.5. The megaron at Jericho

facade of wooden pillars reconstructed by the excavator. Nearby, fragments of human statues modeled in lime plaster were found. Their discovery moved Garstang to interpret the building as a shrine. A similar rectangular structure was uncovered by Kenyon at the same site. A niche in one of its short walls contained a monolithic pillar, about forty centimeters high, made of bituminous limestone of the type found in the Judaean desert. A similar discovery of a stone pillar, or stela, set in a niche has been reported by J. Perrot from his excavations at Munhata.

For the present, these finds may be considered to convey a promise of surprises yet in store. The recent discoveries at 'Ain Ghazal reveal that sites where objects of unfired clay, modeled in lime plaster and organic materials, have been preserved may yet cast new light upon the spiritual life of Neolithic people.

An important question, in terms

of both the history of research and the discussion of structures and architecture of this period, is that of the origins of the population. The marked difference between the house plans of the Pre-Pottery Neolithic A and B, the invention of plaster floors, and the difference in the lithic assemblage of the two periods led Kenyon to the conclusion that the people of the PPNB represent a new settlement wave, with origins in the northern Levant. However, anthropological analyses have shown no differences between skeletons from Jericho in the PPNA and PPNB. Furthermore, there is hardly any difference between the human types of the Natufian and the Neolithic periods. The minor differences (which may indeed have been important, but their significance cannot be estimated) are reflected in the build, with the Natufian population showing more gracile characteristics in relation to the Neolithic folk. Both populations, however, belong to the same proto-Mediterranean group.

A further objection to Kenyon's proposal was raised during the analysis of the finds from Beidha. The Beidha excavations revealed a most interesting stratigraphic sequence. In the earlier levels (VI–IV) buildings were round, oval, or polygonal. They were built of sandstone slabs, and in some cases traces remained of wall supports (in preparation for roofing), consisting of wooden posts placed at fixed intervals. It was the use of these posts in construction that gave the structures their polygonal outline. In the upper layers (III–I) the buildings, including the corridor houses, were generally rectangular or square. The change, according to carbon-14 dates, took place during the first half of the seventh millennium B.C.E.

Detailed analyses carried out P. Mortensen on the rich flint assemblages from Beidha showed that there was no essential difference between the earlier and later levels. This means that the change in the shape of the structures does not indicate settlers of a different origin but rather a change adopted by the local population. Beidha, which lies 150 kilometers south of Jericho, provides an insight into the pace of the diffusion of knowledge, or the rate of cultural influence. Similar rectangular structures may be found at the sites of 'Ain Ghazal, also about 160 kilometers from Beidha, and Abu Gosh.

Another difficulty Kenyon had to contend with was the abandonment of Jericho for hundreds of years, a puzzling situation in view of the copious spring and the agricultural potential in that oasis. The archaeological record has shown that no Neolithic settlement was spared a period of abandonment, and indeed, an agricultural system based on continued single-crop cultivation in nonmanured fields may exhaust the soil and cause salinization. The low density of settlement characterizing the southern Levant in this period enabled the inhabitants of Jericho to move on to another spot and establish a new settlement there.

BURIAL CUSTOMS

Excavations at Jericho, Abu Gosh, Beisamun, Nahal Oren, and elsewhere have shown that there were no changes in the burial customs between the PPNA and PPNB periods. Graves were found between the houses, in abandoned structures, or under the floors (probably by chance, the house having been built later above the grave). There are both individual interments and communal graves containing the remains of several skeletons. The corpse was usually placed on its side, in a flexed position. In a number of adult burials, the head was removed. A small number of modeled skulls, with the features fashioned in plaster, have been found at Jericho, Beisamun, Tell Ramad, and 'Ain Ghazal. Elsewhere, groups of adult skulls were discovered on house floors (Jericho, 'Ain Ghazal). These testify to a certain pattern of behavior that will be discussed presently.

Little is known of the life expectancy of the people of this period. The finds at Jericho indicate that more than half of the deceased were under the age of twenty. Among the adults, however, there were some long-lived individuals (over fifty years). Generally speaking, the health of the Neolithic population was good, in relation to later periods, and not drastically different from that of the hunter-gatherer populations.

LITHIC ASSEMBLAGES

The technology of flint knapping during this period is distinctive. Out of natural flint nodules, Neolithic craftsmen produced cores with two parallel striking platforms. In this manner it was possible to produce by direct blows, using a hammer, or indirect blows, using hammer and punch, flint blades from both sides of the core. The advantage of this technique lay in the production of blades with a straight, though not particularly long, profile; that is, when viewed from one side, they appear to have one long flank. Some of the produced blades were heat treated.

From the many blades struck off the cores, craftsmen fashioned sickle blades, arrowheads, awls and borers, burins, endscrapers, denticulated blades (saw-edged), and other artifacts. Many blades were used as tools without altering their basic form. Their use left its traces in the form of retouch on one or two sides or even in the form of wear and slight polish clearly visible to the naked eye.

This production technique characterizes the Pre-Pottery Neolithic B period in an area extending from the Euphrates to southern Sinai, and from the Mediterranean shores to the heart of the Arabian Peninsula. The technique remained in use at least until the end of the seventh millennium in most places and in some areas into the first half of the sixth millennium B.C.E.

Among the most frequent forms are arrowheads, awls, and borers. Arrowheads (up to 5 centimeters in length) had to be straight. Their length and weight, amounting to a few grams, required a long shaft and a powerful bow. Arrowheads, used primarily for hunting, often served after breakage as knives, burins, or scraping implements. Awls and borers were used to fashion stone beads and pendants, as well as to bore holes in small stone artifacts, hides, reeds, and wooden objects. Some of them were obsolete sickle blades or arrowheads readapted for use as borers.

Another tool that had to be straight was the reaping knife, fitted in a wooden haft. Both blade edges were used in the reaping of cane, reeds, or even grain. As the task of reaping or cutting the cane and reeds (or other fibers) grew easier, fine denticulation was applied to one of the edges. The shorter sickle blades were sometimes fitted in crescent-shaped hafts, as attested by the whole sickle found at Nahal Hemar cave.

Other flint tools include the axe-adze group. The most common axe-adze of the Pre-Pottery Neolithic B had an elongated almond shape, and its cutting edge was formed by transversal blows. This type gave way toward the end of the seventh millennium B.C.E. to a bifacial axe-adze formed in the usual manner. These were sometimes polished, using sand and water, thus improving the effectiveness of the tool. The

cutting edge could be repolished when it was damaged. Polishing was not an innovation of this period, as polished axes appear already in the Pre-Pottery Neolithic A.

Axes and sickle blades are not found in every Neolithic site. They appear, as may be expected, in places where they could be used for clearing undergrowth, producing wooden artifacts, or reaping grain or cane. This means that they are frequent in areas of Mediterranean or Irano-Turanian vegetation: the Galilee, the valleys, and even in the western Negev and Negev Highlands.

The artifact shared by all Neolithic assemblages is the arrowhead. Typological studies covering thousands of arrowheads have revealed that changes in form can be observed in the course of the period.

Important changes occurred at this time in the stone tools used for processing grain. Grinding bowls became flat, oval, and sometimes stepped. In the latter type, flour could be accumulated on the lower step as the grain was ground. The grindstones took on the shape of bread loaves, characterized by a plano-convex cross-section. The use of mortars and pestles continued but to a much lesser extent than in the previous period.

WHITE WARE AND THE APPEARANCE OF POTTERY

The term "white ware" is used to describe vessels resembling simple pottery types—bowls, cups, and footed bowls. They give the impression of being made of soft limestone, but in fact they contain a mixture of lime and ash. Vessels of this type, both whole and fragmentary, have been discovered at many sites in southeast Anatolia, Syria, Lebanon, and Jordan, sites dated to the late seventh and early sixth millennium B.C.E., the late Pre-Pottery

Neolithic period. A few fragments have been found in the Land of Israel, in the Hula and Jordan valleys. The main distribution area of white ware seems to be limited to Syria, Lebanon, and part of Jordan.

At about this time, the first pottery was being produced; the sites of Bouqras on the Euphrates and later Umm Dabaghiyah in northern Mesopotamia furnish some of the earliest specimens. The question of which came first, the production of white ware or of pottery, cannot be answered without further excavations and radiocarbon dates. Experimenting with clay vessel production began as early as the eighth millennium B.C.E., as evidenced by isolated finds from Tell Mureybet, in the Euphrates valley. However, only in the final centuries of the seventh millennium B.C.E. did the use of fired, and therefore durable, vessels become widespread, for example in Bouqras. Remnants of such vessels are abundant at sites of the period, but the interpretation of cultural phenomena such as pottery production cannot rely on the chance discovery of a few artifacts or the mere utilization of clay.

OBJECTS MADE OF ORGANIC MATERIALS

The heading may be somewhat misleading, as bones are organic, and bone tools are present, though few in number, in all periods and sites. What is here referred to are the other, exceptional finds not often discovered in excavations, though their existence may be assumed. The mat impressions found on the floors of Neolithic Jericho, the traces of cane matting on other floors, and the wooden boxes, textiles, and threads found in Anatolia may be taken as a hint of the discoveries that lie ahead in the Land of Israel.

A chance discovery of this kind

was made at the small cave of Nahal Hemar, about ten kilometers southwest of the Dead Sea, apparently used as a storeroom for a considerable length of time during the seventh millennium B.C.E. Remains of at least four archaeological layers were discerned in the cave. In the earliest phase a complete sickle bearing three blades affixed with asphalt was found, as well as a conical knotted headdress of linen threads, known to have been domesticated at this time. The other levels provided an abundance of twined plant fibers and grain stalks. Wooden beads were carved of rootstocks of monocotyledonous plants, and arrowheads were fashioned in wood. Fragments of mats and basket bottoms were found, as well as round containers made of rope lined with asphalt and simply woven cloth napkins. There is little evidence of the use of looms of the type known in later periods.

Alongside these rare artifacts, which testify to various methods of twining rope and thread made of various plant fibers, as well as to the use of asphalt, to woodcarving, and to the utilization of various kinds of wood (including a type of tamarisk apparently brought from Transjordan) for the manufacture of arrows and other implements, further tools and objects were found. They included, in brief, a cache of bone tools including spatulas, flint arrowheads, a special type of knife, a stone mask, and skulls molded in asphalt.

ECONOMY

What is known of the economic base of this period is a direct result of the methods of recovery of animal bones and plant remains practiced in each excavation. The picture is therefore skewed, at present. In the older excavations, such as Jericho, mostly bones were recovered,

though deposits were not regularly sifted. On the other hand, in the Beidha excavations the participation of H. Halbeek, one of the pioneers of paleobotanical research in the Near East, led to an abundance of data about the botanical remains from that site.

In general, the period may be characterized as having a diverse economy: wild game was hunted in accordance with the local environment or obtained from hunter-gatherer groups; herd animals (sheep and goats), introduced into the Levant by the end of the eighth millennium B.C.E., were slaughtered; fruit and other plants were gathered; and cereals and legumes were cultivated.

DOMESTICATED ANIMALS

SHEEP. The origin of the domesticated sheep (*Ovis aries*) is in the wild sheep (*Ovis orientalis*), still to be found in the rolling highlands of southwestern Asia. Wild sheep is encountered extremely rarely in the bone assemblages in sites of Syria, Lebanon, and the Land of Israel during the Epipaleolithic era (about 17000 to 8500 B.C.E.). It is therefore clear that the presence of sheep bones in some Pre-Pottery Neolithic B sites in the Levant must be the result of the later introduction of sheep into the region, following their domestication elsewhere.

In two sites of the Zagros and Taurus zones (northwestern Iran and southeastern Turkey) dated to 9000–8500 B.C.E., a large proportion of bones of young sheep was found. This proportion has been interpreted, according to the principles of this field of research, as signifying control of the herd and is thus seen as the earliest proof of domestication.

GOATS. The domestic goat (*Capra hircus*) originates in the wild goat (*Capra aegageus*), whose geo-

graphical distribution is somewhat similar to that of wild sheep. In Syria and Lebanon many goat bones have been identified in Paleolithic strata, though only a few have been found in the Land of Israel. Hence, hypothetically at least, goats could have been domesticated in the Land of Israel or in nearby regions. Clear archaeological evidence for the domestication of the goat, however, is to be found once more in Iran and Turkey, where it is dated around 7000 B.C.E. or somewhat earlier. Sometime after 7000 B.C.E. there is clear evidence from Jericho, and lately from 'Ain Ghazal, with the proportion of sheep and goat bones exceeding fifty percent of all bones collected at the sites.

It may be suggested that goat domestication occurred simultaneously over the entire region stretching from Iran to the Land of Israel. However, insofar as a close acquaintance with the animal to be domesticated must precede domestication, the process may be attributed only to the northern Levant but more particularly to the Zagros and Taurus regions.

CATTLE. It is not known how wild cattle (*Bos primigenus*) were domesticated, as this large animal is known for its aggressivity. Interestingly enough, the earliest domestic cattle have been found in Greece and Turkey, at sites dated to about 6200–5800 B.C.E. The cattle were identified as domesticates on the basis of two criteria: they were smaller than wild cattle, and over fifty percent of the bone assemblage came from young individuals.

Domesticated cattle (*Bos taurus*) found their way into the Near East a few hundred years later, according to finds from Anatolia and Khuzistan (southwestern Iran). Frequent occurrence of domesticated cattle is reported from many sites only toward the end of the fifth millennium, but the evidence of milking comes from Mesopotamia and Egypt not earlier than the fourth millennium.

It is widely acknowledged that the domestication of cattle occurred only after people had gained experience in domesticating sheep and goats. The main impetus for domestication seems to have been connected with ritual and religious belief, in consequence of the intense adoration accorded to cattle. Evidence for this adoration are the clay bucrania, crowned with real horns, found at Çatal Hüyük in Anatolia.

PIGS. The domestication of the pig (*Sus scrofa*) is attested to in areas north of the Land of Israel. The earliest evidence comes from the Pottery Neolithic layers at Jarmo (Kurdistan) of the late seventh millennium. Domestication reduces the length of the pig's jaws, as revealed in bone deposits from a site on the Zagros fringes of the sixth and fifth millennia. In the Amuq valley and the Lebanese Beqa', evidence has been revealed of the raising of pigs beginning in the sixth millennium. It is currently thought that the first centers of domestication were in southeast Europe, Anatolia, and the northern Zagros (Kurdistan).

In contrast to herds of sheep, goats, and cattle, which can migrate and graze seasonally in varied topographical zones of hill and valley, the domestic pig cannot travel far. It therefore appears that the societies that preferred the domestication and raising of flocks were not the first to domesticate pig.

In the Land of Israel there are few clear attestations of pig breeding, and though bones of the domestic pig have been found in the Pottery Neolithic period (Sha'ar Ha-Golan), it seems that it was only during the Chalcolithic period that

this occupation became routine in the sedentary villages.

TRADE

During the eighth and especially the seventh millennium, the foundations were laid for the developed trade network that characterizes later periods. Trade and barter among agricultural societies, including pastoralists, or between such societies and groups of hunter-gatherers involve the enhancement of social ties but essentially respond to dietary needs. In this sense, barter differs from gift-giving mainly in the amount exchanged, and to some extent in the nature of the goods, as well as in the radius of their geographical distribution. It may be assumed that the barter of this period involved basically the exchange of food and everyday items, made mainly of perishable materials, as well as precious commodities. Groups of hunter-gatherers could supply agriculturalists with hunted meat, plants, and fruits of desert plants (from which simple medicines could be made) and could receive in return grains and household artifacts, such as linen cloth, difficult to manufacture in arid zones. Among agricultural societies, various food products could be exchanged, along with household items, nonperishables (grinding tools, arrowheads), and decorative objects (stone pendants, seashells). As organic objects generally leave no trace, we cannot determine with certainty what the bartered objects were that were made of these materials.

Counted among the products that traveled great distances are obsidian, asphalt, greenstone, and salt. Obsidian is the item most commonly found. Provenance studies, based on the analysis of radioactive minerals in this material, have clearly indicated eastern

Anatolia as the prime source for the obsidian objects found in the Land of Israel and Transjordan.

One indication of the exchange of agricultural products is the wide distribution in the Land of Israel of einkorn wheat, which originated in Anatolia, northern Syria, and the margins of the Zagros.

The introduction of sheep and goats provides further evidence of relations with the northern Levant. From the region of domestication in Zagros, these animals spread first to the Levantine interior (Syria, Lebanon, Transjordan, and the Land of Israel) and later to Anatolia. Cattle could also have been domesticated in the Levant, but the clearest evidence for their domestication comes from Anatolia and Greece. It is therefore quite possible that cattle too were introduced into the Levant from the north.

The existence of interrelations over a wide geographical expanse is also reflected in the diffusion of arrowhead and sickle-blade forms. In this manner, it is possible to distinguish cultural zones—Sinai and southern Transjordan, the central regions of the Land of Israel, northern Syria—and at the same time to observe the presence of shared archaeological characteristics.

ART AND CULT

We have already mentioned in this regard the possible small shrines or cult places discovered at Beidha, Jericho, and apparently at 'Ain Ghazal, and Tell Ramad as well. The picture cannot be said to be conclusive, because of the narrow scope of excavations. Yet it is not unlikely that cult was practiced mainly within the extended family or clan, so that it would be reflected more in the realm of small finds than in public architecture.

Evidence should be forthcoming of the existence of cult or public ritual. In a village society that has developed a social hierarchy, religious ritual is considered one of the institutions that preserve the social fabric. Even if the cult was expressed only by public rituals enacted in an empty plaza, this plaza can be discovered in excavations. The identification of remains of household cults and the uncovering of a series of shrines at Çatal Hüyük or the discovery of caches of lime-plaster statues at Jericho and 'Ain Ghazal hint toward further discoveries that may still lie ahead.

It is generally considered that anthropomorphic and zoomorphic figurines, made of clay, bone, or stone, constitute religiously motivated art. Schematic male and female figurines have been found at Jericho, Munhata, Beidha, Nahal Hemar cave, 'Ain Ghazal, and elsewhere. It may be said that in most cases the emphasis is on the portrayal of women, and it has thus been the tendency of scholars to interpret such figurines as cult objects accompanying the worship of the mother goddess. It should, however, be emphasized that other interpretations are certainly feasible. For example, ethnographic research has shown that such figurines may have been used as teaching aids for women introducing their daughters to the mysteries of life.

Clearer cultic significance is present in the lime-plaster statues found first at Jericho and recently, in a better state of preservation, at 'Ain Ghazal. These statues come in a variety of shapes and sizes, some fashioned as busts, others reaching full length, down to the feet. The statues were fashioned on a reed frame. The similarity between their form and the story of the creation of man as told in the Sumerian myth Enki and Ninmah or in the Babylo-nian creation myth Enuma Elish reveals that the complex world of beliefs known from later periods had its roots in Neolithic societies. They were the foundation on which the civilizations of the fourth and third millennia grew and the well-spring that nourished them.

Among the statues of 'Ain Ghazal, portraits of men, women, and children may be discerned. The face and body were painted in green (probably ground malachite), red (ocher), and black. The eyes were inlaid with shells from the Mediterranean or Red Sea, as were some of the modeled skulls. Preliminary reports indicate that the statues belong to the same cultural milieu as the Jericho statue fragments. For exam-

Fig. 2.6. Clay figurine from Munhata (height 3.6 centimeters)

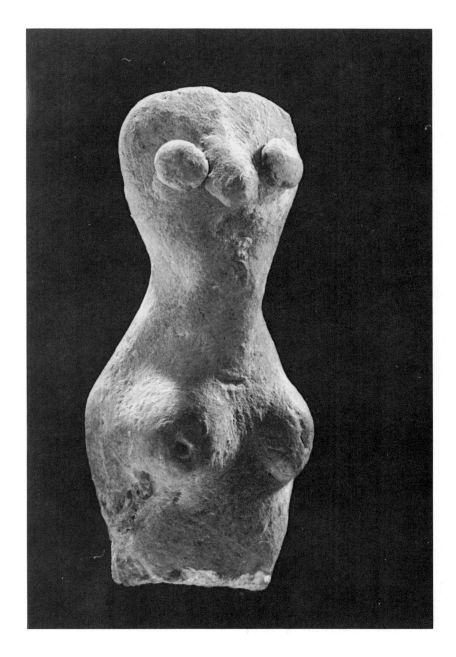

ple, in both sites a six-toed foot was discovered. Remains of a similar statue have also been recently found at Nahal Hemar. This resemblance of finds seems to indicate the existence of a uniform Neolithic culture, ranging perhaps as far as the Damascus plateau, with a developed system of beliefs. It is possible that at this early stage of social development, the cult centered around a group of deities.

Modeled skulls, either in asphalt such as those from the Nahal Hemar cave or in lime plaster, have been discovered at Jericho, 'Ain Ghazal, Beisamun, and Tell Ramad. They are all adult skulls, usually lacking the lower jaw, to which plaster modeled in the form of human features has been applied. The plaster usually covers only the face and the lower part of the skull, the base of which is flattened or slightly arched. The eyes are often inlaid with shells, cowrie or dog-cockle. The skulls

were found in deposits, though it is not clear whether these were sacred places or mere storage deposits. At Tell Ramad, clay pedestals were found on which the skulls could be placed. The skulls from Nahal Hemar cave are exceptional. Judging by its contents (a small, dark chamber full of boulders and crammed with objects of wood, straw, linen, bone, and flint), the cave served as a storeroom in the Neolithic period. Six skulls were found, each covered with asphalt. The covering was applied in two layers: the skull was first coated in asphalt, then a net pattern was fashioned by applying cords of asphalt to the first layer.

Modeled skulls are commonly thought to represent ancestor worship. Those skulls that were analyzed generally proved to belong mainly to adult (over the age of twenty) males. It may be that in a Neolithic society, which carefully nurtured familial ties even as social hierarchy developed, there was a place for an ancestor or hero cult.

Further objects possibly related to this cult are stone masks. They were first discovered in the southern Hebron hills, and they were attributed to the Neolithic period on stylistic grounds. At Nahal Hemar, a complete stone mask was discovered, with apertures for the eyes, nose, and mouth. The forehead is striped vertically, and the cheeks diagonally, with green, black, and red paint. There are eighteen perforations along the edge of the mask, intended perhaps for lacing, as well as traces of asphalt coating with hairs attached. It is difficult to imagine how such a heavy mask could have been worn, and it was perhaps carried as a standard or attached to one of the modeled skulls—but the power of belief knows no limits.

The similarity between the masks and the style of the facial features on the plaster statues, the clay figu-

Fig. 2.7. Head of clay figurine from Jericho (height 22.5 centimeters)

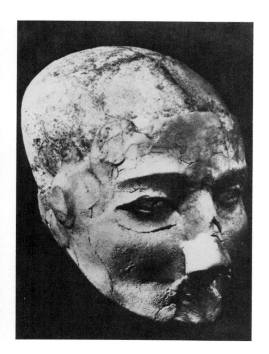

Fig. 2.8. Modeled skull from Jericho (height approx. 20 centimeters)

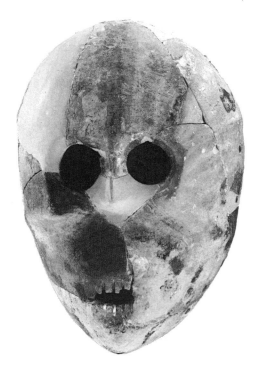

Fig. 2.9. Stone mask from Nahal Hemar (height 26.5 centimeters)

rines, and particularly the modeled skulls should be emphasized. The presence of stone masks should be taken to indicate the possible existence of masks made of organic materials. Together they testify to the practice of public rituals in which these objects were used.

Out of the various archaeological interpretations of sacred place, storeroom, or sacred deposit of cult objects, the latter two possibilities seem the more likely in the cases so far studied, especially when the archaeological context of the objects from the Land of Israel is compared with the shrines of Çatal Hüyük in Anatolia. Only the discovery of cult objects in situ (preserved by a collapse or destruction by fire) can provide a clear example of a Neolithic shrine.

The Pottery Neolithic Period

The period known as the Pottery Neolithic is, without doubt, one of the lesser-known periods in the Land of Israel. In contrast to the abundance of information about this time coming from northern Mesopotamia, Syria, and Anatolia, our knowledge of the southern Levant is fragmentary. From the outset, little effort was directed to the recovery and interpretation of remains of this period. The study of the Neolithic period as a whole was conducted by two groups of scholars. One group belonged to the Paleolithic school, or in other words, they were students of earlier periods, for whom the Neolithic was the extreme later limit of their interest. Their excavations at Neolithic sites, however, were generally conducted on the most rigorous standards. The second group included scholars whose primary interest lay in early cultures, chiefly of the Bronze Age or the Chalcolithic period, at the earliest. Their excavations were conducted according to standards

prevalent in the excavation of mounds. It was in this manner that Kenyon reached, rather by chance, the Neolithic strata at Jericho. There have been few scholars whose interest has centered on the Neolithic period and its margins. The unavoidable result has been that Neolithic sites or strata have been exposed in a fragmentary manner or have been reached in small areas at the base of the large mounds.

Another element in the scarcity of information is the want of carbon-14 dates from this period. This too is the result of the selectivity of the work of the various excavators. Those who reached strata or pits of this period preferred to rely on pottery typology to date its phases. Others were not especially interested in precise dating. Consequently, the number of radiocarbon dates from this period is minute when compared either with earlier (Epipaleolithic, Pre-Pottery Neolithic) or with later (Chalcolithic and Early Bronze Age) periods.

Part of the blame for the fragmentary data may be placed on the character of the remains themselves. There was undoubtedly a marked change in the settlement pattern, in terms of the location of the sites and their internal organization. The change in location means that few of the stratified sites excavated have revealed remains of the period, much less a full stratigraphic sequence. At the same time, many of the Pottery Neolithic sites are single-culture sites; that is, there are no further remains above or below them.

The architectural features of the sites further complicate the picture. Most of the remains consist of pits of various types: house pits, storage pits, or pits dug while excavating for clay, which were soon filled naturally or by occupation debris. Where such pits were excavated in virgin soil, it is not difficult to trace their outline and distinguish their content. But when they were excavated into mound deposits, as in Jericho, their backfilling caused the mixing of finds of several periods, and the problem of distinguishing between Pottery Neolithic and older objects became most complex. Needless to say, the continued reexcavation and overlapping of such pits increase the confusion.

A final difficulty lies in the determination of relative age on the basis of changes in shape and decoration of pottery vessels. In later periods, characterized by a combined chronological base (based on inscriptions, comparisons with Egypt, and an accumulation of identical or similar typological sequences), pottery can usually be used as a good criterion for dating a given stratum. However, an attempt to apply such a criterion to the Pottery Neolithic, without independent control over the results, may lead to many errors. Furthermore, the early stages in pottery production seem to have been based on independent manufacture in each household at each site, as it may be assumed that the fragile products did not achieve a wide distribution. One must therefore not draw hasty conclusions about intersite relations only on the basis of similar forms, as these are the most natural forms, imitating hide vessels, baskets, stone containers, or gourds. Thus, the presence of shared ceramic forms throughout the Near East should not surprise us. Nevertheless, a resemblance in decoration, such as the herringbone pattern, may be considered a result of information flow within a region or between regions. All of the above does not come to suggest that formal similarity should be ignored, but only that it should be treated with caution and

that hasty conclusions should be avoided.

One archaeological unit that has been clearly identified is that termed the Yarmukian culture. It was first defined by M. Stekelis, following his excavations at Sha'ar Ha-Golan. The diverse finds, including an abundance of flint tools, pottery sherds, stone and clay figurines, and traces of dwellings, formed the basis for his definition. Since then other sites have been discovered, and at one of them, the site of Munhata about four kilometers southwest of Sha'ar Ha-Golan, a similar archaeological assemblage was found. Isolated finds and surveys have shown that sites of this culture are distributed over the eastern Jezreel valley, the middle Jordan valley, and perhaps even beyond. Considerable resemblance between the finds of Byblos, on the Lebanese coast, and those of Sha'ar Ha-Golan shows that the Lebanon and Galilee, the Jezreel and Beth Shean valleys, and part of Transjordan (a territory about 250 kilometers in diameter) may have constituted one cultural zone.

In conclusion, the lack of clear stratigraphic sequences that might provide precisely dated pottery, the scarcity of radiocarbon dates, the limited areas of excavation, and the flimsy character of the remains discovered do not exclude a chronological subdivision on the basis of the flint tools, which were still produced in quantity.

CLIMATIC CHANGE AND ENVIRONMENTAL CONDITIONS

The data accumulated so far in the Near East, supplied by boreholes from lakes in the Near East and geomorphological evidence from the Nile valley, indicate that a relatively sharp climatic change took place at the beginning of the sixth millennium B.C.E. It was not a sudden event in this area alone but

rather a change that affected the entire northern hemisphere, leading in each zone to different climatic conditions. The southern Levant seems to have suffered a protracted series of droughts and the prevalence of warm climatic conditions, at first dry and later somewhat more moist. The rise in precipitation that seems to have occurred during the fourth millennium was a result of the penetration of the monsoon belt into the country.

If the reader has received the impression that the general climatic picture is clear, that is not, in fact, the case. It should be emphasized that it is only the transition, the major change, that constitutes the clear phenomenon. The contrast between the flourishing settlements of northern Mesopotamia, Syria, and Anatolia and the impoverished sites of the Land of Israel reveals that only the southern Levant suffered from the environmental change.

The new environmental conditions led, at first, to the desiccation of water sources, to the downcutting of streambeds, and to the spread of plant species more resistant to comparatively dry conditions, such as pine and olive. The deepening of the streambeds enabled settlements such as Sha'ar Ha-Golan (the type site for the Yarmukian culture) to be established on wadi terraces, which were subsequently reflooded and covered with deposits of sand and pebbles. Similarly, sites on the coastal plain, whether situated near wadi beds or in the elongated basins formed between the kurkar ridges of the coast, were covered over the years by silt deposits. Sites between the present coastal ridge and the ridge since destroyed by the sea, of which only islands now remain, are currently submerged (Neve Yam).

During the fifth millennium, ameliorated climatic conditions enabled the development and existence of societies subsisting on pastoralism, agriculture, and hunting (and perhaps gathering) throughout the Land of Israel and the neighboring desert areas. Moreover, this period, known in the European climatic sequence as the Atlantic period, permitted subsistence even in the heart of the arid zones, as evidenced by the many finds discovered in surveys in Arabia and Transjordan.

DISTRIBUTION OF SITES

Climatic conditions were not the only factor governing site distribution. Social factors too began to play an important role in the formation of the settlement pattern of the Near East.

In the Land of Israel, sites have been identified mainly in the Jordan valley (Sha'ar Ha-Golan, Munhata, 'Ain Soda, Tel Eli, Jericho, etc.), the Jezreel valley (Tell Qishyon, and a cluster of sites around Ha-Zorea), and the Coastal Plain (Neve Yam, Herzliya, Givat Ha-Parsa), including its southern reaches, the Gaza Strip (Qatif), and northern Sinai. The situation in the hills is less clear, perhaps because many sites are yet buried at the base of settlement mounds or in alluvial deposits. Little is known of the Negev Highlands as well, on the margins of which one site has been excavated, near Kadesh Barnea. The fragmentary character of the data also impedes the analysis of settlement patterns. In any case, it should be kept in mind that in Syria, Anatolia, and northern Mesopotamia there are many large and important sites of this period.

For the presence of sites in desert zones, two possible explanations may be offered: the first, that these were solely campsites of hunter-gatherers who continued to exist on the margins of the developing civilizations, and the second, that at least some of the sites should be interpreted as the remains of pastoral communities. If future research

should confirm the second suggestion, which is presently based on slender evidence, then it will be possible to state that the origins of pastoral societies (the ancestors of the beduin of today) lie in the sixth and fifth millennia.

Map 2.2. Pottery Neolithic sites

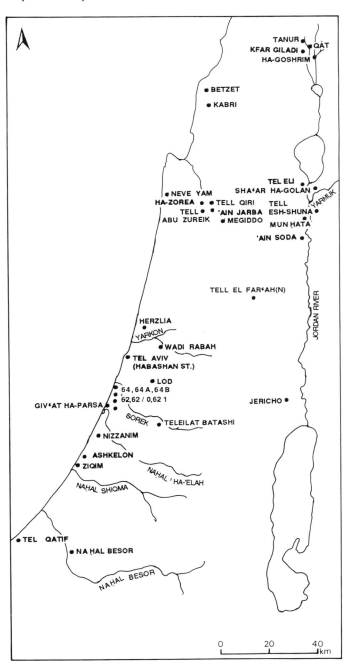

Fig. 2.10. Munhata: rectangular structure (left), silos and storage pits (right)

ARCHITECTURE AND BURIAL
CUSTOMS

The subtitle is rather pretentious,
as the remains of habitations found
so far in the Land of Israel are few
and consist mainly of pits of various
kinds and indirect evidence for the
existence of huts and shelters. It

appears that all the remains attribut-
able to the sixth millennium B.C.E.,
discovered at excavations in Sha'ar
Ha-Golan, 'Ain Soda, Tel Eli, Munhata, Jericho, Nizzanim, Ashkelon,
Givat Ha-Parsa, and Herzliya, can
be included in the general category
of pit settlements.

House pits were 3–4 meters in
diameter and 1 meter in depth. In a
house pit at Munhata, a bench,
hearth, and paved area were uncovered. The upper parts of the
structure were made of mud and
reeds or a thatch of branches, reeds,
and straw, and perhaps hides as

well. Similar pits, later filled with ash, were found at Givat Ha-Parsa. Some of the deep and narrow pits appear to have been silos, and some were probably a by-product of quarrying for earth and clay. The lack of stone foundations has no doubt impeded the identification of walls. Pebble and stone floorings, which could have served as foundations for thatched huts, were found at Nizzanim and Kadesh Barnea 3. Many finds were discovered in these pits and in the deposits around them, including pottery, flint tools, animal bones, and more.

Few graves were uncovered at the sites excavated. An outstanding find is the burial at Sha'ar Ha-Golan, marked by a cairn of river pebbles. A number of jar burials of infants have also been found, beneath occupation surfaces of the fifth millennium B.C.E. It appears that the impermanence or seasonality indicated by the dwelling remains influenced burial customs. Seminomadic societies, which spend part of the year in migration, tend to bury the dead in a central site, practicing primary burial and secondary burial (of bones collected some years after death) at the same site. In addition, clear archaeological evidence of central burial places lying outside the permanent settlements dates from the Chalcolithic period. It is not unlikely that the origins of this practice, which marks an important change in relation to burial customs of the Pre-Pottery Neolithic, lie in the sixth millennium, a time when new social systems were evolving.

LITHIC ASSEMBLAGES

The wealth of flint artifacts found in most Pottery Neolithic sites in the southern Levant allows us to trace the changes in the manufacture of flint tools.

At the beginning of the period, the knapping technique typical of the Pre-Pottery Neolithic B continued in use, namely, the production of blades from cores with two opposed striking platforms. The short, straight blades were used to fashion arrowheads, denticulated sickle blades, awls, and borers. Axe-adzes, often with a polished edge, were fashioned with bifacial flaking. The axes are generally trapezoidal or almond-shaped. The adzes with a plano-convex cross-section, characteristic of the following period, have yet to make their appearance.

A transition in the production of blades from bipolar cores to cores with one striking platform occurred during this period. From the resulting flakes and blades, arrowheads of similar shape to those of the PPNB, but smaller, were produced. They were often fashioned by pressure flaking. In desert regions, the use of these small arrowheads continued into later periods, as late as the fourth millennium B.C.E.

In the latter part of the Pottery Neolithic period, the transverse arrowhead first appears. It has a trapezoidal or triangular shape and is usually made of a blade segment. This type of arrowhead also continued in use in the fourth and third millennia, with one of its subtypes even taking the form of a lunate.

The differences between the earlier and later phases of the period are also reflected in the form of the sickle blade. The coarse denticulation characterizing the earlier part of the period disappears, to be replaced by a fine denticulation or by a straight, undenticulated blade. This type of sickle blade is also characteristic of the following Chalcolithic period.

The later axes do not offer distinctive features. Trapezoidal and triangular forms are common and are accompanied by plano-convex

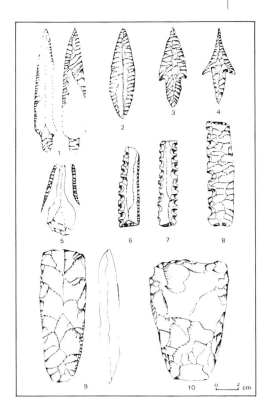

Fig. 2.11. Pottery Neolithic flint tool assemblage: arrowheads (1–4), awl (5), serrated sickle blades (6–8), axes (9–10)

adzes. The latter were attached to wooden handles with the cutting edge set at right angles to the haft, as in a hoe.

Finally, those scrapers generally, though imprecisely, termed fan scrapers seem to have appeared at a late stage in the period. Their frequent appearance in the fourth and third millennia is well documented, but on the basis of finds from excavations on the coast and at Byblos, it appears that they were introduced somewhat earlier.

POTTERY

The pottery of this period, which marks the beginning of the production of clay vessels in the Land of Israel, has yet to be thoroughly studied. As noted, few sites supply a stratigraphic sequence of assemblages, and this has led to several differences of opinion regarding the dating of various vessel types. Other analyses, such as thin-sections for petrographic analysis, are few and far between. It may therefore only be assumed that most pottery vessels were manufactured at the sites where they were found or in the vicinity. There are no characteristic signs of the presence of potters' workshops or production centers from which the vessels could have been distributed. The quality of the vessels is also generally not of the highest and is well below that of the following periods.

The conclusion from such an assumption must be that the craft of pot-making was not distributed throughout the Near East by expert potters but rather through the diffusion of ideas, by personal contact, among village communities. Something akin to trade routes or communication systems had already been established through which materials, objects, and livestock could be transported from one area to another. The limited geographical distribution of the vessel types and the styles of decoration suggest that there is substance in this assumption. Had the craft of pot-making been spread by migrant potters, one may expect that they would have been more successful in imparting their preferred range of shapes and decorations.

The spread of the potter's craft may explain the presence of pottery vessels among hunter-gatherers and pastoralist-gatherers of the Syro-Arabian desert. Such an assumption requires further serious study. Modern nomads do not produce pottery vessels. The archaeological record—for example, the pottery produced by Japanese hunter-gatherers of the Jomon culture some ten thousand years ago—shows that this was not always the case.

Yarmukian pottery vessels, the earliest in the Pottery Neolithic sequence as shown by the excavations at Munhata, predate those discovered in the Early and Middle Neolithic of Byblos. They consist mostly of bowls, loop-handled pots, or deep kraters with knob handles. The vessels are decorated with zigzag bands of red paint or with an incised herringbone pattern. This decoration is limited to bands, which are themselves either straight or zigzag and are at times bordered in red.

In the next phase, called the Munhata phase, the use of red decoration increases, and mat impressions may be found on the base of the vessel. New forms include ring-based bowls and possibly chalices as well. In any case, there is considerable similarity between the vessels of this phase and of the preceding one, and a general resemblance to the assemblages of the Early and Middle Neolithic of Byblos.

ECONOMY

Judging from the admittedly few animal bones recovered from sites such as Sha'ar Ha-Golan, Munhata, Beisamun, Ha-Goshrim, and Jericho, there was little difference between the economy of this period and that of the preceding one. About 60 percent of the bone assemblage is made up of domesticated animals, especially sheep and goats. They are accompanied by cattle and pigs, which had been by then domesticated. Hunting of wild species (or the supplying of meat by hunter-gatherers who continued to subsist outside the cultivated areas) is also represented. If this fragmentary evidence may be used to assemble a complete picture, it seems that the economic base did not change, despite the dramatic shift in the settlement pattern.

Little is known of the plant diet, but there are several hints to its composition. First, there are many grinding tools, accompanied by

Fig. 2.12. Pottery Neolithic vessel from Munhata (height 11 centimeters)

sickle blades, some of which could have been used to reap grain. Furthermore, pottery vessels, especially the larger ones, may attest to grain storage, though some could have been used to store liquids in the dwelling huts. These finds indicate that agriculture continued, if only as a seasonal activity of the Pottery Neolithic inhabitants of the Land of Israel. In any case, the evidence in hand is insufficient to determine conclusively whether the differences between the seventh and sixth millennia B.C.E. were caused by the seminomadic way of life pursued by the inhabitants of the arable zones, or whether the altered character of the sites signifies changes in social organization.

TRADE

Sixth millennium evidence for trade is meager indeed. The resemblance between the material culture

of the Yarmukian sites (Sha'ar Ha-Golan and Munhata) and that of Byblos attests to relations with the Lebanese coast.

The bulk of the evidence for trade relates to obsidian, the sources of which become varied and include both central and eastern Anatolia. A most impressive find is the enormous obsidian core from Kabri, which was brought whole to the country; it is accompanied by tools manufactured abroad and then imported, also found in cist tombs at Kabri. Obsidian tools are largely attributed to the Wadi Rabah culture.

ART AND CULT

The most interesting collection of objects of this period is without doubt that found at Sha'ar Ha-Golan. Most of the site is in present-day fishponds dug into the right bank of the Yarmuk River. When

Fig. 2.13. Clay figurine with coffee-bean eyes from Munhata (height 11 centimeters)

Map 2.3. Extent of the obsidian trade

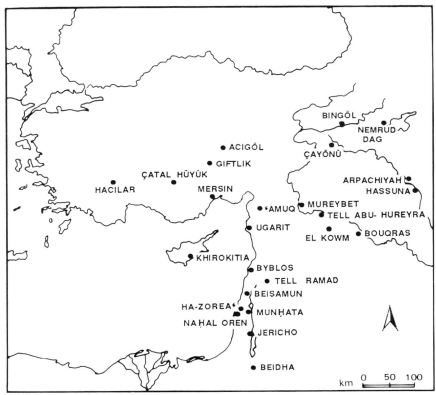

the ponds are cleaned and scraped every few years, many finds are exposed in them or on the surrounding earthen ramparts, including clay figurines and an abundance of pebbles bearing a variety of incisions.

The dominant figure among the clay figurines is that of a woman in a seated posture, wearing a headdress and mask with slanted eyes resembling grains of wheat (sometimes termed coffee-bean eyes). The hands rest on an ample breast and belly. A complete figurine of this type was found at Munhata, four kilometers southwest of Sha'ar Ha-Golan, and another in excavations at Tel Aviv.

Fig. 2.14. Pebble figurine from Sha'ar Ha-Golan (height 9 centimeters)

tility cult is further reflected in animal figurines, such as those found at Munhata and Jericho. They generally portray horned animals or a figure reminiscent of a fattened sheep. As sheep, goats, cattle, and pigs were all domesticated by this time, it is not surprising to find their figures fashioned in clay, whether as an expression of cult or merely of play.

In contrast to previous periods and as a further reflection of the fragmentary architectural picture, there are no building remains that might be interpreted as a shrine or a public place of cultic activity.

The Wadi Rabah Culture

The study of the sixth and fifth millennia B.C.E. (according to uncalibrated carbon-14 dates) has so far been less systematic and intensive than that of the preceding or succeeding periods. As a result of insufficiently understood changes in the settlement pattern, fewer single-phase sites of this period have been excavated than in the Chalcolithic or Pre-Pottery Neolithic B periods. It is therefore characterized by some archaeologists as Late Pottery Neolithic or Early Chalcolithic, while others would attribute the remains found in central and northern parts of the Land of Israel to the Wadi Rabah culture. This term was coined by Y. Kaplan, following his excavations at the site of Wadi Rabah, near the Yarkon headwaters at Rosh Ha-'Ayin, where he found structural remains accompanied by a new pottery assemblage beneath the Ghassulian Chalcolithic layer. Establishing the precise age of this culture is difficult because of the paucity of carbon-14 dates, particularly for the northern and central regions, although the arid zones of the Negev and Sinai have provided in recent years a considerable number of dates. However, the difference in material culture between the desert and the

The emphasis on the female form is present in the incised pebbles as well. Their character is more restrained, and the degree of detail varies, from a conical pebble depicting hands, slanted eyes, and legs to pebbles bearing only two diagonal incisions, representing the eyes. Many of the pebbles have one vertical incision, interpreted as female genitalia. Others bear series of parallel incisions and, rarely, a net pattern. It has been suggested that these pebbles were used in initiation rites. After being heated in fire, they would be applied to the youth's face, their incisions leaving patterned scars on his cheeks or forehead.

The general emphasis on the fer-

sown does not permit the dating of the northern sites on the basis of the Negev carbon-14 dates.

The distribution of sites attributed to the Wadi Rabah culture, in its narrow sense, does not extend south of Nahal Sorek. The sites are on plains or alluvial terraces, the largest being 2–4 hectares. The building foundations indicate rectilinear architecture, apparently of broadrooms, as is common in the later Ghassulian period. Installations include a round grain silo discovered in the submerged site of Kfar Samir, off the Carmel coast. Stone-lined silos have been discovered at other sites as well, such as Tell Qiri.

The pottery vessels of the Wadi Rabah phase are reminiscent of the north Syrian "dark-faced burnished ware." This term includes both red and black slipped vessels bearing a high burnish. Forms include carinated bowls, platters, and closed vessels, among which the bow-rimmed type is prominent. Chalices or pedestal bowls are considered successors to the white ware encountered chiefly in Syria and Lebanon. Ledge handles appear on the large vessels, as do loop handles. The pottery often bears an incised, stippled, or combed decoration; applied decoration in the form of ropes or snakes is also found. One vessel from 'Ain Jarba (near Ha-Zorea, in the Jezreel valley) bears an applied anthropomorphic decoration, interpreted as the figure of a goddess at childbirth.

Sherds of the Halaf culture of northern Syria and Mesopotamia were discovered at the site of Ard Tleili in the Lebanese Beqa', and imitations of this ware were found at Tel Zaf (near Kfar Rupin, in the Beth Shean valley). In the northwest of the Land of Israel, in the western Galilee and along its coast, there is evidence of the influence of the Byblite ceramic culture.

The Wadi Rabah flint tool assemblage is dominated by types that become frequent in the following period, including adzes with a plano-convex cross-section) and long blades that sickles (sometimes finely serrated along the cutting edge) were fashioned on by abrupt retouch. Fan scrapers bearing cortical remains also appear.

Unique vessels found at Kabri apparently originate in disturbed tombs. They include an obsidian mirror, a bow-rimmed jar, highly polished limestone pedestal bowls, a large obsidian core, granite maceheads, and more. The finds testify to contacts with Anatolia on the one hand and apparently Egypt on the other.

Needless to say, we have only an imperfect impression of the settlement pattern of the Wadi Rabah culture. The majority of the remains appear to indicate developed agriculture accompanied by the raising of sheep and goats, cattle, and pigs (in their appropriate environments). Pottery was manufactured by local potters, though central village industries may also have existed. The ability to acquire imported objects appears to stem from the existence of social stratification either within the settlements or between settlements in the general settlement system.

The desert sites of this period retain to a large extent many of their earlier features; for example, the curvilinear construction indicating the utilization of tents and huts. The appearance of seasonal campsites furnished with large yards or pens suggests, alongside the meager faunal remains, pastoral pursuits. Pottery was not yet being used for cooking by the desert dwellers of this period, and flint tools continued to be employed for everyday needs (the removal and processing of hides, the fashioning of wood artifacts). The presence of arrowheads shows that hunting was still practiced.

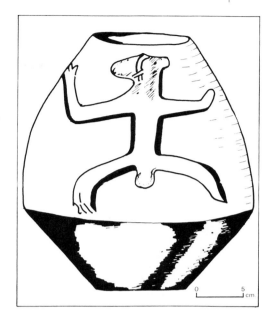

Fig. 2.15. Ceramic vessel with animal relief from 'Ain Jarba

3

The Chalcolithic Period

RIVKA GONEN

In the archaeological sequence of the Land of Israel, the Chalcolithic period lies between the agricultural societies of the Neolithic on the one hand and the urban societies of the Bronze Ages on the other. Its character, to a great extent, reflects this intermediate position. The very name of the period testifies to its transitional character, "Chalcolithic" being composed of the two Greek words *khalkos* (copper) and *lithos* (stone). This indicates that while the Chalcolithic was still largely a stone-using age, a major technological advance occurred, signaled by the introduction of copper into widespread use.

The widespread use of copper attests to considerable technological development, which has its origins in the recognition of the salient quality of metals—their ability to change physical characteristics when heated to melting point. Indeed, in earlier eras people used lumps of various native metal ores to make artifacts, but these were viewed merely as stones; they were drilled, polished, or incised. The crucial stage in the utilization of metal came when it was recognized that these stones could be brought to a liquid state and cast in molds. This discovery, the origin of which must

remain obscure, opened a new era in the history of human technological evolution. From that point on, metal occupied a position of growing importance among the raw materials; new methods of casting were developed, alloying was attempted, and new tools and objects came into existence. The development of agriculture, warfare, trade, and many other realms of human culture cannot be understood without an appreciation of the stage of the search for, and the discovery of, the characteristics of metals; in other words, the Chalcolithic stage.

Furthermore, metals, and in our case copper, cannot be found everywhere; they must be sought out in their natural beds and extracted from the bowels of the earth. The organization of search parties, the allocation of manpower for mining, the setting up of transportation and trade networks, all require an economic, transportation, and social infrastructure extending beyond the level of the subsistence economies that characterize previous periods. The establishment of such networks and the know-how for transmuting raw metal into tools and objects required the allocation of manpower devoted exclusively to these pursuits. Thus there came into being strata or classes of miners, trades-men, or artisans. We must therefore view Chalcolithic society as a complex and even stratified society, divided into professional fraternities and perhaps social classes. These social and economic developments required the establishment of institutions of centralized leadership, which would coordinate the activities of the social and professional groups that composed the community and fulfill public needs. These extended horizons and the implications thereof are an outstanding feature of the period.

The Chalcolithic culture was discovered by chance. A search for the Five Cities of the Plain, instigated in the 1920s by the Pontifical Biblical Institute of Jerusalem, led scholars to a group of low mounds, called Teleilat Ghassul, about seven kilometers northeast of the point where the Jordan River enters the Dead Sea. Pottery fragments, as well as stone and flint tools, were gathered from the surface. It soon became apparent that they were traces of a previously unknown culture. The simple and sometimes crude character of the pottery and especially the abundance of flint tools testified to the relative antiq-uity of this culture and to its inclusion within the sphere of prehistoric cultures. Excavations revealed a number of copper tools and objects, and the term "Chalcolithic period" was coined. Though the ancient character of the culture was obvious, the excavators were not able to place it precisely within the cultural sequence, as it had not been identified in a stratigraphic sequence of mound deposits, which would permit the determination of its relative position. And indeed, since the excavation of Teleilat Ghassul, many other sites of the same cultural sphere have been discovered, nearly all of them single-period sites with no prior or subsequent deposits. Eventually,

however, it became clear that this culture followed the Neolithic period and that at a number of large mounds it appeared at the base of Early Bronze Age strata. In this manner, its position in the general cultural sequence was established.

Teleilat Ghassul was excavated by three different expeditions for a total of fourteen seasons. The Jesuit fathers of the Pontifical Biblical Institute conducted eight seasons of excavation between 1929 and 1938; R. S. J. North renewed the excavations in 1960, and J. B. Hennessy followed in 1967 and in 1975–78. The site thus became a key site for the Chalcolithic culture, and the array of similar cultural assemblages was termed the Ghassulian culture. As more sites were excavated in different parts of the country, it became apparent that regional variants of this culture existed; they were named, after the region in which they were identified, the Golan and Beersheba cultures.

In earlier excavations in the lowest levels of some of the large mounds of the north, Ghassulian pottery was found together with sherds of an altogether different type—red and gray burnished ware. These wares had not been found in any unmixed Ghassulian assemblages of the south. It thus appeared that a cultural phase had been identified that retained Ghassulian traits while introducing new pottery types that were to become dominant as Ghassulian traces gradually disappeared. This phase was termed by some excavators Late Chalcolithic. However, later studies showed that the red and gray burnished pottery had nothing to do with the Ghassulian culture but rather represented the onset of a new period, the Early Bronze Age (see discussion in Chapter 4). Its presence alongside Ghassulian pottery was caused by the intermixing of two unrelated strata.

In the forthcoming pages, the term "Chalcolithic" indicates the Ghassulian culture with its regional variants, and our discussion will concentrate on that period alone.

Once the relative position of the Chalcolithic period between the Neolithic and Early Bronze ages was fixed, scholars began the attempt to establish an absolute chronology. As a prehistoric, preliterate period, it can provide no intrinsic historical dates. An absolute chronology must therefore rely on clear, firm contacts with a well-dated culture or on carbon-14 analyses, and indeed, both types of dating may be successfully applied to the period in question.

As we shall see, the foreign relations of the Chalcolithic period range far and wide. Raw materials were acquired from all over the Near East, and objects, techniques, and artistic styles of various origins all flowed into the Chalcolithic settlements. For chronological purposes, relations with Egypt are of the greatest importance, as Egyptian chronology is relatively well established.

Objects of undoubted Egyptian provenance have been found at a number of Chalcolithic sites. An alabaster goblet dated to predynastic times was discovered at the En Gedi shrine, and a site in northern Sinai provides typically Egyptian vessels dated to the early predynastic period, around 3700–3500 B.C.E. Objects of Egyptian origin have also been found at Gilat and Tel Aviv.

Many carbon-14 analyses have been performed for Chalcolithic strata. Following is a sample of dates obtained from the site of Bir Safadi, near Beersheba:

Stratum A, 5420 ± 350 B.P. = 3770–3070 B.C.E.
Stratum B, 5270 ± 300 B.P. = 3570–2970 B.C.E.
Stratum C, 5210 ± 350 B.P. = 3510–2810 B.C.E.

They provide an average date of 3420, 3270, and 3120 B.C.E. for the respective strata at the site. A textile fragment from Nahal Hever provided a date of 5460 ± 125 B.P., or between 3624 and 3374 B.C.E., with an average date of 3460 B.C.E. The mat from the Cave of the Treasure was examined by several different laboratories, and the following dates are among those obtained: 5390 ± 150 B.P., 4880 ± 250 B.P., 4780 ± 100 B.P., with the average date ranging between 3390 and 2780 B.C.E. Samples from the village of Shiqmim date 5750 ± 180 B.P. (upper village) and 5250 ± 140 B.P. (lower village), that is, 3930–3570 B.C.E. and 3390–3110 B.C.E. respectively.

On the basis of this corpus of dates, the average span of the Chalcolithic period was placed between the mid fourth millennium and about 3300 B.C.E., with the possibility of an upward extension to about 3700 B.C.E. New carbon-14 dates from the excavations of Hennessy at Ghassul (1975–78) imply a date in the first half of the fourth millennium for the Ghassulian culture. These dates, as well as all the others mentioned above, are in uncalibrated radiocarbon years.

The calibration of radiocarbon dates effected since the early 1970s requires a revised approach to the chronology of the period. The dates now proposed push the Chalcolithic period back by several hundred years, roughly to the interval between the fifth millennium and about 3600 B.C.E. These new dates mar the balance with the chronology of predynastic Egypt, leaving a gap between the end of the Chalcolithic and the beginning of the Early Bronze Age. Only further analyses and a wide-ranging comparative chronology will enable a satisfactory resolution of the chronological problem.

Recent surveys and excavations have begun to reveal an interesting pattern of chronological variation between the northern and southern parts of the Land of Israel. In the north, the Ghassulian phase seems to be of short duration, and it is soon replaced by the next cultural phase. In the south, the Ghassulian phase is more dominant and extended, and when it comes to an end, it disappears without a trace, its sites abandoned and their inhabitants gone. It is conceivable that at a certain time the northern Ghassulian culture had already been replaced by the culture of the beginning of the Early Bronze Age, while the southern Ghassulian culture continued to exist. This possibility further complicates the question of the absolute chronology of the Chalcolithic period by adding the regional component.

Site Distribution

The years that have passed since the first identification of Chalcolithic culture at Teleilat Ghassul have witnessed constant addition to the site distribution map of the period. Excavations, chance discoveries, and surveys in various parts of the country have added much information on the location, number, and density of settlements of the period.

Map 3.1 shows excavated Chalcolithic sites as well as areas of intensive surveys. The data obtained in these surveys are presented in Table 3.1. They represent extensive systematic research and thus reflect a picture of the Chalcolithic settlement pattern as we know it today, beyond what is known from the excavated sites. The data reveal some significant features. First, the Negev, south of Beersheba, is virtually devoid of sites. Farther north, the Chalcolithic sites are spread evenly throughout the country. The central hills of Galilee, Samaria, and Judaea are sparsely settled. In contrast, the valleys and plains ringing the hill country to the east, west, and south reveal a considerable density of settlement. The central Golan Heights may also be added to the areas characterized by an open, level terrain. It therefore appears that the people of this period avoided hilly regions, choosing more level areas for settlement. Such a settlement pattern is of great interest and is unique in the history of the land.

Furthermore, the people of this period showed marked preferences in their choice of climate. Some of the densest areas of settlement are marginal areas, where precipitation is low and drought common. Three explanations may be offered for this unique settlement pattern. A: The site distribution map might not reflect the true pattern of Chalcolithic settlement. In other words, it may present an unreliable picture,

Table 3.1 Survey Data from Areas of Chalcolithic Settlement.

Region	Area	No. of sites
Central Golan Heights	about 25 sq km	14
Middle Jordan valley, from the mouth of the Yarmuk to Tirat Zvi	about 20 sq km	40
Atlit Region	about 10 sq km	17
Ramot Menashe	about 10 sq km	33
Northern Samaria	about 2000 sq km	2
Southern Samaria	about 1000 sq km	2
Judaean hills	about 800 sq km	6
Judaean desert and Jericho valley (En Gedi and northward)	about 1400 sq km	22
Beersheba and Besor valleys	about 30 sq km	63

stemming from the selective preservation of archaeological remains. Chalcolithic settlement may have been better preserved in the marginal areas, where later occupation was intermittent, than in the continuously occupied central areas. B: Climatic conditions may have been different from today's. Areas now defined as marginal may have been more moist and better suited for settlement. If this was indeed the case, the rainier hill country could have been covered with vegetation or even forests too dense to be cleared with the technical means then available. C: Natural conditions may not have changed since that time; rather, the economy of the people may have been particularly suited to plains or plateaus with a relatively dry climate.

Another feature evident in the distribution map is the concentration of burial caves along the Coastal Plain, from Palmahim in the south to Hadera in the north.

A review of the areas of Chalcolithic settlement follows, in geographical order from north to south, noting the features peculiar to each area.

THE GOLAN HEIGHTS

This area has been added to the Chalcolithic site distribution map since the 1970s, as a result of intensive research by Claire Epstein.

The central Golan is a basaltic plateau characterized by heavy soils. The relatively plentiful rainfall, 500–600 millimeters per annum, is not quickly absorbed in the clayey soil, and flooding is common.

So far, only the central Golan has been intensively surveyed, with fourteen Chalcolithic sites counted as of the early 1980s. The largest of these is Rasm Harbush (map grid 2213-7/2592-8), which numbers about fifty dwelling units. Other sites are smaller and have fewer dwelling units. There are also occasional, isolated structures near fields. The inhabitants of the area seem to have adapted well to its peculiar characteristics. They cultivated fields near natural drainage channels, erecting dams and walls to direct the surface runoff to the fields. These finds indicate that the inhabitants were farmers who resided near their fields for at least part of the year. The agricultural pursuits of the population are further evidenced by the remains of grain, legumes, and many olive pits in the houses, as well as by the large proportion of cutting and grinding tools and the numerous storage jars found in each house. This was an extensive agricultural settlement, though it has been suggested that the inhabitants did not reside in the area all year round but only in the sowing and reaping seasons, migrating east to the desert margins during the rainy months.

Map 3.1. Chalcolithic sites in the Land of Israel

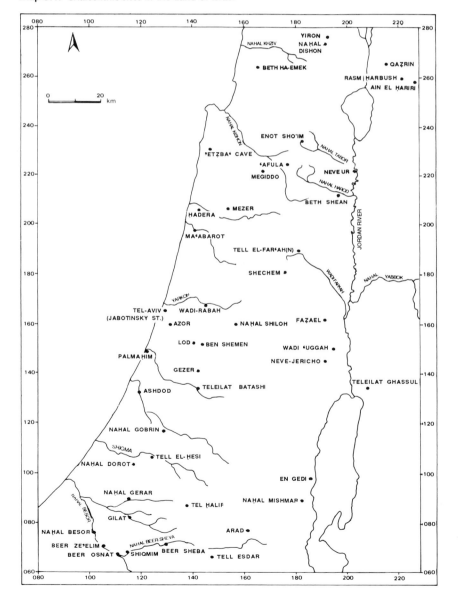

THE WESTERN GALILEE AND ACCHO VALLEY

Four sites have been identified in the western Galilee and Accho valley. None have been widely excavated, and the information about them is therefore quite meager. Nevertheless, the variegated character of the Chalcolithic settlement in the area, in contrast to the uniform character of the Golan settlements, may be noted. In the lowest levels of two sites where limited salvage excavation was performed—Beth Ha-Emeq and Horvat 'Uza—Chalcolithic sherds were found in pockets in the bedrock. The character of the settlements remains unknown, though the lack of architecture may be taken to indicate transient settlement. Unlike most of the Chalcolithic sites of the country, but like some important sites of the north, the two sites continued to be inhabited in the Early Bronze Age. It would be interesting to see whether the sites of continuous settlement are different in character from those sites occupied only in the Chalcolithic period and whether their economic base was different, but only further information will cast light on that question.

A similar situation may be observed at the large coastal mound of Akhziv, but apart from the mere mention of Chalcolithic finds, no information about the settlement is available.

The cave site at Abu Sinan is of interest, as it seems to have been a cave dwelling of the type found in the hill regions. The excavators of this site state that the finds indicate connections with southern cultures, as well as with cultures of the north Syrian coast.

THE JEZREEL VALLEY

Only two Chalcolithic sites have been excavated so far in the Jezreel valley. They consist of pockets in the bedrock found at the base of the mounds of Megiddo and 'Afula. The limited extent of the excavations precludes an appreciation of the character of these early settlements, but the lack of building remains suggests that they were no more than transient settlements.

THE JORDAN VALLEY

If the Golan Heights are characterized by a unique flowering during the Chalcolithic period, the fertile Jordan valley presents a different picture, as this area has attracted human settlement from early Paleolithic times. The warm climate is ideally suited to various cultivations. Rainfall varies from 300–400 millimeters in the north to 100–150 millimeters in the south. The northern, rainier part of the Jordan valley is also watered by Lake Kinneret and the Yarmuk River, but the southern part is barren, its streams are dry most of the year, and springs are few and far between. It is therefore not surprising to find in the Beth Shean valley, between the confluence of the Yarmuk and Jordan rivers in the north and Tirat Zvi in the south, a concentration of more than forty Chalcolithic sites, including pits found at the base of the mound of Beth Shean. The area from the edge of the Beth Shean valley southward is more thinly settled. Yet it should be pointed out that in this semiarid region no fewer than seventeen sites have been counted, including a large settlement on the alluvial fan of the streambeds descending from the Samarian hills near Faza'el. Many of these sites are situated east of the Jordan.

Oddly enough, the mound of Jericho, near the largest spring of the southern Jordan valley, in the midst of a fertile oasis, was abandoned during the Chalcolithic period. Remains of the period were discovered outside the mound itself, along the water channels. It seems that the people of the period congregated mainly around the site of Teleilat Ghassul, across the Jordan River from Jericho, about seven kilometers northeast of the point where it flows into the Dead Sea. Ghassul, which recent excavations show to have been occupied as early as the fifth millennium B.C.E., was abandoned at the end of the Chalcolithic period.

This phenomenon may imply that the period was generally quite humid, with considerable amounts of rainfall distributed evenly over the year and a water table higher than at present. The remains of agricultural products found at Ghassul, which include many date and olive pits, might support such an assumption.

THE COASTAL PLAIN

The coastal plain, between Hadera in the north and Palmahim in the south, is perhaps the most fascinating area of Chalcolithic settlement. A large majority of the finds come not from the few settlement sites but rather from burial caves. The caves were carved into the kurkar ridges running parallel to the shore, and within them the dead were disposed of in various ways. The most interesting and well-known manner of burial is secondary interment in decorated clay ossuaries. Tens of burial caves have been found, most of them centered around the Tel Aviv area. Each cave contained a great number of burials. Such a concentration of tombs in a relatively limited area, when contrasted with the scarcity of burials in other areas of Chalcolithic settlement, has led some archaeologists to propose that the coastal plain served as a central burial ground for the inhabitants of the entire country. Indeed, a regional burial pattern, in what may be called villages of the dead, is suited to the nomadic life-style practiced by at least part of the people of this period.

The few settlement sites excavated in the region have revealed only scant finds. The Jabotinsky Street site in Tel Aviv was a pit settlement; at the site of Azor traces of habitation were found in a disused burial cave, as well as on the nearby hill. The character of some of the sites was certainly temporary. Nevertheless, the identification of seventeen Chalcolithic sites in the Atlit survey suggests that the number of sites on the coastal plain was in fact much larger than what might have been assumed.

The number of sites increases as one moves toward the eastern fringes of the coastal plain, toward the inner plains and the foothills. Here, a series of sites stretching from Mezer in the north to Tel Nagila in the south was found. Most are typical of the period—pits or pottery deposits unrelated to building remains, evidence of ephemeral settlement. Only at Mezer were building remains found, possibly indicating a sedentary settlement, which, it may be noted, continued to exist in the Early Bronze I period.

THE CENTRAL HILLS

In the hill regions of the upper and lower Galilee, a number of so far unexcavated Chalcolithic sites have been found. Few sites have been identified in the Samarian and Judaean hills. Some sherds of the period have been noted at the base of Tel Dothan and in pockets in the bedrock of the City of David in Jerusalem, while at Tell el-Far'ah North traces of meager habitation were found in natural caves. There is little doubt as to the transience of these settlements. Ossuary fragments found in a cave near Shechem

show that this type of burial was practiced in the hill country as well.

An intensive survey of Ramot Menashe, a northeastern extension of the Samaria hills, has revealed the presence of 33 Chalcolithic sites. None has been excavated, so little can be said of the character of this settlement.

THE JUDAEAN DESERT

The Judaean desert was another area of Chalcolithic settlement. Natural caves abound in this arid region, concentrated mainly along the gorges leading down to the Dead Sea. At various times—most prominently during the second revolt against the Romans, in the second century A.D.—the caves sheltered refugees and fugitives. Extensive surveys carried out in the caves in the search for remains of the revolt revealed traces of Chalcolithic habitation in every cave as well as on the plateaus above them. Even if we were to assume that the climate of the period was more humid and the desert less barren than it is today, the topographic difficulties are in themselves sufficient to make habitation in these caves difficult and dangerous. The inhabitants came to the caves fully equipped to carry on a normal life; they had tools and vessels, implements of work and industry, and also plenty of food, remains of which have been remarkably preserved. It cannot be said how long they lived in the caves, but it was no doubt for a short while only.

Of special interest is an isolated shrine, unrelated to any settlement, found near the oasis of En Gedi. It is in a well-watered spot, with breathtaking views, and must have been a place of pilgrimage from near and far. What appear to have been the treasures of the shrine were found in a parcel in the cave of Nahal Mishmar, now known as the Cave of the Treasure.

THE WESTERN NEGEV—THE BEERSHEBA AND ARAD VALLEYS

This area harbors the largest concentration of Chalcolithic sites in the Land of Israel. In a strip sixty kilometers long and half a kilometer wide, running along the banks of Nahal Beersheba and lower Nahal Besor to the edge of the Gaza Strip, 63 sites have been identified. They are concentrated in three or four groups: the lower Nahal Besor cluster, the lower Nahal Beersheba cluster, and a cluster in the environs of the town of Beersheba. In the latter cluster three sites have been excavated—Bir Matar, Bir Safadi, and Horvat Beter—whose distinctive material culture has been termed the Beersheba culture. Large site concentrations have also been found along Nahal Gerar and Nahal Patish. Thirty sites were surveyed along Nahal Gerar, between Tel Sera' and Tel Haror, at least one of which is spread out over a half-kilometer stretch. Another concentration of sites lies at the eastern end of the Beersheba valley, around Tel Arad, where traces of a large pit settlement of a transient character were found. The Chalcolithic period was, undoubtedly, a golden age of settlement in this region. In no other period were so many settlements established here. As in the other parts of the country, all the sites are single-period sites.

The character of the sites varies. Most are small, some even minute. Many, especially in the Nahal Besor area, have a transient character and appear to represent seasonal campsites of a seminomadic population. On the other hand, there are large and very large sites. The site of Gilat, for example, extends over ten hectares, and the site of Shiqmim approaches a similar size (9.5 hectares). Both the smaller and larger sites are dispersed, which appears to relate to a pastoralist life-style in which the inhabitants pitch their tents or build their homes at intervals large enough to accommodate their livestock. Even in settlements of a more sedentary character, such as the Beersheba sites, there is clear evidence for repeated abandonments. At Bir Safadi, four superimposed occupation levels were found, and at Shiqmim seven. The abandoned strata show no signs of destruction or conflagration. The impending abandonment can be sensed at Bir Safadi, where objects were stowed and entrances blocked prior to the exodus.

A life-style alternating between nomadism and sedentism is well suited to the semiarid character of the region. The mean annual precipitation drops from 200–300 millimeters in the areas nearer the coast to only 150 millimeters in the Arad region. Rainfall is not only slight but also irregular, and droughts are common. Under such conditions, pastoralism is the most profitable economic mode.

The large number of sites in this region has moved scholars to put forth a number of interesting theories. It has been proposed to trace the gradual penetration of the Chalcolithic groups from the coast southward to the Nahal Besor area and thence east and northeast to Nahal Gerar, Nahal Beersheba, and, finally, the Beersheba and Arad areas. In this final stage, Chalcolithic settlement would have reached its zenith both in the number of sites and in their size. An attempt has also been made to identify within the region tribal-territorial units centering around major settlement sites, which would have been centers of power and ritual. Around such a center, smaller settlements would have been established, and beyond them, at the periphery, yet smaller sites. Such a settlement pattern bears, in the opinion of some scholars, the germ of urban development, which

was to ripen only hundreds of years later, in the Early Bronze Age.

THE SINAI COAST

Surveys conducted along the ancient coastal route of northern Sinai have revealed three concentrations of Chalcolithic sites, the westernmost of which lies west of El Arish. Other sites appear farther west, as far as Qantara on the Suez Canal. The region is one of active dune formations, which have in recent years covered known sites, and other unknown sites no doubt lie buried beneath them. The Sinai sites are small, short-lived, and probably seasonal. The assemblages found, including many flint sickle blades and stone grinding tools, attest more to an agricultural than to a pastoral way of life. The northern Sinai sites may well have belonged to the Nahal Besor settlement system. The inhabitants would spend the sowing and reaping seasons in northern Sinai and the rest of the year in the pasturelands of the northern Negev. Such a migratory pattern was practiced until recent years by the Beduin tribes of this region. Alongside their relations with the western Negev sites, the people of northern Sinai maintained trade contracts with Egypt, and a number of fragments of Egyptian objects have been found in two of the sites.

Having reviewed the site distribution map of the Chalcolithic period, we may reexamine the hypotheses put forth at the start of the chapter.

The first hypothesis spoke of the accidents of preservation. It was suggested that at sites continuously occupied over many generations, the traces of the earliest occupation would be obliterated, in contrast to the situation in marginal areas. Such a proposal would imply a much denser settlement map than that described above. Can such a

proposition be contradicted by the regional review? Apparently, yes. If we examine the few mounds where Chalcolithic remains have been found at the base, it is evident that traces of the ancient settlement have survived despite the constant building activity at the site. True, the character of these settlements cannot be established with certainty, but the existence of the remains proves that individual settlement traces are not easily obliterated, not to speak of entire regions of settlement. In the Beth Shean valley, a fertile and densely settled region since earliest times, traces of at least forty Chalcolithic sites have been identified. It must therefore be affirmed that a site exhibiting no traces of settlement was indeed not settled, and that if only a few settlements were counted in the hill zones, such indeed was the case during the period in question.

The second hypothesis suggested that the Chalcolithic climate may have been more humid and the distribution of rainfall over the year more even than it is today. The botanical remains found at various sites support such a proposal. Considerable numbers of olive pits were found both in the Golan sites and at Teleilat Ghassul. The olive flourishes in the cooler, rainier hill country of the Galilee, Samaria, and Judaea and requires 400 millimeters of rain per year or, alternatively, irrigation. The presence of the olive pits must therefore weigh heavily in favor of this hypothesis. But it should be kept in mind that a drastic change is not necessarily indicated. A slight rise in rainfall can lead to a rise in the water table and the consequent emergence of springs and wells where they had not previously existed.

On the other hand, keep in mind that Chalcolithic settlement in areas that are today semiarid was of a temporary and largely pastoral character. That type of activity is well suited to semiarid zones and shows that such was the character of these areas in those times as well. It is therefore feasible that the slight rise in precipitation in the Dead Sea area did not leave its mark on the western Negev. It is also possible that the evidence for an abundance of water at Ghassul represents a local phenomenon, related to frequent tectonic activity. Such activity is evidenced by the destruction pattern of the strata demonstrated at this site and only at this site. Such local tectonic activity could have led to the appearance of springs exploited by the inhabitants for the irrigation of their olive orchards.

Additional evidence may be gathered from the settlements of the Aravah and Sinai. Despite the climatic hardships, what may be termed an economic impulse drove people to settle in these areas. One need not suppose climatic amelioration to explain the settlement. Given good reason, they could adapt to existing conditions. It therefore appears that the archaeological evidence in itself provides insufficient foundation for the hypothesis regarding a more humid climate in the Chalcolithic period. Careful laboratory analysis of soils and pollen from various sites has not provided any conclusive answers.

We are thus left with the third hypothesis, which views the Chalcolithic settlement pattern as determined not by natural conditions but by factors operating within the society itself. In other words, in a socioeconomic system suited to semiarid conditions, people would deliberately choose to inhabit marginal areas. If we review the settlement descriptions in the regional survey, we find that the terms "pit settlement" or "temporary character" often appear. And indeed it seems that the settlements of the Chalcolithic period were often not sedentary settlements. The dispersal of sites, their sometimes surprising size, and their impermanence all point to a preoccupation with pastoralism or seasonal agriculture. It seems that a large proportion of the people of this period were not interested in or capable of sedentism, and even in areas well suited to cultivation, extended settlement was not practiced. The preference for a seminomadic way of life led to a preference for regions appropriate to such a way of life. True, there are sedentary settlements in the Chalcolithic period, the largest of which is Teleilat Ghassul. The nine strata encountered there, all of the Chalcolithic period, testify to an extensive, recurring habitation. The three sites excavated near Beersheba were also permanent settlement sites, but their lifespan was not so long, and it was marked by periods of abandonment. The third hypothesis thus remains valid.

Site Organization and Types of Dwellings

It has already been hinted that there were several kinds of settlements in the Chalcolithic period, depending on the life-style of the inhabitants and the character of the environment.

CAVE DWELLINGS

The basic, primary form of settlement is undoubtedly the cave dwelling. Some of the people of this period—a small minority, as far as we know—lived in natural caves in the hills. That was not the general custom of the period, and it should not be seen as a form of permanent habitation. It is conceivable that groups used such sites in the early stages of their settlement process, or perhaps they represent nomadic offshoots of a sedentary population, such as far-ranging shepherds. Support for the latter assumption is provided by a comparison between the finds of two excavated caves, Cave U on the southern slope of Tell el-Far'ah North and a cave in the village of Abu Sinan in the western Galilee. The pottery in the first cave resembles that of the Beersheba culture. Two burials were found in this cave, one of the rare cases of onsite burial. In the cave of Abu Sinan the pottery resembles that of the south, but there are also sherds reminiscent of north Syrian coastal ware. Thus, each cave dwelling is related to a different cultural unit.

In contrast to the dearth of cave dwellings in the central hill zones, a large and interesting concentration of inhabited caves was discovered in the barren reaches of the Judaean desert, particularly along the rock cliffs leading down to the Dead Sea, between Wadi Murabba'at in the north and Masada in the south. Other cave dwellings were discovered in the plateaus above the rock cliffs. The caves were investigated in the 1960s, in the course of the search for remains of the first and second revolts against the Romans. To the surprise of the archaeologists, traces of Chalcolithic presence were found in almost every cave. In a 35-meter stretch on the north bank of Nahal-Mishmar, for example, three caves with Chalcolithic remains were found; one was the famous Cave of the Treasure, and the other two served as burial caves. A fourth cave was discovered on the opposite cliff. Access to most of the caves is difficult. To reach them, archaeologists had to scale the cliffs or descend with ropes from the cliff tops. Though narrow paths, which have since disappeared, may once have led to the caves, it is still a mystery why anybody should have preferred such difficult living conditions in an area that has since served mainly as a refuge for rebels and refugees.

The Judaean desert presents an

area of concentrated cave settlement, differing from what has been found in the central hills of the Land of Israel. Furthermore, while the inhabitants of the isolated cave dwellings in the hills left behind poor traces of domestic life, indicating a seminomadic life, the Judaean desert caves provide evidence of a sedentary, though short-lived, settlement with a surprisingly rich cultural heritage. The assemblage of ceramic, stone, leather, metal, and bone artifacts uncovered in the few excavated caves, and especially the hoard of Nahal Mishmar, constitute one of the high points in the material culture and art of the period. As for the caves themselves, they were not modified by the inhabitants and were used in their natural form. There are no traces of quarrying, enlargement, blockage, or division of space within the caves—evidence of the limited duration of Chalcolithic occupation.

The disparity between this type of cave dwelling and the wealth of material culture found within the caves suggests that the inhabitants reached the caves in extraordinary circumstances. They may not have been seminomadic shepherds but rather bearers of a developed culture forced to leave their homes, perhaps from fear of enemies or of an epidemic. The anthropological study of the skeletal remains also indicates as much: "each of the skeletons belonged to an aboriginal, permanently settled population. We surmise that these cases were not members of a nomadic people, but rather that they were wanderers only during their own generation" (Haas and Nathan 1973).

TEMPORARY SETTLEMENTS

Judging from the finds of surveys and excavations, this type of settlement seems to have been the most common in the Chalcolithic period, especially in the south. Its frequency appears related to the central role of pastoralism in the Chalcolithic economy.

The temporary settlements were seasonal settlements in which nomadic pastoralists resided during their annual migration. At the end of the season the sites were abandoned and never resettled. Their size and depth are therefore small and the material culture poor. The inhabitants of these sites erected no permanent structures, but traces of domestic artifacts, such as various types of pottery vessels, flint tools, fireplaces, and grinding tools, testify to habitation at the site.

One example of an open-air seasonal settlement is the site of En Yahav in the Aravah. The excavators of this site report the presence of dozens of pits along the north bank of Nahal Neqarot, each with a depth of about 60 centimeters and an average diameter of 1.2 meters. An ash layer at the bottom of the pits showed that they functioned as hearths, and a grinding stone lay near the edge of each. Flint tools and pottery fragments were found as well. All the artifacts from the site are typical of the Ghassulian culture.

The absence of structures at these sites is marked. This implies either that the site was inhabited only during those parts of the year when the climate permitted open-air habitation or that the inhabitants built temporary structures, such as tents or shelters, of which no trace remains. Both possibilities reflect the transitory character of the settlement. The presence of hearths, grindstones, flint tools, and sherds shows that the sojourn of the ancient inhabitants at the site, though temporary, was of considerable duration. It is curious that the hearths are not merely outlined on the surface but are placed in pits of no mean depth. The need for fire pits may be related to the prevailing winds at this site or may show that the pits were used not for the preparation of food but for an industrial process related to the search for copper in this area. The pits may also have originally served for food storage.

Pits of various sizes are often found in the seasonal sites. Where conditions permitted, the pits were dug into the soil. On rocky terrain, the inhabitants tended to utilize natural pits or pockets but sometimes carved into the rock. The pits contain the bulk of the finds from these sites, as is the case, for example, in the basal layers of mounds such as Megiddo, Beth Ha-Emeq, Beth Shean, and Arad. It may be that these pits and pockets also served as dug-out foundations for huts or tents.

The great size of the En Yahav site, which occupies ten hectares, is worthy of note. As we have seen, there are other sites of similar size, which are usually considered central sites of territorial units. En Yahav is thus far an isolated site in the region. All sites of this type reveal a dispersed internal structure, further evidence of their transient character and of the chiefly pastoral pursuits of the inhabitants.

PERMANENT SETTLEMENT SITES

In contrast to the transient seasonal settlements, we assign to the permanent settlement type those sites where traces of massive architecture of long-term domestic function can be identified. Their superior construction ensured the improved preservation of these sites, compared with the temporary sites, and they have therefore attracted excavators. In fact, the bulk of our knowledge of the Chalcolithic period is drawn from these few sites.

The best known among the built-up sites is without doubt Teleilat Ghassul. A group of twelve

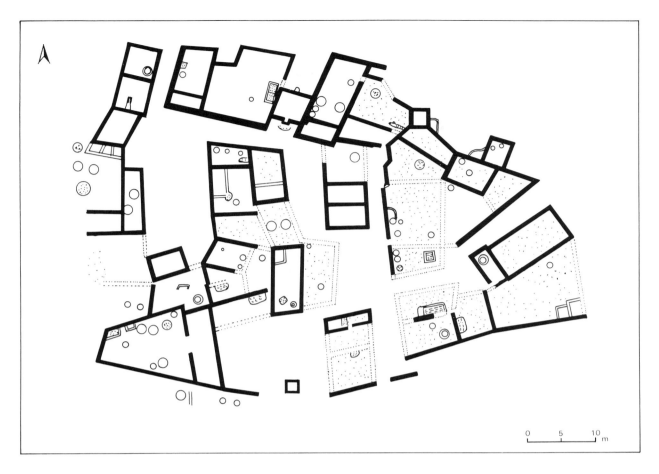

0   5   10
⊢————⊢————⊢ m

Fig. 3.1. Teleilat Ghassul: plan of settlement

small mounds combine to form a large settlement of at least six hectares, and possibly much more. The site has been excavated by three expeditions, who have dug three of the mounds and a few squares between them. Nine major building phases have been identified in a deposit four meters thick. Many floor layers were uncovered, separated by fills of collapsed mud brick. Although the major strata were destroyed by the frequent earthquakes visited on this area, it is not clear what caused the brick collapse on the floors, which necessitated constant resurfacing. Hennessy, the last to excavate at the site, has proposed that the multiple floor surfaces indicate that settlement there was seasonal and that the inhabitants migrated to the hills during summer.

This is a surprising conclusion in view of the density of construction at the site and the thickness of the debris, factors that have led others to conclude that settlement at the site was of a sedentary nature. Thus it may be seen that even the presence of structures is insufficient to determine conclusively the sedentary character of a settlement site.

From the relatively extensive areas excavated, both the common form of dwellings and the spatial organization of the site may be inferred. The houses have a more or less fixed plan of simple design. The house consisted of one rectangular room, which probably served as the habitation unit, fronted by a large walled court. Various installations are found in the courtyards—hearths, pits, small areas set off by walls—all

functioning in the processing of agricultural produce and the preparation of food. In those places where the room entrance can be identified, it is in the long wall, so that the house may be termed a broadhouse. The poor preservation and the density of construction make it difficult to distinguish between the units and between open courts and roofed rooms. Many of the dwelling units are conjoined in various manners, forming dense building clusters bordered by alleys or passageways.

The houses are built of sun-dried mud brick on a foundation of unworked fieldstones. The brick are handmade and set in mortar. It is unlikely that so simple a construction method could have withstood heavy rains, if such there were. This may support the propo-

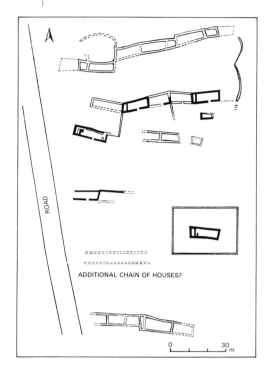

Fig. 3.2. Rasm Harbush: plan of settlement

sition that the Chalcolithic climate was no different than today's. All the excavated houses resemble one another in their construction and basic plan, but a few structures are larger than average. It is thought that they may have a public function, indicating the existence of a community centered around a ruler or a shrine. It is unfortunate that their poor state of preservation has left no clue of unusual details of construction or furnishing. The one detail that stands out in relation to the simple building standard is the white plaster coating on the interior walls, and especially the colorful murals adorning the plaster. Plaster fragments were found in many houses, indicating that the decoration of house walls was not uncommon. Furthermore, the decoration and replastering of the walls was an ongoing activity, as evidenced by fragments with multiple layers of plaster and paint.

It is particularly important that the site of Ghassul was never walled. The absence of fortification is often viewed as evidence that the Chalcolithic period was one of the rare periods of relative peace in the Land of Israel. It may, however, testify less to the objective situation and more to the unwillingness or inability of the inhabitants to organize an extensive communal venture such as the construction of a defense wall. If they were semi-nomads, as Hennessy suggests, the inhabitants may have preferred to abandon the site in times of trouble and escape to hideouts rather than fight for their homes and villages, which were conceived of as having but transient value. Indeed, the abandonments evidenced in many of the settlements excavated may have been a response to attacks by enemies or looters. Instead of defending themselves, the inhabitants took flight until the storm had passed and

then returned to reinhabit their homes.

Built-up sites have been found elsewhere as well, in the Golan, the Jordan valley, and the Beersheba region. In all the regions the basic house plan is the same.

Widespread settlement was found in the central Golan, with a variety of data attesting to its seasonal-agricultural character. All the Golan sites are built in the local basalt, and they may be divided by size into three types: large sites with thirty to fifty structures, smaller sites near the fields, and isolated structures scattered over broad areas near the fields and pastures. The scattered structures were no doubt occupied by shepherds or by farmers in times of agricultural activity.

Regardless of variations in site size, the stone house type is always the same. All the houses consist of a room and courtyard, and all are broadhouses; that is, the entrance is set in one of the long walls. All the structures are oriented similarly; the long walls run east-west, and the entrance always faces south. The narrow roofed living room, sometimes divided in two, lies west of the court. The houses are built parallel to the direction of the surface runoff, in a manner that no doubt served to protect them from flooding in times of heavy rains. In the large and middle-sized sites, the houses are joined on their short end, thus forming chains. The central Golan site of Rasm Harbush, for example, contains fifty house units arranged in six such chains, in more or less parallel ranks, each containing seven to nine houses.

Some of the courtyards had benches lining one or two of the walls, as well as low walls setting apart functional areas, such as animal pens. Large stone slabs set in the courtyards served as work tables. Other installations were found as well. Almost no pits were found, doubtless because of the rocky Golan terrain. The lack of storage pits was compensated for by stone-lined grain bins and large numbers of ceramic pithoi. Small, carved basalt pillars, termed house idols, were often found on the courtyard benches, opposite the entrance.

Another built-up site was found at Faza'el in the middle Jordan valley, a site on the alluvial fan of streams descending from eastern Samaria. The rounded, medium-sized stones deposited on the alluvial fans were used for construction by the ancient inhabitants. The house plans resemble those described above, consisting of a broadroom fronted by a large courtyard with many agricultural installations. Though the site has not been fully excavated, it appears that each house stood well apart from its neighbours. Houses of the same type were found at the site of Mezer, about twelve kilometers east of Hadera.

The broadhouse typifies the northern Negev sites as well. Recent excavations at Shiqmim and at sites on Nahal Patish have revealed a number of broadhouses. Remarkably, individual house plans were maintained over many years, spanning several building phases; when a house was demolished, a new one of identical design was built on its remains. Each structure revealed a series of floors, indicating a long lifespan. The houses were built of mud brick on stone foundations. In one excavation area, an alleyway lined with houses was identified.

One of the fascinating discoveries in the northern Negev sites is the presence of subterranean tunnels excavated in the loess soil and integrated in the building system. The tunnels probably served as

Fig. 3.3. Subterranean dwelling at Bir Safadi

silos and storerooms. A similar phenomenon was encountered in the Nahal Beersheba settlements, Bir Safadi, Bir Matar, and Horvat Beter. Excavations revealed remains of oval subterranean chambers, approached by broad stepped corridors. In a later phase, small round chambers connected by low corridors were added. It was at one time thought that these finds represented a system of underground settlement, but in light of the finds at Nahal Patish, it appears that they too were integrated in the superstructure, serving more for storage than for habitation. In any case, the people of Beersheba used the subterranean systems for a time, before they were abandoned. The abandonment was orderly. Vessels and objects were placed in caches, and entranceways were blocked with stones.

Surface structures were preserved only of the final phase of settlement, their plans resembling those of the other sites described. The structures were built of the raw material most abundant in this area, sun-dried mud brick, and their preservation is therefore quite poor.

At these sites, as at Teleilat Ghassul, one structure considerably larger than the rest was found. A similar structure was found at the site of Gilat in the western Negev, which has been excavated only in a preliminary manner. The size of these structures indicates with a fair degree of certainty that they had a public function, and they therefore provide evidence for the existence of communities organized around a ruler or a shrine. The preservation of these structures is generally poor, and little can be said of the details of their construction and furnishings.

To sum up, the varied forms of settlement testify to the diversity of Chalcolithic society, which was basically a seminomadic society exhibiting various levels of sedentism. An outstanding characteristic is the cultural uniformity evident throughout the country, as exhibited in the house plans, with local and regional variation dictated by climatic conditions and available raw materials. Variety within uniformity is a characteristic that will reappear as we consider other facets of Chalcolithic culture.

Tools and Objects of Daily Use

The Chalcolithic period is extremely rich in tools and objects made of many different materials. This section will treat everyday items, leaving aside for future discussion those objects that may have had a ritual function. It is sometimes difficult to decide whether an object is of ritual

significance, as religion and cult were no doubt an integral part of everyday life, and the same type of artifact could be used in both realms. The distinction has been based either on the context in which the objects were found or on the rarity of the material or the degree of sophistication required to prepare the object, assuming that people invested more effort to serve their gods than to serve themselves. The variety of materials, techniques, and forms is even greater among cult objects than among objects of everyday use.

POTTERY

Following its introduction in the Neolithic period, the craft of pot-making became an integral part of the life-style of all human societies. People of the Chalcolithic culture made widespread use of pottery, creating objects for a wide range of basic needs, especially those related to food. They made containers for the storage of dry foods and liquids, vessels for the stages of food preparation, and tableware. Thus, an assemblage was formed reflecting both the requirements of this society and the technical standards of its craftsmen.

We will begin with technical considerations. The vast majority of Chalcolithic ceramic vessels were handmade, generally in the coil or strip method. The base was prepared by pressing the wet clay onto a flat stone, plank, or mat. Many bases bearing mat impressions witness the extensive use of mats in the production of pottery. While building the vessel, the potter would flatten the walls until a relatively uniform thickness was attained. In this manner, vessels could be manufactured from the smallest to the largest size needed. Small, simple vessels

were often made by pinching a hand-held lump of clay. Alongside those two simple methods, which require no implement save the potter's hands, there is evidence that potters began to use tournettes, which provided rotary motion. They were slow wheels, used chiefly to fashion the rim edges of smaller vessels and to give a uniform thickness and shape to the upper parts of small bowls. After being formed, the vessel was often decorated. Most common are rope decorations, made of strips or coils of clay attached to the vessels and imprinted with the finger or a twig. These strips have the appearance of ropes binding the vessels, and they may recall the ropes actually used to support the vessels while they were being built. Alongside the plastic decoration, a wealth of decoration was imprinted with a thumbnail or small twig on the body of the vessel itself.

Painted decoration on the body of the vessel is less frequent. It usually consists of single bands or line groups of red paint on the rim or body, as well as other patterns such as wavy lines, circles, semicircles, and often triangles and rhombuses, sometimes filled in with a net pattern. The patterns are applied carelessly. The painting of the vessels indicates that the firing was fairly sophisticated, in kilns with two chambers, a combustion chamber and a firing chamber. The separation of the fuel from the vessels allows the latter to attain a uniform hue and brings out the painted pattern.

Another type of decoration, if it may be considered a decoration and not a functional element, is the addition of small lug handles applied haphazardly to various types of vessels, especially small and middle-sized jars. The holes pierced in these handles are so small that it is difficult even to pass a string through them for the purpose of suspension.

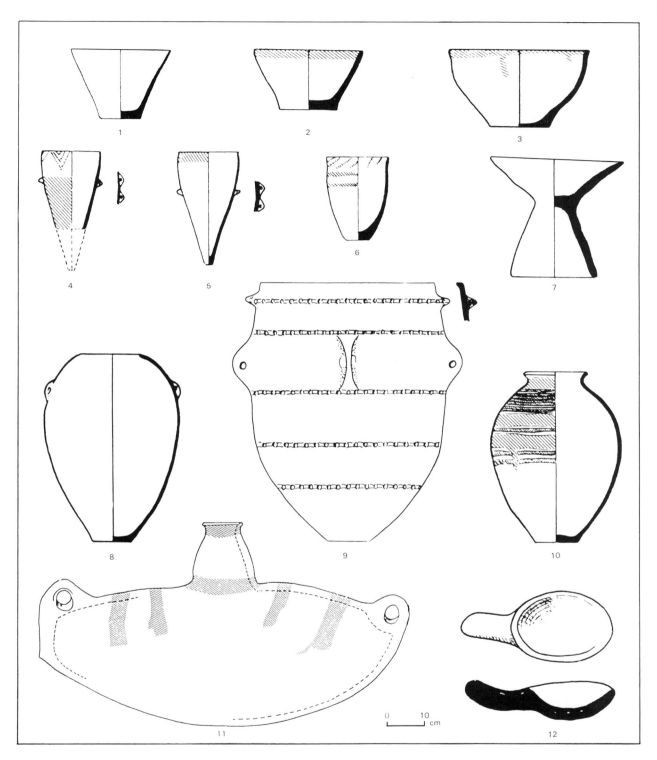

Fig. 3.4. Chalcolithic pottery

Their random distribution enhances their decorative character.

Following is a review of characteristic pottery types of the Chalcolithic period.

STORAGE VESSELS

VERY LARGE STORAGE VESSELS (PITHOI) (fig. 3.4:9). Such vessels are required in any agricultural society with a food surplus. The storage of harvested food enables subsistence throughout the year, until the next harvest is brought in. The yield may of course be stored in pits, but the drawbacks of the pits are manifold, as they are subject to moisture and the predations of rodents and insects. Furthermore, pits cannot be dug at every site. The large storage vessel can overcome these difficulties. Its walls are dry and impermeable. It can be moved about and set down anywhere, and it may be partly embedded in the floor for stability and easy access. It is therefore not surprising that pithoi were among the most common and characteristic vessel types of the period.

The pithos has an elementary shape: a flat base, high walls, a wide mouth, and a generally thickened rim. The largest pithos discovered to date was found partly embedded in a pit at the site of Dalhemiya, near Ashdot Yaacov. The vessel was preserved to a height of 1.53 meters. Its maximum diameter was one meter. Nearly all pithoi are found in rather thick coils of clay modeled in a rope pattern. The bands probably provided added strength to the large vessels as they were being dried and fired. Some pithoi have two or four large loop handles.

STORE JARS (fig. 3.4:10). These are smaller than the pithoi and therefore more easily carried when full. They were no doubt used to store small to moderate amounts of food for immediate use. Two types of store jar were common—a jar with a rounded body, a base slightly wider than the mouth, and a tall upright neck; and a rounded, neckless jar. The latter vessel is termed a holemouth jar. A spout is often found below the rim of the holemouth, indicating its function as a container of liquids. The two jar types, in a variety of sizes, are among the most common vessel types at all sites. Large groups of jars were found in the Golan. They are made of the characteristic basaltic clay of that region and bear a rope decoration.

Another special group of medium and small store jars has been named cream ware. These vessels, of exceptional quality, are made of an oily white clay containing a high proportion of Negev kaolin. This group is characteristic mainly of the Beersheba valley sites.

KITCHENWARE

This group includes vessels employed in the preparation and cooking of food.

BOWLS (fig. 3.4:1–3). These are open vessels (widest at the rim), with a diameter of 15 to 35 centimeters. They have a flat base and their walls are usually splayed at a 45-degree angle. Larger bowls of similar form are sometimes called kraters or basins.

COOKING POTS (fig. 3.4:8). The medium-sized, round- or flat-based holemouth jars may have served this purpose, for they are often found coated with a thick layer of soot.

PANS. These are flat vessels with thick walls, a round or oval outline, and a horizontal handle along each of the shorter sides. The simple, coarse vessels resemble frying pans, but as they bear no fire or oil stains their function remains uncertain.

SPOONS (fig. 3.4:12). One of the unique forms of the Ghassulian assemblage, the oval spoon has a short, thick handle, either round or flat in section. This special kitchen utensil was no doubt used for mixing food.

CHURNS (fig. 3.4:11). This vessel too is peculiar to the Chalcolithic culture, though at Ghassul itself it is less common than at other sites of the period, particularly those of the Beersheba valley and the western Negev. The churn has an unusual shape: its body resembles an elongated, horizontal barrel. One end of the vessel is flat, the other pointed, and to both a loop handle is attached. The neck is inserted into the middle of the vessel. When fragments of this vessel were first found, scholars were sorely puzzled, as no artifact of similar appearance was known. Only when a complete vessel of the type was found and its form established was it seen to resemble the goatskins used by Beduin to churn milk into butter and cheese. The churn is found in various sizes, ranging from large functional vessels 70 centimeters long to miniature objects only 12–13 centimeters long. It is not clear whether the latter had a functional or a ritual purpose.

The churn is an artifact of the pastoral economy. The milking season of sheep and goat is brief, and the warm climate would bar the utilization of milk were it not possible to process it into a less perishable product. Fresh milk, after being boiled and fermented, was poured into the churn for the next stage of processing. The rhythmic motion of the churn separated the fat, and after straining there remained butterfat, from which butter was produced; this could be preserved for a year. The watery part of the milk was used to make cheese.

This type of vessel has no successors in the pottery assemblages of the following periods, though flock husbandry remained without doubt an important part of the economy. This may indicate a division in later times between the sedentarists, who made pottery, and the pastoral nomads, who reverted to the use of skins.

TABLEWARE

The term "tableware" refers to small vessels that could have been used by individuals. These consist mainly of cups, goblets, and saucers.

THE CUP AND GOBLET (fig. 3.4:4–6). These are among the most common vessels of the period. There are rounded cups with a wide or narrow flat base, pedestal cups (which better deserve the name goblet), and pointed horn-shaped vessels termed cornets. The cornet is peculiar to the Ghassulian culture and has many variant forms. It is so typical of the period that a site may be assigned to the Chalcolithic period solely on the basis of the presence of such vessels. The cornet, like the churn and spoon, is entirely absent from the pottery series of later periods.

SAUCERS. These vessels too are quite common. They are deep, with a flat base and V-shaped walls. Their form suggests that they, like the cups and goblets, were used for drinking. Some saucers exhibit traces of smoothing on a slow wheel.

PEDESTAL BOWLS (fig. 3.4:7). A special group of vessels includes bowls placed on a high, fenestrated pedestal. The function of the ped-

estal bowl, whether domestic or ritual, is unclear, so that it is difficult to assign the bowls to one of the main vessel categories. It should be noted that basalt vessels of identical form have been found at various Chalcolithic sites.

The pottery assemblage described above is typical of Chalcolithic sites throughout the country. Accompanying the usual vessel types that appear in all periods (jars and bowls) there is a group of vessels peculiar to the Chalcolithic period. These vessels serve as an excellent means of identifying sites of the period and may provide a key to the understanding of its special character.

The function of the spoon is insufficiently clear, and it has been suggested above that it served as a kitchen utensil. Why were clay spoons no longer produced in later periods? Perhaps simply because the long-handled clay spoon was fragile, and a wooden spoon preferred. The special status of the cornet and churn is clearer. Both vessels express the supreme importance of flocks in Chalcolithic economy. The close relation to the flocks and the dependence on their products are reflected in the invention of these two vessels, the one a drinking vessel shaped like a goat or ram's horn, the other a churn imitating the form of a goatskin. The preparation of food or its imbibition from the body and horns of an animal must have had particular significance for the people of the period. This significance finds its clearest expression in three ceramic figurines found in two temples: a figure of a woman carrying a churn on her head, a zoomorph bearing two churns on its back, and a ram carrying three cornetlike vessels on its back.

Though all the pottery types appear in all sites of the period, there are regional differences in the relative proportions of the different ves-

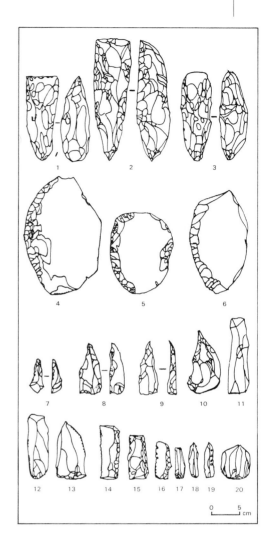

Fig. 3.5. Chalcolithic flint tools: awls, borers, scrapers, knives, and adzes

sel groups. Jars and pithoi are more frequent in the Golan than in other areas, cornets are found in greater numbers in Teleilat Ghassul than in the sites of the western Negev and Beersheba regions, and large churns are more characteristic of the latter area than of Ghassul. Cream ware also characterizes the Beersheba sites, accompanied by a proliferation of perforated lug handles. Painted decoration is more characteristic of Ghassul, and rope decoration of the Golan. These quantitative differences permit the division of the Chalcolithic sites into three main groups: sites resembling Teleilat Ghassul, those resembling the Beersheba sites, and the Golan group. The differences may be regional (related to human groups with different cultural traits who live in different parts of the country) or chronological (involving a temporal sequence of groups). It is now thought that the Beersheba group is somewhat later than that of Ghassul. The Golan group is closer to Ghassul, though it has its own characteristic elements and appears to have extended to the northern Jordan valley, the eastern Galilee, and the Hauran. The pottery assemblages thus reflect the regional variation within the easily recognized cultural unity.

FLINT TOOLS

Flint tools make up an appreciable part of the objects of daily use in the Chalcolithic period, which is among the last stages in human evolution in which widespread use was made of flint tools.

AXES, ADZES, AND CHISELS. All these tools share a common form. They are elongated and trapezoidal in section. Their function relates to the various stages of woodworking: the axe was used for felling trees, removing their branches, and splitting wood; the adze was used to strip the bark and to give basic form to objects such as posts and beams used in construction, canoes, or bowls; and the chisel was used for final touches and finish. In the axe, the blade is aligned parallel to the haft, while the adze blade is perpendicular. It is also possible that adzes were not hafted at all. The chisel is narrower than the other two tools, and it is not known in what manner it was attached to its haft.

PICK. This rare tool has a pointed end and a roughly triangular section. Easily handled, it was probably used for digging or for boring holes.

HAMMERS AND HEAVY CUTTING IMPLEMENTS. These are made of modified cores. Hammers are rounded, whereas cutting tools have sharp edges at each end.

BLADES. These include knives and sickles, the latter being very common in Chalcolithic sites. Sickles made of flint blades set in a wood or bone haft were no doubt used for reaping grain, as well as for the cutting of reeds and cane needed for basketry. Many blades bear the characteristic sheen caused by the friction between the flint blade and the plant stalks.

SCRAPERS. These are made on thick flakes and have retouched edges. Side and end scrapers are found, as well as round, perforated ones, but the best known of the Chalcolithic scrapers is the so-called fan scraper. The fan scraper is made on fine tabular flint, often preserving part of the cortex on one side. Scrapers are assumed to have been used in the processing of hides. In a pastoralist society like that of the Chalcolithic, widespread use was no doubt made of the hides of sheep and cattle for the manufacture of vessels, clothing, footwear, and so on. The fan scraper is one of the most characteristic flint tools of the period.

Many coarse blades and flakes of unspecified form bear signs of modification along one edge, ranging in character from fine retouch to coarse denticulation. These were probably used as knives of various types or as scrapers.

AWLS. These are rather thick flakes, pointed at one end. They were probably used to perforate hides.

STAR-SHAPED TOOLS. This is a tool peculiar to the Chalcolithic period. It is a round flake fashioned so as to have a series of points around its perimeter. The center of the tool is perforated. It has been suggested that this artifact served in the combing and processing of sheep's wool.

AN OUTSIZED FLINT TOOL. At a site in Nahal Besor, a complete flint tool of remarkable size was discovered. It is elongated, with a triangular section, and ends in a point. At 76 centimeters, it is the longest flint tool discovered in the Land of Israel and in the Near East. The tool shows excellent workmanship; it is fashioned by consecutive transversal blows, a common technique in the Chalcolithic period. The function of the artifact is not known, but its great size may indicate that it was not a domestic one.

It is worth noting that there is no artifact in the entire corpus of flint tools that may be termed an arrowhead or spearhead. As only small amounts of wild animal bones were found in some sites, it may be concluded that hunting was of secondary importance in this period.

STONE ARTIFACTS

Stone, particularly basalt and limestone, was a convenient and readily available material used to fashion various artifacts, ranging from coarse work tools to sophisticated and delicate vessels.

TOOLS

Tools made of limestone or basalt were used for various purposes. Stone axes and hammers are relatively common, and they were used alongside similar flint objects. Their form is simple: a long and narrow block served as an axe, a round stone as a hammer. An important stone tool with no flint counterpart is the hoe—a rectangular basalt stone, perforated at one end for the insertion of the handle. A flat stone incised with a groove was used to whet flint and metal blades. Small flat perforated disks were probably used as loom weights.

GRINDING STONES

The extent of crop cultivation is reflected in the rich and variegated assemblage of grindstones and mortars. Grindstones include a quern in the form of a shallow bowl and a stone pushed back and forth over this surface, which grinds the grain into flour. Stone mortars and pestles were used for the same purpose. Basalt was the preferred material for the two types of object, though items made of the softer limestone are also in evidence.

BASALT BOWLS

A unique and outstanding product of Chalcolithic craftsmanship is the basalt bowl. Basalt is one of the more difficult materials to work with, and it is a wonder how the Chalcolithic craftsmen managed to

Fig. 3.6. Ivory artifacts and basalt bowls as found, Bir Safadi

bore into the basalt and create such precise and sophisticated vessels. They may have used a drill of a type in use in Egypt at a somewhat later date.

All the bowls have a V-shaped section. Some have a flat base, others stand on a pedestal, either solid or hollow. Their form resembles that of the ceramic vessels described above. The greatest number of basalt vessels was found at Teleilat

Ghassul, but the most beautiful ones were found in the subterranean storerooms at the sites of Bir Safadi and Bir Matar, near Beersheba. The Beersheba basalt bowls are large and deep, with a diameter of up to 50 centimeters. The wall of the vessel is about one centimeter thick and is uniform to its entire height. The vessel is well smoothed and usually decorated with fine, incised triangles descending from the rim.

Fig. 3.7. Assemblage of basalt vessels from Bir Safadi, including two bowls and a pedestal bowl (height 22 centimeters)

In some of the subterranean storerooms, the basalt vessels were found in sets of three, two plain bowls and a pedestal bowl. This arrangement raises the question whether the vessels might have had a function other than a domestic one, especially in view of the effort invested in their production and acquirement, which is inestimably greater than that required for similar pottery vessels.

Many basalt vessels were found in the Golan sites, some bearing relief representations.

MACEHEADS

Another stone object, usually made of limestone, is a perforated spherical or pyriform artifact with an average height of 5–6 centimeters. Such objects, found at sites throughout the country, are generally termed maceheads and are assumed to have had a wooden handle inserted in the vertical perforation. This weapon, used in hand-to-hand fighting, is similar to artifacts common in Egypt and Mesopotamia at about the same time. Maceheads would thus be the only known weapon used by the people of this period.

A large group of identical artifacts, cast in copper, was found in the Cave of the Treasure in Nahal Mishmar. These may have had a cultic function.

BONE TOOLS

Animal bones were used extensively in the Chalcolithic period for preparing tools such as needles, pins, awls, and handles of stone or copper artifacts. The bone tools are competently carved and are delicate and symmetrical, providing further evidence of the developed aesthetic sense and consummate skill of Chalcolithic artisans.

MATS AND STRAW ARTIFACTS

Straw, reeds, and palm fronds were used for a variety of objects. Remains of such objects come chiefly from the dwelling caves of the arid Judaean desert; they are supplemented by the impressions of mats or trays often found on the bases of pottery vessels.

The treasure trove of Nahal Mishmar was wrapped in a reed mat. Measuring 120 centimeters by 80 centimeters, it has a densely laid warp caught up in a stitched weft drawn through the warp. The joint is thus invisible and is stronger and more attractive than the usual weave. The edge of the mat is wound with straw cordage. This type of matting is unusual, recorded only in two other mats from the same cave. Another type of matting consisted of dense bundles of straw joined by a stitched straw cord.

The most common method for the manufacture of trays and baskets was coiling, in which bundles of straw in a spiral coil are bound by dense strips of straw. In addition to the trays and baskets found in the caves, many impressions of such basketry have been found on pot bases. A twill-woven basket was also found, and the method is recorded on pot bases. This flat weave, usually made of palm fronds, is found chiefly at Ghassul and is entirely unknown in the more arid Beersheba region, where palms were not cultivated.

A particularly fine object is a wickerwork sieve having the form of a shallow bowl with a diameter of 38 centimeters and a depth of 6 centimeters. The sides of the sieve are made of coiled bundles of rushes, and the base is a loose weave of rushes. Many grains of wheat and barley were found near and under the sieve, illustrating its function. This is the earliest sieve known.

Cords made of twined or plaited straw were also present.

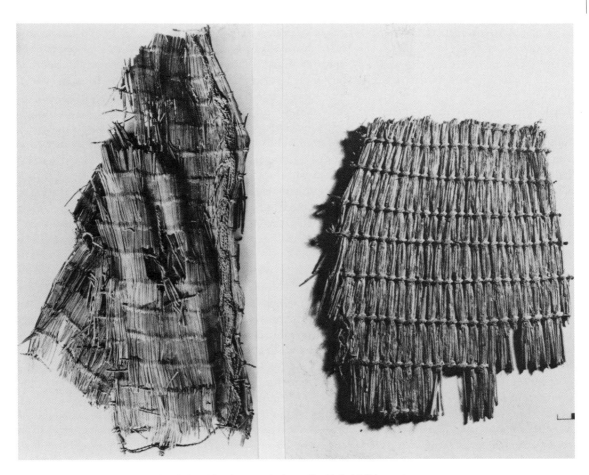

Fig. 3.8. Mat fragments from the Nahal Mishmar treasure

Fig. 3.9. Textile fragments from the Nahal Mishmar treasure

COPPER TOOLS AND THEIR MANUFACTURE

All the tool types and materials thus far discussed were used before Chalcolithic times. Artifacts of clay, flint stone, and bone had been in human use for many generations, and even basketry and weaving had been introduced long since. But while simple copper implements had indeed been produced at the Neolithic site of Çatal Hüyük in Anatolia, it was only in the Chalcolithic period that the methods of mining and processing copper became common knowledge. The coppersmiths of this period attained, within a relatively short span, extremely impressive results, creating sophisticated artifacts with complex techniques.

Few everyday copper items have been found in Chalcolithic sites of the Land of Israel; those that have been found have simple forms: round-sectioned awls or picks and axe or chisel blades. These tools are made of pure copper, from the mines of Timna or Wadi Fenan.

In the copper-rich valley of Timna in the southern Aravah, galleries and installations related to the extraction of copper have been discovered. Miners' settlements were found as well, the inhabitants of which may have supplied copper to the population centers of the north. Another possible copper source is in Wadi Fenan, east of the Aravah valley. Only raw ore was provided by the mines, and processing was completed elsewhere. Thus, at the site of Bir Matar near Beersheba, installations for all phases of copper-working were found. Two flat flint slabs served as worktables for crushing the ore; a few kilograms of copper ore were found nearby. Red stains on the ground containing copper powder mixed with wood charcoal and slag indicate roasting on an open fire. The ore was smelted in small, coarse ceramic crucibles located in round ovens made of earth mixed with straw. No stone or pottery molds were found, and it therefore appears that the copper was cast into sand molds.

Alongside the casting technique, the smiths also practiced annealing. In this technique the copper is hammered while cold, reheated to a medium temperature (500–600°C), then cooled and hammered again. These steps are repeated until the required thickness and form are achieved.

The discovery of the Nahal Mishmar hoard first revealed the full extent of copper technology and the high technical and artistic standard of Chalcolithic craftsmen. The artifacts found in the hoard are made in the lost-wax (cire-perdue) method, a technique far more sophisticated and complex than simple casting. A model of wax or fat in the precise shape of the required object was prepared and wrapped in damp clay, perforated in some places. When the clay dried, the molten metal was poured into the mold through the uppermost hole, melting the wax. As the wax ran out through the other holes, the metal filled the interior of the mold. Once the metal cooled, the clay mold was broken and the object removed. The lost-wax method requires metal of controlled viscosity, so that all the spaces within the mold can be filled in a uniform manner. The pure copper used to make tools was not suited to this technique. And indeed, analysis of the copper composition of the items in the treasure revealed that they contained 4 percent to 12 percent arsenic, an element that lowers the viscosity of the copper and hardens it as well. This has brought up the question of whether the arsenical copper is natural or an intentional alloy. The former possibility seems the more likely, as it is quite difficult to identify and extract native arsenic. Arsenical copper does occur naturally, not in the copper mines in or near the Land of Israel but rather in the Caucasian mountains, as well as in Anatolia and Iran. Here, further questions may be raised: was this special copper mined in any of those regions and sent in its raw state to the Chalcolithic smiths of the Land of Israel, or were the artifacts themselves made in the mountains of the far north and then brought away? And if the objects were brought away, how was it done? Did they arrive by way of trade or by way of the migration of those who made them? In the present stage of knowledge, there are no definite answers to any of these questions, and much depends on the outlook of the scholar who attempts to answer them.

The end of the Chalcolithic period signaled the end of a golden age of metallurgy. In the following periods metal tool production was limited to a small number of objects. Arsenical copper disappeared, and hundreds of years were to pass until the secret of improving copper by the addition of tin was discovered. Chalcolithic copper work represents a unique industrial and artistic high point.

Economic Base

Having reviewed the distribution of Chalcolithic settlements, their character, and the assemblage of artifacts and objects used by their inhabitants, the time has come to attempt to understand the subsistence resources exploited by the people of this age.

AGRICULTURE

There is no doubt that the great majority of the Chalcolithic population subsisted on the two major branches of agricultural activity: the cultivation of crops and the raising of flocks.

Many remains of field and orchard cultivations, as well as faunal remains, have been found in Chalcolithic settlements, and these enable us to determine what the ancient inhabitants raised. The most important crops were domesticated wheat and barley. They had been domesticated in the Neolithic period and since then had undergone thousands of years of cultivation. Grains and spikelets of a two-kerneled domesticated emmer wheat were found in the Judaean desert caves. The discovery is of great importance for the understanding of the history of wheat domestication, as this emmer wheat forms the connecting link between the two-kerneled wild emmer and the domesticated bread wheat. Kernels of einkorn wheat, the most primitive of the domesticates, and of two-rowed barley were also found. Wheat and barley can be successfully grown throughout the country, provided there is sufficient rainfall, and there is no doubt that they were raised during this period as a staple food from the Golan to Beersheba.

A most important implement related to the cultivation of cereals is the sickle, and flint sickle blades have been found in most sites of the period. There are, however, some sites, such as Bir Safadi, where virtually no sickle blades occur, raising the possibility that the inhabitants did not grow their own basic foods but obtained them elsewhere. This may be indirect evidence for the specialization of some settlements in the manufacture of goods exchangeable for food and other basic products.

Alongside wheat and barley, lentils and vetch were raised, carbonized remains of which were discovered in the Beersheba sites, at Teleilat Ghassul and in the Cave of the Treasure. The latter site also provided a few heads and cloves of garlic.

The great innovation of the Chalcolithic period in terms of horticulture is the domestication of a number of fruit trees. The Golan sites, Ghassul, and the Judaean desert caves provide the earliest evidence of olive pits and olivewood. The olive is a characteristic Mediterranean tree requiring at least 400 millimeters of rainfall per annum. The pomegranate, of which bits of rind with the seeds still attached have been found in the Judaean desert caves, is, like the olive, a Mediterranean plant. This period is also the first to cultivate the common date palm, a tree that can grow in more arid climates. Date stones have been found in the Judaean desert caves and at Ghassul. Basketwork employing palm fronds testifies to the diverse utilization of this tree. A long period of experimentation no doubt preceded the domestication of fruit trees and their incorporation in the agricultural economy. The Chalcolithic people planted orchards, thus establishing permanent farms, to which they must have returned year after year. The people of the period also ate wild fruits, such as the pods of the desert broom, acorns, and the nut of *Pistacia atlantica,* all of which were found in the caves of the Judaean desert.

Flax, used to make thread for woven fabrics, was another important crop of the period, evidenced by linen cloth found in the desert caves. The plant itself has yet to be found in a site context.

In addition to the floral remains themselves, implements such as sickles and hoes, pounding and grinding tools, and the straw sieve all testify to the agricultural character of the society.

ANIMAL HUSBANDRY

Alongside vegetable products, flocks were raised to provide food and other products. It has recently been proposed that the Chalcolithic period saw the second and crucial stage of animal utilization in human economy. In the first stage, which occurred in the Neolithic period, animals were domesticated for their meat. Now flocks began to be utilized for their secondary products, milk and wool, without being slaughtered. This development can be proven by determining the age of the animals at death. The greater the age, the longer the period of their secondary exploitation. This second stage is even more important, in economic terms, than the first, as it broadens the variety of uses of livestock and the economic base of those who breed them.

The major species represented in the Chalcolithic household were sheep and goat. Their bones constitute 90 percent of all the bones found in the northern Negev sites and not less than 50 percent at the other sites. The special vessels produced in imitation of parts of animals (the goatskin-shaped churn and the horn-shaped cornet) also testify that a life-style revolving around sheep and goat husbandry was typical of the Chalcolithic period. At some sites it was even more important than agriculture. Various cult remains, particularly horned figurines and objects and figures that carry churns and cornets, indicate the special importance attached to the raising of flocks.

At some sites, especially to the north of Beersheba, about 20 percent of the animal bones proved to be cattle and 30 percent pig. Many pig bones were also found at Ghassul. Pig breeding differs widely from that of flocks or herds, as pigs do not graze and do not migrate. At those sites where pigs were bred there was, therefore, a sedentary component in the population.

Further faunal remains of domesticated species include those of horse and donkey found at Ghassul and of camel found at Shiqmim. This is therefore the first period during which animals were used as beasts of burden, and indeed the existence of foreign trade, particularly the importation of raw materials, cannot be imagined without the assistance of those animals. Thus, by making important innovations in animal domestication, the people of the Chalcolithic period made a vital contribution to the evolution of human society.

Most of the faunal remains found at all sites were of domesticated species, though some remains of game animals, particularly gazelle, appear as well. The Chalcolithic communities were therefore almost entirely dependent on the flocks for their supply of meat, milk, hides, bone, and horn. The absence of weapons, particularly arrowheads and spearheads, confirms that observation. It is noteworthy that in the ritual art the heads of wild species are often depicted, especially ibex. The wild animal, rather than the domestic one, seems to have been a symbol of the deity.

CRAFTS, INDUSTRY, AND TRADE

The use of raw materials from disparate sources, as noted in the review of the objects and tools used by the Chalcolithic population, testifies to the existence of a wide-ranging trade network. Thus, for example, the people of Beersheba had at their disposal basalt or basalt vessels of a northern origin, shells from the Red Sea and the Nile, turquoise from the mines of southern Sinai, copper from Timna, arsenical copper from Anatolia, Iran, or the Caucasian mountains, elephant tusks from Africa or from North Syria,

and hippopotamus tusks, perhaps from Egypt. How these items were traded is not known. It seems likely that it was a slow process of exchange carried on at various stations along the route, the raw materials being exchanged at each stop for finished products and agricultural surplus. It may be supposed that trade was conducted by people who specialized in this occupation.

Some communities also must have initiated their own search for raw materials, especially copper. The copper prospectors of the Aravah and the miners of Timna may have belonged to communities of the more northerly areas, such as the Beersheba valley, spending only part of the year at the mining sites. The turquoise miners of southern Sinai may also have been a distant offshoot of a site or of a group of sites in the Land of Israel, though their products were chiefly for the Egyptian market.

The search for raw materials and the creation of a trade network opened the small communities to external influence. We can no longer speak of independent settlements carrying on a closed, traditional way of life. There must have been a fairly continuous relationship not only between adjacent communities but also with inhabitants of distant or even very distant areas. These economic relations led, in the nature of things, to cultural relations.

Raw materials were processed into many different objects. The processing of materials, and of copper in particular, requires specialization, know-how, and experience. In the manufacture of copper objects there are several phases of expert craftsmanship, so it must be assumed that there were several persons in the Bir Matar community, for example, who were expert coppersmiths and whose sole occupation was the manufacture of the required objects. Likewise, the

sculptors of the ivory statuettes at Bir Safadi must have been experts. We have therefore a situation involving craft specialization, division of labor, a marked rise in the standard of living, and perhaps also the establishment of social hierarchies.

Evidence is gradually accumulating for the existence of settlements that specialized in the various crafts. Thus, at Bir Safadi an ivory workshop for the manufacture of statuettes and other items was discovered, as was, lately, evidence of copper-working. The concomitant lack of sickle blades would also suggest that the inhabitants were craft specialists who obtained their food in exchange for the items they manufactured.

Copper with a high arsenic content, possibly of Armenian origin, was used to cast the objects found at Nahal Mishmar. Further analyses have revealed that similar objects found at other Chalcolithic sites were made of the same copper. Hence the trade in raw copper or in finished products was widespread. The weight of the arsenical copper composing the Nahal Mishmar hoard comes to nearly 140 kilograms, a large amount in view of the early stage of copper technology that it represents and the distant origin of the metal.

Chalcolithic society was based on an extensive network of prospecting and trade in raw materials, production, and exchange of goods—all on the broad economic base of diversified food production and the manufacture of other items of animal and vegetable origin. There is no doubt that this forms the incipient economic base and perhaps the seminal social organization of urban life.

Shrines and Cult

Among the many Chalcolithic sites surveyed and excavated, some can be identified as shrines because of their unusual form, location, or find assemblage.

THE EN GEDI SHRINE

The best-known shrine of this period is the structure excavated at En Gedi. It stands on a rock terrace 30 meters above the spring of En Gedi, on the slope between Nahal En Gedi and Nahal David. Its location near a fertile and well-watered oasis and the breathtaking view it affords of the Dead Sea and the mountains of Moab lend an air of mystery and awe to the spot, as befits a place of religious worship. The shrine is an isolated structure, there are no settlement remains nearby, and it therefore seems likely that it was a place of pilgrimage for the inhabitants of the region and perhaps of more distant areas.

The shrine consists of a large walled enclosure. It is entered from the south, from the direction of the spring, through a gatehouse—a bench-lined room with one doorway facing outward and the other into the enclosure. Inside the gate is a broad court, about 350 square meters, in the middle of which stands a round stone installation about 3 meters in diameter. Inside this installation is a basin composed of seven smooth stones; here a cylindrical object made of Egyptian alabaster was found. A channel ran from the installation toward a stone drain that pierced the eastern wall of the enclosure. The installation seems to have been connected with libations, perhaps the water from the nearby spring. Incorporated in the eastern wall of the enclosure is a rectangular chamber, approached by a paved path. This room was found empty, and its function remains unknown.

Fig. 3.10. The shrine at En Gedi and its surroundings

Opposite the entrance, on the north side of the court, lies the major structure of the sacred enclosure. It is a long and narrow room (5.5 × 20 meters), entered from the southern long wall. Opposite the door is a horseshoe-shaped installation, in the back corner of which stood a round, dressed-stone base, 25 centimeters high, made of white crystalline calcite—perhaps a pedestal for a statue or other sacred object. The installation itself was found full of ash, remains of the offerings burned within it. It also contained burned twigs, bone fragments, chunks of bitumen, many beads and snail shells, and a broken clay zoomorphic figurine, perhaps a bull, carrying two churns on its back—finds suggesting that the installation was an altar. In the center of the room, on either side of the doorway and of the installation, are long narrow benches on which offerings may have been placed. At the two ends of the room rows of small, round pits, about half a meter deep, were dug in the floor. They contained fragments of cornets, pedestal bowls, and small bowls, as well as ibex horns and snail shells.

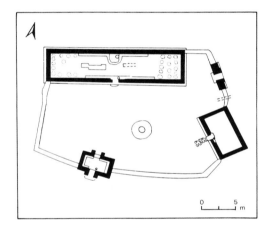

Fig. 3.11. Plan of the En Gedi shrine

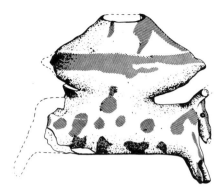

Fig. 3.12. Pottery figurine of animal bearing churns, from the En Gedi shrine (height 11.5 centimeters)

All the enclosure walls are built of mud brick on a foundation of a few courses of stone. A painted plaster fragment found in the debris of the superstructure suggests that the brick walls were plastered and painted in a manner similar to the house walls of Teleilat Ghassul. Unfortunately the fragment is small, and there is no way of reconstructing the painted design.

The scant finds unearthed within the sacred enclosure suggest that it was abandoned and most of the movable objects removed. Evidence of abandonment is characteristic of many Chalcolithic sites. It has been suggested that the cache of copper objects hidden in the Nahal Mishmar cave originated in the En Gedi shrine. The priests at the shrine, faced with the impending abandonment, wrapped the sacred objects and hid them in a nearby and virtually inaccessible cave.

Among the objects in the shrine, special mention should be made of the zoomorphic churn-bearing figurine, which points to the ritual aspects of milk and its special containers. Also of interest are the horn cores of ibex, a wild species of the En Gedi area and the forebear of the domestic goat. No evidence has been found in the settlements for the hunting of ibex for food, but it may have been hunted for ritual purposes and its horns brought as an offering to the shrine. Ibex heads and horns also decorate the cult objects of the Cave of the Treasure, which may have come from the En Gedi shrine. The Chalcolithic people may have considered the ibex to be the embodiment of the godhead and worshiped it to ensure the well-being and fertility of the flocks.

THE GILAT SHRINE

The fields west of Gilat in the western Negev have long been known to cover a Chalcolithic site. At this site, and especially on the low mound in its center, objects of special interest were collected over the years, including sandstone and limestone stelae and violin-shaped stone figurines, indications that the central mound was once the site of a cult center. The site was excavated in 1975, and four superimposed strata were cleared. The uppermost layer had been badly damaged by agricultural activity, but in the second stratum remains of two broadrooms built of mud bricks on a stone foundation were found. They seem to have been part of an extensive enclosure with a large central courtyard bordered by rows of rooms. In contrast to the En Gedi shrine, the shrine at Gilat stands in the center of a large settlement site of about ten hectares.

In both the upper, damaged stratum and in the stratum beneath it (of the two lower levels little is known), a wealth of finds was unearthed: the pottery included common vessels such as bowls, storage vessels, cornets, and churns but also unique loop-handled cylindrical vessels. Many flint tools were also found, as well as basalt artifacts, grindstones, and other stone objects, such as granite and basalt maceheads, and an iron discoid macehead. This abundance shows that the shrine was not divested of all its objects, as was the case at En Gedi, but was abandoned suddenly.

Two ceramic objects were found in the eastern chamber of the shrine. One portrays a seated woman carrying a churn on her head, the other a ram laden with three cornets. The two objects are not statuettes; rather, they are hollow containers, used perhaps in the temple ritual. Both churn and cornet were found in a ritual context at En Gedi, and they are doubtless related to the cult of milk and of the horned animals that provide it. Some view this cult as an early form of the cult of a deity resembling Dumuzi, the Mesopotamian god of fertility and fields, before whom milk was libated. The objects testify to the greater importance of flock husbandry over agriculture in the cult and may reflect their relative importance in the Chalcolithic economy.

The forms of the statuettes are of the greatest interest. The woman's body takes the form of a churn. The body members are attached in an offhand manner and include spindly arms and legs, a large protruding nose, small ears, small pointed breasts, and a navel. The right hand supports the churn on the head, and the left rests on the thighs, cradling in the crook of the elbow a vessel resembling a shallow bowl on a pedestal. The woman is seated on a stool, or in fact within it, as it too has the form of a shallow pedestal bowl. Her legs are quite short and dangle over the edge of the stool. The sexual organs, fingers, and toes are delineated by deep grooves. The entire body of the woman, including the stand cradled in her arm, is decorated with parallel stripes of red paint. Red circles with a dot in the middle represent wide-open eyes, from which two parallel vertical stripes descend between the breasts to the abdomen. The stripes may

Fig. 3.14. Pottery figurine of ram bearing cornets, from Gilat (height 27.5 centimeters)

Fig. 3.13. Pottery figurine of woman bearing churn, from Gilat (height 30 centimeters)

represent a veil covering the mouth, which is not indicated. The woman's hair, also indicated in red paint, appears as two curls on either side of her face and eight more hanging down over her neck and back. The hair is gathered at the top of the head in a sort of headdress composed of three bands. The ram is also fashioned in the form of a churn. Its small head bears horns that curve downward, and a hairy roll of fat is realistically depicted on its breast. The ram's eyes are identical to the woman's—a painted circle with a dot in the middle. Each flank is decorated with ten large red triangles pointed downward and three cornets, painted red, are perched on the back of the ram.

The two vessels may perhaps be seen as a representation of the two most common deities of the period—the female deity represented by the churn, and the male deity in the form of a ram and its attribute, the cornet. Both deities are closely linked to flocks and milk products. In this connection we might recall the figurine found at En Gedi, a bull or perhaps a ram bearing churns, that is, the male deity bearing the female attribute. The ibex horns found in the same context may be another symbol of the male deity.

The female deity is represented at Gilat not only in realistic form. A number of stylized violin-shaped figurines were found as well. All are made of special, nonlocal stone. One is especially large, more than twenty centimeters high, and is made of a red-veined crystalline limestone. These figurines may perhaps be viewed as a schematic representation of the female form. We

cannot know whether the two figures represent two separate deities or different aspects of one goddess. As the violin-shaped figurine also appears on the ossuaries of this period, the subject will be discussed below. Violin-shaped figurines have also been found in the Nahal Besor sites, at a coastal site in northern Sinai, and in large numbers at Ghassul. They were found in domestic, rather than cultic, contexts and seem to have been used in a personal cult, together with other cult-type objects found in what appear to be regular living rooms.

We have thus seen that people of the Chalcolithic culture worshiped their gods in distant, isolated shrines and in shrines within their settlements. In both excavated shrines a divine couple, related to the fertility of the flocks, was apparently worshiped. Sacred objects seem to have been displayed in ritual processions, whereas the ritual itself consisted, it seems, of libation, perhaps of milk, from special vessels, of the libation of water into courtyard installations, of sacrifices, and of offerings. Neither shrine contained elements that may be associated with agriculture. This indicates the great importance of animal husbandry in the Chalcolithic economy.

Alongside the public cult there is much evidence for an extensive household cult, as attested by the many finds of cultic nature from domestic contexts. The coexistence of the two kinds of cult may indicate the belief in a divine hierarchy, in which personal gods were distinguished from the central, cosmic deities of the entire community.

Artistic Expression and Its Context

Many objects and art items that were not found in a clearly sacred context nevertheless suggest cultic significance in their form, standard of workmanship, motifs, and sometimes their findspot. As far as we know, Chalcolithic society was a communal society, and the art that it fostered was chiefly of a religious nature, serving the requirements of cult, whether public, as enacted in the central shrines, or household and even personal, as performed within tribes or scattered settlements.

THE TREASURE OF NAHAL MISHMAR

This survey begins with the magnificent hoard discovered by chance, hidden in a niche in a distant corner of a Chalcolithic dwelling cave in the north face of the gorge of Nahal Mishmar in the Judaean desert. The hoard was wrapped in a mat and contained 442 different objects, 429 of copper, 6 of hematite, 1 of stone, 5 of hippopotamus ivory, and 1 of elephant ivory. It is a strange and unique collection of finds, and it appears to have been hurriedly collected and cached in the final days of settlement in the cave. In view of this, it has been plausibly suggested that the hoard is the sacred treasure

Fig. 3.15. Nahal Mishmar treasure as discovered

of the En Gedi shrine (found virtually devoid of finds), which lies only twelve kilometers away.

Most of the objects in the hoard are made of a copper containing a varying but always high percentage of arsenic (4%–12%). What is most surprising is that this special copper was used only in the objects made by the lost-wax technique and not in the simple chisels and hammers, of which sixteen were found. This distinction is present in other sites as well. A scepter found at Bir Matar and resembling those of the treasure contained 12 percent arsenic and a macehead from Nahal Zeelim had 4.6 percent arsenic, whereas an axe head from Nahal Zeelim had only a trace of this element. There is therefore a clear-cut separation in the employment of the two kinds of copper. For tools nearly pure copper of the kind found at Timna was used, though it is softer; for the special objects, an arsenical copper, harder and more easily cast, was used. That distinction alone is sufficient to set the interesting and artistic objects apart from the other items in the treasure.

CROWNS. Ten cylindrical objects resembling crowns, with a diameter of 15.6–19 centimeters and a height of 7–11.7 centimeters, were found in the cache. Two are provided with small feet. The body sometimes bears incised decoration of varying pattern: parallel lines, triangles, herringbone bands. One crown has a unique design in the form of a carelessly executed seven-pointed star. On the same object, opposite the star, a small human face is carved in relief, with a protruding nose and two round eyes with round irises. The mouth is not shown. The features resemble those of the goddess with the churn from Gilat, and this seems to have been the common manner of depicting human features in all forms of Chalcolithic art.

Some of the crowns have projections from the rim. They are independent elements soldered onto the body, and many were broken off and lost before the deposition of the cache. One crown preserves the remains of four flat bands curving inward, which may have joined to form a kind of cap. The crown with the features retains what resembles a bent, flat-topped nail, as well as six other protrusions. One crown, preserved completely, bears two small, schematic horned animal heads of an unidentified species. Another crown has four hornlike knobs bent inward.

One more crown was nearly perfectly preserved and is the most interesting of all. A wide aperture in the body is flanked by two flat knobs. Above the right doorpost, a shaft with two discoidal protrusions springs from the rim. A small broken protuberance above the left doorpost indicates that there was originally another such shaft at this point. On the opposite side of the crown, two schematic representations of birds are soldered to the rim, their bodies decorated with incised lines simulating feathers. Both birds face right. Between the shafts and the birds stand two gate-shaped structures. Each gatepost is decorated with four flat knobs, and a rectangular addition over the gate is furnished with a pair of horns.

Fig. 3.16. Crown from Nahal Mishmar (height 17.5 centimeters)

This crown is a repository of religious symbolism. The opening in the body suggests that it was intended as a model of a round structure, perhaps a hut built of branches, and the shafts with the flat top may represent the upper part of the branches, converted from a structural element to one of decorative symbolic significance. As no round structures have been found in any of the Chalcolithic settlements—neither a dwelling house nor a temple—the round structure may recall a period of migration and wanderings before settlement in the Land of Israel. The gate-shaped structures as a whole—the opening, the knobs, and the rectangular addition—closely resemble the facades of ossuaries of this period. The rectangular gable is also reminiscent of the violin-shaped figurines, and the horns recall the horned animals and horn cores from the shrines of En Gedi and Gilat.

The combination of symbols suggests several avenues of interpretation. The entire assemblage may be related in essence to the concept of death and afterlife, with the gate an emblem of the gateway to the world of the dead. The gate is fashioned as a schematic goddess but bears male attributes as well; the latter may symbolize the hope for a power of reincarnation and revival. Further speculation may be attempted, but unfortunately we have no information other than that provided in the objects themselves.

SCEPTERS. This is a diverse group of 118 objects, their lengths ranging from 7 centimeters to 40 centimeters. Some of the scepters preserved traces of wood or reed hafts, and in some a black adhesive substance remained. This has led archaeologists to conclude that the objects were carried on long poles, perhaps in sacred processions. A flax thread found in one of the scepters may indicate that light materials, such as ribbons, were tied to the scepters.

The scepters are all similar in form but differ widely in size and the details of their decoration. All have a flat, discoid rim, and most have a spherical or pyriform bulge under the rim, giving the appearance of a complete mace, with its head and handle. The body is decorated with parallel horizontal, diagonal, or zigzag incisions, net patterns, spiral fluting, and small spherical knobs. The rounded bulge is also decorated, usually with diagonal or horizontal fluting or with horizontal incised lines. At times flat knobs project from the bulge.

One of the scepters has four branchlike arms springing from the bulge, giving it the appearance of a tree. Another is dotted with spherical knobs of different sizes, resembling knots on a branch. These vegetal motifs may have had cultic significance.

Fig. 3.17. Scepter decorated with ibexes from Nahal Mishmar (height 27.5 centimeters)

Three scepters are adorned with horned animal heads. Four knobs sprout from the head of another scepter, ending in a schematic animal head with straight horns, a protruding snout, and a cloven beard. In another scepter, a miniature animal head with large down-curved horns emerges from the spherical bulge.

The most magnificent of the scepters bears five animal heads. Three short shafts emerge from the bulge, each ending in a finely formed head whose ears, mouth, and eyes are indicated by small knobs. Two of these are ibex heads, with thick, grooved, down-curving horns; the third is of an animal with smooth, sinuous horns. From the flat rim of the scepter springs a pair of smaller ibex heads.

A unique scepter has, on its pyriform bulge, human features depicted in relief, with a prominent aquiline nose, eyes marked by incised circles, and only a hint of an incised mouth. All these elements conform to the traditional portrayal of human features in Chalcolithic art. Two elongated knobs replace the ears on each side of the head, and the remains of another knob may be observed on the back of the head.

It should be noted that similar scepters have been found at other sites. A fragment was found at Bir Matar, and the burial cave at Palmahim revealed a short scepter, complete, with a pyriform bulge and a discoid rim. Metallurgical analysis shows that the two items were made of copper with a high arsenic content (12 percent for the Bir Matar scepter and 8.3 percent for the scepter from Palmahim), the same kind of copper used in Nahal Mishmar. Another scepter has been discovered in a structure at Shiqmim.

WANDS. This term describes a group of slender, long, solid scep-

ters. Three appear to be refined versions of scepters—long rods with various bulges at their ends. The fourth resembles the stalk of a plant, and the fifth has a flat, hooked head.

DECORATED STANDARDS. The three splendid standards in this group were no doubt mounted on a pole. The first is a hollow, pear-shaped object bearing twin ibex with one body, four legs, and two heads.

Each ibex faces a large arm springing from the pear-shaped body, the one shaped like an axe, the other like a knife. The second standard has a short hollow shaft with a rectangular panel spreading out from the center, modeled as a vulture with outspread wings. The bald head is modeled in the round and has a gaping beak. The feathers of the body and wings are marked by zigzag grooves. The third standard is more modest; from its bulge spring

Fig. 3.18. Scepter decorated with human features from Nahal Mishmar (height 13.2 centimeters)

four flat knobs in four different directions.

HORN-SHAPED OBJECTS. Three objects in the shape of a curved horn emphasize the importance of horns in Chalcolithic ritual. Two of the horns bear, on their narrow end, schematic figures of birds, one with wings outspread and the other perched upright.

CONTAINERS. A tall-necked pitcher of comely proportions, a pot or deep bowl, and three basketlike vessels with a high looped handle are the only containers found in the treasure.

MACEHEADS. The largest group of objects, numbering 261 artifacts, includes thickened objects of varying description—round,

pyriform, elongated, or disk-shaped—generally called maceheads. All have a hole in the center suitable for the insertion of a handle. Indeed, in some examples were found remains of wooden handles, traces of a black adhesive, and in one case a piece of flax cloth. These artifacts should not, perhaps, be seen as weapons, though the macehead was a common weapon in Mesopotamia and Egypt during this period. Their presence in the treasure would seem to indicate, rather, a ceremonial use. Their similarity to the bulges on the standards and scepters supports this assumption.

Six maceheads were made of hematite, a natural iron oxide. They were not cast but drilled, for the technology of iron-working was yet unknown. One macehead is made of

hard limestone. All the maceheads have a well-polished, undecorated surface.

Similar maceheads have been found at many settlement and burial sites of the period. Those that have been analyzed have all proven to be of arsenical copper.

OBJECTS MADE OF HIPPOPOTAMUS TUSK. Five mysterious objects were cached together with the copper objects: hippopotamus tusks, sliced lengthwise into scythe-shaped objects. They are perforated by three rows of round holes, and in the middle of each is a hole with a raised border.

AN IVORY BOX. A final unique find is an ivory box, 38 centimeters long, made of part of a well-pol-

Fig. 3.19. Macehead decorated with double ibex from Nahal Mishmar (height 11 centimeters)

ished but otherwise unmodified elephant tusk.

The hoard as a whole is a magnificent collection of art objects. The objects are made of valuable materials, maintain a high technological standard, and bear a superior finish. Their forms testify to a developed aesthetic sense. It may be assumed, in view of the decorative motifs, that they form a rich repository of religious symbolism.

WALL PAINTINGS FROM TELEILAT GHASSUL

Another art form with probable religious content is wall painting, as discovered in houses at Ghassul. Small fragments of painted plaster found at En Gedi indicate that this art form had a wider distribution. Fresco fragments were discovered in many rooms, and it was assumed

that the paintings were executed in a domestic context. These wall paintings, it should be noted, were not single creations. Rather, they were continuously plastered over and repainted. Some fragments preserve more than twenty painted layers. It has recently been speculated that the painted rooms were in fact shrines situated within the dense building clusters.

No complete wall segments were preserved, only small fragments reconstituted by the excavators to form the larger segments. The most remarkable segment is the star fresco. It consists of a large eight-pointed star, 1.84 meters in diameter. Its center is composed of concentric circles and contains two more eight-pointed stars. The innermost star is white on a black ground; the second is white, bor-

Fig. 3.21. Mask wall painting from Teleilat Ghassul (height 18 centimeters)

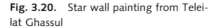

Fig. 3.20. Star wall painting from Teleilat Ghassul

dered with black, on a red cross-hatched ground; and the outermost star has alternating red and black rays. The execution is most precise. Around the star hover fragments that do not form a coherent picture, and they appear to belong to different layers of painting. Left of the star is an animal with a colorful wing; opposite it is part of a horned animal. Both animals have large eyes. Between them a masklike face appears, with large round eyes, a long nose, and long red fangs. A yellow halo surrounds the head. A similar mask with nose and fangs is portrayed on other fresco fragments. This is, therefore, a figure of special significance. Under this mask is another goggle-eyed figure, and above it a gnarled hand joined to an incompletely preserved body garbed in a long red robe. In the lower right corner, superimposed on part of a black ray of the large star, is a fragmentary depiction of what may be a structure, resembling the aperture of an ossuary or a gate such as that on the crown from the Cave of the Treasure.

Another fresco fragment shows a crouching animal, perhaps a leopard, with large eyes, and above it two concentric semicircles. Another fragment consists of the lower part of a scene of which only the paws and feet of animal and human figures remain. This scene has been interpreted as a procession in which sacrifices are offered to a pair of deities.

The wall paintings of Teleilat Ghassul are an exceptional phenomenon in the realm of artistic expression in the Land of Israel. Neither in earlier periods nor in later ones—until the Late Bronze Age—is there evidence for wall painting. This lends credence to the hypothesis that the creators of the frescos came from a region in which this form of artistic expression was known and common, perhaps Mes-

opotamia, where wall paintings of the period have been discovered. With the disappearance of the Chalcolithic culture, the art of wall painting disappeared as well.

STATUETTES AND IVORY OBJECTS FROM THE BEERSHEBA SITES

Another of the many facets of Chalcolithic art is the realm of ivory sculpture, the products of which have been found at the Beersheba sites. At Bir Safadi, an ivory workshop was discovered, with a stone table slab, a complete unworked tusk of an elephant, and a pointed tool with a bone haft. The origin of the elephant tusk is unknown; it may have come either from Africa via Egypt or from northern Syria,

where elephants were hunted as late as the first millennium B.C.E.

The most fascinating group of carved ivory objects is without question that of the anthropomorphic statuettes. We have already seen some of the ways in which the human figure was represented in art objects: the female statuette from Gilat, the human features on the scepter from the Cave of the Treasure. Here we have a representation of the human figure in a different material, which, despite variations inherent in the different character of the material, displays a remarkable resemblance to the other attempts at depicting the human form. This suggests that a uniform concept governed the depiction of the human figure at all sites and in all materials.

Fig. 3.22. Ivory figurines from Bir Safadi (male, height 33 centimeters; female, 12 centimeters)

A tall (33 centimeters), thin statuette depicts a male figure in a frozen attitude. The head is large in relation to the body, and its upper portion is hollowed out to form a small vessel, as it were. The nose of monumental proportions, the large round eyes, and the lack of mouth are all basic conventions of human representation in the Chalcolithic period. The face is bordered by holes, no doubt for the insertion of a hair or straw beard. The eyes were apparently inlaid. The shoulders and chest are narrow, the arms spindly, and the hands rest upon the belly. The body broadens somewhat below the waist, and the proportions of the legs are fairly realistic. Fingers and toes are marked by incisions.

In another house, a nearly identical, though smaller (25 centimeters) male statuette was found. Its head is quite large, and the enormous nose is paralleled by the large member, covered in a sort of pouch. This figure had no beard. Here too the hands are held over the belly. The two figures do not grasp or carry an object of any kind and have no identifying features.

The excavator of the site, Jean Perrot, has suggested that the attitude of the figures implies awe and submission, and he therefore sees them as representing ritually naked worshipers, making obeisance to their gods. Other scholars believe the figures to be divine, particularly on the assumption that the art of this period was intended, first and foremost, to present religious concepts and not the community of worshipers.

A nearly complete female statuette found at Bir Safadi, styled the Beersheba Venus, shows the now headless figure of a pregnant, nude woman standing 12 centimeters tall. The sexual organs are heavily emphasized, and the navel and nipples are represented by holes. Here, as in the male figures, the hands are clasped over the belly and the figure carries no identifying objects. The figure is softer and more supple than the frozen male figures. The knees are slightly bent in a nearly natural stance. The emphasis on the sexual organs may indicate the function of a fertility goddess, though this may also be a depiction of a naked worshiper. The head and breast of another female figurine was found. A perforated ivory disk was inlaid in one of the large eyes of this armless figure. Two further heads with piled-up hairdos have also been identified as female. A recent fortuitous find of a female statuette may be added to this group. Complete but for the feet, the figurine stands 29 centimeters high. The upright attitude resembles that of the male figures, and the thin hands rest on the belly. As usual, the head is large and schematic, with a prominent nose and no mouth. In this statuette, however, the eyes are also not shown. Unlike the Beersheba Venus and the Gilat figure, the breasts are large, and the sexual organs are not depicted at all.

In one house at Bir Safadi (next to two basalt bowls, a male figurine, and the head of a female figure), two sickle-shaped ivory objects were found, one of them whole and the other broken. The complete sickle is 40 centimeters long and undecorated. The fragmentary sickle bears a stippled pattern of lines, a flower, and an hourglass. The perforations were filled in with a material identified as bitumen. A similar fragment was found in another house at the same site, decorated in a stippled zigzag pattern. The ivory sickle doubtless had a ceremonial function, perhaps in connection with a ritual for increasing the fertility of the fields. If this is the case, it is the only cult object so far that can be related to agriculture rather than flock husbandry. It is of interest that the Beersheba sites reveal no cultic use of the horn or churn symbols. It is even more interesting that no flint sickle blades were found at Bir Safadi, so at this specific site cereal cultivation was not practiced. This may indicate that the Bir Safadi workshops created the ivory sickles solely for export.

A solid bell-shaped object, a fine schematic portrayal of a pelicanlike bird, and amuletlike disks complete the rare collection of ivories from Beersheba.

We do not know for certain whether the rooms in which the ivory objects were found were cult areas or workshops. It is also difficult to tell whether the other objects found there, such as the basalt bowls, fulfilled a cultic function, raising questions similar to those surrounding the Ghassul wall paintings.

The ivory object assemblage, particularly the male and female statuettes, generally resembles ivory statuettes found in tombs of this period in southern Egypt. Though the quality of the Beersheba ivories is higher, there must have been some connection between the glyptic art of the two regions.

BASALT HOUSE IDOLS FROM THE GOLAN

The cultic component in the life of the inhabitants of the Golan sites is expressed in an assemblage of more than forty basalt statues, averaging 20 centimeters in height. They resemble round pillars with a bowl-shaped top (compare the heads of the male ivory figurines). Schematic human features are carved on them, the most prominent being the large aquiline nose. Some pillars present depictions of eyes, hair, beard, and horns, in varying combinations. Others have only a beard and horns, and it is suggested that these represent animals. Many of the elements mentioned in connection with other art forms are here repeated, and they all appear to have a similar intent, the portrayal of the adored and vital gods who protect the fields and flocks.

The basalt pillars were found in and near the houses, and one was found in situ, on a pedestal facing the house door. In view of their shape and findspot, the excavator of the Golan sites, Claire Epstein, termed them house idols and suggested that offerings were placed in the bowl-shaped heads. This view has been called into question, particularly in view of comparative study with neighboring cultures, where divine representations are not abbreviated by the depiction of one or two body members. It has therefore been suggested that the pillars were stands or portable altars, or perhaps merely decorated mortars.

Fig. 3.23. Basalt house idol from the Golan (height 29 centimeters)

Burial Customs

In their burial customs as in their life-style and cult, Chalcolithic people differ from all those who came before or after. The most common burial custom in the Chalcolithic period is that of secondary burial, in which the deceased must pass two stages before reaching a final resting place. In the first stage, the corpse is laid out until the flesh decomposes; then the bones are gathered and placed in their final place of interment. In this manner the anatomical structure of the body is dislocated and the bones laid in jumbled fashion or in an order prescribed by custom and ritual. This is not the first occurrence of secondary burial. We have seen that in the Pre-Pottery Neolithic B, skulls were buried separately from the rest of the body. This is also not the last we shall see of the prolonged treatment of the dead; secondary burial was customary in the Land of Israel during most ancient periods, including the periods covered in this volume.

The kind of secondary burial that first appears in this period is the disposal of the bones in small ceramic containers called ossuaries. These ossuaries give Chalcolithic burials their singular, mysterious air. Ossuary burials were placed in caves, often artificial caves, carved specially to serve as tombs. They were entered by a vertical or diagonal shaft. At times the walls were lined with ledges, where the ossuaries could be placed. Most of the caves have collapsed, and the ossuaries have been found in fragments, scattered over the cave.

The greatest geographic concentration of burial caves is in the kurkar ridges of the middle coastal plain, between Hadera in the north and Palmahim in the south, with an especially high density in the Tel Aviv area. In recent years it has become apparent that the distribution of the ossuaries was wider. They have been found in natural caves in the hill regions (at a site near Shechem, at Mesilat Zion near Jerusalem, and at Umm Qatafa in the Judaean desert) and in cist tombs in the cemetery site of Shiqmim in the western Negev. All the same, the proliferation of tomb caves in the coastal region raises many questions, as virtually no settlements have been discovered nearby, and cemeteries are not in evidence in or near large settlements of other regions. It cannot therefore be established whether the caves of the coastal region served the population of the entire country, that of part of the country, or perhaps only a local population that lived in structures so ephemeral that nothing has remained of them. The absence of cemeteries near Teleilat Ghassul and Beersheba lends weight to the first hypothesis, especially considering that the assemblages of the burial caves belong to the sphere of the Ghassul-Beersheba culture. Recent years, however, have seen the discovery of a cemetery near the site of Shiqmim in the western Negev, and a proposal has been mooted—though proof is yet to come—that each site cluster had a central burial ground.

The ossuaries themselves are fascinating objects. They are large enough to contain the bones of an adult, especially the skull and long bones. And indeed these are the bones, of adults only, that have been found in ossuaries. The ossuaries average 70 centimeters in length, 30 centimeters in width, and 60 centimeters in height. They are usually made of coarse clay and are modeled by hand. The ossuaries were fired at low temperatures and are therefore quite fragile. From this we may infer that they were made near the burial sites and not transported from afar.

Most of the ossuaries take the form of a plain rectangular box, but a large group has been preserved that resembles, thanks to a few additions, a house. The most important addition is the roof, which is usually a tall gable roof but is sometimes arched. The walls are sometimes pierced with windows. One ossuary from Azor has one window in one of the broad walls in addition to three windows in the upper part of the narrow gabled wall. Some ossuaries are mounted on what appear to be stilts. There are many plastic and painted decorations that add realistic detail to the house form, such as a red net pattern painted on a slanted roof, simulating the beams and rafters of which roofs were made. Some ossuaries have a projecting ledge running around the entire house, under the eaves, and others have pierced projections on either side of the door to which a clay or wooden door could be attached. There are also many projecting

Fig. 3.24. House-shaped ossuary (height 60 centimeters)

knobs resembling those in the facade of the crown from the Cave of the Treasure, which may represent beams.

The modeling of ossuaries after the form of houses could have taught us a great deal about the dwelling structures of the period, especially since only the foundations and lower wall courses have survived in most of the structures excavated. They do not, however, resemble excavated structures. In ossuaries, the doorway is on the narrow side, while in the excavated structures it is always on the broad side. This may be because long bones had to be inserted in the ossuaries and may not indicate the existence of another house type. The tall slanted roof, however, is surprising for as far as we know, house roofs were flat, as was the custom in the Land of Israel in all periods. It has been suggested that the slanted roofs indicate structures suited to regions of heavy rain or even snow, and some would have liked to see them as a hint of the origin of the Chalcolithic population. More recently it has been suggested that the ossuaries, particularly those with the arched roof, are imitations in clay of reed huts of the type still used for habitation in marshlands such as those of southern Mesopotamia; this too has been taken as a hint of the origin of the population. Notably, there are some ossuaries shaped like a round hut, and it may be surmised that part of the Chalcolithic population lived in similar structures. As such huts would have been built of perishable materials, no trace of them has remained in the archaeological record.

In addition to the realistic details that raise associations of house or reed huts, the ossuaries abound in details that, by comparison with similar details in other places and on other objects, may be interpreted as religious symbols. First and foremost is the raised panel above the door of the ossuary, which is usually rectangular or trapezoidal but is sometimes rounded or pointed. Such a panel has been encountered on the crown from Nahal Mishmar and in the fragmentary wall painting from Ghassul. Y. Yadin suggested the connection between the shape (and hence the concept) of this raised panel and the violin-shaped, stylized female figurines found at the Gilat shrine and elsewhere. Might not the entire facade be intended to represent the gateway to the realm of the dead, guarded by a limbless, faceless goddess? Further symbols are sometimes attached to the panel, the most common of which is the prominent aquiline nose, perhaps the most characteristic symbol of the period. Large round eyes, either painted or applied, appear on some of the panels, and as in the anthropomorphic statuettes, there is no trace of a mouth. It has been suggested that the anthropomorphic ossuary facade was intended to represent the deceased or, in another interpretation, the breath of life, symbolized by the nose; or perhaps it is the symbol of the god who protects the dead. This does not exclude the possibility that the facade as a whole is connected with the limbless violin-shaped goddess. The panel sometimes bears horns, themselves symbols of a potent godhead. The act of burial evokes a world of associations revolving around the fate of the dead and the spiritual travail of the survivors, and these find expression in many different symbols. Archaeologist Jean Perrot prefers not to see religious symbolism in the ossuaries and views the features as a warning sign against potential enemies of the deceased. He believes that they may well have been copies of similar symbols that were affixed to the facades of the actual dwelling houses.

Fig. 3.25. Ossuary facade, adorned with eyes and nose (height 30 centimeters)

Accompanying the house-shaped ossuaries were the zoomorphic and storejar-shaped ossuaries. As both animals and stored foods were part of the vital domestic needs of Chalcolithic people, ossuaries imitating their forms may, perhaps, have been intended to insure the abundance of provisions in the afterlife.

Another ossuary form is the coverless stone coffer, a type found at Azor, Bene Braq, Ben Shemen, and Palmahim. In one tomb at Ben Shemen there were found two rather large stone ossuaries, one 1.1 meters long and the other 95 centimeters long. In the larger ossuary, seven skulls were placed on one side and the long bones on the other. This group burial included adults, adolescents, and children. It is unique in the number of individuals interred and in the presence of children in the ossuary and may thus indicate unusual circumstances of death. In the three nearby caves, clay ossuaries of the usual kind housed individual burials.

In some tombs were found small or miniature ossuaries, modeled in the same way as the full-sized objects nearby. If ossuaries are models of houses, installations, and everyday objects, are these small items to be seen as models of models?

The burial caves also contained objects and vessels left for the use of the deceased. The most common vessels are the V-shaped bowls, and they are accompanied by typical pottery of the period—and of the Beersheba culture in particular—including pedestal bowls, various pots, and holemouth jars. There are virtually no cornets or churns, vessels charged with religious symbolism. Flint tools were also found in the burial caves, as well as a few other items. A cave at Palmahim provided two unusual vessels shaped like birds, probably doves. These hollow vessels have only one aperture in the back, which rules out the possibility of libation, so it is difficult to guess what purpose they served. Their presence in a tomb testifies to a relation between birds (or specifically doves) and the realm of the dead. A schematic portrayal of a bird in flight also appears on a jar ossuary from a cave near Mesilat Zion.

Primary burial (that is, permanent interment, from which the bones are not removed) was less common in the Chalcolithic period and, as far as can be ascertained, was limited mainly to infants and children or to adults who died in unusual circumstances. Children were buried inside the houses, either under the floors or in grain pits. In the Beersheba sites infants and children were buried in a fetal position on their right side. Some were provided with fine pottery vessels. Nineteen graves of children and infants were found in houses at Teleilat Ghassul, ranging from stillborn to eight or nine years old. Many were placed inside ceramic pithoi in a contracted

Fig. 3.26. Jar-shaped ossuary

10 cm

position, in almost precise imitation of the position of the fetus, which may well have been in the mind of those who buried them. Pithos burials of children were also found in the Nahal Besor settlements.

At Bir Safadi, five primary burials of adults were found, but four seem to have been buried after the site was abandoned. Only the fifth, found in a contracted position at the bottom of a bell-shaped pit and accompanied by gifts, may be attributed to the period of habitation at the site. Three of the Nahal Mishmar caves also had primary adult burials. The story of these individuals is unique. The anthropologists who studied the 21 skeletons from the caves determined that they belonged to a population of sedentary origin. They reached the caves after suffering physical traumas inflicted by cruel blows and died only a short time later. The dead seem to have been buried in family groups. In Cave 2, a man, a woman, and four children aged two to six years were buried. They were wrapped in bloodstained linen cloth and covered with mats. The right hand of the man was severed, and its binding was heavily stained with blood. The individuals buried in Cave 1 also apparently belonged to an extended family, but no such relation was indicated for those buried in Cave 3. This description attests to death under unusual circumstances, perhaps in warfare, and in these circumstances the cave dwellers practiced unorthodox methods of burial.

Origin and Fate of the Chalcolithic Population

Archaeologists have long struggled with the question of the origin of the bearers of Chalcolithic culture and the place where their outstanding technological and artistic achievements were developed. The range of answers has reflected the weight assigned by different scholars to various types of contact with neighboring lands.

Many agree that there is continuity in some basic cultural elements between Chalcolithic culture and that which preceded it, the Pottery Neolithic, observed chiefly in the flint tool industry and in some of the most basic ceramic forms. This has led some to presume a continuity in the population from one period to the other. Supporting evidence is adduced from the skeletal remains at various burial and settlement sites. There is no doubt that some of the population was of a proto-Mediterranean type that inhabited the country before this time and continued to do so in following periods. This was, it is suggested, an indigenous stratum of population and culture that received an influx from without and thus evolved locally in a unique synthesis of old and new elements.

What is the source of the innovations of the Chalcolithic period? A common view is that this local population, which continues from one period to another, was reinforced by one or more population waves bearing a new culture, identified as the Chalcolithic culture, comprising the unique, interesting, or even spectacular features described in detail in this chapter. There are two major schools of thought concerning the origin of these new groups; one looks to the north, the other east.

Anthropological study of the various burials has shown that alongside the indigenous group, a new group may be identified. This group is described as "a tall population, dolicho-mesocranic, ovoid pentagonoid with high brain-cases, broad frontal bones. The facial skeleton is long and robust. Lower jaws are high and wide. The occipital region is more or less rounded. . . . The inferior nuchal plane is elongated and almost horizontal. . . .

Groups with similar anthropological features . . . have been designated the Proto-Mediterranean type in its Southern variant" (Haas and Nathan 1973). Anthropologist D. Ferembach defined a broad-skulled population, found at the site of Bir Safadi and in the cemeteries of Azor and Ben Shemen, as being of the Armenoid or Anatolian race, whose origins lie in the Caucasus.

Could these people be the bearers of the varying facets of Chalcolithic culture? The distant north is the source of the arsenical copper used in the artifacts of the Nahal Mishmar treasure and similar objects, and it is feasible that finished products, rather than raw copper, were brought from that region, perhaps by the bearers of the culture that arrived and settled in the Land of Israel. Some scholars do in fact hold that the origin of Chalcolithic culture lies in eastern Anatolia-Caucasia (P. Bar Adon, D. Ussishkin). This hypothesis is undermined by the absence of finds in those areas presumed to be the cradle of this culture in any way resembling those of the Chalcolithic culture of the Land of Israel.

Other scholars indicate "the North" as the origin of the Chalcolithic culture. P. Lapp suggested an origin in the distant steppes of south Russia, which he saw as a source of population waves in various periods, including the Chalcolithic, some of which reached the Land of Israel. J. Mellaart preferred to employ a generalized term for the direction of origin, saying only that the Chalcolithic people came from "the North."

Another view (Hennessy, C. Elliot) is that the origin of the newcomers lies in an imprecisely defined East. According to this view, there were population movements from east to west around the start of the Chalcolithic period, introducing new cultural elements into Mesopotamia, Syria, southern Anatolia, Byblos, and the Land of Israel, which lay at the extremity of this expansion. Perrot may also be included in this school of thought. In his view there was a migration of people, who may have originated in southern or northern Mesopotamia, through the Syrian steppe and Transjordan to the Land of Israel, where they finally settled.

Both theories are based largely on evidence concerning trade in raw materials or on a similarity of form in some elements of the material culture, though the northern theory is also supported by some anthropological evidence. Neither provides an answer to basic issues in the understanding of Chalcolithic culture, such as the question of the origin of the practice of ossuary burial, a practice with no counterpart in the entire region, or that of the context of the strange symbolic world of the period, which is also exceptional in the entire Near East. The strongest connection on the symbolic plane is with western Anatolia and the Aegean, which are not generally considered a possible source of the Chalcolithic population. Perhaps it was the other way round, and the Chalcolithic survivors migrated westward from the Land of Israel at the end of the period, as has been suggested by A. Jirco.

An interesting possibility recently broached is based on anthropological evidence alone. B. Arensburg, in a comparative study of Neolithic and Chalcolithic populations, found that the Neolithic population of the Land of Israel was sparse and that it consisted of small, isolated communities. Under those conditions, marriage ties were limited; this led to the eventual emergence of clear genetic differences among the different groups, though all were of the same origin and of the same proto-Mediterranean race.

Thus, small separate groups of dolichocephalic and brachicephalic, taller and shorter people may be identified, all as a natural result of the social organization of the period.

In the Chalcolithic period the barriers between the isolated groups collapsed. For reasons as yet undetermined the population grew and people began to live in larger mixed communities. That is why we find in the same settlements and burial grounds different human types; natural internal developments caused a considerable increase of population and the creation of an open society, in contrast to the closed, isolated groups of the preceding period. Therefore we need not seek an external origin for this or that population group, as has been attempted by most scholars.

It is reasonable to assume that a similar process occurred in all parts of the Near East at roughly the same time, leading to increased interaction between the inhabitants of this part of the world. These contacts consisted primarily of trade in raw materials and finished products, a natural consequence of which was the transfer of ideas, styles, and modes of expression. This extensive network of contacts was perhaps effected by traveling merchants, who would have formed a new, separate social class, or perhaps by mobile tribes, who encountered other tribes along their fixed, traditional migratory routes and traded objects and information with them, to be passed on again in the next encounter. Movements of entire populations need not be assumed to explain the emergence of the Chalcolithic culture of the Land of Israel. Rather, at least part of the impressive technological development of the period may be credited to an internal evolution brought about by the rise in the standard of living and the availability of raw materials,

supplemented no doubt by ideas from without. We are therefore witness to the release of internal forces, latent in the local population, in the wake of socioeconomic processes both within the society and in the entire region. It is also possible that the symbolic world of this period evolved in reaction to conditions of social stress and in an attempt to ensure, on an ideological plane, the community's continued existence and success. Here too it may be preferable not to seek external sources of influence but to attempt to understand the essence of these symbols, as far as possible, and the part they played in the new social and economic system.

If the origins of the population and culture are shrouded in obscurity, so too does the end of the period present grave difficulties. The survey of settlement sites noted that most of the sites were abandoned, with no evidence of violent struggle. Most were not resettled in the following period or in any succeeding period. This is especially true of the sites of the south and of the Golan. The impression is created of a sudden end to the period as a result of a catastrophe of some sort, either natural or inflicted by man, which forced the inhabitants to abandon their settlements and move on elsewhere.

Several suggestions have been offered to explain the disappearance of the people and culture of the Chalcolithic period. Hennessy believes that they were forced to give way to a new group migrating from the north, along the coast or through the Lebanese Beqa', the group bearing the culture of the beginning of the Early Bronze Age. Indeed, some of the mounds of the northern and central regions have remains of the new culture superimposed on those of the Chalcolithic period. The Chalcolithic layers of these sites are poor and relatively thin. Chalcolithic settlement may have lasted there for only a short while before being replaced by the new settlers. However, the Chalcolithic layers may have been damaged as a result of their location at the base of the mounds.

M. Dothan has suggested that the southern areas suffered a severe drought, which drove their inhabitants north to settle at sites such as 'Afula, Megiddo, and Beth Shean. Although there is little difficulty in accepting the first part of this suggestion, in view of the marginal climate of the southern regions, it is harder to prove that the northern sites were inhabited only after the abandonment of the southern sites. The opposite is true. The latest phases of Chalcolithic culture have been identified in the Beersheba valley and the Judaean desert caves, rather than in the sites of the north, which may be attributed to the earlier part of the period.

A further suggestion was broached by Yadin, who sought a circumstantial connection between the disappearance of Chalcolithic culture and the early expansion of Egypt in the first stages of its unification under Narmer. He viewed some objects found in Egypt associated with Narmer and the presence of some vessels bearing the name of this king in sites of the southern Land of Israel as proof of the existence of Egyptian expansionist initiatives. If Yadin's view is correct, it is not impossible that in an early stage of this expansion the Chalcolithic culture, unequipped to withstand the growing power of the Egyptians, was annihilated. The fugitives—those who reached the Judaean desert caves and lived there for a while, and those who died of wounds inflicted before their arrival—may bear silent witness to the raids of Egyptian troops on the open, defenseless sites of the Chalcolithic population. Some scholars, however, view the Egyptian finds in the south as evidence of trade connections rather than military campaigns.

Where did the refugees of the famine, wars, and perhaps the concomitant epidemics disappear to? Perrot has suggested that they returned to the places they had come from, that is to the desert plateaus of Transjordan and Syria. Ruth Amiran has suggested that they did not disappear but rather merged with the bearers of the new culture, introducing some of the characteristics of their culture. These were not necessarily the special, attractive features, the artistic and technical achievements, but rather a few details of the pottery industry, such as the continued tradition of hole-mouth jars, the decoration of small bowls with red paint, and especially the continued, short-lived use of a variant churn form. Can such details, which appear to be marginal in the assemblage of Chalcolithic culture, be taken as proof of continuity into the following period? If so, what is it in these details that allowed them to survive in preference to other elements, which would appear to be of greater significance? And where did all the know-how, sophistication, and originality of the Chalcolithic people in so many realms of creativity go? Those who followed them seem to have started from scratch, with the exception of some basic ceramic forms. All that had been attained during the Chalcolithic period disappeared, never to return, and the following generations never reached similar achievements, not even after hundreds and thousands of years.

The Chalcolithic period thus remains a mysterious period from beginning to end. If no significant breakthroughs in the appreciation of its true essence are forthcoming, we will be left only to contemplate its creations, admire them, and wonder who their creators were, how they lived, in what manner they interpreted the world around them, and why they finally disappeared from the stage of human history.

4

The Early Bronze Age

AMNON BEN-TOR

Two difficulties attend the term "Early Bronze Age." The first concerns the early use of bronze, an alloy of copper with 5–10 percent tin. Being much harder than copper, its introduction brought about an improvement in the quality of tools and weapons and was thus a great step forward in the history of civilization. However, it was not used widely in Palestine until the early second millennium B.C.E., or about a thousand years after the beginning of the so-called Early Bronze Age. The term, however, has taken root and become accepted, inaccurate though it may be from the purely technological aspect. The second difficulty concerns the method used in defining periods. Later periods, such as the Persian, Hellenistic, and Roman, may be delimited by fairly accurate dates; the Hellenistic period, for example, may be said to begin in the year 332 B.C.E., with the conquest of Alexander the Great, and end in the year 37 B.C.E. with the accession of Herod. But such a definition, justified though it may be from the political-historical point of view, is not an archaeological one, for archaeology deals with the history of material and spiritual culture, not with that of political change. Archaeologically,

each period is firmly bound to its predecessor and overlaps with its successor, so that it is difficult to tell exactly when one period ends and the next begins. Those periods of transition (such as the period from the Chalcolithic to the Early Bronze) are the most problematic and therefore most often studied and debated. In addition, there are many questions concerning the subdivisions within the principal periods. As far as the subject treated in this chapter is concerned, the question may be put thus: when and how did the Early Bronze Age begin and end, and can this period be subdivided?

In 1937, G. E. Wright, in an extensive study of the pottery of the period, laid the foundations for the definition and subdivision of the Early Bronze Age. His division of the period into four phases was widely accepted and remains in force to this day. As may be expected, most of the discussions and suggested revisions of his study, including those by Wright himself, have been devoted to the first and last phases of the period (the transitional phases) while relatively few changes have come about in the understanding of the two middle phases.

In conducting a survey such as this, spanning approximately one thousand years, a question of method arises: should a vertical approach be taken, which deals separately with each of the cultural characteristics as they develop over the entire Early Bronze Age, or should a horizontal approach be preferred, in which complete cultural assemblages are discussed, phase by phase? This chapter combines both methods: the cultural arrays of the first and last phases are discussed separately, whereas the two middle phases are treated as one unit, using the vertical approach. This methodological approach takes into account the special complexities of the transitional phases (special importance is attached to the first phase, in which the seeds of all the characteristics of the following phases are sown), and it reflects the current state of research, which has concentrated mainly on the first and last phases, with the middle phases often treated as one unit.

SOURCES OF INFORMATION

The lack of written documents in Early Bronze Age Palestine forms the main obstacle to its study. Written sources, it should be said, are not completely absent. In the third millennium faint signs of literacy were in the air, with isolated hieroglyphic signs (mainly royal names) occurring here and there; and there are, perhaps, vague references to Palestine in Egyptian texts of the period. Also, the recent discovery of an archive of the mid third millennium at Tell Mardikh (ancient Ebla) has brought Early Bronze Age Syria into the historic age, though it is not yet known whether Palestine is mentioned in any of its documents. Thus the picture of Palestine in the Early Bronze Age must be founded on an interpretation of the silent evidence, that is, objects uncovered in excavations, and the resulting working hypotheses must be con-

stantly subjected to the test of new discoveries.

CHRONOLOGY

The absolute chronology of Palestine in the Early Bronze Age is drawn from carbon-14 analysis and the chronology of Egypt and Mesopotamia. Carbon-14 dating is most important for periods more than six thousand years before the present, but its usefulness declines for later periods, until by the second millennium the method is almost useless. For the Early Bronze Age, carbon-14 dating can still be useful, especially where there are many samples from one site. However, where there is textual evidence, and this increases in quantity during the third millennium in Mesopotamia, Egypt, and now in Syria, the importance of carbon-14 dating diminishes. Carbon-14 dates from the Early Bronze Age in Palestine now total nearly one hundred, and the scholarly attitude toward them may be characterized as mixed or cautious. There is a clear tendency to prefer dates based on written records; these dates, however, are far fewer in number and do not always allow firm conclusions to be drawn. The Egyptian chronological framework remains the main anchor of Palestinian chronology for the whole of the Early Bronze Age. In Egypt itself there is some chronological uncertainty, due to varying interpretations of the written sources, especially in regard to the first two dynasties. Many scholars therefore prefer to avoid mentioning absolute dates and use relative dates, such as "the First Dynasty period" or "the period of Dynasties I–II." We will here attempt, for the sake of clarity, to mention specific dates. They will be based on the middle chronology, which is one of several possible Egyptian chronologies. The difference between Egyptian chro-

nologies may be as great as two hundred years at the beginning of the period (3100/2900 B.C.E.), but it rapidly dwindles until by the twenty-eighth century it is nearly non-existent. The contacts between Palestine and Mesopotamia during this period are much less direct. Concerning absolute dates in the last centuries of the fourth millennium and the beginning of the third, Mesopotamian chronology labors under difficulties similar to Egypt's. At times chronological reasoning enters a vicious circle, where the chronology of Mesopotamia is dependent on that of Egypt, and vice versa. We shall therefore favor Egyptian chronology.

Taking the year 3000 as the approximate date for the founding of the First Dynasty in Egypt, the chronology of the four phases of the Early Bronze Age is as follows:

> Early Bronze Age I, 3200/3100–2950/2900 (Late Predynastic–Early First Dynasty)
> Early Bronze Age II, 2950/2900–2700/2650 (end of First Dynasty–Second Dynasty)
> Early Bronze Age III, 2700/2650–2350 (Second–Fifth Dynasties),
> Early Bronze Age IV, 2350–2200 (Sixth Dynasty).

The proposed dates should, of course, be treated with circumspection and be taken mainly as indicators of the relative length of each phase. Also, the nature of transitions between archaeological periods should be kept in mind: they are gradual, prolonged, and therefore difficult to date, in contrast to political events such as the rise and fall of dynasties.

The Early Bronze Age I

In the late fourth millennium B.C.E., the Chalcolithic culture in Palestine disappears under unclear circumstances, and a new epoch in the history of Palestine begins. Questions concerning the causes of the decline of Chalcolithic culture, the character of the transition between periods (Was it gradual and peaceful or sudden and violent?), or the population groups in Palestine (Were they newcomers? If so, where did they come from, how many were they, and what happened to the indigenous population?) have been the center of scholarly focus for many years. The answers given by various archaeologists affected their understanding of the period and hence the name by which they called it.

During the period in question, and particularly in the final two centuries of the fourth millennium, there occurred a series of developments that were to have far-reaching consequences in the history of the land. They affected basic features such as settlement patterns and population density, economy, foreign relations, crafts, art, and religion. So wide a range of human activity was affected, at so great a pace, relatively speaking, that the change may be called a revolution. At the end of it, the land took on a character completely different from that of the Chalcolithic period.

THE SETTLEMENT PATTERN

In contrast to the Chalcolithic period, when semiarid and steppe zones were preferred for settlement (with the exception of the Chalcolithic Golan culture), the Early Bronze Age saw the establishment of settlement zones in hills, plains, and valleys where the Mediterranean climate prevails and where average annual rainfall exceeds 300 millimeters. The reasons for this transition are not clear, though one possibility is that the climate of Palestine at the end of the fourth millennium and the first half of the

third millennium was somewhat warmer and more moist than in the preceding and succeeding periods. In any case, the story of the Early Bronze Age (and of Palestine in general from this point and on) is the story of sites such as Dan, Hazor, Beth Yerah, Beth Shean, Ta'anach, Megiddo, Tell el-Far'ah North, Ai, Gezer, Jericho, Yarmuth, Lachish, Tell el-Hesi, Arad,

and many others. Jerusalem too was first settled in this period, though the information on the character and size of the settlement is meager. The many Chalcolithic settlements of the northern Negev and of the Golan were permanently abandoned. There are some exceptions, such as Arad, Tell el-Far'ah North, and Megiddo, where a settlement of sorts did exist in the Chalcolithic; but they were

Map 4.1. Early Bronze Age sites

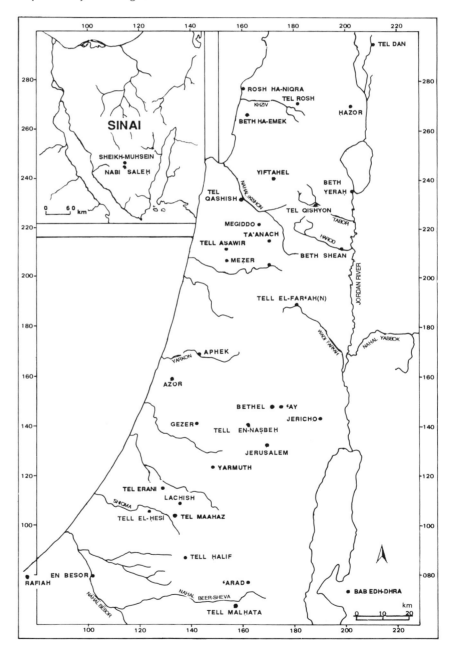

small, poor, and entirely different from settlements of the same sites in the following period. They may be said to be exceptions that prove the rule, for of the three hundred or so known Early Bronze Age sites (and undoubtedly there are more to be discovered), 90 percent are in the new settlement areas—where the average annual rainfall is above 300 millimeters—and the location of the remaining sites may be explained by local factors, such as the proximity of oases (Jericho, Bab edh-Dhra) or other abundant water sources (the settlements of the middle Jordan valley).

The fertile soils in Palestine are the alluvial soils of the valleys and the coastal plain and the *terra rosa* of the hills. However, of the Early Bronze Age settlements, 40 percent are on the alluvium and a further 40 percent on chalky soils, with only 10 percent situated on *terra rosa* soils. This may be explained by the difficulty of clearing the natural cover from the hills, by the necessity of terracing to prevent erosion, and by the scarcity of water sources. Still, important settlements were founded in the hills during the Early Bronze Age, usually confined to hilltops near small interior valleys, for example, Tel Rosh in the Galilee, Shiloh, Bethel, Tell en-Nasbeh, and Ai. As the art of storing water in plaster-lined cisterns was not yet known in the Early Bronze Age, the hill population, and others who were distant from their water sources, were in a difficult position. They overcame it by constructing reservoirs at the lowest point in the towns, which collected enough runoff to enable the existence of some of the most important settlements of the Early Bronze Age, such as Ai, Arad, and, apparently, Yarmuth.

The coastal plain is conspicuously absent from the settlement zones of the Early Bronze Age. The sites of Akhziv, Accho, Dor, Jaffa, Yavne-Yam, and others were first settled only in the early second millennium B.C.E. The absence of ports on the Mediterranean coast of Palestine during the third millennium stands in stark contrast to the situation in Syria (Byblos, Ugarit, etc.) and had a decisive influence on the coastal trade of Palestine during this period.

ECONOMY

Our knowledge of the economy and particularly of animal husbandry and agriculture is meager and random, both because organic remains (with the exception of bones) are poorly preserved in the Palestinian climate and because sufficient attention has not so far been given to the retrieval of the relevant data. Despite these limitations, a number of conclusions may be drawn from the information in hand.

It seems that at the end of the fourth millennium, there was a return to agricultural patterns prevalent before the Ghassulian Chalcolithic, that is, to the economy characteristic of late fifth and early fourth millennium settlements. In this respect, as well as in others, the Ghassulian-Beersheba Chalcolithic may be seen as an intrusive culture in Palestine, whose disappearance is followed by a continuation of interrupted processes. Yet there are important differences: herds, mainly sheep and goat, do not play so central a role as in earlier periods, and the distribution of cattle and pigs is drastically reduced. Of great importance is the appearance of the donkey and the ox in the domestic assemblage; as draft and pack animals they allowed better cultivation of the soil and larger harvests on the one hand and improved communications and transportation on the other. The ox and donkey were central factors in the improvement of the standard of living, in the accumulation of surplus, and in the promotion of trade.

In agriculture, there is a noticeable increase in the importance of previously known crops such as cereals, vegetables and legumes (lentil, chickpea, bean, and pea), and various fruits (walnut, almond, fig, plum, date, pomegranate). These, and especially the fruits, varied and enriched the diet of the people, but they also constituted, with their by-products, an important part of the export trade of Palestine.

Most important are two crop plants that were first widely cultivated in the Early Bronze Age, the olive and the vine. The immense contribution of these plants to the history of Mediterranean civilization has often been remarked: the olive and vine adapt well to poor soil, require relatively little attention (and that mainly in convenient seasons of the year), produce highly nutritious fruit and by-products (mainly oil and wine) that keep well for long periods. It is not surprising that oil and wine soon occupy a prominent position among the exports of Palestine.

The concentration of Early Bronze Age settlement in Mediterranean zones led to the establishment of the so-called Mediterranean economy, which was the basis of economic life in Palestine for thousands of years, from the beginning of the third millennium onward. This economy is based on a combination of goat- and sheep-herding with cultivation, especially of the olive, the vine, and other fruit trees. The product of these labors served to raise the people's standard of living, increase the number of persons who could live off a given plot of land, and bring about an accumulation of surplus, a precondition for trade. These results had a far-reaching influence on every aspect of daily life and on the material and spiritual culture from the beginning of the Early Bronze Age and on.

POPULATION AND URBANIZATION

The two basic facts concerning the population of Early Bronze Age Palestine—its size and ethnic composition—cannot be satisfactorily ascertained, largely because of the complete absence of written sources. Comparative anthropological study of Chalcolithic and Early Bronze Age burials has been of limited scope, and the once commonly held notion that the bulk of the Chalcolithic population was of the broad-headed Armenoid type and that it was replaced at the beginning of the Early Bronze Age by a dolichocephalic proto-Mediterranean population has been shown to be unfounded. Rather, it appears that the bulk of the Palestinian population, or at least that part represented by the few skeletons studied, belongs, both in the third and in the fourth millennia, to the Mediterranean type, though there are small groups belonging to the Alpine, the Euro-African, and the Armenoid types. If there were migrations of new populations into Palestine in the fourth millennium that could be held responsible for all those changes mentioned above, they were not migrations of a race different from that of the bulk of the indigenous population of Palestine. We must therefore try to trace the source of these populations with the aid of criteria other than those of physical anthropology.

As for population size, various methods of estimating rural and urban populations in a given period have been developed over recent years. These estimates must overcome certain limitations, chiefly two. First, we are not, nor are we ever likely to be, acquainted with all the Early Bronze Age sites that

ever existed; many sites, particularly the smaller ones, have disappeared over the years as a result of human or natural activity, and few of the known sites have been fully excavated. Second, in every age, the third millennium included, there was a nomadic and seminomadic population existing alongside the sedentary population. No data allowing an informed estimate of the size of this population, which lived principally in the marginal areas, is currently available. Despite those limitations, the question of population size cannot be ignored, for the number of persons in each site, as well as in the country as a whole, has far-reaching implications concerning, for example, economic and military power, resources for the development of arts and crafts, and so on.

Archaeological research clearly indicates a progressive increase in population at the end of the fourth millennium and the beginning of the third, which peaked in the mid third millennium. The clearest sign of this increase is not a growth in settlement size, for that remained virtually unchanged throughout the Early Bronze Age; rather, there was a marked increase in population density within the settlements. The many open spaces in the sparsely built-up settlements of the earlier part of the period were filled in with time and nearly disappeared. Population increase was also spurred by the improvement in the carrying capacity of the land, that is, by the greater number of persons who could subsist on a given area.

A calculation based on an estimate of the total settled area in the towns and villages of Early Bronze Age Palestine multiplied by 30 persons per dunam (representing the maximal density) indicates a population no greater than 150,000 persons. This, of course, is only a rough estimate, and it is important

mainly because it provides a point of departure for comparison with the estimated populations in the periods preceding and succeeding the Early Bronze Age. The figure must be supplemented by the nomadic and seminomadic population, the size of which is even more difficult to estimate, though it may be assumed that it did not exceed some thousands or a few tens of thousands.

At the beginning of the third millennium the population of Palestine was undergoing urbanization. This is not to say that the entire population moved into towns; on the contrary, it may be assumed that the majority continued to live in the tens and hundreds of villages scattered over the countryside, as they did in later periods. However, the crystallization of the city or town as a form of settlement is the single most important social phenomenon during this period in the Near East as a whole and appears to be one of the essential conditions for the development of civilization. The definition of the city or town is a subject often studied and much debated. Its intricacies cannot here be fully treated, but it seems that some conditions—such as size, fortification, population density, public building, social stratification, a part of the population engaged in nonrural pursuits—are essential for the definition of a settlement as urban, though not all of them are required in every case. In regard to size, which is the easiest datum to ascertain, the settlements of Early Bronze Age Palestine may be divided into three categories: 1. Small settlements, or farms, up to 2 dunams (one dunam is one tenth of a hectare). There were probably many such sites, but as they leave no topographical trace, they are difficult to identify. It is also likely that many of them have been destroyed over the years by human and natural agencies. 2. Villages, which range from 5 to 20 dunams, the majority being about 10 dunams. 3. Towns, which range from 40 to 150 dunams (some towns, such as Beth Yerah and Tel Erani, exceed 150 dunams). Among the towns may be included small towns, less than 70 dunams (Megiddo, Lachish, Jericho), and large towns, more than 70 dunams (Yarmuth, Gezer, Aphek, Arad, and others). Multiplying the area by the coefficient of 30 provides a population estimate for each site.

The urban unit dictated the political organization of Palestine for the following two thousand years. The city-state was a unit in the center of which stood the city or town surrounded by villages and farmsteads, which formed its agricultural hinterland and for which the town provided protection and services. Historical sources of the second millennium show that city-states were often allied or at war with one another, and there is no reason to doubt that this was the case in the third millennium as well. The little that has been revealed on this subject from the archives of Ebla in Syria (dating to the second half of the third millennium) certainly points in this direction.

How did urbanization evolve in Palestine? Was it a result of internal development? Was it imported as a concept or, as is more likely, introduced by immigrants from the North? These are some of the questions that still engage scholars. The best-known model of urbanization is the Mesopotamian one, which apparently began in the south of that land, in Sumer. Here, the phenomenon may be clearly and firmly defined, for art and literature were highly developed, and the cities attained an area of 400 (Khafajeh), 600 (Ur), and even 4000 (Uruk) dunams. Some believe that cities evolved independently in different areas, when conditions ripened. Others suggest that urbanization should be seen as a diffusive process, emanating from a single center. If the latter is the case, then Sumer should be seen as the center, and the process as similar to the effect created by a stone thrown into a pond. In this analogy, Palestine is at the edge of the pond, and only small ripples from the processes occurring in Sumer arrive there, and even those by way of Syria. The high urban culture of Syria may thus be explained by the direct contact between the Mesopotamians and the people of northeastern Syria, especially those of the Middle Euphrates region (for example, the site of Habuba Kabira). From there the phenomenon spread to the Syrian interior and thence to Palestine. This hypothesis cannot yet be proven, though there are various indications that it is highly probable. In any case it is generally agreed that the phenomenon of urbanization in Palestine, with all its importance to the history of that land, is but a faint echo of what was happening in Mesopotamia.

Finally, it should be remarked that urbanization did not occur simultaneously at all sites. One example is provided by the excavations of Arad and Tel Erani. At both sites, the strata of the beginning of the Early Bronze Age were dated by finds to the early First Dynasty period. However, while Tel Erani was at this time a fortified and apparently urban site, Arad was no more than a poor, unwalled village. Only in the following phase (Early Bronze Age II) did Arad become a fortified town. The same is true for most of the towns in Palestine, which achieved urban status only at the beginning of the Early Bronze Age II; some places, however, such as Erani, Ai, and Tell el-Far'ah North, preceded the others and may be called towns already at the end of the Early Bronze Age I.

ARCHITECTURE

DWELLINGS. The private structures of the Early Bronze Age I are rather unimpressive, being built for the most part of bricks on a low foundation of fieldstones, with walls of 0.6–0.7 meter in width (the breadth of two bricks or the length of one). They do not have a fixed plan and generally consist of a few small rooms and a courtyard. The most common domestic installation is a pit dug into the ground, sometimes lined with stone, which served as a silo. The spread-out character of the settlements, the relatively small areas cleared in excavations, and the destruction wrought by the intensive construction activity of the urban settlements built atop the Early Bronze Age I villages have combined to reduce the number of houses known from this period.

An exception is an Early Bronze Age I village of about five dunams currently being excavated at Yiftahel, in the southern part of the Lower Galilee. This village, apparently abandoned toward the end of the Early Bronze Age I, not long after its foundation, was never resettled. Its houses were thus not destroyed by later construction, and a relatively large portion of the village could be exposed. The character of other, more poorly preserved villages can probably be inferred from the site of Yiftahel. The houses, fifteen of which have been excavated, were built of bricks on a low foundation of fieldstones. The structures are relatively large, with an average area of 50 square meters, and single-roomed, a feature characterizing many of the Early Bronze Age houses in Palestine. Some are oval, others are rectangular with rounded corners. Structures of an identical plan have been found at Megiddo and Tell el-Far'ah North in Palestine and at Byblos, on the Syrian coast. In light of the varied connections between the important center at Byblos and sites of northern Palestine revealed in the archaeological finds, it may be suggested that Byblos was the origin of these types of structures.

APSIDAL STRUCTURES. These are rectangular structures with three straight walls and one (short) curved wall. The resulting form resembles the apse of a church, hence the name. They have one or two rooms, with the entrance set either in the short straight wall or in one of the long walls. The position of the doorway is significant, as we shall later see. Apsidal structures have been found at sites in Palestine: Megiddo, Beth Shean, Mezer, Yiftahel, and elsewhere. Such structures have also been found at Byblos (where they first appear earlier than in Palestine) and in Asia Minor and Greece. Regarding their age, origin, and function, only the first can be established with any degree of certainty: they have a relatively short span of existence in Palestine, and all the examples so far uncovered clearly date to the Early Bronze Age I. Their origin is a matter of debate, though it should probably be sought on the Syro-Lebanese coast (Byblos). Every sort of function has been suggested for these structures—regular dwelling houses, patrician houses, temples—but in the present state of research the question had best be left open.

TEMPLES. Remains of cult structures of the Early Bronze Age I have been discovered at Jericho, Ai, and Megiddo. Of these, the most impressive and well preserved is the double temple of Megiddo stratum XIX, which was built before the site was walled and perhaps served as the core around which the town developed.

The temple plan is that of a single-roomed rectangular structure,

entered through one of the long walls. A rectangular structure entered through one of the short walls, on its longer axis, is a longroom structure, whereas the opposite is a broadroom structure. Each of the Megiddo temples is thus a single-roomed broadroom structure with a platform (or altar) set against the wall directly opposite the doorway. The temple abuts a wall, which surrounds the sacred area. Such boundary walls are common in ancient Near Eastern temples and are termed temenos walls, the area within the walls being termed a temenos. The temenos wall in fact served as the rear wall of the temple. The temenos itself was paved with flagstones, some of them inscribed with rather crude drawings of humans and animals. Only one of the two broadrooms of the Megiddo double temple is well preserved, and the other almost completely destroyed. Between the two rooms is a small annex, which probably served for storage.

The plan of the Megiddo temples is remarkably similar to that of the Chalcolithic temple at En Gedi. The broadroom concept, which lies at the foundation of the double temple at Megiddo and of later Early Bronze Age temples, is characteristic of houses of the period but also appears in the plan of the En Gedi temple and in houses of the Chalcolithic period (for example, at Ghassul and in the Golan). The continuity in temple design, in which tradition gave less rein to the builder's imagination than in domestic construction, has great significance as far as the transition from Chalcolithic to Early Bronze Age is concerned. It would seem to indicate that at least part of the Chalcolithic population of Palestine remained there during the Early Bronze Age, transmitting building traditions to the newcomers and merging with them to comprise the

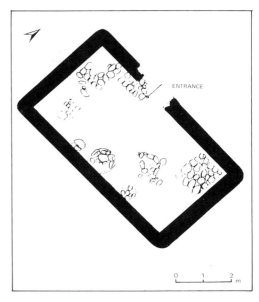

Fig. 4.1. Byblos: structure with rounded corners

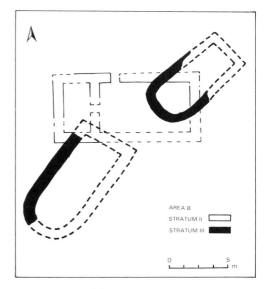

Fig. 4.2. Apsidal structures at Mezer

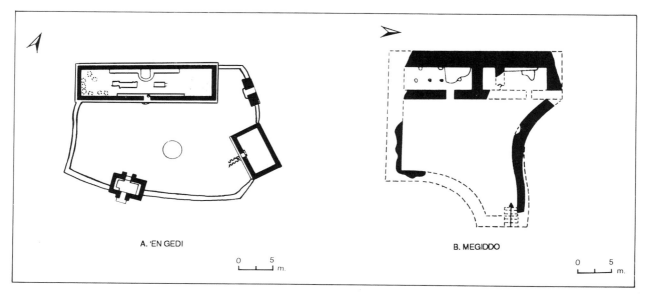

Fig. 4.3. Comparison of En Gedi and Megiddo temples

population of Early Bronze Age Palestine.

BURIAL PRACTICES

Tombs provide important information on the Early Bronze Age I. Large cemeteries have been discovered at a number of sites, the most important being the cemeteries of Bab edh-Dhra, Jericho, Ai, Tell en-Nasbeh, Azor, and Tell el-Far'ah North. The most common form of burial is in caves, whether specially cut for this purpose (Jericho, Azor) or natural (Ai, Tell en-Nasbeh). The use of shaft tombs (with a vertical entry shaft to the burial chamber) observed at Bab edh-Dhra is exceptional; only a thousand years later, in the Middle Bronze I period, do such tombs become common in Palestine.

Burial customs, which are—like temples—closely linked to religion and cult, provide important information on the composition of the population. The lack of uniformity in important aspects of burial seems to suggest a heterogeneous population but not the existence of separate groups, that is, a population with some important joint characteristics but with variants representing differences of region, tribe, and the like.

The number of interments in each tomb ranges from a few individuals (five to ten) to nearly two hundred. Usually the remains of a few dozen individuals were placed in one tomb, and it is clear that they do not represent one interment but rather the continuous use of one cave over a long period by one tribal or familial unit. In most cases burial is primary (the body was interred soon after death). The considerable mixing of bones noticeable in the tombs is the result of the repeated pushing aside of the bones to make room for new interments. Nevertheless, some cases of secondary burial have been observed, where the bones were gathered after decarnation. This practice was observed chiefly in the cemetery of Bab edh-Dhra, where not all the bones were interred, skulls and long bones being preferred. In some cases there are clear signs of cremation, for example, at Gezer and Azor. But this practice was not widespread and did not even include all the tombs of any site; in two adjacent tombs at Azor, cremation was observed only in one.

The burial gifts placed alongside the deceased consisted chiefly of pottery and occasionally small amounts of jewelry, weapons, and other personal goods. In view of the poor state of preservation of the settlement sites of the Early Bronze Age I, it is the many tombs, with their wealth of finds, that provide most of the data concerning the material culture of the period.

POTTERY

The pottery of this period may be divided into two principal groups: the tomb pottery—the vast majority of the assemblage—and the pottery from occupation layers. British archaeologist Kathleen Kenyon, who excavated the large Early Bronze Age I cemetery at Jericho, divided the pottery found in the tombs into three families: Proto-Urban A, B, and C ("Proto-Urban" is the term Kenyon used to describe the Early Bronze Age I). The A and B families are composed mainly of saucers, amphoriskoi, and teapots;

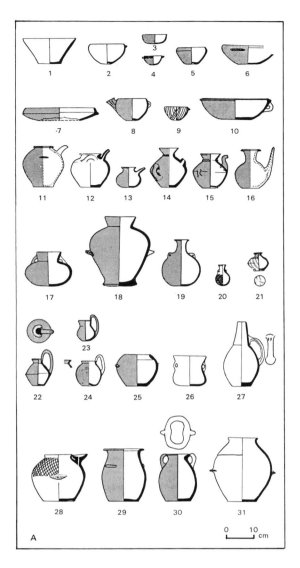

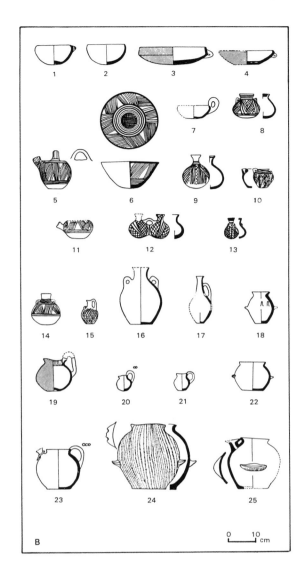

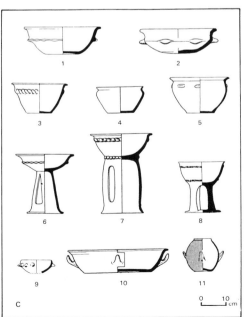

Fig. 4.4. Pottery of the Early Bronze I: Proto-Urban A, B, and C

the vessels are small and clearly not intended for everyday use but rather as burial gifts. The principal difference between the two groups is their decoration: vessels of the A family are undecorated or carry a red slip, and the B vessels are decorated with groups of lines painted in red over the entire vessel. The C pottery consists of two forms only—bowls and chalices (high-footed bowls), slipped in various shades of gray and finely burnished.

The vessels found in occupation layers are mostly storage and cooking vessels, forms rarely found in tombs. They are large, their clay is usually coarse, and they consist mainly of holemouths, jars with large ledge or ear handles, and pithoi. Some of these are decorated with applied relief decoration and others with bands of slip in a peculiar style termed band slip or grain wash, a mode of decoration especially common in northern Palestine. The variability noted in the burial practices may also be discerned in the pottery, again indicating a heterogeneous population with regional variations.

The continuity of ceramic traditions from the preceding period is most noticeable in the holemouths, cooking vessels that clearly continue Chalcolithic prototypes. Continuity is also evident in some bowls, in details of form such as ledge handles, and in the gray burnished ware: the gray color of these bowls and chalices is reminiscent of the Chalcolithic basalt vessels, which also appear only in the form of bowls and chalices. The identical color and typology of the Chalcolithic basalt vessels and the gray burnished vessels of the Early Bronze Age I clearly attest a continuity of tradition, which apparently represents a continuity of population.

The remaining vessel types are new, and it is not impossible that at least part of the new forms originated in the Syro-Lebanese coastal area (Byblos) and arrived in Palestine with population groups emigrating from there. A much debated question is that of the source of Kenyon's A and B groups. Apart from isolated occurrences in Egypt and perhaps in Tarsus in Asia Minor (results of trade with Palestine), such vessels, so common in Palestine, are unknown outside the country, and all the attempts to locate a northern source for them have thus far failed. It is true that the bent spout that sometimes appears on Proto-Urban A teapots is reminiscent of Mesopotamian spouts and may be an example of the borrowing of one type or a part of a form—a spout in this case—from the Mesopotamian ceramic assemblage. But even if this were the case, which is not at all certain, it concerns only a single component of a large assemblage of so far unparalleled vessels. Northern parallels that have been adduced for gray burnished ware have also proved unconvincing, as the similarities between the vessels are not significant, and the technique of burnish on a gray slip appears over a wide geographic and temporal range. It seems, therefore, that the source of these ceramic groups should not be sought outside Palestine. The phenomenon of Proto-Urban A and B ware is specific and defined—small pottery vessels manufactured for use as burial gifts—and should therefore be seen as an original creation. The forms are so unique, with no precursors and no successors (excepting a few types), the technique so uniform, and the geographic distribution so limited that these two pottery types may perhaps be seen as the creation of a limited number of itinerant potters who went from one site to another, producing burial-gift ware for the inhabitants.

METALLURGY

Compared with the Chalcolithic finds in the Cave of the Treasure, which represent an unprecedented and unsustained peak in the history of metalworking in Palestine, the metallurgy of the Early Bronze Age represents a decline. If, however, we leave out that Chalcolithic treasure trove, which is after all an anomaly, then some of the metal objects of the Early Bronze Age I may be said to show a development of Chalcolithic traditions, with improvements and variations of undoubted northern origin and some a continued production of early tool types. Continuity between the Chalcolithic and Early Bronze Age I is evidenced in the axes, adzes, and awls, which are so similar in form and technique that no typological differentiation can be made between the earlier and later objects. The difference between the two periods is shown in the marked decline in the distribution of the maceheads so typical of the Chalcolithic and in the introduction of spearheads (Azor) and daggers. The latter, found in a number of tombs, exhibit a variety of types, from the untanged dagger with a rhomboid section to the relatively developed type, with tang and midrib.

Tombs have also provided an important group of silver and gold beads and, most important of all, a silver bowl found at Tell el-Far'ah North. While the gold may have originated in Africa, arriving either directly from Egypt or via Syria-Lebanon, the silver (then more rare and precious than gold) must have come from the north, the nearest source of silver being in the mountains of Asia Minor.

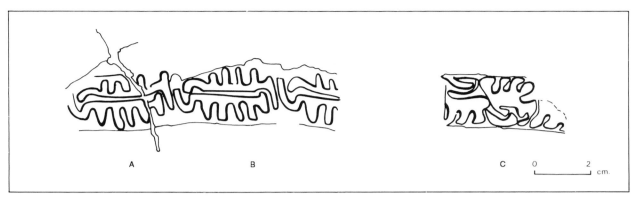

Fig. 4.5. Cylinder seal impressions from Megiddo Stage V

ART AND CULT

The art of Early Bronze Age Palestine is poorly attested to, especially in the earlier part of the period. The most important of the art objects that do occur belong to the realm of seal carving; chief among them are a number of cylinder seal impressions on pottery vessels found at Megiddo. The cylinder seal is a small cylinder, one to four centimeters high, usually made of stone, though examples in wood, ivory, or clay are known. A scene, accompanied at times by an inscription, is engraved on the cylinder, and when the cylinder is rolled over soft clay the scene is impressed on it in relief. The cylinder seal was invented in Mesopotamia some time during the fourth millennium, and the idea soon spread throughout the ancient Near East. In some places imported Mesopotamian cylinder seals have been discovered, but usually the seals were made in the different lands by local artisans, the scenes being derived from local theme assemblages. In their land of origin, cylinder seals were used chiefly for the signing and legal confirmation of official documents. In Syria and Palestine, however, it became customary during the third millennium to decorate pottery vessels with them. The impressions found at Megiddo belong to this type, and they fit in well with similar finds from Syria, and especially from Byblos. The seals themselves have not survived, as they were evidently made of wood, a characteristic feature of third millennium Syro-Palestinian glyptic art. One of the Megiddo impressions is composed entirely of animal heads, in a manner reminiscent of Mesopotamian glyptic. Most of the remaining impressions portray what seem to be lions and various horned animals. Their technique, style, and composition highly resemble those of seal impressions from Byblos. A seal from Tel Qishyon in which a long-horned animal is portrayed indicates contact with North Syria. The material of the seal, its form, and the style in which the animal is depicted all testify to a foreign origin, in the region of Syro-Cilicia.

Seal engraving is the principal expression of the artistic impulse in Early Bronze Age Palestine. It is supplemented by drawings incised on stone or, occasionally, potsherds, which usually portray human or animal figures. Such drawings have been found at Arad and Jericho, and the largest group at Megiddo. There the figures, depicting armed persons (hunters or warriors, perhaps) and various animals, most of them long-horned, were incised on the paving stones of the sacred area (described earlier in the section on architecture). The scenes may be taken as one of the few indications of the nature of cult practice in the Early Bronze Age I. The important cult structures of this period are the Megiddo double temple and the so-called Babylonian shrine at Jericho. These are considered to be temples because of the quality of their construction, their plan, cult installations found in them (for example, platforms), and the temenos wall that surrounds them. At Megiddo the double temple marks the start of a long-lasting cultic tradition; for centuries to come, the temples of Megiddo were erected in one place, termed the sacred area. The most difficult task faced by scholars is to understand the nature of the cult actually practiced both within these structures and by the people of Palestine in general. Not only are there no written documents but there is also a dearth of silent evidence—archaeological artifacts that can be clearly defined as cultic. There is thus no choice but to attempt to reconstruct a partial picture using logical inference and objects whose cultic nature, though highly probable, is uncertain.

A continuity of temple design is evident between the Chalcolithic and the Early Bronze I, particularly in the temple plans of Megiddo and En Gedi, and the same principles of design are followed in temples of the later part of the Early Bronze Age. This long-lived temple plan may be explained not only by a continuity of population groups and by the conservative nature of cultic architecture but also by a continuity in the character of the cult. Finds of the Chalcolithic period have revealed a widespread fertility cult with a strong emphasis on the fertility of flocks. This may not have been the only cult, but it is the one we know best and was no doubt of central importance. Finds of the later phases of the Early Bronze Age reveal that the fertility of land and vegetation joined that of flocks as central elements in the cult. This is no doubt related to the growing importance of field crops, which began to play a greater role at the beginning of the Early Bronze Age. If fertility cults were practiced in

Palestine both before and after the Early Bronze Age I, it is reasonable to assume that they were practiced during this period as well and pertained to the fertility of flocks or to that of crops or, as is most likely, to both. The depictions of horned animals on the flagstones of the Early Bronze Age I temple at Megiddo cannot but remind us of the depictions of these animals so common among the cult objects of the Chalcolithic. Incised drawings of such animals were also found on pottery vessels at Bab edh-Dhra, along with a graffito of a palm tree bearing fruit and a vessel decorated with a unique scene: four figures with hands upraised portrayed on either side of a pattern resembling a palm branch. On the rear of the vessel, more palm branches, perhaps bearing fruit, are depicted. The figures' attitude, par-

ticularly the upraised hands, have led to the assumption that they are engaged in a cultic activity such as prayer or dance. A similar scene from the same period was found on a pottery vessel from Egypt, where branches may clearly be seen springing out of the heads of figures with upraised hands. These scenes may be the artistic expression of a vegetation cult. An indication of the continuance of this cult is found on a stela from Early Bronze Age II Arad. A thread of continuity is also evident in the clay figurine assemblage of vessel-bearing animals. This type of figurine first appears in the Chalcolithic period. At Azor an animal described by the excavator as a donkey bearing a pair of vessels was found. In the Chalcolithic shrine at En Gedi a figurine of a horned animal bearing a pair of churns was

Fig. 4.6. Animal bearing vessels, from Azor (height 7 centimeters)

found; it has been noted that churns are closely connected with the milk cult of the Chalcolithic period. Two figurines of an animal bearing a pair of vessels dated to the Early Bronze Age I were found at Aphek, and a similar figurine was found in Early Bronze Age II Arad. It thus appears that the same continuity shown by cult structures, where the basic plan is carried over from the Chalcolithic period through the earlier and later phases of the Early Bronze Age, is demonstrated by cult objects such as vessel-bearing figurines. It is therefore likely that the cult itself, a fertility cult of flocks and vegetation closely linked to the economic life of the people, continued to be practiced.

FOREIGN RELATIONS

The suggestion that some of the people of Palestine in the Early Bronze Age I were immigrants from the north, whose place of origin was somewhere in Syria-Lebanon, can-

not yet be proved, and obviously no estimate can be made as to the size of the incoming groups or to their relative proportion in the general population. Nonetheless, it is likely that such a population movement did take place, and finds from the realms of pottery, metallurgy, and glyptics are clearly related to developments in countries to the north of Palestine. It also seems as if the immigrants played a role, perhaps a central one, in bringing about or speeding up processes occurring in the country at this time, processes that herald a new era in the history of Palestine. Yet it should be emphasized that this subject has not yet been thoroughly studied, and suppositions still outweigh certainties.

In contrast, the relations of Palestine with Egypt have aroused great interest, and the subject has been widely discussed. Evidence for relations with Egypt, in the form of Egyptian objects found at Palestinian sites, first appears in the Chalcolithic period and perhaps even

earlier. However, there is a sudden and drastic change in the number and character of these relations at the beginning of the Early Bronze Age. A large number of Egyptian artifacts, especially ceramic vessels, have been found in Palestinian sites of this period, particularly in southern sites such as Tel Erani, Tel Maahaz, and Tel Halif, where Egyptian pottery constitutes the greater part of the Early Bronze Age I assemblage. The finds are in part truly Egyptian (imported) and in part locally produced in Egyptian forms. Some of the vessels are medium-sized containers, but the great majority are small vessels. Notable are the simple crude vessels used for baking or cooking and the tableware. Two are of particular interest, one from Tel Erani and the other from Arad. They are fragments of two large closed vessels of Egyptian manufacture; each bears an incised design in the form of a rectangular frame containing the name of Narmer, the founder of the first

Fig. 4.7. Egyptian pottery from En Besor

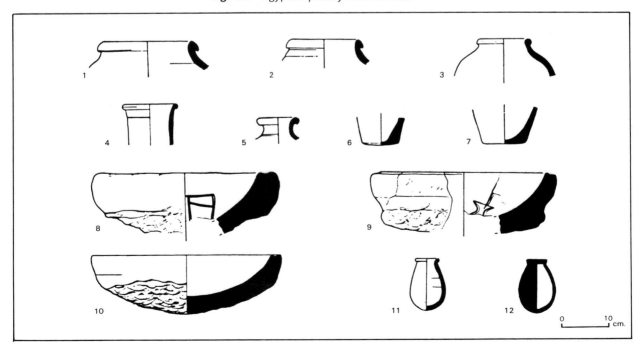

Fig. 4.8. Incised serekh signs of Narmer on pottery vessels: Arad (1), Egypt (2), Tel Erani (3)

Egyptian dynasty. The inscribing of the king's name within a rectangular border—a schematic representation of a temple facade—was a widespread practice in the third millennium B.C.E., and this design is termed a *serekh* in Egyptian. The two inscribed serekhs from Tel Erani and Arad are of great importance in establishing the absolute chronology of the period and contribute much to the discussion of the nature of the ties between Egypt and Palestine. Other serekhs of the Archaic period in Egypt have been found inscribed on Egyptian pottery vessels in Palestine: at En Besor an incised serekh apparently bearing the name of Hor-Aha, Narmer's successor, was discovered, and further serekhs (with the names of unidentifiable kings) have been found in sites of northern Sinai and the Gaza Strip (Rafiah) and at Tel Malhata in the Beersheba valley. At En Besor there were discovered, in addition to the Egyptian vessels and the incised serekh, tens of seal impressions of Egyptian officials, impressed on clay stoppers used to seal various containers, apparently sacks and skins. There is some uncertainty concerning the identity of the officials and their dates, but there is little doubt that the seals belonged to Egyptian administrative officials ranging in time over the whole of the First Dynasty period.

In the important cemetery of Azor, Egyptian finds included pottery vessels, a cosmetic palette decorated with figures of birds, beads, and a beautifully worked flint knife. Anthropological study of the skeletal remains has shown that although most were of the local type (as was the majority of the pottery in the tombs), some were of African origin. The Egyptian finds in the tombs allow us to assume that the latter were in fact Egyptians. Isolated Egyptian finds from other sites include a cosmetic palette from

Jericho and a clay cylinder seal from Gezer engraved with scenes derived from the Egyptian glyptic. As one proceeds northward the quantity of Egyptian artifacts diminishes. Among the few items found are a closed vessel and a macehead from Megiddo, a stone vessel from Tel Yoqneam, and beads and a stone amulet from Tell Asawir.

Palestinian imports into Egypt, though fewer in number and less varied than the Egyptian exports to Palestine, must not be overlooked. First and foremost is the not insignificant number of medium-sized vessels of Palestinian origin, which stand out in the Egyptian assemblage with their wide, flat bases and their large ledge and ear handles. Such vessels have been found both in sites of the eastern Delta, such as Minshat Abu-Omar, an area that has always maintained close relations with Palestine, and in sites of the Egyptian interior, such as El-Gerze, Naqada, and Abusir el-Melek. They are also portrayed on small plaques made of wood or ivory discovered in tombs of the early First Dynasty in Egypt. These vessels are shown carried on the heads or in the hands of men with non-Egyptian features and clothing, and it is likely that the bearers of the vessels are inhabitants of Canaan.

Another group of finds includes pottery vessels of Kenyon's Proto-Urban A or Proto-Urban B groups, so common in tombs of the period in Palestine. They have turned up both in the eastern Delta and in the Egyptian interior. It is improbable that any kind of merchandise was carried in these miniature vessels, and if there was any, it would have been of minute quantity. Rather, it may be suggested that these vessels, originally intended for use as burial gifts, were imported into Egypt by merchants from Palestine and were interred with them in Egypt when they died.

Thus it can be proven that ties existed between Egypt and Palestine in the Early Bronze Age I, as attested by the great number of objects from each land found in sites of the other. Scholarly debate has centered not on the question of the existence of ties but on the nature of the ties: did Egypt control Palestine, or at least the southern part of it, during this period, or were the ties between the two lands only commercial? One of the well-known finds from the time of Narmer, the founder of the First Dynasty, is a slate palette discovered some decades ago in Egypt bearing scenes carved in relief describing important events from the reign of this monarch. Nearly thirty years ago Y. Yadin proposed to interpret one of the signs on the palette as referring to Palestine and expressing Egyptian domination of that land. Those who support this interpretation explain the presence of Egyptian artifacts in southern Palestine, such as the vessels bearing the name of Narmer or the Egyptian seal impressions, as evidence of garrisons or of trade colonies protected by Egyptian troops, which exploited the economic resources of the land. Other scholars have not accepted Yadin's interpretation and thus do not accept the idea of Egyptian domination of southern Palestine. They prefer to see the relations between Egypt and Palestine as trade relations. Therefore, they interpret the pottery-bearing figures depicted in the wood and ivory plaques found in Egypt as merchants, while those who support the theory of Egyptian domination see them as tribute bearers. As for the goods themselves—especially those exported from Palestine to Egypt—whether tribute or merchandise, they will be dealt with in the following section, for the relations between the two countries continued in the Early Bronze Age II.

Fig. 4.9. Egyptian ivory plaques depicting Canaanites bearing ceramic jars (height 7.5 centimeters)

CHRONOLOGY

The archaeological finds do not seem to justify dating the beginning of the Early Bronze Age I to more than one hundred years before the reign of Narmer, at about 3100 B.C.E. The end of the Early Bronze Age I is fixed mainly by the appearance of a certain type of pottery vessel imported from Palestine into royal tombs in Egypt, dated to the reign of Djer (the third king of the First Dynasty), around 2950/2900 B.C.E. The multitude of approaches and proposals that archaeologists have applied to those two hundred years demonstrate that the period generates more questions than answers. Most difficult of all is the question of the relation between the Early Bronze Age I and the Ghassulian Chalcolithic. Was there an overlap between the two cultures, when the earlier had not yet disappeared and the later had not yet crystallized? How long did the overlap last? Did it occur throughout the country or only in parts? Or perhaps there was no overlap but rather a gap between the two cultures.

The current state of knowledge seems to present the following picture. The Early Bronze Age I begins with the disappearance of the Ghassulian Chalcolithic, which was an extended process, as were all the cultural transitions in Palestine. There is no question of a catastrophe involving the extermination of one population and the appearance of a new one, thus it is only natural that certain elements of the Ghassulian Chalcolithic should have been carried over into the Early Bronze Age I and even later. The material culture of Palestine during the period is quite varied. On one hand traditions seem to continue from the preceding period, and on the other new pottery assemblages are clearly defined, appearing more or less simultaneously, side by side, or even mixed. The period may be divided into, at most, two phases, of approximately equal length. In the first, which ends with the unification of Egypt under Narmer, ceramic traditions of the Ghassulian Chalcolithic are still strong and relations with Egypt are still weak. In the second, Chalcolithic traditions decline, and the ties between Egypt and Palestine increase, thanks apparently to the unification of Egypt.

The Early Bronze Age II–III

The important developments incipient in the Early Bronze Age I—the penetration into new regions, the establishment of a Mediterranean economy, the accumulation of surplus, and the increase in population—reached maturity in the Early Bronze Age II–III. The transition between the periods was gradual, without a break. Only a few Early Bronze Age I sites were abandoned or destroyed (for example, Mezer) and no longer settled. Most of them continued into the following phase, among them Hazor, Beth Yerah, Beth Shean, Megiddo, Ai, Jericho, Tel Erani, Lachish, and Arad, and many became urbanized. Characterizing this process is the erection of fortifications and public buildings, the development of urban planning, and the apparent social stratification. The towns of Palestine can be seen as a modest version of the urban society of Mesopotamia. The difference between the societies is most evident in the small size of the Palestinian towns, which is comparable to that of Mesopotamian villages, and in the absence of writing. Nevertheless it seems permissible to speak of the development of an urban society during this period in Palestine, and of towns of considerable size, compared with the nearby villages. Agricultural improvement, the higher standard of living, and the resultant increase in popula-

tion also led to the foundation of many small settlements—farmsteads or villages. These unwalled settlements were sometimes near the large fortified towns, such as the agricultural villages around Tell el-Far'ah North or those of the Beersheba valley (related no doubt to Arad), and sometimes a great distance away from them, for example the many sites of the Negev Highlands, Uvda valley, and Sinai. Of the latter, some were seasonal settlements of pastoral nomads (mostly goatherds), some were agricultural settlements (part of the Uvda valley sites), and some (the settlements of southern Sinai) were workers' villages whose inhabitants were engaged in the mining of copper and its supply to the urban regions north of the Negev Highlands. The phenomenon of coexisting urban and nonurban populations, the latter residing near the towns and in the marginal areas, is thus well known in the Early Bronze Age II–III. Strong bonds undoubtedly existed between these two components of the population; some may be observed in the archaeological record, and others only inferred from documents of the second millennium B.C.E., when the population of Palestine and indeed of the entire Near East was composed in a similar manner. Towns provided villagers and seminomads with various spiritual and material services, with a market for their produce, protection in times of danger, and perhaps a political framework and a sense of community. The villagers and seminomads, in return, brought their surplus produce into the urban settlements, and played an important part in intersite communication and in the trade network. Sometimes the very existence of the villages depended on the urban markets, as was the case with the miners' settlements of southern Sinai, and in any case they

were clearly subservient to the large towns, their culture at best a poorer version of urban culture. Comparison of the ceramic assemblages of villages of the Jezreel valley with that of Megiddo, villages of the Beth Shean valley with that of Beth Shean, or villages in the valley east of Shechem with that of Tell el-Far'ah North reveals in each case that the village assemblage is poorer, the range of forms narrower, and the quality of the vessels often lower than in the adjacent towns. A strong bond was also observed between the miners' settlements of southern Sinai and the town of Arad, 180 miles to the north. This relationship is reflected, for example, in the identity of the house plans and of the flint and copper tools in the miners' settlements and in Arad. Clay analyses have revealed that some of the southern Sinai vessels were made of clay that originated in the Arad valley (or were imported as vessels from that region), while in return, some of the vessels at Arad were made of clay that originated in southern Sinai. There are, however, some differences: though the plans of individual houses in southern Sinai resemble the Arad house, the circular outline of the settlement as a whole contrasts with that of the town of Arad. Also, the ceramic assemblage in the southern Sinai settlements is poorer in variety and in quality than that of Arad.

Not all the settlements appearing at the start of the Early Bronze Age II–III existed until the end of that period. On the contrary, every site excavated has provided evidence that the period was one of great unrest. In all sites a number of phases or strata of the period were observed, often separated by conflagration layers testifying to destruction, probably the result of wars. Also, many additions and repairs were found to have been made in the fortifications erected at the start of the period, further evidence of unrest and preparation for war. The fortifications of Jericho, for example, underwent no fewer than sixteen phases of repair and alteration from the time of their construction until the destruction of the town in the latter part of the Early Bronze Age.

There is a marked decrease in the number of sites between the Early Bronze Age II and III. The important towns of Arad and Tell el-Far'ah North, and perhaps also Tel Erani and Aphek, were abandoned at the end of the Early Bronze Age II and remained unoccupied in the Early Bronze Age III. Their rural dependents, the miners' settlements of southern Sinai and the villages of the valley east of Shechem, were completely abandoned with the demise of the two towns. The Israel Archaeological Survey has revealed a general decline in the number of Early Bronze Age III sites in comparison with the preceding period. This phenomenon, evident throughout the country, is especially conspicuous in the south. In the Negev Highlands, the Aravah, and Sinai the entire settlement system, composed solely of rural settlements, collapsed, and these regions lay deserted for hundreds of years. The causes of the phenomenon are not altogether clear. We do not know if towns like Arad or Tell el Far'ah North were destroyed in war or merely abandoned following a gradual decline. It has been suggested that the attrition wrought by frequent warfare among the towns of Palestine affected the entire urban system, with the weaker towns expiring first, but Tell el-Far'ah North and Arad were hardly weak. Others have suggested climatic change, pointing to a gradual process of dessication, decreased rainfall, and a lowering of the water table that reached its peak at the end of the third millennium B.C.E. Clearly such a process would affect the settlements in the southern desert fringes first, explaining, if only partially, the abandonment of these regions at the end of Early Bronze Age II. Economic factors may also be considered: the disruption of trade relations with Egypt in the Early Bronze Age II would have had a greater effect on the southern sites, which stood in close contact with Egypt, than on the sites of northern Palestine. It would perhaps be best to see the causes of the change in settlement pattern as a combination of the factors described here, accompanied by others as yet unknown to us. A different factor may have been decisive in each town or region, and one explanation need not be sought for all cases.

Despite what has been said, not all the villages of Palestine were abandoned, and many continued to exist in the Early Bronze Age III, as did most of the towns. In fact, the Early Bronze Age III is considered the high point of urban culture in the Early Bronze Age. All those towns that have been thoroughly studied—notably Beth Yerah, Megiddo, Ai, Yarmuth, and Jericho, as well as sites such as Dan, Beth Shean, Lachish, Tell el-Hesi, and Bab edh-Dhra—now reached the height of their prosperity. This is attested by their size, the public buildings erected in them, and their developed material culture, which has provided evidence for, among other things, relations with centers far distant from the borders of Palestine. It may be assumed that the inhabitants of the towns and villages abandoned at the end of the Early Bronze Age II found their way to sites that were not affected and were assimilated into those towns, stimulating their growth and prosperity.

ARCHITECTURE

FORTIFICATIONS. As we have seen, a few sites such as Ai and Tell el-Far'ah may have been fortified late in the Early Bronze Age I, permitting them to be characterized as towns at a relatively early stage. They may not have been the only sites fortified at the time, but the transition from unwalled to walled settlement in the majority of Palestinian sites occurred in the Early Bronze Age II, the outstanding examples being sites such as Arad, Megiddo, and Ta'anach. These sites had been sparsely inhabited in Early Bronze Age I, and though cult structures had been built in them in that phase (Megiddo, Jericho), they cannot be considered to have been planned, organized settlements. In the Early Bronze Age II a sudden transformation seems to occur; impressive fortifications are constructed and, as far as may be discerned, the foundations of the urban layout that was to characterize these towns are laid. It is difficult to accept the view that an invasion from abroad and a deterioration of security conditions were responsible for this sudden erection of fortifications. The social changes of the Early Bronze Age I, which matured earlier in some places than in others, led as a matter of course to the rise of towns in most of the Palestinian sites, many of which reached this phase more or less simultaneously. The accumulation of means and the development of construction technology, accompanied by the rivalry between the different settlements, were the reasons for the deterioration in security and the erection of fortifications. It was thus an internal development, the causes of which should not be sought elsewhere, especially as there are no signs of change in other components of the material culture that would indicate the arrival of newcomers.

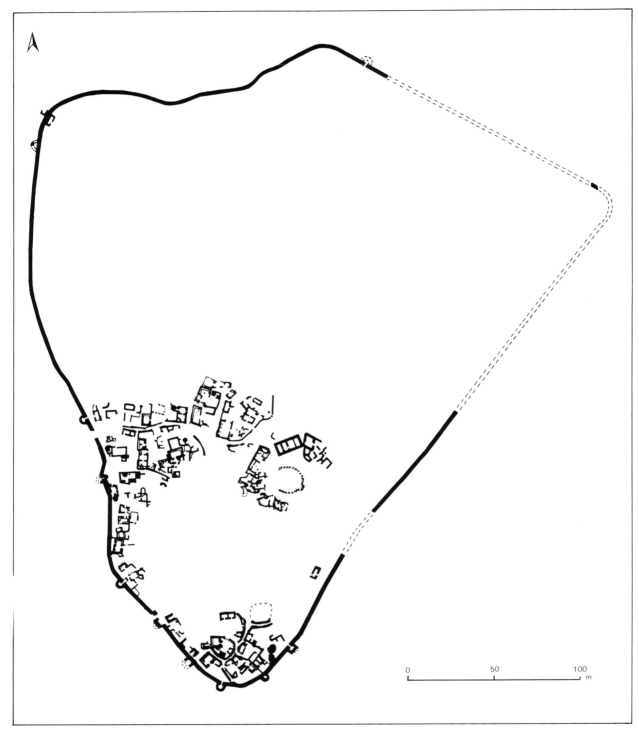

Fig. 4.10. Plan of Arad in Early Bronze II

The heart of the fortifications was the town wall. As the walls have not been preserved to their original height, we have no knowledge of the superstructure (balustrades, battlements, crenellations, and the like). At some sites, such as Megiddo, Tell el-Far'ah North, and Ai, the stone walls were preserved to a considerable height, often exceeding 2 meters, and it is difficult to say whether they were built of stone to their full height or whether, as seems likely, their upper parts were made of mud brick. At sites where stones are not so abundant, such as Jericho, only the foundations were made of stone and the walls themselves of brick. At some sites the walls are 2–3 meters thick (Arad, Aphek), while at others they are more than 8 meters (Beth Yerah, Megiddo). This tremendous width brought about structural problems involving the stability of large masses of masonry, but the ancient builders overcame the problems to construct fortifications that stood for hundreds of years, sometimes for the entire length of the Early Bronze Age. Buttresses and additions to the walls, as well as glacis added to protect their base, were no doubt intended not only to confront the enemy but also to overcome problems of everyday maintenance. Another measure observed at Megiddo, Jericho, and elsewhere was the building of the wall in separate segments, with a clearly visible seam between each segment. This method (which may also reflect a degree of social organization, each segment being built by a different crew) made the wall more flexible and minimized damage that might be caused by human or natural agencies, such as earthquakes. As no means of battering and piercing walls are known to have been used by the armies of this period (the battering ram was not introduced before the second millennium), the main func-

tion of the walls was to prevent sapping and scaling. The thicker the walls were, the higher they could be built; thus both breadth and height served to counter the possible means of enemy attack.

The defensive capabilities of the walls were improved by the construction of projecting towers. These were either semicircular, as seems more characteristic of the earlier part of the period (Arad, Jericho, Ai), or rectangular (Tell el-Far'ah North, Megiddo, Ta'anach). The most impressive gate is that

discovered at Tell el-Far'ah North, where the entryway is set between two strong towers that protect it. The western gate of Arad, in the Early Bronze Age II, is a gap in the wall defended by two semicircular towers. A fortification system of the Early Bronze Age III, including a gate approached by a ramp of beaten earth and an impressive wall built of huge stones, was excavated at Tel Yarmuth. The principle of narrowing the entrance by the construction of internal piers, typical of gates of the Middle Bronze Age and beyond,

Fig. 4.11. Megiddo city wall in Early Bronze II

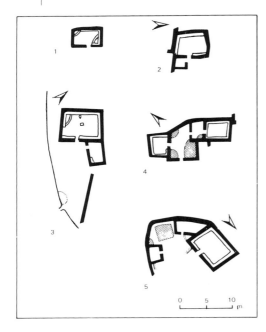

Fig. 4.12. Variants of the Arad house

was not yet known in the Early Bronze Age. At some sites (Arad, Ai, Tell el-Far'ah North, and elsewhere), postern gates—small passages 1–1.5 meters wide—were set in the walls to provide the inhabitants with convenient passage to the nearby fields. In times of danger they could be blocked easily and quickly with stones, and indeed several of those excavated were so blocked.

DWELLINGS. As private structures were conceived, planned, and built by the families that resided in them, it is difficult to define fixed types of dwellings, many of them being devoid of any discernible design. Nevertheless, the apparent existence of building fashions or traditions allows us to single out from among the dwellings of the Early Bronze Age II–III two types of

structures with fixed principles of design.

The first group consists of structures often called Arad houses, after the site where they appear in the greatest number and most complete form. Their plan is that of a broadroom structure, or broadhouse, with the doorway set in the middle of one of the long walls. The entry is thus along the short axis of the structure, with the interior space extending along the breadth, to the left and right. The house contains one main dwelling unit, sometimes accompanied by a small, cell-like room, which probably served for storage. The floor is below street level and is therefore approached by several steps. The door, located by the stone socket upon which it turned, opened inward and to the left. Benches are set along part or all of the walls; various installations

Fig. 4.13. Clay model of the Arad house found at Arad (height 21 centimeters)

and platforms furnish the rooms. Stone slabs are set in the floor, some serving as installations for domestic use and others as socles for posts that supported the roof. A clay model of such a house, found at Arad, reveals details of the unpreserved superstructure. The structure had one story and was windowless or had, at most, narrow slits for windows, suited to the harsh climate (sun, dust, sandstorms); the roof was flat with slightly raised edges to collect rainwater.

This plan is repeated many times at Arad, and structures of the same types have been observed in other Palestinian sites and in Sinai, where they characterize miners' settlements such as Nebi Salah and Sheikh Mohssein. The broadroom design is typical of dwellings of the Ghassulian Chalcolithic and is present in the Chalcolithic temple of En Gedi; it is also represented in the temples of Megiddo and Jericho in the Early Bronze Age I and now in the dwellings and temples of the Early Bronze Age II–III. It is, therefore, one of the clear manifestations of the traditionalism and of the continuity of the population in Palestine over more than one thousand years.

The second type of dwelling is less distinctly characterized by fixed design components, though it remains well defined. It may perhaps be termed the front-room house. The house consists of a courtyard and a dwelling unit behind it. The apparently open courtyard (the front room) contains installations such as the hearth and silo; through it the dwelling unit was approached. Typical examples of this type of structure may be seen, for example, at Tell el-Far'ah North, in the Early Bronze Age II, and Tel Qashish, in the Early Bronze Age III.

TEMPLES. The broadroom plan also characterizes the temples of the Early Bronze Age. The design common to the abode of both man and god (cf. "the house of the Lord," I Kings 6:1–2) was apparently used by the king, the most important citizen of the town, who was intermediary between man and god, or perhaps the gods' representative on earth. Palace remains are rarely found in Palestine in general and in the Early Bronze Age in particular. But the relation in plan and concept between palace and temple is readily perceived in Mesopotamia, and it may be assumed that a similar relation existed in Palestine. The king has a house, with male and female servants providing above all for his food and drink; so too has the god a house, with priests and priestesses providing sacrifices and libations. The house of the king is set off from those of his subjects, access to it is limited, and the throne room is the heart of the palace; so too is the house of the god surrounded by a wall that sets off the sacred area from the rest of the town; only a chosen few may enter that area, and fewer still the house itself, at the heart of which lies the cella, the holy of holies. If the complex of buildings south of the double temple at Arad is a palace, as the excavators believe and as indeed seems to be the case, then it is a good example of the surprising resemblance between the layout of private dwellings and the palace, on the one hand, and between that of the palace and the temple (Fig. 4.14) on the other. Adjacent to the palace on the north there appears to be a pair of small temples, which may be interpreted as a royal chapel, in contrast to the large double temple, which served the general population. The palace and its annex are almost identical to the Chalcolithic temple at En Gedi. The broadroom plan also appears in charnel houses (man's abode in

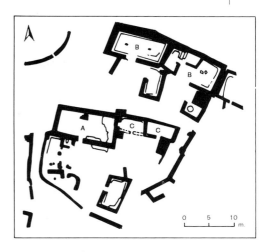

Fig. 4.14. Palace (A) and two pairs of twin temples (B-B, C-C) at Arad

death) excavated at Bab edh-Dhra. These are again single-room broadhouses, in which the floor is lower than street level and is approached by several steps. Such tombs have yet to be discovered in western Palestine.

The double temple first appears in the Early Bronze Age I, at Megiddo. There is no way of knowing whether this indicates the worship of a pair of deities, perhaps male and female. In any case, the large double temple at Arad bears a close resemblance in plan to the Early Bronze Age I double temple at Megiddo: in both cases the rear wall of the temple adjoins the temenos wall, making it quite thick, which is also the situation in the Early Bronze Age I shrine at Jericho and in the Chalcolithic temple of En Gedi. At Arad as at Megiddo, a small annex (probably a storeroom) lies between the two structures. In both cases entry to the temple is from the east. The principal difference between the temples of Megiddo and Arad is that in the former the platform (altar) is within the sanctuary, opposite the entrance and abutting the rear wall, whereas in the latter, it appears that the sacrifices and libations required by

the cult were performed in the court east of the temples themselves, as evidenced by the basin and altars found outside both the large and small double temples. The benches built along the walls of the Arad temples are also absent at Megiddo.

Another important temple was discovered at Ai. It is a monumental building of fine stone construction, situated at the highest point of the site, hence its name, the Acropolis Temple. This temple had a long span of existence; it was founded in the Early Bronze Age II and abandoned some time during the Early Bronze Age III. During this extended period a number of changes were made in the structure, though the building remained fundamentally the same throughout. It is a solitary temple (as opposed to the double temples discussed above), designed as a single-roomed broadhouse of impressive dimensions, with the entrance in the east. An annex (storeroom) was later added to the main structure. The principles so well known from Arad and Megiddo are thus repeated here. Yet the Ai temple differs in some features from those structures, particularly in the organization of the courtyard or sacred area east of the structure. It is

bounded, at least for a time, by two walls jutting out of the east wall of the temple proper, which function as antae of a megaronlike structure (cf. the Megiddo temples). Likewise, the rear wall of the temple is not, in this case, part of the temenos wall, as in the temples of Jericho, Megiddo, and Arad; rather, a narrow corridor separates the temple from the temenos wall. The main hall of the sanctuary contains a number of stone pillar bases, and it is devoid of any cult installations. It has been suggested that a sacrificial altar be reconstructed in the courtyard east of the structure, as at Arad. The Acropolis Temple was abandoned after a fire some time in the course of the Early Bronze Age III, and the cult, along with the cult objects, removed to a lower building north of the acropolis, adjacent to the town fortifications.

The new temple was no more than a dwelling house converted for use as a temple. The house was the last in a series built on that spot since the Early Bronze Age I, and it was the only one that served a religious function. This explains why the structure so little resembles other known temples (though it is a broadroom structure, with two

Fig. 4.15. Acropolis Temple at Ai

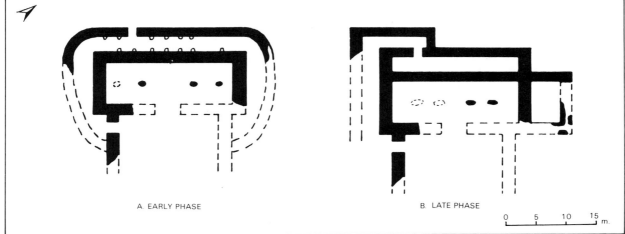

A. EARLY PHASE

B. LATE PHASE

0   5   10   15 m.

units in file, the rear one containing the altar), to the point that some scholars have denied its being a temple at all.

A most important group of temples was discovered at Megiddo. After the double temple of the Early Bronze Age I went out of use, the sacred character of the area was maintained. The still extant monumental remains of the Early Bronze Age III temples prevent a clear understanding of the character of the area in Early Bronze Age II. However, toward the end of that period a round stone platform 10 meters in diameter and 1.5 meters high, with a flight of steps leading to the top from the east, was constructed. Ashes and remains of sacrificial victims found in large quantities near the platform indicate that it served as an altar. Nothing else like it has

so far been found in Palestine. Shortly after the construction of the platform, a temple was built nearby, and the platform was encircled by a temenos wall adjoining the temple. Some time later two more temples were built. The entire array—the three temples and the platform—served for a while and then gradually went out of use, so that by the end of the Early Bronze Age only the platform and the first temple remained, having undergone many changes.

This array of cult structures is the most magnificent and complex in Early Bronze Age Palestine, presenting several intriguing issues. The singularity of the platform has been noted; to this should be added the problem of the orientation of the temples. A clear preference for an eastern orientation of cult structures

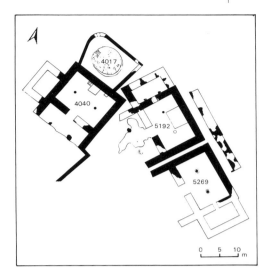

Fig. 4.16. Early Bronze III temples at Megiddo

Fig. 4.17. Cult platform in Megiddo sacred area

has been noticed; the oldest of the three Megiddo temples has an orientation different from that of the two adjacent and somewhat later temples. Is this difference linked to the nature of the cult? We do not know, but it must have had some significance, for cult traditions are binding, and no detail is accidental.

Another issue is the number of the temples. We have already seen double temples; now we are presented with a group of three temples functioning simultaneously in close proximity, a unique phenomenon in the history of temples in Palestine. Whether three deities were worshiped cannot be known, no more than we can know whether two were worshiped in the double temples, for not only are there no written texts of the period but the temples themselves were empty of any finds indicating the nature of the cult practiced within them. In addition to the round platform in the temenos courtyard outside the temples, each temple had a platform adjoining its rear wall, opposite the entrance. This sets the Megiddo temples apart from those of Arad and Ai and firmly within the tradition of the double temple in Early Bronze Age I Megiddo, and perhaps even that of the Chalcolithic period, as evidenced in the En Gedi temple.

Finally, the plan of the temples, especially of the two later temples and their temenos wall, reveals a clear resemblance to the Acropolis Temple at Ai. The Ai temple may be regarded as a precursor of the Early Bronze Age III temples at Megiddo and as a link between the concepts governing the organization of the sacred area at Arad and at Megiddo. The temples of Megiddo and Ai are single-roomed broadroom structures. At both sites an annex was attached to the main hall. The plan of the Ai temple approached that of the megaron, and the three Megiddo temples are undoubtedly structures

of this type. The megaron, whose origin lies in Greece or Asia Minor, is a longroom structure with an entrance porch bordered by extensions of the two long walls of the hall. The extensions are termed in classical architecture *antae*. The precise source of this plan is a matter of dispute, but such structures appear in the early third millennium in Asia Minor and Greece, and they belong undoubtedly to public structures—palaces or temples. Over the years the plan was confined to temples and often served as the core of the classical temple. The megaron no doubt came to Palestine as a result of relations with the north, for examples of such structures have been discovered in various sites in Syria-Lebanon (such as Byblos and Tell Chuera). In the process of adopting it, the temple builders at Megiddo made one significant alteration: the principle and tradition of the broadroom was so deeply ingrained in Palestine that the builders turned the megaron, a typical longroom structure, into a broadroom structure.

OTHER PUBLIC BUILDINGS AND TOWN PLANNING. The most impressive public building in Early Bronze Age Palestine was excavated at Beth Yerah and dates to the Early Bronze Age III. It is a structure of great size (30 × 40 meters), with walls nearly 10 meters wide. The building is not well preserved, having sustained extensive damage as a result of later construction. Nevertheless, enough of the structure has survived so that its plan may be almost fully reconstructed. The circles set in the thick walls should be reconstructed as silos of a cylindrical or conical form, in which grain was stored in bulk. It was therefore a public granary of enormous capacity, possibly exceeding the production capability of the town of Beth Yerah. If such was the case, the

granary must have served as a depot for the harvest of the entire region, the town and its rural hinterland, with all the political and social implications of such a function. Interestingly enough, similar structures of the same period appear in Egyptian wall paintings and on a stone model dated to the late third millennium, discovered on one of the Aegean islands. The public granary of Beth Yerah is so far the only one found in Palestine. Whether it was unique or whether more will yet be discovered, and whether its builders were influenced by the designs of similar buildings in neighboring countries, yet remains to be seen.

Further evidence of public works are two water supply systems, one of the Early Bronze Age II at Arad and the other of the Early Bronze Age III at Ai. In Arad a reservoir, situated at the lowest point in the town, was excavated in the soft Cretaceous limestone, apparently reaching the water table but in any case serving to collect the runoff from town slopes. The structural remains adjacent to the reservoir differ in character from the dwelling houses, and they clearly were connected with the administration and upkeep of these central public works, on which the welfare of the entire population depended. The reservoir at Ai was also built at the lowest point in the town. It was lined with stone slabs and caulked to retain the floodwaters efficiently, and its capacity is estimated at 2000 cubic meters. There can be little doubt that more water systems of this type await discovery in other Early Bronze Age sites.

In most Palestinian sites, the Early Bronze Age levels are hidden deep beneath the debris of later eras. This greatly impedes the broad exposure of Early Bronze Age strata, so that these are usually reached only in narrow trenches. Such narrow exposures provide but scanty information, especially where issues such as that of town planning are concerned. Hence the great importance of sites such as Arad, where the third millennium strata are not covered by later remains and wide areas of the Early Bronze Age strata may be cleared. And indeed at this site the outlines of the town plan may be followed.

The town occupies the slopes of a natural, saucerlike depression, with the wall set along the rim of the saucer at its highest point. A main street crosses the town from east to west, and peripheral alleys follow the course of the wall, with allowances made for topographical variations. Public buildings (the temple, palace, and water system) are in the center of the town, adjoining the main street.

Features of town planning were also observed at Tell el-Far'ah North. From the beginning and throughout the existence of the Early Bronze Age II town, two main streets bisected the town, one running east-west and the other north-south. Another street wound parallel to the town wall. A drainage system was built along the main streets. In time a new wall was built along the north side of the town, inside the previous wall; concurrently, in a wide-scale planned operation, house levels were changed to facilitate drainage through a new sewer running under the wall. Urban planning is also attested in the layout and delimitation of the sacred area at Megiddo and in the organization of access to it from other parts of the town. The sites just described are no doubt illustrative of the situation at other sites, where broad exposure is barred.

POTTERY

The ceramic assemblage of the Early Bronze Age II–III is, in the main, a continuation and development of the assemblage of the first phase of the Early Bronze Age. The Early Bronze Age I assemblage is, however, largely a tomb assemblage, whereas most of the Early Bronze Age II–III vessels in our possession originate in occupation levels, though tomb vessels play an important role. Thus, the assemblages differ significantly in that the majority of the known vessels of the first part of the period are small votive vessels, while those of the two phases here discussed are generally vessels for everyday use. Among the votive vessels, Kenyon's Proto-Urban C group now disappears entirely. The distribution of her Proto-Urban A and Proto-Urban B groups also declines radically, though some types, particularly of the Proto-Urban A family, continue to exist and even to develop and influence ceramic forms, particularly in Early Bronze Age II. The characteristic band slip of the Early Bronze Age I is also no longer present in Early Bronze Age II–III, though the vessels decorated in this fashion continue to exist. Continuity is also evident in a number of forms, such as storejars, neckless cooking pots (holemouths), and various types of bowls, and a great deal of continuity is seen in details such as the ledge handle, so characteristic of the entire Early Bronze Age, and in ceramic technology: most vessels are handmade, though as time goes by the number of wheel-made vessels increases. At Tell el-Far'ah North, for example, about 20 percent of the vessels were made on the wheel in the Early Bronze Age I and some 35 percent in Early Bronze Age II. The quality of the clay improves as well; its preparation is more meticulous, and the bonding materials are well

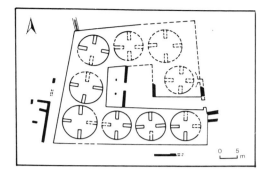

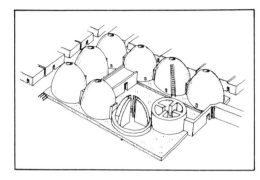

Fig. 4.18. Public granary at Beth Yerah: plan and suggested restoration

Fig. 4.19. Egyptian wall painting portraying granary

sifted. Finally, the firing of the vessels improves considerably. All the above led to the production of finer vessels, having thinner walls and a more regular outline, compared with the vessels of the previous phase. The improved craftsmanship suggests the establishment of a class of craft specialists, another feature of the urbanization of Early Bronze Age society.

Further elements suggest standardization and specialization. The variety of ceramic decoration prevalent in the Early Bronze Age I decreases and gives way to the widespread use of red slip and burnish. Of the decorated vessels, the vast majority are decorated in this fashion. Using this technique, potters attained new heights of craftsmanship; the red slipped vessels with net or pattern burnish are among the finest ever produced in Palestine. The variety of forms also diminishes in relation to early periods. Different sites have rendered closely similar groups of platters,

jugs, and jars, apparently testifying to the existence of potters' workshops that produced more than the immediate needs of the site in which they functioned. Another phenomenon that fits in well with the apparent industrialization of the potter's craft is the presence of workshops that served an entire region. Tell el-Far'ah North is the only site in which a workshop of the period has been discovered. Two kilns, which had evidently seen extended use, were found there. Indirect evidence that the potters produced vessels for their own site and for the nearby region is given by a number of local-regional variants that appear in ceramic assemblages of the Early Bronze Age II–III, for example, the pottery characteristic of Tell el-Far'ah North and the nearby Wadi Far'ah sites, the pottery characteristic of Jericho and of the lower Jordan valley, and the pottery characteristic of Tel Yarmuth

and of the nearby Shephelah (inner plains) sites.

The rise in the standard of pottery production and craft specialization was perforce dependent on increased demand for pottery vessels due both to population increases and to the new requirements of the Mediterranean economy, such as the need to store and transport oil and wine. It must, however, be emphasized that there was no ceramic revolution, and the changes indicated did not affect the entire assemblage at once. On the contrary, the old "archaic" pottery forms still played an important role, in some places even comprising the greater part of the assemblage. But even if at the beginning of the Early Bronze Age II many potters continued to produce in the old traditions, it is clear that new times had arrived.

Among the many pottery groups characterizing the Early Bronze Age II–III assemblages, the following

Fig. 4.20.   Abydos ware from Canaan (6–10) and Egypt (1–5)

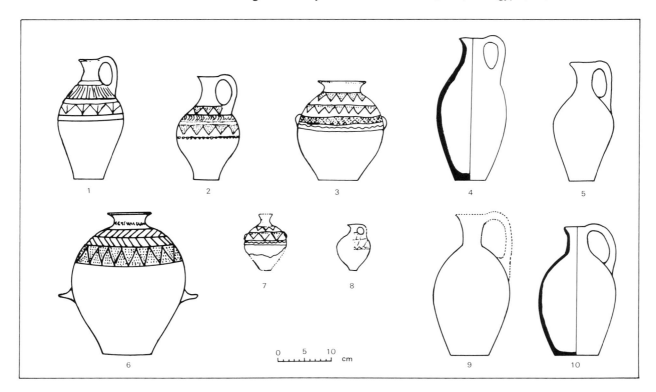

three are of special significance, as they shed much light on the economy and production techniques as well as on the chronology and the foreign relations of Palestine during this period.

ABYDOS WARE. This term refers to a class of pottery consisting mainly of jugs and juglets, as well as one type of store jar. Technically this pottery group represents the best in the potter's craft of the period. The vessels are made of well-levigated clay, they are finely and elegantly formed, many are wheel-made and highly fired. Most are covered with a burnished red slip, and some with a painted decoration limited to the upper part of the vessel consisting of triangles, arches, concentric semicircles, and dots, all in a red color that stands out against the pale surface of the vessel. These vessels are of great importance not only because they comprise a defined and widely distributed class in the ceramic assemblage of Early Bronze Age II–III Palestine but also because of the central role they play in determining an absolute chronology of the period. The appearance of this ware may with certainty be dated to the Early Bronze Age II; some jugs that may be considered prototypes of the Abydos ware jugs appear in Early Bronze Age I assemblages, but they are few and of poorer quality than the jugs of the following phase. The occurrence of this class of vessels in Early Bronze Age II assemblages has been observed in every relevant site in Palestine. This is especially marked at Arad, a key site for the study of these vessels. Stratum IV at Arad represents the preurban village and is dated to the Early Bronze Age I; Abydos ware is entirely absent from this stratum. In stratum III of the Early Bronze Age II, when Arad becomes a town, this ware appears in all its glory and

with a full range of variants. It is named after the site of Abydos, in Egypt, where the vessels were first discovered many years ago in the tombs of kings and high officials of the First Dynasty. The excavators of these tombs recognized the vessels as foreign to the Egyptian repertoire, and it soon transpired that they were the containers in which liquid products—apparently scented oils, medicines, and cosmetics—were imported to Egypt for the use of the governing classes in life and after death. It must be emphasized that the name comes after the site in which the vessels were first identified, though it is clear that they were not made there, nor is it the

only site in which they have been found. In Egypt itself this ware has been found in tombs at Saqqara, Abusir el-Melek, and elsewhere, and in Syria and Palestine it is present in large quantities at many sites.

What region was it within this wide expanse that exported the products stored in these containers to Egypt? The products originated, in all probability, in the southern part of their distribution area: in Palestine. In the first place, there is no evidence for relations between Egypt and Syria in the First Dynasty, whereas relations with Palestine were close. Second, all the variants of Abydos ware found in Egypt are known in Palestine but

Map 4.2. Distribution of Abydos ware in Canaan and Egypt

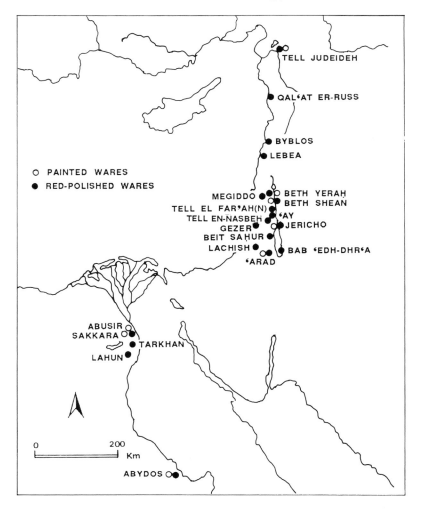

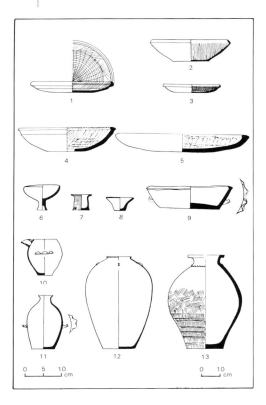

Fig. 4.21. Burnished and combed metallic-ware vessels

not in Syria; this is true especially of the decorated store jars, which have been found in Egypt and Palestine (Arad) but not in Syria. Finally, chemical analysis shows the clay of the vessels found at Abydos to be almost identical to that of the vessels found in Palestine.

The Arad excavations have provided the most conclusive evidence regarding the absolute chronology of the Early Bronze Age. Abydos ware does not appear in Egypt in tombs ascribed to the period of the first two kings of the First Dynasty, Narmer and Hor-Aha, but only during the reign of the third king, Djer. Similarly, at Arad, in stratum IV of the Early Bronze Age I, where an Egyptian vessel bearing the serekh of Narmer was found, Abydos ware does not yet occur; it appears only in stratum III of the Early Bronze Age II, which must therefore be dated from the reign of Djer onward. Finally, Abydos ware had a rather long lifespan in Syria-Palestine, and it continued to be produced there long after its importation into Egypt had ceased. Certain changes occurred during the Early Bronze Age III: jug bases became elongated, juglets grew more common, and the painted decoration disappeared.

METALLIC WARE. This term has been applied to a class of exceptionally well fired vessels. The higher the firing temperature, the harder, stronger, and more durable a pot becomes; it takes on a reddish hue and gives off a high-pitched metallic sound when struck with the finger. The firing temperature of this ware is about 900°C, much hotter than the 500°–700°C characteristic of the ware of the previous phase. Improved kilns and firing techniques were hallmarks of the Early Bronze Age II–III ceramic industry, and the number of highly fired vessels steadily increases, until they constitute

one fifth of the Early Bronze Age III assemblage at some sites. The vessels thus treated include chiefly store jars, jugs (including a large proportion of the Abydos ware vessels), and large, flat bowls called platters. The store jars are of particular interest, being the largest group in the metallic-ware assemblage. Palestinian agricultural produce, particularly wine and oil, was stored and traded in these jars. To fulfill this function, the jars would have had to meet certain standards, and it appears that they did so admirably. Vessels made with aluminum-calcite clay (the majority of those produced up to this time) are not resistant to acidic liquids such as wine. Furthermore, such vessels are more porous and tend to sweat, in the manner of Middle Eastern water jars, in which water is stored and kept cool by the evaporation of the moisture on the exterior of the vessel. In wine jars such a process would cause the wine to ferment and spoil and therefore had to be avoided. Analysis of metallic-ware jars has revealed that most were made of aluminum-silicate clay; they were thus resistant to acids and did not sweat. The vast majority of the metallic-ware jars were not decorated, except by combing. The widespread combing decoration was performed before firing when the vessel was at a leather-hard stage. A toothed, comblike instrument was used to incise groups of parallel lines on the vessel exterior. So-called pattern combing was produced when the line groups were short and ran in different directions. Combing may have been intended merely for decoration, but it seems more likely that another function was served. In some cases, particularly on jars found in hill and Shephelah sites (Ai, Lachish, Yarmuth, and others), the exterior of the vessel shows traces of a white lime wash, possibly related to waterproofing, insulation, and maintenance of a fixed temperature, which improved the preservation of the liquids in the vessel. The wash did not always adhere well to the vessel, and many of the vessels found without it may have originally been covered with it.

The open metallic-ware vessels—mostly platters, as well as bowls and saucers—were not, of course, meant to carry liquids and were not shipped abroad as containers. They were vessels for local, domestic use, and in some the potter's art is revealed at its best, the vessels being red slipped and burnished with star or net patterns.

BETH YERAH WARE. Beth Yerah ware presents a phenomenon entirely different from that of the two groups just described. The latter consist chiefly of closed vessels intended for the storage of liquid products; they have been found in Egypt, and they range in time over the entire length of the Early Bronze Age II–III. Beth Yerah ware vessels are, in the vast majority, open forms, certainly not intended for the storage of liquids; they have not been found in Egypt, and they appear only in the Early Bronze Age III. In view of the considerable degree of continuity between the assemblages of the Early Bronze Age II and III phases, the presence of Beth Yerah ware often serves as an important criterion for the attribution of a given assemblage to the Early Bronze Age III.

Beth Yerah ware consists mainly of bowls, saucers, and cups, which make up over 90 percent of the finds in this group. There are also a number of utensils not encountered in other ceramic groups; these include lids and pot stands. Profiles are soft and sinuous, and the bases very small in proportion to the diameter, so that the vessels are unsteady, which explains the widespread use of pot stands. The vessels are never

wheel-turned; the clay is poorly levigated and mixed with large grits and straw. All the vessels are covered with a thick slip, which may be either red, black, or bichrome. In the latter case, the interior and upper exterior surfaces are red, and the rest of the exterior is black. Finally, the entire vessel is highly burnished and thus provided with a brilliant sheen. The play of colors was induced by a change in the firing atmosphere in the kiln: during firing, the potter passed from an oxidizing atmosphere, which produced red hues, to a reducing atmosphere (an oxygen-poor atmosphere produced by allowing smoke to enter the firing chamber), which resulted in shades of black. This unusual and striking finish, though serving primarily as decoration, enhanced the impermeability of the vessels, which would otherwise have been kept quite low by the poor levigation of their clay.

The vessels are also often decorated in relief, some with ribbing, others with nipplelike protuberances and circles. The thick, burnished slip covers these decorations as well. A few of the vessels, particularly lids and pot stands, bear incised decoration, which sometimes takes the form of a human face.

In each of these features—the profiles, details of form, hand-forming, poor levigation, poor firing, thick slip, and bichrome coloring—Beth Yerah ware stands out as completely alien to the ceramic traditions of Palestine. In contrast to Abydos ware and metallic ware, which were deeply rooted in local traditions both in form and technique, Beth Yerah ware appears suddenly and disappears as suddenly, leaving no trace.

This class of pottery was named Beth Yerah ware (or Khirbet Kerak ware) after the site of Beth Yerah (Khirbet Kerak), near the Sea of Galilee, where it was first identified

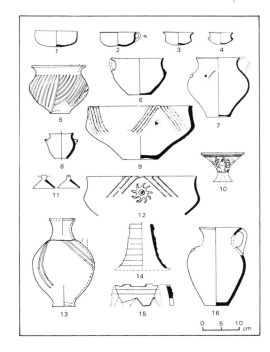

Fig. 4.22. Beth Yerah (Khirbet Kerak) ware typology

Fig. 4.23. Beth Yerah ware: bowl (height 24 centimeters) and mug (27 centimeters)

and defined. The ware is found mainly in the valleys—the Jezreel, Jordan, and Beth Shean valleys—at sites such as 'Afula, Beth Yerah, and Beth Shean. From these sites Beth Yerah ware comprises a significant part of the Early Bronze Age III assemblage. Far smaller quantities of Beth Yerah ware are present at sites such as Hazor in the upper Galilee, Jericho in the lower Jordan valley (often regarded as an extension of the northern valleys), Ai in the hill country, Yarmuth in the inner plains, and Tel Nagila in the northern Negev, which marks the southernmost extent of its distribution.

The Beth Yerah ware phenomenon as a whole requires explanation. How did these vessels reach Palestine? (That they are alien to local pottery traditions is obvious.) Did they arrive through trade? Were they the property of an invading population arriving at the beginning of the Early Bronze Age III, or did only a few foreign potters arrive in Palestine at this time? In this context the existence of Beth Yerah ware north of Palestine should be noted. In Syria the ware is also found chiefly in valley sites, for example, in the Orontes and Amuq basins. The Beth Yerah ware found in these regions is identical to that found in Palestine and constitutes a considerable proportion of the ceramic assemblage where it occurs. Beyond Syria, the resemblance to Beth Yerah ware diminishes. In the Anatolian plateau vessels akin to Beth Yerah ware were found, but the resemblance is less vivid than that of the Syrian and Palestinian wares, with the exception of one type: the pot stand of Anatolia is identical to those found in Syria and Palestine. Another region apparently connected with the Beth Yerah ware family lies between the Caspian Sea and the Turkish border. Here, in Armenia and Georgia, many Bronze

Age sites were discovered with pottery bearing familiar features: S-shaped profiles, small bases, highly burnished decoration, and some patterns of ribbed and relief decoration that appear in Beth Yerah ware. Again, these vessels are not identical with the ware of Syria and Palestine, but a certain bond no doubt exists.

The forms and ware of Beth Yerah vessels made them unsuitable for trade and inconvenient to transport, and it may be assumed that they were produced locally. Chemical analysis of the clay has revealed beyond doubt that the Beth Yerah ware found in Palestine was not imported and that the bulk of it was produced in the sites where it was found. However, as its presence is alien to Palestine (and to Syria), we must look northward for its sources of influence and inspiration. Such influence could have arrived in one of three ways: population move-

ments (the vessels were the property of immigrants), the immigration of potters who came from somewhere in the north and continued to produce pottery in the traditions of their homeland, or importation of ideas (local craftsmen producing pottery under foreign inspiration). Opinion is divided over these possibilities, but the second seems the most plausible. On the one hand, there is no evidence of massive migrations into Palestine in the Early Bronze Age III, though a migration not accompanied by hostile acts and destructions is difficult to trace. On the other hand, it is hard to believe that a local potter would abandon everything he was accustomed to in favor of an imported concept. If Beth Yerah ware was created by local potters, one would expect to find hybrid features, reflecting the coexistence of local traditions with foreign characteristics. This is not

Map 4.3. Suggested migration route of bearers of Beth Yerah culture

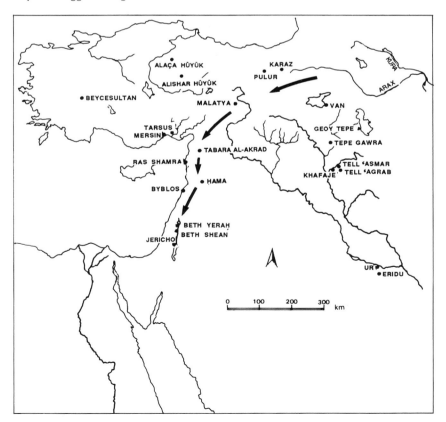

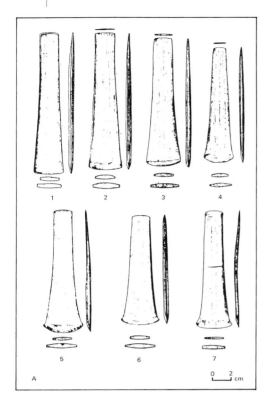

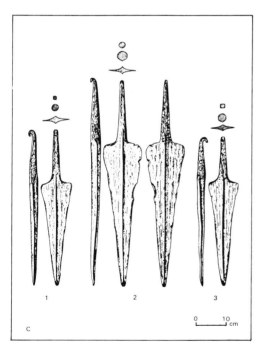

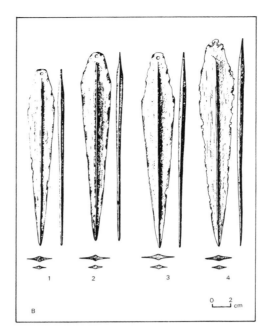

Fig. 4.24. Kfar Monash hoard: axes and adzes (A), daggers (B), spearheads (C)

the case; Beth Yerah ware is entirely alien to Palestinian traditions. The remaining option is thus to be preferred—the immigration of potters, who continued to create their unique pottery in Palestine. During their stay, they had some interaction with local craftsmen; here and there, vessels made in the local tradition bear a feature of Beth Yerah ware, such as the sinuous profile or the relief decoration. But the Beth Yerah tradition was so foreign to Palestine that it had no chance of acclimatization, and as it appeared, so did it disappear: abruptly, in the midst of the Early Bronze Age III, leaving no trace.

METALLURGY

A hoard of metal objects found in a field near Kfar Monash in the Sharon constitutes the most important metallurgical find of third millennium B.C.E. Palestine. The hoard contains a large number of artifacts, most of them weapons and tools, including six axes, eleven adzes, three chisels, a saw, two long knives with curved ends, four spearheads, four daggers, a knife, a macehead, a stake, a crescent-shaped object, a few hundred copper plaques, fragments of a silver mirror, and a number of carnelian beads. The most important questions regarding the so-called Kfar Monash hoard are: How may we explain the findspot of the hoard, far from any ancient site? What was the precise function of the implements, some of which (especially the spearheads) are exaggerated in size, exceeding that of any other known tools? Were these implements made in Palestine or were they imported? If they were made locally, what is the source of the metal? Finally, what is the date of the group?

There are no data relating to the first question. The Sharon was sparsely settled in the Early Bronze Age, and it is generally assumed that it was covered by swamps and dense thickets. The only explanation thus far offered for the odd location of the hoard is that of S. Yeivin, who believed the hoard to be the equipment of a detail of Egyptian troops (four soldiers and an officer) who came to the Sharon to fell timber and send it to Egypt. For reasons unknown—perhaps a surprise attack, or the need to be rid of the heavy burden to ease their retreat— the soldiers had to bury their gear. Needless to say, such a theory cannot be verified, and as things stand, the first question must remain unanswered. Yeivin's theory assumes an Egyptian origin for the implements, and a date in the days of Narmer, in the early First Dynasty (this date was first advanced by the original publishers of the hoard). We will here attempt to show that both the Egyptian origin and the Early Bronze Age I date are highly improbable.

The most problematic of the implements, in regard to function, are the giant spearhead, 66 centimeters in length and 2 kilograms in weight, and a group of 800 thin copper plaques, measuring 5 × 11 centimeters each. It has been suggested that the spearhead was the head of a battering ram (the metal point attached to a long wooden pole intended to batter walls) and the copper plaques pieces of scale armor, which would have been sewn onto a leather garment. Neither suggestion seems plausible: battering rams and scale armor appear hundreds of years after the latest date possible for the hoard, the supposed scales have no eyelets that would allow them to be sewn to the garment, and the battering ram is of a material too soft to batter a wall. It would therefore be best to leave the question of the function of these implements open as well.

As for the question of origin, comparative typological study (the comparative study of the forms of the various artifacts) does not point to any of Palestine's neighbors as a likely source for the objects. The unique objects, whether those mentioned above or objects such as the two long knives with the curved ends, have no parallel in or out of Palestine, while most of the remaining implements are typologically at home both in Palestine and in the neighboring lands. It must be kept in mind that tools and weapons throughout the eastern Mediterranean have much in common. The forms of metal implements may be said to be more international and the number of variations much smaller than, for example, among ceramic wares, no doubt because the scarcity of raw material and the technical difficulties involved in obtaining and working metal resulted in there being far fewer metal-working centers than there were pottery-producing centers. Pottery centers were present at almost every site, whereas metal working depended on the presence and coexistence of several factors. It may thus be assumed that there were itinerant smiths who manufactured their wares in various places or permanently settled craftsmen who sold their products far and wide. There is no evidence that the Kfar Monash hoard was imported, and it need not be assumed that the artifacts are of foreign manufacture. The source of the raw material for the objects has also been studied. Chemical analysis has shown that it came from different parts of the Near East, such as the Sinai, northern Syria, Anatolia, and Armenia, and may be seen as evidence of contact with those areas.

The most hotly debated question is that of the hoard's date. As the group was not found in an archaeological site and is not related to ceramic or other finds, the only way

to date the artifacts is by comparative typological study with objects discovered in datable contexts. The main difficulty with this method is that the valuable and durable metal implements are slow to change, and an artifact type may have a lifespan of hundreds of years, as opposed to pottery, in which typological change is relatively swift and serves as a convenient chronological indicator. Usually, when the tools and weapons indicate a broad temporal range, a more precise date may be provided by the context in which they are discovered; this, as noted, cannot apply to the Kfar Monash hoard. The axe and adze group, the largest group in the assemblage, excepting the copper plaques, is the most difficult to date. These simple tools are of so basic a form that they may be paralleled in assemblages ranging from the Chalcolithic to the second millennium, a period of 1500 years. All attempts at a subdivision of this artifact into types according to proportions, the shape of the cutting edge, and so on have been unsuccessful. Clearly, then, such artifacts cannot date the Kfar Monash group. The same is true of the daggers, the range of which, though more limited than that of the axes and adzes, covers the whole of the Early Bronze Age. The spearheads are indeed unique, but their shape and prominent midrib seem to point to a relatively advanced stage in the Early Bronze Age. The most important object for determining the date of the Kfar Monash hoard is the one with the shortest range: a battle-axe of the type known as the crescentic axe (or epsilon axe, for its similarity to the shape of the Greek letter). This axehead, discovered some distance away from the hoard itself, was probably part of it originally. It matches the hoard in its metal content and has no conceivable archaeological context apart from that of the nearby hoard. It was most likely

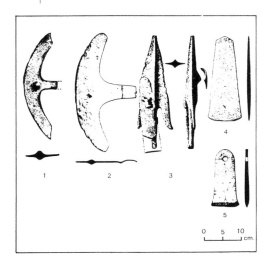

Fig. 4.25. Axe from Jericho (1), axe (2), spearhead (3), and adzes (4–5) from Tell el-Hesi, Early Bronze III

Fig. 4.26. Cylinder seal impression depicting animal procession, from Jericho

dragged across to its findspot when the field was plowed. Similar axeheads have been found in Palestine, but in Early Bronze Age III contexts. The Kfar Monash axe is a prototype of these axeheads: it lacks the small knob in the middle of the blade and is of somewhat poorer workmanship. A date somewhere toward the end of the Early Bronze Age II is thus indicated. This date is, in effect, a mean between the (late?) Early Bronze Age I date proposed by R. Hestrin and M. Tadmor, who first published the find, and the Early Bronze Age III date proposed by several other scholars.

Apart from the crescentic axe discovered at Kfar Monash, three such objects have been found at Tell el-Hesi, Jericho, and Bab edh-Dhra. At the latter two sites, the axeheads clearly come from Early Bronze Age III contexts, and this appears to be the case at Tell el-Hesi as well. The crescentic axe belongs to the family of tanged axes. The middle and longest of its three tangs served to fix the axehead firmly in place when inserted through, then twisted round the haft. This was the first step toward the development of a socket for the attachment of the axehead to the haft, a development evidenced in the fenestrated axes of the Middle Bronze Age I, and is a further indication of the relatively late Early Bronze Age date of the crescentic axe. Another improvement is the knob in the middle of the blade, which prevents the penetration of the axehead too deeply into the haft with repeated blows. The knob is lacking in the Kfar Monash find, hence the earlier date proposed for it. Crescentic axes have been found outside Palestine. At Byblos a mold for casting crescentic axes was discovered, identical in every detail to the axes discovered in Palestine, though unfortunately in an undatable context. Similar axes have been found in Anatolia and Mesopotamia, but the resemblance, though great, is not as great as that between the Byblite and Palestinian examples. We have, therefore, a phenomenon somewhat similar to that encountered in the case of Beth Yerah ware. The source of inspiration is somewhere in the north, perhaps in Upper Mesopotamia, and thence the concept migrated to the Levant. Syria and Palestine present an identical variant, the outcome of a northern influence on both lands.

Metal objects have been encountered in nearly every site where Early Bronze Age II–III layers have been excavated. They include daggers, which are usually short and have rivet holes in their bases; adzes, similar in every way to those of Kfar Monash; pins, awls, and hammers. Unique objects include a probably ceremonial spearhead of the Early Bronze Age II, partly plated with silver, from Megiddo; a spearhead, apparently of the Early Bronze Age III, found with the crescentic axe and a number of adzes at Tell el-Hesi, which also seems to bear a resemblance to objects from Syria (Amuq, Ugarit); and a small saw, of the Early Bronze Age III, found at Hazor. Metal jewelry—rings, bracelets, pins, and beads—was generally made of copper, but fragments of a silver mirror from Kfar Monash, gold beads from Lachish, and a gold brooch from a tomb near Kinneret have also been found.

No workshops have yet been discovered, but examination of the artifacts themselves has shown that some (especially the daggers and pins) were fashioned by hammering and annealing, and others were cast in open molds, as evidenced by the planoconvex section of most of the adzes and by two such molds discovered at Megiddo (Early Bronze Age III). Some of the objects, such as the spearheads and daggers with the prominent midrib from Kfar Monash and the crescentic axes with the central knob, were probably cast in closed molds.

The principal raw material was copper; far smaller amounts of gold, silver, and lead (a by-product of silver) are also represented. Unfortunately, only a few chemical analyses of the various objects have been conducted, and there is little data available regarding the source of the copper. Analyses have revealed that some artifacts were made of Sinai copper, including those made of copper with no nickel content (if part of the Kfar Monash hoard was indeed made of copper from Sinai, it would support the dating of the hoard, as there is no evidence for the utilization of the Sinai mines before the Early Bronze Age II). Some objects were also found to be made of copper that apparently originated in Anatolia and Trans-Caucasia, as indicated by the high nickel and lead content. The same source may be indicated by the arsenic content in some of the Kfar Monash artifacts. This does not necessarily testify to the importation of the objects themselves from those regions; it is just as reasonable to assume that only the raw material was imported and that the objects were manufactured in Palestine.

ART AND CULT

The number of art objects of the Early Bronze Age found in Palestine is very small. Evidently, the carving of seals was the principal mode of artistic expression, and the seals and seal impressions form the principal group of art objects found to date in Palestine. They number more than a hundred finds, almost every excavation or survey of Early Bronze Age sites having produced a few. Of the two types, stamp seals and cylinder seals, the latter are the more numerous.

Stamp seals, which appear in great numbers in the northern countries (Syria and Mesopotamia) are rare in Palestine, for reasons yet unknown. Stamp seal impressions have been found on a jar from Tell el-Far'ah North dated early in the Early Bronze Age II. The impressions were evidently produced by wooden seals and were repeated a number of times to create the illusion of a cylinder seal impression. One seal portrays a snake and the other an animal with long horns, apparently an ibex. Both are depicted rather schematically in low, flat relief. The snake and the horned animal are known as symbols of fertility and are often portrayed in ancient Near Eastern art, particularly in countries north of Palestine, either separately or together. The inspiration of the Tell el-Far'ah North seals is therefore northern, close parallels having been found at Byblos, at various sites in North Syria and on the borders of Mesopotamia, and even in distant Elam. One stamp seal of local limestone was discovered at Arad and dated, like the Tell el-Far'ah North seals, to the Early Bronze Age II. It is larger than average (3.5 × 8 centimeters) and of rather crude workmanship. Its pattern resembles two large eyes and has good parallels both at Byblos and in upper Syria. As at Far'ah, northern inspiration may be sought for this locally made seal.

The cylinder seals include a stone seal from Arad, a seal from Megiddo, a bone seal from Jericho, and some stone seals whose precise provenance in Palestine is unknown. The scene on the Arad seal consists of highly schematic animals and a geometric pattern; the remaining seals bear linear geometric patterns. The seals all share an Early Bronze II date (this is less than certain in the Arad and Jericho seals) and, like the stamp seals, draw their inspiration from northern Syria and northern Mesopotamia.

The vast majority of Palestinian cylinder seals are represented only by their impressions on ceramic vessels. The seals themselves were apparently made of wood, as attested by the flat relief and the crude linear outline of the patterns, and have not survived. The custom of decorating ceramic vessels, particularly jars, with cylinder seal impressions seems to have originated in Palestine, where it is especially widespread. It has also been observed in some parts of Syria, in Greece, and in isolated cases in Mesopotamia and Elam. It is not clear whether it developed independently in each place or whether one region influenced the others.

One class of impressions is characterized by scenes of animal processions, generally consisting of alternating lions and horned animals. Such impressions have been discovered at Jericho, Hazor, and Dan. In none of these sites have they been discovered in Early Bronze Age strata, and thus their precise date within the Early Bronze Age is open to doubt. The impressions closely resemble cylinder seal impressions from Byblos; some designs are almost identical. This site has produced the largest number of seal impressions and the largest number of variants of this group. It is thus probable that the concept of the Palestinian seals, if not the seals themselves, came from Byblos. Unfortunately, the stratigraphic attribution of most of the Byblite impressions is not clear either, and while some certainly belong to levels of the Early Bronze Age II, it is not clear to what extent, if at all, the production and use of these seals continued into Early Bronze Age III. Not one of the impressions of this type from Palestine can with certainty be ascribed to Early Bronze Age III levels. Rather, the levels have provided a wealth of seal impressions of different types. It is

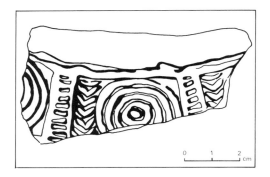

Fig. 4.27. Geometric cylinder seal impression from Hazor

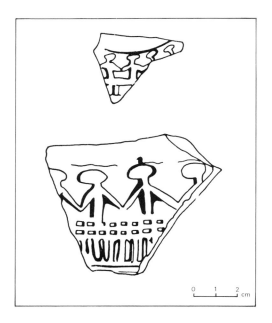

Fig. 4.28. Cylinder seal impressions depicting cultic scenes from Rosh Ha-Niqra and Beth Yerah

therefore probable, though not certain, that the impressions showing animal processions are to be dated, at least in Palestine, to the Early Bronze Age II.

Two main classes of cylinder seal impressions belong to the Early Bronze Age III. The first bears geometric patterns, and the second cult scenes. In broad terms, these two classes of seal impressions have much in common with those portraying animal processions. All three classes were produced by wooden seals that have not survived; they exhibit low relief and a schematic representation of the figures and were used to decorate store jars.

Geometric seal impressions are the most common, having been found in considerable quantities in the Golan Heights, Tel Dan, Beth Ha-Emeq, Beth Yerah, Tel Qashish, and elsewhere. The seals are variously composed of herringbone, net, lozenge, and spiral patterns. It is a homogeneous class, with a great degree of uniformity and resemblance among the seals from various sites. It is also particularly characteristic of Palestine and was probably produced by local craftsmen. Few geometric seals are known from Syria; their patterns are usually different from those common in Palestine, and any connection between the seals of the two lands must have been minimal. However, a large group of geometric cylinder seal impressions was found at the site of Lerna in Greece. The impressions were produced by wooden seals larger than those common in Palestine, but their similarity to the geometric patterns of Palestine is great. It is not clear whether this similarity between the two centers of geometric seal production (Greece and Palestine) is accidental or whether there was some sort of contact, and the impressions from Greece are the result of Palestinian influence. The practice of decorating

vessels with wooden cylinder seals has a much longer history and a wider distribution in Palestine than in Greece, so that if the impressions of Lerna (and a small number of impressions from other Greek sites) are related in some way to those of Palestine, it is likely that the direction of influence was from Palestine to Greece and not the other way round.

The most interesting class of cylinder seal impressions is that bearing cult-related scenes. Such impressions have been found, among other places, at Rosh Ha-Niqra, Tel Dan, Beth Yerah, and Bab edh-Dhra. The scenes are composed of human figures holding hands and apparently dancing, a long-horned animal generally standing on its hind legs, and a net pattern in the form of a building facade. In the latter detail, windows and paneled construction appear, typical of temple architecture, and this is how it is often portrayed throughout the ancient Near East. Some impressions show all three components; others contain only two, usually the human figures and the temple facade. Of all the seal impression scenes discussed here, these tell the most revealing tale. What exactly this tale may have been can only be surmised, in view of the lack of written sources for the period in Palestine. Similar scenes, where human figures appear next to temples, are known from many art objects discovered in Syria and Mesopotamia. They are most common in glyptic art, from which we learn that the subject was a favorite one among seal carvers. In most cases the human figures appear to be engaged in a cult dance near the temple, in front of it, behind it, or on its roof (in Syrian seals). The strong bond between the horned animal and the fertility cult is often expressed in ancient Near Eastern art. The appearance of long-horned animals on the seals may show that the cult was a fertility cult. In some scenes the horned animals stand on their hind legs; their stance suggests that they are not really animals but masked human figures. In one of the impressions from Har Rabi (near Sepphoris), the animal appears seated on a chair. A human figure in the guise of a horned animal, shown dancing near a horned animal or a temple, clearly appears on stamp and cylinder seals found in North Syria and Mesopotamia. Palestinian seal impressions showing scenes related to cult are therefore a local variant of a scene common in areas north of Palestine: they portray a cultic dance, related apparently to fertility, performed near a temple, with the participants sometimes shown in the guise of horned animals.

The vast majority of the seal impressions come from northern Palestine; the Jezreel valley marks the southern reaches of their distribution, and only a handful of finds come from sites south of this line. Jericho and Bab edh-Dhra, despite their southern location, should be seen as northern sites or extensions, via the Jordan valley, of northern culture. The concentration of the vast majority of the finds in sites of northern Palestine reflects the strong bond and close resemblance between the scenes portrayed in Palestinian seals and those depicted in seals of regions to the north, from Byblos to northern Syria.

The one hundred and more seal impressions in the Palestinian assemblage, though falling into three major classes—animal processions, geometric patterns, and cult scenes —share many features (raw material and carving technique) and reveal a strong family resemblance. The uniformity is remarkable, considering the long existence of these groups, spanning the entire Early Bronze Age II–III (more than 500 years).

This indicates considerable conservatism on the part of workshops or seal cutters, who must have been few in number.

Another group of Palestinian art objects, the ivory bulls' heads, is quite small: one bull's head was discovered at Beth Yerah, a second at Jericho (where a similar object made of stone, possibly a model for the ivory bulls' heads, was also discovered), and a third at Ai. Another head from Ai and two from Bab edh-Dhra have been reported but have not yet been fully published. This class of objects also reveals a high degree of homogeneity. All the objects are dated to the Early Bronze III, and all resemble one another in technique and form. The resemblance is so great that all may have been produced by one artist (possibly at Jericho) or one school of artists. What these objects decorated, whether furniture, scepters, or the like, is not known. Neither has their origin been established. The lack of such finds outside Palestine suggests that they were local productions, but whether their concept was local or foreign is not known. A number of Mesopotamian objects bear some resemblance to the bulls' heads, particularly in the triangular design on the forehead. If the Palestinian artist was influenced by an extra-Palestinian source, the northern regions must again be considered.

The single most important art find of the Early Bronze Age in Palestine is undoubtedly the cultic stela from Arad. This plaque, made of local limestone and standing about 24 centimeters high, was found near one of the temples in the Early Bronze Age II town. Two figures, human and nearly identical in form, were crudely but distinctly incised on the plaque. One is shown lying flat within a rectangular frame (a bed?), and the other stands beside it. The most interesting feature is

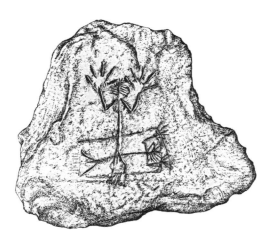

Fig. 4.29. "Dumuzi" stela from Arad (height 24 centimeters)

the head of the two figures, which is not human but rather takes the form of a plant. R. Amiran, the excavator of Arad, is no doubt correct in stating that the scene described is related to the myth of Dumuzi (Tammuz), as reported in Mesopotamian texts. The summer heat, when all things wither and dry up, represents the death of Dumuzi, the vegetation god. His death must be mourned ("there sat the women bewailing Tammuz," Ezek. 8:14), and his resurrection—and with it, that of plant life—prayed for. The precise interpretation of the Arad stela is not entirely clear. Is Dumuzi here shown in two states, those of death and resurrection, or does the plaque portray the act of mourning for the dead god? Neither is the local name of this deity known, in the absence of texts ("Dumuzi" is a Sumerian name, "Tammuz" a later Babylonian name). These questions, however, are secondary; what is certain is that the scene relates to the cult of the god of plenty, here in his capacity as vegetation god.

An apparently related cult object was found in Sanctuary A at Ai. It consists of fragments of a stone vessel shaped like a waterskin. Sumerian texts tell us of the goddess Bilulu, who was accused of killing Dumuzi and was sentenced to become a waterskin. The object from Ai may thus represent the Bilulu aspect of the Dumuzi cult. It is one of a group of vessels of the early part of the Early Bronze Age II, which were originally part of the Acropolis Temple assemblage at Ai. The cult may have survived into the Early Bronze Age III, for when the Acropolis Temple was abandoned, the objects were removed to the new cult place of that phase.

Dumuzi was responsible for the fertility of the flocks as well as that of the fields. Perhaps the figures in the guise of horned animals depicted in the seal impressions described above represent a cult of the fertility of the flocks, parallel to the vegetation cult depicted in the Arad stela and no doubt present in other sites in Palestine.

The continuity evident in the plans of cult structures has been noted, beginning with the Chalcolithic temple at En Gedi, through the temples of the Early Bronze Age I (Megiddo), the Early Bronze Age II (Arad), and the Early Bronze Age III (Megiddo, Ai). It is quite probable that the cult practiced within these structures exhibited a similar continuity; lacking texts, however, the only evidence is circumstantial, based on the interpretation of silent finds. If this is indeed the case, then fertility occupied a central, if not solitary, position in the Palestinian cult at least from the Chalcolithic period to the end of the Early Bronze Age. Paralleling the development of the economic substructure from a pastoral economy in the Chalcolithic to a Mediterranean economy based on a combination of pastoralism and agriculture in the Early Bronze Age, the fertility cult developed from a cult connected with the fertility of the flocks and with milk products in the Chalcolithic to one connected with the fertility of both fields and flocks in the Early Bronze Age.

FOREIGN RELATIONS

The network of relations between Egypt and Palestine begun and established in the Early Bronze Age I continued in the Early Bronze Age II. Those settlements of southern Palestine in which a wealth of Egyptian pottery had appeared—Tel Erani, Tel Halif, and others—continued to flourish. The seal impressions of Egyptian officials found on clay stoppers at En Besor indicate uninterrupted activity at the site nearly until the end of the First Dynasty. These settlements should be viewed as Egyptian trade stations, where Palestinian export shipments to Egypt were prepared. Goods were transported along the main road between the two countries, which passes through northern Sinai. A large number of way stations that protected and provided for the caravans have been discovered along the highway. The ceramic finds at the way stations reveal a predominance of Egyptian pottery at some and of Palestinian pottery at others. Evidently it was in the interest of both the Egyptians and the inhabitants of Palestine to maintain this important trade route. When the network of relationships between Egypt and Palestine collapsed during the Second Dynasty, in the latter half of the Early Bronze Age II, the way stations were abandoned, and the road remained unused for hundreds of years.

The difference in political organization between the two countries (which can only be inferred from what is known of later periods) leads one to assume that Egyptian trade was far more centralized than that of Palestine and that those engaged in it were the representatives and officials of the central authority (the royal court). This may explain the serekh-bearing Egyptian vessels found in Palestine and the sealed stoppers from En Besor. Palestinian trade was probably freer than Egyptian trade, and the merchants citizens or representatives of various city-states.

Import and export are directly related to the natural resources of the land on the one hand and the standard of living of the population, or of select groups within it, on the other. In the absence of mineral resources, apart from Sinai copper, agricultural produce and its by-products formed the main export potential of Palestine. The lack of written documents and the perishability of the organic agricultural goods impedes the compilation of a list of Palestinian exports. Nevertheless, such a list may be reconstructed, mainly by inference from later texts (of the first and second millennium) that mention exports and also by tracing the pottery vessels that contained some of the export products. Another factor influencing Palestinian trade involves ways and means of transport. Because of the difficulties attending long-distance transport, the most lucrative trade was in products of the smallest weight and volume, such as spices, gold, silver, and the like. As these were not produced in Palestine, Palestinian trade could not have been very profitable. Exceptions to this rule were cosmetic items such as scented oils and resins of various kinds, and they were among the luxury products of the land. A further limitation of Palestinian trade was that it was exclusively landbound; not one port is known to have existed before the second millennium, and all trade to and from Early Bronze Age Palestine went overland. This severely limited the size and weight of the cargoes, precluding, for example, the export of wood from Palestine, a product in great demand in Egypt.

Palestine exported mainly wine, oil, and date honey, shipped in jars of the type described above; cosmetic products such as scented oils, shipped, apparently, in jugs and juglets of Abydos ware; and materials such as bitumen (extracted from the Dead Sea and exported perhaps via Arad) and resins used for sealing and embalming. Invisible exports (organic products packed in perishable containers such as sacks, baskets, or skins) would have included small amounts of wheat, barley, and vegetables (chiefly pulse), dried fruit (dates, figs, and raisins), textiles, and perhaps (by inference from later periods) some livestock (sheep and cattle) and slaves.

What did Palestine import from Egypt? Most of the Egyptian vessels found in Palestine are not suited to serve as containers, and the few Egyptian jars that have been found were probably brought by the Egyptian merchants and officials living in Palestine for their own use. It would appear that Egypt did not grow crops that were in demand in Palestine. Ancient lands were for the most part economically self-sufficient, except in metals, and most of the trade was intended to supply the demands of the governing classes—kings, ministers, high officials, priests. The imports required by the higher classes of Palestine, which were limited in number and in means, were perforce few, consisting mainly of luxury items such as Egyptian stone vessels of alabaster or granite (for example, those of the Ai temple treasures) or jewelry made of gold, silver, and semiprecious stones, which was presumably stolen over the years or melted down and recast, leaving no trace in the archaeological record. Invisible imports, which may have comprised the greater part of the import trade, could have included exotic items from Africa, like those echoed in the tales of the trade with Ophir and the visit of the Queen of Sheba—spices, monkeys, parrots, animal hides, ostrich feathers, and the like. None of course have survived.

Signs of a decline in relations between Egypt and Palestine are observable in the course of the Early Bronze Age II. Canaanite vessels in Egypt occur for the most part in First Dynasty contexts and are rare in Second Dynasty ones. It is not known what caused this decline, but by the end of the Early Bronze Age II the process had run its course, and the network of trade relations between Egypt and Palestine had utterly collapsed.

One of the probable causes of the disruption of relations was the

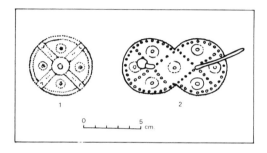

Fig. 4.30. Gold disks from Kinneret (1) and Anatolia (2)

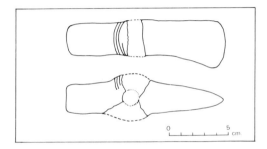

Fig. 4.31. Stone ceremonial axe from Ai

increasing demand for wood in Egypt. This demand brought merchants to the coast of Syria and Lebanon, where they found both wood in quantity and the great port of Byblos. The wood, the port, and perhaps also the rise of a central authority in Syria—the kingdom of Ebla, which provided stability and security—may have all combined to make the region attractive to Egypt. Once Egypt's relations with Syria-Lebanon were established, it began importing from that country all those agricultural products that had previously been imported from Palestine, a shift attested to by the vessels in which the goods were shipped, quantities of which have been found in Egypt in Old Kingdom assemblages. Despite the resemblance of the vessels to metallic-ware jars of Palestine, their more northerly origin is noticeable.

As trade with Egypt had been limited, its interruption did not have a particularly harsh effect on the economy of Palestine, though it may have been a decisive factor in the decline of towns such as Arad and Tel Erani and in the abandonment of the miners' settlements in southern Sinai and the stations on the North Sinai caravan route. In most of the towns of Palestine, however, the Early Bronze Age III, characterized by a complete absence of relations with Egypt, was a period of prosperity.

The foreign relations of Palestine were now directed northward. This was not a novelty; it is possible that northern immigrants in the Early Bronze Age I brought with them new ideas and objects, and there were relations in the realm of glyptics between Syria-Lebanon and Palestine. In broad terms, though the bulk of Palestine's economic contacts were with Egypt as the main market for its produce, the source of spiritual-cultural inspiration remained always in the north. There is a marked correlation in the ceramic assemblages of Palestine and the north, true both of the common wares and of the three families, Abydos ware, metallic ware, and Beth Yerah ware.

Metallurgy provided a further impulse for relations with the north. The origin of at least some of the copper used in the tools and weapons of Palestine lay in Anatolia, the Caucasus, and Armenia. There is also a family resemblance among the tools found in Palestine and in those regions, best evidenced in the crescent axe, which has close parallels in Lebanon and Asia Minor.

It seems as if these longstanding relations with the north were intensified in the course of the Early Bronze Age III and spanned ever greater distances. Apart from the pottery and metal artifacts just mentioned, there are six object assemblages of clear northern origin, all of the Palestinian Early Bronze Age III:

A GOLD PLAQUE. The finest third-millennium gold object so far found in Palestine comes from a burial cave near Kinneret, belonging apparently to the settlement at Beth Yerah. The plaque is made in a technique identical to that used in creating gold objects of the same period found in Asia Minor, such as the brooches from the royal tombs at Alaca Hüyük. This resemblance, as well as mounting evidence that Anatolia was at this time an exporter of gold, strongly suggests that the gold plaque found in Palestine was imported from Asia Minor.

CEREMONIAL AXES. Two axes made of greenish stone were discovered in the Ai temple. As the stone is foreign to Palestine and as great numbers of similar axes have been discovered in Asia Minor, there can be no doubt that that country is the source of the axes found in Palestine.

IVORY BULLS' HEADS. This group has been mentioned in the preceding section, "Art and Cult," and the possibility of its foreign, perhaps Mesopotamian, inspiration has been noted. In contrast to the gold plaque and the ceremonial axes, which were physically imported, these objects suggest the importation of a concept.

MODELS OF CULT BEDS. The same process is suggested by a group of small model beds made of fired clay, which seem to have had a cultic purpose. Such objects have been found at Ai, Beth Yerah, and elsewhere. It is not likely that they themselves were imported, but the discovery of similar objects in North Syria and Mesopotamia seems to indicate those regions as the source of the concept.

CARVED BONE HANDLES. At some sites, among them Ai, Jericho, and Beth Yerah, bone handles with incised decoration were discovered. Their function is not known. Identical handles have been found in Syria, Asia Minor, and the Greek Islands. The distribution of this class of finds over so wide an area, the same area through which objects such as the axes and the gold plaque passed, is of great interest. If these carved handles were not physically imported, the inspiration for their production must be sought somewhere in Asia Minor or the Aegean.

CYLINDER SEAL IMPRESSIONS. There is a striking resemblance between geometric seal impressions from Palestine and those from Greece. The similarities in motifs and in the use of the seals for the decoration of pottery vessels apparently indicate contact between Greece and Palestine in the Early Bronze Age III, as do other finds, such as the gold plaque, the ceremonial axes, and the bone handles.

The relations with Syria and, through Syria, with more northerly regions characterize the international relations of Palestine in the Early Bronze Age III. However, even when actual imports are identified (the gold plaque or ceremonial axes), it cannot be determined whether an import trade existed or

Fig. 4.32. Ivory bull's head from Jericho

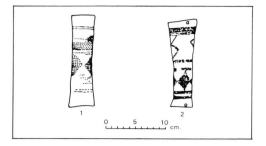

Fig. 4.33. Decorated bone handles from Jericho and Ai

whether all or most of the objects represent contacts of a different sort—the exchange of gifts, personal property of foreigners in Palestine, or the like. If actual trade relations did exist, we do not know what it was that Palestine exported. If it was agricultural produce, it was not of the sort shipped in pottery containers, as vessels of Palestinian origin have not been found in the north; we must therefore assume it was invisible exports, such as textiles or food products shipped in sacks or skins.

CHRONOLOGY

The date of the beginning of the Early Bronze Age II is closely linked to that of Narmer, the first king of the First Dynasty. Abydos ware, characteristic of the Early Bronze Age II, appears in Egyptian tombs that date, at the earliest, to the reign of Djer, the third king of the First Dynasty. The year 3000 has here been taken as the approximate date of Narmer's accession; Djer and the appearance of Abydos ware in Egypt must therefore be dated about 2950-2900 B.C.E. The importance of Arad for the chronology of the Early Bronze Age I–II must here be reaffirmed: the vessel bearing the incised serekh of Narmer appears in stratum IV, dated on ceramic grounds to Early Bronze Age I; Abydos ware appears in stratum III at Arad. The table below sums up this Palestine-Egypt synchronism.

The disruption of contacts between Palestine and Egypt during the Early Bronze Age II makes the chronology of the end of this period and of the Early Bronze Age III difficult to establish. At this stage the Egyptian synchronisms are still the most reliable data points in Early Bronze Age chronology. Many Egyptian objects bearing names of Old Kingdom rulers of the Fourth and Fifth Dynasties have been found at Byblos (no Third Dynasty objects appear there, however); unfortunately, most of these were not found in context, nor has a comparative study of the ceramic assemblages of Byblos and Palestine yet been performed. Despite these difficulties, there are sufficient grounds to ascribe stratum III at Byblos to the Early Bronze Age II, and strata IV–V (and perhaps part of stratum VI) to the Early Bronze Age III. This synchronism is of the greatest importance, as there is much in common between this rich site and the assemblages of Palestine.

Albright proposed a three-part division of the Early Bronze Age III based on the presence of Beth Yerah ware: a phase preceding its introduction, a phase in which this ware flourishes, and a post Beth Yerah ware phase. More recent research suggests that the phase preceding the appearance of Beth Yerah ware cannot be substantiated, whereas the phase following the disappearance of this ware should probably not be included in Early Bronze Age III.

The date of the beginning of

	Palestine	Egypt
Early Bronze Age I	Arad IV; Narmer *serekh* No Abydos ware.	Narmer founds Dynasty I No Abydos ware.
Early Bronze Age II	Arad III; Abydos ware first appears.	Reign of Djer; Abydos ware first appears

Early Bronze Age III (and the end of Early Bronze Age II) is thus dependent on the dating of the appearance of Beth Yerah ware. As this ware has not yet appeared in a context dated by Egyptian finds, its range has been difficult to determine. A date around 2700 B.C.E. for the end of Early Bronze Age II and the beginning of Early Bronze Age III is widely accepted. Four carbon-14 dates from Early Bronze Age II destruction layers at Ai have provided an average date of 2700 B.C.E. An object bearing the name of the last king of the Second Dynasty was found at Byblos in an early Early Bronze Age III context (the object should be attributed to late stratum III or early stratum IV at that site). The date of this king has been set at about 2700–2680 B.C.E. Finally, the Beth Yerah ware family is related to population movements originating in the Armenia and Caucasus regions. Carbon-14 analyses from these regions indicate that this type of pottery flourished in southwest Russia about 2800 B.C.E. A date one hundred years later is thus plausible for the appearance of this style in Syria-Palestine.

The dating of the end of the Early Bronze Age III is also quite difficult. Most of the sites excavated indicate that the period was a long one, revealing several phases of building and destruction, for example, the six phases at Jericho, subdivided into two main stages. A subdivision into two phases is indicated at other sites such as Megiddo, Beth Shean, Beth Yerah, Ai, or Tell el-Hesi. It has therefore been suggested that the period be split into the Early Bronze Age IIIA and IIIB, allotting each phase a similar span of about 200 years. Where Beth Yerah ware appears (at Beth Yerah itself, Beth Shean, and Ai), it is found in both phases. A split in the period has also been observed

in sites of Syria and the Lebanon, for example, in the Amuq and at Byblos. If the beginning of Early Bronze Age III has been fixed around 2700-2650 B.C.E., the two divisions may be dated thus:
Early Bronze Age IIIA, 2700-2650–2550 (Third and Fourth Dynasties)
Early Bronze Age IIIB, 2550–2350 (late Fourth and Fifth Dynasties).

The Early Bronze Age IV: The Decline of Urban Culture

This phase is the most problematic of the Early Bronze Age phases. A phenomenon so central in Palestinian history as that of the formation of an urban society, with all its consequences for the material and spiritual culture of the country, dissolves before our very eyes. Some have suggested that this phase be excluded from the framework of the Early Bronze Age; others prefer to see it only as the first of three subphases labeled Early Bronze Age IVA, IVB, and IVC, a period of transition from the urban culture of the Early Bronze Age to that of Middle Bronze Age Palestine. Those who have pointed out the continuity between this phase and the preceding phases are no doubt correct: all three subphases share in the general process of the decline of urban culture and the rise of nomadic and seminomadic societies subsisting mainly in the marginal zones of Palestine; they also share components of material culture, such as the pottery assemblage and metallurgy. Nevertheless, it seems preferable to consider only the first of the subphases as part of the Early Bronze Age (designated Early Bronze Age IV) and to assign the other two subphases to the period termed Intermediate Bronze or Middle Bronze I. This is not merely a semantic distinction, for differences in terminology (for example, "Early Bronze

Age I" versus "Late Chalcolithic") reflect differences in the conception and understanding of a period. It is true that the Early Bronze Age IV is related to the following period, but that is true of every period in the history of the land. Some periods are more firmly interrelated, some less; but in no case is there an absolute break between periods.

The Early Bronze Age IV should be seen as the phase during which the process of the desertion of the towns reached its peak; some of the towns had been abandoned during the Early Bronze Age IIIB, and others were abandoned during this phase. By the end of the Early Bronze Age IV, there were no urban settlements left in Palestine. What were the causes of the decline of urban culture? Which sites were abandoned in the Early Bronze Age IIIB, and which survived into the Early Bronze IV? Which were destroyed, and which merely deserted? Too little data are available regarding these questions, and their answers remain largely in the realm of hypothesis.

Three alternate explanations of the events in Palestine during this period have been offered. Some scholars have proposed that a wave of northern invaders (part of the Amorite migration to this region) or a campaign of Egyptian Fifth Dynasty kings was responsible for the destruction of the towns. The supporters of this theory tend to emphasize the wave of destruction that overtook some of the sites, while the undestroyed sites are understood to have been abandoned in terror. Others prefer an ecological explanation, pointing to data indicating a decrease in rainfall and a lowering of the water table, which would have doomed many settlements. The third approach sees the city-state system destroyed by attrition, a result of the constant warfare between the city-states evidenced in the repeated destructions and reconstructions visible in the Early Bronze Age II–III layers. This process would have been aggravated by the severing of trade relations with Egypt and the loss of the chief market for Palestinian produce at the end of the Early Bronze Age II. At present, the available data do not decisively support any one of the three approaches, and it seems that an approach integrating the three, along with additional reasons that are not yet manifest, should be preferred in explaining the demise of urban culture.

In other lands throughout the Near East, this is a period of increasing unrest, which culminates in the collapse of existing political structures. In Egypt, the period parallels the sixth and last dynasty of the Old Kingdom. Mesopotamia is in the last days of the dynasty of Akkad. Egyptian and Mesopotamian texts reveal the unrest and the population movements that threatened the borders. Destruction and desertion are visited on many sites in Asia Minor, perhaps at the hands of new peoples, the forefathers of the Hittites, who penetrated the region. The great towns of Syria, however, were seemingly unaffected by the turmoil overtaking the Near East; Byblos (stratum VI?) prospered, as did Ebla, Hama, and Qatna, among others. The reason for the conspicuous difference between Palestine and Syria is not known and may be added to the long list of unresolved questions concerning the Early Bronze Age IV.

Some of the towns in Palestine survive through the Early Bronze Age IV and are destroyed or deserted only at its end. Among them may be included Beth Shean, Megiddo, Beth Yerah, and perhaps Ai, Yarmuth, and Jericho, though it seems that the northern towns held out longer than those of the south. The pottery assemblage of this period clearly preserves the ceramic traditions of the Early Bronze Age, but some marked changes occur: Beth Yerah ware disappears entirely, Abydos ware continues to be produced but in a limited range of types and in degenerate forms, and the same holds true for metallic ware. Among the metallic ware, one type of jar characterized by an applied rope decoration around the base of the neck occurs in Early Bronze Age IV levels. Stone imitations of such vessels have been found in Egypt in Sixth Dynasty contexts. There is a marked decline of slipped and painted decoration, and a number of forms dominant in the following periods first appear. The ceramic picture thus reflects the historical character of the period; it is a transitional period, with the old traditions still in force—though often in a weak and degenerate form—and signs of a new era beginning to appear.

The Early Bronze Age IV lasted 100–150 years, corresponding to the Sixth Dynasty, the last of the dynasties of the Old Kingdom in Egypt. Despite signs of the impending crisis, Egypt was still powerful enough to maintain relations with Syria; the many Egyptian vessels bearing names of kings of this dynasty found at Byblos and Ebla are ample evidence of Egypt's influence.

More evidence of Egyptian activity in Asia is provided by texts and artworks. Unfortunately, not one contains a clear and unequivocal reference to an identifiable event or site. A place named Wenet, which is usually identified with a fortress in southern Canaan (perhaps Rafiah), is mentioned in documents of the Sixth Dynasty, as are battles with Mentiju, Amu, and Shasu, identified as peoples or tribes living in the Sinai and southern Canaan. Two well-known depictions of battles between Egyptians and Asians adorn tombs of the late Fifth Dynasty in Deshashe and Saqqara. The best known and most widely debated of the documents is in the tomb of a man by the name of Weni (or Uni), who was a general in the army of King Pepi I (2330–2280 B.C.E.) of the Sixth Dynasty. The inscription describes a series of military campaigns (or plundering raids) "to carry off the property of the Asiatics." Six such campaigns were undertaken by Weni, five by land and one by sea. The Asiatics attacked in these campaigns are called Sand-dwellers, and the sea raid brought the Egyptian army to a place called "the nose of Gazelle's head," or Antelope's Nose. Opinion is divided as to the identity of the Sand-dwellers and Gazelle's head, though there seems to be no doubt that the text refers to places north of the Sinai, as it speaks of the destruction of fortified towns, of fig trees, and of vines, none of which occur in Sinai. On the other hand, it is not likely that such raids were conducted against parts of Syria or the Lebanon, as the archaeological record attests to good relations between Egypt and Syria-Lebanon at this time. It thus appears that the southern Palestine coast was the objective of Weni's campaigns.

As the inscription of Weni is the oldest document mentioning place-names and events related, most probably, to Palestine, it seems proper to bring a full translation of the passage describing the campaigns themselves:

This army returned in safety,
It had ravaged the Sand-dwellers'
land.
This army returned in safety,
It had flattened the Sand-dwell-
ers' land.
This army returned in safety,
It had sacked its strongholds.
This army returned in safety,
It had cut down its figs, its vines.
This army returned in safety,
It had thrown fire in all its
[mansions].
This army returned in safety,
It had slain its troops by many
ten-thousands.
This army returned in safety,
[It had carried] off many [troops]
as captives.
His majesty praised me for it
beyond anything. His majesty
sent me to lead this army five
times, to attack the land of the
Sand-dwellers as often as they
rebelled with these troops. I
acted so that his majesty
praised me [for it beyond
anything].
Told there were marauders (?)
among these foreigners at the
nose of Gazelle's head, I
crossed in ships with these
troops. I made a landing in the
back of the height of the
mountain range, to the north
of the land of the Sand-dwellers, while half of this army
was on the road. I came and
caught them all and slew every
marauder among them.
(Lichtheim, Vol. I: 20)

These booty raids of Weni's, and perhaps other campaigns unknown to us, may have been made possible by and may have taken advantage of the weakness of Palestine in Early Bronze Age IV. By the same token, such campaigns may be seen as among the causes that weakened the city-state system and accelerated its decline and utter collapse around the end of the twenty-third century B.C.E.

5

The Intermediate Bronze Age

RAM GOPHNA

The culture of the Land of Israel in the late third millennium B.C.E. took form in the shadow of the dissolution of the urban culture of the Early Bronze Age. The twenty-fourth and twenty-third centuries B.C.E. were a period of crisis of settlement, culture, and demography, chiefly in Canaan; Syria and Lebanon were not so severely affected. By the time the abandonment of the towns had run its course, the population of the Land of Israel had declined to such an extent that broad areas, especially west of the Jordan, were almost entirely depopulated. From this time, and until the beginning of the second millennium B.C.E., the inhabitants of the country lived in unwalled settlements, where they practiced agriculture, herding, and hunting.

Archaeological study of the late third millennium has been concerned with the identification of the environmental factors (such as climatic change) and the socioeconomic processes that led to this crisis of urban culture. The endeavor resembles the attempt to understand sudden changes that occurred in previous protohistoric periods, such as the end of Chalcolithic culture and the start of the Early Bronze

Age or the socioeconomic transformation during the Early Bronze Age that brought about the first towns. As in those cases, the archaeologist studying the events of the late third millennium must recognize the causes and processes of change and define the essential qualities of the new or transformed culture. The archaeological evidence does not yet furnish a precise date for the abandonment of the last of the Early Bronze Age towns. Did the towns exist only until the first half of the twenty-fourth century, when the Fifth Dynasty ruled in Egypt (as implied, for example, in Hennessy's Early Bronze IIIB), or might some towns have continued to exist until the mid twenty-third century, during the rule of the Sixth Dynasty (as proposed by R. de Vaux, Wright, Ben-Tor, and others)? The accurate dating of the final dissolution of urban life is essential for any estimate of the rate of the processes that led to the emergence of the new society. The ambiguity regarding the circumstances and precise dating of the end of urban culture has contributed to the formation of varying and contrasting views on the demographic composition of the country and on its material culture at the time. Also debated is the mysterious population's social and cultural affinity for the Early Bronze Age on the one hand and the Middle Bronze Age on the other, leading to disagreement over the appropriate terminology for this era of the country's history.

More than fifty years have passed since Albright (following his excavations at Tell Beit Mirsim) first coined the term "Middle Bronze I" for the period in question. He believed that the material culture of the late third millennium B.C.E. was a prelude to the urban culture that was to evolve during the first half of the second millennium B.C.E. and was therefore to be called the Middle Bronze Age II.

Today it is the scholarly consensus that an evolutionary relation can hardly be posited between the culture of the inhabitants of the villages of the late third millennium and the urban culture of the second millennium. Nonetheless, many continue to employ Albright's term "Middle Bronze I," as it is deeply rooted in the archaeological literature. Over the years, many names were offered for the culture of the Land of Israel during this period. W. F. Petrie, the first to recognize the distinctive character of this culture, termed the period the Copper Age because of the high frequency of copper objects he uncovered in the cemetery adjacent to Tell el-Ajjul. The resemblance observed between some cup-shaped pottery vessels, common during this period, and vessels found in Syria moved O. Tufnell, the excavator of Lachish, to term the culture the Caliciform culture. K. Kenyon, following her excavations at Jericho in the fifties, asserted that no affinity need be sought between the culture of this period and the two urban cultures of the Bronze Age. In her view, it is an intrusive intermediate culture, which should therefore be termed Intermediate Early Bronze–Middle Bronze Age.

J. H. Iliffe had employed that term many years earlier, while preparing the exhibits in the Palestine Archaeological Museum in the thirties. It was also accepted by Hennessy in the sixties but for reasons diametrically opposed to Kenyon's; in his view, there were affinities between this culture and those of both urban periods. R. H. Smith later abbreviated the term to Intermediate Bronze Age, emphasizing the transitional character of the period. It has recently been adopted by some Israeli archaeologists as well (Kochavi and Amiran), who assert that despite the preservation of some degree of affinity to the cultural tradition of the Early Bronze Age, the nonurban culture evolved independently, during the gap between the two urban cultures. The phase therefore deserves a name of its own, suitable to its position.

In the wake of new excavations at late third millennium sites, particularly in Transjordan, W. G. Dever has called for the readoption of the term "Early Bronze IV," applying it to the last four hundred years of the third millennium. The term was used by Wright in the thirties to define a meager assemblage from the end of the Early Bronze Age, attributed by him to approximately the second half of the twenty-fourth century and the twenty-third century. Dever has maintained that the cultural history of the Land of Israel in the twenty-second and twenty-first centuries cannot be dissociated from the Early Bronze Age sequence, despite the abandonment of the towns and the dispersal of the inhabitants in seminomadic, unfortified settlements. In his view, remains of the material culture from those two centuries should be incorporated in a subphase of the Early Bronze IV, as the decline of the urban system had already gained momentum by the twenty-fourth and twenty-third centuries. In my

view, "Early Bronze IV" does not do justice to the singularities of the rural settlement patterns and the material culture assemblage that appeared in the Land of Israel in the late third millennium. We have therefore chosen to adhere in this chapter to the term "Intermediate Bronze Age."

CHRONOLOGY

The chronological framework of the Intermediate Bronze Age is dependent on internal archaeological considerations, spanning as it does the interval between the Early Bronze Age and the Middle Bronze Age. If the urban culture of the Early Bronze Age did last into the days of the Sixth Dynasty of Egypt, the beginning of the Intermediate Bronze Age may be fixed to the twenty-third century. As for the end of the period, archaeological consensus puts it at the beginning of the second millennium (around the year 2000 B.C.E.), the time of the establishment of the Twelfth Dynasty in Egypt, when the Middle Kingdom was founded and the contacts between Egypt and the Levant, severed during the Intermediate Bronze Age, were resumed. These considerations suggest a span of 200–250 years for the Intermediate Bronze Age in the Land of Israel. Dever has proposed a span of 400 years. Until recently, there were no Egyptian finds that could help determine the chronology of the Intermediate Bronze Age, as they did for the Early Bronze Age. Recently, however, Egyptian pottery has been identified among the finds of the North Sinai survey conducted by the Ben Gurion University in the seventies (led by E. D. Oren). The Egyptian sherds were found together with pottery typical of the Intermediate Bronze Age in Israel at 45 campsites of the period discovered during the survey. The

Egyptian sherds belong to a type of ware common in Egypt during the latter part of the Old Kingdom and the beginning of the First Intermediate Period, from the twenty-third century to the twenty-first century. This discovery may support the previously accepted assumption that the Intermediate Bronze Age in the Land of Israel more or less corresponds to the First Intermediate Period and the Eleventh Dynasty of Egypt (the twenty-second and twenty-first centuries). Further support comes from excavations conducted in the eastern Nile Delta (for example, at Tell ed-Daba). It appears, contrary to what was supposed until recently, that relations did exist at least between northern Sinai and Egypt during this time, implying that population groups that originated in the Land of Israel and migrated as far as the threshold of Egypt maintained contacts with the Egyptians.

Comparative studies of Intermediate Bronze Age objects (pottery and copper implements) from the Land of Israel and from sites in northern Syria (such as Hama, Qatna, Ebla, and Ugarit) suggest that the Intermediate Bronze Age spanned chiefly the twenty-second and twenty-first centuries, or the later days of the dynasty of Akkad and the neo-Sumerian Third Dynasty of Ur in Mesopotamia. Carbon-14 dates obtained at Hama (from Phase J, which has eight subphases) place the start of the period between 2310 ± 140 and 2210 ± 120 B.C.E., but these dates refer to the beginning of an extensive period of settlement at the site. The determination of the internal chronology of the Intermediate Bronze Age is a task for the future, as the attempts to devise an internal chronology on the basis of typological pottery studies have yet to succeed. Nonetheless, Dever has proposed dividing the period, which he believes to

have lasted four hundred years, into three parts:

Early Bronze IVA,
2400–2200 B.C.E.
Early Bronze IVB,
2200–2100 B.C.E.
Early Bronze IVC,
2100–2000 B.C.E.

This division is consequent to the approach that posits a twenty-fourth-century date for the start of the Intermediate Bronze Age, for Dever believes the decline of the urban culture began as early as the mid third millennium. Others, this writer among them, suggest that the events of the twenty-fourth century should fall within the Early Bronze III period, as the last towns were destroyed during the twenty-third century.

Settlement Features: Geographic Distribution, Site Organization, and Architecture

There seems to be no correlation between the large number of cemeteries discovered, with their impressive tombs, and the relatively small number of habitation sites investigated and the poor remains unearthed within them, which may lead to underestimation of the importance of the system of unwalled settlements that came into being during the Intermediate Bronze Age. A collation of old and new evidence shows, however, that in the limestone regions of the Land of Israel, for example, the more than one hundred shaft-tomb cemeteries are matched by a similar number of habitation sites. Though it often happens that an Intermediate Bronze Age cemetery is discovered with no traces of a related settlement, there are also traces of settlement with no adjacent cemetery. Presumably, cemeteries that cannot be attributed to a known habitation site reflect an invisible component in

the settlement system, which may be beyond the reach of archaeological recovery. Because many of the Intermediate Bronze Age sites were small and short-lived, their material remains were so slight as to have disappeared over the centuries. Other settlements were buried by alluvium or absorbed in the debris layers of the multiperiod mounds. Another explanation offered for the "orphan" cemeteries (those with no adjacent habitation site) views at least some of them as evidence of central burial grounds for seminomadic population groups that have left no architectural remains (Dever, Kenyon). According to this view, there is little point in searching for settlement remains at these sites.

The following extensive review of the settlement data for the Intermediate Bronze Age is essential to evaluate the position of the Intermediate Bronze Age in the history of the land in the third millennium B.C.E. It forms the basis for the study of the economy, the social system, and life-style of the inhabitants of the desert and the sown during the late third millennium, as well as for any estimate of the population, in comparison with the Early Bronze Age. The review divides the regions of the Land of Israel and Transjordan into two main groups—west of the Jordan and east of it—to accommodate quantitative considerations: the data regarding the sites of the Jordan valley and regions to the west are inestimably greater than those concerning the Transjordanian plateau. Also, recent discoveries indicate that the settlement history of some parts of the Transjordanian plateau in the posturban period was different from that of the Land of Israel. The order of the regional review is not intended to indicate directions of the settlement dynamic during this period. They may perhaps be reconstructed by means of

regional subdivisions of the pottery
type groups.

THE JORDAN AND JEZREEL VALLEY AREAS

Some of the unwalled settlements
in the Jordan valley and the large
valleys of the interior during the
Intermediate Bronze Age were built
on abandoned mounds, where fortified towns of the Early Bronze
Age had existed. Excavations reveal
a stratigraphic-occupational discontinuity between the fortified towns
of the Early Bronze and the Intermediate Bronze Age villages built on
their ruins. The latter were not confined to the abandoned mounds and
tended to extend beyond their
boundaries. However, most of the
unwalled Intermediate Bronze Age
settlements were built at new and
previously uninhabited locations or
at village sites of a much earlier era,
pre-dating the urban centers of the
Early Bronze Age (of Neolithic,
Chalcolithic, or Early Bronze I
date). Sites of this type thus reveal a
gap of between one thousand and
several thousand years from their
first occupation to the Intermediate
Bronze Age settlement. Most of the
sites were small, and at the few large
sites, tens or hundreds of dunams in
area, the density of settlement was
low, because dwelling units were
constructed at some distance from
each other. The burial grounds
of these settlements were found
nearby.

The typical dwelling structure
was the rectangular broadhouse.
The frequency of this plan in Intermediate Bronze Age architecture
testifies to the continuity of a building tradition with roots in the Pre-
Pottery Neolithic B period, a tradition revived in the Chalcolithic period and maintained during the
whole of the Early Bronze Age.
Courtyards and pens adjoined the
houses, which were built of mud

Map 5.1. Intermediate Bronze Age sites and cemeteries

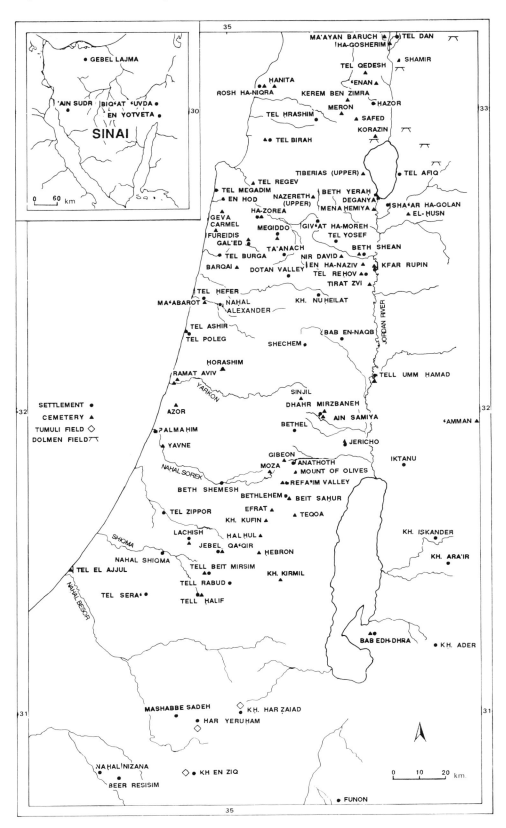

brick on a stone foundation. Floors were made of beaten earth, stones, gravel, and potsherds. Clusters of dwellings were sometimes joined to form residential quarters, divided by narrow alleyways. The alleys were paved with stone, gravel, or beaten earth. The architectural details (floor levels, benches, doorways, installations) of the broadhouses of the period have not yet been elucidated, as, for example, is the case with the typical Early Bronze Age house. Such features, were they known, could help explain the functional division of the structures.

Some sites revealed internal stratigraphy, representing several phases of construction. The irregular dispersal of occupation over wide areas may well indicate, however, that the lifespan of the settlements should not be estimated solely on stratigraphic grounds; the process of horizontal expansion, which may have been lengthy, should also be taken into consideration. Some archaeologists have interpreted the thin deposits in some of the larger sites as indicative of the transitory character of some of the settlements (Kenyon, K. Prag), but the unwalled settlements of the Jordan valley in the Intermediate Bronze Age may also be taken to represent a sedentary village system.

In excavations in the upper Jordan valley (the Hula valley), at the mounds of Hazor and Dan, traces of Intermediate Bronze Age settlements were found; they consisted, at Hazor, of pottery alone, not linked to any architectural remains, and were termed Stratum XVIII. Pottery alone was found at Tel Dan as well. In the same region, shaft-tomb cemeteries were discovered at Ma'ayan Baruch, Ha-Goshrim, 'Enan, and Shamir.

In the middle Jordan valley (between Lake Kinneret and the southern Beth Shean valley) and in the Jezreel valley, about 35 settlement sites and 20 cemeteries have been recorded. A few have been excavated.

At Beth Yerah, on the shores of Lake Kinneret, remains of a settlement were unearthed by P. Bar Adon in the fifties. Three building phases of a pebble-and-gravel street, flanked by houses and courtyards, were recorded. The houses were well built, on a rectangular plan. Their walls were 0.6–0.7 meter thick and had limestone foundations. The doorways were set neither in the center of the wall nor near one of the corners but rather at about the one-third mark. Not far from the mound, within the perimeter of Kibbutz Deganya A, were two stone-lined tombs, which must have belonged to one of the cemeteries of this settlement.

On the northern bank of the Yarmuk River, where the fishponds of Sha'ar Ha-Golan now lie, traces of a large, Intermediate Bronze Age settlement were discovered in the early fifties (this is also where M. Stekelis discovered and excavated a Pottery Neolithic site, which gave its name to part of the cultural assemblage of the period, known as the Yarmukian culture). Further building remains of the Intermediate Bronze Age were excavated in the late seventies, and it was found that the site extends over an area of about fifteen hectares. In the earlier excavations, conducted by Stekelis, a house with two or three courses of basalt foundations was uncovered. It had four square rooms and an internal courtyard, inside which was a round stone installation. The average room dimensions were 1.6 × 2 meters. The structure was paved with flat basalt slabs and cobblestones and plastered with a mixture of clay, crushed limestone, and gravel. In the recent excavations, conducted by E. Eisenberg, three house clusters, situated at sixty-meter intervals, were investigated. Work was concentrated on the westernmost cluster, where about ten adjoining rooms, square in plan, were cleared. Finds included pottery vessels, basalt grinding tools, and various installations. The foundations were built of one or two courses of large river pebbles, which apparently supported a mud-brick superstructure. The floors were generally of yellowish beaten earth. The excavator notes that though the walls were not preserved, the doorways were probably in the long walls, making the structures broadhouses.

Few Intermediate Bronze Age remains have come to light in the excavations of Beth Shean. North of the mound, however, a cemetery of the period has been discovered, containing about two hundred shaft tombs. Archaeologists believe that the bulk of the settlement extended outside the mound proper.

On the southern ridge of Giv'at Qumi, east of Tel Yosef, on the northern edge of the Harod valley, lie the remains of a large Intermediate Bronze Age settlement. The site, also known as Murkhan, was discovered in the thirties and excavated by N. Zori. It occupies an area of one square kilometer. A small portion of the site was excavated, consisting of a large multi-roomed structure adjoined by a large animal pen, a round structure, and three tombs. The large structure has seven rooms and measures 7.5 × 9.5 meters. Stone wall foundations, one course high, were preserved. The exterior walls are 0.4 meter wide, and the interior walls 0.25 meter. A stone door socket was found in one of the rooms. Floors were made of beaten earth or small stones, mixed with potsherds. Many basalt grinding stones, pottery vessels, flint tools, and copper weapons were found at the site.

East of Nahal Tirzah (Wadi Far'ah) and the Jordan River, in the triangle bounded by the Yaboq

(Wadi ez-Zarqa) and Jordan rivers, the remains of a large Intermediate Bronze Age site, Tell Umm Hammad, have been subject to study since the forties (Glueck's survey). The site lies in an area suitable for farming and grazing, with abundant water sources. Recent excavations by S. Helms have revealed shaft tombs of the Intermediate Bronze Age, belonging to a large cemetery. Glueck reported an Intermediate Bronze Age ceramic scatter over an area one kilometer long and half a kilometer wide, but it included no structural traces on the surface. Helms's excavation revealed a large structure with many rooms. K. Prag, who summed up the state of research on this site in the early seventies, believes that the deposits at Tell Umm Hammad indicate prolonged settlement. The sherd scatter (consisting of typical domestic ware) extends east and west, far beyond the boundaries of the site. Various scholars who explored the site thought that it may have served as a campsite, which gradually expanded as time went on. Prag wonders whether the remains might indicate a seasonally inhabited campsite. In any case, the extent of the Intermediate Bronze Age settlement remains at Tell Umm Hammad testify to the dispersed character of the site organization.

The settlement unearthed by Kenyon in her excavations at Jericho and the cemeteries adjacent to the mound serve as an example of an Intermediate Bronze Age village founded on the abandoned ruins of an Early Bronze Age III town, and of the stratigraphic and occupational gap between the settlements of the two periods. According to the excavator, some time passed between the destruction of the town and the renewal of settlement in the Intermediate Bronze Age, as the Intermediate Bronze Age houses were founded on an erosional deposit 2.5

meters thick. The eroded soil filled in the moat that had protected the Early Bronze III fortifications. The houses of Intermediate Bronze Age Jericho were rectangular, with mud-brick walls on stone foundations. Three building phases were observed in the excavations, and houses of this settlement were scattered not only on the mound and its slopes but on the neighboring slopes as well. It thus appears that in the course of the period, the site extended over various parts of the Jericho oasis, and only a small part lay within the compass of the abandoned mound overlooking the spring. Furthermore, Kenyon believed that there were two stages of Intermediate Bronze Age occupation at Jericho, the first preceding the construction of the houses and consisting of a nomadic campsite. The cemeteries lay on the hill slopes to the north and northwest of the site, where 345 tombs have been excavated.

Thirty-five kilometers southeast of Jericho, in the steppes of Moab east of the Jordan, lies Tell Iktanu. Prag's excavations at the site have revealed an unwalled site of the Intermediate Bronze Age, resembling that of Jericho. Prag describes the remains of a "rather large" site, extending not only over the abandoned Early Bronze Age mound but also on a low ridge adjoining it. In the first stage of settlement the houses were built of terre pisee on half-meter-high river-pebble foundations. In the second stage they were built of mud bricks on similar foundations. The houses were rectangular in plan, and large yards adjoined them. Remains of roofing were uncovered, made of clay, twigs, and straw. The village houses were built in clusters, divided by unpaved alleyways running from the top of the mound to the streambeds at its foot.

The remains of another large In-

termediate Bronze Age site were discovered at Bab edh-Dhra on the Dead Sea plain (east of the Lisan) and excavated by W. Rast and R. T. Schaub. A fortified town had existed at the spot in the Early Bronze III (as at Jericho and Beth Shean), and most of the remains were found outside its ruins. Northeast of the ruined town (in the excavators' Area X), four architectural phases were found of mud brick structures built on fieldstone foundations. The excavators conjecture that some of the structures belonged to a walled industrial compound. There were, in any case, many millstones and stone mortars scattered over this area. South of the abandoned town (in Area IX), deposits of the Intermediate Bronze Age were shallow. A domestic quarter, where the stone foundations of a number of houses remained, was identified. The house plans of Bab edh-Dhra correspond to the house plans of the Intermediate Bronze Age Jordan valley sites of Beth Yerah, Tel Yosef, Sha'ar Ha-Golan, Tell Iktanu, and Jericho. One of the houses was described as a rectangular structure with the entrance placed off-center. The excavators clearly state that the structure is of the broadhouse type, characteristic of the architecture of the Early Bronze Age II–III. They believe it indicates continuity between the architectural traditions of the town dwellers of the Early Bronze II–III and those of the Intermediate Bronze Age. In an area excavated on the northern flank of the ruined Early Bronze town (Area XVI), building fragments were found, showing that Intermediate Bronze Age occupation did extend over part of the abandoned urban site. Four building phases were observed. The remains associated with the final phase were interpreted as a shrine: a large, flat slab set on a foundation of smaller stones, in a walled enclosure. Nearby were about a dozen horns of domestic cattle, which appear to have been sacrificed. The excavators of Bab edh-Dhra view the Intermediate Bronze Age remains as evidence of the habitation of a sedentary population, which erected a planned group of structures unrelated to the Early Bronze Age town limits. At the neighboring site of Numeira, about thirteen kilometers south of Bab edh-Dhra, the fortified site of the Early Bronze Age III was never resettled after its destruction.

THE HILL REGION

Traces of Intermediate Bronze Age habitation sites and cemeteries have been found throughout that part of the hill country of the Land of Israel within the Mediterranean vegetation zone. The geographical distribution of settlements in this region was wider than in the Early Bronze Age and covered semiarid regions of the Samarian and Judaean deserts. Occupational-stratigraphic gaps between the Early Bronze urban system and the Intermediate Bronze village system are also characteristic of the hill country. Some ruined city mounds of the Early Bronze Age II–III exhibit traces of Intermediate Bronze Age occupation, but they are in the minority, and settlements were generally established at new sites.

The outstanding characteristic of the hill settlements in the Intermediate Bronze Age is the utilization of caves for habitation, storage, and industry. Cave entrances were often walled, and various installations, such as grain bins, have been found within, as well as much pottery. The caves were integrated in the layout of the sites, which also included residential quarters with rectangular broadhouses. The size of the hill sites was often quite small, their lifespan short, and the dispersal of dwelling units within the large sites wide.

Cemeteries of the period have been discovered at upper Galilee sites where no traces of habitation have yet been identified, such as Hanita, Safed, Kerem Ben Zimra, and Meron. The cave discovered near Tel Qedesh may have belonged to a settlement on the mound itself. M. Tadmor, who published the finds from the cave, believes that it was used not for burial but for a burial cult, hence the small number of bones found within. Finds included a pillar and ledge carved in the rock and an abundance of cooking pots and pedestal lamps. Many of the vessels are wheel-made, which is significant to relations between the Land of Israel and Syria.

The excavations of Bethel revealed traces of an Intermediate Bronze Age settlement, but its size and character were not ascertained. Further remains in the central hill region have been identified at Tell el-Ful (Giv'at Shaul), north of Jerusalem, and at 'Emeq Refaim, Bethlehem, and Efrat, to the south. The Tell el-Ful excavations showed that the earliest occupation at the site dates from the Intermediate Bronze Age. On the rock terraces of Giv'at Masuah, verging on 'Emeq Refaim, structures and shaft tombs were discovered along a two-kilometer stretch. Excavations revealed rectilinear houses of the Intermediate Bronze Age, with mud-brick walls built on stone foundations. Inside the houses pottery and stone vessels, flint tools, and bones of sheep and pigs were found. The excavations at Efrat revealed a series of long walls and a stone structure, adjoined by a cemetery containing more than thirty shaft tombs.

Many shaft-tomb cemeteries, some adjacent to settlements of the period, have been investigated in the hill country of Ephraim and Judaea: at Gibeon, Silwan, the Mount of Olives, 'Ain Karem, Beth Sahur, Khirbet Kufin, El'azar, Halhul, and Ras Tawra. It appears that the settlement of the central hill region in the Intermediate Bronze Age extended as far south as the southern Hebron foothills, approaching the Arad valley, but no traces of the period have as yet been discovered among the ruins of the Early Bronze II–III towns at Ai and Tell el-Far'ah North.

Intermediate Bronze Age campsites have also been discovered south of Nahal Tirzah. Large shaft-tomb cemeteries are known to have existed in the area of the large spring of 'Ain Samiya, in upper Wadi Auja. More than three hundred shaft tombs were recorded there, especially in the area called Dhahr Mirzbaneh and near Khirbet Samiyeh. In the cemetery discovered on the northern slope of Jebel Taamur, about twelve kilometers south of 'Ain Samiya, two hundred shaft tombs were counted. As in the other limestone hill zones, it appears that part of the population lived in caves; excavations in Cave II in Wadi ed-Daliyeh, northeast of 'Ain Samiya, brought to light a pottery assemblage of characteristic Intermediate Bronze Age cooking and storage vessels.

THE JUDAEAN SHEPHELAH AND THE COASTAL PLAIN

The excavations conducted at Lachish (by J. L. Starkey and O. Tufnell) and Tell Beit Mirsim (Albright) between the two world wars and the recent excavations at Jebel Qa'aqir (by Dever) and the Tel Halif terrace in the Judaean Shephelah (by D. Alon) have contributed much toward the revelation of the dwelling customs and the life-style in the hill regions of the Land of Israel in the Intermediate Bronze Age.

Though traces of occupation (consisting only of a few sherds) were revealed in the large section excavated at Tel Lachish, settlement at this site was concentrated mainly on a hill about 500 meters west of the mound (Area 1500). This occupation again illustrates the discontinuity between the ruined fortified settlement of Early Bronze III Lachish and the Intermediate Bronze Age village established some distance away. Excavations in Area 1500 revealed dwelling structures, dwelling caves, and garbage pits of the Intermediate Bronze Age. The houses were of the rectangular broadhouse type, with fieldstone foundations. Among the remains excavated was a central courtyard flanked by two rooms. A shaft-tomb cemetery, called the 2000 Cemetery, was found nearby.

At Tell Beit Mirsim, stratified deposits of the Intermediate Bronze Age were identified, sandwiched between Early Bronze and Middle Bronze Age strata. As in the 1500 Area at Lachish, the inhabitants of Tell Beit Mirsim lived in caves as well as in freestanding structures.

On a spur called Jebel Qa'aqir, about twelve kilometers southeast of Lachish, within the furrow valley separating the Shephelah from the Hebron hills, an Intermediate Bronze Age settlement consisting of dwelling structures and cave habitations was excavated in the late sixties. At the foot of the spur, on a rock terrace, entrances to about eighty shaft tombs were observed, and some of the tombs were excavated. On the ridge itself, six cairns were explored, and building remains were found buried under one of them. Surrounding the cairns, a stone wall, interpreted as a large animal pen, was discovered, with a pottery kiln nearby. In a survey conducted during the eighties along the furrow valley (by Y. Dagan),

remains of further Intermediate Bronze Age settlements and cemeteries were recorded, among them a site one kilometer southwest of Khirbet Qe'ila. Its remains extend for about twenty hectares on an elongated rocky knoll. Domestic remains of the Intermediate Bronze Age were also recovered in caves on the terrace of Tel Halif, at the southwest edge of the Shephelah.

The Intermediate Bronze Age site distribution on the coastal plain resembles that of the Jordan valley. A few sites have been recorded on the eastern margins of the Galilean coastal plain. In Kibbutz Yas'ur, a cemetery and traces of settlement founded on virgin soil were discovered under a Middle Bronze Age stratum.

The Intermediate Bronze Age sites of the Carmel coast, the Sharon and Philistia are located along the flood basins of the streams. About

Fig. 5.1.   Dwelling cave at Jebel Qa'aqir

fifteen sites have been recorded so far, among them sites extending over several hectares; they include Tell Burga near Nahal Taninim, the Nahal Alexander site, Tel Zippor on Nahal Lachish, and a site near Tel Sera' on Nahal Gerar. Smaller sites, sometimes indicated only by the presence of a handful of sherds, have been discovered at Tel Megadim, Tel Poleg, Tel Aphek, near Palmahim, in Nahal Shiqma, and in Nahal Besor. About a dozen shaft-tomb cemeteries have been discovered in the Sharon and Philistia, concentrated for the most part along the kurkar ridges and to a lesser extent in the limestone hills on the eastern fringe of the coastal plain. These include the sites of Tel Esur, Khirbet Ibreiktas, Eliashib, Ma'abarot, the Tel Aviv area, Horashim, Azor, Yavne, Gedera, Nahala, and Tell el-Ajjul.

SETTLEMENTS OF THE ARID ZONES: THE NEGEV AND SINAI

The Intermediate Bronze Age settlements of the Negev Highlands and Sinai, like the Early Bronze Age II settlements in these regions, are virtual open-air museums, thanks to their fine state of preservation. Excavations in the Negev Highlands have uncovered entire settlements of the Intermediate Bronze Age, an achievement not yet accomplished in more northerly areas. But as in the "settled land" north of the Beersheba-Arad valley, the evidence in the arid zones of the Negev Highlands and Sinai indicates a stratigraphic discontinuity between the Early Bronze and Intermediate Bronze Age settlements. This gap was observed not only in excavations but also in the divergent settlement pattern in part of the area. Surveys in the Arad and Beersheba valleys of the northeast Negev recorded no Intermediate Bronze Age remains within the valleys but only along their margins, on the slopes of the Hebron hills to the north. To the south, old and new surveys (and particularly the Emergency Survey of the eighties, headed by R. Cohen) revealed hundreds of unwalled sites in the Negev Highlands and Sinai, of both Early Bronze and Intermediate Bronze Age dates. Through the northeastern Negev (a semiarid region in the Irano-Turanian vegetation zone) runs the 200-millimeter isohyet, which marks the border for dry farming. It is an area of nonsaline loess soil, suited for grazing and agriculture, and indeed it saw extensive rural settlement in the Chalcolithic and Early Bronze I periods. During Early Bronze II, the city of Arad and its dependencies flourished. Arad was situated between the settled zone of the Hebron hills and the Dead Sea plain to the north and east, and hundreds of unfortified sites spread over the Negev Highlands and the frontiers of southern Sinai. The Intermediate Bronze Age settlement pattern suggests that in the late third millennium, the valleys of the northeastern Negev formed an uninhabited partition between the sites of the Hebron and Judaean hills to the north and

Fig. 5.2. Har Yeruham, plan of settlement

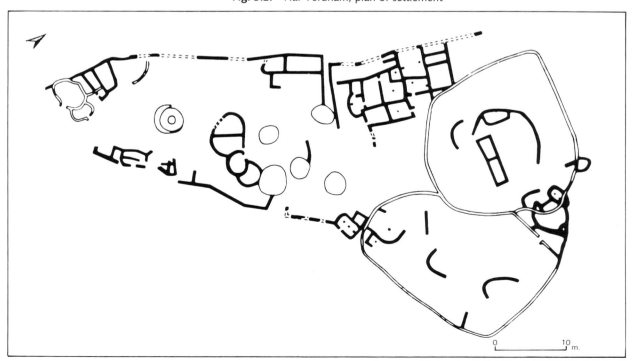

0 ⸺ 10 m.

the hundreds of settlements of the Negev Highlands to the south.

More than five hundred sites have been recorded thus far in the Negev Highlands. Settlement clusters have been studied in the Dimona and Yeruham hills, near Sede Boqer, and in the regions farther west, toward Nahal Nizzana and the Shunra and Agur dune belts. Southward, settlements have been investigated north of Makhtesh Ramon, near Har Ha-Me'ara and Har Saggi, and farther south near Har Karkom, the Uvda valley, and the southern Aravah (near Yotveta). West of the Negev Highlands lie the sites of northern Sinai (Jebel Hilal, Jebel Maghara, and near 'Ain Sudr). Along the northern Sinai coast, between Rafiah and the eastern border of the Nile Delta, more than two hundred campsites were recorded with finds of the Intermediate Bronze Age. The settlement pattern of the Intermediate Bronze Age sites in the Negev Highlands and Sinai corresponds only in part to that of the Early Bronze Age. Thus, for example, no Intermediate Bronze Age sites were discovered in the mountains of southern Sinai, an area of fairly dense settlement in the Early Bronze II, and this region henceforth remained outside the Canaanite sphere of influence. In most of northern and central Sinai, however, many Intermediate Bronze Age sites were found in areas only sparsely inhabited during the Early Bronze II. Furthermore, even in the Negev Highlands, where site distributions of the two periods overlap, Intermediate Bronze Age sites were often established at new sites and not on the ruins of the Early Bronze Age sites. The site and house plans of the Intermediate Bronze Age also changed in relation to the Early Bronze Age. Only a few Intermediate Bronze Age sites preserved the broadhouse plan characteristic of the Early Bronze Age.

Information provided by surveys of the Kadesh Barnea area may illustrate the change in the settlement pattern within a limited region. The Early Bronze Age settlement was concentrated on the plateaus to the north and south of the oasis, just above the springs, whereas during the Intermediate Bronze Age, the sites were distributed over the plateau east of the oasis, far away from the water sources. The excavations in the Uvda valley illustrate the stratigraphic discontinuity between the Intermediate Bronze Age and Early Bronze Age settlement and the difference in site and house plans. At Site 17, Y. Bet Arieh excavated a dwelling house of the sunken broadhouse type, dated to the Early Bronze II, the remains of which were covered with a thick layer of sand. Above the sand cover, a series of joined round structures, not sunk into the ground, were built in the Intermediate Bronze Age.

The Negev sites of the Intermediate Bronze Age were usually built on hilltops or on slopes. Settlements established in the valleys between the hills are rare. Of the hundreds of sites explored, few are large. The vast majority are medium to small, that is, 0.1–0.5 hectare. The large sites were built near water sources (springs or wells), and sometimes contained more than two hundred structures. The large sites include Horvat En Ziq, 2 hectares; Beer Resisim, where about 150 dwelling units were counted over an area of 1.5 hectares; Horvat Mashabbe Sade, about 1.2 hectares; Horvat Nahal Nizzana, about 1 hectare; Horvat Har Yeruham, 0.5 hectare; and Horvat Har Zayyad. The middle-sized sites, such as the Nahal Boqer site, contained house clusters with about fifteen units. Most sites, however, were small and situated at a distance from available water. They consisted of two or three houses adjoined by sheep pens. Be-

Fig. 5.3. Beer Resisim, plan of settlement

sides the hundreds of open-air settlements, there were in the Negev Highlands some cave sites of the Intermediate Bronze Age that had been inhabited during the Early Bronze II, such as the site of Nahal Ahdir.

The most common dwelling for the nuclear family was a round or oval stone structure, with a diameter of two to four meters. Its roof was supported by a central column, made of one or more stones. The roof was built of beams laid radially between the central column and the walls, which supported flat stone slabs, subsequently covered with mud or lime plaster. The doorway had a stone threshold and lintel. Rarely, broadhouses are found, with right-angled or rounded corners, as at Har Yeruham and Horvat Mashabbe Sade.

The site organization of the Intermediate Bronze Age settlements of the Negev Highlands also differs, for the most part, from that common in this region during the Early Bronze Age II. In the Early Bronze Age, sites consisted of a group of dwellings and service structures arranged around a communal courtyard. In contrast, during the Intermediate Bronze Age the houses were usually built as independent units, bunched together and often abutting each other. This created, in the large sites, large beehivelike clusters, such as Beer Resisim and En Ziq. In some sites these house aggregates were bisected by alleyways to form residential quarters of a sort, as at Horvat Nahal Nizzana.

At Har Yeruham, two strata of Intermediate Bronze Age settlement were excavated by M. Kochavi. This is the only site in the Negev Highlands with two clearly separate occupations. The strata differ in the general site plan and in the house plans. The first settlement was surrounded by a stone wall. Houses were of the rectilinear broadroom

type and abutted the perimeter wall. House roofs were supported by round, segmented stone columns. The columns were placed either in the center of the room or in a row of two or three along the longer axis. Part of the house served as a work area, as evidenced by the presence of stone mortars and hammers. Stone benches were found in some structures. Following the abandonment of the first stratum, a new settlement was erected, consisting of round houses organized in a manner consistent with most of the Negev sites of the period. Open courtyards and animal pens adjoined the round structures. Tumuli containing cist tombs were scattered over the site. Some were built above the remains of the earlier settlement. On a nearby hilltop, a cult place was discovered. The cemetery found on a nearby ridge contained eighty tumuli.

SUMMARY: SETTLEMENT IN THE WESTERN REGIONS

Remains of unwalled settlements and cemeteries of the Intermediate Bronze Age at sites already inhabited during the Early Bronze Age have been discovered in most parts of the land lying east of the Transjordanian plateau. However, the distribution of sites in the arid and semiarid regions, such as the Samarian desert, the margins of the Judaean desert, the Negev, and Sinai, differs from the pattern of settlement in these areas during the Early Bronze Age. In the arid Negev Highlands, entire sites of the Intermediate Bronze Age have been excavated, whereas in the more humid northerly regions, sites of the period have been only partially exposed. In excavations of multilayered mounds, remains of unwalled Intermediate Bronze Age settlements have been revealed, founded on the ruins of the fortified towns of the Early

Bronze II–III. Such excavations have revealed stratigraphic gaps between the settlement remains of the two periods. This indicates a chronological gap and cultural discontinuity between the urban system of the Early Bronze Age and the new system of village settlement established during the Intermediate Bronze Age. Furthermore, only a small portion of the new unwalled sites were erected on the ruins of the abandoned Early Bronze Age towns. Most were established at sites not settled during the Early Bronze II–III. Some were established at sites of unfortified settlement during the Neolithic, Chalcolithic, or Early Bronze I (preurban) periods, but more were established at new, previously unoccupied sites.

The differences observed in the desert regions (the Negev and Sinai) between the unfortified settlements of the Early Bronze Age II and those of the Intermediate Bronze Age (in settlement pattern, site organization, and architecture) testify to a decline in the influence of the material culture of the northern regions on the desert population. During the period in question, the nomadic population of central southern Sinai was cut off from the influence of cultures of the Land of Israel, in contrast to its surprising degree of integration with those cultures during the Early Bronze II, when it fulfilled a central role in the supply of copper to the Land of Israel.

On the eastern margins of the hill country of Samaria and Judaea, within the Mediterranean and Irano-Turanian vegetation zones, the exploitation of semiarid regions on the desert margins increased, in relation to the Early Bronze Age.

The dwelling structures of the arid zones (which had generally been, during the Early Bronze Age, of the broadhouse type, as in the settled regions of the north) reverted during the Intermediate Bronze Age to the curvilinear plan, which had been the dominant plan in the desert before the Early Bronze Age. The broadhouse continued to be in use in the villages of the north.

Despite a general resemblance in the geographic range of settlement in these two periods in the western part of the Land of Israel, many factors indicate that the rural settlement system of the Intermediate Bronze Age was unrelated, from its inception, to the urban system of the Early Bronze Age II–III. The study of the thin deposits of the Intermediate Bronze Age sites shows that they did not have a long lifespan. A considerable proportion may therefore be termed transient settlements.

THE SETTLEMENT OF THE EASTERN REGION: THE TRANSJORDANIAN PLATEAU

Since Nelson Glueck's pioneering effort in 1932–47 and until the present, intensive surveys of the Transjordanian plateau, south of the Yarmuk River (the lands of Gilead, Ammon, and Moab), have brought to light much data regarding the Intermediate Bronze Age settlement pattern in this region. The surveys show that the extent of settlement in the Transjordanian plateau was no smaller than that of the hill regions west of the Jordan. Furthermore, systematic surveys and excavations of the dolmen fields in the Hauran and the Golan have provided data concerning the settlements and cult sites in the basaltic regions in northern Transjordan and on the edge of the Syrian desert, such as the site of Khirbet el-Umbachi, about seventy kilometers south of Damascus. The site included, among other things, a bone pile extending over one thousand square meters, containing the remains of forty thousand animals: sheep, goat, cattle, and deer.

It should, however, be pointed out that no Intermediate Bronze Age sites have yet been excavated in most parts of the Transjordanian plateau, with the exception of burial sites in the Gilead (El-Husn) and at Amman and the three southern sites of Khirbet Iskander, Aroer, and Ader. As the study of the fortified towns of the Early Bronze II–III in this area has also been neglected, there is no information regarding the stratigraphic relationship between the remains of these towns and the remains of the late third millennium settlements. In other words, it is not clear whether there was a time lapse here too between the destruction of the Early Bronze Age towns and the settlements of the Intermediate Bronze Age, or whether the settlements of the two periods follow in a close sequence, with no stratigraphic gap. Only lately have excavations begun at Early Bronze Age sites north of Amman. The results may clarify this question.

The classification of the pottery collected in the surveys and tomb excavations in northern and central Transjordan (in the Golan, Gilead, and Ammon) indicates a geographical-typological subdivision into northern regions and southern regions, similar to that observed across the river.

In light of the incomplete data, the northern and central areas on either side of the Jordan may be pictured as forming, in the Intermediate Bronze Age, one cultural-geographical unit, differing from southern Transjordan. The latter region may be viewed, in light of the newest evidence, as a geographical unit with a different settlement history. Data gathered in the sites mentioned above indicate that the history of the sites of southern Transjordan was somewhat different from that of the sites of the Jordan valley and the Land of Israel (and perhaps

also from those of the northern and central Transjordanian plateau).

The ruins of the large (four hectares) Byzantine site in the village of Ader, seven kilometers northeast of Kerak and 950 meters above sea level, have been surveyed twice: once by Albright in 1924 and again by Glueck in 1933. Their surveys also revealed the remains of a late third millennium occupation. The site had previously been known for the remains of a shrine with four menhirs (standing stones), each about four meters high. Albright excavated the site and, in one of his soundings (4 × 10 meters), identified three architectural layers of a late third millennium settlement. The earliest was ascribed to the Early Bronze Age and the latter two to the Intermediate Bronze Age. The pottery of all three phases was in the ceramic tradition of the Early Bronze Age (red burnished slip and applied plastic decoration). The excavators did not succeed, however, in dating the temple and menhirs.

The 1964–66 excavations of a Spanish expedition headed by E. Olavarri at Khirbet 'Ara'ir (biblical Aroer), north of the Arnon River, revealed two consecutive occupation strata of the late third millennium B.C.E. The earlier deposit had a depth of two meters. As no remains of permanent structures were found within it, the excavator concluded that the site was first occupied by seminomads who also practiced farming. The pottery and flints indicate continuity from the Early Bronze III (the continued use of red burnished slip on the pottery). The remains of the later stratum included some poor construction, and the pottery found included some types defined by the excavator as the caliciform ware of the Land of Israel.

Khirbet Iskander is on a hilltop on the northern bank of Wadi el-Wala, a tributary of the Arnon, 480 meters above sea level. The site cov-

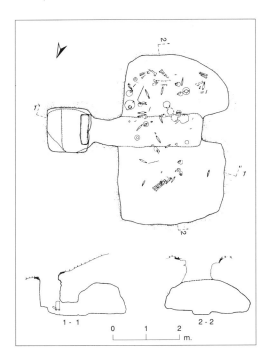

Fig. 5.4. Plan and sections of shaft tomb

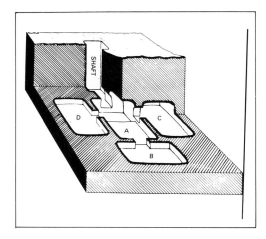

Fig. 5.5. Isometric view of shaft tomb at Megiddo

ers about four hectares. Glueck described an enclosure surrounded by a wall with houses built up against it, as well as stone circles and standing stones in the vicinity. The site was first excavated by P. Parr in 1955, and three phases of Intermediate Bronze Age settlement were revealed, including remains of houses and a defense wall. Traces of an earlier settlement dating from the Chalcolithic and Early Bronze I periods were found as well. An American expedition headed by S. Richard and R. S. Boraas excavated the site in 1981–84 and reported the discovery of monumental architecture, fortifications, and residential quarters of the Intermediate Bronze Age. The published data indicate that the houses, of the broadhouse type, were built of stone and mud brick. The pottery discovered at the site was coarse and decorated with a red slip. This ware was determined to be in the Early Bronze Age ceramic tradition (coarse clay, mixed with large grits used for temper). Among the remains attributed to the latter phases of the site's existence were pottery vessels of a thin, greenish metallic ware, bearing a combed decoration characteristic of the Intermediate Bronze Age in the Land of Israel.

The three sites of the late third millennium excavated in southern Transjordan reveal a different picture from that of the Jordan valley and westward, in the Land of Israel. Their pottery (form, decoration, and technique), the presence of fortifications (Khirbet Iskander), and their extended lifespan combine to suggest that part of the urban population of Early Bronze III Transjordan moved to new sites in the late third millennium, establishing new settlements, some even fortified. Such a process, possibly indicating a relative continuity of late third millennium settlement in at least part of the Transjordanian plateau, as well

as continuity in the material culture, has not been discovered to the west, in the Land of Israel. The latter region is characterized by clear-cut occupational and stratigraphic discontinuity between the fortified settlements of the Early Bronze Age III and the unfortified settlements of the Intermediate Bronze Age.

It may be predicted that future excavations in northern and central Transjordan will clarify the geographical extent of the area in which the material culture sequence of the late third millennium was not interrupted, as appears to be the case in the southern Transjordanian plateau, both to the north and to the south of the Arnon River. At any rate, there seems to be no correlation between the tripartite chronological division of the late third millennium proposed by Dever (which may correspond to the stratigraphic data from the southern Transjordanian plateau) and the clear stratigraphic situation revealed in the Land of Israel. The latest evidence points to an occupational gap between the towns of the Early Bronze III and the settlements of the Intermediate Bronze Age.

It would appear, therefore, that the evidence from the Land of Israel does not justify the subdivision of the Intermediate Bronze Age there according to the evidence from the Transjordanian plateau, as Dever proposes. The lack of correlation between the settlement history of the Land of Israel and of the Transjordanian plateau (as revealed by the archaeological evidence) in the Intermediate Bronze Age poses difficult questions to the archaeologist, as it implies that the settlement history of the late third millennium varied from one region to the next. This variability must influence the characterization of the culture of the period and the terminology and chronology adopted.

Tombs and Burial Customs

The interment of individuals or of nuclear families in shaft tombs or megalithic monuments and the time, effort, and care invested in tomb construction characterize the burial customs in the Land of Israel during the late third millennium, in contrast to the Early Bronze Age practice of mass burial, over prolonged periods, of many families or entire clans in caves. The varied burial customs of this period afford many interpretations. Sometimes the bodies were interred whole within the tomb, in a flexed or extended position; this is known as primary burial. Mostly, however, the bones were gathered after decomposition and placed, either piled up or scattered, in the tomb, called secondary burial. The sites of the primary burial and the rites accompanying it (in the latter case) still await discovery. In the cemetery adjacent to Jericho, 80 percent of the burials were secondary burials of individuals. Many variations have been found in the location and orientation of the remains within the tombs. At times, different customs have been observed to characterize different tomb groups within a single cemetery, such as the cemeteries of Jericho and Tell el-Ajjul. At these sites, the shape of the tomb was correlated with the type of burial (primary or secondary) and burial gifts. The varying interpretations of these phenomena relate to the realms of chronology, beliefs, cult, society, and economy.

The limited number of individuals buried in each tomb led to the creation of many large cemeteries during the Intermediate Bronze Age, to the extent that their remains constitute one of the hallmarks of the period.

Tens of cemeteries have been discovered throughout the country, and hundreds of tombs have been excavated. The burial gifts interred in the Intermediate Bronze Age tombs do not excel in wealth or diversity. The typical assemblage consists of pottery vessels, metal (usually copper) tools and weapons, and personal ornaments (metal pins and bracelets, as well as beads). The high proportion of metal objects among the tomb gifts is conspicuous.

SHAFT TOMBS

Shaft tombs were carved either in the limestone regions or in the kurkar (sandstone) ridges of the coastal plain. There are also some shaft tombs excavated in the soil and lined with stone slabs. The shaft tomb is considered one of the characteristic features of Intermediate Bronze Age culture, though shaft tombs of the first phase of the Early Bronze Age have been discovered in the cemetery of Bab edh-Dhra. The basic form of the shaft tomb consists of a subterranean chamber approached by a vertical shaft. The entrance leading from the bottom of the shaft to the burial chamber was usually blocked with a large stone. The forms of the shafts and chambers are varied, ranging from rectangular to round and to amorphous. The shaft tombs excavated at the foot of Megiddo are among the most elaborate discovered in the Land of Israel. These burial caves

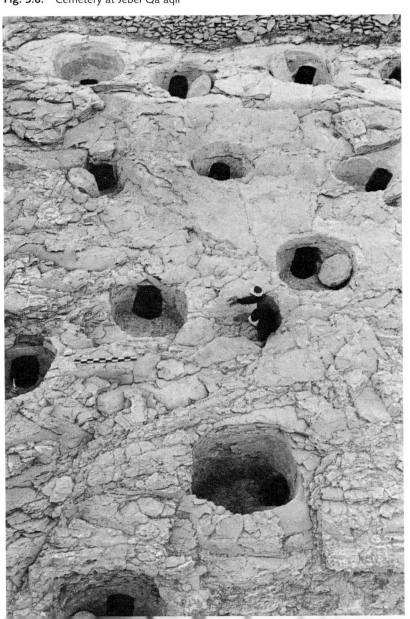

Fig. 5.6. Cemetery at Jebel Qa'aqir

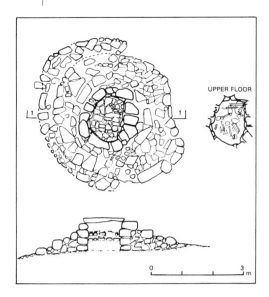

Fig. 5.7. Plan and section of Har Yeruham tumulus

had deep square shafts, leading off to a system of three or four large rectangular chambers.

Many of the shaft tombs were used for individual burials, but some served for entire families, such as the tomb at 'Enan. The condition of the skeletons found in the shaft tombs indicates that many of the deceased were not given an orderly burial; rather, their bones were gathered and reinterred in the tombs following decomposition. There are also some instances of articulated burials of complete skeletons, usually laid in a flexed position.

Shaft tomb cemeteries have been investigated in the Galilean hills (Safed, Hanita), the Hula valley (Shamir, Ha-Goshrim, Ma'ayan Baruch, 'Enan), the Jezreel valley (Megiddo, Ha-Zorea), the middle Jordan valley and the Beth Shean valley (Tiberias, Menahemiya, Beth Shean, En Ha-Naziv, Tirat Zvi, Tel Rehov), the coastal plain (Barqai, Khirbet Ibreiktas, Ma'abarot, Tel Aviv, Azor, Yavne, Tell el-Ajjul), Ramot Menashe (Gal'ed), the cen-

tral hills (the 'Ain Samiya region, Gibeon), the Judaean hills (Khirbet Kufin, Efrat, Tekoa, Khirbet Kirmil), the Judaean Shephelah (Lachish, Jebel Qa'aqir), the lower Jordan valley (Jericho, Bab edh-Dhra). Shaft tombs have also been discovered in the Transjordanian plateau (northern Gilead and Amman).

On the banks of the Jordan River, in Kibbutz Deganya A south of the Early Bronze Age mound of Beth Yerah, a cemetery belonging to the settlement built on the ruins of the town was discovered. Two shaft tombs of rectangular plan were excavated. Dug into the marl soil (*huwwar*) of the Jordan valley, the tombs were lined with limestone and basalt slabs. The entrance shaft occupied half the tomb, and the burial chambers were roofed and paved with basalt slabs. The joins between the slabs were filled in with thick, coarse mortar. Remains of juveniles and adults were found in the tombs, indicating family burial.

Fig. 5.8. Plans and sections of Golan dolmens

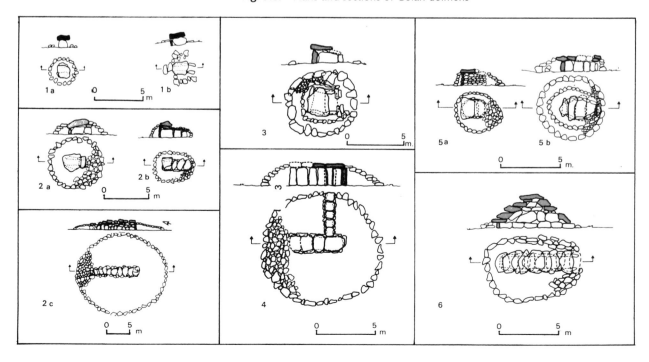

MEGALITHIC TOMBS

Another tomb type characteristic of the late third millennium belongs to the family of megalithic monuments. The term is composed of the Greek words *megas* ("great") and *lithos* ("stone") and describes tombs built of large, unworked boulders (though other stones are sometimes used), often covered by mounds of earth or stone piles. Megalithic tombs were constructed in the Land of Israel during various phases of the Chalcolithic and Early Bronze periods. In the late third millennium, two types of megalithic tombs, extant already in the Early Bronze Age, became widespread: stone or earthen tumuli, and dolmens.

TUMULI. In this tomb type, the corpse was laid either in an articulated or disarticulated state within a stone cist, covered with a mound of stone and earth. Tumulus fields of the Intermediate Bronze Age are found in the Transjordanian plateau, in the basalt regions of the Hauran and Golan, in the Jordan valley, and in the Negev Highlands, where thousands of tumuli have been discovered in large concentrations on mountain ridges, on hilltops, and near or even within habitation sites (for example, Har Yeruham and Beer Resisim). Similar tombs have been found in excavations at Chorazin in the upper Galilee, near Talpiyot (Jerusalem), in Wadi et-Terfeh (northeast of the Dead Sea), and Bab edh-Dhra, east of the Lisan.

A description of the tumuli excavated in Har Yeruham, for example, illustrates the method of construction. A stone cist, resembling a coffin, built of large slabs was constructed on the bedrock and paved with small flat stones. The deceased, or some of his bones (in the case of secondary burial), was then placed in the tomb with burial offerings (pottery, copper artifacts, beads).

The stone coffin was covered with flat stones and encircled by a ring of standing stones. The space between the outer stone circle and the cist was filled with stones, thus creating a tumulus 0.5–1.5 meters high.

DOLMENS. Dolmens are enlarged versions of tumulus-covered cists. "Dolmen," in Breton (the large dolmen fields of Brittany were among the first studied), means a stone table. A simple dolmen may be constructed of six large unworked slabs. The average size of dolmen stones in the Land of Israel is $0.9 \times 0.7 \times 4$ meters, and each weighs over a ton. Four are arranged in a rectangle, the fifth stone serves as a base, and the sixth, the largest of all, is the table slab, placed atop the rest. The entire structure served as a burial chamber and was covered with a cairn of stone or earth to form a tumulus. The base of the tumulus was bounded with one or more rings of small stones, intended, perhaps, to support the tumulus and prevent its collapse.

Fields containing thousands of dolmens may be found in Transjordan and the Golan. Dolmen remains have also been discovered in the basalt regions of the eastern Galilee (near Chorazin) and even in the limestone regions of the central Galilee (near Mount Meron and 'Alma). It is difficult to determine the precise date of construction of the various dolmen types, as they were repeatedly reused long after their construction. Thus, excavations in a dolmen field near Damiyah, in the Jordan valley, have shown that the custom of burial in dolmens was common as early as the Early Bronze Age I. In excavations conducted by Claire Epstein in dolmen fields of the Golan, clear evidence has been found dating the construction and first use of a great part of the dolmens to the late third millennium. Despite differences in size and

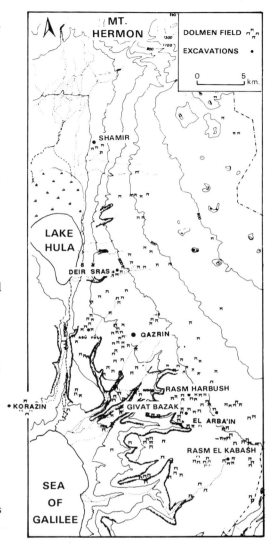

Map 5.2. Dolmen fields in the Golan

style, most of the Golan dolmens were built on the same basic design, involving fieldstones, a rectangular or sometimes trapezoidal burial chamber, orthostats (stone slab lining) for the lower part of the walls (cf. the tomb at Deganya), paving, and stone slabs for roofing. The dolmen is generally enclosed in an oval tumulus and is sometimes entirely buried beneath it. Sometimes the roof just emerges from the stone pile; elsewhere, it towers high above it. Burials within the dolmen chambers were secondary. Weapons, bracelets, beads, and pottery were placed alongside the dead.

Pottery

The study of pottery is the essence and touchstone for the evaluation of the distinctiveness of the culture of the Land of Israel in the late third millennium. Any attempt to clarify the internal chronology of this culture must also rely on the study of pottery. A currently accepted approach is that the pottery of the period concludes, from many aspects, a long ceramic tradition that evolved in the Land of Israel from the beginning of the Early Bronze Age. There is, however, disagreement over how traditional the assemblage in fact was, for many new elements were incorporated in its technology, formal concepts, and typological array. The study of this pottery is based on the rich tomb finds of the period and on material from habitation sites. Recent work seems to have reduced the data gap (quantitative and typological) between the assemblages appearing in tombs, which represent burial gifts, and the household ware (such as cooking pots, various bowls, and pithoi) generally found at habitation sites. This imbalance long hindered an accurate characterization of the assemblage as a whole. The recent discoveries now permit a more considered evaluation of the pottery of this period.

R. Amiran was the first to attempt to describe and analyze the technology, forms, decorations, and types of late third millennium pottery and to determine its internal chronological divisions. Her typological analysis, based on tomb finds (without stratigraphic control), resulted in the division of the as-

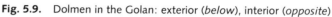

Fig. 5.9. Dolmen in the Golan: exterior (*below*), interior (*opposite*)

semblage into several families common in different parts of the country. A division into three regional families was first suggested: one southern, one northern, and one of the Megiddo area. As finds accumulated, the subdivisions were refined into the south (the southern coast, the Shephelah, the Hebron hills, and the Negev), the north (Galilee and Gilead), the Megiddo–Ha-Zorea region, and the central hills (from Samaria to Jerusalem). Still later, additional finds resulted in a re-evaluation of the families and their reduction to two or three in number: one northern, one southern, and one of the Bethel hill region. It thus appears that the basis for Amiran's typological-regional division was and remains the distinction between pottery of the northern and southern regions. It has, however, proved impossible to draw clear boundaries between the regional subfamilies.

Amiran also suggested, at first, internal chronological divisions, corresponding to the regional divisions, while attempting to trace the pro-

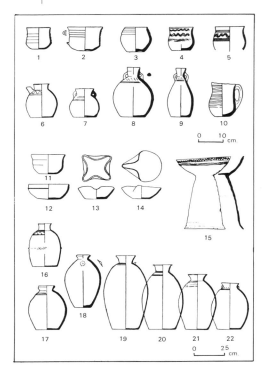

Fig. 5.10. Intermediate Bronze Age pottery, the southern family

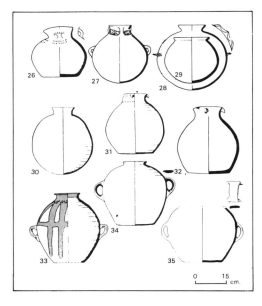

Fig. 5.11. Intermediate Bronze Age pottery, the northern family

posed relation between the pottery of the Land of Israel and that of Mesopotamia of the Akkadian period and immediately following that period. With time, Amiran took a more skeptical position regarding the use of regional families to determine the internal chronology of the period, for it became increasingly clear that there is a great deal of overlap between the ceramic families of the north and of the south. She therefore tended to focus on the essential and formal unity characterizing the pottery of the period throughout the country. Amiran analyzes the integration of new elements in the ceramic tradition of the Early Bronze Age and their influence in molding the character of late third millennium pottery as a distinctive ceramic culture, emphasizing the difference in many aspects, some of them crucial, between Early Bronze and Intermediate Bronze Age pottery.

Dever and others of his school believe that household vessels, such as holemouth cooking pots and various types of bowls, show direct formal continuity with the Early Bronze Age vessels and that the pottery of southern Transjordan contains clear elements of the Early Bronze Age tradition. They have tended to attribute little weight to the new ceramic elements, whose source lies outside the Land of Israel, while emphasizing the elements indicating, in their view, continuity of ceramic traditions with the Early Bronze Age. Thus, they see the entire pottery assemblage of the late third millennium B.C.E. as a direct continuation of the Early Bronze Age ceramic culture. Following repeated typological analyses, Dever proposed a regional subdivision of the pottery distributions on both sides of the Jordan River into seven groups: north (the upper Galilee), north-central (lower Galilee and Jezreel valley), coastal, Jordan val-

ley–Jericho, central hills, south (south of the Jerusalem–Tel Aviv line), Transjordan. On the basis of his diagnosis of regional characteristics of the pottery assemblages (as well as metal objects, burial types, and even settlement types), but without stratigraphic control, Dever offered his tripartite chronological subdivision of the period.

In conclusion, a combination of factors still bars any attempt to employ the pottery assemblage of the late third millennium B.C.E. in constructing a reliable relative chronology for the period. These factors include, first, the many and varied ceramic characterizations that come to light with each new excavation; second, the want of assemblages from sites with an extended stratigraphic sequence; and third, the lack of typological uniformity between assemblages originating in cemeteries and those exposed in the adjacent settlements. Amiran states that we cannot determine with certainty whether the regional pottery groups are contemporaneous but of varying temporal range, or whether each occupies a separate chronological niche in the internal development of the period. There seems to be no answer to the question of whether the typological variation between the regional pottery groups of the Intermediate Bronze Age stems from chronological differences, tribal boundaries, or both.

TECHNIQUE

The clay composition, the manner of its preparation, and its firing may be held responsible for the pale color (greenish gray, yellowish gray, or pinkish gray) characterizing the Intermediate Bronze Age pottery, in contrast to Early Bronze Age pottery, in most parts of the Land of Israel. Pottery was handmade, and the use of the wheel, which had become common in the Early

Bronze Age, nearly ceased. The wheel was employed only in the finishing of the vessels, such as in the joining of the rim to the neck. It has even been claimed that the finishing too was done by hand, with the aid of simple rotary movement. This mode of manufacture is reflected in the unpolished appearance of the vessels, with potters' fingermarks in evidence in the not uncommon dents found in the vessels. Certain vessel types, found in the north, were wheel-made, but they appear to have been imported from Syria.

Pottery kilns of the Intermediate Bronze Age have been found at five sites: Beth Yerah, Tel Yosef, Tell el-Hayyat, Jebel Qa'aqir, and Har Yeruham.

FORMS

Most vessels have a flat base and a globular or barrel-shaped form. They usually lack shoulders. The holemouth cooking pots have a round base, as do a group of jars of a northern type. Jars have a bag-shaped body, differing from the form common in the Early Bronze Age. This change testifies to a new formal conception, as the flat base of this jar is far greater in diameter than the neck. The absence of handles on many of the vessels is another characteristic of late third millennium pottery. Though some jars are equipped with degenerate folded ledge handles, a vestige of Early Bronze Age traditions, they no longer serve any useful function. Ribbon loop handles are also sometimes attached to jars and jugs, and diminutive loop handles to amphoriskoi in particular. These too are a vestige of earlier ceramic traditions.

DECORATION

The most common decorations consist of fine incisions and stippling and constitute an innovation in relation to Early Bronze Age decoration. This decoration blends well with the pale tint of late third millennium pottery. It was effected with the aid of a pointed stick (or metal pin) and a three- or five-toothed comb. The comb created groups of straight or wavy parallel lines. Alongside the incised decoration, decorative techniques of the Early Bronze Age persisted, though their execution changed: reddish-brown slip, painted brush strokes, and some burnishing (mainly in the southern Transjordanian plateau). Applied plastic decoration is also common.

TYPOLOGY

New pottery types appearing in the late third millennium include the goblet, the mug, the teapot, and the jug teapot. Vessels showing continuous development from the Early Bronze Age are globular holemouth cooking pots and holemouth jars, large bowls, and spouted vessels.

BOWLS. Common in domestic assemblages are large bowls, deep and open, with inverted ridged rims. Also common are the small, deep bowls (rounded or carinated), often found as burial offerings in tombs. The domestic assemblages also include large basins, some with vestigial ledge handles, which may be termed kraters. Bowls generally have flat bases, though among the smaller bowls there are some round bases, particularly in the north.

CHALICES. This vessel is rare in the assemblage of the period. Large chalices with unfenestrated conical pedestals have been found. The chalice is decorated mainly with incised horizontal wavy lines. Amiran believes these vessels reflect North Syrian influence.

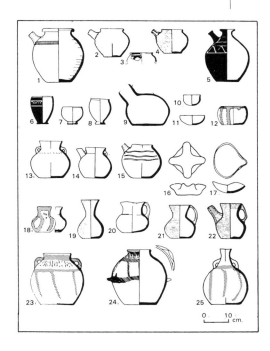

Fig. 5.12. Intermediate Bronze Age pottery, the Megiddo family

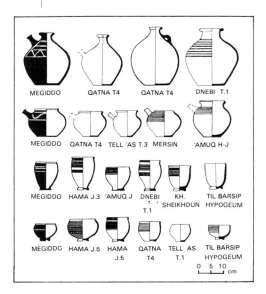

Fig. 5.14. Caliciform ware: comparison of forms from the Land of Israel and Syria

Fig. 5.13. Wheel-made goblet from Qedesh

GOBLETS. The goblet, with its subtypes, is one of the new vessel types appearing in the late third millennium assemblage. Tufnell's Caliciform culture takes its name from this vessel.

Different goblet types were used in the northern and southern regions of the Land of Israel. Among those found in the north, for example, Megiddo and Kedesh, some may be taken to indicate the Syrian origin of this vessel. At these sites, both tall and squat goblets (the latter resembling small bowls) were found. They are wheel-made, of a dark ware—black, gray, or reddish brown—and have a metallic ring. They are decorated with painted bands of yellowish white or are incised in such a manner that the light fabric of the clay is exposed. There are also some handmade goblets, apparent imitations of the wheel-made ware.

It has lately become evident that the wheel-made goblets, as well as teapots and other forms, were im-ported to the north from north-central Syria, where similar vessels have been encountered (for example, at Qatna, Hama).

The goblets common to the southern regions are all handmade. They bear a grooved decoration and are characterized by an inverted or everted wall, which sometimes has a handle attached at the lower point of carination.

MUGS. The mug belongs to the southern ceramic assemblage, and it too is a new type peculiar to the period. The vessel has a long, thin loop handle resembling a ribbon and bears grooved decoration.

TEAPOTS. The teapot is common throughout the country. It is a spouted vessel, usually without handles, though sometimes it has a handle or knob opposite the rim.

Characteristic to the north is a hybrid vessel, a teapot superimposed on an amphoriskos. One of the two handles bridges the spout and neck, thus creating the teapot jug. There are also holemouth teapots with vestigial folded ledge handles. In northern regions, wheel-made teapots of a dark gray ware occur. Like the wheel-made goblets of similar ware, the teapots bear a painted yellowish-white decoration of wavy or straight lines. It may be assumed that these vessels, like the goblets, came by way of trade from central Syria.

ASKOS. This is an unusual vessel discovered in northern assemblages (Safed, 'Enan). It has been termed an askos because of its similarity to late third millennium vessels found in the Aegean islands and Crete. The vessel has a hemispherical body and a broad ribbon handle attached to the short, wide spout.

JARS. In the south, jars are usually barrel-shaped, though some holemouths appear as well. Northern jars are more globular or bag-shaped and are sometimes pinched. Many jars have vestigial ledge handles. Painted jars occur in the Jordan valley.

AMPHORISKOI. These are among the most common vessels of the period, appearing throughout the country. Some of the northern varieties have pinched rims, which form a kind of spout.

BOTTLES. Handmade bottles have been found in the north, some of them red slipped or painted. Wheel-made bottles of a gray ware have also been found, decorated with horizontal white bands. Similar bottles occur at the site of Hama, in Syria. Farther south, particularly in the Bethel area, the amphoriskos bottle may be found, its form being close to that of the amphoriskos, with two small loop handles.

JUGS. Jugs are among the types characterizing the northerly regions. Ribbon handles occur, as well as simple and carelessly executed painted decoration and red-brown slip. Jugs have been found in the south as well, some bearing incised decoration.

COOKING POTS. The southern regions continue to employ globular holemouth cooking pots, with a squared or rounded rim. In the north, cooking pots are globular and have a short everted rim. Some bases are round, and others flat. Shallow, coarse cooking pots resembling flat-based bowls occur in the north, while in the south (on both sides of the Jordan) some fragments have turned up of straight-sided cooking pots with applied decoration. These belong to a cooking-pot type that

characterizes the Middle Bronze Age assemblage.

LAMPS. The most common lamp of the late third millennium features four spouts and is found throughout the country. Southern sites have also provided some single-spouted examples, a type that was to continue to evolve from the Middle Bronze to the Iron Age. Pedestal lamps have been found at northern sites (Ma'ayan Baruch, 'Enan, and the Golan dolmens). The average height of this lamp is 9.7 centimeters, and it is furnished with several spouts.

Metallurgy

The abundance of metal artifacts is an outstanding characteristic of Intermediate Bronze Age culture in the Land of Israel. Astonishing quantities of metal artifacts continue to be found, and recent years have seen the accumulation of new data on the metal technology employed during this period. Most metal objects have been discovered in tombs, but some have been found among settlement remains. Daggers are the most common type of weapon found, whereas the number of metal tools is small indeed.

The comparative abundance of metal artifacts in the Intermediate Bronze Age and the advanced technology evidenced in their manufacture are especially remarkable in view of the wretched appearance of most sites of this period. The conspicuous role played by metal artifacts among the poor settlement remains is enhanced when compared with the modest quantities of metal objects recovered in the tombs and settlements of the Early Bronze Age. Chemical analyses of Intermediate Bronze Age artifacts have shown that tin-bronze technology was introduced in the late third

millennium in the Land of Israel, though the traditional pure copper or arsenical copper technologies remained in widespread use. Arsenical copper probably originated in Anatolia. The two dominant elements used to create copper-based alloys (bronze) were arsenic and tin, for both have a similar hardening effect on the cast metal. However, it is generally thought that arsenic, unlike tin, was not processed independently but existed as a natural component of certain copper beds. Arsenical copper had been in use in the Land of Israel since the Chalcolithic and Early Bronze Ages (arsenic bronze), alongside the nearly pure copper generally employed by local craftsmen. The technology used to prepare an alloy of two different metals, copper and tin (tin bronze), spread throughout the Levant chiefly during the Middle Bronze Age, in the first half of the second millennium. It therefore appears that as far as metallurgy is concerned, the Early Bronze Age should be considered still a copper age, whereas the Intermediate Bronze Age culture of the late third millennium crossed the threshold of the true bronze age. Furthermore, only a few of the tools and weapons common in the Intermediate Bronze Age evolved out of Early Bronze Age types (axes, adzes, and some types of daggers). Most of the weapons were new.

The metallurgy of the Land of Israel during the late third millennium conforms to the conception of the culture as an intermediate culture, for during this period there coexisted two metal technologies. The artifacts in the archaeological assemblage made with the new tin-bronze technology are, however, limited in quantity and in the number of types.

J. Muhly, R. Maddin, and Tamara Stech are of the opinion that the Intermediate Bronze Age technology of the Land of Israel represents an imported Anatolian tradition, without roots in the local metallurgy of the Early Bronze Age, raising some questions that must be addressed in future research. Who were the metal craftsmen of the late third millennium, and what was their position in society? What role did local craftsmen play in the manufacture of metal objects found in the Land of Israel? Were complete objects imported by way of trade, or only raw materials (ingots of arsenical copper and tin), the objects themselves being manufactured locally? Were the traditional copper beds of the south (Timna, Fenan, and southern Sinai) exploited in the Intermediate Bronze Age as well? If so, which of them, and to what extent?

Against the background of these questions, the discovery at Lachish and Har Yeruham of cylindrical clay vessels, perhaps crucibles, used to melt copper stands out. Excavations at Intermediate Bronze Age sites, particularly in the south (Jericho, Lachish, Har Yeruham, Beer Resisim, En Ziq, and Har Zayyad) uncovered a significant number of copper ingots, which appear to have a standard form. Ingots of this type were also found among caches bought from antiquities dealers, such as a cache from the southern Hebron hills and another exhibited in the Hecht Museum at Haifa University. The ingots are 8–10 centimeters long and 2–3 centimeters wide. Maddin and Stech, who analyzed some of the ingots from Har Yeruham and the Hebron hills, state

Fig. 5.15. Copper ingots from the vicinity of Hebron (length 18–21 centimeters)

that ingots of this type are the result of the recasting of larger ingots made of pure ore or of the recycling of discarded copper implements, of the same source. Dever suggests that the ingots were brought by itinerant coppersmiths, who used them to cast tools, weapons, and ornaments at the same sites where they were discovered. However, the question of the origin of the copper ore has yet to be resolved. Recent evidence indicates the utilization of local copper ores: on a hill in Nahal Timna, B. Rothenberg found pounded copper slag and other waste material of copper industry in an Intermediate Bronze Age context. He also reports the discovery of large grinding tools and, nearby, unsmelted copper ore. Also, a large Intermediate Bronze Age site was discovered in the seventies near the Yotvata springs, about fifteen kilometers north of Timna.

Excavations and surveys conducted by a German expedition in 1983–84 at Fenan, east of the Aravah, revealed evidence of the exploitation of the local copper beds in the Chalcolithic, Early Bronze, and Intermediate Bronze ages. The copper beds of southern Sinai, however, were no longer exploited in the Intermediate Bronze Age.

WEAPONS

Artifact types carried over from the Early Bronze Age metallurgical tradition include one variety of dagger found in the Intermediate Bronze Age repertoire. Most dagger types, however, are new. The spears, javelins, and battle-axes are also new, and the copper arrowhead is first introduced in this period.

DAGGERS. The short, straight, untanged dagger, with rivet holes in the base for attaching the haft, common in the Early Bronze Age, remained in use in the Intermediate

Bronze Age. Most dagger types, however, were new and could be used for slashing and beating, as well as stabbing. They are common throughout southwest Asia in the late third millennium B.C.E. They are relatively long (30–40 centimeters), some long enough to be classed as swords, and feature a pronounced midrib and a tang through which several rivets were driven to improve the attachment of haft and blade. Chemical analyses of the dagger groups from Deganya and from 'Enan show that they were made of tin bronze. The amount of tin added to the copper ranges from 3 percent to 7 percent. Daggers of the same type have been found in tombs at Jericho, Menahemiya, and Moza but were not chemically analyzed.

JAVELINS. This weapon, lighter than the spear, was usually thrown. Three types of javelin heads were found in Intermediate Bronze Age contexts. The first, featuring a long blade with midrib and curled tang, has been found in tombs from the northern part of the country (Ginnosar, Tiberias, Beth Shean, Menahemiya, Geva Carmel, Fureidis, Barqai, and Ma'abarot). A second type, more common in southern regions, has a short and narrow blade with a midrib and an elongated curled tang. The third type is elongated and square in section. Yadin suggested that it was a spear butt, permitting the spear to be thrust into the ground when at camp, an interpretation that illustrates the biblical passage from 2 Samuel 2:23: "When he refused to desist, Abner struck him in the belly with a backward thrust of his spear." This type of javelin appears to be a local innovation, as it is characteristic only of the weapon assemblages of the Land of Israel. The curl at the end of the javelin tangs testifies to the manner in which they were attached to the shaft. The shaft was split and the blade inserted in it. The lower end of the tang was then bent and curled round the shaft, after which the area of the join was bound with twine or with a thin copper coil (remains of such coils have been found on javelin heads from tombs at Moza and 'Ain Samiya).

Fig. 5.16. Copper daggers from 'Enan

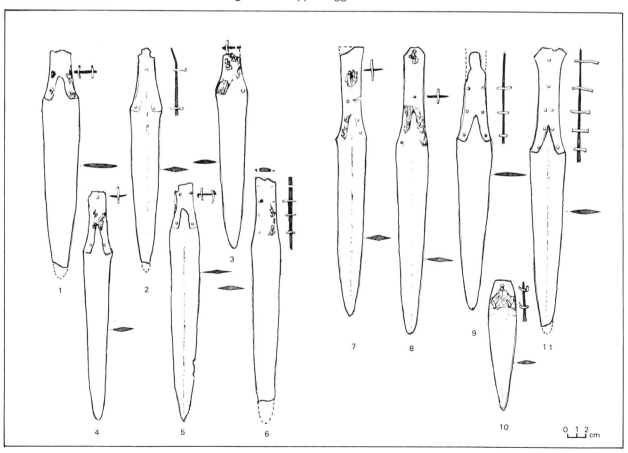

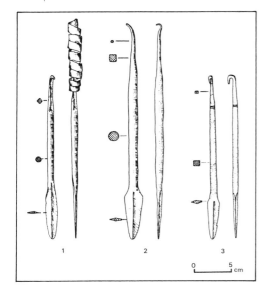

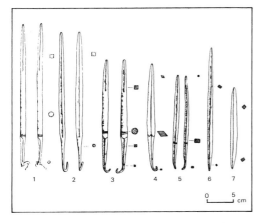

Fig. 5.17. Javelin heads (*top*) and butts (*bottom*) from 'Ain Samiya

In dolmens of the Golan, socketed javelin heads have been found, similar to those in the shaft tombs at Megiddo. This type was widespread in Syria in the late third millennium.

SPEARS. Spears were heavier and longer than javelins and were used mainly for jabbing. A type of spear discovered in tombs ('Enan, Ma'ayan Baruch) and habitation sites (Tel Yosef) of the north is of a variety found in large quantities in Byblos, among the foundation offerings of a temple. It resembles a dagger in shape, but the tang is different—long, narrow, and affixed to the shaft with two rivets. The weight of the spearheads found at 'Enan is double that of the daggers. The function of these artifacts may be deduced from their location in the tomb near 'Enan; although most of the daggers were placed by the waist of the adult male skeletons, the spears were placed in or near a niche broad enough to accommodate the long (unpreserved) shaft.

ARROWHEADS. Small, thin copper arrowheads have been discovered in tombs mainly of the north (Ma'ayan Baruch, the Golan dolmens, Tiberias, Menahemiya, and Megiddo). They are leaf-shaped, with a short, pointed, square-sectioned tang. They have no Early Bronze Age parallels.

BATTLE-AXES. Fenestrated axes have been found in the shaft tombs of Megiddo and Ma'abarot and in a cache from Jericho, along with typical Intermediate Bronze Age finds. In a tumulus in northern Transjordan (near Der'a), a somewhat different type of axehead, with a cylindrical socket, appears.

The fenestrated axes are socketed. They take their name from the apertures or windows in the blade. They were cast whole in closed molds and may be classed among

Fig. 5.18. Fenestrated axe from Ma'abarot (height 11.6 centimeters)

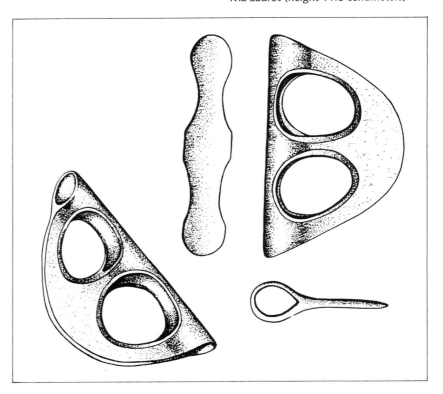

the most complex metal artifacts ever designed in the ancient Near East. Apparently the introduction of tin-bronze technology, with its improved properties for casting, promoted typological improvements such as those reflected in the fenestrated axe. The socketed axe eliminated the need to affix the blade to the haft by riveting and binding. The fenestrated axe appears to have been developed in the Levant, though its precise centers of production are difficult to determine (the Lebanese coast has been suggested).

The scant artifacts found in the Land of Israel may indicate that they arrived from the north by way of trade. At any rate, battle-axes of this type remained in use, judging by finds in Syria and Lebanon, into the early Middle Bronze Age (the twentieth century B.C.E.). A similar period of use is indicated by the wall paintings of Beni Hassan, Egypt, from the twentieth century, which portray two types of battle-axe, the

Fig. 5.19. Assemblage of weapons from tomb at Barqai: fenestrated axe, daggers, javelin spear heads and butts

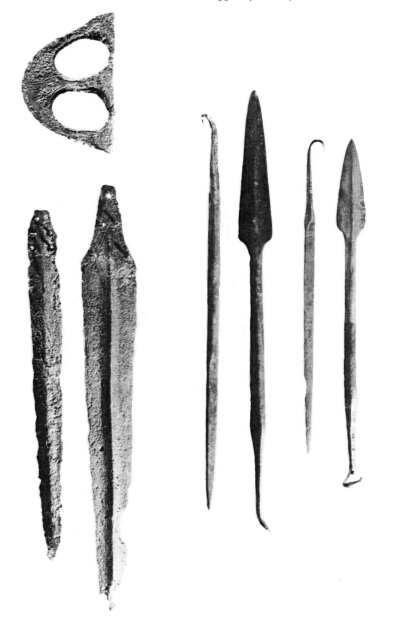

fenestrated axe and the duckbill axe. The latter soon became the dominant form.

SHIELDS. Indirect knowledge of the form of warriors' shields in the Intermediate Bronze Age is provided by a rock drawing found in a shaft tomb at Jericho. The shields portrayed are rectangular, similar to those characteristic of southwest Asia. A group of short copper nails (2.5–3.5 centimeters long) and cap-shaped objects found in tombs at Moza, Jericho, and Dhahr Mirzbaneh may have belonged to shields, which would have been made of hides nailed onto a wooden frame.

TOOLS

Metal tools of the Intermediate Bronze Age are for the most part typologically similar to those employed in the Chalcolithic and Early Bronze Ages. They include axes, adzes, and chisels. The number of artifacts of this type so far found in Intermediate Bronze Age contexts in Israel is still quite small. Most were discovered in hoards, with other metal implements. Eleven axes and adzes were found inside a jar at Jericho; four axes and adzes, as well as a few chisels, were found in a cache from the Hebron hills; and objects of this type are part of the cache exhibited in the Hecht Museum in Haifa. Adze marks left in the soft limestone walls of tombs at Jebel Qa'aqir and elsewhere reveal one of the uses of this tool in the Intermediate Bronze Age.

TOGGLE PINS, AWLS, AND COPPER ORNAMENTS

Pins are often found in tombs throughout the country. Most are simple short pins: unperforated, square-sectioned, and pointed at both ends. Such pins were used mainly to fasten clothing, but some were found set in bone handles and may well have served as awls. In the Galilee, northern Transjordan (Gilead), and the Golan there appear, alongside the simple pin, toggle pins of a different variety, common in Syria and Lebanon in contexts dated to the twenty-second and twenty-first centuries (Hama, Byblos, Ugarit, and elsewhere). Some have eyelets and knobbed or hemispherical heads. Especially long pins, 34–35 centimeters, have been found at Ma'ayan Baruch, as well as a curl-headed toggle pin also found in northern contexts.

ORNAMENTS. Copper ornaments—bracelets, earrings, and rings—have been found, for the most part in northern tombs.

Society and Economy

The study of the society and economy of the Intermediate Bronze Age has attempted to determine the relative roles of sedentism and mobility in the posturban society of the Land of Israel in the late third millennium B.C.E. and to define the position of this society within the social fabric of the Near East. In this context, the need to understand the interrelation between sedentary and semisedentary communities in Mediterranean as well as semiarid zones arises. Can the characteristics of these posturban communities be compared, for example, with the preurban communities of the Chalcolithic and Early Bronze I societies? For unlike the earlier periods, posturban settlement spread over almost every geographical zone (moist and arid) that had seen urban settlement in the Early Bronze Age.

The social and economic study of the period has, in recent years, availed itself of models borrowed from the social sciences. These are based on data obtained from ethnographic studies of seminomadic

pastoralists of recent or even of present times, in the Middle East and in other parts of the world, as well as on studies of ancient Near Eastern societies of the first half of the second millennium.

ECONOMIC BASE

The primary archaeological data for the study of the economic base of the Intermediate Bronze Age population include the faunal and floral remains, pounding and grinding stones, and flint tools unearthed in excavations. These may testify to the relative importance of crops, herds, and hunting in the economy of the period. Other finds, such as metal artifacts and jewelry, provide information about crafts and trade. The investigation of the settlement pattern and of burial customs may also aid in explaining the economic foundations of the posturban society.

DOMESTICATED PLANTS. Few remains of edible plants have so far been identified either in cemeteries or in habitation sites, and they provide only a hint of the types of cultivation practiced during this period. They include varieties of cereals and legumes already cultivated in the Early Bronze Age. At Jericho, grains of wheat and barley, peas, lentils, and chickpeas were found; Khirbet 'Ara'ir yielded charred grains of wheat, and Har Yeruham olive pits. Information regarding the cultivation of orchards is as yet insubstantial.

FAUNAL REMAINS. Bones of domesticated species and of hunted species have been found at fairly many sites of the Intermediate Bronze Age. There is a marked difference between the kinds of domesticated animals found in the Negev Highlands and those found in settlements of the moister regions: in the

desert zones, only sheep and goats have been found, but in the Jordan valley, Jericho, for example, has provided remains of sheep, goats, cattle, pigs, and gazelles, and Tell Iktanu has provided sheep, goats, small cattle, and gazelles. The site near Gal'ed provided sheep and goats, cattle, and pigs, and the site of 'Emeq Refaim remains of sheep, goats, and pigs. From the site of Nahal Alexander in the Sharon, pig, cattle, sheep, goat, gazelle, and antelope have been reported, and sheep and goats have also been reported at the Shephelah site of Jebel Qa'aqir. The faunal remains from Beer Resisim in the Negev Highlands consisted of 90 percent bones of small stock, mostly Negev black goat. Gazelle bones were found as well. Har Yeruham also had bones of sheep and goats.

The role of hunting in the economy is suggested by a hunting scene carved on the wall of a tomb cave at Jericho. Two hunters are depicted, bearing spears and shields, in the midst of a herd of ibex.

GRINDING AND POUNDING STONES. Grinding and pounding stones, usually interpreted as tools for the processing of crops, have been found at many sites of the Intermediate Bronze Age throughout the country. They are usually made of basalt and sometimes of limestone. Large numbers have been found at Sha'ar Ha-Golan, Tel Yosef, Nahal Alexander, Bab edh-Dhra, Tell Iktanu, and Khirbet 'Ara'ir.

FLINT TOOLS. Many flint tools have been discovered in habitation sites of the period. In technique and form, the flint industry of the Intermediate Bronze Age carries on the Early Bronze Age traditions. Assemblages of sites of the moist zones (Sha'ar Ha-Golan, Tel Yosef, Lachish, and Jebel Qa'aqir) are characterized by long blades, used as knives and sickle blades. In contrast, the flint industry of the Negev Highlands sites (such as at Har Yeruham) exhibits inferior workmanship, and long blades are rare.

TRADE. The importation of metal and pottery has been noted above. A magnificent silver cup from a tomb near 'Ain Samiya, which bears a relief containing mythological scenes, probably came to the Land of Israel via the international trade routes of northern Syria. Trade in Nubian sandstone, which came from the southern Negev or Sinai, is evidenced by whetstones found at the sites of Nahal Alexander and Har Yeruham. Shells from the Red Sea have been discovered in habitation sites and tombs.

SETTLEMENT PATTERNS AND BURIAL CUSTOMS AS A REFLECTION OF SOCIAL AND ECONOMIC CONDITIONS

The review of the Intermediate Bronze Age settlement pattern offered at the beginning of this chapter reveals certain features suggestive of an economy based on pastoralism and seasonal agriculture: extensive settlement in the relatively moist zones on the margins of the deserts and the Mediterranean forests of Samaria and Judaea, areas nearly devoid of settlement in the Early Bronze Age; cave habitation; the presence of what appear to be animal pens within habitation sites; the limited lifespan of most settlements (they were inhabited for only two or three generations, in contrast to the sites of the Early Bronze Age, which existed for hundreds of years). Against those indicators stand what appear to be sedentary village remains, with well-built broadhouses in the tradition of Early Bronze Age agriculturalists. They occupy sites of the moister parts of

the country (Sha'ar Ha-Golan, Tel Yosef, Beth Yerah) and the oases of the lower Jordan valley (such as Jericho and Tell Iktanu).

The burial customs of the Intermediate Bronze Age also illustrate both the sedentary and mobile facies of the period: primary burials alongside secondary burials, individual burials and family burials, cemeteries adjacent to habitation sites and far from habitation (especially megalithic burial fields). Ethnographic research has shown that sedentarists practice secondary burial and that nomads may also practice primary burial.

SOCIOECONOMIC STRUCTURE

The archaeological record has given rise to definitions and generalizations regarding the socioeconomic structure of the Intermediate Bronze Age population in the Land of Israel. Until the mid-sixties, before the recent intensification of research, contrasting definitions of the society and economy of the period were prevalent. Glueck saw the Transjordan sites as representing an advanced agricultural civilization. Kenyon considered the inhabitants of the country pastoral nomads. Kochavi, in the sixties, described the economy as nomadic, based on hunting, herding, and plundering.

The excavation of Intermediate Bronze Age sites in the Jordan valley (for example, Tell Iktanu), the Shephelah (Jebel Qa'aqir), and the Negev Highlands (Har Yeruham and Beer Resisim) on the one hand and the analysis of cemetery finds on the other have recently given archaeologists the tools to analyze and reconstruct the socioeconomic structure of the Intermediate Bronze Age population. However, even the increased use of anthropological and ethnographic research is insufficient to clarify such issues as the significance and validity of the term "pas-

toral nomadism." This term is employed by Dever and others to define the life-style prevalent in this period throughout the country, in both arid and humid regions. The interaction between the inhabitants of the wetter north and the drier south, in comparison with Early Bronze Age relations between the urban population of the north and the seminomadic population of the south, has yet to be sufficiently investigated. The results of the recent extensive studies of the Intermediate Bronze Age settlements of the Negev Highlands seem to have overshadowed the study of settlement in more northerly regions, possibly leading to an imbalanced view of the social structure and the interaction between the two areas. There may have been differences in social structure between the two regions, as was the case in the Early Bronze Age, although towns no longer existed.

Dever has excavated in two regions, at Jebel Qa'aqir in the furrow valley between the Shephelah and the Hebron hills and at Beer Resisim in the Negev Highlands. The results serve as the basis for his reconstruction of the social structure, economy, and life-style of part of the country's Intermediate Bronze Age population. Citing the beduin life-style of recent generations, Dever has reconstructed a society that spent the winter months in the Negev Highlands and in summer descended to the Judaean Shephelah. Dever concludes that the settlement excavated at Beer Resisim was a seasonal camp of an extended family or a small clan, with a mixed subsistence economy based mainly on sheep and goat herding and to some extent on hunting and gathering, primitive dry farming, and an irregular trade in Red Sea shells and Sinai copper. From the site organization and the function of the structures, Dever determines that there is

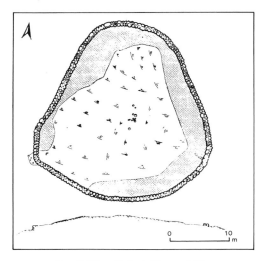

Fig. 5.20. Cult platform at Har Yeruham

no evidence for social stratification and that the social structure was egalitarian.

K. Prag, who dug at Tell Iktanu, confronts the data from the moister regions, giving greater emphasis to the sedentary agricultural elements in the economy and society of the Intermediate Bronze Age. She sees a mixed economy of small villages based on seasonal agriculture, some vegetable cultivation, orchard cultivation, grazing, and hunting and emphasizes the raising of cattle, noting that the society of this period contained a sedentary element, as well as groups who lived in both permanent and seasonal sites. In both site types there is clear evidence for seasonal agriculture; if there was any migratory activity, its range was limited.

Cults

Information on cult practices related to burial is provided by excavations in shaft tombs and megalithic tombs. Two open-air cult sites of the Intermediate Bronze Age have also been excavated. One was discovered in the fifties near Har Yeruham, in the Negev Highlands; the other was excavated in 1982 at Tel Ashir, in the Sharon. The Har Yeruham site lies on the ridgetop. It resembles a *bamah* (high place) and consists of an exposed rock platform 0.1 hectare in size, dotted with cupmarks and enclosed by a wall. The site at Tel Ashir lies on a hill overlooking the southern bank of Nahal Poleg, with a view of the Sharon plain as far as the Samaria and Carmel ranges. Excavations revealed about a dozen large kurkar stones. They are round, flat, and thick (0.5–1.6 meters in diameter) and surrounded by smaller stones. Ten such stones were found arrayed in a line. Alongside them were long flat stelae embedded in the ground, made of Samarian limestone. Both the kurkar

and limestone slabs were embedded in a thick layer of ash, containing pottery of the Intermediate Bronze Age, carnelian beads, and shell ornaments, as well as copper implements—a knife, dagger, awls, and pins.

Two animal figurines (one of clay, the other of stone) were found at Har Yeruham in the ash layer adjacent to the pottery kiln.

A unique female figurine, possibly a household cult object, was found at Jebel Qa'aqir. Dever sees a resemblance between this figurine and figurines found in this period at sites of the Middle Euphrates region.

The silver cup from 'Ain Samiya is decorated with a relief containing mythological scenes. There is little agreement over the geographical and cultural origins of these compositions, nor has it been decided to what extent, if at all, the scenes reflect the beliefs and cult of the inhabitants of the Land of Israel or of Syria-Lebanon during the period in question. Yadin and others interpret the scenes as representations of the Babylonian creation myth, the Enuma Elish; M. H. Carre-Gates suggested that the cultural milieu should be sought not in Mesopotamia but in the realm of Hurrian iconography. According to this view, the provenance of the cup, which must have been imported, lies not in Mesopotamia but in the broad expanse between the northern Caucasus and central Asia, hinting at the penetration of northern populations into the Land of Israel in the late third millennium. T. Jacobsen, however, postulates a coastal Syrian source for the Marduk and Tiamat (thunder god and sea goddess) battle motif; he suggests it was introduced into Mesopotamia by western Semites. Jacobsen's suggestion may be used to support the view that the source of the 'Ain Samiya cup was in fact Syria. A further possibility is that the mythological scene on the cup is but a Syrian rendering of a Babylonian-Mesopotamian motif.

Population

A few attempts have been made to estimate the size of the population inhabiting certain sites or regions of the Land of Israel during the Intermediate Bronze Age. T. Shai has estimated the number of inhabitants at the desert oasis of Jericho—using variables based on cemetery finds, such as the short life expectancy of the inhabitants, the length of time that the cemetery was in use, and the degree of sedentarism evidenced in the occupation—at 70–120 persons. Kenyon, who excavated the site, rejected any attempt to estimate the population of Jericho during this period, for she believed that the cemetery was used by seminomads

who transported their dead from their area of migration to their winter camp for burial.

The exposure of an entire settlement at Beer Resisim allowed Dever to attempt to estimate the size of that community using the family-coefficient method, based on traditional nonurban societies of the present. He postulated that there were five inhabitants in each roofed dwelling unit and concluded that the average population of Beer Resisim, one of the largest Negev Highland sites of the period, was no greater than ninety persons.

In another study, R. Gophna and Y. Portugali estimate the Chalcolithic and Bronze Age populations of the coastal plain south of the Carmel. This region falls within the Mediterranean zone and occupies about one quarter of the Land of Israel. They based their calculation

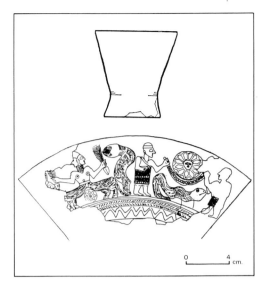

Fig. 5.22. 'Ain Samiya goblet: outline and drawing

Fig. 5.21. 'Ain Samiya goblet (height 8.2 centimeters)

of the Intermediate Bronze Age population on a flexible coefficient of 120–150 persons per settled hectare, in accordance with the relative size of the settlement. Their result, about 2000 persons, is based on incomplete evidence and should be seen as a tentative estimate.

These estimates show that the posturban population fell far short of the Early Bronze Age II–III population. It was supposedly 10,000–15,000 persons, or a mere 10 percent of the Early Bronze II–III population. The inhabitants congregated in small to minute communities scattered throughout the countryside, and not in large population centers. Apart from the arid and semiarid regions, the settlement remains had little impact on the archaeological landscape.

ORIGIN AND IDENTIFICATION

All the suggestions regarding the origin and ethnic identification of the people of the Land of Israel during the Intermediate Bronze Age have confronted the archaeological record of the Near East and tried to relate the archaeological finds to Akkadian historical documents from Mesopotamia. Was there a massive migration of people from the north in this period, or were most of the inhabitants descendants of the Early Bronze Age people? If there was a migration, where did the newcomers originate, in Syria or in more distant parts? Did the old and new inhabitants belong to Semitic or other ethnic groups? To what degree does the archaeological record reflect the relative size of the incoming population versus the remnants of the indigenous population remaining after the dissolution of the urban society? Perhaps the singular material culture of the Intermediate Bronze Age in the Land of Israel should be seen as the result merely of foreign influences, originating in the Syrian trade

routes, rather than of large-scale population movements.

A view adopted by many scholars (Wright, Kenyon, and Vaux) was that the Intermediate Bronze Age was marked by large-scale incursions of nomadic tribes to be identified with the Amorites, the west Semitic tribes mentioned in Akkadian texts. According to these texts, the Amorites first appeared on the Near Eastern stage in the mid third millennium B.C.E., and some assign them a major role in the disintegration of urban culture in Syria, the Land of Israel, and Egypt. Kenyon held the Amorite invaders responsible for the utter destruction of the urban culture of the Early Bronze

Age and attributed to them the tribal organization, pottery, and new burial customs of the Intermediate Bronze Age.

A different and far-reaching proposal, put forth by Lapp and Kochavi in the sixties, placed the origin of the invaders in the Trans-Caucasian cultures of central Asia. Kochavi saw this invasion as the first wave of a great population movement of Indo-European tribes, the nomads of the Eurasian steppes—an invasion that brought on, directly or indirectly, the decline of Egypt and the destruction of Mesopotamian and Anatolian cultures. This bold hypothesis was based on a similarity between the culture of the Indo-

Map 5.3. Key Intermediate Bronze Age sites in the Land of Israel, Syria, and northern Mesopotamia

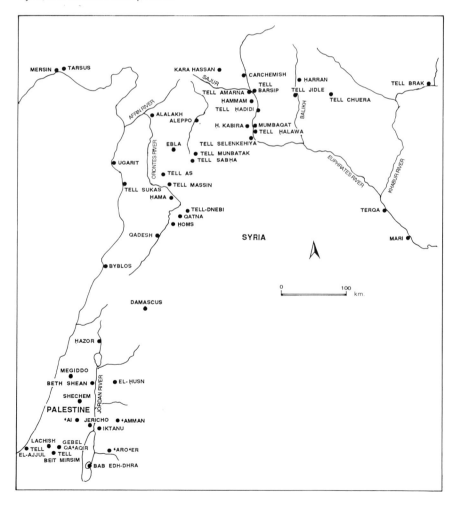

European nomads and the nomadic culture of the Intermediate Bronze Age in the Land of Israel, a similarity that extends even to such details as shaft and tumulus tombs and advanced metallurgy. The theories of Lapp and Kochavi did not gain many adherents, and most scholars continued to search for the origins of Intermediate Bronze Age culture in Syria and Mesopotamia. Thus, for example, Amiran had previously suggested the Orontes valley as the area of origin, in view of the resemblance of ceramic elements in the Land of Israel to the ceramic tradition of the same period in northern Syria. Oren sought the origins of the culture in the Syro-Lebanese coast.

Excavations in the important mounds of central Syria (Hama) and northern Syria (Tell Mardikh), as well as at mounds on the Middle Euphrates, made it more and more apparent that in stark contrast to the Land of Israel, urban culture continued to flourish in broad areas of Syria. Thus, outstanding improvements were made in the manufacture of pottery in Syria, expressed in the standardization and industrial production of many pottery types that achieved wide distribution. However, in contrast to the situation in inner Syria, important urban centers of the Syro-Lebanese coast such as Ras Shamra (Ugarit) and Byblos were utterly destroyed, as were all the Early Bronze Age towns of the Land of Israel. Apparently, the Land of Israel as a whole became the most backward part of the Levant, a land inhabited only by poor settlements of farmers and herders. In this manner, the increasingly detailed picture of the settlement pattern in different parts of greater Syria permits the reassessment, within a broad perspective, of the question of the origin and ethnic identification of the population of the Land of Israel during the Inter-mediate Bronze Age. The place of the Land of Israel within the broad pattern of settlement in the Levant and northwest Mesopotamia may now be established, and the interrelations between the people of the urban and nonurban zones may be investigated.

Dever has vacillated among various solutions to these questions; his pronouncements therefore suffer from internal contradictions, and his definitions and historic scenarios remain ambiguous. While he does reject the theories of large-scale invasions of the Land of Israel, stating that the culture was of a local rather than an intrusive character, he nevertheless admits that the new elements appearing in the pottery and metallurgy, as well as the new tomb types, were introduced by semi-nomads of Syrian origin. He suggests that they were people who escaped from the Early Bronze Age urban centers when they collapsed, and that a hybrid culture came into existence, first in Transjordan, then in the Land of Israel. He also notes that southbound population movements had always existed between the fertile and steppe regions and that they need not be seen as incursions of foreign elements.

A straightforward approach was adopted by his student S. Richard, who states that the ceramic continuity over the last centuries of the third millennium B.C.E. indicates an internal development, or degeneration, within the confines of the Land of Israel and that there is no basis for assuming that an invasion, migration, or movement of population took place. In her opinion, the new elements present in the ceramic assemblage may be explained merely as external influences. A similar approach is taken by S. Mazzoni, who studied the late third millennium pottery found at Ebla, in northern Syria. She views the Syrian features found in Intermediate Bronze Age pottery of the Land of Israel (for example, caliciform vessels and teapots) as results of the diffusion of advanced techniques from Syria by way of trade. She sees the southern Orontes valley as the source of direct or indirect cultural and technological influences (cf. the opinion of R. Amiran, above).

A cautious approach, which runs along similar lines to that of Dever, is adopted by Prag. She suggests that mobile pastoralists and agriculturalists indeed penetrated from Syria, but as long as no documents from the period are forthcoming, it cannot be stated whether they were Amorites. The new groups, she suggests, did not wipe out the previous population but rather were assimilated into it, while contributing to the dissolution of urban life and the reversion to a nomadic life-style. Also, they did not introduce an entirely new ceramic tradition; rather, they made marked innovations in the previous techniques and introduced new burial customs.

Anthropological examination of skeletal remains from Jebel Qa'aqir, Gibeon, and Efrat has revealed that as far as physical and biological traits are concerned, the Intermediate Bronze Age population of the Land of Israel resembled that of the Chalcolithic and Early Bronze Ages. This population, termed by anthropologists "gracile Mediterranean," characterized the entire Syro-Mesopotamian expanse.

Judging from the discoveries made at Ebla, at least part of the people of Syria and the Land of Israel spoke a Semitic language resembling that of the Early Bronze Age people. (The tablets found in the royal archives of Ebla reveal that the Early Bronze Age inhabitants of northern Syria spoke a Semitic language whose precise place within the family of Semitic tongues of the third millennium B.C.E. has yet to be established.) It is therefore likely that the population of the Land of Israel in the Intermediate Bronze Age was an integral part of the nonurban Semitic population residing in parts of Syria, in the shadow of those regions where urban life—and even city-states such as Ebla—continued to exist.

The new elements in the late third millennium population, probably of Syrian origin, were responsible for the refashioning of the material culture of the land, which came into its own as the culture here termed the Intermediate Bronze Age culture.

6

The Middle Bronze Age

AHARON KEMPINSKI

Although the tendency of recent years has been to regard the Middle Bronze Age II as a period of uninterrupted development, in which the material finds, including pottery, undergo slow typological change, that inclination has not reached the stage where a consensus regarding a new terminological and chronological scheme may be formed. The present discussion will retain the traditional scheme, which divides the period into two phases, labeled IIa and IIb. (A third phase IIc—adopted by some American archaeologists, especially those who participated in the renewed excavations at Shechem—will be incorporated within the Middle Bronze IIb, as it does not possess, in my opinion, sufficient characteristic features to merit a separate designation.)

The reconsolidation of Canaanite urban civilization at the beginning of the second millennium B.C.E. ushers in an era for which many historical documents are available from the two main sources of written documentation in the Near East, Egypt in the south and Syro-Mesopotamia in the north. These historical documents and references allow us, for the first time, to relate the Land of Israel to the historical framework of the neighboring lands and to establish a more reliable sequence of events, which can be related to the material finds. Thus, reference to an identifiable site in one of the sources invites the archaeologist to identify the stratum and finds of that town and to correlate them chronologically with the written documents. Written material, both Akkadian and Egyptian, from the sites themselves, though rare, makes its first appearance in this period and contributes much to the dating of strata and finds. We are, therefore, with the onset of the Middle Bronze Age, firmly in the realm of historical archaeology, and the principal means for dating the strata and finds are the chronological and historical data from the neighboring literate civilizations.

At the start of the twentieth century (1991 B.C.E., according to Egyptian chronology), the Twelfth Dynasty was established in Egypt. This dynasty reunited the land of the Nile and extended the frontiers of Egypt's political influence toward Canaan, the Lebanese coast, and Syria.

The earliest written documents of this era are the so-called Execration Texts. To enhance their control over the local rulers in Canaan, Syria, and Nubia, the kings of the

Fig. 6.1. Canaanites in Egypt, tomb painting from Beni Hassan, Egypt, nineteenth century B.C.E.

Fig. 6.2. Group of scarab seals from Tell el-Ajjul and Lachish

Twelfth and Thirteenth Dynasties resorted to magical texts. The earliest Execration Texts are incantation bowls inscribed with the names of the settlements and their rulers. This group of texts (the Berlin group), published by K. Sethe and dated to the beginning of the Twelfth Dynasty, refers to the towns of Ashkelon, Rehov (in the Accho valley), Beth Shean, and Jerusalem, the only site of the Canaanite interior. Byblos, Ullaza, and 'Arqatum, all on the Lebanese coast, are also mentioned, as well as a number of unidentified sites. The sites mentioned in the texts are often attributed three or even four rulers, indicating that a tribal system still prevailed there.

A fascinating document, revealing much of the life of the inhabitants of northern Canaan (called in Egyptian Retenu), is the biography of Sinuhe. It describes events in the mid twentieth century B.C.E., during the population's transition from seminomadic to sedentary life. Alongside this population (the Aamu) lives a still fully nomadic population, the Setjet. Inscriptions preserved on Middle Kingdom stelae tell of military campaigns to Canaan. The best known is that of Khu-Sobk, who commanded the Egyptian army under Senusret III (in the mid nineteenth century). This stela reports the siege of Shechem. When Shechem fell, we are told, all of "wretched Retenu" fell with it, indicating that Shechem was the chief town of the region. This is the only written record of the siege and capture of a town in Canaan by Egyptians in Middle Kingdom times.

A further important find from the days of Senusret III comes from Megiddo: a statue of Thut-Hotep, a senior Egyptian official who served at Megiddo. Though the statue was found out of context, in a later stratum, it should probably be attributed to stratum XII or XIII at the site. The appointment of this official at Megiddo seems to indicate that during the rule of Senusret III, a first attempt was made to incorporate Canaan into the Egyptian empire. Scholarly opinion, however, is divided over the precise character of the relations between Egypt and Canaan at this time. Some go so far as to assert that Egypt actually ruled over the region, while others describe the relations merely as trade contacts.

To the reign of Senusret III, and to the same attempt to incorporate Canaan within the framework of his extended kingdom, we may ascribe a second group of Execration Texts, the Brussels group, published by G. Posener. This group contains many place-names from all over the Land of Israel and Transjordan. Each site has one ruler, instead of several. Some of the major sites are Hormah and Ashkelon in the south; Jerusalem, Shechem, Aphek, and Lod in the central region; Megiddo (as read by Goerg), Beth Shean, and Shumunu in the valley region; Akhshaph, Mash'al, Rehov, and Accho in the Accho valley; Beth Shemesh, Hazor, Kedesh, Laish (Dan), and Abel in the Galilee. The mention of these sites in a list dated to the mid nineteenth century permits the dating of specific strata in each site. Further

Table 6.1 Middle Bronze Age IIa Chronology.

Date	Pottery	Other indicators
2200 BCE	Late EBIII pottery Late IB pottery	
2000/1950	Early MBIIa pottery	Beginning of the Twelfth Dynasty
1900/1850	Middle MBIIa pottery	
	Late MBIIa pottery	Byblos royal tombs; Amenemhet III, IV
1800/1750	Transition to MBIIb	Jericho tombs, phase ii

material evidence for the hegemony or influence of the Egyptians in Canaan has been discovered.

Wall paintings from Middle Kingdom tombs in Egypt form another important source of information. The well-known paintings from Beni Hassan, in upper Egypt, portray a caravan of Semites, apparently from northern Transjordan, led by their chief Abishar to Egypt. Their dress and accoutrements reveal many details of Canaanite life in the nineteenth century. Of particular interest are the weapons carried by the men. Their tools, primarily the duckbill axes, show that these were people of the Middle Bronze Age IIa. The title of the chief, *heka khaswt* (Ruler of a Foreign Land), is also most important: in the second part of the Middle Bronze Age II, rulers bearing this title dominate Egypt and establish a Semitic-Canaanite dynasty.

Toward the end of the first phase of the Middle Bronze IIa, the Thirteenth Dynasty replaced the Twelfth. Concurrently, Egyptian historical references to Canaan diminish; only at Byblos on the Lebanese coast have inscriptions of Thirteenth Dynasty kings been discovered. Most important among them is Nefer-hotep I (ca. 1760 B.C.E.), who is portrayed in relief facing Prince Yantin (Amu?) of Byblos; this find may imply Neferhotep's control at least of coastal Canaan and Lebanon. But the principal evidence for Egyptian contacts comes from small finds, especially the scarab seals, which become increasingly abundant in the assemblages of the Land of Israel. The scarab is an oval seal in the form of the dung beetle, which was sacred to the Egyptians. Carved on the flat underside of the seal—usually made of stone or faience—are hieroglyphs and various designs, often including the name of a king or an official. A number of scarabs bear the names of Thirteenth Dynasty kings and are of the greatest importance in dating the various assemblages.

At about this time, the first half of the eighteenth century, Canaan first came within the sphere of influence of the Amorite kingdoms of north Syria and northern Mesopotamia. These kingdoms used clay tablets inscribed in the Akkadian cuneiform script for their correspondence. A large archive of this period was discovered at Tell el-Hariri, the ancient city of Mari, on the Middle Euphrates, particularly important for its mentions of towns of northern Canaan (Laish-Dan and Hazor have been identified). A number of letters mention the names of the rulers of these towns. The Mari evidence shows that toward mid-century, with the decline of Egyptian influence in Canaan, the powerful Amorite kingdoms of northern Syria began to exert influence, particularly in the regions lying north of the valley of Jezreel. This change finds expression in the material culture as well, placing the transition from the Middle Bronze Age IIa to the Middle Bronze Age IIb around the year 1750.

Pottery Typology of the Middle Bronze Age IIa

The pottery of the Middle Bronze Age II undergoes slight, slow changes, and its forms and development can be studied with relative ease. We will first review the characteristic types of the Middle Bronze IIa and their typological development.

BOWLS, KRATERS, MUGS, AND GOBLETS

To the earliest group belong the rounded, combed-faced bowls, in the Byblite tradition (Fig. 6.3:1).

The carinated bowl with a disk base (Fig. 6.3:2) also originated in the same part of the Lebanese littoral. During the Middle Bronze IIa it develops into the later form, with a concave disk base. The earlier form is red slipped (including the base) and well burnished, whereas the later type is usually not slipped and is burnished either partially or not at all (Fig. 6.3:3). Amiran has pointed out the origins of this vessel in the Byblos assemblage, illustrating its metallic prototype (a silver bowl, in this case).

The platter bowl in Fig. 6.3:4 is clearly in the tradition of the Early Bronze Age platters. In early assemblages at Byblos it still bears the pattern burnish so typical of the early prototype (Fig. 6.3:5). The later type is deeper, without pattern burnish, and sometimes has a disk base.

Another type of open bowl, often found among burial offerings, is marked by the elongated bar handles along the rim (Fig. 6.3:6). These bowls were made in imitation of wooden vessels, such as those

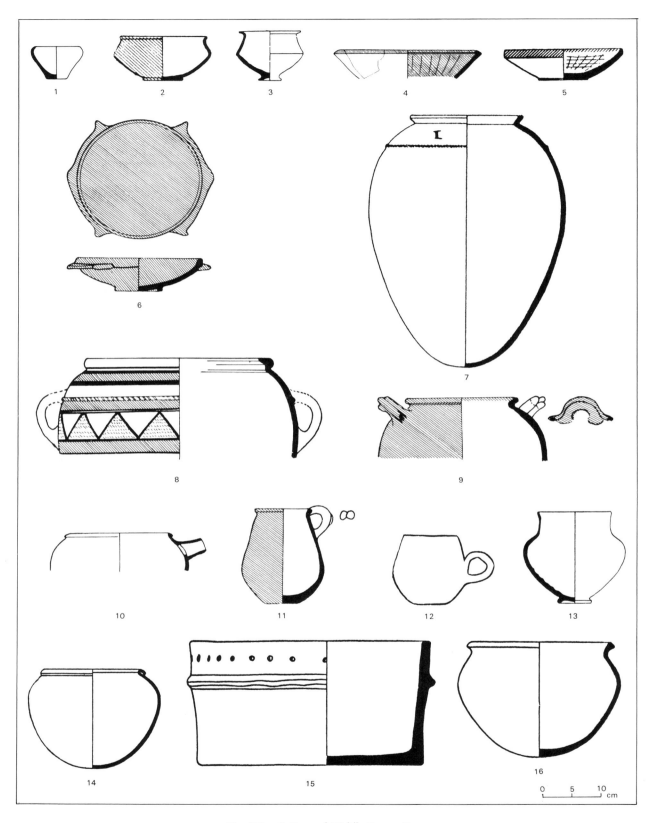

Fig. 6.3.   Pottery of Middle Bronze IIa

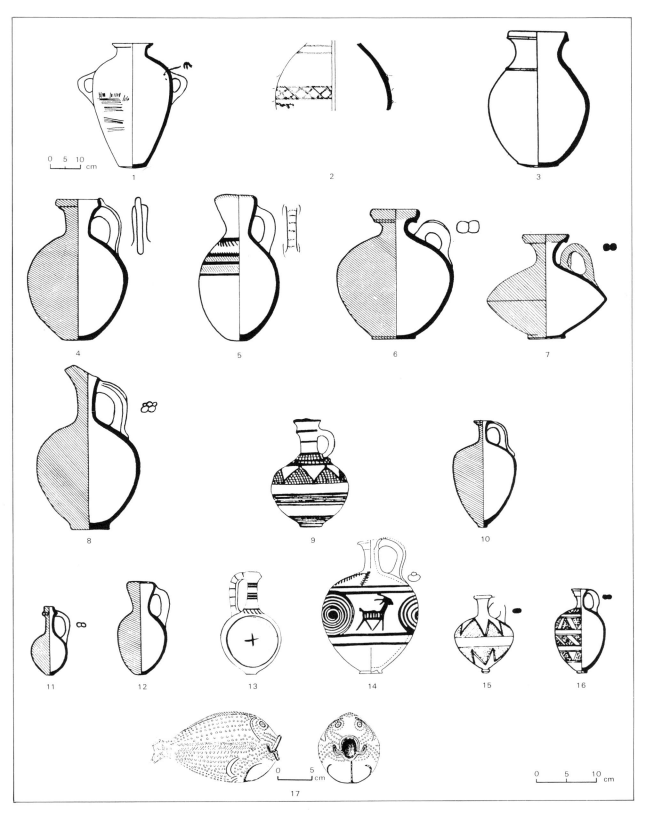

Fig. 6.4. Pottery of Middle Bronze IIa

unearthed by Kenyon in the Jericho tombs.

The kraters (large deep bowls, sometimes equipped with handles) of the Middle Bronze IIa are of a singular shape, which was generally not carried over into the second phase of the period. The form and decoration of the holemouth krater found at Aphek (Fig. 6.3:7) are reminiscent of Intermediate Bronze Age tradition. This may be seen as proof of the assimilation of the early population into the incoming groups. Fig. 6.3:8 shows a krater type that continues to appear in Middle Bronze IIb, whereas Fig. 6.3:9, with horizontal handles no doubt influenced by north Syrian or even Anatolian forms, illustrates a type that does not outlive the Middle Bronze IIa. The spouted krater (Fig. 6.3:10) appears to be related to the teapot of the Intermediate Bronze Age.

Two traditions may be discerned among the mugs and goblets: the Byblite Intermediate Bronze tradition, exhibited in Fig. 6.3:11 and 12, and a second tradition, rooted in central and northern Syria of the late third millennium B.C.E.. This tradition is reflected in the handleless goblet (Fig. 6.3:13), particularly common at Jericho from this phase on, which may be related to identical forms from northern and central Syria. The type is a latecomer to the local pottery repertoire, and there is clear evidence for its attribution to the final phase of the Middle Bronze IIa.

This group of pottery contains, alongside some new pottery types, forms that appear to be the offspring of Early Bronze III types, seeming to bridge the gap between the Early Bronze III and the Middle Bronze IIa. They, in turn, coexist with vessels that appear to preserve Intermediate Bronze Age traditions.

COOKING POTS

Three main types of cooking pots may be observed in this period, two of which have their origin in earlier assemblages: The holemouth cooking pot preserves the traditions of the Early Bronze Age III and of the Intermediate Bronze Age as well (Fig. 6.3:14). The straight-walled cooking pot with the thumb-impressed decoration and perforations beneath the rim originates, as shown by Amiran, in the Intermediate Bronze Age (Fig. 6.3:15). A form that later develops into the characteristic cooking pot of the Middle Bronze IIb has an everted and sometimes concave or channeled rim (Fig. 6.3:16).

JARS

This vessel too can be traced back to the two regions considered as the ceramic, and to some extent cultural, source of the period.

The local jar (referring to Canaan and the Lebanese coast) represents the direct continuation of the Early Bronze IIIb jars. Fig. 6.4:1 is but a reincarnation of the combed metallic store jar of the later part of the Early Bronze Age. The workshops that produced this vessel, apparently located along the northern coast (the Accho valley and Lebanese coast), continued its production without interruption during the Intermediate Bronze and Middle Bronze IIa periods. The small jar (up to 45 centimeters in height) with prominent loop handles, shown in Fig. 6.4:2, which often bears painted decoration (parallel or, rarely, crossed lines, or crosshatched triangles on the shoulder), is common at Byblos, and it seems that its origin, like that of the carinated bowl, is to be sought on the Lebanese coast.

The foreign jar (Fig. 6.4:3) is a handleless jar in the ceramic tradition of northern Syria. It is often decorated with concentric circles or broad horizontal bands.

The presence of the two jar types demonstrates in a most convincing fashion the origins of the Middle Bronze IIa ceramic tradition. One source is the coast of Lebanon and perhaps of northern Israel (the Accho valley); the other is central and northern Syria. These two ceramic traditions, which appear together from the start of the period, apparently reflect the migration of populations from the two regions to the Land of Israel.

JUGS AND JUGLETS

The jugs bear a number of characteristic features of the period, the most important of which is the dense, continuous burnish applied to a dark red slip. The style of burnish and the color of slip link wide areas of the ancient Near East, whereas the technique with which they are applied indicates ceramic traditions borrowed from Anatolia and the Cilician coast. The surface finish was intended to give the pots the appearance of copper vessels. It may be assumed that alongside the ceramic jugs there was a significant distribution of copper jugs imported from Anatolia, where the copper industry flourished.

Two main groups of jugs characterize the period. The origin of the earlier group lies in forms common in the Land of Israel and the Lebanese coast at the end of the Early Bronze Age. Fig. 6.4:4 should be seen as the successor of the polished jug common at the end of the Early Bronze Age. At the beginning of the Middle Bronze IIa, with no clear sequence of development, the jug appears in the form here illustrated: somewhat squat, with a triple handle particularly characteristic of the Middle Bronze IIa. Fig. 6.4:5 also has its antecedents in a Byblite vessel of the Early Bronze Age IIIb.

Fig. 6.4:6 represents an entirely new phenomenon, which, to judge by Syrian parallels from the environs of Aleppo, shows the influence of this region on the local potter. The jug in Fig. 6.4:7 exhibits Anatolian influence, notably the sharp carination. This vessel is closely related to the Hittite jugs of the Assyrian colony period in Anatolia, as is Fig. 6.4:8, which shows Anatolian inspiration not only in its form but also in its cut-away neck. Jug 9, also of northern Syrian origin, is occasionally, and mistakenly, termed Habur ware. It appears rarely in some Middle Bronze IIa contexts. Similar vessels have been found in recent years at sites on the Lebanese coast and in central Syria.

The pyriform juglet (Fig. 6.4:10) also has strong links to Early Bronze III traditions, while the dipper juglet in Fig. 6.4:11, the prototype of all dipper juglets of the Middle Bronze II, originates in the Byblite group already mentioned in relation to the jugs (Fig. 6.4:5). This vessel, as well as Fig. 6.4:12, has a flat base. All the juglets mentioned thus far bear a dark red burnished slip.

The decorated juglets of the period did not originate locally; their source, as shown by C. Epstein, lies in the middle Orontes valley. Juglets 13 and 14 are characterized by a decoration of concentric circles on a white or cream ground, with 14 bearing an added animal motif. These types appear toward the later part of the Middle Bronze IIa, as do juglets of the Tell el-Yahudiyeh type (named after the Egyptian delta site where they were first identified). Tell el-Yahudiyeh juglets usually take the form of the standard juglet (Fig. 6.4:15 and 16). They are made of black clay and bear a geometric decoration formed by rubbing lime or white pigment into incisions on the surface of the vessel. A special variant of this type, usually dated to the Middle Bronze IIa, is the zoomorphic vessel, exemplified by the fish-shaped vessel from Tel Poleg (Fig. 6.4:17). Tell el-Yahudiyeh ware was to remain in use during the Middle Bronze IIb but underwent typological changes both in form and decoration. The decorations lose their complexity and become simple bands running the length of the vessel.

Three sources of inspiration for the potters of the Middle Bronze IIa may thus be discerned. First is the Byblite source, which developed along the Lebanese coast. At Byblos, ceramic tradition developed

Fig. 6.5. Fish-shaped vessel in the Tell el-Yahudiyeh style (length 19 centimeters)

directly from the Early Bronze Age III to the Middle Bronze Age IIa, bypassing completely the ceramic traditions of the Intermediate Bronze Age culture of inner Syria, Transjordan, and the Land of Israel. The second source is a local one, from within the Land of Israel, consisting of a limited continuation of the Intermediate Bronze tradition. Vessels of this type are rare and appear chiefly in village assemblages. They are represented mainly by the straight-walled cooking pot. The third source is related to the migratory movement from north Syria and the Orontes, and it is reflected in the importation of ceramic traditions of northern Syria and even southern Anatolia.

THE ASSEMBLAGE AND THE FOSSILE DIRECTEUR

When attempting to date archaeological strata with the aid of pottery, two important factors should be taken into account. The first is the assemblage, that is, a group containing several types of vessels—bowls, kraters, jugs, juglets, jars, cooking pots, and so on—that may be dated to the same time span. When there is doubt, particularly in cases of transition from one period to the next, we may consider only those vessels within the assemblage that are typologically characteristic of a given phase and that disappear or change in the next. Such vessels are called guide fossils (from the French *fossile directeur*) or diagnostic forms. Among the diagnostic forms are channeled-rim burnished carinated bowls, the open pattern-burnished bowls, and the holemouth kraters, all diagnostic for the early part of the Middle Bronze IIa. Jars indicative of the early phase include the jar with an applied rope decoration at the base of the neck and the pattern-burnished or wheel-burnished jar; among the jugs and

juglets there are those vessels closest to the Byblite type. Diagnostic forms for the later part of the Middle Bronze IIa are the unslipped and burnished carinated bowls, the thickened rim bowls, cooking pots with a fashioned or concave rim, Anatolian-type jugs, and light-faced decorated juglets (the Ginnosar assemblage).

The Settlement Pattern in the Middle Bronze Age IIa

Until the early sixties, most archaeologists agreed that because the Middle Bronze IIa was poorly represented at the large mounds, and at small sites and single-period sites its remains generally consisted of one occupation layer lacking significant architectural remains or fortification, the period must have been short-lived. But research conducted during the sixties and seventies by scholars such as Mazar and Gophna led to a revised view of the period. According to the revision, an early phase of the period was indeed marked by the appearance of small unfortified sites, but in the second and third phases, some of the sites became fortified city-states. These were bounded by rural settlement, which depended on the large towns for their political and economic welfare. Gophna counted, within his survey area, seven such city-state units. The phases of development posited by Gophna were given substance by the excavations at Aphek. Thanks to those excavations, a stratigraphic-chronological sequence can be created for central Canaan.

Four stratigraphic phases were uncovered at various sites on the mound at Aphek and may be summed up as follows: (A) The earliest phase, termed the pre-Palace phase by the excavators, marks the first unfortified settlement at the site. (B) The first fortification wall was built, with adjoining houses.

(C) The second fortification as well as the western palace was constructed. (D) The western palace was destroyed; pottery types of this phase show some characteristics of the Middle Bronze IIb.

A similar stratigraphic sequence can be seen at Megiddo. Stratum XIIIB marks the first wave of settlement, which remained unfortified. In the next stratum, XIIIA, the previous construction is continued and improved, and the city wall is erected. In the following stratum, XII, the city wall is broadened and the town becomes a planned, organized site. The end of this stratum marks the transition to the Middle Bronze IIb.

A similar picture may be obtained from the Accho valley, where two major mounds have been excavated so far. Settlement at Tel Kabri and Tel Accho appears to begin at the very start of the Middle Bronze IIa. With the arrival of newcomers from the Lebanese coast, the two sites grew in size, and the establishment of fortifications at Accho may date to this period.

It thus appears that the first stage of settlement in the Middle Bronze Age IIa occurred, first and foremost, along the coast and in the adjacent valleys. This settlement pattern corresponds well to the early Execration Texts, which mention chiefly coastal sites. Settlement expanded toward the interior later on, near the end of the nineteenth century B.C.E. Evidence of late Middle Bronze IIa settlement may be seen at mounds in the hilly interior of the Land of Israel—Shechem, Tell el-Far'ah North, Laish-Dan, and Hazor. The spread of settlement throughout the entire country, however, took place only in the Middle Bronze Age IIb.

The marked cultural discontinuity between the Intermediate Bronze Age and the Middle Bronze Age IIa confirms their designation as two entirely separate periods. In the realms of material culture, settlement pattern, and religious and spiritual life, the differences are great. The population of the Intermediate Bronze was seminomadic, originating in the periphery of the urban culture of the Early Bronze Age, whereas the Middle Bronze IIa population originated from within the sphere of the urban culture and the related village culture of the central and northern Lebanese coast and the Orontes valley of central Syria. Kenyon proposed that the Middle Bronze IIa (MB I in her terminology) emerged from the Intermediate Bronze Age culture of Byblos.

Map 6.1. Middle Bronze Age II sites in Canaan

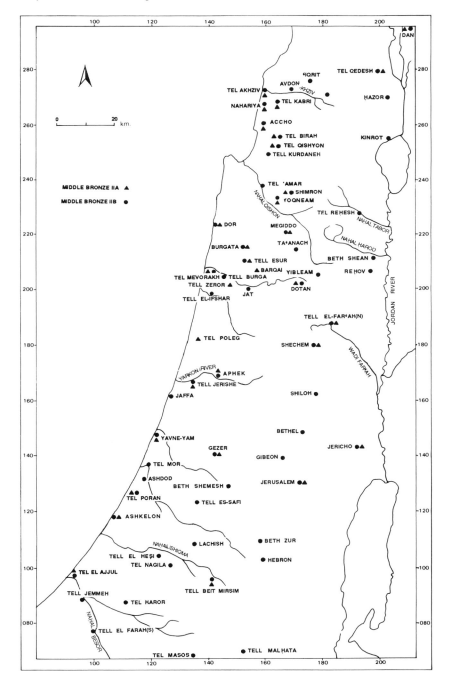

Though that observation must be broadened to include the entire Lebanese coast and perhaps the Accho valley as well, her initial intuition seems to have been correct. Dever was among those who proved the existence of a population group with contacts in the Orontes region, rather than the Habur as others had posited. These contacts indicate that in the early part of the period, migrant populations were largely responsible for the emergence of a new cultural assemblage in the Land of Israel and for the form it took. What then happened to the seminomadic Intermediate Bronze Age population? I believe that it was to some extent absorbed, particularly in the new rural population. Evidence is provided by a number of pottery types, particularly in village wares, that remained in use in the Middle Bronze IIa and by a few architectural residues. The rest of the population was again driven to the periphery, where it formed the nucleus of the nomadic groups of the Middle Bronze Age IIb and of the Late Bronze Age.

CHRONOLOGY

Middle Bronze IIa chronology is established through the analysis of the pottery of the period (Table 6.1). The introduction of the earliest assemblage is determined by the final date of the latest pottery of the preceding Intermediate Bronze period, with a degree of overlap between the two. In terms of absolute chronology, this early phase may be attributed to the beginning of the Twelfth Dynasty, that is, the beginning of the twentieth century B.C.E.

The date of the later phase of the Middle Bronze IIa is determined by two factors: first, the presence of characteristic pottery types found in the royal tombs of Byblos, which are dated by Egyptian finds to the days of Amenemhet III and IV (the late nineteenth and early eighteenth centuries; second, the discovery of pottery typical of Middle Bronze IIa–b transition alongside cylinder seals attributed to the days of Hammurabi (1792–1750 B.C.E.) in phase ii tombs at Jericho.

Sites

MEGIDDO. Megiddo stands out as one of the early sites most characteristic of the coastal plain and the valleys. This mound, which lies in the western part of the valley, near the mouth of Nahal 'Iron (Wadi 'Ara), enjoyed important topographic advantages. It was well defended, thanks to the massive Early Bronze Age fortification that added considerable height to the natural hilltop where the site was first established; two springs lay nearby; and an important international route connecting Egypt, Syria, and the Lebanese coast passed by the foot of the mound. Such were these advantages that as early as the latter part of the Intermediate Bronze Age, settlers from the coastal area arrived at Megiddo and established their settlement. At first, this bore the character of an unfortified town (stratum XIIIb). The remains of their houses, the first courtyard dwellings to appear during this period in the Land of Israel, have been discovered grouped round the Early Bronze III temple, which was the focus of development for the new settlement. The slowly expanding settlement soon became a fortified town, with a narrow inset-offset wall and a gate. It consisted of a maze of alleyways converging on a walled courtyard, which functioned as an open-air temple. At this time, the lower city of Megiddo was established on the northeastern terrace of the mound, and the site attained an area of thirteen hectares. The gate, in its earlier phase, served the citadel area of the town, and it may be assumed that a main gate was situated at the north end of the lower city.

The fortified town soon became a city. The fortifications were doubled in width, and a town plan was layed out, with a perimeter road and a ring of houses abutting the city wall. The sacred enclosure was walled and stelae were erected within, as well as a cult chamber. To this period we should ascribe the statuette of Thut-hotep, a senior official of Senusret III at Megiddo. Alongside the statuette were found (in a context from the late twelfth century B.C.E.) the statuette of a woman (perhaps his wife) and the remains of a third Egyptian statue. West of the enclosure a large palace was built, measuring about thirty meters by sixty meters, with two central courts. A road led to the sacred enclosure from the west, and the enclosure was entered through a bent-axis gateway.

An important characteristic, which reveals the northern origin of the new population of Megiddo, is the custom of intramural burial. At first, shallow graves were dug under the house floors; later on more elaborate tombs, virtual burial vaults, were excavated under the houses. This burial custom, which differs from the local custom of both the Early and Intermediate Bronze Ages, is of northern Syrian origin, where it is traced in turn to the influence of Mesopotamian cultures. The burial customs, as well as the northern character of the pottery, hint at the ethnic origins of the population—the Amorites, a Syrian people, whose existence was recorded as early as the mid third millennium.

The absolute chronology of the Megiddo strata is based, like most Middle Bronze Age chronology, on the dates of the Egyptian scarabs and Syrian and Babylonian cylinder seals. The tombs constructed under the floors are also of great assistance in determining the chronology. In many cases these tombs can be securely dated because they were built over wall remains of earlier periods. One such tomb was found in the gate area, overlying walls of stratum XIIIa. The scarabs found in this tomb are identical to those found in the phase i tombs at Jericho, as classified by Kenyon. Phase iii at Jericho provided a royal scarab of Ka-hotep-ra (Sobk-hotep V), dated to the final third of the eighteenth century (around 1730 B.C.E.). This find dates the scarabs of the first group at Jericho, and those resembling them, to about 1830–1800 B.C.E., allowing some time for the phase ii finds. Support for this date comes from a scarab belonging to Iw.f.seneb, who was the Chief of the Bureau of Cattle-Counting, found in another tomb. The title of this Egyptian official, who may have served at Megiddo, is known from the Middle Kingdom period. Alongside the official scarab was another scarab, which has a nearly identical parallel in phase ii at Jericho. This tomb may therefore be dated to the end of the nineteenth century, a date supported by yet another find from the same tomb, an early Syrian cylinder seal. It may be assumed that this town (Megiddo XII) is the same Megiddo mentioned in the later group of Execration Texts and that the Egyptian control evidenced here is related to Senusret III's domination of Canaan after the conquest of the Shechem area and Retenu. As this event took place in the fourth decade of the nineteenth century, the planned construction at Megiddo may be related to increased Egyptian interest in Canaan in the second half of the century.

Strata XIIIa and XIIIb, also attributed to the Middle Bronze II and pre-dating by nearly a century the foundation of the stratum XII city, fix the date of the first settle-

Plate 1. Natufian jewelry

Plate 2. Modeled skull from Beisamun

Plate 3. Head of clay figurine, Jericho

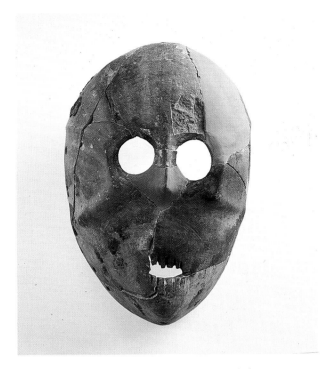

Plate 4. Stone mask from Nahal Hemar

Plate 5. Modeled skull, Nahal Hemar

Plate 6. Clay figurine with coffee-bean eyes, from Munhata

Plate 7. Clay figurines from Gilat

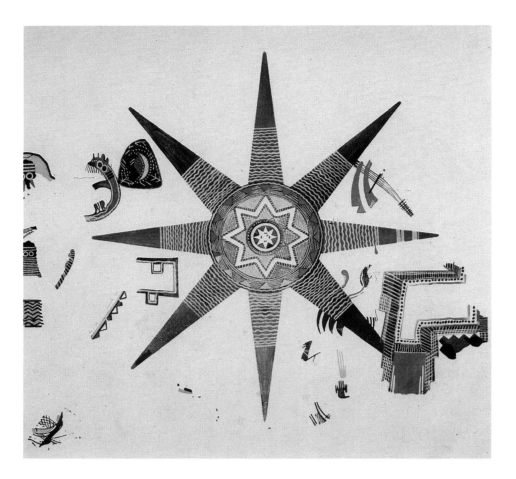

Plate 8. Star wall painting from Teleilat Ghassul

Plate 9. Mask wall painting from Teleilat Ghassul

Plate 10. Ossuary facade adorned with eyes and nose

Plate 11. The Nahal Mishmar treasure

Plate 12. Chalcolithic ivory figurines

Plate 13. Abydos jar from Arad

Plate 14. Arad House

Plate 15. Flint knife from Azor

Plate 16. Clay bulla from En Besor

Plate 17. Egyptian clay vessels from Azor

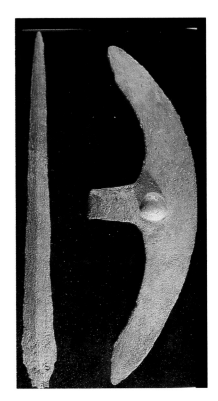

Plate 18. Early Bronze Age copper weapons

Plate 19. Cult platform at Megiddo

Plate 20. Khirbet Kerak bowl

Plate 21. Intermediate Bronze Age pottery

Plate 22. Pottery from dolmens

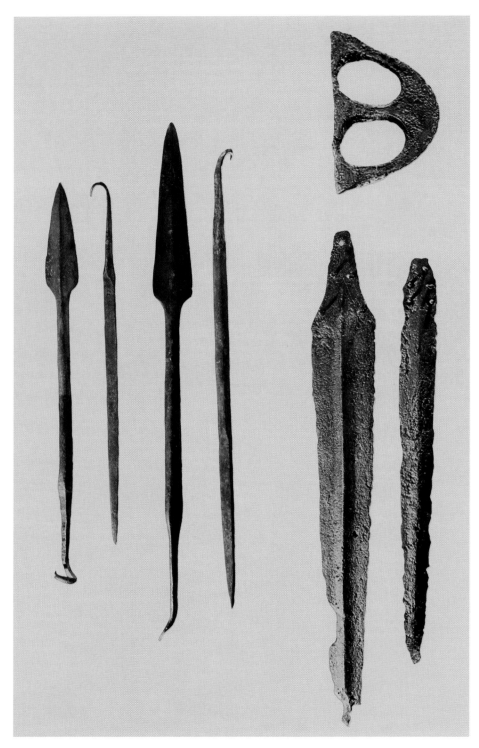

Plate 23. Intermediate Bronze Age weapons

Plate 24. The 'Ain Samiya goblet

Plate 25. Middle Bronze Age II serpent-vessel

Plate 26. Anthropomorphic goblet from Jericho

Plate 27. Storage jars from Shiloh

Plate 28. Section through glacis at Shiloh

Plate 29. Metal figurines from Nahariya

Plate 30. Fish-shaped vessels in clay and alabaster

Plate 31. Gold jewelry from Tell el-Ajjul

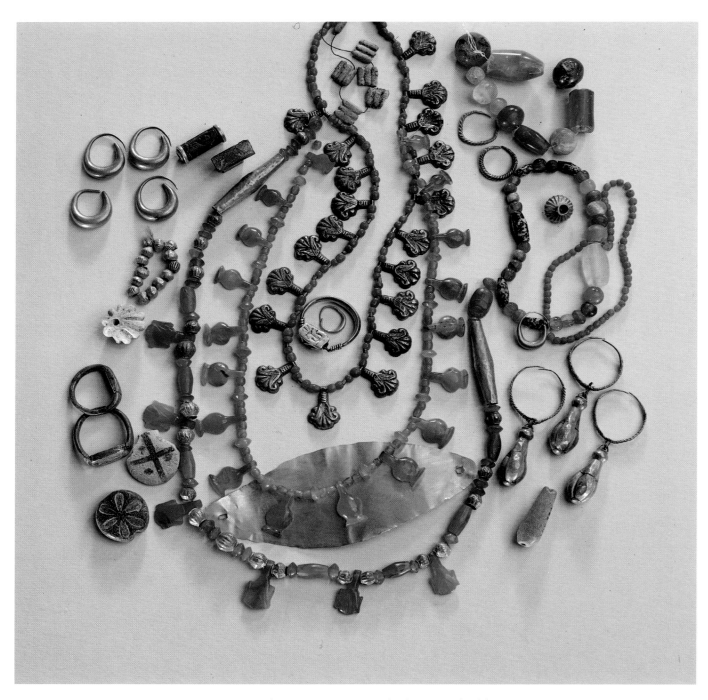

Plate 32. Canaanite jewelry from Deir el-Balah

Plate 33. Tel Lachish, aerial view

Plate 34. Ivories from Lachish

Plate 35. The Orpheus jug from Megiddo

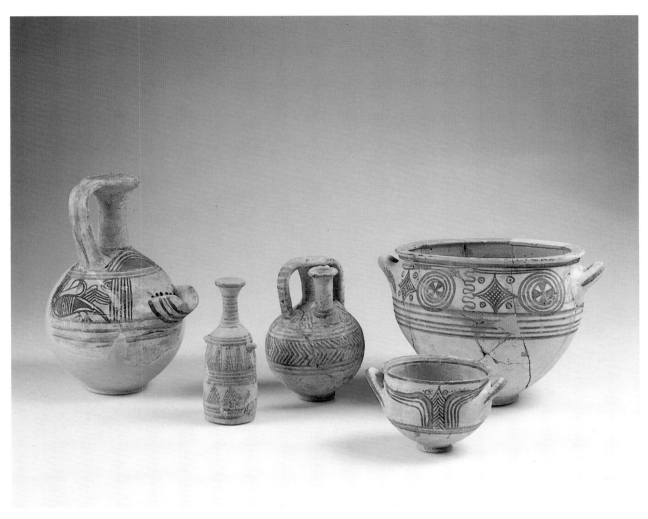

Plate 36. Philistine pottery

Plate 37. Lid of anthropoid coffin

Plate 38. The Ta'anach cult stand

Plate 39. Ivory lions from Samaria

Plate 40. Ivory sphinx from Samaria

Plate 41. Ivory stopper from Lachish

Plate 42. Head of horned deity from Qitmit

Plate 43. Heads of clay figurines from Qitmit

Plate 44. Siege and conquest of Lachish as portrayed on the walls of king Sennacherib's palace at Ninveh

Plate 45. Akhziv ware

Plate 46. Pillar figurines

Plate 47. Figurine of pregnant deity, Akhziv

ment at Megiddo at the start of the Middle Bronze II, to the first half of the twentieth century B.C.E.

ACCHO. The foundation of Accho may also be securely dated to the beginning of the twentieth century. It is not yet possible to compare the size of the area uncovered at Megiddo with that uncovered at Accho, as the excavations at Accho are still in progress and it will be some time before they are published. The Middle Bronze II is particularly well represented in the Accho valley as a whole, and this area preceded other parts of the country in the development of its settlement system. Two fields have been excavated at Accho itself. The first lies at the summit of the mound, where the rampart was sectioned and the earliest fortification and glacis of the mound discovered, consisting of a cyclopean wall, preserved to a height of nearly four meters. In the second area of excavation on the western slope of the mound, a gate, styled the Sea Gate, was cleared. I believe that two phases are to be distinguished in this gate, both related to the early glacis (the excavator noted only one phase). The western gate was covered by the later rampart of the Middle Bronze IIb. The pottery found in the two principal phases of the Middle Bronze IIa at the site allows the conclusion that the site was founded when the Twelfth Dynasty of Egypt first established its influence over Canaan, probably during the reign of Senusret I. Also, a scarab bearing the name of this king was found on the surface of the mound. The mention of Accho in the second group of Execration Texts indicates the importance of this town in the late Twelfth Dynasty.

THE PORT OF NAHARIYA. North of Accho, near the mouth of Nahal Ga'aton, lies the port town of Nahariya, about two hectares in size, only a small fraction of which has been excavated. These excavations revealed a wall and remains of a tower. About nine hundred meters north of the settlement, I. Ben Dor and M. Dothan excavated a temple and high place, which existed during the greater part of the Middle Bronze Age II. The temple was founded at the very beginning of the period, as may be gathered by the presence of vessels in the earliest phase, such as the four-spouted lamp and fragments of wavy-combed jars, which may be dated to the twentieth century.

TEL DAN. Tel Dan (Canaanite Laish) lies in the northernmost part of the Jordan valley, in an area directly influenced, through the Orontes valley, by Syria. Here, as in Accho, a city gate has recently been discovered entirely covered over by a later rampart of the Middle Bronze IIb. The burial of the gate within the later rampart ensured its complete preservation, and it is thus the best-preserved Bronze Age gate in the Land of Israel. The gate has two chambers and three piers, a plan of apparent Syrian origin. Two phases were discerned in the approaches to the gate—evidence, as at Accho, of an extended period of use. The interior of the Middle Bronze IIa city has not yet been excavated. Laish is also mentioned in the later Execration Texts and contemporaneously in commercial texts from Mari, in the third decade of the eighteenth century. This evidence correlates well with the date of the later phase of the Middle Bronze IIa.

HAZOR. South of Laish-Dan is the city of Hazor. We now have evidence—a tomb discovered in the upper city—for the existence of the upper city and its eastern extension as early as the end of the Middle Bronze IIa. Hazor is mentioned only in the later group of Execration Texts and, like Laish, in the Mari archives; however, judging by the frequency with which Hazor appears in the Mari letters, the town was an important trade center in northern Canaan as early as the mid eighteenth century.

TELL BURGA AND TEL MEVORAKH. On the coastal strip, south of the Carmel, a chain of sites adjacent to the shore or in inland ports on riverbanks may be distinguished. One site, Tell Burga, has been thoroughly surveyed and, owing to its present situation underneath an orchard, cannot be further excavated. The pottery collected on the mound is of the later phases of the Middle Bronze IIa, but the Middle Bronze IIb is not represented. The site, estimated at 25 hectares, was surrounded by a low rampart. The site's size suggests that it was the chief city of the Sharon at this time.

A fortified port uncovered at Tel Mevorakh probably served the city of Tell Burga as a fortress, protecting the coastal route that approached Megiddo and the Jezreel valley via Wadi Milh, and as a harbor for small vessels, which could navigate Nahal Taninim as far as the mound. In the earliest phase at the site, stratum XV, a brick-walled fortress was erected, which continued to serve in a later phase, still at the start of the Middle Bronze IIa. In the later phase of stratum XIV the settlement expanded. Domestic structures were built over against the fortress, and the latter underwent a number of changes. The two phases of the Middle Bronze IIa are identical, in ceramic terms, with neighboring Tell Burga. The fortress of the Middle Bronze IIa was covered and buried, in a manner reminiscent of Accho and Tel Dan, by a rampart of the Middle Bronze IIb.

Another fortress guarding the coastal route was that of Tel Poleg, south of Netanya. Here, R. Gophna spent a number of seasons excavating the remains of a broad wall and a related gate, identical to those of Tell Burga and Tel Mevorakh. A similar situation was found at Tel Zeror, not far from the entrance to Nahal 'Iron (Wadi 'Ara).

TEL APHEK. The central Middle Bronze IIa site in the Yarkon basin is, without doubt, Tel Aphek. Extensive excavations carried out since 1972 by M. Kochavi and P. Beck have uncovered a stratigraphic and ceramic sequence that provides, like Megiddo in the north, a complete picture of the development of the site from the early stages of the period to the transition to Middle Bronze IIb. Two fortification systems were uncovered, testifying to prolonged habitation during Middle Bronze IIa. Simultaneously a large building was cleared, termed a palace by the excavators, though it appears to be no more than a patrician dwelling, with a central court and a porch. The palace of the ruler of Aphek was at the summit of the mound, under a series of palaces or fortified mansions of the Middle Bronze IIb and the Late Bronze Age. Domestic structures preceded the construction of the first city wall and the patrician house, under the foundations of which their remains appeared. This is the earliest stratum at Middle Bronze Age Aphek, and ceramically it represents the early part of the Middle Bronze IIa at the site. The next phase saw the construction of the patrician house, with its especially thick walls. During its first phase a portico was built in the back of the courtyard, similar to the structure excavated by Albright at Tell Beit Mirsim, stratum G. The rear of the building was destroyed, but it is reasonable to assume, by virtue of comparison with Tell Beit Mirsim, that it contained a range of rooms. In the latter phase of the building, the portico

was dismantled and a thick lime floor laid over the central courtyard. This thick lime floor is most characteristic of Middle Bronze IIa and IIb palaces and patrician houses. Following the destruction of the patrician house, private dwellings were built on its ruins; this stratum (D) represents the transition to the Middle Bronze IIb. At Aphek as at Megiddo, the custom of burial under house floors was adopted, apparently introduced by the new settlers of the early Middle Bronze IIa. A series of burials in Area A, the area of the patrician house, permits the establishment of a chronology, relative to the house, according to pottery types appearing in tombs.

TELL JERISHE. In line with the model of a major inland town serviced by a river-mouth port, as in the case of Tell Burga and Tel Mevorakh, the port of Tel Aphek may be identified at nearby Tell Jerishe. This mound, on the banks of the Yarkon River within the modern city of Ramat Gan, was an excellent port. It was founded in the Middle Bronze IIa, though recent excavations at the site by Z. Herzog and A. Rainey have proven the importance of the site throughout the Middle Bronze Age II. The existence of many ports during this period all along the coast testifies to the great importance of the coastal trade, which linked the Land of Israel to the Syro-Lebanese coast. The rise of trade in this period may stand in direct relation to the rapid growth of settlement at the start of the period, especially along the coast.

Farther south, along the southern coastal plain and in the Judaean Shephelah, the settlement pattern becomes sparse. The most important sites are Gezer, Yavne-Yam, Tell Beit Mirsim, and Tell el-Ajjul.

GEZER. At Gezer, tombs excavated early in this century by R. A. S. Macalister were found to contain the well-known Habur ware, Syrian vessels. The American expedition excavating at Gezer in the sixties cleared areas rich in finds of the Middle Bronze IIa. It seems that the earliest town fortifications were erected at this time, and on the acropolis fragments of a statuette of the Egyptian princess Sobk-neferu were found. Both Senusret I and Amenemhet III had a daughter by this name. As the pottery belongs to a late phase of the Middle Bronze IIa, it seems likely that the statuette belonged to the daughter of Amenemhet III (1842–1797 B.C.E.). Macalister, the first excavator of Gezer, also found two Egyptian Middle Kingdom statues, but they cannot be attributed with certainty to a specific monarch. This series of statuettes joins the statuette of Thuthotep and those found with it at Megiddo to indicate the importance of these two sites and the strong bonds between them and the Egyptian administrative system of the time.

YAVNE-YAM. The Middle Bronze Age site lying on the coast opposite Gezer is Yavne-Yam (Minat Rubin). Here in the late sixties Y. Kaplan excavated a huge enclosure surrounded by a rampart containing pottery of the Middle Bronze IIa. At Ashkelon (mentioned in the early Execration Texts) as well as at nearby Tel Poran sherds of the period were found. But until these coastal sites are more widely excavated, little can be said of their character.

TELL BEIT MIRSIM. This small site is the first site where Albright identified the Middle Bronze Age IIa. Two strata, G and F, were excavated. The earlier Middle Bronze IIa phase, stratum G, was like Aphek unfortified and had a series of struc-

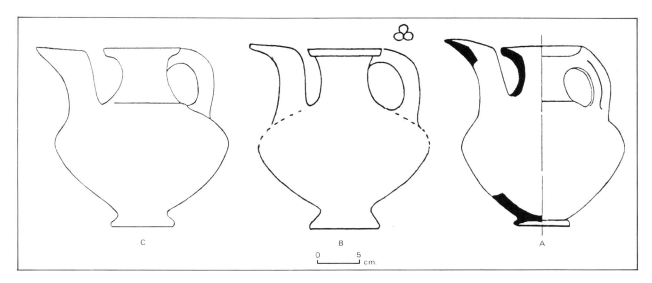

Fig. 6.6. Spouted jugs from Byblos (A), Tell el-Ajjul (B), and Accho (C)

tures ranged around its perimeter. The most interesting building is the patrician house; it contained a broad anteroom with three columns and a rear section consisting of a number of rooms. The building has a certain resemblance to the patrician house at Aphek. In the next stratum, F, the town wall was built, with towers at about twenty-meter intervals. The patrician house was replaced by a monumental structure of which little remained save a few massive wall fragments; two courtyard houses were uncovered to the southwest.

TELL EL-AJJUL. The large site of Tell el-Ajjul was also established in this period. At various points in the town W. M. F. Petrie uncovered deposits belonging to what he termed City III, as well as a cemetery in the courtyard of the earliest of the palaces uncovered at the summit of the mound. The stratigraphic relationship between the cemetery and the palace indicates the relatively early date of the cemetery, which seems to have belonged to a small structure dismantled when the large palace was erected toward the end of the Middle Bronze IIa. A hint of an early phase of this kind may be found in a cluster of houses

west of the palace, where a vessel of late Twelfth Dynasty date, probably imported from Byblos, came to light. A similar vessel was found at Accho, and a closely related vessel was found at Byblos, in a tomb dated to the days of Amenemhet III and IV. These discoveries establish a clear correlation between these Egyptian kings and the ceramic assemblages at the three sites. British archaeologist O. Tufnell, who was one of Petrie's assistants, published an innovative study of the courtyard cemetery and was the first to establish, on the basis of the tombs, the internal ceramic sequence of the Middle Bronze IIa.

Among the finds indicating settlement at Ajjul as early as the beginning of the Twelfth Dynasty are a large carnelian bead bearing the name of Amenemhet I and a statue of an Egyptian official belonging to the Middle Kingdom type found at Gezer and Megiddo. The floruit of Tell el-Ajjul occurred, however, in Thirteenth Dynasty times and during the reign of the Hyksos kings.

JERICHO AND JUDAEA. The central hill settlements, in the Judaean and Samarian hills, are few and date to the later phase of the Middle

Bronze IIa. This category includes Jericho, whose settlement and economic welfare were highly dependent on the Judaean hills and Transjordan. At Jericho, which achieved major importance only in the Middle Bronze IIb, remains of Middle Bronze IIa occupation were found on the mound and in the cemetery. The poverty of the remains indicates that only a small settlement existed here. Surveys of recent years have shown that Middle Bronze IIa populations infiltrated the northern and central hills fairly early, but they never achieved the broad settlement pattern of the large valleys and along the coast. The sites were usually unfortified, and their urbanization came late, at the end of the Middle Bronze IIa and mainly in the Middle Bronze IIb. Exceptions do, however, exist.

At Jerusalem, on the ridge known as the City of David, sherds of the period were found in pockets in the bedrock. They may be linked to the mention of the city in both the earlier and later group of Execration Texts. The intensive construction works of later periods prevent the uncovering of even the slightest structural remains of this early town.

A village of the late Middle

Bronze IIa was discovered at Giv'at Sharet, about one kilometer south of the mound of Beth Shemesh. This village, where characteristic courtyard houses were preserved, illustrates the continued presence of seminomadic populations that survived the Intermediate Bronze Age. Two characteristics of the earlier period remain: the house plans, which resemble the rectilinear courtyard houses at the Intermediate Bronze site of Har Yeruham in the northern Negev, and the large quantity of straight-sided cooking pots.

THE CENTRAL HILLS. The major settlement of the central hills was Shechem. This site dominated the entire hill country throughout the whole of the Middle Bronze Age, as well as the Late Bronze Age, as may be learned from later historical sources. It was not an isolated settlement but was linked to a series of rural settlements that had penetrated into the hill country earlier in the Middle Bronze IIa. At

Shechem itself, two strata (XXII and XXI) belonging to the early phase of settlement were discovered, with a wealth of Middle Bronze IIa pottery. These strata were defined by the excavators as unfortified. According to the Khu-Sobk inscription, the city must have been fortified at least by the time of Senusret III. Indeed, the excavators attribute the destruction layer intervening between the two phases of the Middle Bronze IIa to the campaign of Senusret III reported by Khu-Sobk.

Certain concepts were universally accepted in the sixties, during the excavations of Shechem. One was that there were no fortifications during Middle Bronze IIa, and that if there were such fortifications, they were built at the very end of the period. Ramparts and glacis were attributed to the Middle Bronze IIb alone, and it was agreed that they certainly did not exist during Middle Bronze IIa. Following the excavations at Hazor, Megiddo, Yavne-Yam, Laish (Dan), and Ac-

cho—sites with hints and sometimes clear proof of the existence of glacis and ramparts during Middle Bronze IIa—the process of fortification at Shechem may be understood in a different way from that adopted by the excavators. The first phase should probably be seen as a settlement defended by a low defensive rampart topped with an unpreserved brick town wall. This town was destroyed by the armies of Senusret III and then rebuilt. Evidence of Egyptian administration at the site is provided by a seal impression of Amenemhet the (royal) overseer, imprinted on a jar handle. It may be assumed that after the withdrawal of the Egyptians and the decline of their influence in the Canaan during the second half of the eighteenth century (the end of the Middle Bronze IIa), considerable architectural changes took place in the town and in its defenses. At Tell el-Far'ah North, lying east of Shechem on the road leading from the hills to the Jordan valley, slight remains of the Middle Bronze IIa were discovered, but there is as yet no evidence of the

Fig. 6.7. Patrician houses at Megiddo

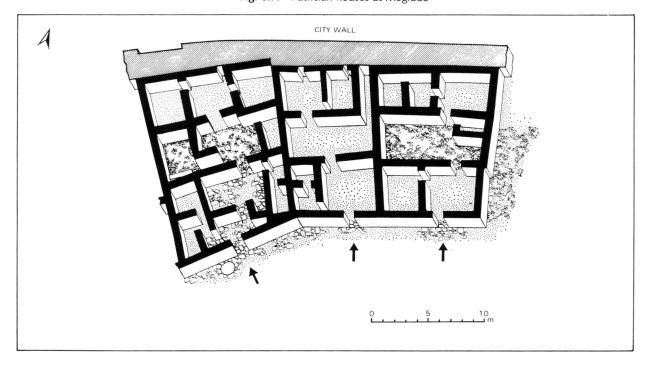

site's having been fortified before the Middle Bronze IIb.

Architecture

DWELLINGS

Two main types of dwellings may be distinguished, the village dwelling and the urban dwelling. The differences between the two types are not great, as a large component of the town population engaged in farming. Another type of dwelling attributed mainly to urban architecture is the patrician house, which will receive detailed attention in the section on the Middle Bronze Age IIb.

The village house resembles in plan the houses of the Intermediate Bronze Age. The houses excavated at Giv'at Sharet near Beth Shemesh were planned as room clusters, with a courtyard near one of the sides, adjacent to a terrace wall built along a slope. A number of rooms had segmented columns to support the roof. Their planning (corner courtyards on one side of the building) and building technique (segmented columns) closely resemble the village structures excavated at the Intermediate Bronze Age site of Har Yeruham.

The evolution of the urban dwelling from the nomadic one is evidenced at Megiddo. The first houses at the site were erected when the site was unfortified and still bore a rural character. At Megiddo, the courtyard house first appears, that is, a house consisting of rooms ranged round a courtyard in the center or in a corner of the structure. This type of structure became the standard dwelling in a somewhat later phase. A few examples of the developed courtyard house (about 12 × 17 meters) remain, with a forecourt and an inner court flanked by rooms. A column at one end of the forecourt supported a cross-beam, which in

turn supported the roof beams of the court. In stratum XII the area was laid out as a residential quarter of corner-court houses. The houses were smaller than their predecessors, measuring about 8 × 10 meters, but judging by the thickness of the walls at least some were two-storied. This is further proof of the rapid urbanization of Megiddo between stratum XIIIA, when it was still a small town, and stratum XII, when it became a city.

In the gate area of Megiddo, standardized patrician dwellings abutted the wall during this phase (stratum XII). Each unit was about 8 × 12 meters, and it contained two rooms at the front, one of which was probably used to house livestock. A central court afforded access to the rooms in the rear. The inner court often contained an oven. These houses were, it appears, also two-storied.

Remains of patrician dwellings were found at Aphek in the Sharon as well. Here, the forecourt of a building was uncovered, with four pillars indicating a roofed area in the rear. This seems to have been the entrance to the dwelling rooms, of which only traces remain. Some resemblance to the Aphek residence may be seen in the patrician house of Tell Beit Mirsim. Here too is the characteristic forecourt with its central pillars and with the access to the dwelling rooms. The thickness of the walls suggests that at least its rear section was two-storied.

PALACES

There is, so far, little evidence for the existence of palaces in the early part of the Middle Bronze IIa. A later structure preserved only in the most fragmentary manner is the palace of stratum XII at Megiddo. Apparently, a palace measuring some 60 meters in length and 30 meters in width is to be reconstructed;

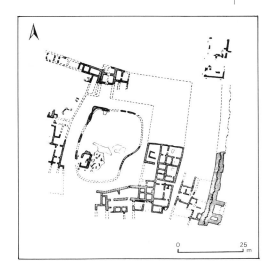

Fig. 6.8. The high place at Megiddo

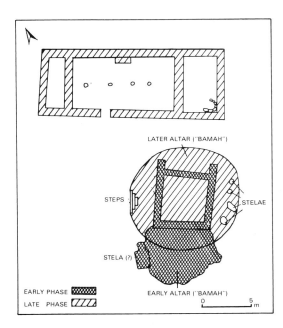

Fig. 6.9. The high place at Nahariya

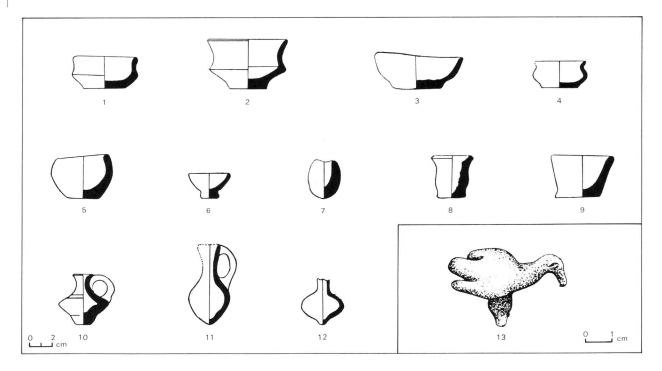

Fig. 6.10. Finds from the high place at Nahariya

the ground area of 1800 square meters would have included two major courtyards, surrounded by chambers. The palace may have been built under the influence of Syrian architectural styles of the period, as revealed at Tell Mardikh (Ebla) in northern Syria. Another structure, the function of which is debated, was excavated at Shechem. It is a central-courtyard structure, surrounded by a thick boundary wall. The central courtyard has a portico resembling those of Aphek and Tell Beit Mirsim. The excavator of Shechem, G. E. Wright, believed the structure to be a temple, but the remains may possibly be those of a palace or patrician dwelling.

TEMPLES AND CULT SITES

One of the important characteristics of the Middle Bronze IIa is the presence of open-air cult places containing stelae (*masseboth*). The temple structure itself was of secondary importance in this period. The open character of the cult is in

the spirit of the cult and religion practiced during the Intermediate Bronze Age, when open-air cult places were common. Gradual changes in the cult area used during the Intermediate Bronze Age may be observed at Megiddo, where, alongside the still-functioning Early Bronze III temple, a small cult platform is erected. At the beginning of the Middle Bronze IIa, the cult cell seems to have been finally abandoned, and a large high place (*bamah*) is established on the ruins of the temple. In the following strata the area receives its final form: house clusters are built around it, the platform itself is surrounded by a fence, and a new cult cell is constructed at its southern end. East of this cell, masseboth are erected. The cult area is separated from the residential quarters by a surrounding plaza and a bent-axis gateway.

At Nahariya, about 900 meters north of the Middle Bronze IIa-b site, a temple dating mainly to the Middle Bronze IIa was discovered. Two building phases were identified.

In the early phase, a shrine or cult cell measuring about 5.5 × 5 meters was built, with an annex to its north. To the south, a small high place was constructed, at the western edge of which was an altar. This temple was destroyed at an unknown date, but the area remained sacred, becoming a large high place some 12 meters in diameter. A row of masseboth was erected on its east side, and to the west stood an altar, approached by three steps. A large rectangular structure was built north of the high place, with four central roof pillars. Annexes were later added to this structure on the east and west. Many votive and cultic vessels were found on the later high place, one of the rare cases where the votive vessels have been well preserved. They consist mainly of miniature versions of larger pottery vessels, silver figurines, and gifts such as beads and miniature weapons offered to the local goddess (apparently Ashtoreth).

At Gezer, a row of masseboth and a basin, possibly attributed to the Middle Bronze IIa, were excavated by Macalister. W. G. Dever, who directed renewed excavations at the site, dates the cult place to phases b and c of the Middle Bronze II, a view not accepted by the present author. The Egyptian statuettes mentioned earlier were found near the cult site.

Outside Canaan similar cult places have been discovered. At Byblos the Temple of the Obelisks, an open-air cult place adjacent to a temple, is dated to the same period. Here too a cultic installation resembling that at Nahariya was found, with cultic and votive vessels of a type identical to those found at Nahariya.

FORTIFICATIONS

Two kinds of fortification were current throughout the entire Middle Bronze Age: the city wall and

the rampart. The city wall continued the form and construction technique of Early Bronze Age architectural traditions, except that at the beginning of the period, the walls were markedly thinner than those of the third millennium.

At Megiddo, Aphek, and Tell Beit Mirsim, and perhaps at Tel Zeror as well, inset-offset walls, sometimes furnished with towers, were built; they consisted of mud-brick superstructures on a stone foundation. The intervals between towers varied, from about twenty meters at Tell Beit Mirsim to only four meters at Aphek. The Megiddo walls were not furnished with towers; rather, the wall was built in offsets (in stratum XIIIA) placed at three-meter intervals. In a later phase of the wall (stratum XII), the interval was about five meters. At Megiddo and Tel Poleg a glacis protected the base of the wall and pre-

vented its being undermined by enemy forces.

The rampart took various forms, but in principal it consisted of a nucleus built of stone, bricks, packed earth, or any combination. This nucleus formed the center of a double-sloped rampart, with the exterior slope serving as a glacis for the city wall. The rampart was generally crowned by a wall, which because of erosion is rarely preserved; the few that remain are in poor condition. The width of the ramparts, at the base, varies from forty meters to eighty meters, and their height is estimated at ten to twenty meters.

The glacis is a single-sloped fortification element (as opposed to the double-sloped rampart). It was built, like the rampart, of different combinations of soil and fills and sloped from the top of the mound outward, covering the outer face of the mound. A wall was usually built

Fig. 6.11. Fortifications of the Middle Bronze Age II: glacis (1–2), earth ramparts (3–4)

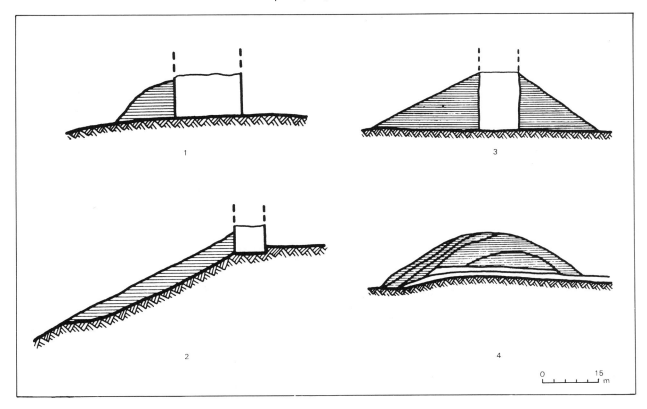

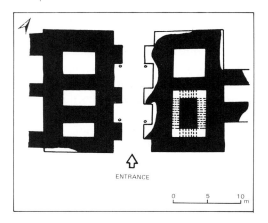

Fig. 6.12. City gate at Yavne-Yam

at the top of the glacis, and the double function of the glacis, therefore, was to consolidate the slope and prevent the undercutting of the wall, and to impede the approach of the enemy to the wall.

It seems that glacis fortifications began in the Early Bronze Age, as at sites such as Ta'anach and Tell el-Far'ah North. Rampart fortifications, which could be constructed rapidly, were most suitable for cities established on level ground. This was the case at Yavne-Yam, Accho, and Tel Dan. The wall-and-glacis system was better suited to mounds such as Megiddo and Tell Beit Mirsim.

Toward the end of the Middle Bronze IIa, or during the transition to Middle Bronze IIb, thick stone facings were added to the outer rampart slopes. Such, it seems, was Wall C at Shechem, which was a sloped support wall for the early glacis.

Middle Bronze IIa walls were sometimes furnished with bastions. The smaller type consisted of two small chambers; they were ten meters long and projected five or six meters from the wall. Examples have been preserved at Megiddo, Tell el-Far'ah North, and Tel Zeror, while at Gezer a large bastion twenty meters long was found. Rectangular in plan, the bastion jutted out two meters from the city wall. A well-built stairway lay on the east side, and four rooms were built to its west. The excavator, Dever, dates the tower at Gezer to a late phase of the Middle Bronze IIb. A similar type of bastion was found at Tell Mardikh (Ebla) in northern Syria, where it was dated unequivocally to the Middle Bronze IIa. This type of tower seems to have been introduced from central Syria.

The Middle Bronze IIa also saw the introduction of the straight-axis gateway, flanked by two or three piers. The cities of Megiddo XIII–XII were served by a bent-axis gate, but this gate is the only one of its kind so far discovered in Middle Bronze Age Canaan, and it seems that it served as the gateway only of

Fig. 6.13. Reconstruction of gate at Tel Dan

the citadel. It is likely that the lower city of Megiddo, which extended to the northeast of the mound (in the area of the modern park and museum), had a straight-axis gateway.

The Sea Gate at Accho is contemporaneous with the gate at Megiddo. This gate had, in my opinion, two phases. Its earlier phase was built of mud brick on a low stone foundation. The gate was connected to the city wall, which adjoined the earlier rampart of Accho. The gate originally had a single chamber framed by two piers on each side. In the second phase of construction, an elongated stone-built antechamber was added, creating a two-chambered gate with three piers on each side and measuring about fifteen meters long by eight meters wide. The intent behind the transformation of the gate seems to have been to conform to the Syrian gate plan common in the period.

The most common type of gate from the later part of the Middle Bronze IIa on was thus the Syrian gate, with a straight axis of entry and three piers on each side. The name is derived from its apparent origin in northern Syria, where gates of the type, such as the gate at Tell Mardikh, are dated to the Middle Bronze IIa. These gates in Canaan generally measure 15–20 meters long and 8–10 meters wide in each chamber. The passage is 2.5–3 meters wide, wide enough for chariots to pass between the piers. A typical gate of this type was discovered in the Middle Bronze IIa enclosure at Yavne-Yam. It had a staircase in one tower. A gate dating to the end of the period, which has been preserved to its entire height, including the roof vault, was discovered at Tel Dan. This gate had three piers on each side and was roofed by a mud-brick barrel vault in north Syrian and Mesopotamian style. The height of the entranceway was 3.5 meters.

The Transition to Middle Bronze IIb

The transition between the two parts of the Middle Bronze Age was gradual. In the pottery assemblage (one of the main features used to define any period or cultural phase) the change was quite slow; typical Middle Bronze IIa forms disappear or undergo typological change, while new types, or types that evolved out of Middle Bronze IIa prototypes, take their place. In addition, regional differences in the development of the ceramic culture of the Middle Bronze IIb are noticeable, particularly between northern and southern assemblages and between assemblages of the coastal plain, the hill country, and the Jordan valley. This process may be indicative of the dominance of certain trade systems or potter's workshops over their respective areas of distribution.

Chronologically, the transition from Middle Bronze IIa to IIb should be fixed at a date following 1800 and before 1750 B.C.E., as the culture of the second part of the Middle Bronze Age was well established after this date. Absolute dates are determined according to synchronisms with Egypt, the Mesopotamian and north Syrian synchronisms being insufficient to provide definite chronological determinations, though gradual headway in this direction has been made in recent years.

CANAAN IN 1800–1720 B.C.E.: ABSOLUTE CHRONOLOGY AND ITS RELATION TO ARCHAEOLOGICAL ASSEMBLAGES

As at the beginning of the Middle Bronze IIa, in the transitional period local chronology is dependent on that of Egypt. The most important assemblages in this respect are those of the Royal Tombs III and IV, discovered in the twenties at Byblos. These magnificent tombs contained Egyptian objects bearing the names of Amenemhet III and IV, the last kings of the Twelfth Dynasty in Egypt (1828–1798 B.C.E.) alongside locally made objects and pottery vessels closely resembling finds from Canaan. These gifts to the local Byblite rulers were interred in the tombs between 1828 and 1798 B.C.E. or a short time later. The pottery retains some of the characteristics of the

Table 6.2 Synchronisms between the Main Assemblages of the Land of Israel and Neighboring Lands in the Eighteenth Century.

Date	Assemblage	Remarks
1842–1790 (Amenemhet III and IV)	Byblos royal tombs	still MBIIa
Before c. 1780	Jericho tombs, phase i, Hazor lower city, stratum pre-IV (see below)	still MBIIa
c. 1760	Jericho tombs, phase ii	four Babylonian cylinder seals, beginning MBIIb
c. 1750 (Nefer-hotep I)	end of Megiddo stratum XII	early MBIIb
After c. 1730, Ka-hotep-ra (Sobk-hotep V; Thirteenth Dynasty)	Jericho tombs, phase iii	MBIIb

latter Middle Bronze IIa phase, such as closed and carinated bowls, platters, jars, and jugs. An analysis of the assemblage shows, therefore, that round the year 1800, or somewhat later, ceramic forms typical to the Middle Bronze IIa still prevailed, at least along the Lebanese coast, and doubtless farther south as well. The next chronological synchronism, related to the first kings of the Thirteenth Dynasty, is made possible by the discovery of a royal scarab of Ka-hotep-ra (Sobk-hotep V) in a phase iii tomb at Jericho. As the reign of this king was short and is dated to approximately 1730 B.C.E., and as the pottery of phase iii at Jericho may be considered typical of the Middle Bronze IIb, the transition must precede the year 1730. Even if the Ka-hotep-ra scarab was kept as an heirloom for a generation or two, it was found in a phase iii tomb, belonging to fully developed Middle Bronze IIb. Even the preceding phase ii tombs have features, though not prominent ones, of the later Middle Bronze phase. The following sequence may be deduced:

> phase i of the Jericho tombs, late Middle Bronze IIa (about 1800 B.C.E.);
> phase ii, early Middle Bronze IIb (about 1760–1750 B.C.E.);
> phase iii, Middle Bronze IIb (after 1730 B.C.E.).

The chronological framework of the eighteenth century may also be established with the aid of the chronology of the first Babylonian dynasty, whose most famous king was Hammurabi. Astronomical observations of Venus in the eighth year of Ammisaduqa, the great-grandson of Hammurabi, permit the precise calculation of Ammisaduqa's reign. The precise number of years between the beginning of Hammurabi's rule and the accession of Ammisaduqa is known, thanks to the preservation of the Babylonian date lists, in which the outstanding event of each year was recorded. That event became the year name and appeared in all official documents. The sum of the year names dates Hammurabi's reign to 1792–1750 B.C.E., according to one calculation, called the middle chronology. These dates are of crucial importance for the relations and chronological synchronisms between the Land of Israel and northern Syria. Also, Babylonian cylinder seals, stylistically dated to the reign of Hammurabi or somewhat earlier, appear in Jericho in the phase ii tombs, from the first half of the eighteenth century. As the scarab of Ka-hotep-ra (c. 1730) was found in a phase iii tomb, we have further support from Egyptian chronology for the dating of the reign of Hammurabi to the first part of the century.

Another important synchronism is the mention of the cities of Hazor and Laish (Dan) in texts found at Mari, dating from the reign of Zimrilim, a contemporary of Hammurabi. Mari was destroyed by Hammurabi in 1760 B.C.E. (according to the middle chronology), and the towns of Hazor and Laish must therefore have been in existence before then, for the king of Mari could hardly have corresponded with Hazor after the destruction of his city. Evidence accumulated in recent years shows that these two cities were established by the main phase of the Middle Bronze IIa.

HISTORY AND CHRONOLOGY OF THE LAND OF ISRAEL, 1720–1580 B.C.E.

In the interval between the final days of the Thirteenth Dynasty (and the contraction of its dominions to the environs of Thebes) and the start of the reconquest of Egypt and the Canaan by the Seventeenth and Eighteenth Dynasties, local chronology is entirely dependent on that of Egypt. Only at the northern extremity of Syria, where the battles between the Hittite kings and the kingdom of Aleppo took place, is it possible to link finds and strata to Babylonian chronology.

At the start of the Middle Bronze Age IIb a historic event occurred related to the occupation of the city of Avaris (Hwt Wa'ret, Tell ed-Daba in the eastern delta) by a Canaanite dynasty and its transformation into the religious and political capital of that dynasty. The date recorded for this event is 1720 B.C.E., for at about 1320 B.C.E. Horemhab, the founder of the Nineteenth Dynasty, commemorated the enthronement of the Semitic god Baal-Seth in a stela, known as the Stela of Year 400. Clearly, the stela represents a religious tradition based on a round figure that is not precise; nonethe-

Table 6.3   Chronology of the Fifteenth Dynasty.

1680–1650	Sheshi (Ma-ib-re); scarabs bearing the name of this king have been found at Tell el-Far'ah (S), in City II at Tell el-Ajjul, in a tomb at Barqai identical to the assemblage of Megiddo stratum XI, and in the Jericho tombs, phases iv–v.
1660–1650	Yakub-her (II); he is not recorded in Cannan.
1650–1630	Khyan (Khyran); known from a scarab found in an MBIIb deposit at Gezer and a sealing found on the surface of Tell es-Safi.
1630–1620	Ianasas-Adan; not recorded in Canaan.
1620–1580	Apophis; scarabs at Ajjul in destruction assemblages of the Eighteenth Dynasty.
1580–1575	Khamudy; not recorded in Canaan.

(The regnal years and dates are estimated, except for Apophis, who is known to have reigned for forty years.)

less it serves as an indication of the coming to power of the Semites in the northeast delta and the installation of the Baal cult there. The cult of Baal-Seth was denounced in the Eighteenth Dynasty, and only during the Nineteenth Dynasty, which had a Semitic-Canaanite orientation, was it restored to importance.

The Semitic dynasties that seized control of the northeast delta are sometimes termed the Hyksos dynasties, but we shall apply this name only to the Fifteenth Dynasty, which was so styled by the Egyptian historians themselves, as in the Turin Papyrus. "Hyksos" is the Greek form of the Egyptian for "rulers of foreign lands," an epithet originally used to designate the heads of Canaanite families and tribes in Asia and then, in the course of the seventeenth century B.C.E., applied to the Canaanite rulers of Egypt. The Egyptian historian Manetho, who lived in Hellenistic times, misunderstood the term and supposed that it meant "shepherd kings," thus transmitting the Greek term "Hyksos," with historical overtones of the invasion of Egypt by shepherd tribes and their chiefs, to modern historiography. It is now recognized that there was no single invasion of foreign populations but a gradual infiltration of Canaanite immigrants into the eastern delta, leading to their ultimate control of the greater part of Egypt in the second and third decades of the seventeenth century. The Fifteenth Dynasty ruled just over one hundred years. Because it came to an end in the second decade of the sixteenth century when Ahmose, the founder of the Eighteenth Dynasty, completed the expulsion of the Hyksos forces from Egypt and eventually from their center in Canaan, it is clear that the dynasty came to power sometime around 1680 B.C.E. Egyptian sources (the Turin Papyrus) and Manetho mention six rulers, some of them known

from finds in the Land of Israel (listed in chronological order in Table 6.3).

Thanks to the discovery of scarabs bearing names of kings of this dynasty in clear ceramic contexts, an absolute chronology of a number of ceramic groups is possible. Tombs containing scarabs of Sheshi belong to a group with late Middle Bronze IIb features; finds are confined mainly to cylindrical juglets and open carinated bowls on a high foot. The scarabs of the fifth king of the dynasty, Apophis, appear in assemblages belonging already to the transition to Late Bronze I, characterized by bichrome ware, of major diagnostic importance for this transitional period. The transition seems to correspond to the end of Apophis' reign and the reign of Khamudy, and of course to those of the first kings of the Eighteenth Dynasty. On the basis of this information, the cultural boundary of Middle Bronze IIb may be established at about 1600 B.C.E., after which date the Late Bronze I begins. The guide fossil for this transition is bichrome ware and the related pottery known as chocolate-on-white ware.

Confirmation is provided by the north Syrian site of Alalakh, an important city in the kingdom of Aleppo. Alalakh was destroyed in the campaign of Hattusilis I, at about 1615–1610 B.C.E., according to the middle chronology. The destruction level (stratum VII) contained no bichrome ware, whereas the succeeding stratum, VI, has this type of pottery. The appearance of this type of pottery along the Syro-Canaanite littoral may therefore be dated to about 1600 B.C.E.

The capital of the Fifteenth Dynasty was Avaris. Here the dynasty established control over the greater part of Egypt and over southern and central Canaan, as far north as the Jezreel valley. Beyond this boundary lay the regions under the direct con-

trol of Hazor and within the sphere of influence of the Syrian-Amorite kingdoms of Qatna and Aleppo. Southern and central Canaan were administered by the kingdom centered in the Nile Delta and therefore called the Delta Kingdom. This kingdom was ruled by a local Canaanite population, and large parts of Canaan were under the cultural influence of the Semitic population of the Delta, which was in turn undergoing a process of assimilation into Egyptian culture. This state of affairs left a clear impression on the material culture: the second phase of the Middle Bronze Age is marked by a wealth of Egyptian imports. They consisted for the most part of scarabs set in the seal rings of members of the upper and middle classes, faience and alabaster vessels, and bone-inlaid boxes that reveal Egyptian influence, though they were manufactured in Canaan. Objects made of gold, whose nearest source is in the Sudan, also show a dramatic increase in the Middle Bronze IIb, with caches found principally at Tell el-Ajjul, Gezer, and Megiddo and at other sites as well.

The increasing cultural and economic influence of Egypt over southern Canaanite populations stems from the close links between this population and the Canaanite population of the Delta, which had been subject to powerful Egyptian influences for some time. The close relation with Egypt may also arise from close commercial ties between Canaan and the Delta and from the recruitment of mercenaries into the armies of the Fifteenth Dynasty kings, who had to fend off, particularly toward the end of the dynasty, pressure from the Egyptian rulers of the south (the Seventeenth Dynasty).

Pottery Typology of the Middle Bronze Age IIb

Most pottery forms of the Middle Bronze Age IIa constituted prototypes of the Middle Bronze IIb forms. The following discussion will therefore take particular note of the degree of conservatism or innovation evident in the main Middle Bronze IIb forms.

BOWLS, KRATERS, AND GOBLETS

The open and rounded bowl of the earlier phase replaces its disk base with a low ring base (Fig. 6.14:1). This base grows taller during the Middle Bronze IIb, especially toward the end of the period, until the bowl takes on the form of a chalice (Fig. 6.14:2). This type of bowl tends to be burnished on the outside, though the unburnished type becomes more common toward the end of the period. The closed carinated bowl of the Middle Bronze IIa becomes more rounded (Fig. 6.14:3), though the closed carinated type remains in use in the south during the greater part of the period.

The most characteristic bowl of the Middle Bronze IIb is the open carinated bowl. At first it has a low foot (Fig. 6.14:4), but toward the end of the period it becomes goblet-like, on a high pedestal and with sharp carination (Fig. 6.14:5).

The two principal types of kraters are the deep krater with two handles attached to the rim (Fig. 6.14:6) and the deep, rounded krater furnished with handles at mid-body (Fig. 6.14:7), a characteristic Middle Bronze IIb vessel. This vessel is a typological successor of the type B kraters of the previous phase.

Continuity is also evident among the goblets. The Middle Bronze IIa type (Fig. 6.3:13) undergoes slight changes (Fig. 6.14:8). In the Jericho tombs and in the southern ceramic repertoire, which gradually takes form toward the end of the period, the closed goblet is accompanied by an open form (Fig. 6.14:9).

COOKING POTS

All the cooking pot types of the Middle Bronze IIa continue into the next phase, with three typological variations: The holemouth cooking pot becomes a closed pot with a folded rim (Fig. 6.14:10). In the straight-walled cooking pot, the holes beneath the rim disappear and the impressed decoration climbs up toward the rim; this type is more common in the south than in the

Fig. 6.14. Pottery of the Middle Bronze IIb

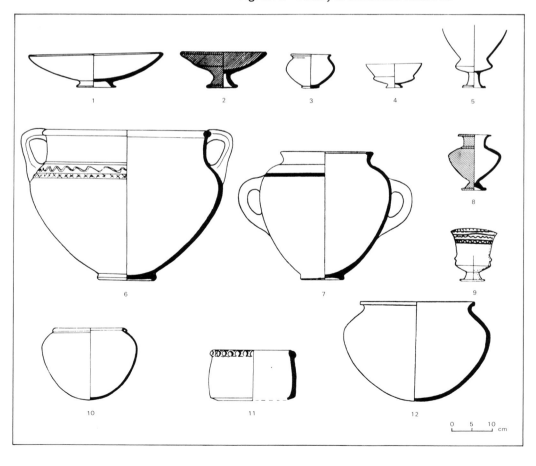

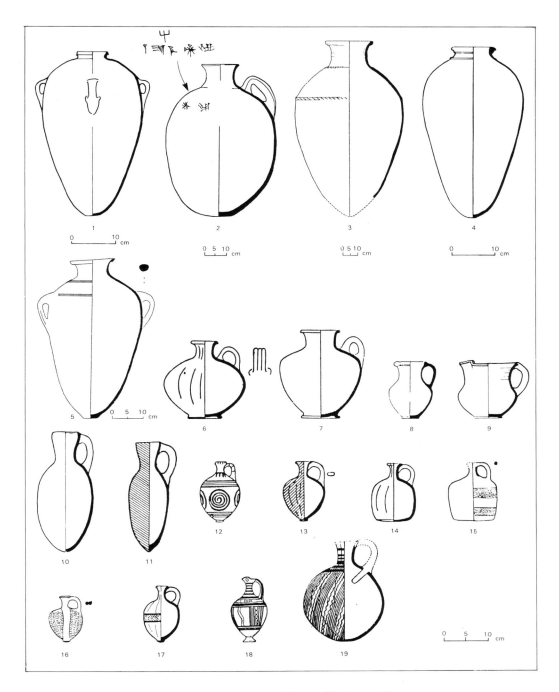

Fig. 6.15. Pottery of the Middle Bronze IIb

north (Fig. 6.14:11). The everted-rim cooking pot becomes common, and its rim takes on a triangular shape toward the end of the period (Fig. 6.14:12).

JARS

The two-handled jar with a modeled rim encountered in the previous period tends to be larger in the Middle Bronze IIb and is sometimes covered with a white wash or decorated with a wavy line near the shoulder. An offshoot of this type is the large four-handled storage jar (Fig. 6.15:1). A new type is the one-handled jar (Fig. 6.15:2). The vessel here illustrated is from Hazor; the name of the owner, Is-me-Adad ("Hadad has heard," a reading first proposed by A. Shaffer) is incised on the jar in Akkadian cuneiform characters and is accompanied by a trident, the emblem of the god Hadad. The practice of carving the owner's name on the vessel is otherwise unknown in the Land of Israel before the Iron Age, making the Hazor jar an exceptional find. The storage jar most typical of the north is the handleless pithos (Fig. 6.15:3). Another storage vessel of the period is the torpedo-shaped pithos (Fig. 6.15:4), 1–1.2 meters high. Finally, a jar that appears mostly in southern Canaan and clearly carries on earlier traditions is the two-handled jar with wavy combed decoration on the shoulder (Fig. 6.15:5).

JUGS AND JUGLETS

Most of the jug types exhibit clear continuity with types of the earlier phase, except for a sharp decrease in the number of red slipped and burnished vessels. This tendency increases as the Middle Bronze IIb progresses and is more marked in the south. There are also new jug types carried over into Late Bronze I.

Jugs 6 and 7 in Fig. 6.15 retain the form of the shoulder-handled jugs of Middle Bronze IIa (Fig. 6.4:6–7). The carinated type disappears, giving way to the rounded vessel. Jug 8 (Fig. 6.15) is characteristic of the Middle Bronze IIb and continues into Late Bronze I, as does the jug pot illustrated in Fig. 6.15:9, which is relatively rare and a diagnostic form.

The dipper juglet (Fig. 6.15:10) continues in the tradition of the earlier period, though it is larger and more elongated. The handle, which in Middle Bronze IIa was joined to the midneck, tends in Middle Bronze IIb to join near or at the rim. In Fig. 6.15:11 the base becomes pointed instead of flat or button-shaped. In the first part of the Middle Bronze IIb juglets are still generally red-slipped, but they lose their slip toward the end of the period. The juglets in Fig. 6.15:12 continue, at the beginning of Middle Bronze IIb, the northern juglet types of the Ginnosar assemblage, but they soon disappear. The pyriform juglet with a button base (Fig. 6.15:13) is the most characteristic form of the major part of the Middle Bronze IIb, along with the cylindrical juglet (Fig. 6.15:14), a fossil guide of the period. The ratio of cylindrical juglets to pyriform juglets gradually increases as the Middle Bronze IIb progresses, especially in the south. These changes in the ceramic assemblage have great chronological significance. A high frequency of cylindrical juglets indicates a late date for a given assemblage, and vice versa: the smaller the proportion of cylindrical juglets to pyriform juglets, the earlier the date within the Middle Bronze IIb.

Typological changes also occur in the Tell el-Yahudiyeh juglets. Juglets bearing a complex decoration, or one that imitates shapes of fruit (Fig. 6.15:15 and 16), dominate the start of the period, whereas later juglets are characterized by only a single band of decoration (Fig. 6.15:17). Also, the cylindrical Tell el-Yahudiyeh juglet (Fig. 6.15:15) becomes increasingly popular as the pyriform juglet gradually disappears. Eventually, Tell el-Yahudiyeh juglets cease to appear in southern Canaan, while continuing to appear in northern Syria, Cyprus, and apparently in Nile delta sites with a Semitic population (Tell ed-Daba and Tell el-Yahudiyeh). At this stage (about 1600 B.C.E.), Cypriot imports in Canaan begin to increase. Juglets 18 and 19 are containers of Cypriot produce imported to Canaan; their small size suggests that they contained valued ointments or cosmetics.

To sum up, there is a gradual disappearance of red slip and burnish; the rarer these elements in a given assemblage, the nearer their date to Late Bronze I. Also, new types appear, increasing in numbers as the year 1600 B.C.E. approaches. The phenomenon is more clearly marked in the south than in the north, possibly because the south was more industrialized and hence had fewer potter's workshops than the north.

The Settlement Pattern in the Middle Bronze Age IIb

The infrastructure of settlement established in the Middle Bronze IIa formed a firm basis for the continued expansion of settlement during the second phase of the Middle Bronze Age. The large increase in Canaanite sites mentioned in the Posener group of Execration Texts reflects a process that was well under way by the end of the Middle Bronze IIa.

Several site groups included in the later Execration Texts are: In the Accho valley, Accho, Mash'al, Akhshaph, and Rehov. Among these, Accho and Mash'al (Tell Keisan) have been excavated, and Rehov (probably Tel Kabri) has seen two seasons of excavation. Each excavation has revealed occupation spanning the whole of the Middle Bronze Age II. In the Jezreel valley, Shumunu (Shimron), Beth Shean (written E-Shean), and Megiddo. The latter two sites have been excavated. At Beth Shean, however, the Middle Bronze Age stratum has been only slightly excavated; Megiddo, of course, is one of the key sites for the period. In the Galilee and the upper Jordan valley, Kedesh, Beth Shemesh (of Galilee), 'Iyon, Abel (Beth Ma'achah), Laish (Dan), and Hazor. Only the last two sites have been excavated, revealing layers of the late Middle Bronze IIa and a full Middle Bronze IIb sequence. On the coast, Ashkelon and Aphek (at the Yarkon headwaters). Both sites have been excavated and the various phases are all represented. In the central hills, Shechem, Jerusalem, and apparently Hebron (under the name Ya'nak). In each site Middle Bronze II remains have been revealed. There are also tens of names that have not been identified with a site; the lifespan of these sites was short, and was limited to the Middle Bronze II alone.

Comparison between the earlier and later Execration Texts reveals the great development in the distribution of sites during the interval between the two lists (between the start of the Twelfth Dynasty and its end). As opposed to about 10 settlements identified in the earlier list (out of a total of 19), about 40 have been identified in the later list (out of 64). Thus, a considerable leap in the density of settlement may be observed over less than two hundred years.

Intensive archaeological surveys conducted over recent years provide further evidence for this trend. While in the early part of the period settlements are ranged chiefly along the coast and in the valleys, by the end of Middle Bronze IIa the pen-etration into the hilly areas had begun, first in the more easily settled zone of the intermontane valleys, such as northern Samaria, and later to harsher environments, such as the hills of Ephraim and Judaea. In the Judaean hills, two exceptions to the rule appear in the earlier Execration Texts. The first is Jerusalem, where ceramic remains of the early Middle Bronze Age IIa have been found. The motive for occupying this site, which was economically and politically significant before the Late Bronze Age, may have been its religious standing, with origins in the period under discussion. The second center is Ya'nak (Hebron), where a seminomadic occupation crystallized into a sedentary settlement only at the end of the Middle Bronze IIa or the beginning of Middle Bronze IIb. The ancient name of this site, containing the element " 'Anak," is preserved in the book of Joshua (21:11, "Kiriath-arba . . . that is, Hebron . . . together with the pastures around it. [Arba was] the father of the Anokites." See also Num. 13:22).

Archaeological surveys add much information concerning the distribution of settlement; their results are summarized here.

THE VALLEY OF ACCHO. The sites founded in the Middle Bronze IIa continued to exist throughout the following period. At the beginning of the Middle Bronze IIb Kabri and the related site at Nahariya were flourishing, together with the northerly sites of Akhziv and Abdon. In the southern valley, the sites of Accho, Tell Keisan (Mash'al), Tel Kurdani (Aphek), Khirbet Da'uk, and Tell er-Ras remained inhabited. The density of settlement thus remained unchanged, but the center of gravity shifted at the end of the Middle Bronze IIb to the city-state of Accho, which replaced Kabri as the principal site of the area.

THE JEZREEL VALLEY. The centers of habitation here were Megiddo, Tel Shimron, Ta'anach, Yoqneam, and Tell Harbaj (Akhshaph). A survey of the western Jezreel valley showed eleven sites dated to the Middle Bronze IIa, increasing to eighteen Middle Bronze IIb sites. It appears that control of the valley was divided between Megiddo and Tel Shimron. At Tel Shimron, gates and a rampart (dated possibly to the Middle Bronze IIb) have been discovered, and an extramural cemetery has been revealed in recent years.

THE SOUTHERN CARMEL. The survey conducted in this area provides evidence of 45 sites attributed to the Middle Bronze II; about a third are tumuli dated to Middle Bronze IIa. The remaining sites are village sites. Along the Wadi Milh corridor, on the route between Yoqneam Bat-Shelomo and Zikhron Ya'aqov, 8 Middle Bronze IIa sites are concentrated. In the Middle Bronze IIb, settlement along this corridor increased and extended to the south. The pattern observed in the Jezreel valley is thus repeated in the marginal zone bordering the Carmel range.

THE GALILEE AND THE CENTRAL HILLS. Aharoni's Galilee survey, conducted in the fifties, recorded five settlements in the heart of the Galilee, the great majority being of the Middle Bronze IIb. A recent survey of the lower Galilee revealed fourteen sedentary settlements of the same period, with no settlements of the earlier phase. A survey conducted in the sixties near Shechem did not distinguish between the two phases, but the period as a whole was observed to be one of increased settlement. Kenyon, who examined the ceramic finds from hill sites excavated up to the seventies (Tell el-Far'ah, Gibeon,

Bethel, and others), noted a phase of destruction at the end of the period, which she attributed to a campaign of an Egyptian army headed by Ahmose, the founder of the Eighteenth Dynasty. The ceramic picture, however, does not seem at all homogeneous, and some of the hill sites may well have been abandoned in the course of the Middle Bronze IIb.

THE COASTAL PLAIN. Here too there is no conspicuous change, though local shifts in settlement occur; the Tell Burga enclosure is abandoned, and the fortress at Tel Mevorakh, now surrounded by a rampart, grows smaller. Similar phenomena affect the Yarkon River sites of Tel Aphek and Tel Gerisa (Tell Jerishe). These abandonments are offset by a flowering of settlement in the middle and later parts of the Middle Bronze IIb in southern Canaan. The principal sites are Ashdod and its port Tel Mor, Tell el-Ajjul (Sharuhen), Tell el-Far'ah South, Tel Nagila, Tell Jemmeh (Yurza), Tel Sera' (Ziklag), Tel Haror (Gerar),

and two related sites of the Beersheba valley, Tel Masos (Hormah) and Tel Malhata.

It thus appears that the shift of the focus of settlement to the southern coastal plain is closely linked to the establishment of the Canaanite Delta Kingdom, which became, in 1670 B.C.E., part of the Fifteenth Dynasty, or Hyksos, extended kingdom. The concentration of population in the south, particularly along the coastal plain, suggests that the Canaanite Delta Kingdom wished to establish a stable economic and political hinterland. The retreat of the Fifteenth Dynasty armies to Sharuhen (probably Tell el-Ajjul) after their defeat at Avaris, and their ability to withstand a three-year siege by the Egyptians, indicate the economic and military strength of this province. Incentives for settlement in more southerly areas seem to have been among the causes of the increasing impoverishment of the central hill country and parts of the inner plains, which occurred from the second half of the seventeenth century B.C.E. and on. The

incentives may at times have been accompanied by force, so that the destruction of certain sites in the middle of the century may be related to the resettlement policy.

Sites of the Middle Bronze Age IIb

HAZOR. This city was, without doubt, the most important city in northern Canaan during the Middle Bronze IIb. Its relations with the trading cities of northern Syria and Mesopotamia are revealed in the royal Mari archives. The cultural and political ties of Hazor and neighboring Laish (Dan) with Syro-Mesopotamia in the Middle Bronze IIa and the beginning of the Middle Bronze IIb could suggest that in later times too, the kingdom of Hazor maintained links with the Syrian political and economic system, rather than with the Canaanite Delta Kingdom. The Jezreel valley may be seen as the border zone between these two political units and their cultural spheres of influence.

The role of Hazor as a trading center in northern Canaan and the wealth amassed by its traders and rulers resulted in the creation of the largest Bronze Age city of Canaan and southern Syria, with an area of 74 hectares. As the size of the urban unit generally reflects the size of the dependent territorial unit, the Middle Bronze IIb kingdom of Hazor probably dominated northern Canaan as far north as the southern Beqa' valley, and perhaps as far east as the Golan and northern Transjordan.

Several stages in the urban development of Hazor may be observed. The early mound, whose occupation dates from the Early Bronze Age, formed the nucleus of urban development following the Intermediate Bronze Age. At the start of the Middle Bronze IIa the city expanded

Table 6.4 Stratigraphy of Upper City of Hazor.

Stratum	Period	Remarks
pre-XVII	Middle Bronze IIa	According to Yadin, MBIIa–b transition
XVII	Middle Bronze IIb	Inner citadel wall palace remains
XVI	Middle Bronze IIb	As above; also, Area A temple founded
post-XVI	Middle Bronze IIb	

Table 6.5 Stratigraphy of Lower City of Hazor.

Stratum	Correlation with upper city	Remarks
pre-4	pre-XVII	Partly MBIIa, in deposits unrelated to structures.
4	XVII	Dated MBIIb by excavators, city surrounded by rampart.
3	XVI and post-XVI	MBIIb; Area H temple and Area F palace (temple)

to the eastern ridge, and the first rampart may have been constructed at this time. Toward the end of the nineteenth or at the start of the eighteenth century B.C.E. the large, nearly rectangular lower city was established north of the earlier site. Yadin's excavations in the upper city reached Middle Bronze Age strata only in narrow trenches, revealing the stratigraphy outlined in Table 6.4. Only three strata, listed in Table 6.5, have so far been recorded in the lower city (the enclosure).

The nucleus of the site, the ancient mound, apparently included an internal citadel and palace, probably built at the end of the Middle Bronze IIa. (The excavator dated them to Middle Bronze IIb, though the changes in terminology and the phase termed pre-XVII may indicate some ambiguity in the interpretation of the stratigraphy.) In a later phase, when the focus of commercial and economic activity shifted to the lower city, followed by centers of public activity, the Area F palace

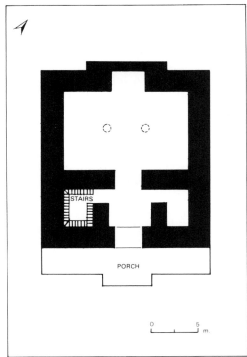

Fig. 6.17. Area H temple at Hazor, stratum 3

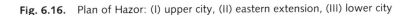

Fig. 6.16. Plan of Hazor: (I) upper city, (II) eastern extension, (III) lower city

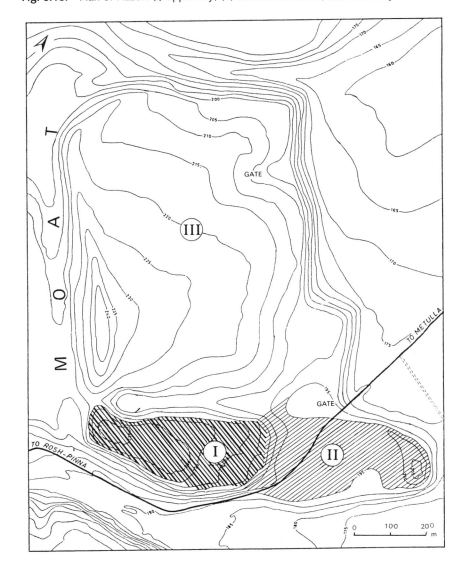

and the Area H temple were constructed.

The plan of the Area F structure is strongly reminiscent of the great palace recently discovered in the lower city of Ebla and of the stratum XII palace at Megiddo. The Hazor palace had two matching courts, each surrounded by a range of rooms. It measured about 48 meters long and 23 meters wide, and beneath it extended a maze of corridors carved in the rock, at least some of which were intended to serve as tombs (cf. the subterranean tomb system found under the palace at Ebla).

The temple discovered in Area H abutted the northern rampart, the southern slope of which was partly cleared. The excavators attributed the temple's construction to stratum 3, though it could well have been built in a late phase of stratum 4. The temple, planned as a longhouse, has a broadroom as its central cult chamber (hekhal). The hekhal continues an ancient temple-building tradition in the Land of Israel. The bases of two pillars were found in the middle of the room. At the northern end of the hekhal was a niche where the sacred cult objects were placed. The cult niche was built on the axis of entry into the

structure. On either side of the entrance, a flight of steps led to flanking towers, one of which served as a stairwell. There is a great deal of similarity between the plan of this temple and that of the temple excavated at Shechem.

In Area C, two houses were excavated in a residential quarter that abutted the eastern rampart. The houses were of the courtyard type, each with an anteroom. Their plan resembles that of the houses of Megiddo stratum XII. It thus appears that building traditions were retained from the Middle Bronze IIa through the later part of the Middle Bronze II. Burials (mainly of infants) were found under the floors; this practice, present in the earliest phase of the period, continued to its end and even into the beginning of the Late Bronze Age. Near the two houses, in a structure that may have been a cult niche dismantled during Middle Bronze IIb, three identical jars were found, one with the name "Is-me-Adad" incised in cuneiform script. The jar probably originated in stratum 4 (see Fig. 6.15:2). The close resemblance noted by A. Malamat and P. Artzi between the style of this inscription and the cuneiform script of the Mari archives suggests

that the date of stratum 4 cannot be far from that of the Mari correspondence (the first half of the eighteenth century B.C.E.). The Hazor scribal school, which must have been established during the time of the Mari correspondence, continued to flourish during the eighteenth and early seventeenth centuries, as gathered from a fragment of a Sumerian-Akkadian vocabulary and an Akkadian tablet recording legal proceedings found in the dumps of the upper city. There is no doubt that the Middle Bronze Age archives are still buried somewhere within the upper city palace or citadel.

MEGIDDO. The transition to Middle Bronze IIb occurred toward the end of stratum XII, and in stratum XI a change in the town plan also reflects the transformation of Megiddo from an Egyptian dependency to the capital of an independent city-state. The architectural development in strata XI and X gave Megiddo the urban character it was to retain until the end of the Late Bronze Age.

Only a few elements remained of the stratum XII city. The mud-brick walls were completely destroyed, public buildings underwent drastic

Fig. 6.18. Megiddo temple and its surroundings

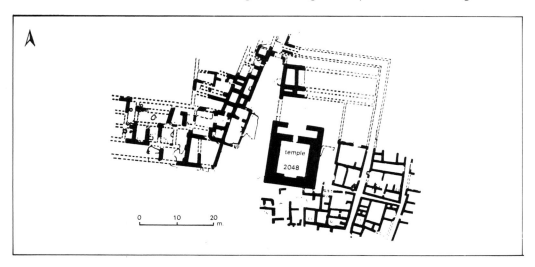

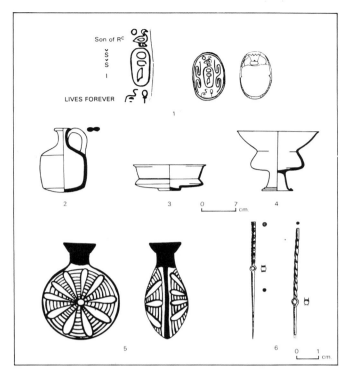

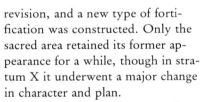

Fig. 6.19. Finds from tomb at Barqai

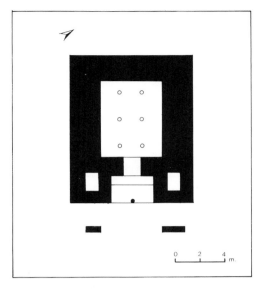

Fig. 6.20. Temple at Shechem

revision, and a new type of fortification was constructed. Only the sacred area retained its former appearance for a while, though in stratum X it underwent a major change in character and plan.

The fortifications consisted mainly of a series of glacis, probably topped by a brick wall. The town gate was also rebuilt and now took the form of a straight-axis entrance. These changes in the fortification system enlarged the area of the city to about eight hectares on the top of the mound (the citadel), in addition to about five hectares in the lower city; in terms of size, Megiddo thus approaches Tel Dan.

West of the sacred area a new palace was built in stratum XI. The residential quarter east of the sacred area preserved, more or less, its stratum XII layout. In stratum X the palace was reduced in size, while a building was constructed near the new Syrian-style gateway. The new

building served as the nucleus for the Late Bronze Age palace.

Sometime during the existence of stratum X a Syrian-style temple was constructed. It resembles the temple of Hazor but is most closely related to the Syrian temple found in Level VII at Alalakh (Tell Atchana, in the Orontes valley near the modern Syrian-Turkish frontier). In its first phase the temple had a broad anteroom instead of flanking towers, which were added only during the Late Bronze Age. The main room is a longroom and thus retains its Syrian quality.

The absolute chronology of strata XII–X is based on synchronisms with the Barqai tomb, where a royal scarab of Sheshi, the first ruler of the Fifteenth Dynasty, was discovered. The pottery of the Barqai tomb being identical to that of the late stratum XI and early stratum X at Megiddo, the transition between the two levels seems to

have occurred between 1670 and 1650 B.C.E. The end of stratum X is marked by the appearance of bichrome vessels, whose date, according to the evidence from Tell el-Ajjul, can be fixed to the reign of Apophis, one of the last kings of the Hyksos dynasty (about 1620–1580 B.C.E.). Megiddo X was apparently destroyed during his reign. Stratum IX is ceramically within the compass of the Late Bronze Age.

In strata XI and X the practice of burial under house floors reached its apex. Tomb structures resembling vaults, built in the corbeling technique, often remained in use over more than one stratum. They had entrance shafts and corridors leading into the tomb. Generations of families who lived in the houses above were interred in these conveniently located vaults, which often contained a wealth of pottery vessels, jewelry, and weapons.

Fig. 6.21. Wooden objects from Jericho tombs

BARQAI (TOMB). Figure 6.19 presents objects characteristic of the latest phase of the Barqai tomb: 1. The royal scarab of Sheshi, who was probably the first ruler of the Fifteenth Dynasty (1680–1650 B.C.E.). 2–4. Three pottery vessels characteristic of the late Middle Bronze IIb. 5. A faience flask. Faience juglets are present in Egypt from late Twelfth Dynasty times. The flask appears rarely in tomb contexts in Canaan, especially in the later phase of the Middle Bronze IIb. The form of the vessel is not Egyptian. 6. A peg-shaped toggle pin, with a threaded decoration at the top. This type replaces the bulbous-headed type of the Middle Bronze IIa and is characteristic of the whole of the Middle Bronze IIb. The selection from the Barqai assemblage is a good example of the complete chronological correlation between the ceramic contents of the tomb and the other objects found there, particularly the royal scarab, dated to the later part of Middle Bronze IIb.

APHEK. The information presently available on the Middle Bronze IIb levels at this site is still limited. Excavations within the royal fortress area have revealed a stratigraphic sequence of two similar Middle Bronze IIb palaces. Both were built over the remains of a huge palace (not fully excavated) of the Middle Bronze IIa. In the town itself the residential quarters apparently dwindled in size.

SHECHEM. The city of Shechem remained the most important political center in the central hills with the advent of the Middle Bronze IIb. The published evidence has focused on the fortifications and the temple, which resembles the temples of Megiddo and Hazor. It was built on the inner slope of the rampart, a portion of which was leveled to create a raised platform, and comprised a longhouse with two rows of Egyptian-style octagonal pillars. In the earlier phase, the holy of holies was integrated in the main room, but in a later phase a niche was constructed at the northern end, apparently to accommodate a cult image. As at Hazor, the entrance to the temple faces southeast. The construction of the temple and dismantling of the rampart were carried out at the same time as the construction of wall A, which is built of huge boulders in polygonal construction. This wall was furnished with a characteristic Syrian gateway. As at Hazor, a cuneiform tablet dating to Middle Bronze IIb was found here, containing a complaint of a local clerk concerning his wages. This tablet testifies to the spread of Akkadian writing throughout the important city-states of Canaan.

TELL EL-FAR'AH NORTH. The available information on this site is also meager and concerns mainly the fortifications and tombs found inside the city. The city wall, with internal buttresses, was constructed at the start of the Middle Bronze IIb using a technique identical to the wall of Megiddo stratum XI. The gate built into this wall differs somewhat from other gates of the period. The town was abandoned or destroyed before the end of the seventeenth century.

JERICHO. The importance of Jericho increases during this period, mainly because it is on the main route between Transjordan and the Land of Israel. The town was surrounded by a rampart faced, at least in the last phase of use, with a stone glacis. The glacis was crowned by impressive remains of a brick wall. Within the city, Garstang excavated a residential area in the thirties and termed it "the palace store rooms," mainly because of the large numbers of storage jars he found filled with carbonized wheat. Kenyon, who renewed excavations at Jericho in the fifties, interpreted the finds as a residential quarter with flour and grain shops lining the streets.

The large cemetery discovered to the north and west of the site is one of the largest so far excavated. The inhabitants of Jericho rarely buried their dead within the town confines, that is, under the house floors, suggesting that powerful local traditions prohibited intramural burial, a custom that took root in Canaan following the penetration of north Syrian populations (mainly in the north). The tombs at Jericho are mostly shaft tombs of the Intermediate Bronze Age, cleared to accommodate the new burials, but there are also many tombs cut in the Middle Bronze IIb. Kenyon divided the assemblages found in the tombs into five chronological phases.

The absolute and comparative chronology of the phases was established by the scarabs of Thirteenth and Fifteenth Dynasty kings, as well as by Babylonian and Syrian cylinder seals. Finds of the greatest importance, unparalleled at any other cemetery of the period in the Land of Israel, are the objects made of perishable materials, preserved by the dry climate of Jericho. They include stools, chairs, beds, and bowls—all of wood—and mats. These finds permit a more accurate reconstruction of the household objects and daily life of the Middle Bronze IIb.

GEZER. The results of Macalister's excavations at this site were reexamined and corrected in the sixties by the American expedition headed by Dever. A large area was excavated near the Middle Bronze II gate uncovered at the beginning of this century by Macalister, and it was discovered that two fortification systems existed within the span of the Middle Bronze II. The earlier system adjoined the citadel built at the end of the first part of the period, while the later fortifications, consisting mainly of a glacis and a double-chambered gateway, appear to have been built in the second phase of the Middle Bronze Age.

The destruction of these fortifications should be dated to the early sixteenth century, when the rulers of the Eighteenth Dynasty invaded southern Canaan. The destruction deposits contained a seal ring bearing the royal name of Khyan (Khyran), the third king of the Fifteenth Dynasty (about 1640 B.C.E.). The presence of this gold-inlaid ring in the destruction layer shows that it remained in use until the days of Apophis or possibly later, until the reign of Khamudy (about 1570 B.C.E.).

The most important find was a clay envelope inscribed in cuneiform characters, containing two personal names. The names are Hurrian, and as the envelope has been epigraphically dated to the late Middle Bronze IIb, the arrival of Hurrian groups in Canaan during the seventeenth century may be inferred.

SOUTHERN TOWNS

The political unit that encompassed the towns of the northern Negev, the Shephelah, and the southern coast was dominated by the city of Sharuhen, probably to be identified with Tell el-Ajjul. Sharuhen was the last stronghold of the Fifteenth Dynasty (Hyksos) armies, pursued from Egypt into Canaan and southern Syria by Ahmose, the founder of the Eighteenth Dynasty—which serves as a historical anchor for a discussion of the chronology and stratigraphy of the region.

TELL EL-AJJUL. Two main areas of excavation were opened on the mound, the area of palaces and fortresses, and the city proper. Petrie employed a different stratigraphic terminology in each area: the city and palace strata are correlated in Table 6.6.

Table 6.6 Tell el-Ajjul Stratigraphy and Chronology.

City	Palace/Citadel	Period	Remarks
III	pre-I and I (courtyard cemetery)	Late MBIIa	Twelfth and Thirteenth dynasties
II	Palace II	MBIIb (and early LBI)	Sheshi (1670) to Ahmose (1570)
I	Citadel III	LBI	

Table 6.7 Synchronisms between Northern and Southern Sites in the Seventeenth and Sixteenth Centuries.

	Megiddo	Barqai	Mevorakh	Tell Beit Mirsim	Tell el-Ajjul	Jericho	Tell el-Far'ah (S)
1670 (no bichrome ware)	XI	Tomb (Sheshi)	XII	D	Early II (Sheshi)	phase iv (Sheshi)	500 (Sheshi)
1600	X				II	phase v	
1570	IX				End II (Apophis)		
1500							

City III was dated to the period between the mid-late Twelfth Dynasty and the early Thirteenth Dynasty. Two scarabs of Nefer-hotep I (about 1730 B.C.E.) date the stratum, testifying that the city was at least within the influence of this king until the end of his reign.

City II was built during the reign of Sheshi, probably the first of the Fifteenth Dynasty kings (about 1680–1650); one of his scarabs was discovered in the construction fills of this stratum. The destruction of the stratum occurred after the reign of Apophis (1620–1580), as may be inferred from the discovery of scarabs bearing his name in the destruction layers or in related deposits (tombs from late in the City II sequence). The fall of Tell el-Ajjul during the campaign of Ahmose in Canaan, after a three-year siege, is related in the biography of one of the officers who participated in the siege. The identification of Tell el-Ajjul with Sharuhen is not based solely on the presence of the scarabs but also on the size of the site, the discovery of gold treasures unparalleled in size in the Land of Israel, the location of the site, and its subsequent history until the days of Thutmose III.

The destruction layers of City II contained relatively large amounts of bichrome and chocolate-on-white wares, as well as Cypriot pottery dated to the early sixteenth century. This shows that by the year 1570 the Late Bronze Age had already begun and that the transition from Middle Bronze IIb must have occurred twenty or thirty years earlier. The scarcity of bichrome ware in stratum X at Megiddo and its complete absence in stratum XII at Tel Mevorakh indicate that those two strata ended at about 1620 B.C.E. The synchronization between the south, where absolute dates based on Egyptian chronology are available, and the north, where the only absolute date is furnished by a single scarab bearing the name of Sheshi (from Barqai), is outlined in Table 6.7.

Large-scale exposures such as those conducted by Petrie permit a relatively close look at the Middle Bronze IIb city. The palace was built at the northwestern edge of the site. East of it lay the gate, which was built of mud brick and has almost completely washed away. Tunnels bored through the kurkar rock under the gate seem to have

served as sally ports. The city was defended by a rampart and a deep ditch, which was apparently filled with water from nearby Wadi Ghazzeh (Nahal Besor). On the southern side of the city, on the banks of the Besor, there was probably a jetty, which was later moved to the nearby site of Tel Zanem. The rampart was preserved only in small segments.

The city itself was divided into quarters. Excavation was concentrated in two of these, the southeast quarter and the central quarter. The residential area had patrician houses ranged alongside lower-class dwellings. The influence of Egyptian construction techniques in City II is conspicuous. The burning of the city by the Egyptian attackers covered it with a thick layer of ash, preserving some of the patrician houses to the ceiling level of the first story, in some cases the doorposts and beams remained intact, a rare phenomenon in the archaeology of the Land of Israel.

City II is also the city of the gold caches, the largest ever found in a Bronze Age city in the Land of Israel. They lead to two important conclusions: first, that the inhabi-

Fig. 6.22. Plan of Tell el-Ajjul

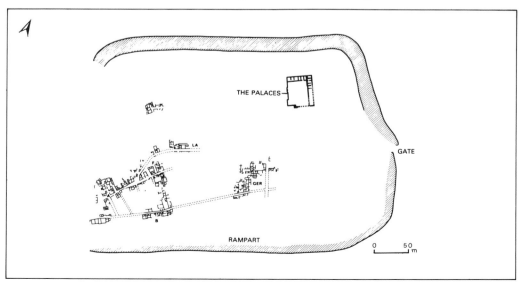

tants of City II had considerable material wealth, largely of Egyptian origin (Nubia was the main source of gold in the Bronze Age), and that the city was therefore one of the most important towns of Canaan at the time; second, that the inhabitants had sufficient opportunity to hide some of their valuables under the house floors and in the brick walls before abandoning the site, suggesting a siege of considerable duration. These conclusions support the identification of Tell el-Ajjul with Sharuhen, the Canaanite capital of the Fifteenth Dynasty.

In the palace area, Palace I was built along Syro-Canaanite lines. It formed a rectangle about 35 × 50 meters, with a large court in the center and rooms ranged round the sides. The walls of the palace were lined with orthostats at their base and had a brick superstructure. This technique is in the traditional Syro-Canaanite style.

Above this palace, after its destruction, a patrician house, or a small palace (Palace II), was built. This palace was made entirely of mud brick, without orthostats, a technique reflecting the influence of the Fifteenth Dynasty on local architecture. The palace was destroyed together with City II during the campaign of Ahmose around the year 1570 B.C.E. The destruction layer contained much bichrome ware, and a tomb later cut into its northwest corner also contained pottery typical of the late Middle Bronze IIb or the early Late Bronze I. Thus Albright's contention that both City II and Palace II were destroyed by Thutmose III runs contrary to the weight of archaeological evidence both from the lower city and the palace area.

As at Megiddo, the practice of intramural burial, under house floors, was common at Tell el-Ajjul; but as at Jericho, there were burial grounds outside the city as well. These were extensive cemeteries, some of which made secondary use of Intermediate Bronze Age tombs. A new tomb type appeared later in the Middle Bronze IIb, featured so far in Canaan only at Tell el-Ajjul. It was an oval or rectangular tomb, with a large central courtyard carved in the earth or kurkar, furnished with niches to accommodate the deceased. One of these courtyards contained the complete skeleton of a donkey or horse, buried, no doubt, to accompany one of the deceased. Another tomb contained remains of three equids, as well as a human burial. This phenomenon reflects the addition of the horse to the inner circle of domesticated animals and may even indicate the introduc-

Fig. 6.23.   Horse burial, Tell el-Ajjul

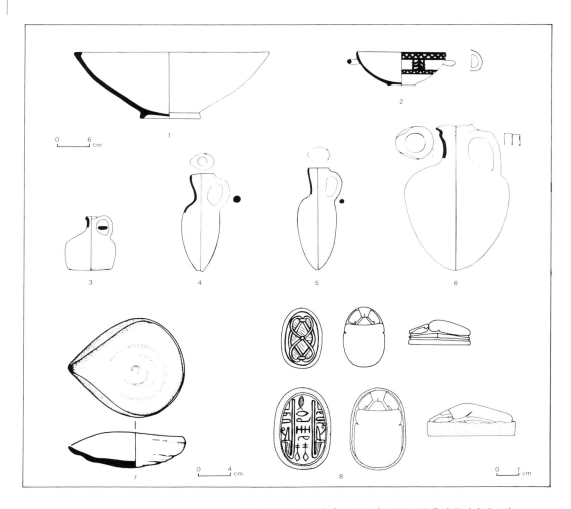

Fig. 6.24.   Finds from tomb 569 at Tell el-Far'ah South

tion of the light chariot into Canaan. A similar phenomenon has
been observed in contemporary
strata at Tell ed-Daba. In several of
the Middle Bronze IIb tombs there,
donkeys or other equids were interred together with humans.

TELL EL-FAR'AH SOUTH.
This mound, in upper Wadi Ghazzeh, was previously identified with
Sharuhen, but it is smaller and less
important than Tell el-Ajjul. This
site too was excavated by Petrie, and
like Tell el-Ajjul was surrounded by
a rampart and moat carved in the
kurkar bedrock. The earliest occupation of the site dates from the
Middle Bronze IIb. The most prom-

inent structure is the gatehouse,
constructed in typical Syrian style.
Tombs of the Middle Bronze Age
were found in cemeteries surrounding the site. The 500 Cemetery is
one of the more important cemeteries; it was established before the
reign of Sheshi and remained in use
until the end of the Middle Bronze
IIb, before the introduction of bichrome ware at about 1600 B.C.E.
The earlier tombs are shallow, single-chambered shaft tombs; the later
tombs consist of a stepped shaft
leading to a short dromos, and
thence to two parallel chambers,
giving the tomb the form of a kid-
ney. This tomb type was to remain
in use throughout the Late Bronze

Age and into the Iron Age I. The
typological-chronological sequence
provided by the 500 Cemetery
matches almost precisely the sequence of habitation at the site. The
tombs themselves were used for the
interment of up to five bodies, with
modest burial gifts: a bowl, a jar, a
dipper juglet, a lamp, and a saucer.
In addition, the personal scarab seals
of the deceased were buried with
them, and in some cases weapons.
These modest gifts suggest that the
people buried in the 500 Cemetery
were of the lower middle class; no
luxurious tombs or tomb contents
were found. Faience juglets containing kohl may indicate the burial of
women.

LACHISH. The section excavated by Starkey through the rampart deposits at Lachish showed that it was constructed in the Middle Bronze IIb. Proof is provided by the discovery of an early Middle Bronze IIb tomb underneath the earliest rampart deposits. The renewed excavations at the site under the direction of D. Ussishkin concentrated on the place where Starkey believed the Late Bronze Age palace would be located. As it turned out, a palace was found of the Middle Bronze IIb. Only a few rooms of the palace have been cleared so far. The rooms, clearly destroyed in a conflagration, had walls up to two meters thick, lined, as in the Tell el-Ajjul palace, with orthostats. The latest pottery pre-dates the introduction of bichrome and chocolate-on-white wares and must therefore be dated to before 1620 B.C.E.

TELL BEIT MIRSIM. At this site, which has particular importance for the history of archaeological research in the Land of Israel, the transition between the first and second phases of the Middle Bronze Age was attributed to stratum E. A residential quarter bisected by a street was excavated, as well as a Syrian style gateway, of which only fragments remain. Also discovered in stratum E were a scarab seal of a Canaanite king by the name of Ya'qub-['a]mu. Stratum D is subdivided into two phases, and Albright proposed that in stratum D1 the glacis was given a stone facing. The destruction of stratum D corresponds to the end of the Lachish palace. This destruction, which we would date before 1600 B.C.E., is apparently linked to the abandonment of sites in the hills and along their margins, coinciding with the shift of the political and economic centers of Canaan toward the southern coast.

ASHDOD AND TEL MOR. The city of Ashdod and its port at Tel Mor were founded, as far as is known, toward the end of the Middle Bronze IIb. The scant material published from these two sites shows close correlation to City II at Tell el-Ajjul. At Ashdod, a city gate was revealed consisting of a single chamber and two pairs of buttresses. M. Dothan, the excavator of these two sites, ascribed their foundation to Apophis, who would have fortified the southern coast in preparation for the onslaught of the armies of the Seventeenth Dynasty, which had by then begun the reconquest of Egypt. However, the urbanization of the southern coast was probably a more extended process than that envisioned by Dothan, being related to the shift of the focus of settlement toward the southern coast.

THE SETTLEMENT SYSTEM IN PERSPECTIVE: THE CITY-STATES

The 150 years of the Middle Bronze IIb do not represent a period of stability or stagnation, especially insofar as the settlement pattern is concerned. A great urban expansion marked the end of the Middle Bronze IIa and beginning of the Middle Bronze IIb. Following this phase, which also witnessed the abandonment or decline of some earlier centers, a number of local blocs crystallized. In the more advanced stages of the Middle Bronze IIb village sites nearly disappeared. The rural population seems to have gradually been absorbed into the cities or into the fortified settlements or towns such as Tel Mevorakh and Tell Beit Mirsim. The full reurbanization of Canaan reached its zenith during the second part of the Middle Bronze IIb.

This section will review the various blocs of settlement, from north to south, while attempting to define the territorial limits of the city-states

or of regions featuring marked cultural uniformity.

The great size of Hazor probably reflects the importance of the political unit it headed. Its growth was incremental; that is, the city developed from a relatively small nucleus into a metropolis by the beginning of the Middle Bronze IIb, and that process continued throughout this phase. A similar process of territorial expansion may also have occurred in the city-state of Laish-Dan. Hazor and Syria were culturally linked, and the material culture assemblages of Hazor present features that characterize northern Canaan as a whole, so that the state of Hazor may have extended over the entire northern region as well as parts of northern Transjordan.

The central hills state headed by Shechem in Middle Kingdom times shows, like Hazor, continued intensive building activity, the fortifications reaching their greatest size in the Middle Bronze IIb. It would appear that the mound proper (Tell Balatah), which measures five hectares, was merely the center of a much larger city. Traces of the lower city of Shechem, found by the German expedition while conducting sporadic excavations west of the mound, indicate that the site may have covered fifteen hectares. The territory of the hill state lay mostly in the Samaria hills and the adjacent regions and included the towns of Tell el-Far'ah North and Shiloh.

The relation of the city-state of Shechem to the Delta Kingdom of the Fifteenth Dynasty is not known, but the depopulation of the central hills late in the seventeenth century B.C.E. underlines the attraction that the new areas in the south held for the inhabitants of the central hill state.

Southern Canaan witnessed the consolidation of the political bloc headed by Sharuhen, on the basis of urban units founded in Middle Kingdom times, such as Tell el-Ajjul, Ashkelon, Tel Poran, and Tell Beit Mirsim. This urban bloc provided the economic, military, and political hinterland for the delta state in the homeland of the dynasty. We have previously noted the increasing flow of population into this bloc from the mid seventeenth century and on, which finds expression in the foundation of new cities in the region. This political-economic bloc no doubt had interests extending beyond the Coastal Plain and northern Negev. The late Middle Bronze IIb fortress at Tel Malhata, as well as the earlier fortress at Tel Masos, testify to the importance of the route to Transjordan, which passed through the northern Negev, for the southern coastal towns. The Delta Kingdom seems to have had close relations with the Judaean hill region. At Hebron a cyclopean wall, similar to Wall A at Shechem, has been excavated, and the find may be related to biblical traditions concerning Hebron; the name "Sheshi" appears in the list of the Anakites who ruled Hebron and possibly represents a vague recollection of the rule of the founder of the Fifteenth Dynasty in the town: "Caleb dislodged from there the three Anakites: Sheshai, Ahiman and Talmai, descendants of Anak" (Num. 13:22; Joshua 15:13; cf. Judges 1:20).

The distribution of Fifteenth Dynasty scarabs also reflects the sphere of that dynasty's influence. Most of the scarabs originate in the southern bloc of cities under the direct domination of the Fifteenth Dynasty, and a minority from the regions at the periphery of its influence, such as the Jezreel valley or Jericho, the gateway to Transjordan.

The concentration of population in the southern coastal area had far-reaching consequences in the following period, the Late Bronze Age. The concentration of population along the coast and in the valleys,

particularly along the main highways, contrasting with the dispersed character of the hill settlements, eventually resulted in a decisive change in the ethnocultural character of the Land of Israel toward the end of the Late Bronze Age.

Ethnic Groups and Population Size

In the Execration Texts many of the names indicate Amorite ancestry, Amorites being the north-Syrian, western-Semitic population whose non-Canaanite dialect is known more from the corpus of personal names than from actual documents. The north and central Syrian origin of the population is reflected in the pottery as well, particularly by the Syrian forms originating in the Orontes valley. Kenyon tried to associate the population groups entering the Land of Israel during the Intermediate Bronze Age with the Amorites. It now appears, however, that those groups were mainly of Transjordanian origin and only a minority were Syrian groups possibly identifiable as Amorite.

Alongside the new groups we find the Canaanite population of indigenous as well as coastal Lebanese origin. A third element of the population was Hurrian; small groups of Hurrians found their way from northern Syria to Canaan, mainly at the end of the period. Evidence for this process is as yet meager; one example is the decidedly Hurrian name (Waritaldu) of the king of Laish (Dan) during the Mari period, which appears in a document concerning a shipment of tin to Canaan.

The size of the population remains a moot point, as no consensus has been achieved on the correct method of calculation. However, the currently accepted population coefficient is 250 persons per hectare in urban areas, which gives a total of

120,000 persons for the main urban sites of the Middle Bronze IIb. This sum seems reasonable, for the population of Hazor alone, with its 74 hectares at the height of the period, is estimated at 20,000 persons. As this calculation takes only the main sites into account, the population of the smaller towns, the villages, and the marginal areas should be added, bringing the total to roughly 200,000 persons for the entire country in the Middle Bronze IIb.

Architecture of the Middle Bronze Age IIb

DWELLINGS

The dominant courtyard house, developed later in the Middle Bronze IIa, remained in use without marked changes in the Middle Bronze IIb. The Megiddo XI–X dwelling units are larger than those of stratum XII; in both phases the houses are large courtyard houses, with a tomb vault under one of the rooms.

At Hazor, two private dwellings with a central courtyard and anteroom, similar to the units defined in Megiddo stratum XII, were identified.

At Tell Beit Mirsim, houses with corner courtyards were excavated. The houses seem to have retained a rural character, the arrangement of the rooms around the large corner courtyard suggesting that livestock were housed there. Similar houses were uncovered in a residential quarter partly excavated at Tel Nagila by Amiran and Eitan; here too the settlement may have been more a fortified village than a city.

At Tell el-Ajjul much may be learned of the social status of the inhabitants from the architectural fabric of the residential quarter of City II. Patrician dwellings are closely abutted by poorer courtyard houses, with either central or corner courtyards. The patrician houses measure 190–270 square meters on the ground floor, while the poorer dwellings attain an area of 70–100 square meters (both measurements include the internal courtyards). The patrician houses always had a second floor, so their area may have been double that of the ground floor, whereas in the houses of the common folk the ground area represents the entire available living space.

PATRICIAN HOUSES

The term "patrician houses" was introduced into archaeological literature by Albright, who attempted to relate the appearance of well-built and planned structures to the entry of new ethnic elements into Syria and Canaan. These new elements, claimed Albright, established a feudal system that revolutionized the social and political structure of Canaan. The element was defined as Indo-Iranian (Indo-Aryan), and in the Akkadian documents of north Syria it is termed the mariyannu caste (*marya* is the Sanskrit for a noble or a young warrior). It seems, therefore, that the appearance of patrician houses within city limits reflects the accumulation of wealth by the elite, leading to a marked improvement in their standard of living, probably as a result of their involvement in trade, government, and administration in the Nile Delta.

In stratum X at Megiddo the royal quarter moved from near the sacred area to the gate area, beginning with the construction of a patrician house that served as a nucleus for the development of the strata IX–VIII palace. The patrician house was designed as a palace in miniature, imitating the courtyard palace plan of the period. The habitation space in its two stories totaled about 700 square meters, considerably smaller than the contemporaneous

Area BB palace, which covered 1200 square meters on the ground floor alone. The heart of the patrician house was the large, rectangular courtyard. A staircase was built in the southwest corner, which communicated with the second floor. A water installation was set in the courtyard, equipped with a drain. The house abutted the city wall, and its northern wall was in fact part of the fortifications. Judging by its size and plan, this house doubtless belonged to a member of the ruling family.

At the nearby site of Ta'anach another patrician house (the western citadel) was excavated. The palace itself was uncovered in the northern part of the mound. The patrician house dates from about the same time as the Megiddo house, the end of the seventeenth century or the end of Middle Bronze IIb. Renewed excavations showed that the patrician house was linked to a repair in the last phase of the rampart surrounding the town. The plan of the structure differs from that of the Megiddo house, consisting of a corner courtyard adjoined by two rows of rooms. To the west of the courtyard was a stairway joined to a row of rooms built up against the fortifications. The total area of the two-story building was about 570 square meters, including 55 square meters of courtyard.

One of many patrician dwellings found at Tell el-Ajjul was Building AM, from City II. Its northern wing consisted of an enclosed courtyard surrounded by rooms, while the southern wing, which faced the street, comprised a central courtyard flanked symmetrically by four rooms. The ground floor measured 340 square meters. Also from City II, Building TO, incompletely preserved, had a corner courtyard. On its northern and western flanks it had small chambers, probably storerooms or granaries. The building

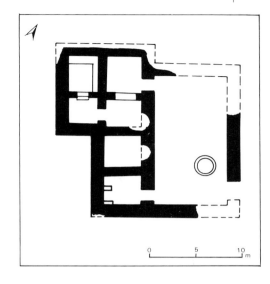

Fig. 6.25. Plan of patrician house, Tell Beit Mirsim

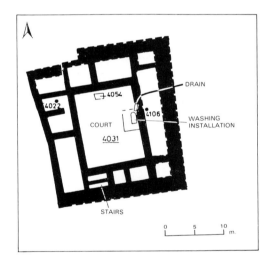

Fig. 6.26. Plan of patrician house, Megiddo

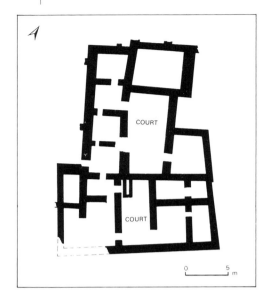

COURT

COURT

0   5
⌐—————⌐ m

Fig. 6.27. Plan of building AM, Tell el-Ajjul

covered about 200 square meters on the ground.

PALACES

Traces of a probable palace were discovered in Area F at Hazor. The estimated area of the ground floor, including the courtyards, was 1100 square meters.

At Megiddo, the stratum XII palace was replaced in stratum XI by a new palace, built on a different plan and architectural concept, which nonetheless utilized part of the external outline of the earlier structure for its outer framework. The new architectural concept was based on a large central court paved with a thick layer of lime. This rectangular court was in the northern part of the structure. To its south lay the ceremonial halls and the main living quarters. This structure covered 750 square meters and served as the nucleus of the palace. Another wing was constructed south of the main structure, but its size and extent are not known. In the east, facing the sacred enclosure, a separate elongated wing was constructed. The rooms facing the sacred area were small and may have served as granaries. In all, the built-up area of the palace, not including the courtyard, was 1500 square meters on the ground floor. The building plan changed in Stratum X. The palace grew smaller, covering 1000 square meters, and incorporated the eastern wing, which had been a separate unit in the earlier phase.

At Tell el-Ajjul the palace sequence corresponds to that of Megiddo XII–X. The earliest palace (I) had a rectangular outline, measuring 35 × 50 meters. Its rooms were arranged along the northern and eastern edges, and the remaining area served as a courtyard, so that only about one quarter of the space was actually roofed. The staircase was in the northeast corner, while

the main entrance to the palace lay on the south side of the courtyard. The wall bases were lined with large orthostats carved out of the local kurkar stone.

Palace II, constructed in about 1650 B.C.E., had a different ground plan. The central courtyard was retained, but the residential quarters were reduced to 10 × 20 meters. This structure was built entirely of mud brick, without stone foundations, apparently an expression of Egyptian influence. The palace plan included an anteroom, a staircase, and service rooms, including baths.

The evolution of palaces in Middle Bronze IIb Canaan begins with the parallel-courtyards plan of Megiddo XII, followed by the palace with the large central court, of the type found at Tell el-Ajjul or in the patrician houses of Megiddo X. Toward the end of the seventeenth century B.C.E. a new type is in evidence, with broader proportions; the courtyard is sometimes situated in the corner and in any case is not as central in the plan as in the earlier palaces.

TEMPLES AND HIGH PLACES

The open-air bamah (high place) and related structures, usually consisting of a cult room or cell, continued to exist in the early days of the Middle Bronze IIb. At Megiddo the high place and cult cell of stratum XII continued to function in stratum XI, while at Nahariya the final phases of the high place and the adjacent broadroom shrine appear to survive into the first part of the second Middle Bronze Age phase. But these all rapidly disappear. At Megiddo, a Syrian-style temple is built over the remains of the high place. At Nahariya as well, traces of a structure built over the high place were found, suggesting that a similar temple stood there. The designation of the new type of temple as Syrian stems mainly from the discovery of the earliest examples at Tell Mardikh in Syria. The three temples of this type found at Hazor, Megiddo, and Shechem share certain features. All continue to serve as the central cult places in their respective cities well into the Late Bronze Age, and the temples of Megiddo and Shechem last until the early days of the Iron Age I. Judging by the architectural continuity, these sites exhibit a continuity of cult from the seventeenth century until the beginning of the Iron Age. What was it, then, that initiated the new cult practice? Was a broad religious reform effected in the Syro-Canaanite expanse (the introduction of the cult of the storm god Hadad [Seth] of the Fifteenth Dynasty)? Or did new ethnic elements arrive in the region, as proposed by B. Mazar? Archaeology cannot, as yet, answer those questions.

The Syrian temple is marked by its excessively thick walls—four meters at Shechem, for example. The two towers flanking the entrance to the temple indicate that it was a multistoried structure. This feature accompanied by the biblical verse, "When all the people of the Tower of Shechem learned of it, they entered the stronghold of the house of El-berith" (Judges 9:46), led Mazar to coin the term "Tower Temple" for this type of structure.

The main cult hall of the temple was the hekhal. A niche or raised platform was built at its far end, where the masseboth (stelae), cult images, and emblems of the god could be placed. The worshipers did not enter the hekhal. As the axis of entry was direct and led to the cult niche, it was possible, when the portals were open, to view the sacred objects from without the temple walls.

Another kind of cult was practiced outside the temple, on a high place (bamah) or an altar. On the Nahariya high place, for example, clear remains of the cult were preserved. The assemblage, including many minute votive vessels as well as beads, miniature metal objects, and of course sacrifices, was placed on the bamah, adjacent to the altar and opposite the masseboth. At Megiddo too there seems to have been, alongside and west of the temple, a high place or an area designated for votive offerings, as may be gathered from the concentration of figurines, votive vessels, and magnificent pottery vessels found there.

Incense burners were rare in the Middle Bronze II; they became frequent in the cult assemblage only later. At Nahariya, however, they were found in large quantities, a unique phenomenon among the assemblages of the time. At Megiddo and Gezer only fragments were found.

The cult images actually recovered in or near temples are quite small, 10–18 centimeters. They were apparently gold-plated. In contrast to neighboring countries, where the divine images were often larger than life, the sculpture of the Middle Bronze Age craftsmen of Canaan was confined to a miniature scale, and no attempt was made at monumental sculpture.

FORTIFICATIONS

The most common Middle Bronze Age gate is the Syrian gate, with three piers and two chambers on each side. Here too, the term "Syrian" is based on the assumption that the origin of this gate type is in Syria, where the earliest examples have been found. The gatehouses found in the Land of Israel vary from 15 meters to 20 meters in length, with a maximum breadth of 10 meters. The entrance was 2.5–3 meters wide, more than enough for chariots. Most gate towers include

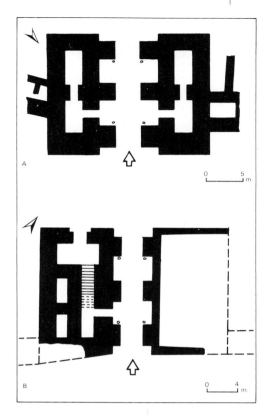

Fig. 6.28. Gateways at Hazor (A) and Alalakh (B)

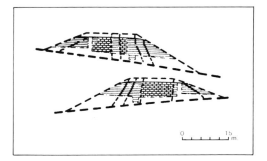

Fig. 6.29. Hazor ramparts, sections

staircases constructed around a central pillar or wall.

At Tell Mardikh door sockets were found in place, permitting a reconstruction of the manner in which the gate was closed: the leaves of the inner and outer doors both opened inward, toward the middle pier. The roofing, as discovered in the intact city gate at Tel Dan, consisted of a mud-brick barrel vault.

Among the typical Syrian gates found in the Land of Israel are those of Laish (Dan), Accho, Hazor, Shechem (the northern gate), Megiddo, Tell el-Far'ah South, Beth Shemesh, and Yavne-Yam. All have an identical plan, in general terms, though they differ in details of the staircases or towers. The near identity of the gates found in the Land of Israel and those found in Syria shows that they were part of a single concept of fortification.

Ramparts came into use during the Middle Bronze IIa. During the Middle Bronze IIb they became the standard fortification of most cities of Canaan.

HAZOR. The ramparts surrounding the lower city and part of the upper city have been well preserved. They were built in various methods, according to the topographical situation and the defense requirements of each area. The western rampart is the most impressive, towering 15 meters, with a breadth of 60 meters. Its external flank was protected by a ditch, presently some 15 meters deep, whence most of the fill of the rampart was obtained.

The eastern rampart of the city was sectioned through to its core. It is anchored to a sturdy inner core built as a structural casemate wall, filled with rubble and earth. The outer sections of the rampart were built in three main blocks, with each tip layer being covered with a lime surface and matting to prevent collapse during the construction. The two blocks of fill nearest the core on each side were built simultaneously, while the third and steepest block was built last of all and covered with a thick layer of lime. The earliest floor level excavated inside the city, cutting the inner rampart slope, included Middle Bronze IIa sherds, but the manner of excavation and scant material preclude a definite pronouncement on the date of the building of the rampart itself. There is a close resemblance, in terms of technique, to the rampart at Laish (Dan), and the Hazor rampart may therefore be dated to a similar period, that is, the Middle Bronze IIa.

MEGIDDO. At Megiddo, two existing features were exploited during the construction of the rampart. First, there was the natural slope of the mound, which could easily be used as a glacis, on the rampart's exterior slope. Second, there were the remains of the wall (strata XII–XIII), which were used, at least in part, as a core for the rampart. Only where the earlier wall could not be utilized was a new core erected, serving also as a foundation for the wall built above it. The inner slope, though moderate, remained uninhabited, unlike Hazor.

SHECHEM. The fortification system excavated at Shechem is extremely complex; this discussion covers only two of its components, the rampart wall designated Wall C by the excavators and a wall designated Wall A. Wall C is the northern wall of a rampart; its outer slope was revetted with stones and thus took on the aspect of a slanted support wall. The rampart itself was excavated only in a few narrow trenches, and it appears to have been about thirty meters wide. It was partly dismantled during the construction of the Tower Temple. On the interior, the rampart was bordered by a wall, dated by the excavator to the Middle Bronze IIa, possibly the foundation date of the rampart as well. In a later phase of the Middle Bronze Age II the rampart was raised, and a new external revetment, Wall A, was constructed. This wall, built of huge boulders, was preserved to a height of some six meters and remains to this day one of the most impressive examples of the art of fortification in the Middle Bronze IIb; it is related to the construction of a new city gate.

JERICHO. The builders of the rampart at Jericho, faced with an existing mound, girdled its slopes with a series of ramparts that fortified the margins of the mound. In its final stage, the rampart features an inclined stone glacis resembling, in concept if not in size, Wall A at Shechem. The last two phases of rampart construction at Jericho, separated by a burned layer, clearly belong to two separate periods. In the final phase, cyclopean boulders were incorporated at the base of the revetment, suggesting that local builders were influenced by the construction methods of Shechem. The evolution of massive revetments, beginning with Wall C at Shechem and ending with Wall A and the massive wall at Jericho, seems to represent an internal development within Middle Bronze IIb Canaan.

Writing, Art, and Crafts

ORIGINS OF THE CANAANITE ALPHABET

Toward the end of the Middle Bronze IIb, Canaanite scribes first attempted a local alphabet, known as proto-Canaanite. Their inspiration came from monosyllabic Egyptian hieroglyphs usually employed by Egyptian scribes to transcribe foreign names and places. The number of deciphered Middle Bronze Age proto-Canaanite signs is small. In a relief inscription from Shechem, for example, the Egyptian hieroglyph for "head" (*rosh*) is prominent; it was adopted by the Canaanites to express the letter *r*. The same is true of the Gezer ostracon; the only sign deciphered so far is the hieroglyph for "house" (*bayit*), which represents the letter *b*. The original relation between the proto-Canaanite alphabet and the Egyptian hieroglyphs shows that the scribe or scribes who invented the Canaanite alphabet were acquainted with Egyptian culture and probably served in one of the centers of the Delta Kingdom, perhaps even in Avaris or Sharuhen.

SCULPTURE

The Middle Bronze Age witnessed the first appearance in the Land of Israel of the stylized sculpture of the Syro-Mesopotamian school. It is present at first on a small scale, limited mainly to two-dimensional reliefs, and only rarely does it take the form of sculpture in the round. The sources of this style are mainly Syrian.

A relief found at Tell Beit Mirsim is known as the Serpent Goddess, an apparent misnomer. The surviving fragment is 42 centimeters high, and the original object must have been about 65 centimeters. It depicts a standing figure with what appears to be a serpent twined round the lower part of its garment. After Albright published this relief, the publication of several north Syrian cylinder seals made it clear that the serpentine relief merely represents the fringes of a long garment. The figure portrayed in Fig. 6.31, taken from a cylinder seal, reveals what the original appearance of the Tell Beit Mirsim relief must have been. A similar relief was found in the Shechem excavations, complete with the fringes

Fig. 6.30. Serpent Goddess relief from Tell Beit Mirsim

Fig. 6.31. Cylinder seal depicting figure clad in long robe

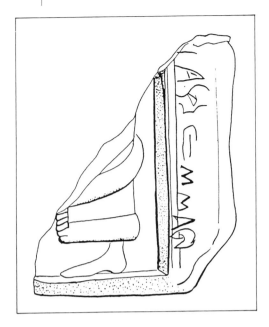

Fig. 6.32. Relief depicting figure clad in long robe from Shechem (height 8 centimeters)

Fig. 6.33. Plaque depicting Canaanite dignitary from Hazor

on the standing figure's garment and tufts on its hair cloak. The relief is accompanied by proto-Canaanite letters, which have yet to be deciphered.

What is the figure represented in the two stelae? The answer to this question may well be provided by a bronze plaque found at Hazor in the Area H temple and by a relief from Ugarit. The Hazor plaque portrays a prince wrapped in a hair cloak and a scarf, with his hand extended in a gesture of obeisance. The Ugarit relief (known as the Baal stela) portrays a prince in similar attire, standing near the storm god (as the lord of lightning), with his hand raised in obeisance. An almost identical scene is shown on a cylinder seal from Alalakh, level VII, where the prince raises his hand in obeisance toward a goddess, apparently Ishtar. The Canaanite reliefs probably portray a similar scene, with the prince placed so that his obeisance is addressed to an image of the local god.

A basalt statue found in the temple at Hazor in a Late Bronze Age context is probably of Middle Bronze Age II origin (the excavator, Yadin, attributed the statue to the Late Bronze Age). It portrays a ruler seated on a throne and is the only statue so far discovered in the Land of Israel that may clearly be ascribed to the Syrian school. The ruler sits with one hand on his knee and the other apparently grasping a cup. His garment exposes one shoulder, a style well known from third and early second millennium Mesopotamia. A similar statue was discovered near the gate of Tell Mardikh. The Hazor statue may have been imported from Syria, at a time when close trade relations existed between Hazor and the kingdoms of northern Syria.

ART OBJECTS

As opposed to the Syrian-oriented realm of sculpture, the fashioning of wooden boxes with bone inlays, faience vessels, and alabaster vessels reflects a close bond between Canaan and Egypt. The presence of these objects from the end of the Middle Bronze IIa and their proliferation as the period advances, especially in the south, testify to the integration of this part of Canaan with the Fifteenth Dynasty delta state. A continuous evolution can be traced from the end of Middle Bronze IIa to the end of Middle Bronze IIb, eliminating the usual division between the two phases.

BONE-INLAID WOODEN BOXES. Most of these appear in the form of burial gifts, though it may be assumed that they served everyday functions as well. The inlay was produced like modern-day Damascene bone inlays, by fitting the inlay into the wood and affixing it with resin or wooden pins inserted at the edges of the bone strips. The boxes range in size from 8 × 12 centimeters to 12 × 18 centimeters. They are local objects, though a number of items appear in Egypt in early Middle Kingdom times. It is at present difficult to say whether the inspiration for this object came from Canaan or Egypt; however, the existence of a tradition of inlaid wooden boxes in Mesopotamia and Syria as early as the late third millennium indicates the original source.

The decorative elements on the boxes are drawn mainly from Egyptian motifs. They may be divided into three groups. The first contains thematic decorations, that is, figures derived from well-known scenes of Egyptian mythology. This group includes the remains of a magnificent box (or bed) from a tomb near El-Gisr, decorated with figures of gods, animals (many of African origin), and humans. A contemporary of these inlays depicts a Canaanite prisoner, found in City II at Tell el-Ajjul. The unique depiction suggests that the inlay was made during the period of Egyptian rule in the late Twelfth and early Thirteenth Dynasty. The second group is limited in its subjects, characterized by Egyptian Djed columns, Egyptian-style fowl, and rare occurrences of cattle, horned animals, and even snakes. The third group is the most schematic and geometric. Animals appear only rarely, and decorations consist mostly of zigzag patterns and concentric circles. This group also rep-

resents the final phase of the boxes, which disappear at the beginning of the Late Bronze Age. An interesting evolution may thus be observed, from the rich realistic-thematic patterns to the later schematic-geometric ones.

FAIENCE. The art of manufacturing faience was known in predynastic Egypt. Faience vessels are made of sand molded over a core, dried, and fired to 800°C, resulting in a semifired core with a glazed surface. Faience manufacture is related to the beginnings of glassmak-

Fig. 6.35. Bone inlays from Megiddo

Fig. 6.34. Bone inlays from El-Gisr

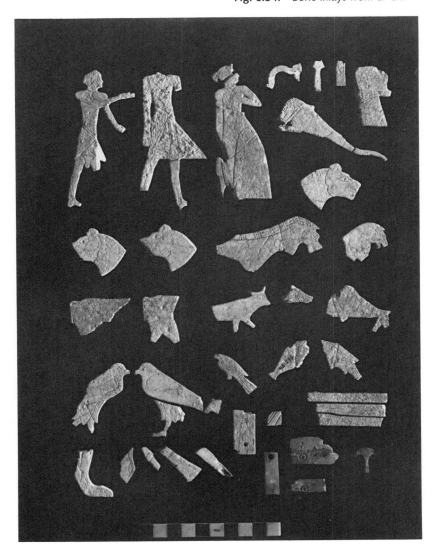

Fig. 6.36. Faience vessels

ing. The colors of the glaze—blue, green, and reddish brown—were produced, as in glass, by the addition of various minerals to the quartz base. Faience objects first appear in Canaan during the Middle Bronze IIb and are more common toward the end of the period.

Several types of faience objects are recorded in the Land of Israel. The most common is a tear-shaped object, which imitates Egyptian forms. The vessel is often decorated with a leaf pattern or a geometric pattern of interlacing knots. Another common type is a miniature slender flask, often decorated with a rosette or a wavy pattern. Faience objects are usually found in tombs. Their appearance toward the end of the Middle Bronze IIb, after the year 1700 B.C.E., reveals the influence of Egyptian burial customs on the inhabitants of Canaan.

ALABASTER. Alabaster vessels were used in Egypt and the ancient Near East as the most suitable containers for ointments and precious perfumes, mainly because the cooling effect of the stone helped preserve the contents.

The importation of Egyptian alabaster began in the Middle Bronze Age. The imports are easily identified by two main characteristics: Egyptian alabaster is calcium carbonate, whereas local alabaster is calcium sulphate (gypsum); and Egyptian alabaster vessels were shaped with a drill, rather than the chisel used on Canaanite vessels. At Beth Shean, considerable quantities of incomplete vessels in local alabaster were recovered, originating in a workshop of the Middle Bronze IIb and Late Bronze Age. The raw material for this workshop was apparently obtained in the gypsum deposits of Menahemiya, about eighteen kilometers north of Beth Shean.

The widespread distribution of alabaster vessels began at the beginning of Middle Bronze IIb, with the larger part of the objects appearing in tomb deposits. The dominant form in the Middle Bronze Age was still the Egyptian bag-shaped vessel or the elongated vessel, considered until much later times as the classic alabaster form, hence the term "alabastron" for ceramic vessels imitating this form. Type C, however, is an imitation of the Canaanite dipper juglet. It was apparently set in a wooden stand, as may be inferred from the knob on the base.

CYLINDER SEALS

The cylinder seal is of Mesopotamian origin and came into use in the Land of Israel by the beginning of the third millennium. Following the establishment of close cultural ties with Syria, particularly in Middle Bronze IIa, there was a flood of cylinder seal imports from Syria and Mesopotamia. One of the earliest cylinder seals in Canaan is recorded in an impression on a jar found at Shechem, which was accompanied by the imprint of a scarab seal of a Twelfth Dynasty Egyptian official. The vast majority of the seals found in Canaan belong to the Syrian group, and only a few (such as the seals found in the Jericho tombs) belong to the peripheral Babylonian group, exhibiting some carelessness in execution.

The Syrian seals are of outstanding beauty, precision, and formal and thematic variety. The subjects are borrowed partly from the Babylonian sphere, but there are Syrian and Egyptian motifs as well. A number of figures appear frequently on the seals; the most common is a Syrian prince wearing a heavy, double-fringed woolen garment, a kind of woolen cloak. At his side is the storm god Hadad, wearing a horned headdress and bearing arms, or the goddess Ishtar, often depicted spreading her robe to the sides to reveal her nude body.

Local seals make up a smaller, distinct group, exhibiting strong Egyptian influence. They include the seal of Yh(i)-set from Tell Beit Mirsim and a cylinder seal from Tell el-Ajjul, engraved in a style identical to that of scarab seals.

FIGURINES AND JEWELRY

The beginning of the Middle Bronze IIa is stamped with the influence of coastal Lebanon, and the city of Byblos and its environs continue to serve as an important cultural center for the newcomers who settled in Canaan. The technique of casting in flat molds, so common in Byblos, made its way to Canaan along with the migrant population. This is conspicuous especially in the manufacture of miniature objects in metal, which were cast in such molds. Metal figurines from Byblos and its environs, most of them representing the goddess of fertility, were found in large numbers at Byblos itself. In Canaan, such figurines

were found at the high place of Nahariya and near the high place at Megiddo. The mold of a magnificent figurine found at Nahariya (Fig. 6.38:1) portrays a nude goddess with a tall conical headdress and horns. Another type, the peg-shaped figurine (Fig. 6.39), has a long history in Mesopotamia, where it often appears in foundation deposits; in Canaan, however, the figurine was a consecrated object, offered to the god at an already existent cult place.

The pendant in Fig. 6.40 reveals the features common to figurines (which were part of the cult at temples or high places) and pendant figurines, which come close to being classified as a personal ornament. The gold pendants from Tell el-Ajjul represent in a schematic fashion the figure of the fertility goddess (possibly Asthoreth) while depicting the main elements of the divinity: the head, breasts, belly, and vulva. More abstract are the gold pendants depicting the star of Ishtar (Fig. 6.41) and likewise the silver pendant

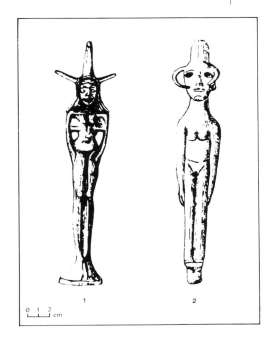

Fig. 6.38. Metal figurines from Nahariya

Fig. 6.37. Syrian-style cylinder seal (height 3 centimeters)

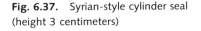

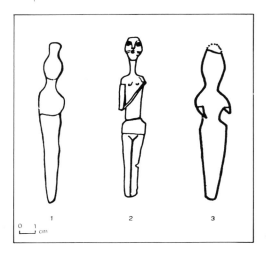

Fig. 6.39. Silver figurines from Nahariya (1), Megiddo (2), and Gezer (3)

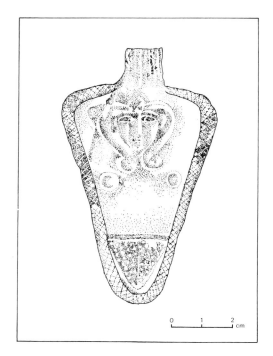

Fig. 6.40. Gold pendant from Tell el-Ajjul

from Shiloh (Fig. 6.42) bearing the emblem of the storm god Hadad. This emblem is quite common in northern Syria.

The earliest molds for the casting of small objects had already arrived in Canaan by the beginning of the Middle Bronze IIa. However, the manufacture of jewelry for personal adornment or of pendants flourished only in a late stage of the Middle Bronze IIb. The best evidence for this comes from Tell el-Ajjul, site of the largest quantity of gold jewelry ever discovered in the Land of Israel. A lack of goldsmiths cannot be the reason for the late appearance of jewelry in the Land of Israel. A lack of wealth, however, would explain it. If there had been a demand for jewelry in Canaan, accompanied by

a concentration of wealth, goldsmiths would have found their way from Byblos or Egypt. But southern Canaan did not achieve the necessary concentration of wealth, and particularly of Nubian gold, until the Fifteenth Dynasty. The assemblage of luxury items is not limited to Tell el-Ajjul; a cache including gold pendant figurines was found in the renewed excavations at Gezer (Fig. 6.43), its date identical to that of the Ajjul assemblage. Technically, the Ajjul assemblage is characterized by the repoussé technique (hammering into relief on a small anvil) and by granulation (the soldering of small grains of gold onto the surface of the ornament). The technique of granulation originated in Mesopotamia and had arrived at Byblos

Fig. 6.41. Gold pendant (star of Ishtar) from Tell el-Ajjul (height 2.5 centimeters)

by the nineteenth century. Its presence at seventeenth-century Ajjul indicates the influence of Syrian goldwork. The forms of the jewelry are also generally characteristic of Syrian art. An exception to this rule are the gold flies and maggots already present in Middle Kingdom Egypt. Unique to Ajjul are the granulated crescents.

A most useful ornament was the toggle pin, used to fasten the garment at the shoulder. A precise depiction of its use is given on an ivory inlay from Mari. Three main types of toggle pin occur in Canaan. The earliest has a bulbous head, is of Syrian or Anatolian origin, and may be found in the Middle Bronze IIa. At the beginning of Middle Bronze IIb it is replaced by the wedge-shaped type, the upper part of which is broad and decorated with incisions. Toward the end of the period a third type appears with an applied decoration, often cast in gold and sometimes inlaid with a precious stone. The ring attached to the pin was intended for the fastening of a scarab seal, as ascertained at Jericho, where many scarabs were found near the shoulder of the deceased, with a toggle pin often nearby. The source of this custom is apparently Mesopotamian; there, a cylinder seal was fastened to the toggle pin.

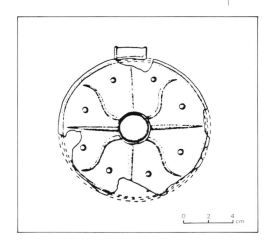

Fig. 6.42. Silver pendant with emblem of storm god, from Shiloh

Fig. 6.44. Gold crescent from Tell el-Ajjul

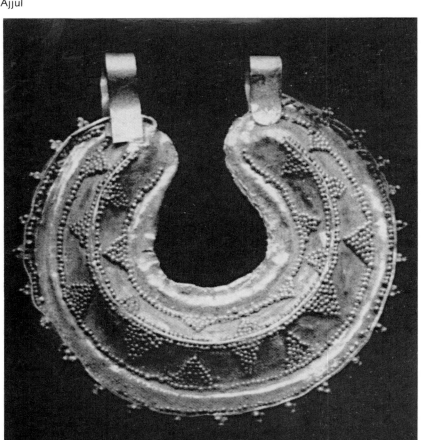

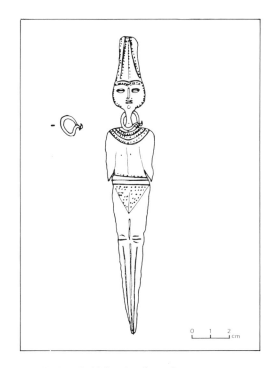

Fig. 6.43. Gold figurine from Gezer

Fig. 6.45. Depiction of use of toggle pin, from Mari

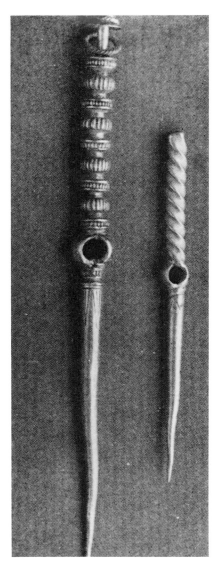

Fig. 6.46. Ornamented gold toggle pins from Tell el-Ajjul

WEAPONS

The invention of new metal-working methods and, above all, the perfection of bronze casting techniques significantly improved the weapons of the Middle Bronze Age. True bronze is composed of about 90 percent copper and 8 percent to 10 percent tin, tin being the element that hardens the metal and transforms copper into bronze. Bronze production was introduced during the third millennium, and by the beginning of the second millennium it had been adopted throughout the Near East. Axes, javelins, and swords, all were of bronze.

At the beginning of the Middle Bronze IIa, the duckbill axe, a typological development from the fenestrated axe of the Intermediate Bronze Age, was in fashion. With time, it was replaced by the long and narrow battle-axe, with a short socket and a notch near the base. This notch permitted the fastening of the axe head to the haft. The characteristic javelin head was socketed, and the sword was broad and finely ribbed. The haft was made of wood and had a stone or bone pommel. The advent of the Middle Bronze IIb did not bring about great changes. The sword itself remained unchanged, with the exception of the replacement of the fine ribbing by a heavy midrib. This sword too was furnished with a stone pommel and a wooden grip. The battle-axe developed a hook or knob near the socket instead of a notch. Toward the end of the period the hand-shaped axe, or finger axe, was introduced.

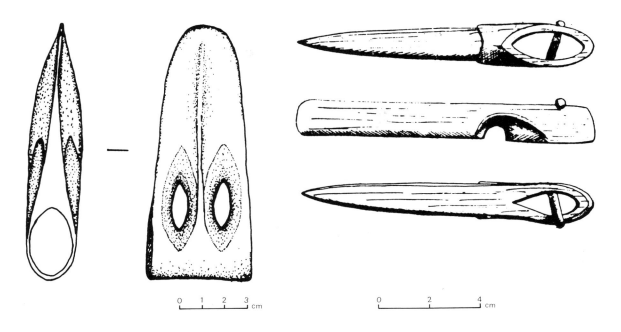

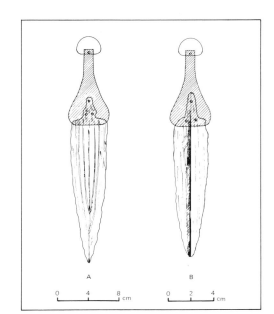

Fig. 6.47. Duckbill axe of the Middle Bronze IIa

Fig. 6.48. Notched axe of the Middle Bronze IIa–b

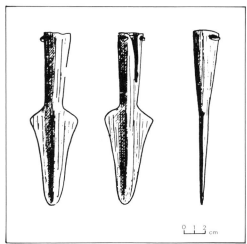

Fig. 6.49. Javelin head of the Middle Bronze IIa–b

Fig. 6.50. Ribbed dagger of the Middle Bronze IIa (A) and dagger with midrib of the Middle Bronze IIb (B)

Fig. 6.51. Axe with hook at base of socket of Middle Bronze IIb

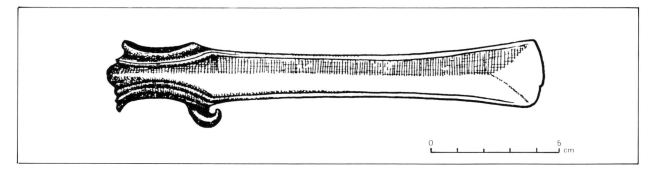

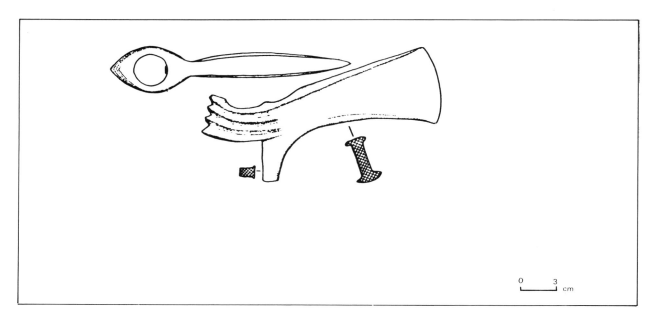

Fig. 6.52.   Finger axe from Shiloh

THE CHARIOT

The war chariot was introduced in Canaan in the second millennium. Though known since the Early Dynastic III period in Mesopotamia (the mid third millennium), it appeared in Syria only in the nineteenth century. The chariot illustrated in Fig. 6.53 comes from a Syrian cylinder seal impression on a document dated to the fourteenth year of King Hammurabi of Babylon (1778 B.C.E., according to the chronology adopted here). Compared with the third millennium chariots, this chariot is light and maneuverable, thanks to the spoked wheel and the single shaft to which both horses were harnessed. The front of the chariot is low, and the ledge at the rear could perhaps accommodate another rider. The revolutionary improvement in the Syrian chariot was the spoked wheel, which replaced the solid wheel of the slow and unwieldy third-millennium Mesopotamian vehicles.

Apart from a harness found at Tell el-Ajjul, no chariot parts have yet been unearthed in excavations in Israel, but the apparent practice of horse burial evidenced at Tell el-Ajjul may testify to the great value accorded to horses in the Middle Bronze II. The adoption of the chariot in Fifteenth Dynasty Egypt could not have come about without the mediation of the Syro-Canaanite population.

The Middle Bronze Age: A Retrospective View

The aim of archaeology is not merely to be "the handmaiden of history," as stated by scholars of an older generation. In their view, archaeology was to supply data from the realm of material culture as supporting evidence for facts already known from written documents. Modern archaeology has set itself a more ambitious goal: to forge an independent discipline that examines, in a process parallel to historic investigation, the theoretical framework, events, and facts processed by the historian.

In periods of meager historical documentation, such as the Middle Bronze Age, archaeology attempts, by describing a developmental sequence, to portray cultural advance (or retreat) in a given period and to formulate its significance in relation to the preceding and succeeding periods. With this portrait in hand the historian can investigate whether his historical reconstruction is founded on acceptable facts. This section will summarize the trends evident in the evolution of this period, not in an attempt to write history but only to point out the advantages archaeology provides for the reconstruction of a most general view. The archaeological picture obviously cannot take the place of a history, which must draw on entirely different methods and techniques.

THE EVOLUTION OF CULTURE. Following the decline of urban culture in the Intermediate Bronze Age, Canaan returns to prosper, for reasons ascribed, in a large measure, to the influence of migrant groups penetrating along the coast from Lebanon and later from the Orontes valley of Syria. This deeply affects the character of the Middle Bronze II, which is, in contrast to preceding and succeeding periods, very much Syrian-oriented. The material culture, particularly in northern sites, is closely bound to that of Syria and the Lebanese coast. Southern Canaan, however, is now linked to Egypt, the cause being not the penetration of Egyptian immigrants but a combination of political and economic interests related to the Delta Kingdom. After the first phase of the period (one of security and calm, judging from the few, thin town walls and many unfortified sites), there occurred toward the end of the first part of the Middle Bronze IIa, and especially at the

start of the later part of this phase, a trend toward massive fortifications coupled with a wide distribution of sites over the entire countryside. It would therefore appear that political conditions and new social trends of the late Twelfth and early Thirteenth Dynasty were the cause of these developments.

HISTORY. Historical data directly concerning the Land of Israel are meager. Historical events, either political or military, are recorded only in the stela of Khu-Sobk and the Louvre stela, both memorial stelae recording Egyptian military campaigns in Canaan. They indicate a degree of subjection to Egyptian rule at the start of the period. Alongside these events, the existence of the Execration Texts reveals a certain degree of Egyptian control, or at least an interest, in Canaan and part of Syria, paralleling the partial domination by Egypt of Nubia and Libya.

There is more information available in the realm of cultural and economic history. The tale of Sinuhe provides an excellent description of the social, economic, and, to some extent, political life in northern Canaan (or perhaps in the Lebanese Beqa'). The portraits of trading or nomadic caravans descending to Egypt preserved in the tombs of Egyptian nobles are greatly informative regarding the dress and accoutrements of the inhabitants.

From the information provided by the Mari archives we may derive by way of analogy knowledge of the seminomadic and rural societies of Canaan, for it may be assumed that the tribal life-style of the middle Euphrates region did not differ considerably from that of the tribes and villages of southern Syria or Canaan. To this day there is a marked resemblance between the Arab agricultural and urban societies of Syria, northern Iraq, and Israel.

Fig. 6.53. Depiction of chariot on Syrian cylinder seal

In the final phase of the period, the later Middle Bronze IIb, we have somewhat more historical information, again from Egyptian sources. The reign of the Fifteenth Dynasty (the Delta Kingdom) over most of Canaan is reflected in the large number of objects (mainly scarabs) bearing the names of kings of that dynasty found in excavations in southern Canaan. In addition to scarabs of Fifteenth Dynasty kings, the seals of high officials have been discovered. Foremost among them is the treasurer Hori, whose tenure covered the early years of the dynasty and whose name ("the Hurrian") indicates Syro-Canaanite extraction. The end of the period is well documented, thanks to the discovery of Egyptian texts relating the overthrow of the Fifteenth Dynasty in Egypt and its entrenchment in Canaan. This permits the reconstruction of the events and hence the interpretation of the intensification of settlement in the south during the seventeenth century.

CULTURAL SIGNIFICANCE. The culture created in the Land of Israel during the third millennium formed the basis for the establishment of Bronze Age culture. This foundation, however, was insufficient, and the inhabitants of the late third millennium, under pressure of ecological and other changes, had to change their life-style and revert to village or seminomadic modes. At the start of the second millennium the urban culture of Canaan was refashioned, or rather restored, mainly owing to the survival of pockets of urban culture on the Lebanese coast and in northern Syria. The dominance of the culture of greater Syria cannot be denied, but it merged with Egyptian cultural influences, which steadily increased as the period drew to a close. The fusion of the two directions of cultural influence represents the classic Canaanite culture as we know it in the Late Bronze Age. The latter period is but a direct continuation of the Middle Bronze Age II, with Egyptian influence gaining dominance.

Another important achievement of Middle Bronze II culture was the reincarnation of the Canaanite city-state. This sociopolitical formation would continue to exist, basically unchanged, along the entire eastern Mediterranean littoral for the whole of the Bronze Age, and in some cases well into the Iron Age. The increasing intervention of Canaanites in the politics of a neighboring land (Egypt) and the contribution of this population to the creation of the Fifteenth Dynasty represent, for the first time, the exertion of political influence by inhabitants of Canaan over regions outside its geographical borders. The population, an amalgam of northern immigrants with indigenous elements, had the potential by the second part of the period to spawn migrant groups that could settle in a neighboring country and even, for a short time, replace its governing elite.

The strength and resilience of Canaanite culture grew out of its ability to fuse Syrian elements, which in themselves contained many Mesopotamian elements, with Egyptian culture. The two systems of writing present in Middle Bronze Age Canaan—Akkadian writing from northern Syria and Egyptian script—are evidence for this process. Only toward the end of the period do Canaanite scribes succeed in fashioning a local script, the proto-Canaanite alphabet, the forerunner of the Canaanite and Hebrew alphabets. The broad foundations of Canaanite culture in the Middle Bronze Age made possible the continued growth and the manifold foreign relations of Canaan in the Late Bronze Age.

7

The Late Bronze Age

RIVKA GONEN

The general sequence of events is thoroughly documented for the Late Bronze Age in Canaan, which corresponds to the New Kingdom in Egypt (the Eighteenth, Nineteenth, and early Twentieth Dynasties). No other biblical era, the First Temple period excepted, is so brightly illuminated by historical sources or provides so firm a historical basis for archaeological investigation.

The entire Late Bronze Age stands in the sign of Egyptian supremacy in Canaan, beginning with the renewal of Egyptian control, following the expulsion of the Hyksos dynasty and the reunification of Egypt under the Theban kings, and ending with the gradual attenuation of Egyptian rule, leading to the retreat of Egypt from the region. For four hundred–odd years, Canaan was part of the Egyptian empire and under its direct administration. But notwithstanding its political and military subordination, Canaan maintained its independence in the realms of material and spiritual culture, reaching the zenith of Canaanite creativity in the fields of religion, literature, and art.

From the historical aspect, the events that terminated the Middle Bronze Age and inaugurated the Late Bronze Age were the over-throw of the Hyksos dynasty and reunification of Egypt under Ahmose, the founder of the Eighteenth Dynasty, and the conquest of Canaan. The overthrow of Hyksos rule began when Ahmose (1570–1546 B.C.E.) conquered the Hyksos capital at Avaris in the eastern Nile Delta in about 1560 B.C.E., ending Hyksos rule in Egypt. Later, in an unknown year, Ahmose marched across the Sinai peninsula and lay siege to the city of Sharuhen for three years before finally conquering it. Sharuhen, long identified with Tell el-Far'ah South, is presently identified with Tell el-Ajjul. Documents contemporaneous with the rule of Ahmose describe a military campaign to Djahi (a broad Egyptian term for Syria and Canaan), the taking of prisoners there, and the taking of booty from Fenkhu (an Egyptian term for the Lebanese coast). These citations indicate military campaigns in Canaan or perhaps even conquest of parts of the country, laying the foundations of the Egyptian empire in Asia and marking the start of the Late Bronze Age.

Ahmose's successors Amenhotep I (1546–1524 B.C.E.) and Thutmose I (1524–1515 B.C.E.) extended the scope of Egyptian interests beyond the borders of Canaan by pursuing a war with the kingdom of Mitanni, called Naharin by the Egyptians, which had only recently established itself in northern Syria. Thutmose I even crossed the Euphrates and erected a victory stela on the opposite shore. But the power of Mitanni did not diminish. On the contrary, the kingdom expanded in the following years. The kingdom of Mitanni was founded by the Hurrians, the hill people of the upper Euphrates. By the end of the third millennium they had established small kingdoms in the region of the Habur River, a tributary of the Euphrates. From the seventeenth century on, the Hurrian kingdoms gained strength, invading Syria and even Canaan. By the last quarter of the sixteenth century a united Hurrian kingdom, Mitanni, had been established in northern Mesopotamia. To the fourteenth century, it was the principal Near Eastern power opposing Egypt. Mitanni continued to expand east, west, and south, reaching its greatest extent under Saustatar, in the early fifteenth century. Considerable portions of Canaan previously occupied by Egypt, perhaps even all of Canaan, passed into the hands of Mitanni.

This was the state of affairs when Thutmose III (1504–1450 B.C.E.), the great Eighteenth Dynasty conqueror, embarked on a series of campaigns that restored and fortified Egyptian domination in Canaan and Syria. The first campaign took place in his twenty-third year (1482 B.C.E.) and was aimed at the pacification of the rebellious cities of Canaan, who were supported by Mitanni. Thutmose III conducted fifteen more campaigns, first against Syria, then against the kingdom of Mitanni itself. In his eighth campaign (1472), Thutmose defeated Mitanni, but the continued struggle of the Mitannian dependencies impeded firm Egyptian control over Syria. In Canaan, however, the Egyptian victory was complete.

The most decisive of Thutmose III's campaigns in Canaan was the first, which culminated in the battle of Megiddo and is described in detail in the annals inscribed by order of the king on the walls of the temple of Amun at Karnak. These annals constitute a rare description of ancient military strategy; they are arranged in chronological order and are assumed to be based on the campaign diary written by the royal scribes who participated in the campaigns. The description of the march on Megiddo is the most detailed of the Egyptian campaign reports. An abbreviated record of the campaign was inscribed on stelae found at Armant in upper Egypt and at Jebel Barkal in Nubia. The coalition of rebellious cities in Canaan and Syria, headed by the Mitannian-supported city of Qadesh, included 119 towns, most of them in the Jezreel valley, the Accho valley, the northern Jordan valley, the Bashan, the Damascus plateau, and the Lebanese Beqa'. These appear to have been the most active regions of opposition. The names of all these towns, as well as other sites on the route of the advancing Egyptian army, are inscribed on the walls of the temple at Karnak.

Map 7.1. Carmel passes and Megiddo battlefield

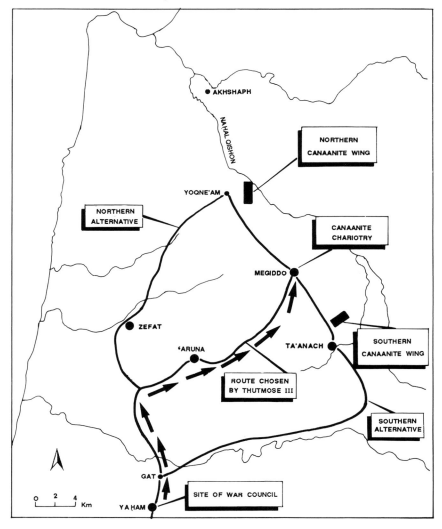

The Egyptian army won a great victory at the battle of Megiddo, but the Egyptian troops fell to looting and did not pursue their advantage. The leaders of the coalition escaped to Megiddo and shut themselves within its walls, forcing the Egyptians to lay a seven-month siege before surrendering; it is odd that no fortifications of that period have been uncovered at the site. The rebellious kings were taken captive, along with much booty. Military equipment figures highly in the booty lists—924 chariots and 2041 horses, 200 coats of mail and 502 bows—and illustrates the power of the coalition opposing Egypt.

After his decisive victory, Thutmose III established an administrative system in Canaan that endured until the end of the Late Bronze Age. Direct authority over the cities remained in the hands of local rulers, but a few key towns were appropriated for the needs of the Egyptian administration. Chief among them was Gaza, which attained the status of capital of the Egyptian government in Canaan. Other administrative centers included Jaffa and Beth Shean, Yeno'am in Transjordan, Kumidi in the Lebanese Beqa', and Ullaza and Sumur on the Phoenician coast. The administration was headed by an Egyptian governor, appointed by the king; officials, aided by small garrisons, assisted in maintaining the peace and collecting taxes.

The death of Thutmose III brought about renewed unrest in the areas of Egyptian domination in Syria and Canaan, requiring his son Amenhotep II (1450–1427 B.C.E.) to conduct three military campaigns. The first (1450 B.C.E.) was directed against the land of Takhshi (the Qadesh region in Syria), which had returned to Mitannian domination. The second campaign (1446 B.C.E.) was also directed against the Syrian kingdoms of Qadesh, Qatna, and

Ni, who were allied with Mitanni. The two campaigns appear to have been only moderately successful, as their descriptions include booty lists but no report of battles or victories. The third campaign (1444 B.C.E.) was limited to the Sharon plain and the Jezreel valley and consisted mainly of small-scale battles, which may represent the pacification of local mutinies.

Despite Amenhotep II's unimpressive record in the battlefield, Egypt attained a balance of power with Mitanni, owed, perhaps, to the attrition of both sides by the extended conflict. Egypt and Mitanni established their respective spheres of influence. The border between the two ran from the Qadesh area to the Lebanese Beqa', with Canaan remaining under Egyptian control. This border marked the limit of Egyptian expansion until the end of the Late Bronze Age and even received biblical sanction as the northern border of the Promised Land (Num. 34; Ezek. 47). The agreement with Mitanni enabled Egypt to secure its grip over Canaan, and the successors of Amenhotep II—Thutmose IV and Amenhotep III—conducted only limited forays into Canaan.

Our knowledge of events in Canaan during the reign of Amenhotep IV, better known as Akhenaten (1364–1347 B.C.E.), is greatly enhanced by the discovery of the royal archives at El-Amarna, the site of Akhenaten's capital. This heretic king, who promoted the god Aten to the supreme position in the Egyptian pantheon, founded his capital, called Akhetaten, on virgin ground. In the seventh year of his reign (1358 B.C.E.) the royal court moved to the new capital, bringing along a part of the royal archives that contained letters from the reign of Amenhotep III. During the sojourn of the king in Akhetaten more letters were added to the archives.

Akhetaten was abandoned in 1344 B.C.E., in the third year of the reign of Akhenaten's successor, Tutankhamen (1347–1338 B.C.E.). The El-Amarna archives thus span 27 years, known as the El-Amarna period. The term in its broader sense includes the whole of the fourteenth century, from the days of Amenhotep III to the end of the Eighteenth Dynasty.

The El-Amarna period is well documented by contemporary Egyptian, Hittite, Ugaritic, and Mesopotamian sources. The major events in the Near Eastern expanse may be summed up as the decline of the power of Mitanni and the concomitant rise of the Hittite kingdom as the major power in the northern fertile crescent. The Hittites were an Indo-European nation who penetrated into eastern Anatolia in the first part of the second millennium or perhaps as early as the late third millennium. By the second half of the seventeenth century B.C.E. the Hittites had established a large kingdom, the Old Hittite Kingdom. Following a brief climax, Hittite power and territorial dominion waned. In the mid fifteenth century a second period of military and territorial expansion began, climaxed by the creation of the Hittite Empire. Shupiluliumas I, the greatest of the Hittite kings (1375–1335 B.C.E.) conducted a series of campaigns against Mitanni, ending with the conquest of the capital Wassukanni. He continued south to Syria, gaining the allegiance of the vassal kingdoms of Mitanni. From then on, until the end of the Late Bronze Age, the Hittite Empire was Egypt's rival for dominion in Syria, a struggle punctuated by campaigns by Nineteenth Dynasty kings who wished to maintain Egyptian interests in that region.

During this era of dramatic change in the north, Canaan remained loyal to Egypt. This and other aspects of Canaan's internal situation in mid fourteenth century Canaan may be gathered from the El-Amarna documents, many of which are letters sent from Canaanite princes to the Egyptian court. They brightly illuminate the Canaanite condition at this time, its settlement, its population, the relations between the Canaanite cities and between these cities and Egypt.

About 350 letters were discovered in the El-Amarna archives. They were written for the most part in Akkadian, the international language of the period. The letters include missives sent by the kings of Hatti, Mitanni, Babylon, and Cyprus (Alashiya), as well as copies of the replies of the Egyptian king, but the great majority were written by local Canaanite princes. In some cases, an extended correspondence of a single ruler is preserved; we know of 6 letters sent by 'Abdu-Heba of Jerusalem, 5 by Milkilu of Gezer, and 4 by his successor Yapahu. In all, 27 Canaanite cities and 25 Canaanite princes are mentioned. Towns of the Syro-Lebanese coast, the Lebanese Beqa', the Damascus plateau, and the Bashan appear as well. From these documents it emerges that only 13 of the towns were city-states of any significance. The rest were minor towns, either directly ruled by the larger cities or otherwise subordinate to them. Though all the city-states were subject to the supreme authority of the Egyptian king, represented by the governor residing at Gaza, they enjoyed autonomy in conducting their internal affairs. Relations among the city-states were strained and marked by repeated attempts to annex territories of neighboring states. In their letters, the Canaanite princes express their loyalty to Egypt in effusive terms and implore the Pharaoh to send Egyptian military units to assist in the defense against their neighbors. The size of the units requested is surprisingly small; the prince of Jerusalem, for example, requested fifty troops. The letters offer a vivid portrait of Prince Labayu of Shechem, an ambitious ruler who threatened the territorial integrity of neighboring states in the hills, the Sharon, the Shephelah, and the Jezreel valley. Following the impassioned pleas for assistance sent to the Egyptian king, Labayu was ordered to present himself at court and was assassinated by his enemies on the way there.

The El-Amarna tablets also mention a group termed 'Apiru, or Habiru, which existed on the periphery of Canaanite society. The 'Apiru lack a clear ethnic identity. They were a motley crowd of social outcasts who coalesced, perhaps in several small, unrelated groups. According to the sources, the 'Apiru had no permanent settlements, social privileges, or property. They played an important role in the rivalries between the city-states, transferring their allegiance from one side to another, according to their own interests.

The small chink opened on the social and political life of Canaan was soon shut. From the end of the El-Amarna age onward, our knowledge is again only general.

The rise of the Nineteenth Dynasty saw renewed Egyptian attempts to stabilize its base in face of the growing power of the Hittite empire, which had conquered northern and central Syria. Nineteenth Dynasty kings embarked on military campaigns to stabilize the northern boundary of the Egyptian empire. References to Canaan are derived mainly from accounts of military operations, from which it may be inferred that social ferment was on the rise, particularly among nomadic elements. The three great kings of this dynasty, Seti I, Ramesses II, and Merneptah, led military campaigns, some aimed at putting down rebellions within Canaan, others directed against the Hittite forces in Syria. Seti I (1291–1279 B.C.E., dates in accord with the chronological tables of Wente and Van Siclen) erected two stelae at Beth Shean; one reports the pacification of the nomadic groups, among them the 'Apiru of Mount Yarmuta (biblical Yarmut, in the lower Galilee), who had attacked neighboring settlements. Information regarding the two other campaigns of Seti I is fragmentary, but they appear to have been directed against the cities of Syria and the Hittite forces and probably did not pass through the heart of Canaan but along the coast.

We do not know what the concrete results of Seti I's campaigns were. His heir, Ramesses II (1279–1212 B.C.E.), whose 66-year reign was one of the longest in history, renewed the war against the Hittites. The campaign of 1275 was intended to be the decisive thrust in the struggle between the Egyptians and Hittites, climaxing in the battle of Qadesh on the Orontes. It is most thoroughly documented in inscriptions and reliefs carved on the walls of temples throughout Egypt. According to the Egyptian sources, the Hittite army consisted of 2500 chariots and 37,000 foot soldiers, while the Egyptian army, for which no precise numbers are given, consisted of four divisions named after the four principal Egyptian gods, Amun, Pre (Re), Ptah, and Sutekh (Seth). The detailed descriptions extol the Egyptian army, and particularly the personal prowess of the king, but between the lines the true picture emerges: the Hittites mounted a surprise attack on two of the Egyptian divisions near Qadesh, and only the timely arrival of the third division and an elite seaborne unit prevented the utter defeat of the Egyptians. Ramesses II conducted further campaigns to Syria and Canaan, but details are not known.

The struggle between Egypt and Hatti ended in 1259 B.C.E. with the so-called Silver Treaty, which established the spheres of influence of each power and fixed their boundary along the line of Lebo Hamat in the Lebanese Beqa'. Normalization of relations between Egypt and Hatti followed and was maintained until the collapse of the Hittite empire.

It was during the reign of Merneptah (1212–1202 B.C.E.) that Egypt entered a decline, which led to its withdrawal from Canaan seventy years later. Merneptah had to fend off not only the Libyans, the traditional enemy of Egypt on its western frontier, but also two new elements, the Sea Peoples and Israel.

The invasions of the Sea Peoples, which brought about the downfall of the Hittite empire and the kingdoms of the Syrian and Canaanite coast, as well as the rise of the Israelite tribes in Canaan, spelled the end of the old order that had reigned in the eastern Mediterranean littoral throughout the second millennium B.C.E. The ascendancy of the great powers came to an end, and in the resulting vacuum small national states came into being. Historically and archaeologically the early days of the Twentieth Dynasty in Egypt mark the end of the Late Bronze Age and the beginning of the Iron Age.

However, the decline was not immediate. The great campaigner against the Sea Peoples was Ramesses III (1182–1151 B.C.E.), of the Twentieth Dynasty. He fought two great battles, in his fifth and eighth years; the first was a sea battle fought in the Nile Delta, and the second a land battle fought at an unknown place. The Egyptian version of these battles contains the usual boasts about the utter defeat of the enemy, but this seems not to have been quite the case. The battle reliefs carved on the walls of the temple of Medinet Habu, near Thebes, show that the Sea Peoples

were a migrating people, traveling with their women, children, and household effects. The Egyptians had to contend with a military force and with an uprooted population. The Harris Papyrus, dating from the days of Ramesses III's successor, describes the settling of the Sea Peoples in border fortresses, thus marking the beginning of the Sea Peoples' settlement in Canaan.

The infiltration of the Sea Peoples—and particularly the Philistines, the best known of these groups—was to deeply influence the turn of events in the Iron Age I. Though the Egyptians continued to control Canaan, or at least parts of it, for another fifty years or so, they were no longer able to prevent the settlement of the Israelites in the hill regions or of the Philistines along

Map 7.2. Late Bronze Age sites in Canaan

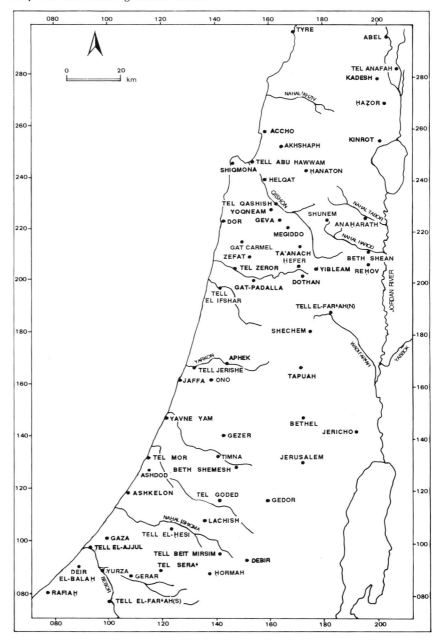

the coastal plain, and by the mid twelfth century, Egyptian presence in Canaan ceased, giving way to new forces and the new order of the Iron Age.

Just as the beginning and end of the Late Bronze Age are fixed by historical events, so too do the various schemes for the subdivision of the period rely on historical events. One common subdivision is into three parts:

Late Bronze I (1550–1400 B.C.E.), the first part of the Eighteenth Dynasty;
Late Bronze IIA (1400–1300 B.C.E.), the El-Amarna period, the latter part of the Eighteenth Dynasty;
Late Bronze IIB (1300–1200 B.C.E.), the Nineteenth Dynasty.

This scheme suggests that the two-hundred-year span from 1400 to 1200 B.C.E. is fundamentally a single period with two subphases, but such is not the case. Although there is considerable cultural continuity between the fourteenth and thirteenth centuries, many changes are evident as well, a result of the increasing involvement of Egypt in Canaan in the face of the Hittite threat from the north and internal sources of unrest, such as the nomadic tribes. The thirteenth century is the most Egyptian in Canaanite history; Egypt tightened her hold on Canaan by establishing a series of administrative centers and fortresses, Egyptian exports to Canaan increased, and Egyptianizing tendencies spread in the local culture. It has therefore been proposed to view the century as an independent phase.

Another scheme for subdivision is that proposed by R. Amiran in her *Ancient Pottery of the Holy Land*. Her subdivision is based on the precise date established for the conquest of Avaris (1570 B.C.E.) and the reigns of Amenhotep II and IV,

and the dates are the same cited in the subdivision of the Mycenaean pottery groups.

Late Bronze I, 1570–1410 B.C.E.;
Late Bronze II, 1410–1340 B.C.E.; and
Late Bronze III, 1340–1200 B.C.E.

There appears to be a consensus regarding the round figure of 1200 for the end of the Late Bronze Age. However, new discoveries at Lachish, Megiddo, Beth Shean, and Tel Sera', including precisely dated inscriptions, and recent reappraisals of terminal Late Bronze Age strata at several sites (such as Megiddo and Beth Shean) indicate that the period should in fact end fifty years later, at approximately 1150 B.C.E. This chapter, therefore, presents a subdivision that takes account of all those reservations, while retaining the simplicity of the first scheme proposed:

Late Bronze I (1550–1400 B.C.E.), the Eighteenth Dynasty;
Late Bronze II (1400–1300 B.C.E.), the El-Amarna period; and
Late Bronze III (1300–1150 B.C.E.), the Nineteenth and early Twentieth Dynasties.

The Settlement of Canaan in the Late Bronze Age

The Late Bronze Age is often thought of as a period of urban efflorescence, though recent research has shown this reputation to be quite exaggerated. The urban image has been based largely on the mention of many sites in Egyptian texts of the period. In the great topographical list of Thutmose III about 75 place names in Canaan and another 40 in the Lebanese Beqa', the Damascus plateau, and the Bashan are noted. The annals of Amenhotep

II's campaign mention 12 to 14 names, the El-Amarna letters 28 names, and the topographical lists of Seti I 6 or 7 names of settlements in Canaan. The texts, particularly the El-Amarna letters, reveal that while some of these sites were capitals of city-states, most were of secondary importance. All were subject to the authority of the Egyptian crown, but their internal affairs were managed by local rulers, who often styled themselves kings. This manner of administration, with its origins in the Middle Bronze Age, was reaffirmed by Thutmose III after the battle of Megiddo and was maintained throughout the Late Bronze Age.

In the light of excavations and surveys, it becomes apparent that the urban system of Canaan underwent a drastic change in the transition from the Middle to the Late Bronze Age. Many sites were destroyed, and most were not soon reinhabited. Those that were resettled did not attain their original size and influence. The causes of the destruction of the Middle Bronze sites have not been adequately clarified, but it is usually ascribed to the Egyptian conquest of Canaan with the ascent of the Eighteenth Dynasty. Though Egyptian sources mention the siege of only one city, Sharuhen, it would appear that Egypt pursued her military advantage northward. The passage of the Egyptian army through the countryside would have been accompanied by siege operations and conquests. Presumably the fugitives from the defeated cities added to the destruction in their search for new dwelling places. They would have been responsible for raids on provincial towns and small outlying settlements, with the Egyptians confining themselves to the towns along the main routes. In any case, hardly a single site escaped massive destruction, including some of the largest and most important sites in the country: Tell el-Far'ah South, Tell el-Ajjul, Tell Beit Mirsim, Jericho, Shechem, Megiddo, Accho, Hazor, and Dan. Such large-scale destruction no doubt impoverished the population of Canaan, so that when reconstruction began it could only be partial. Of the 54 excavated sites existing at the end of the Middle Bronze Age, only 22 were rebuilt during the Late Bronze I. This casts some doubt on the list of 75 Canaanite cities compiled by Thutmose III, and it could be that some of the places were reference points or ruins, rather than existing towns.

During the Late Bronze II the number of sites doubled. Old sites were reinhabited and new settlements were established at previously uninhabited spots. Concurrently, however, several large sites that had been occupied from the Middle Bronze Age were now abandoned. The new settlements were largely clustered along the coast. Sites such as Tell Abu Hawam, Tel Megadim, and Tel Girit were no doubt small ports servicing the greatly increased import trade. The balance of total settled area thus remained stable throughout the Late Bronze Age. A rough calculation of the total area of the Late Bronze I sites provides a sum of about 184 hectares, and the total settled area of the Late Bronze II amounts to about 204 hectares, a difference of only 10 percent. So far, only five sites with a Late Bronze Age occupation of more than 5 hectares have been identified (Tell Keisan, Tell Jerishe, Ashdod, Lachish, and Hazor), but at Dor and Ashkelon, currently under excavation, the strata of the period have yet to be exposed. New discoveries of Late Bronze Age settlements may also be made. All the remaining sites excavated are less than 5 hectares and often measure only a few dunams, reflecting not only the small average size of sites but also the corresponding small size of the population, in which no significant growth may be discerned as the period progresses. A similar situation may be observed in the Late Bronze III. Though new sites were added to the Canaanite settlement system, they were small and their contribution to the total inhabited area was insignificant. The new sites were for the most part Egyptian fortresses or residences, built along the main routes or in regions deemed vital for the maintenance of Egyptian authority. Such structures were sometimes built at new sites such as Deir el-Balah, but for the most part they are found at long-inhabited sites such as Tell el-Far'ah South, which had lain in ruins since the great destruction at the end of the Middle Bronze Age, or Tell el-Ajjul, which was destroyed early in the Late Bronze I. These fortresses and residences were of characteristic Egyptian type, built in the Egyptian construction technique, to serve Egyptian interests. They should not, therefore, be viewed as a significant addition to the Canaanite urban system. Intensive archaeological surveys in various parts of the country round out the observed pattern of a significant decline in the number of sites. Where some 270 Middle Bronze sites were counted, only about 100 Late Bronze Age sites were found, a decrease of more than 60 percent.

Both the surveys and the excavations indicate considerable differences in the distribution of sites in various parts of the country. The coastal plain from the Sinai to the Carmel, the Judaean Shephelah, and the valleys of Jezreel, Beth Shean, and the upper Jordan were all rather densely inhabited during the Late Bronze Age, though the sites were generally small. In contrast, the hill areas remained devoid of settlement. In the central hills, only Tapuah, Dothan, Hefer, Debir, Jerusalem, Bethel, Shechem, and Tell el-Far'ah North were occupied, while in the Galilee hills there appear to have been only a minute number of settlements, and only the sites of Tel Qedesh and Tel Rosh may be attributed to the period with any certainty. The large site of Gibeon was abandoned at the end of the Middle Bronze Age and not resettled in the Late Bronze Age, though the cemetery remained partly in use. Beth Zur was also abandoned, and possibly Hebron as well. Jerusalem, which had been a walled town in the Middle Bronze Age, contracted in the Late Bronze Age into a fortress of no great size on the acropolis of the City of David. The hill areas were apparently inhabited by nonsedentary populations such as the 'Apiru and Shasu, who left their imprint in the form of burial sites. The transfer of the focus of settlement to the plains and valleys and the near abandonment of the hill country had a decisive significance for Israelite settlement.

Fortification of the Late Bronze Age Towns

The transition from the Middle to the Late Bronze Age is also reflected in the radical changes in fortification, one of the most prominent features of urban settlement. The impressive fortifications of the Middle Bronze Age were based largely on glacis systems and huge earthen embankments. In the course of the Middle Bronze Age, and even more so with the destruction of the cities, occupation levels within the fortified enclosures rose nearly to the height of the ramparts. By the time the Late Bronze Age cities were established these fortifications, though still extant, did not provide much protection. This was the case at Accho, for instance, where the enormous ramparts had gone out of use halfway through the Middle Bronze Age. Toward the end of that period the foundations of a citadel were sunk into the summit of the ramparts, and the Late Bronze Age inhabitants established themselves on the ruins of the citadel. The ramparts continued to support the steep slopes surrounding the mound but did not protrude above the occupation level of the Late Bronze site, so that its defensive value was quite limited. An exception to this rule was the city of Hazor. There is no doubt that the Middle Bronze Age rampart at Hazor towered high above the lower city occupation levels through the whole of the Late Bronze Age; it may thus be considered a true Late Bronze Age defensive system.

If most of the Middle Bronze Age defensive works did not continue to protect cities in the succeeding period, how then were the Late Bronze Age cities defended? The answer is rather surprising: most excavated sites have yielded no remains of Late Bronze Age fortification. In some cases, such as at Timna (Tel Batash), or at least at the excavated northeast corner of the site, public structures were built in a continuous line, and their exterior walls provided a degree of protection for the site. At Lachish, however, houses and installations were built on the earlier rampart slopes and even within the defensive ditch at its foot, no new fortification having been constructed.

The absence of defensive systems at the sites and their small average size (and hence population) combine to cast doubt on the magnitude of the urban phenomenon in the Late Bronze Age; it would appear that the towns were for the most part quite weak and impoverished. This state of affairs appears to be related to Canaan's location on the route of the Egyptian armies northward; at times it even served as the theater of battle. It may be assumed that for each military campaign that passed through the countryside, the local population was expected to supply auxiliary forces, labor, and provisions and to clear roadways. The supreme Egyptian interest was to keep the routes open and the Canaanite population submissive. The pressures on the Canaanite population may have been unendurable (witness the occasional uprisings against Egyptian rule), and many inhabitants likely left the towns to avoid the constant Egyptian demand for supplies and manpower. They could have moved to the more thinly settled zones, in scattered settlements that left few archaeological remains, or they could have joined up with the 'Apiru or the other unstable elements in Canaan. Many others may have emigrated to Egypt itself, whether by free choice or as captives and slaves (Egyptian texts mention a Canaanite presence in Egypt). As for the fortifications, it may be assumed that the Egyptians prohibited the circumvallation of towns, which could be interpreted as preparation for revolt. Egypt, a great power through most of the Late Bronze Age, was geographically close to Canaan, maintained an Egyptian governor and Egyptian garrisons, could keep a close watch on the cities, and could bring any attempts to construct fortifications to a halt. Small, unfortified sites were more submissive to Egyptian demands than large fortified ones. The settlement picture in Canaan thus reflects fairly its subservience to Egypt.

Urban Structure

Though the urban system of Late Bronze Age Canaan was not a powerful one, there were nonetheless towns with private dwellings and public institutions. From the meager information gleaned in excavations, a conventional town plan seems to emerge, based on a peripheral range of structures and a core where the public buildings were concentrated. There were also public areas where commerce was pursued. It seems reasonable to assume that these areas—vacant lots rather than built-up marketplaces—were near the city gates. A public structure present in every city was the temple, located either in the core of the town or near the gate. The larger towns had more than one temple.

WALLS AND GATES

Fortified cities were few and far between in the Late Bronze Age. A small number of sites were, however, walled, and a handful of city gates have been discovered as well. Ramparts have been identified at Hazor and Tel Kinrot, both in the upper Jordan valley; at Beth Shean; at Tel Regev and Tell Abu Hawam in the Accho valley; at Shechem, Tell el-Far'ah North, and perhaps Bethel in the central hills; and at Debir (Khirbet Rabud) in the Hebron hills. Hazor was defended by its tremendous Middle Bronze Age ramparts; there is no evidence that they were repaired or enlarged in the Late Bronze Age. At Shechem, the Middle Bronze Age wall was restored, as may have been the case at Bethel as well. Tel Kinrot was first settled at the start of the Late Bronze Age, and Debir in the Late Bronze II; both sites seem to have been fortified from the start. We thus observe no uniform pattern of fortification; those settlements able to construct a defensive wall did so with the materials or earlier structures at hand.

The gates of the period are also largely restorations of Middle Bronze gates, that is, direct-axis entryways flanked by towers and guardrooms. The gate excavated in the lower city of Hazor was first built in the Middle Bronze II, hand in hand with the construction of the great earthen ramparts (stratum 4). It was furnished with a pair of square, solid towers and three pairs of small buttresses on either side of the passage. In the following Middle Bronze phase (stratum 3) the gate was altered to a large gate with two rectangular towers and three pairs of buttresses, the characteristic plan of the gates of this period. This gate was razed in the great destruction of the Middle Bronze Age city and was rebuilt in the Late Bronze I (stratum 2) along precisely the same lines, this time with massive ashlar masonry. This structure survived until the end of the period, undergoing slight repairs and changes, such as the raising of the level of the gate passage and the addition of a threshold of large basalt slabs. The two Middle Bronze Age gates of Shechem were also restored in the Late Bronze Age on an identical plan.

At Megiddo, the large north gate first appears in the plan of the Late Bronze I town of stratum IX; however, the excavators suggested that it was first built in stratum X, at the end of the Middle Bronze Age. The gate retained its form throughout the Late Bronze Age, when it was lined with well-carved stone slabs. An interesting feature is the remnant of a wooden beam between the fourth and fifth masonry courses. This is the earliest instance of the integration of wooden beams in stone walls, and the method was to be employed in the Solomonic gate at Megiddo as well as in the temple of Solomon in Jerusalem, according to the biblical description. The Megiddo gate has no towers and is not joined to a defensive wall, appearing more ceremonial than truly defensive. It seems thus that Late Bronze Age Megiddo was unfortified. This raises serious problems with regard to the interpretation of the Egyptian

account of the siege of the city by Thutmose III.

Another gate of possible ceremonial character was found at Jaffa. The stone jambs were inscribed with part of the name of Ramesses II and five of his titles. No wall was found.

Freestanding gates, though not a common phenomenon, are not inconceivable, for gates served more than a defensive function. The gate was the ceremonial entrance, the town showpiece, and the focus of trade, public gatherings, litigation, news reports, and even cult. Even if the construction of town walls, with their explicitly defensive capacity, was prohibited by the Egyptians, the erection of ceremonial gateways, particularly at key sites, may well have been allowed.

The Late Bronze Age thus produced no innovation in the art of fortification; where fortifications existed, they carried on traditions established during the Middle Bronze Age.

The Late Bronze Age city being a rather feeble entity, it should not come as a surprise that few public structures have been discovered. In fact, the most common public structure in the city was the temple, which was indispensable, as it fulfilled the religious needs of the community. Only a few buildings of governmental or local administrative function have been excavated so far. Structures serving the common welfare, such as public granaries or water supply systems, are as yet unknown. It would appear that the responsibility for food and water supply devolved on the citizens themselves, further evidence of the relative impotence of the municipal governments.

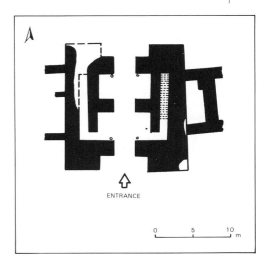

Fig. 7.1. City gate at Shechem

ENTRANCE

0   5   10 m

PALACES

With the political structure of Late Bronze Age Canaan based on the rule of the Egyptian overlord, each urban settlement could be expected to contain a modest palace to serve as the ruler's residence and as the administrative center of the town, with its audience rooms, offices, guardrooms, stables, and storerooms to accommodate considerable provisions both for the ruling family and for the municipal bureaucracy. The palace would also have housed the scribes and the municipal archives and treasury. All these would have required a structure not only larger than the common dwelling but also better defended. It is not surprising to find, therefore, that the buildings identified as palaces are characterized by thick walls that serve both as defense and as support for a second and third story. Two main palace types prevailed during the Late Bronze Age: the courtyard palace, built along the same basic plan of the common dwellings and continuing the Middle Bronze Age building traditions, and the Egyptian-style residency, a type

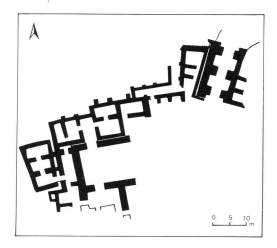

Fig. 7.2. Megiddo palace and city gate

of structure introduced into Canaan mainly during the Late Bronze III, when Egypt intensified its grip on Canaan.

COURTYARD PALACES. The courtyard palace, as its name suggests, consists of a large court with rooms ranged around it. The courtyard may be entirely enclosed by the rooms, which may be ranged in several rows, or only partially enclosed, with rooms concentrated on one or two sides. The courtyard palace was common in the Middle and Late Bronze Ages throughout the Levant and in northern Mesopotamia, the most complete and representative examples being those found in the Syrian cities of Ugarit, Ebla, and Alalakh. In Canaan, Middle Bronze Age courtyard palaces have been unearthed at Hazor, Shechem, Aphek, Lachish, Tel Sera', and Tell el-Ajjul, but only one Late Bronze Age palace has so far come to light—at Megiddo. More Late Bronze palaces may yet be discovered, but for now, their absence provides further evidence for the impoverishment of city life.

During most of the Middle Bronze Age, the Megiddo palace was near the city center, close to the Fortress Temple. The end of the period, however, saw its removal to the city gate area. Here the expansion of the palace and the changes in its plan may be traced through the Late Bronze Age. The palace first built in stratum X, the late Middle Bronze Age, remained unchanged, apart from the raised floor levels, during stratum IX. The salient features of this palace are the thick northern and eastern walls (about 2.5 meters and 3.5 meters, respectively). The southern and western walls were not preserved, and it is unclear whether the exterior palace walls were all of such extreme breadth. The central lime-paved courtyard of the palace measured

about 100 square meters and was surrounded by rooms on every side. A pair of long and narrow rooms in the southwest corner mark the place of the staircase leading to the second floor (and perhaps to a third as well, in view of the extreme thickness of the walls). The west wing of the palace consisted of a maze of rooms and courtyards. A collection of spindle whorls and loom weights found here suggest that these were weaving workshops, a craft that may have been under the patronage of the local ruler.

In stratum VIII of the Late Bronze II the palace attained its greatest extent. The plan changed, but the massive northern and eastern walls remained in use. The preserved palace area is about 1500 square meters, though there appears to have been another wing to the southwest. The main entrance was from the south, leading through a broad portal to the large central court. The courtyard and the surrounding rooms were paved with fine lime plaster. Three broad doorways led off the central court to rooms on the northeast and northwest and to a shell-paved courtyard on the south. This courtyard was probably a bath chamber, with a square basin sunk into the center of the floor and drained by a subsurface channel. A doorway led west to the most magnificent part of the palace, another large courtyard opening onto a series of rooms. Two pillars (only the base of one has been preserved) stood in the wide entryway, no doubt lending it particular grandeur. It opened onto a broad hall, perhaps an audience hall. A small chamber in the northern part of the palace was probably a treasury. Beneath its floors was found a hoard of gold artifacts, jewelry, cylinder seals, and ivories.

East of the gate, the remains of another palace, smaller than that of Area AA but of a similar plan (a central courtyard enclosed by rooms), were recovered. The walls are thinner than those of the large palace, and the structure may have been an outlying wing of the central structure.

In strata VIIB and VIIA of the thirteenth and early twelfth centuries, significant changes took place in the organization of the space surrounding the central courtyard of the large palace, but the courtyard itself, as well as the shell-paved court to the southwest, remained unchanged. The halls and roomy inner courts gave way to smaller chambers. West of the central courtyard, in place of the magnificent apartments, a series of three contiguous rooms led to a hall, in the west corner of which lay a small platform approached by steps, a type of small household shrine. In the stratum VIIA palace of the end of the Late Bronze Age, the three rooms were expanded to form a separate, subterranean building approached by stairs. In this cellar was found a cache of valuables, the most important of which are the many rare ivories. Fragments of painted plaster found in the ruins of this palace indicate that its walls were decorated with frescoes.

EGYPTIAN-STYLE RESIDEN-CIES. Palaces of a completely different kind were established in Canaan during the thirteenth and twelfth centuries B.C.E. These structures, commonly known as residencies, were not built by the Canaanite inhabitants and do not reflect their needs. Rather, they represent the strategic concerns of Egypt, for whom Canaan was an important staging post. The Egyptian effort to consolidate its grip on Canaan was concentrated on the southern coastal strip and along the main international routes. It included the construction of outposts at key points

to house Egyptian officials and fulfill military and administrative functions. Such structures were usually built within existing settlements, but in some cases, such as at Deir el-Balah and Tel Mor, they were unrelated to a habitation site and constituted isolated outposts on the highway, with the defensive character of a fortress. It is, however, possible that habitation sites may yet be discovered at these sites as well.

The residencies, first identified by Petrie in the excavations of Tell el-Far'ah South, were built according to Egyptian architectural and construction principles and therefore stand out as unique in the history of architecture in Canaan. Their plans are uniformly similar to that of private dwellings in Egypt. The buildings are square, with corner entrances. A square courtyard—sometimes identified as a covered hall, if furnished with a base for a pillar that supported the ceiling—lies at the center of the structure. Small chambers surround this square space, and a corner staircase leads to the second floor. The Egyptian mode of construction is reflected in the thick, mud-brick walls with mud-brick foundations or, at times, no foundations at all. Some residencies incorporate other Egyptian architectural features, such as T-shaped doorjambs and thresholds. Fine examples of such details appear in two structures from Beth Shean, known as buildings 1500 and 1700. An Egyptian inscription, found out of context but attributed to building 1500, states that the Egyptian general Ramesses-weser-khepesh occupied the building during the reign of Ramesses III.

Egyptian-style residencies have been excavated thus far at Tell el-Far'ah South, Tell el-Hesi, Tel Sera', Tell Jemmeh, and Tel Mor, all on the southern coast of Canaan. Such structures were also found at Beth Shean, an Egyptian stronghold dur-

ing the Late Bronze and Early Iron ages.

The palace at Aphek reveals an Egyptian influence in its ground plan, though its construction technique is entirely Canaanite. The small fortified palace transformed the small Canaanite town on the Yarkon headwaters into an Egyptian administrative center. Excavations have concentrated on the palace proper, leaving it a moot point whether some contemporaneous remains excavated nearby were part of a habitation site or merely annexes of an isolated palace. The building occupies about 360 square meters. The corner entrance leads to a paved vestibule with a stone bench, perhaps a waiting room. A broad stairway led from the vestibule to the second story, which is not preserved. The ground floor consists of long halls and small chambers; these are not arranged around a central courtyard as is commonly the case in residencies. The walls, or more precisely the foundations, are 1.4 meters thick and are built of stone, in contrast to Egyptian practice. The Aphek palace is thus far the only building of its kind in Canaan.

DWELLINGS

Not many Late Bronze Age dwellings have been exposed in archaeological excavations, and the most important site for the study of this subject remains Megiddo. In the eastern part of the mound a number of houses forming part of a residential quarter were cleared. Their location, size, and plan, first established in the Middle Bronze Age, remained unchanged during the whole of the Late Bronze Age, reflecting a high measure of continuity, extending over hundreds of years. Certain internal changes in the houses did, of course, occur, such as the raising of floors, the removal or construction of dividing walls, and the blocking of doorways, all common alterations reflecting the extended use of the buildings.

Four nearly complete houses were exposed in the excavated area, as well as parts of a fifth. The layout of house 3002 in stratum VIII at Megiddo has been almost entirely recovered and provides a good example of a Late Bronze Age dwelling. It measures about 15 × 16 meters. The area designated 3002 was apparently an unroofed courtyard, and the large room to the west may have been one as well. These two inner courts were not approached directly but were surrounded by many small rooms. Because of the poor preservation of the walls and the schematic ground plans provided in the excavation report, the disposition of the entrances and the manner of circulation within the house are difficult to determine. Some of the rooms had a plastered, beaten earth floor; others were paved with cobblestones. It cannot be said what special function, if any, set these rooms apart from the rest of the house. In nearby house 3003, in the corner of a room with a plaster floor, was an installation in the shape of a quarter-circle, perhaps a bathing installation, drained by a channel flowing under the wall and the floor of the adjacent room to a pit.

The construction of the houses was quite simple. Walls are 0.75 meter wide, the lower, preserved portions being built of fieldstones and the superstructure probably of mud brick. No wall has been sufficiently preserved to provide evidence of windows. Houses arranged around central courtyards can receive light and air through the doorways, so that windows are not indispensable. It is doubtful whether the houses had a second story. Roofs were not preserved at Megiddo, but in contemporary stratum C

at Tell Beit Mirsim a large portion of a roof that had collapsed in a conflagration was found. The ceiling was made of wooden beams spanning the room at 0.6-meter intervals. Above and across the beams were laid smaller branches and beams. This wooden structure was covered by a thick layer of clay, which was then plastered. The underside of the ceiling was also covered by a thin layer of plastered clay. This type of construction suggests that the roof was flat. Stone rollers for the upkeep of the plastered roof were found in Area C at Hazor, indicating that this roof-type was widespread throughout Canaan.

It is a question whether the large floor space of the Megiddo dwellings (about 240 square meters) was characteristic of houses of the period. The houses are near the Fortress Temple, and their inhabitants may have held cultic office or been otherwise of the elite. The houses did, however, also serve for the storage of large amounts of provisions as well as for the pursuit of various household crafts. A dwelling of a different type was discovered at Tel Batash in the Judaean Shephelah. It is rectangular (9 × 11 meters), with thick (1.2 meters) walls. The entrance was from the short south wall. Immediately to the right of the entrance a narrow corridor and a staircase led to the second story, where the living quarters were no doubt situated. The ground floor consisted of one large hall divided by two rows of wooden columns (only the stone bases have remained) and screen walls into three long rooms somewhat reminiscent of the four-roomed house of the Iron Age.

The question of site organization leads back to Megiddo, where a cluster of neighboring houses was uncovered. The houses were arranged on either side of a narrow street, two meters wide, which ran north-south. Another alley

branched off between the houses to the east; the houses on the west side shared a common exterior wall. Because of the poor state of the remains it is not clear whether the houses were entered from the main street or from the side alleys. It may be surmised that the residential quarters of Megiddo were built in a series of rings around the city perimeter. A street would have divided the external row of houses from the internal one.

A residential area was uncovered in Area C at Hazor. Unlike Megiddo, where each house stands apart, the houses at Hazor are clustered in irregular blocks, so it is difficult to determine which units joined to form one dwelling. The walls are not of uniform breadth, are not straight, and do not join at right angles. The house blocks are separated by crooked lanes, giving the area a more plebeian appearance than the Megiddo residential areas.

TEMPLES AND CULT OBJECTS

It is not surprising that many Late Bronze Age temples have been discovered in excavations, since every ancient place of habitation had at least one temple that would have a fair chance of discovery, given sufficiently extensive excavations. The temples found show a marked absence of uniformity. They are of many different types and of varied size, location, and content, reflecting an ethnically diverse population, a variety of influences, and no doubt the multitude of divinities in the Canaanite pantheon, as reflected in the Ugaritic mythology and other writings. Despite their great number, our knowledge of the various deities worshiped in the temples, of the character of the cult and the manner in which it was practiced, and of the function and status of the temple in the community is very limited. The absence of texts and the paucity of cult objects with an obvious function permit a discussion only of the architectural aspects of the temples.

MIGDOL TEMPLES

At three sites in the country—Megiddo, Shechem, and Hazor—temples of a type noteworthy for its monumental dimensions and standard plan have been discovered. They have thick walls, which give them the aspect of a fortress, heightened by the sturdy towers flanking the entrance to the building. The layout is symmetrical along a longitudinal axis, on which the entrances are located. At the far end of this axis, adjacent to or within the rear wall of the temple, was the focus of the cult, the holy of holies, in the form of a niche or an altar. The migdol temples may be divided into two subtypes: structures in which the interior is occupied by a single hall, and structures in which the interior is divided into two or three broadrooms. The origins of both subtypes lie in northern Syria, where they appear in the major cities of Ebla (Tell Mardikh), Tell Mumbaqat, and Alalakh. The mig-

dol temple made its first appearance at the three sites in the Middle Bronze Age and remained in use for the entire Late Bronze Age, with some changes and additions. Four temples of this type have been excavated in Canaan; those of Megiddo, Shechem, and Hazor (Area A) are of the first subtype, and the temple of Area H at Hazor is of the second. The Area A temple at Hazor has no flanking towers at the entrance.

THE TEMPLE OF SHECHEM. This building, near the western gate of the city, was founded on a massive fill accumulated from modifications made in the Middle Bronze Age fortifications. It measures 21.2 × 26.3 meters, and its walls are more than 5 meters thick. Its corners are oriented precisely to the four cardinal points, and the entrance is on the southeast side. Two rows of three pillars supported the roof. The massive entrance towers probably served as stairwells. The column that stood in the middle of the front entrance during the Middle Bronze Age was removed in the Late Bronze Age. On either side of the doorway leading to the main hall were two stones with recesses that

once held, it has been suggested, cultic stelae (masseboth). No traces of these stelae have been recovered, but in the courtyard fronting the temple a fragment of a large stela was recovered and restored by the excavators to its original position. This Shechem temple, which remained unchanged throughout the Late Bronze Age and even into the Iron Age, has been identified with the tower of Shechem (Jud. 9:47).

THE TEMPLE OF MEGIDDO. The history of the monumental temple of Megiddo is more complex. The excavators of the site suggested that the temple was first constructed in stratum VIII of the Late Bronze II, but renewed investigations have attributed its foundation to stratum X of the Middle Bronze Age. The building remained in use until stratum VIIA, the terminal phase of Canaanite Megiddo, undergoing some changes. The Megiddo temple is identical in plan to that of Shechem but much smaller. In its earliest, well-built phase, it measured only 9.6 × 11.5 meters, with walls 4 meters thick. The rear wall, 5 meters thick, contained a shallow niche. The corners of this structure

Fig. 7.3. Three stages of the Megiddo temple

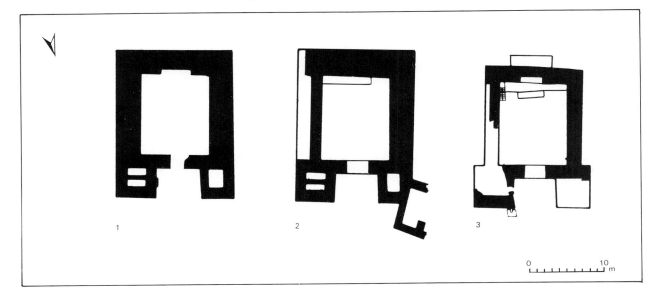

0 _____ 10
m

are not aligned with the cardinal points, and its entrance is on the north side. The tower to the left of the entrance is built of fine ashlar masonry and contains two narrow chambers interpreted as a staircase; the tower on the right side contains a square chamber. In the next phase of the temple's existence the niche in the rear wall was blocked and the focus of the cult was transferred to a narrow platform. In the final phase the temple walls were considerably narrowed, thus detracting from its fortified character. The contents of the temple were meager.

THE TEMPLE OF HAZOR, AREA A. The third single-chambered migdol temple is that of Area A in the upper city of Hazor. This structure, founded in stratum XVI and remaining in use until the end of

stratum XV (the Middle Bronze Age to the Late Bronze I), consisted of one longroom 9 × 16 meters, with walls 2.35 meters thick. In its lack of flanking towers it differs from the other temples. Yadin suggested that the lack of towers may be ascribed to the proximity of the royal palace, which would have made the separate defense of the temple unnecessary. Like the fortress temple of Shechem, the corners of the temple are oriented with the cardinal points. Opposite the entrance, against the rear wall, was a rectangular brick platform covered with a thick layer of plaster. In the Late Bronze I the entrance was lined with orthostats (finely dressed rectangular stone slabs, often carved in relief, commonly used in the northern Levant to line temple walls). Two orthostats

stood on either side of the entrance, and four more formed the threshold. Many fragments of cult vessels, all of the Late Bronze I, were found on the floor of the temple, along with animal bones. The building was destroyed at the end of the Late Bronze I and, unlike other temples of the same type, was never rebuilt. However, the sanctity of the area was preserved, and during the Late Bronze II and III various installations were built around the ruins; rituals were observed, leaving behind heaps of animal bones and votive vessels.

THE MIGDOL TEMPLE WITH BROADROOMS AT HAZOR. The most interesting and opulent of the monumental temples of Canaan is the broadroom temple found in

Fig. 7.4.   Orthostat threshold of the Area A temple at Hazor

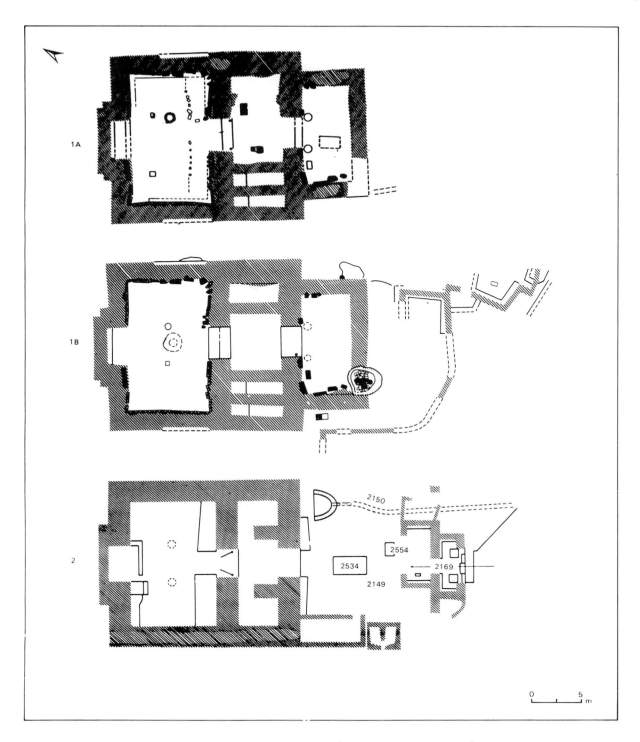

Fig. 7.5. Area H temple at Hazor, strata 2, 1B and 1A

Area H at Hazor. In plan it resembles the temples found at Tell Mardikh and Alalakh in northern Syria, and it is thought that its origins lie in that region. The main cult hall is a broadroom, and the two towers flanking the entrance form a broad anteroom. The walls of the temple are thick and its axis of entry direct. The nearly square structure measures 18 × 20 meters, with walls 2.5 meters thick. As at Shechem, the building is oriented precisely to the four cardinal points, and it is entered from the southeast. The stratum 2 temple of the Late Bronze I is identical to that of stratum 3, of the Middle Bronze Age. In the middle of the main cult room, the holy of holies, are two pillar bases. Benches line the walls on either side of the entrance, and a cult niche is set in the rear wall, with a low wall bor-

dering what was no doubt the most sacred part of the temple. In front of the temple was a large court in which, during this phase, various structures were erected—rooms, water installations, and drainage channels. The center of the court was occupied by a square structure; this may have been a platform or altar, and indeed the surrounding area was strewn with animal bones and ash. A gateway led to this court, and beyond it lay an external courtyard. Cultic finds from the inner courtyard include two small female figurines, one in bronze and the other of silver leaf. Also found here was a clay liver model inscribed with Akkadian cuneiform formulas. This object, used for divination, testifies that the people of Hazor were familiar with the cult practices of the Syro-Akkadian expanse.

In the next phase, stratum 1B of the Late Bronze II, an entirely new structure was built on the ruins of the earlier temple. Its plan was fundamentally similar to its predecessor, only now a third broadroom, narrower than the other two, was added to the front of the building. The former vestibule now became a middle hall, divided into long, narrow chambers, which no doubt served as staircases. The temple thus became a tripartite structure 28 meters long, the largest temple of the period. In the center of the holy of holies a small deep pit was carved, the upper part of which was lined with fieldstones. A headless statue of a seated man was found in the pit. On either side of the pit were two basalt pillar bases, one round and the other square. This asymmetry led the excavators to

Fig. 7.6. Lion orthostat from the Area H temple at Hazor

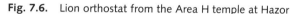

propose that the bases were taken from the remains of the previous temple, apparently a common practice at Hazor. The inner and outer courtyards fronting the temple remained in use, but the cultic installations within them were rebuilt.

After the destruction of this phase, the last in the series of temples was built above it on an identical plan. This structure, attributed to stratum IA of the Late Bronze III, is known as the Orthostat Temple, after the orthostats lining the main hall in a continuous row and placed at intervals along the walls of the vestibule. The orthostats, which were left plain, were carelessly laid and did not form a continuous surface. This led the excavators to assume that the stone slabs, like the pillar bases, were dismantled from one of the earlier temples and reused

here. In view of the discovery of the orthostats in the Late Bronze I temple of Area A, in the upper city, a stratum 2 origin was suggested. To this same stratum was assigned an unusually large orthostat found in an unusual context: in a pit cut into the exterior wall left of the entrance. The orthostat was 1.9 meters long and 0.9 meter high, with a lion carved in relief on one side. Judging by the size of the orthostat and the stance of the lion, it had once lined the right jamb of the main entrance, facing its companion guardian, which was never found. Clearly, the relief had been purposely interred in the pit, but it is unclear when and under what circumstances this was done.

The cult objects scattered on the floor of the holy of holies form one of the largest collections of such

items ever found in Israel. Notable in its absence was the central ritual object, the divine image or emblem, which no doubt stood in the cult niche. Yadin suggested, however, that two fragments of a basalt statue found in the inner courtyard of the stratum 1B temple were remains of the cult image of the temple. One fragment was a torso of a male figure whose breast was adorned with a medallion containing a four-rayed emblem. The second fragment was a base in the form of a bull, on which the male figure may have stood. Yadin suggested that this was the image of Hadad, the Canaanite storm god. The four-rayed emblem is sometimes interpreted as a wheel in the storm god's chariot; others interpret it as a solar disk. If the fragments did belong to the cult image that stood in the niche, they

Fig. 7.7. Cella of the Area H temple at Hazor with finds in situ

Fig. 7.8. Statue fragments from the Area H temple at Hazor: human torso and bull

Fig. 7.9. Offering table with emblem of Hadad (height 105 centimeters)

represent the only identification of a worshiped deity in Canaanite temples. Support for the identification of the four-rayed emblem as a divine symbol comes from a basalt offering table found on the temple floor by the niche. On one side of this object (0.5 × 0.5 × 1.7 meters) was carved a square frame enclosing the same four-rayed solar disk found on the torso. Two elongated depressions

carved beneath the emblem give the offering table the aspect of a three-columned facade. Similar depressions were carved on the two adjoining sides. Nearby lay a large basalt basin (0.5 meter in diameter), and somewhat to the south another, smaller basin decorated with a running spiral of Mycenaean type. Other finds include basalt offering tables, large ceramic basins, and a

wealth of small objects, including cylinder seals, beads, and pottery. Also found were four small bronze figurines, among them a bull figurine, which Yadin viewed as further proof that the temple deity was the figure depicted standing on a bull. Near the doorway of the holy of holies another statue of a seated figure was found. The figure was decapitated, like the one found in the 1B temple, but the head was discovered nearby.

SQUARE TEMPLES

Another type of temple is the square temple, of which three have been found—at Hazor, on the slopes of Mount Gerizim, and near Amman in Transjordan. This type of temple has a square central courtyard with a single entrance. The narrow corridor between the courtyard walls and the exterior walls is divided by thin walls into rooms of equal length. The temple was entered near one of the corners. When the first building of this type was excavated at Mount Gerizim its sacred character was not perceived. Only after the discovery of the Amman shrine was the Gerizim structure reinvestigated and a new temple type proposed. The Amman and Gerizim shrines inspired the interpretation of the stratum 2 building in Area F at Hazor as a sacred structure. This building is so poorly preserved, however, that its reconstruction as a square temple must remain in doubt. In view of the isolation of the Gerizim and Amman temples, at a distance from sedentary settlement, it has been

proposed to attribute this type of shrine to a nonsedentary population. Be that as it may, the origins of the square plan are unknown, nor is there any evidence regarding the nature of the cult practiced in the temple or the identity of the deity worshiped there. The temple at Hazor was empty of finds, further impeding identification, and the temple at Gerizim contained only fragments of an incense stand. The Amman temple provided a large, rich assemblage of objects, including objects of gold, ivory, bone, stone, and pottery—many of them imported—as well as a considerable quantity of weapons, but it is not an assemblage of particularly cultic character. On the contrary, because of the profane nature of the finds it has been suggested that they were booty taken during raids on wealthier populations. Some scholars do not accept the identification of the square structures as temples, viewing them rather as mansions architecturally related to the Egyptian-style residencies. The similarity to the Egyptian structures is underlined by the identification of column bases (rather than altars) in the central space, suggesting that it was a room rather than an open court.

As for the temporal range of the square shrines, the structure at Mount Gerizim was dated by the excavators to the Middle Bronze Age II, that of Hazor to the Late Bronze I, and the Amman temple to the Late Bronze II–III. The square temple thus had a range similar to that of the migdol temple, but each of the square temples was short-lived.

EGYPTIAN-STYLE TEMPLES

Temple remains from three Canaanite sites—Beth Shean, Lachish, and Timna in the Aravah valley near Elath—exhibit Egyptian influence either in their layout or in some details of their construction. This should not come as a surprise; on the contrary, it is astonishing to discover how small the influence of Egypt was on Canaanite temples and cult, despite Egypt's supreme power in Canaan for the whole of the Late Bronze Age.

Inscriptions reveal the presence of temples in Canaan where Egyptian deities were worshiped. One such inscription, carved on an ivory pen case from the Megiddo treasure, mentions a woman minstrel of Ptah in Ashkelon and implies that a tem-

Fig. 7.10. Square temples at Hazor (A) and Amman (B)

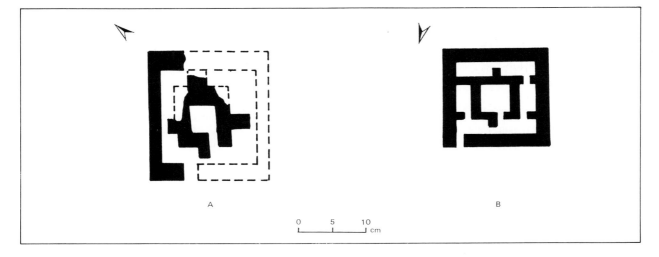

A

B

0   5   10
cm

ple (so far undiscovered) is dedicated to this deity at that site.

At Beth Shean, one of the Egyptian garrison towns, a sequence of temples spanning most of the Late Bronze Age and the beginning of the Iron Age was excavated. The first in the sequence, the stratum IX temple generally attributed to the reign of Thutmose III, is of the courtyard type. Its plan is not entirely clear, and it is not Egyptian in character, but many Egyptian objects were found among its remains. Chief among them is a small limestone stela dedicated by one Pa-re-em-heb to "Mekal, the god of Beth Shean," in memory of his father Amen-em-Opet. There can be no doubt that Pa-re-em-heb and his father were Egyptians, and they are thus portrayed on the stela. However, the god Mekal is recorded neither in the Egyptian nor the Canaanite pantheons; on the stela he is portrayed as a bearded Canaanite deity, with a tall horned headdress and a long ribbon dangling behind. Another unique object from this temple is a basalt orthostat with two scenes carved in relief. Both depict a lion and a dog (or a lioness) locked in combat. The cultic significance of these scenes, if any, is unclear.

Of the stratum VIII temple little can be said, as all that has remained of it are basalt pillar bases. The temple of strata VII and VI was a single structure that underwent some slight alterations between the two phases. It was built in the mid fourteenth century (others suggest a thirteenth-century date). It closely resembles in both plan and construction several Egyptian cultic installations found at El-Amarna, suggesting that the temple served the local Egyptian governor. It remained in use throughout stratum VI, until the days of Ramesses III.

The mud-brick building is oriented north-south. It has a large main hall, nearly square, with two bases for the roof supports at its center. Low benches line the walls. Two chambers lie behind the main hall. The one on the right, the cella, is approached by a flight of steps and has a platform abutting its rear wall. The platform no doubt accommodated the image to whom incense was offered on a small altar that stood in the main hall, just in front of the stairway. The lefthand chamber may have been the temple storeroom. The main hall of the sanctuary was approached via a walled courtyard entered from the west, a bent-axis approach foreign to the Canaanite cultic tradition. Behind this courtyard was another enclosed court. A papyrus capital, common in Egyptian architecture, was found in the temple, as well as a rich variety of objects including a bronze standard in the image of the Egyptian goddess Hathor, crowned with cow horns and a disk, her features sheathed in gold leaf. Also found were Syro-Hittite cylinder seals and a bronze axehead made in the Anatolian metalworking tradition. The advent of stratum VI brought about a slight change in the rear of the temple. The cella and platform were now in the middle of the rear part of the building, flanked by two small chambers. As before, the cella was approached by a flight of steps, in front of which stood an incense altar. The courtyards fronting the temple were also rearranged: the inner court was dismantled, and a new court was added to the former outer court, extending west of the temple facade. One now entered the forecourt through a broad columned portal, turned left toward the inner court, and left again to the main hall and the cella. The environs of this temple were strewn with typically Egyptian architectural elements, including painted cornices and T-shaped thresholds and doorjambs bearing hieroglyphic inscriptions. Two stelae of Ramesses II are at-

tributed to this stratum, as is a lintel inscribed with the name of Ramesses III, which was reused in the stratum V temple of the Iron Age. Smaller finds include many ceramic stands bearing either painted or applied decorations of cultic import.

The temple uncovered at the summit of Tel Lachish, within the citadel or palace precinct, is not a typically Egyptian structure, but it has architectural elements identified as Egyptian. Unlike Beth Shean, Lachish is not mentioned among the cities that served as Egyptian administrative or military centers, but many finds at the site testify to a close connection with Egypt. The temple's phases, all imperfectly preserved, date to the Late Bronze II–III. The structure bears a general resemblance to the strata VII and VI temple at Beth Shean. It has a large central hall, with two column bases set in the center of the mud-brick floor. Many fragments of carbonized wood from the roof beams were found and identified as Lebanese cedar. At the eastern end of the structure, a monumental staircase with a low stone parapet led to a small chamber assumed to be the cella. The large hall, the stairs, and the raised cella recall the Beth Shean temples and are Egyptian in concept. The east wall of the main hall, near the staircase, was decorated with colorful wall paintings, preserved only in fragments of colored plaster found along its base. Along this same wall were ranged three bases of engaged columns. Fragments of slender octagonal columns found thrown on the floor near the staircase may have once stood on the bases. The shape of the columns and the manner in which they were attached to the wall also belong to the Egyptian architectural tradition, as do the light blue hues of the wall paintings.

Somewhat to the north, a large mass of bricks may represent the base of a staircase leading to the second story or to the roof. In the north wall of the main hall there was a monumental doorway, with a threshold built of finely dressed stones; between them lay a wooden plank that supported two wooden posts. The lower parts of the doorjambs were preserved in situ and recesses in them contained carbonized remains of cedar beams. In front of this entrance was a chamber, with graffiti on the floor. If this was the only entrance to the main hall, the temple has an indirect axis of entry, as at Beth Shean.

The most interesting find in the temple was a thin gold plaque originally affixed to a wooden plaque or sewn on cloth or leather, as evidenced by the small perforations around its edges. It was found crumpled and discarded near the staircase leading to the cella. It bears the figure of a nude goddess wearing a headdress in the shape of a flower with two horns at the bottom. The unidentified goddess stands on a horse clad in armor wearing a feathered decoration on its head. She holds two lotus flowers.

The third Egyptian-style sanctuary is the shrine near the copper mines of Timna in the southern Aravah, about 25 kilometers north of Elath. Its construction is no doubt related to the copper mining activity of Egyptians at Timna during the Nineteenth and Twentieth dynasties. The shrine consists of a small room abutting a rock scarp. The entrance on the southeast side faced a small niche carved in the rock wall. The image of Hathor, the patroness of the mines to whom the shrine was devoted, was carved repeatedly on stones and pillars in and around the shrine. Many inscribed objects, some bearing the names of Egyptian kings beginning with Seti I and ending Ramesses V, prove that the shrine was used by Egyptians working the site. Of particular interest is a copper snake, similar to one found at the temple of Tel Mevorakh. The ceramic assemblage includes a large group of decorated vessels known as Midianite ware. In its final phase the shrine was probably covered with a cloth canopy, attested to by textile remains on the floor.

OTHER TEMPLES

In addition to the temples enumerated above, there are several Canaanite temples that do not fall into any clear category. These should be seen as of local, popular Canaanite character, and they may possibly have preserved ancient Canaanite cult traditions.

THE FOSSE TEMPLE AT LACHISH. The moat (fosse) that formed part of the fortifications of Middle Bronze Age Lachish went out of use during the Late Bronze Age, and a temple was constructed inside it, near the northwestern corner of the mound. This building, known as the Fosse Temple, was first constructed in the Late Bronze I and was twice destroyed and rebuilt during the Late Bronze Age, the three phases of construction corresponding to the three phases of the period. Each of the three temples was a simple affair, of rather poor construction. They were oriented north-south, and a cult platform adjoined the south wall of each. The earliest Fosse Temple consisted of a small room (5 × 10 meters), its roof supported by two pillars. A narrow cult platform had three projections. West of the main room was a small chamber near one of the entrances to the temple. A second entrance was in the east wall. The finds in this temple, which included much pottery, a rare Mycenaean vessel, and a scarab of Thutmose III, come from favissae dug into its floors, where vessels that had gone out of use were discarded. The second Fosse Temple was larger than the first and of a different plan. In fact, from the earlier structure only the location of the cult platform, now even narrower and with only a single projection, was retained. The main hall comprised a 10 × 10 meter square, and its ceiling was supported by four pillars, of which only the bases were found. Low benches lined the walls in two or three rows. Two entrances, one from a room at the northwest corner, the other at the southwest corner, led to the main hall. There was another room, also containing benches, on the southeast side of the hall, behind the platform. The latest Fosse Temple, built in the Late Bronze III, is nearly identical to the second, except for the addition of a room at the southwest corner and the enlargement of the cult platform. A large and varied assemblage of objects was found on the temple floors and in the nearby favissae: ivory, bone, glass, metal, faience, and stone, as well as much pottery, a good deal of it imported. A large jug bore the proto-Canaanite inscription "An offering to my Lady Elat." Elat may well have been the goddess worshiped in the temple. The three Fosse Temples at Lachish are completely different from the large and well-built structure revealed inside the town, in the palace area.

THE STELAE TEMPLE IN AREA C AT HAZOR. Another local shrine was discovered in Area C in the lower city of Hazor, abutting the inner slope of the huge rampart surrounding the city. The shrine has two phases, corresponding to stratum 1A and 1B. In both phases the shrine consisted of one broadroom, 2.5 × 3.5 meters. Its corners face the four cardinal points, and the entrance was from the northeast, as in the Area A temple in the upper city. Opposite the entrance a semi-circular niche was carved into the rampart and lined with a row of stones; a ceramic vessel was placed in the center of it. Finds on the temple floor included a considerable amount of pottery and a pair of bronze cymbals in a bronze bowl. The 1A structure, built directly over the 1B shrine, made use of some earlier wall fragments. During this phase, a row of stelae was placed in the niche, earning the shrine the name of the Stelae Temple. The ten stelae were made of basalt; they had smoothly dressed faces, concave backs, and rounded tops. The middle stela bore a relief depicting hands outstretched toward an emblem composed of a crescent cradling a disk, interpreted by Yadin as the emblem of the moon god. The hands were understood to represent the consort of the moon god. This small shrine was thus dedicated to the worship of a divine couple, the moon god and his consort. Yadin found support for this interpretation in the statue of a seated male figure at the southern end of the row of stelae, whose chopped-off head was found nearby. An inverted crescent, the emblem of the moon god Sin, was carved in relief on the breast of the figure. At the northern end of the row of stelae, at a somewhat lower elevation, was a small lion orthostat. Its position suggests that, like its larger counterpart in the Area H temple, it was purposely buried. A rather crude basalt slab in front of the stelae was probably an offering table. Nearby items may have been brought as offerings, including part of a potter's wheel. A few objects found in neighboring houses have also been interpreted as cult objects. One is a silver-plated cult standard, with a crescent and a stylized snake portrayed above the crude figure of a woman holding snakes. Yadin understood the snakes to be related to the cult of the moon

god. Another object, a small terra-cotta mask also found in a nearby building, should be seen, according to Yadin, as a plastic expression of "the face of Baal," a title of the god's consort.

An open-air shrine was excavated in Area F of the lower city at Hazor. Following the destruction of the stratum 2 square temple, the area became an open cult place during strata 1A–1B. Within this area was a large altar made of a single stone, 2.4 × 0.8 × 1.2 meters, with two recesses. Many cattle bones were found strewn about the altar. The altar stood at one end of an open area; a drainage channel ran through the middle of the area, and at the far end ceramic vessels and a bull's skull were found on a raised construction. The area was littered with pottery, including vessels of cultic type.

THE TEL MEVORAKH TEMPLE. In the Late Bronze I stratum of Tel Mevorakh, in the northern Sharon, a small temple was built on the rampart that had defended the settlement in the Middle Bronze Age and had by then fallen into disuse. The shrine consisted of an elongated chamber (5 × 10 meters), oriented east-west. A raised platform in the northwest corner was approached by five steps. The eastern part of the structure has not been preserved, and the precise location of the entrance is therefore not known. Benches lined the walls, which were plastered and decorated with colorful frescoes, as in the Lachish temple. A paved court bordering the shrine on three sides occupied the entire summit of the mound. The sanctuary was therefore not related to a settlement site but should be seen as a roadside shrine for travelers passing on the nearby highway. The temple was gutted by fire and restored in the fourteenth century B.C.E. The later structure is

poorly preserved, because of later massive construction at the spot. Both building phases provided a rich collection of artifacts, especially of ceramic vessels. Among the metal objects is a pair of cymbals, resembling those found in the stratum 1B temple in Area C at Hazor, and a copper snake resembling the one found in the shrine at Timna.

Other temples of a local character or that are difficult to categorize have been found at various sites—Tel Kitan in the Jordan valley north of Beth Shean, Tell es-Sa'idiyeh in the eastern Jordan valley, and Tel Sera' in the northern Negev.

Pottery

The local ceramic ware of the Late Bronze Age is entirely wheel-made. The quality of the local products is generally inferior to that of the Middle Bronze Age II. There is less care taken to balance the proportions and less effort invested in the finishing (the slip and burnish). Deformed vessels, a result of careless handling during the drying process prior to firing, are not uncommon. Painted decoration is relatively common in the Late Bronze Age, though it too is often quite carelessly executed. Pottery types are uniform throughout the country, with the exception of isolated cases of limited regional distribution; this uniformity reflects a standardized industry, concentrated in workshops providing large quantities of pottery to an extensive consumer's market. Alongside the local industry, importation of pottery reached an unprecedented scope during the Late Bronze Age.

As in domestic and public architecture, the local ware exhibits a conspicuous degree of typological continuity with the Middle Bronze Age. The ceramic assemblages of the Late Bronze I preserve the strong traditions of the Middle Bronze Age, though by the Late Bronze II,

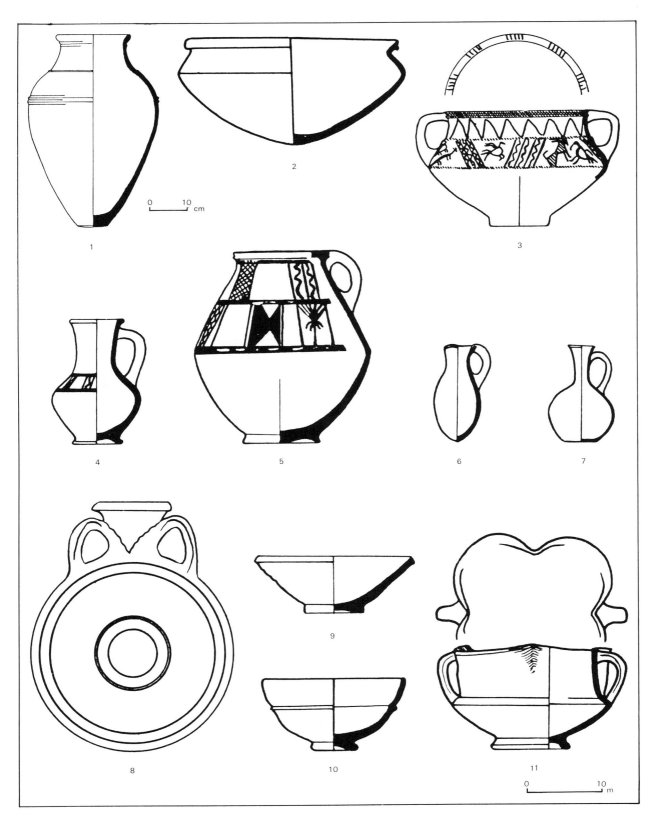

Fig. 7.11. Late Bronze Age pottery

forms were gradually breaking away from these canons. It is difficult to find significant differences between pottery of the fourteenth and thirteenth centuries, and dating is generally based on imported pottery types.

LOCAL POTTERY

PITHOI (fig. 7.11:1). The largest storage vessel of the period was the pithos, a large store jar measuring 1.2 meters or more in height. It has a thick rim, a broad shoulder, a tapering body, and a small base. Pithoi are limited in their distribution to northern Canaan, chiefly to Hazor. A similar type has been found in Syria, relating the vessel to assemblages of the North. It first appears in the Late Bronze II and carries over into the Late Bronze III. It is also one of the vessel types that continues to exist, with some changes, in the Early Iron Age.

JARS. The household jar is the direct descendant of the Middle Bronze Age II jar, and it changes little during the Late Bronze Age. It is ovoid, with a slightly flattened base, and bears two large loop handles. It is often decorated in painted bands or simple painted geometric designs.

A second common jar type has a narrow neck, a broad horizontal shoulder, a tapering body, and a prominent, pointed thick base. This jar, often termed the Canaanite Commercial Jar, has been discovered in tomb assemblages in Greece and Egypt, and it appears to have been used for the exportation of Canaanite produce, perhaps oil and wine, to foreign markets, as part of the extensive international trade network that is the hallmark of the period. Egyptian wall paintings show similar jars with lids, borne by laborers who unload Canaanite trading vessels at Egyptian ports. The commercial jar came into common use in the Late Bronze II and remained in use until the end of the period.

COOKING POTS (fig. 7.11:2). The Late Bronze Age cooking pot is a rounded, handleless vessel, with a triangular rim and a rounded base. This vessel preserves the Middle Bronze II form, which differed only in its rounded rim. In fact, both the rounded and the triangular rim types were extant in the Late Bronze I, before the latter became predominant in the Late Bronze II.

KRATERS (fig. 7.11:3). These are deep broad bowls of varying form. Most have a wide aperture

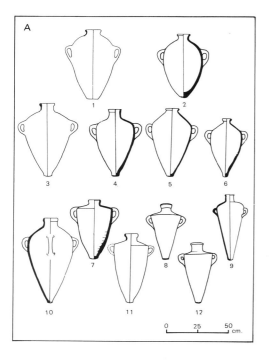

Fig. 7.12. Canaanite jar: typology (A) and Egyptian tomb painting (B) depicting jars being unloaded from ship

and handles drawn from the rim to a carinated shoulder. Some stand on a high foot. Kraters are often decorated, especially in the shoulder area. Incised decoration in the Middle Bronze tradition is common in the Late Bronze I. From the Late Bronze II on, painted decoration in simple geometric motifs (wavy lines or net patterns) becomes widespread. Some kraters bear animal representations, mainly goats or ibex and birds.

JUGS (fig. 7.11:4–5). Jugs are divided into globular and biconical shapes. Globular jugs with one shoulder handle closely resemble vessels of the preceding period and gradually disappear as the period progresses. More common are jugs with a large handle extending from rim to shoulder, often decorated in horizontal bands or zigzags. The biconical jugs, which first appear in the Late Bronze Age, form a distinct group. They are generally larger than globular jugs and have one or two handles. Their prominent feature is the wealth of painted decoration, again largely composed of simple geometric patterns— groups of straight and wavy lines, network or checkerboard patterns painted on the upper part of the vessel. Faunal and floral motifs appear as well. A fine example comes from Megiddo, its shoulder decorated with the ibex and palm motif. This motif, most typical of ceramic vessels of this period, is a popular depiction of the tree of life, a symbol of deep significance in the ancient Near East. The ibex and palm motif appears mainly on biconical jugs but occasionally on jars, chalices, and kraters as well. The Megiddo jug fills out the scene with more ibexes and many different kinds of birds. A crab is depicted in a separate panel beneath the handle.

JUGLETS (fig. 7.11:6). The typical juglet of this period is the dipper juglet. At the start of the period it is quite large, with a long and somewhat swollen neck in the Middle Bronze tradition. With time, the juglet becomes more slender and has a pinched spout. During the Late Bronze I the cylindrical juglet, a legacy of the Middle Bronze Age, was still in common use, but it soon disappeared. Also common in the same early stage of the period is a well-fashioned juglet, gray in color, with a rounded body, a tall neck, and a high burnish. This gray juglet is one of the diagnostic features of the Late Bronze I (Fig. 7.11:7).

FLASKS (fig. 7.11:8). The flask is composed of two wheel-made bowls attached face to face; a wheel-made neck is inserted at the juncture of the two bowls, and finally, two handles are attached in a manner that envelops the neck. Flasks are often decorated, usually in a pattern of concentric circles.

BOWLS (fig. 7.11:9–10). Bowls are the most common pottery vessel. The most frequent types are shallow straight-walled bowls, carinated bowls, and deep rounded bowls. The various bowl categories preserve Middle Bronze Age traditions, and the changes effected during the Late Bronze Age may be observed chiefly in the bases. At the start of the period the ring base, inherited from the earlier period, is most common; it gradually gives way to the disk base and finally to the plain flat base.

In one special bowl type, a rather large carinated bowl, the walls have been pushed in to form a quatrefoil vessel (Fig. 7.11:11). Handles were added on two sides, between the foils. This unique type has been found only in Late Bronze I strata at Hazor, and its sources should apparently be sought in the

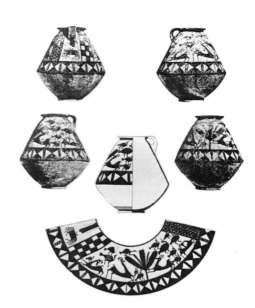

Fig. 7.13. Painted biconical jug portraying palm and various animals, from Megiddo (height 34 centimeters)

Cilician culture of southern Anatolia.

GOBLETS AND CHALICES.
Goblets are tall, narrow vessels, while chalices are rounded or flat bowls; both are furnished with a high foot. The two vessels are not very common and are most often found in temples; their function may thus have been cultic rather than domestic. Goblets are often decorated with straight or wavy lines, semicircles, and net patterns. Chalices are usually not decorated.

LAMPS. The oil lamp is a shallow, wheel-made bowl, with one end pinched to form a spout. The pinched spout becomes increasingly prominent as the Late Bronze Age progresses.

BICHROME WARE

This group of vessels, characterized by a painted bichrome decoration, was until recently considered Canaanite in origin, though many specimens have been found in Cyprus. Analysis of the clay composition of several vessels has revealed that though some were indeed made in Canaan, others came from Cyprus. This family of vessels is therefore discussed between the local and imported wares.

Bichrome vessels are most often jugs or kraters. Locally made vessels are usually of a common local form; the imported Cypriot items generally exhibit variant characteristics, such as a wide neck or a rounded body and base. The typical black and red decoration of this ware is painted in one register on the shoulder. The decorative patterns are usually geometric (crosshatched lozenges, hourglasses, hatched triangles, or running spirals), but

faunal motifs appear as well. The quality of the drawing is usually outstanding. Birds are the most commonly drawn animals, though bulls, fish, and cervids appear. Bichrome ware first appears in Canaan at the end of the Middle Bronze Age, but it is most common in the Late Bronze I. It is, in fact, so typical of this period that it has become a diagnostic feature of it, a *fossile directeur*.

IMPORTED POTTERY

The Late Bronze Age is characterized by a wealth of imported pottery, originating in various parts of the eastern Mediterranean basin —Cyprus, Mycenae, Syria, and Egypt. The presence of imports testifies to the flowering of commerce, to open sea routes, and to a rather high standard of living, which allowed the purchase of imported goods.

CYPRIOT IMPORTS. Base-ring ware, extremely common in Cyprus, is the Cypriot ware most often encountered in Canaan. The vessels of this family feature a number of technical peculiarities. They are handmade of a fine gray-brown clay and are fired to a high temperature. The handle is not applied to the body but inserted into it. The tall ring base gives the ware its name. The vessel's surface is decorated in vertical and diagonal line groups. In vessels of the earlier base-ring I variety, the lines consist of applied strips of clay; in the later base-ring II vessels they are painted in white.

The most common base-ring forms are jugs and juglets. Other forms include a wishbone-handled bowl, a long, slender bottle, and a lentoid flask. Another form, classified as base-ring ware on account of its method of manufacture, is a bull-shaped vessel. Of all the forms, the juglet (no doubt used to convey

Fig. 7.14. Bichrome krater from Tel Nagila (height 25 centimeters)

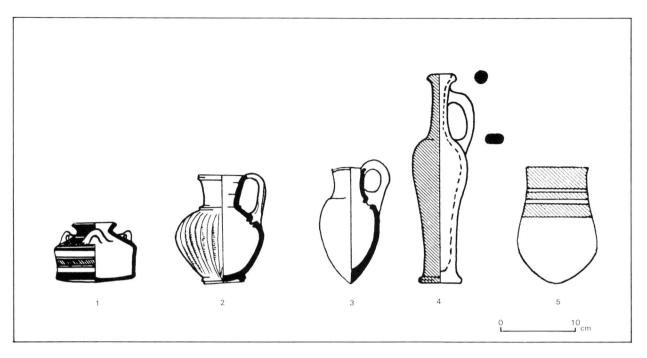

Fig. 7.15. Late Bronze Age imported pottery: Mycenaean pyxis (1), Cypriot Bucchero jug (2) and white shaved juglet (3), Syrian bottle (4), Egyptian vase (5)

Fig. 7.16. Base-ring ware, Cypriot imports into Canaan

Fig. 7.17. Base-ring jugs (bilbils) (A, B) and poppy capsules (C, D, approx. height 2.5 centimeters)

valuable liquids) is the most widely distributed. R. S. Merrillees suggests that the juglet was used for the exportation of opium. Turned upside down, the juglet resembles the poppy capsule from which opium is extracted.

Base-ring vessels are often used as chronological indicators for subphases of the Late Bronze Age; base-ring I vessels are common mainly in the Late Bronze I, and base-ring II vessels in the Late Bronze II. This division is not absolute, for there is an overlap in the use of the two types of vessels in both phases.

For white slip ware the characteristic vessel is a hemispheric bowl with a horizontal wishbone handle (Fig. 7.16:C). The white or grayish-white slip covering the interior and exterior has given rise to the common appellation "milk bowl." The outside of the bowl bears a painted decoration in shades of brown. The earlier white slip I ware has carefully painted designs, horizontal and vertical bands of ladder or cross-hatched pattern. In the later group, white slip II, the designs are debased. Generally speaking, white slip I ware can be dated to the Late Bronze I, and white slip II to the Late Bronze II–III. Another, rarely encountered member of the white slip family is the elegant tankard with its protruding handle.

White shaved juglets (Fig. 7.15:3) have the form of common Canaanite dipper juglets, but their technique is typically Cypriot. They are handmade and have an inserted handle, as in base-ring ware. They are made of whitish clay, and the body is pared with a knife. White shaved juglets appear in considerable numbers in Late Bronze II–III Canaan.

MYCENAEAN POTTERY. Alongside vessels of Cypriot origin, large quantities of Mycenaean pottery from Greece or Mycenaean-style pottery manufactured in Cyprus were marketed in Canaan during the Late Bronze Age. These vessels are all expertly wheel-made and highly fired. The surface is decorated with simple geometric patterns painted with great precision.

The earliest vessel imported to Canaan is a kylix (drinking cup) of Mycenaean II ware, found in Fosse Temple I of the Late Bronze I at Lachish. Mycenaean imports greatly increased during the Late Bronze II, when vessels of Mycenaean IIIA ware were brought to Canaan. They included, for the most part, stirrup vases, pyxides, and pyriform jars. In the Late Bronze III they were replaced by vessels of the Mycenaean IIIB family. The differentiation between the two groups of Mycenaean

Fig. 7.18. Imported Mycenaean pottery

ware is of extreme chronological importance, as it permits us to distinguish between assemblages of the fourteenth and thirteenth centuries.

In a class of their own stand the Mycenaean chariot kraters, large kraters that portray chariot processions. A complete krater of this type was found in a tomb at Tel Dan, and fragments have appeared at various sites.

SYRIAN IMPORTS (fig. 7.15:4). A comparatively rare vessel among those imported to Canaan is a tall, slender bottle, red slipped and highly burnished. The origin of this vessel, called Syrian bottle, is in northern Syria or southern Anatolia, and it first appears in Canaan during the Late Bronze II.

EGYPTIAN IMPORTS (fig. 7.15:5). The considerable influence of Egypt on the southern coast of Canaan is faintly reflected in the importation of limited numbers of Egyptian ceramic vessels. A few Egyptian vessels, particularly handleless bag-shaped jars, appear already in assemblages of the Late Bronze II, but the bulk of the Egyptian finds come from Late Bronze III contexts, for the most part in Egyptian fortresses and residencies.

A mixture of pottery vessels of varying origin characterizes burial offerings of the period. In tombs one might find Canaanite jars sealed with Cypriot bowls and Mycenaean vessels alongside Canaanite and Egyptian ones. Such phenomena testify to the flourishing trade among the disparate parts of the eastern Mediterranean basin.

Tombs

Two main tomb types predominate in Late Bronze Age Canaan: burial caves and pit graves. Other forms of burial were practiced as well, some carried over from earlier times and others, of apparently foreign origin, introduced only in the Late Bronze Age. The investigation of burial customs and their origins can reveal a great deal about the population of Canaan and the social processes that it underwent.

BURIAL CAVES

The interment of dead in caves was practiced in Canaan since Early Bronze times, and it was the most common form of burial in the Middle Bronze Age. Cave burials were always multiple burials. The tombs, used over a long period, accommodated many bodies. In the Middle Bronze Age, it was the custom to push the bones of the earlier burials toward the sides of the cave and to inter the newly deceased in the center. In this manner the walls became lined with bone heaps and burial offerings, which were moved along with the bones of their owners. This custom continued unchanged during the Late Bronze Age. The preservation over many generations of a basic burial custom shows that the Canaanite inhabitants of this period were direct descendants of the earlier populations.

The term "cave" refers principally to natural or man-made caves specifically set aside for burial, though it may include chambers carved for other purposes, such as water cisterns, which were adapted for use as tombs. All these cave types saw use during the Late Bronze Age, but the salient characteristic of the period was the reuse

Fig. 7.19. Mycenaean charioteer vase (height 39 centimeters)

of burial caves hewn in earlier periods; there are but few caves first cut during the Late Bronze Age.

As pushing aside skeletons led to the accumulation of many bodies in one chamber, each cave is in effect a cemetery. It is usually difficult to discover the number of interments in each cave, as the bones in most of the tombs excavated are not well preserved and those that have been preserved have often received too little attention. Offerings placed alongside the deceased gradually accumulated, too, with each added interment, until the objects numbered, in some cases, in the hundreds—most of them ceramic vessels.

In contrast to the clear continuity evidenced in the use of caves and in the manner of interment, there were significant changes in the geographic distribution of this mode of burial. During the Middle Bronze Age, cave burials were the most common burial type, and cave tombs were present throughout the country. In the Late Bronze Age, the burial caves of the coastal plain were abandoned, never to be reused. In the hill and Shephelah regions, cave burials were renewed, though often following a considerable time lapse. Only rarely was there continuous use of a cave from the Middle to the Late Bronze Age. Middle Bronze Age cave tombs reused after a lapse have been found at Safed, Hanita, Damun in the Carmel, Megiddo, Beth Shean, Tell el-Far'ah North, Gibeon, Gezer, Jericho, Lachish, and Tell Rumeideh in Hebron. Caves first used in the Late Bronze Age have been excavated at Kafr 'Ara, Jerusalem, Tell Jedur, and Khirbet Rabud.

Burial caves such as those at Safed, Hanita, Damun, Gibeon, Jedur, and Hebron are not adjacent to any settlement site. The hill zones were virtually devoid of settlement during the Late Bronze Age; a review of the distribution of burial sites, however, reveals a denser pattern. This may comprise archaeological evidence of a nonsedentary population of the unstable kind exemplified by the 'Apiru of the El-Amarna letters and other texts, which harassed the settled population. This unsettled population, which may have been disenfranchised and therefore unable to maintain its own burial grounds, buried its dead wherever it could—in caves cut by earlier generations or natural caves in the hills—and preserved the traditional burial practices of the Middle Bronze Age, being unexposed to new influences.

The burial offerings in the caves were usually modest, consisting mainly of domestic pottery: cooking pots, kraters, store jars, jugs, juglets, and a great many bowls. The choice of household objects and the lack of special burial vessels suggest a strong bond between the home and the tomb and perhaps a belief that the tomb was now the home of the deceased. Luxury items such as imported pottery, metal objects, precious jewelry, and weapons are rare, indicating that the standard of living of the Late Bronze Age hill people was quite modest.

Multiple cave burial, so conspicuously preserving the burial customs of earlier generations, implies a conservative attitude, with little attempt to change long-standing behavioral patterns. It appears that in the hill area, well away from the coastal and valley highways, it was easier to maintain a traditional life-style, uninfluenced by the new and strange customs that penetrated the more susceptible regions.

PIT BURIALS

In contrast to the continuity of tradition shown in the tombs of the hill and Shephelah populations, the burial practices of the inhabitants of the coastal plain, and gradually of the interior valleys, underwent a radical metamorphosis. In the Late Bronze Age, the coastal populations no longer buried their dead in traditional cave tombs, which were abandoned. They were replaced by burials in rectangular pits excavated in the sand or the kurkar rock. Sometimes the pits were lined with stone slabs, termed cist graves. Most often burials were solitary, one body to a grave. Once sealed, the tomb was never reopened, and the repose of the dead was not disturbed. Occasionally two or three bodies were placed in one grave, implying a relation between the deceased. The difference between undisturbed single pit burials and multiple pushed-back cave burials is so fundamental that it must be assumed that the inhabitants of the coastal regions radically changed their outlook on death and burial. The change may be ascribed to the infiltration of Egyptian ideas regarding the need to preserve the body, ideas that arrived at their fullest expression in the custom of embalming. It should not be surprising to find Egyptian influence at its most potent along the Coastal Plain, and later in the valleys of the interior, where the main international routes, closely guarded by Egypt, passed. The inhabitants of these regions were exposed throughout the entire Late Bronze Age or even earlier to Egyptian ideas (a small number of pit burials appear in the Middle Bronze Age). In contrast, the inhabitants of the hill regions were outside the scope of Egyptian interests and thus were free to maintain local cultural traditions.

Pit burials appear in extensive cemeteries. The largest are those of Tell el-Ajjul, which constantly expanded as the period progressed. Cemeteries have also been identified at Tell Ridan and Deir el-Balah in the Gaza Strip, at Tell el-Far'ah

South, at Horvat Humra and Palmahim on the banks of Nahal Sorek, at Tel Zeror in the northern Sharon, Tell Abu Hawam on the banks of Nahal Qishon, the Persian Garden near Accho, and at Kibbutz Gesher Ha-Ziv. Toward the end of the period the custom spread to the interior valleys, and cemeteries of this type have been found at 'Afula and at Tell es-Sa'idiyeh in the Jordan valley. A number of cemeteries reveal a dominant alignment of burials, with the head pointed west, a typically Egyptian orientation.

Unlike cave burials, where the tomb offerings are replicas of household effects, pit burials provide a distinctive assemblage. The most important component is one jar or two, placed upright in the grave and covered by bowls, sometimes of imported ware, which contain dipper juglets. Another typical offering group consists of a jug and a few bowls. The sealed jars no doubt contained liquids and the bowls food; in fact, bowls have been found to contain the remains of joints of meat. Pit burials also contain more luxury items than cave tombs: imported pottery, beads and jewelry, weapons, and metal pins. It may be inferred that the coastal dwellers understood the needs of the departed differently from the hill people. Furthermore, the coastal people seem to have enjoyed a higher standard of living, doubtless due to their proximity to international land and sea routes.

OTHER FORMS OF BURIAL

Various sites have yielded tombs that differ from the usual types in form, manner of construction, or inclusion of new elements (benches or niches). In some tombs the corpse was interred in a container— a coffin, box, or urn. Most of these elements first appear in Canaan during the Late Bronze Age, though some may be found at the end of the Middle Bronze Age. They have no precedent in local tradition, and their origins must be sought outside Canaan, tracing diverse influences from throughout the region.

BENCH TOMBS. These are caves in which burial benches were left along one or more of the walls as they were cut. Sometimes, especially in cases where an earlier cave was reused, the benches were constructed of stone. It appears that the intent was to leave the bodies on the benches, and several tombs have been found with complete skeletons still in that position. However, in other cases the bones were gathered into a heap in the center of the cave to make room for later burials. The presence of such benches indicates planning and specific intent in fashioning the tomb chamber, as opposed to the random choice evident in the usual type of burial cave. The intention of interring each body separately, on its own shelf, testifies to a different view of burial, though in some cases the original intent was confounded, and the burials took on the character of the usual cave tombs.

The best-known instances of bench tombs come from the cemeteries of Tell el-Far'ah South, found in two groups. One dates from the thirteenth and twelfth centuries. The other group (which the excavator Petrie called "the tombs of the lords of the Philistines" after discovering anthropoid coffins and Philistine pottery on the floor between the benches) was dated to the twelfth century. When it became apparent that anthropoid coffins need not be linked to the Philistines, a date in the thirteenth century became feasible, and the Philistine vessels could be attributed to a later phase in the use of the tombs. Because of the supposed relation between the bench tombs and the tombs of the lords of the Philistines, a Mycenaean origin for this tomb type was assumed. A number of archaeologists pointed out the resemblance between the bench tombs and the Mycenaean chamber tombs and suggested that the bench tomb was introduced into Canaan by an early wave of Aegean immigrants, preceding the main wave of Philistines and other Sea Peoples. A reappraisal of the characteristic features of bench tombs and a comparison with the Mycenaean chamber tombs showed that the two types are not alike. At Mycenae, the tombs have no benches and are approached by a sloping dromos. It was discovered, however, that the bench element and the broad, stepped shaft entrance are characteristic of Cypriot tombs from the Middle Cypriot period onward, reflecting the infiltration of small groups of people from Cyprus. Bench tombs have been excavated at Sarepta, north of Tyre, at Gezer, Lachish, Tell 'Eitun, and Tell el-Ajjul, all sites of the Coastal Plain and the Shephelah.

TOMBS WITH NICHES. These tombs have niches cut into the walls where the dead were laid. The burial concept here resembles the original intent of the bench tombs, as each body was interred separately in a well-defined area. In these tombs too, however, the bones were sometimes removed from the niches and cast onto the floor of the chamber.

Niche tombs have been found at only three sites in Canaan, Tell el-Ajjul, Lachish, and Megiddo. The most interesting group, the so-called "horse and loculi" tombs, comes from the Tell el-Ajjul cemetery and dates to the very end of the Middle Bronze Age, approximately 1600 B.C.E. The tombs take on various shapes, round, oval, or rectilinear. They are entered from above, through the center of the chamber, which thus serves also as a shaft.

Recesses cut into the walls accommodate one or two bodies, which have remained complete and in situ. Some tombs contain a skeleton of a horse with some bones removed, placed in the center of the tomb. The meaning of this custom remains a mystery. A jawbone of a horse was also found in a niche tomb at Lachish, one of four such tombs discovered at that site. Only two niche tombs were found at Megiddo; one of them had only one niche, proving that the tomb was cut to accommodate only one person, an unusual phenomenon in itself.

Like the benches, burial niches are known in Cyprus from the Middle Cypriot period onward. The combination of horse burials with niches, however, is known neither in Cyprus nor in any other neighboring land. Burials of parts of horses are known from contemporaneous sites in Greece, but they occur in tombs of a different type. There is as yet insufficient evidence to relate the disparate scraps of information, other than to suggest that the people buried in the niche tombs, with or without horses, have some relation to the Cypriot-Aegean region.

BUILT TOMBS. Tel Dan and Aphek, separated by a considerable distance, each provide one instance of a built tomb. Built tombs feature a structural chamber, a rare phenomenon in any period in Canaan. The Aphek tomb was damaged by later construction, but the Dan tomb has been preserved to a height of 2.4 meters, and its manner of construction may be observed. It consists of a small chamber, 2.2 × 2.4 meters. The walls are corbeled and were probably sealed with a large roof slab, which has not been preserved.

Within the small chamber of the Dan tomb were the remains of 40 individuals, of whom 25 were identified as males (mostly young), 7 as

females, and 5 as children. They were interred with a large assemblage of pottery vessels and other objects. There is a prominent group of Mycenaean imports, among them a complete chariot vase, as well as weapons, gold plaques and earrings, ivory objects, and other bronze, bone, and basalt artifacts. The Dan tomb dates to the fourteenth century B.C.E., and the Aphek tomb (found in a poor state of preservation) belongs to the thirteenth century.

SMALL CERAMIC COFFINS (LARNAKES). Two terra-cotta larnakes have been discovered thus far in Canaan. One, a multihandled chest with a flat lid, was found in a bench tomb at Gezer dated to the fifteenth century. It contained two primary child burials, along with the disarticulated bones of ten more children and an adult. This tomb contained the remains of another 89 individuals, strewn over the benches and the floor of the tomb. The second larnax, in the shape of a small, open tub, was found overturned in one of the pit graves in the Persian Garden near Accho,

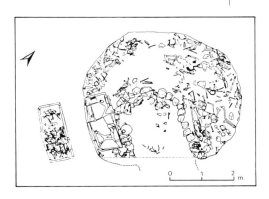

Fig. 7.21. Larnax burial at Gezer

Fig. 7.20. Built tomb (the Mycenaean tomb) at Tel Dan

Fig. 7.22. Gezer larnax (length 175 centimeters)

with the bones of a young male scattered about. It has been dated to the fourteenth century.

Larnakes were in common use as small coffins for secondary burial on the island of Crete, and they are closely linked to Minoan culture and its offshoots. The presence of larnakes in Canaan may imply some relation with the Minoan world, but it cannot have been a very significant one.

JAR BURIALS. Adult burials in store jars, not to be confused with the infant jar burials under house floors characteristic of the Middle Bronze Age, were common in the Hittite kingdom, especially in the last phase of its existence. The discovery of adult jar burials in Canaan testifies to the arrival of a small population bearing a foreign burial custom. As the jar burials are dated to the early twelfth century (the end of the Late Bronze Age or the beginning of the Iron Age), the bearers of this custom may have been refugees from the disintegrating Hittite Empire.

Jar burials have been encountered at four sites in Canaan, Kfar Yehoshua in the Jezreel valley, Tel Zeror in the Sharon, Tell el-Far'ah North in the Samaria hills, and Azor, near Tel Aviv. The finest ex-

ample comes from Kfar Yehoshua. The deceased, a man of about forty, was laid full length within two jars sheared off at the shoulder and laid face to face. Three flasks were placed inside the jars, and vessels were placed round them, as well as a bronze knife or sickle and the remains of a goat, ox, and pig.

ANTHROPOID COFFINS. The discovery many years ago of large pottery coffins of anthropoid form in the cemeteries of Beth Shean, Lachish, and Tell el-Far'ah South attracted much interest, and it was commonly assumed that they were the burial coffins of the Philistines dating to the twelfth century. Since then, many coffins have been discovered at Deir el-Balah in the Gaza Strip accompanied by vessels and objects of undoubted thirteenth-century date, and it has been established that there is in fact no relation between anthropoid coffins and the Philistines. Rather, the coffins are linked to the strong Egyptian presence in Canaan toward the end of the Late Bronze Age. Many of their representational details relate to the Egyptian world of beliefs concerning the needs of the dead and are found on coffins in Egypt. Most prominent are the lotus flowers on the forehead, the Osiris beard (Os-

iris is the Egyptian god of the dead), and the emblems of Osiris grasped in the hands. However, in those coffins found whole there were two complete adult burials and the bones of one or two other adult or juvenile individuals, a departure from the Egyptian practice of separate interment for each person. Anthropological analysis of the skeletal remains from Deir el-Balah has revealed a resemblance to the population of lower Egypt in the Eighteenth and Nineteenth dynasties and a dissimilarity to Canaanite populations of the same period. It thus appears that the people buried at Deir el-Balah were Egyptians who lived and died in Canaan. The grave gifts in the Deir el-Balah cemetery include, alongside the usual assemblage of Canaanite, Cypriot, and Mycenaean vessels, Egyptian pottery and other objects of Egyptian origin or form.

Like the larnakes, anthropoid coffins are not linked to a specific tomb type. At Deir el-Balah the coffins were found in pit graves, in a cemetery that had many similar graves without coffins. At other sites, the coffins were placed in cave tombs already in use, either in hewn burial caves of the usual type (Beth Shean and Lachish) or in bench tombs (Tell el-Far'ah).

The analysis of tomb types has shown that the Canaanite population of the Late Bronze Age was directly descended from that of the Middle Bronze Age. This population gradually became divided into two groups, the conservative hill dwellers, who continued to bury their dead in multiple cave burials, and the more cosmopolitan coastal inhabitants, who were more susceptible to innovation and external influences and buried their dead in single pit graves. Burial within the settlement, a practice deeply rooted in Middle Bronze Age traditions, declined at the beginning of the Late

Map 7.3. Distribution of different forms of burial in the Late Bronze Age

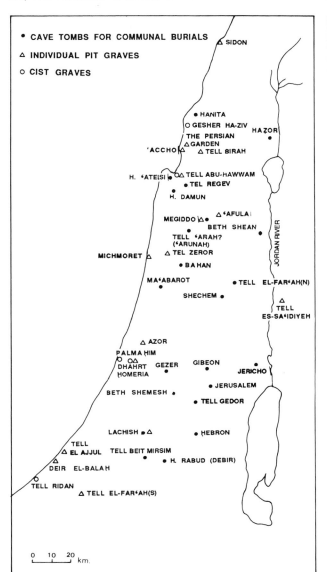

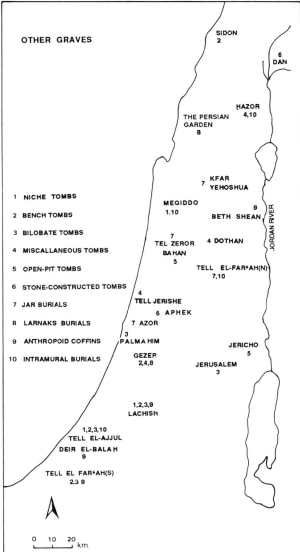

Bronze Age and was eventually discontinued. Alongside the stable population, small groups of immigrants from parts of the Near East—Cyprus, Crete, Egypt, and Anatolia—arrived. Their forms of burial did not leave a lasting impression on the basic modes of burial in Canaan.

Warfare

The study of ancient warfare is based on written sources and a wealth of pictorial documents—tomb paintings and reliefs carved on

the walls of temples and palaces. The archaeological evidence for warfare, however, is limited mainly to the weapons unearthed in excavations. The decisive innovations in the Late Bronze Age battlefield consisted of two new weapons, the light horse-drawn chariot and the long-range composite bow. Their extensive use gave the Egyptian armies a decisive advantage, fully exploited in Egyptian imperial expansion.

The Late Bronze Age chariot was a light chariot harnessed to two horses and mounted by two per-

sons, a driver and a combatant. The origin of the horse-drawn chariot has yet to be elucidated. The Egyptian word for chariot clearly indicates that it was brought to Egypt from Canaan, though Canaan was merely a way station on the route of its diffusion from the original source. Egyptian depictions show that the Canaanite chariots were lighter than those of the Egyptians, so light that one man could carry a chariot on his shoulder. The Canaanite chariot wheel had four spokes, in contrast to the six-spoked

Fig. 7.23. Depiction of Canaanite chariot in an Egyptian wall painting

Egyptian wheel, and the axle was set
somewhat forward of the rear of the
chassis.

The second battlefield weapon,
the composite bow, was constructed
of various kinds of wood and ten-
dons and had an effective range of as
much as four hundred meters, the
greatest range of any ancient weapon.
Though composite bows have
not been found in Canaan, where
organic materials are not usually
preserved, they are mentioned in
Egyptian booty lists from Canaan.
In addition, a multitude of bronze
arrowheads have come to light,
some flat and leaf-shaped, others
reinforced by a midrib. Whether the
two types were used for different
bows is not clear, though it appears
that the Canaanites employed a simple bow alongside the composite
bow.

Javelins and the heavier spears
served for medium-range combat.
The tips of both weapons, resembling the arrowhead in form, are
often difficult to tell apart. Swords
and daggers were used in hand-to-
hand combat. The most characteristic Late Bronze Age sword is
the sickle-shaped sword; unlike the
sickle, its cutting edge is on the
exterior. A considerable number of
sickle-shaped swords have been
found in Canaan and in Egypt, and
they are typical of the Late Bronze
Age in both places, though they
were introduced toward the end of
the Middle Bronze Age. At close
range, short, straight daggers were
also employed. Like the sickle-
shaped swords, the daggers often
exhibit high standards of metalworking. The blade and haft are
generally cast in one piece, in a flat
mold. The handle was often designed with a recess in which wood
or ivory could be inlaid. The Canaanite soldier wore a coat of mail
made of scales of armor sewn onto a
leather or cloth jacket. Such metal
scales have been found in excava-

tions, complementing the depictions
in Egyptian wall paintings. A helmet
completed the protective gear of the
foot soldier.

If the art of battle in the open
field saw dramatic advances during
the Late Bronze Age, the art of siege
warfare remained stagnant. Egypt,
the prime factor in the battlegrounds
of the period, did not excel in siege
warfare. The conquest of the city of
Sharuhen, which paved the way for
Egyptian dominion in Canaan and
marks the transition from the Middle to the Late Bronze Age, dragged
on for three years, according to
Egyptian sources. A siege of three
years implies a tactic of protracted
attrition rather than direct attack,
and that seems to have been the
usual Egyptian approach. Egypt did
not develop or make use of the
battering ram, a decisive weapon in
Iron Age battles. Though the archaeological evidence shows that
few towns were encircled by walls,
Egyptian artists portrayed conquest
scenes of fortified towns, attacked
by scaling ladders and other simple
hand-operated means in use as early
as the third millennium B.C.E. In
view of the lack of archaeological
evidence, these scenes should be understood as artistic conventions
rather than true representations.

Economy and Trade

There is no doubt that agriculture
comprised the basis of the Canaanite
economy. The fame of Canaan's
"seven kinds" of produce is no exaggeration; the land was suitable for
raising cereals, fruits, and vegetables, as well as for breeding livestock such as small and large cattle,
donkeys, and horses. We cannot say
whether the land was always sufficiently productive to supply all the
subsistence needs of its inhabitants.
In years of sufficient rainfall, agricultural produce may well have been
sufficient for subsistence and even

for exchangeable surplus, but in dry years, part of the population was forced to look elsewhere for its sustenance, especially to Egypt, whose fields were watered by the Nile floods. Biblical and Egyptian sources describe the descent into Egypt during extended droughts, and their stories seem to reflect a fairly common reality.

The only mineral of marketable value in Canaan was the copper of the Timna region. However, there is no evidence that copper was extracted during most of the Late Bronze Age. No settlements of the period have been found in the Negev or Aravah, and in view of the weakness of the local authorities it is hardly likely that any of them would have had the political power or economic initiative to operate the mines. Only at the end of the period is there evidence for mining at Timna, by a state-run Egyptian concession. The Egyptian presence was underlined

by the erection near the mines of a temple dedicated to Hathor.

Despite the dearth of raw materials, or perhaps for that reason, Canaan excelled in its crafts. The potter's craft was advanced, and the textile industry (particularly the use of a purple dye processed from the murex seasnail) may have been well developed in Canaan by the Late Bronze Age. Heaps of split murex shells were discovered in a late Late Bronze Age stratum at Accho. Canaanite craftsmen seem also to have excelled in metalwork in general and in the manufacture of weapons and chariots in particular. The protective headgear used by Canaanite soldiers (as portrayed on the Megiddo ivories) was of apparently local manufacture, for nothing like it has been encountered elsewhere. Canaanites also seem to have been expert jewelers, and various types of uniquely Canaanite ornaments have been identified. Further proof of the ex-

pertise of the Canaanite craftsman may be found in Egyptian texts, which tell of Canaanite craftsmen engaged in building and decorating tasks in Egypt.

The Late Bronze Age was marked by intensive international trade, compassing the entire eastern Mediterranean basin. Canaan took an active part in this traffic, if only because of its location on the main arteries of overland trade. The archaeological record reveals far more evidence of foreign imports in Canaan than of Canaanite export abroad. As trade in this period was based on exchange, Canaan must have manufactured a considerable quantity of exportable goods that have not been preserved. As far as can be ascertained, agricultural surplus constituted the bulk of the Canaanite export trade. This may be deduced from the wide distribution of the Canaanite jar, a jar specifically designed for trade and trans-

Fig. 7.24. Sickle sword

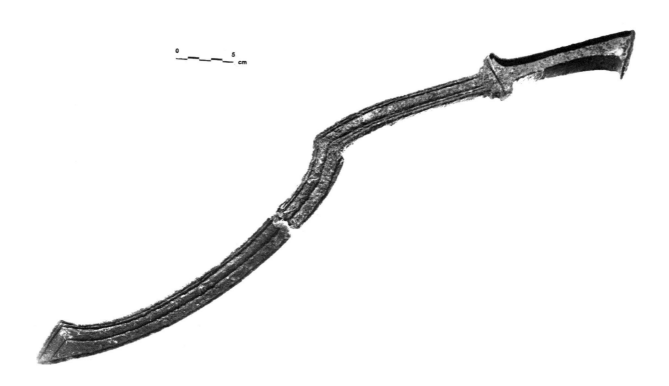

port of liquids, probably the wines and oils for which Canaan was famous. Valuable testimony to the extent of such trade is provided in an Egyptian tomb painting of a Canaanite merchant ship docked in an Egyptian port and unloading a cargo of jars. The Canaanite jar reached Greece as well, even finding its way to a tomb in Athens.

In the Late Bronze II–III, the quantity of imported wares becomes so great that there is hardly a tomb or an excavated room without at least one imported vessel. A com-

bination of vessels from various sources (Mycenae, Cyprus, Syria, and Egypt) is characteristic of ceramic assemblages, particularly tombs, of the period. Though little is known of the content of these vessels or why they were purchased in such large quantities, their numbers constitute a unique phenomenon in the history of the region. In addition to the pottery, many different raw materials were imported into Canaan. Copper, the basis of all metallurgy of the period, was undoubtedly the most important, and

it is probable that copper-rich Cyprus was the principal source. To prepare bronze, the metal most commonly employed by the smiths of the Late Bronze Age, an alloy of 10-percent tin was needed. The source of tin has yet to be determined, though it clearly was imported. Other imported raw materials for the manufacture of luxury items include gold, silver, and elephant tusks for the preparation of carved ivories.

It is not clear whether this extensive international trade was carried out through direct contacts between the diverse regions or via intermediaries, merchants who traveled the land or sea routes, loading and unloading their goods at each stop. An ancient wreck discovered some years ago at Cape Gelidonya, off the southeastern coast of Turkey, provides evidence of intensive maritime trade. This small ship, which was apparently headed west, contained many copper ingots of apparent Cypriot origin, as well as many copper implements, most of them broken, which were no doubt meant to be recast; it may have been a kind of traveling copper foundry. The form of the ship suggests that it was a Syro-Canaanite vessel, though little can be said of its crew or owners. The cargo of the ship, which was wrecked toward the end of the thirteenth century, reflects the cosmopolitan character of Late Bronze Age trade. Lately, another wreck has been found off the cape of Kas in southern Turkey. Its excavation will no doubt provide much new information concerning the character and extent of international trade in the Late Bronze Age.

A trade network as extensive as that of the Late Bronze Age undoubtedly depended on the maintenance of open land and sea routes and on reliable modes of transport. The land routes were the same highways that had been in use since early

Fig. 7.25. Necklaces of gold (length 44 centimeters) and carnelian (43 centimeters) beads from Deir el-Balah

times. The main trade route of the ancient Near East was that later known as the Via Maris (the Way of the Sea), which passed along the coastal plain and interior valleys of Canaan. The settlements along the highway enjoyed the advantages of being on the caravan routes, and they have been found to contain a larger proportion of imported vessels and objects than do the settlements of the interior and the hill zones. Secondary routes crisscrossed the country, servicing the sites of the interior. As for conveyances, the donkey appears still to have been the main beast of burden, and donkey caravans bore the main burden of trade. Horses were domesticated mainly for military use, to draw chariots. Though there is no evidence for the use of ox-drawn carts, such as appear in the reliefs of the migrant Sea Peoples, their use cannot be ruled out.

The arts of maritime navigation and shipbuilding had to be greatly developed during this period, for it is difficult to imagine the pursuit of the intensive trade with Cyprus and Greece without the benefit of advances in sea transport. Little is known of the ships of the period, as the number of ships so far discovered is not great. The Cape Gelidonya and Kas ships have provided invaluable data on the structure of Late Bronze Age ships and the character of ancient seafaring. It would appear that a considerable proportion of sea travel was coastal. Movement was generally by day, maintaining eye contact with the shore; at night the ships anchored at small ports. This method of maritime transport, based on frequent anchorage, may explain the rise of small port towns along the Canaanite coast, such as Tel Nami, Tel Megadim, and Shiqmona. Another part of the sea trade was pursued on the open sea; traffic between Crete and Egypt, for example, could hardly have taken another route.

Fig. 7.26. Portrayals of Canaanites in an Egyptian wall painting

Canaanite Culture

The Late Bronze Age marks the zenith of Canaanite culture. During this period of high living standards and flourishing international trade, Canaan was open not only to innovations in art and religion but also to material achievements attained throughout the west Asian and eastern Mediterranean expanse. In two important facets of cultural achievement, art and writing, Canaan made a vital contribution to the advancement of human culture as a whole.

SCRIPTS AND THE INVENTION OF THE ALPHABET

Owing to the cosmopolitan character of Late Bronze Age Canaan, all forms of writing prevalent in the Near East were extant in Canaan. The predominant script was the Akkadian cuneiform, Akkadian being the international language of diplomacy at the time. Even the king of Egypt used this language and script in his correspondence with the kings of independent states of equal standing and with the vassal rulers of the Canaanite cities. The El-Amarna letters, as well as the somewhat earlier Ta'anakh letters, were all written in Akkadian cuneiform script. As literacy, particularly in foreign tongues, was not widespread, every ruler, great or small, must have employed scribes and interpreters who aided him in conducting his foreign affairs. Another interesting document written in Akkadian cuneiform is a fragment of a tablet bearing a portion of the famed Mesopotamian Epic of Gilgamesh found at Megiddo, which appears to have been employed in teaching the Akkadian language. This tablet shows that literary works were available in Megiddo and suggests that a scribal school existed at the site.

Another script used in Canaan at

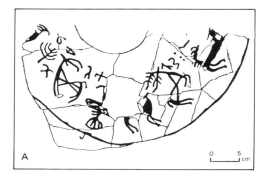

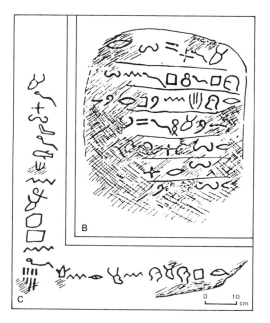

Fig. 7.27. Proto-Canaanite and proto-Sinaitic inscriptions from Lachish (A) and from Sinai (B, C)

this time was the Egyptian hieroglyphic script and its variants. Formal hieroglyphic script was used in official texts, such as the stelae erected by kings of the Nineteenth Dynasty at Beth Shean to commemorate their victories in the region or a fragment of a stela from Tel Kinrot. Monumental hieroglyphic inscriptions containing the names of Egyptian monarchs appear on stone doorjambs at Beth Shean and at Jaffa. The name of Ramesses III was inscribed on a metal object in the destruction layer of Lachish. Royal scarabs have been found all over the country. Most common are the scarabs of Thutmose III, Amenhotep II, and Ramesses II, the kings who reigned when Egypt's presence in Canaan was the strongest. A considerable number of Egyptian documents written in hieratic script, the cursive Egyptian script, have been discovered, particularly in the southern sites of Lachish and Tel Sera'. These are notes and administrative lists reflecting the activity of the Egyptian government in Canaan.

A so-far undeciphered script was found incised on elongated clay tablets from the site of Deir 'Alla in the Jordan valley. These signs are reminiscent of the Minoan linear script. A clay bulla from Aphek (a lump of clay used to seal rolled up letters) bears a seal impression with Hittite hieroglyphic characters. These instances all bear witness to the extent of the international relations of Canaan in the Late Bronze Age.

The local Canaanite tongue was late to develop its own script. In the Late Bronze Age two different writing systems came into being. Though the two systems use different characters, they share an important feature—both are alphabetical scripts, that is, each character represents only a single phoneme. There was no longer any need for the hundreds of signs used in contemporary writing systems such as cuneiform or Egyptian hieroglyphs, where each sign represents a complete word or syllable or serves as a determinative. In the alphabetical script there are few signs, corresponding to the small number of phonemes used in speech. The alphabet liberated script from the concrete concept expressed in the word and made it an abstract tool, allowing expression in stylized characters that bear no relation to the meaning of the words. The invention of the alphabetic script is the most vivid expression of the intellectual bent of the Canaanites and of their positive attitude toward abstract expression.

The earliest alphabetic system of writing known is that termed the proto-Sinaitic script, a group of such inscriptions having been found in the eastern part of the peninsula, in and about the Egyptian temple adjacent to the turquoise mines at Serabit el-Khadim. A series of characters was inscribed in an unskilled hand on Egyptian stelae dedicated to Hathor of the mines. Some of the characters, such as those that depict a hand or a fish, may be interpreted as pictographs and are reminiscent of hieroglyphs. But when scholars added up the different characters appearing in the inscriptions, there were only 27; the small number suggested that the script was alphabetic. The deciphering of the proto-Sinaitic inscriptions proved that their language was Canaanite and that they consist of benedictions dedicated to a goddess called Elat or Ba'alat, perhaps the Canaanite name of the Egyptian goddess Hathor. Accompanying inscriptions mention various persons by name, title, and position. They may have been inscribed by Canaanite slaves or workmen employed by the Egyptians in the turquoise mines of Sinai. They are generally dated to the fifteenth century.

At Ugarit, the large Canaanite city on the northern coast of Syria, an alphabetic script was developed during the Late Bronze Age based on cuneiform signs. As far as we know, Ugaritic writing developed independently of the proto-Sinaitic and proto-Canaanite scripts of southern Canaan. The independent invention of two systems testifies to the urgent need for a new system of writing, perhaps because of the unprecedented development of international trade, in which the Canaanites were prime movers. The Ugaritic alphabet contains 30 characters, of which 27 are consonants and 3 are vowels. It was employed in Ugarit during the fourteenth and thirteenth centuries and has been preserved in a rich archive of literary, religious, economic, and legal texts found at the site. Isolated inscriptions in this script found in southern Canaan (Beth Shemesh, Ta'anach, and Aphek) show that it was disseminated outside Ugarit. Unlike the southern Canaanite scripts, Ugaritic had no successors, and it went out of use when Ugarit was laid waste at the end of the Late Bronze Age.

ART

The rulers of Canaan did not customarily immortalize their achievements in monumental sculptures and reliefs such as those commissioned by the great kings of the neighboring kingdoms. This is no doubt a corollary of the subordinate status of the Canaanite princes, who at no time during the Late Bronze Age were independent or capable of determining the political and military policies of their kingdoms. There is, therefore, no monumental Canaanite art treating of historical subjects, and we must make do with the ornamental and miniature arts and with the few instances discovered in excavations of monumental religious sculpture.

Fig. 7.28.   Lachish ewer and its inscription

The proto-Sinaitic script underwent development during the Late Bronze Age at the Canaanite urban centers. This script has become known as proto-Canaanite, and some of its earliest inscriptions date possibly to the end of the Middle Bronze Age. Judging from the few proto-Canaanite inscriptions so far unearthed, this method of writing was altered conceptually after its invention. The development was for the most part graphic, the characters gradually losing their resemblance to pictographs and becoming progressively linear. The proto-Canaanite script gave rise, in the Iron Age, to paleo-Hebrew, Phoenician, and Aramaic scripts, each of which fathered subbranches that eventually developed into scripts still in use to this day. Thus, the proto-Canaanite was the father of all alphabetic scripts, and its invention was without doubt Canaan's most significant contribution to world culture.

STONE SCULPTURE AND RE-LIEFS. Monumental sculptures and reliefs in stone have been discovered so far only at Hazor and Beth Shean. The objects are made of basalt, the durability of which has no doubt contributed to their preservation. They were discovered in the various temples excavated at the site, and their subject matter was religious.

The largest item of sculpture discovered so far in Canaan is the lion orthostat from the Area H temple at Hazor. The lion is portrayed by a combination of two techniques: while the body is shown in high relief, the head and forelegs are shaped in the round and protrude from the front of the orthostat. The unfinished rear of the orthostat and the round dowel holes drilled along its upper edge indicate that the lion was set into the wall of the temple, as the right doorjamb of the main entrance. The Hazor lion excels in its naturalistic design and in the high quality of its workmanship. The lion's head is a powerful three-di-

mensional portrait, sparing in details, which gives the impression of majestic calm. The body is executed in high relief, with simple, well-defined contours. Details include the mane, which tapers to a stylized horn-shaped tip, and the tail, which curls under the hindleg and around the lion's back. The hindleg is small in proportion to the rest of the body and is the only limb of unnatural proportions. The most interesting aspect of this work of art is the transition from the flat modeling of the lion's body to the three-dimensional execution of the head and forelegs. The point of transition is camouflaged in a sophisticated way by the mane, which covers both the sculptured neck and the relief shoulder of the lion. The problematic transition is further masked by the pattern of incised triangles representing the mane.

Another, smaller lion (33 × 44 centimeters), also carved on a basalt orthostat, was found in the Area C temple at Hazor. Like the larger lion, the body is carved in relief on

one side of the orthostat, while the head and forelegs project to the fore, but the execution is less refined, and the artist confined himself to outlining the contours of the body and the limbs. The stance is different from that of the large lion; the smaller lion is not crouched in repose but appears to be raised on its haunches, perhaps about to leap, its mouth open in a roar. The mane again terminates in a horn and is accentuated with incisions.

The head of yet another lion, or rather lioness, as it has no mane, was found in Area A in the upper city of Hazor. This could be the remnant of a pair of lionesses guarding the entrance to the upper city palace or temple. The three Hazor lions prove that the lion was of particular significance in the conceptual world of the people of the Late Bronze Age, perhaps as a symbol of potent protective power.

Lions are also portrayed on a basalt stela found at Beth Shean. The stela, 92 centimeters high, is composed of two rectangular registers, each containing a separate scene. The upper register depicts a battle between a dog and a lion, or perhaps a lion and a lioness engaged in courtship. The two animals are raised on their hindlegs and form a triangular composition. They are of equal size, and the lion's mane is modeled, as in the Hazor orthostats, by triangular incisions. On the lion's shoulder is a star, of unknown significance. In the lower scene the lion faces left, in apparent triumph, while the other figure, shown behind the lion, bites his rump.

The motif of the lion, particularly the relief lion guarding the entrance to palaces or temples, is well known in north Syrian and Hittite cultures. An example appears in the city of Alalakh in northern Syria. The Alalakh lions resemble those of Hazor in some important details, the tail passing through the

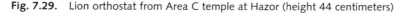

Fig. 7.29.   Lion orthostat from Area C temple at Hazor (height 44 centimeters)

hindlegs and curling over the back or the incised mane terminating in a horn, which indicates that the workshop responsible for the lion reliefs at Hazor and Beth Shean was related to artistic schools of northern Syria and the Hittite kingdom. The Alalakh lions are crude and schematic, and their execution is far less refined than that of the Hazor lions, proving that though the Canaanite artist may not have been imaginative in his choice of theme, his artistic standards were high.

Two small basalt statues of male figures from Hazor might be attributed to the same school of sculptors; they too are reminiscent of statues from Alalakh. One comes from the Area H temple and the other from the temple in Area C. The Area C statue retains the character of the basalt block of which it was fashioned. The features are extremely schematic, and the statue is blocklike, without open spaces. The features of the second statue are far more natural, and there is a hollow under the seat, giving the statue a less massive aspect. The two figures are seated in a calm, erect pose, the Area H statue on a tall-backed chair and its counterpart on a stool. The two males are smooth shaven; the Area H figure wears a wig or headdress, while the Area C figure is bareheaded. Both hold their hands on their knees, though the latter appears to be grasping a vessel or object of some kind. The Area H figure bears no identifying features, and it has been suggested that it represents a king. The Area C figure has the emblem of the inverted crescent on its breast and so may be identified as a deity, perhaps the moon god. The heads of both statues were purposely removed and cast a short distance from the bodies, clearly attesting to the deliberate desecration of the sacred objects, as does the burial of the large lion orthostat. The burial of disused statues in or near temples is also known at Alalakh, further evidence

Fig. 7.30. Lion and dog orthostat from Beth-Shean (height 89 centimeters)

Fig. 7.31. Statue of seated deity from Area H temple at Hazor (height 40 centimeters)

of the close ties between Hazor and the North.

Other basalt reliefs from the Hazor temples include the Area C temple stelae (particularly the one bearing the relief of the upraised hands, crescent, and disk) and, from Area H, a large bowl with a running spiral design, a pattern characteristic of the Mycenaean world, where it appears on pottery vessels and other objects.

IVORY CARVING. The Late Bronze Age, especially the one hundred years or so between the end of the fourteenth century and the early twelfth century B.C.E., is rich in ivory objects. They are small artifacts, usually flat plaques inlaid in wooden furnishings or boxes to add to their value and beauty. There are also three-dimensional objects made entirely of ivory, such as pyxides, bottles, or stoppers carved in the likeness of small figurines. Ivory comes from elephant tusks, and it was brought to Canaan from Egypt

or from North Syria, where elephants were hunted as late as the early first millennium, as described in various Assyrian documents. Ivory was a precious commodity, and it was collected and hoarded by potentates as a highly valued exchange item. In Canaan, ivory carving is first encountered in the Chalcolithic period, but after that time there is a long lapse in the art of ivory-working, ending only in the Middle Bronze Age II. During that period, and to a greater extent during the Late Bronze Age, ivory carving was reinstated as one of the most important branches of Canaanite art.

Canaanite ivory work exhibits the hallmark of all Canaanite art, eclecticism. While the art of basalt sculpture characterizing northern Canaan was linked to artistic traditions of northern Syria, the art of ivory carving echoed several traditions, first and foremost the Egyptian school. The Canaanite ivory carver was acquainted with the techniques and themes prevalent in

Egypt and was able to imitate them in his own workshop. However, the Egyptian themes are accompanied by motifs copied from objects imported into Canaan from diverse lands such as Mycenae, Cyprus, or Anatolia and hoarded in the treasuries of the Canaanite rulers. The mixture of elements is the leading characteristic of Canaanite art.

The most important collection of ivories was unearthed in the treasury of the king of Megiddo, the cellar west of the stratum VIIA palace. Strewn on the floor of the cellar were 380 objects and fragments collected over about 150 years. One of the outstanding objects in this treasure is a square pyxis adorned in high relief with the figures of lions on three sides and sphinxes on the fourth. The lions, like those of Hazor, exhibit northern (Syrian or Hittite) influence, and the object may have been imported from Syria. On the fourth side, two facing sphinxes are portrayed. Their heads are missing and, to judge by the holes remaining in the neck, they were modeled separately.

A fascinating group of objects includes elongated ivory plaques engraved with scenes. Of particular renown is a victory celebration depicted on a knife handle. A procession moves from right to left toward the king, who is seated on a throne decorated with winged sphinxes. Two women face the king; one offers him a beverage and lotus flowers while the other plays a lyre. Behind the women is a battle scene: a warrior stands in a chariot drawn by two horses to which two nude prisoners are tied. They are led by a soldier bearing a round shield and a spear. Behind the king, two servants serve a beverage from a large jar decorated with animal heads. A winged solar disk hovers between

Fig. 7.32.   Ivory pyxis from Megiddo (height 12 centimeters)

Fig. 7.33. Ivory plaque (knife handle) from Megiddo (length 26 centimeters)

Fig. 7.34. Hittite ivory from Megiddo (height 10.2 centimeters)

Fig. 7.35. Aegean ivory from Megiddo (height 9.2 centimeters)

the chariot and the horse. This motif, along with the general character and composition of the scene, suggests considerable Egyptian influence on this Canaanite creation. Scenes of battle and of victory banquets appear on other ivory plaques in the Megiddo hoard. Some plaques are executed in a different technique, that of cutout relief. One such plaque bears the portrait of the Egyptian deity Bes; another portrays a sphinx with large wings, a hybrid of elements of Egyptian (the coiffure and feathered headdress) and Aegean (the wings) origin. The stylized palm motif becomes a central theme in Iron Age Phoenician art, a tradition grounded in the hybrid Canaanite style.

In the Megiddo cache there are also objects of obvious foreign origin. Such is a plaque with a typical Hittite scene consisting of two kings or gods portrayed antithetically; they are dressed in characteristic Hittite garb, a close-fitting cap and a long robe, and they grasp a curved object. These figures are borne on row upon row of Hittite divinities with the aspect of hybrid animals. Above the kings appears the solar disk motif. The plaque is one of a handful of Hittite objects found in Canaan.

There are also some objects from the Mycenaean sphere, among them a plaque depicting a sphinx, and combs of apparent Cypriot origin. A number of items, including a

pen case inscribed with the name and titles of the scribe who owned it (dated to the days of Ramesses III), are original Egyptian objects brought to Megiddo.

Another collection of ivories was found in the last of the Lachish Fosse Temples. It is more or less a contemporary of the Megiddo cache but is more homogeneous, revealing more clearly the Egyptian sources of Canaanite glyptic art. A prominent item is a bottle in the form of a

standing woman. The lower part of the bottle is made of a large intact section of elephant tusk. The upper part, which includes the hands, neck, and head of the female figure, was made separately. A spoon, into which the contents of the bottle (perfumes or cosmetics) could be poured, was inserted into the head. Such objects are held by Canaanites or Syrian tribute bearers portrayed in Egyptian wall paintings. Another object from Lachish is a fragment of a carved pyxis. It portrays animals locked in combat, including a charging bull in the upper register reminiscent of the bulls shown at the bottom of the Hittite plaque from Megiddo.

From the governor's residence at Tell el-Far'ah South come the remains of an ivory-inlaid wooden box. There is a banquet scene and a depiction of a Nilotic environment. Here too, style and theme are closely linked to the Egyptian tradition,

Fig. 7.36. Bronze bull figurine from Hazor (height 4.3 centimeters)

yet a number of local motifs reveal that this is a typical hybrid Canaanite product.

METALWORKING. Canaanite metalwork was largely confined to small objects. A bull cast in bronze, found in the Area H temple at Hazor, has minuscule dimensions (length 5 centimeters), but its naturalistic and powerful stance give it an almost monumental character. This statuette, reminiscent of Syrian moldwork, testifies to the high standards of the Canaanite craftsman. That standard also finds expression in a number of small idols, particularly in a group from Megiddo. Apart from these, the products of Canaanite metalworking are not impressive, and they consist mostly of figurines of gods and goddesses cast in flat molds. Stylistically, as in the realms of stone and ivory carving, Canaanite metalworking exhibits a mixture of Egyptian, Syrian, and Aegean elements. Precious metals were rarely used for objects other than jewelry. An engraved gold plaque was found crumpled in the Lachish acropolis temple; once opened, it revealed the portrait of a goddess standing on a horse, embossed in the repoussé technique. The goddess is nude and wears a headdress based on floral motifs. She holds large lotus flowers, and the horse wears a coat of mail.

Conclusion

Late Bronze Age Canaan was influenced by two main factors: Egypt, and the cultures of the eastern Mediterranean basin. Politically, Canaan was part of the Egyptian empire, and the influence of Egypt is perceptible in many realms. On the one hand, Egypt brought about the decline of the Canaanite city and a significant reduction in the population of Canaan. On the other, Canaan was opened to Egyptian religious and artistic values, and these left their mark in the form of changes in burial customs and in the development of artistic styles. The lands of the eastern Mediterranean basin influenced Canaan through intensive commerce rather than by imperial domination. Canaan was susceptible to developments in its vicinity and received many cultural elements from its neighbors in the realms of religion, architecture, ceramics, and art. Absorbing and alloying the diverse influences, Canaan forged a culture of its own, which reached its zenith in the Late Bronze Age.

8

The Iron Age I

AMIHAI MAZAR

A similar version of this chapter appears in *Archaeology of the Land of the Bible (10000–586 B.C.E.)*, by A. Mazar. New York: Doubleday, 1990.

TERMINOLOGY

The term "Iron Age" covers the period between the end of the Late Bronze Age (about 1200 B.C.E.) and the destruction of the First Temple in 586 B.C.E. The study of the Iron Age in the Land of Israel has been largely motivated by the constant search for the link between archaeological discoveries and historical sources, both biblical and extra-biblical. That such a link should exist is only to be for the period spanning the settlement of the Israelite tribes and the existence of the First Temple forms a major part of history; however, the attempts to discover this link have given rise to severe methodological problems, some of which will be touched on in the course of this chapter. The Iron Age is sometimes called the Israelite Period, in view of the dominant role played by the Israelites. However, other nations, with a distinctive material culture of their own, resided both in Transjordan and the Land of Israel in the biblical period. It is therefore preferable to retain the commonly accepted term "Iron Age," which continues the series beginning with the Stone and Bronze Ages.

Various suggestions for the subdivision of the Iron Age have been offered over the years. The one used by many archaeologists until the late sixties was:

Iron Age I—1200–920/900 B.C.E.
Iron Age II—920–586 B.C.E.

The first part of the Iron Age includes, according to this subdivision, both the periods of the Judges (twelfth and eleventh centuries) and of the United Monarchy.

In 1958, following the excavations at Hazor, Aharoni and Amiran proposed a new scheme for the subdivision of the Iron Age. The main division suggested by them was

Iron Age I—1200–1000
Iron Age II—1000–586 B.C.E.
(for further subdivisions of Iron II, see next chapter).

The Iron Age I here includes the period of the Judges and of the Iron Age II the whole of the monarchic period, up to the destruction of the First Temple. In the present chapter we will follow this subdivision.

At the end of the Late Bronze Age, a grave crisis overtook the political, social, and economic structure that had existed in the ancient world for hundreds of years. In the Late Bronze Age, and particularly in the thirteenth century, a balance had been achieved between the Egyptian empire and the Hittite Empire, which controlled large portions of the Near East, while the Aegean came largely under the influence of Mycenaean civilization, which maintained close contacts with the Levant. Within this balance of power, Canaanite towns managed, despite Egyptian domination, to maintain their cultural distinctiveness. This state of affairs came to an end in the late thirteenth century. Within a short time the Hittite Empire collapsed, a wave of destruction engulfed the centers of Mycenaean culture, and Egyptian power declined, putting an end to Egyptian rule in Canaan. The destruction did not spare the Levant. Ugarit and Alalakh, two important cultural centers of North Syria, were destroyed at the end of the Late Bronze Age. In Canaan, many towns were destroyed; some, notably Hazor, the largest of the Canaanite cities, and Lachish, lay in ruin for many years. In a process parallel to the destruction of the ethnopolitical structure of the Bronze Age, new peoples began to enter the area, some of them immigrants from distant lands, bringing about distinctive changes in the material culture.

Various theories explain the destructions and the influx of new populations. The destruction of the Mycenaean civilization was once seen as a result of Doric invasions from the north; today it is generally thought that economic difficulties, particularly an extended series of droughts, brought on the collapse of the Aegean culture. Responsibility for the destruction of the Hittite empire was pinned on the invasion of the so-called Sea Peoples; it now appears that the empire also suffered from extended droughts and famine. The final blow, to Hattusha, the Hittite capital, was apparently struck by invading bands from the west (the Phrygians) and the north (the Kaska). There is no clear explanation for the decline of the Egyptian empire. Ramesses III's wars with the Sea Peoples (in the early twelfth century) did not cause an immediate diminution of Egyptian power, but shortly after Ramesses III, Egypt declined, perhaps as a result of the more profound consequences of these wars and of the settlement of the Sea Peoples in areas under Egyptian rule.

In the short transition period between the Late Bronze and Iron Ages, significant changes occurred in the material culture of Canaan and in the ethnic composition of its inhabitants. These changes resulted in the establishment of new nations, which founded a series of neighboring kingdoms in different parts of the country: the Philistines and other Sea Peoples, Israelites, and Canaanites-Phoenicians in the Land of Israel; the Edomites, Moabites, and Ammonites in Transjordan. Each of these nations developed a distinctive material culture.

TERMINOLOGY AND CHRONOLOGY

The term "Iron Age" covers the period between the end of the Late Bronze Age (about 1200 B.C.E.) and the destruction of the First Temple in 586 B.C.E., a period that spans the settlement of the Israelite tribes in Canaan and a major part of biblical history. Various subdivisions of the Iron Age have been proposed over the years. In 1958, following the excavations at Hazor, Aharoni and Amiran suggested that it be divided at 1000 B.C.E., with the Iron Age I (1200–1000 B.C.E.) including the period of the Judges and Saul, and the Iron Age II–III (1000–586 B.C.E.) including the whole of the monarchic period up to the destruction of the First Temple. This chapter will follow their subdivision.

As in earlier periods, the determination of the absolute chronology of the material culture of the Land of Israel in the Iron Age I is largely dependent on Egyptian chronology. The transition from the Late Bronze Age to the Iron Age I overlaps with the final phase of Egyptian domination in Canaan, so Egyptian finds bearing royal names in strata of this period are an important source of information. Table 8.1 presents several dates based on the two most commonly accepted methods for determining the chronology of the Nineteenth and Twentieth dynasties. Column A presents the chronology adopted by the editors of the *Cam-*

Table 8.1 Two Chronologies of the Nineteenth and Twentieth Dynasties. A: *Cambridge Ancient History.* B: Wente and Van Siclen.

Dynasty 19	A	B
Ramesses II	1304–1237	1279–1212
Marneptah	1236–1223	1212–1202
Seti II	1216–1210	1199–1193
Tewosret	1210–1200	1187–1185
Dynasty 20	A	B
Ramesses III	1198–1166	1182–1151
Ramesses VI	1156–1148	1141–1133
Ramesses VIII	1147–1140	1127–1126

bridge Ancient History, while column B presents a lower chronology proposed by Wente and Van Siclen of the University of Chicago, which has since been accepted by other Egyptologists. The chronology of the transition from the Late Bronze Age to the Iron Age I has been determined on the basis of the dates of these Egyptian monarchs, particularly those of the Twentieth Dynasty.

The Decline of Egyptian Domination in Canaan

The first fifty years of the Iron Age I (ca. 1200–1150 B.C.E.), when the characteristic features of the new period had not yet appeared, are considered transitional between the Late Bronze Age and the Iron Age. The material culture in this transition varies in different parts of the country. In some sites, the transition may be linked to the decline of Egyptian domination in Canaan.

Many Canaanite towns were destroyed toward the end of the Late Bronze Age: Hazor (stratum XIII), Beth Shean (stratum VII), Megiddo (stratum VIIB), Aphek (the Egyptian Residency), Beth Shemesh (stratum IV), Gezer (stratum XV), Tell Beit Mirsim (stratum C), Lachish (stratum VII and Fosse Temple III), and others. Some of these towns were rebuilt along similar lines and survived until the mid twelfth century, when Egyptian hegemony in Canaan ended. There is no scholarly consensus regarding the attribution of the phase between the late thirteenth century and the mid twelfth century either to the Late Bronze Age or Iron Age I. The considerable cultural continuity evidenced at key Canaanite sites of this period has led D. Ussishkin to include the phase within the Late Bronze Age. Despite the logic underlying that method, we prefer to retain the division determined by Albright and Wright,

beginning the Iron Age at the end of the Nineteenth Dynasty of Egypt, which corresponds to the destruction of some of the Canaanite cities and the disruption of the international trade system. The Twentieth Dynasty does represent, however, the final phase of Egyptian rule in Canaan. It is a transitional period deserving of a specific designation. Following Wright and many other scholars, it shall here be termed the Iron Age Ia. During this time span, Canaanite culture survived in the rebuilt towns, mainly in the coastal and valley areas (for example, Megiddo and Beth Shean) and in the northern Negev (for example, Tel Sera' and Tell el-Far'ah South). However, certain characteristics of Late Bronze Age Canaanite culture (such as the international trade reflected in pottery imports from Cyprus and Greece) disappeared, and some towns of central importance in the previous period, such as Hazor, remained in ruins.

CHRONOLOGICAL FACTORS

The transition between the Late Bronze and Iron ages is not sharply defined in every part of the country. A dividing line, however, may be related to the date when the importation of Cypriot and Mycenaean pottery ceased. International trade contacts characterized the Late Bronze Age, and the severance of those contacts may be considered a true expression of the end of the period. Using this criterion, the borderline between the two periods may be determined by the archaeological assemblages containing datable Egyptian finds.

At Tell Deir 'Alla, identified by some as Succoth (in the Jordan valley east of Damiyah Bridge), a rich assemblage of the end of the Late Bronze Age has been discovered; it contains many Cypriot and Mycenaean imports and a faience frag-

ment bearing the cartouche of Queen Tewosret. Thus trade with Cyprus and Mycenae must have flourished during, and perhaps a short time after, the one-year reign of Queen Tewosret. At Lachish, the greatest wealth of Late Bronze Age finds comes from Fosse Temple III, outside the town proper, excavated by the Wellcome-Marston expedition in the thirties. This temple, which contained many imported vessels, must have been destroyed at the same time as stratum VII on the mound proper, whereas stratum VI represents the Iron Age Ia, within which falls the reign of Ramesses III. This stratum has provided no Mycenaean or Cypriot imports, though the material culture as a whole is fundamentally Canaanite. The dividing line between the Late Bronze Age and the Iron Age I may thus be fixed at a point later than Queen Tewosret and earlier than Ramesses III. Rowton's chronology, used in the new *Cambridge Ancient History*, puts the one year of Tewosret's independent reign at 1200 B.C.E.; Wente and Van Siclen's method dates Tewosret to 1185 B.C.E. The occurrence of a new type of Mycenaean ware (Mycenaean IIIC) probably coincides with the reign of Ramesses III and may have lasted until the reign of Ramesses VI.

BETH SHEAN, STRATUM VI, AND MEGIDDO, STRATUM VIIA

The fifty-year period termed the Iron Age Ia may be clearly identified at sites where Canaanite culture and Egyptian activity were reaffirmed following a destruction at the end of the Late Bronze Age. Five of these sites are of special interest: Beth Shean, Megiddo, Tel Sera', Tell el-Far'ah South, and Lachish.

Beth Shean was an Egyptian administrative center during the greater part of the Late Bronze Age. The town was destroyed toward the end of the thirteenth century (stratum VII) but was soon rebuilt (stratum VI). The rebuilt town retained the outline of the previous stratum, and some new buildings were added. This process is best evidenced in the temple, which was rebuilt along the same lines as its predecessor, while incorporating a number of changes: the cella was given a broad, open facade, and an anteroom, creating an indirect entrance, was added. Several Egyptian-style architectural elements were used in the temple, for example, papyriform capitals and decorated cornices. Nearby, a structure (building 1500) that must have served as an administrative center or as the residence of a high Egyptian official was built on a typically Egyptian plan, with characteristic Egyptian elements, such as T-shaped thresholds. Further finds of this stratum attest to Egyptian presence. In building 1500 a lintel was found bearing a dedicatory inscription dating to the reign of Ramesses III. A statue of Ramesses III, found in secondary use in a later stratum, no doubt originated in stratum VI as well.

The wealth of finds from stratum VI, including hundreds of ceramic vessels, may be attributed to the twelfth century. Mycenaean IIIB or Cypriot imports do not appear. The continued Egyptian presence in the first part of the Iron Age, at least through the reign of Ramesses III, is thus indicated. In the northern cemetery of Beth Shean, burial caves of this period were discovered, containing anthropoid coffins similar to those found in the Late Bronze II cemetery at Deir el-Balah. Most of the Beth Shean coffin lids are fashioned in a naturalistic manner, and they seem to have been made for Egyptian soldiers or officials or for mercenaries serving in the Egyptian army, who may have lived in Beth Shean. The religious syncretism of

Beth Shean at this time is attested to by a miniature stela of an Egyptian official. It is made in a thoroughly Egyptian style, showing the official worshiping the Canaanite god Mekal, who is portrayed with typical Canaanite garb, headdress and emblems.

In contrast to Beth Shean, which was an Egyptian stronghold, Megiddo remained a Canaanite city-state throughout the Late Bronze Age. The thirteenth-century town (stratum VIIB) was destroyed toward the end of that century but, like Beth Shean, was soon rebuilt. The cause of the destruction of these two towns is not known, but their rapid recovery is evidence of the survival of Late Bronze Age culture into the first half of the twelfth century. In the restored town of Megiddo (stratum VIIA), the buildings of the previous phase were rebuilt—the royal palace near the gate, the temple in the eastern part of the town, and dwelling houses. The palace was constructed along lines similar to those of its predecessor, the most important changes being the construction of a basement annex on the west side of the building consisting of three rooms in file. In this annex, which may have served as the palace treasury, a rich hoard of ivories was discovered, the fruit of many years' collecting, as it represents the art of the Late Bronze Age. One of the ivories, the cover of a pen case, bears a cartouche of Ramesses III. A bronze Egyptian-style statue base also found at Megiddo bears the cartouche of Ramesses VI. The pedestal was found in an unclear stratigraphic context, but it may be assumed that it originated in stratum VIIA, which is chronologically suitable. Stratum VIIA itself exhibits considerable continuity of Canaanite culture: red and black decorated pottery, bronzes, jewelry, and other objects of Canaanite character. Mycenaean and Cypriot imports, how-

ever, are entirely absent. A few such vessels seem to have been mistakenly attributed to this stratum, as were one vessel and a number of sherds of Philistine ware.

EVIDENCE FOR EGYPTIAN PRESENCE IN SOUTHERN CANAAN

At Tel Sera' on Nahal Gerar, and at Tell el-Far'ah South on Nahal Besor, important evidence concerning the Iron Age Ia in the south has come to light. At Tel Sera', Oren uncovered the remains of a mud-brick fortress erected in the Late Bronze Age (stratum X). The finds of this structure include a wealth of Egyptian and Canaanite pottery, as well as Mycenaean and Cypriot imports. Shortly after its destruction in the late thirteenth century, the fortress was rebuilt (stratum IX) along similar lines. The rich destruction layer of this fortress, built in the early twelfth century and destroyed near the end of Egyptian rule in Canaan, contained many Egyptian and Canaanite vessels, including bowls with hieratic Egyptian inscriptions written in ink, but no Mycenaean or Cypriot imports. The most important inscription contains the date "year 22." The inscriptions are probably dedications of offering bowls presented in a cultic context, and they suggest the presence of Egyptian troops and officials. "Year 22" seems to refer to a regnal year, and archaeological and paleographic studies confirm the attribution of the inscriptions (hence the Egyptian presence at the fortress of Tel Sera') to the reign of Ramesses III. A similar sequence appears at Tel Mor, at the mouth of Nahal Rubin on the Mediterranean coast near Ashdod. In the Late Bronze Age, a small mud-brick fort (11 × 11 meters) was constructed here. It was destroyed toward the end of the thirteenth century and rebuilt in the Iron Age Ia (strata VI–V).

At Tell el-Far'ah South Petrie excavated a large mud-brick fortress that also seems to have been erected by the Egyptian administration. Its history is not clear, but it appears that it continued to serve the Philistines in the later part of the Iron Age I. The cemeteries adjacent to the mound are of great importance for the study of the Late Bronze–Iron Age transition. Cemetery 900 contains a series of solitary burials, rock-cut tombs with stepped dromos, and a burial chamber with broad benches. The finds in these tombs include many vessels made in the Late Bronze Age tradition but no Mycenaean or Cypriot imports. Scarabs of Ramesses III, Ramesses IV, and perhaps Ramesses VIII were found, thus dating the cemetery to the final days of Egyptian rule in Canaan. Philistine pottery appears in the following phase, represented in cemetery 500.

Stratum VI at Lachish provides a good example of the cultural sequence of the first half of the twelfth century. This stratum follows stratum VII and Fosse Temple III, in which Cypriot and Mycenaean imports appeared, and has been dated to the Twentieth Dynasty, on the basis of the discovery of a bronze object bearing the cartouche of Ramesses III. Votive bowls bearing hieratic inscriptions, similar to those found at Tel Sera', are dated to the same time, as is a tomb containing a clay anthropoid coffin inscribed in Egyptian hieratic script, which probably belonged to an Egyptian official. The temple found in Area P at Lachish resembles a temple of the same period at Beth Shean; both contain many Egyptian elements.

Egyptian activity in Canaan is also well documented at the Timna copper mines in the Aravah valley. The Egyptian finds in the temple at the foot of Solomon's Pillars indicate that the temple and the mines as a whole continued to function until the days of Ramesses V. Cartouches of Ramesses III inscribed on the face of the rock in Timna and near Beerot Oded in the southern Negev indicate the route followed by the Egyptians across the Sinai desert and the southern Negev to Timna.

Settlement of the Philistines and other Sea Peoples in Canaan

HISTORICAL SOURCES

One of the most fascinating episodes in the history of the Iron Age I is that of the arrival and settlement of the Sea Peoples in Canaan. The term "Sea Peoples" is commonly used to designate peoples who arrived in the eastern Mediterranean littoral in this period. Inscriptions on the walls of Ramesses III's mortuary temple at Medinet Habu in Egypt (west of Luxor) record the names and much of what is known of "the peoples of the sea and of the north." The best known among these peoples are the Philistines, often mentioned in the Bible. Their settlement on the southern coastal plain of Canaan is merely a part of a broader migration and settlement of Sea Peoples on the Levantine coast, a product of the deep crisis that overtook the Aegean and Anatolian civilizations at the end of the thirteenth century.

Egyptian mention of contacts with Sea Peoples, either as mercen-

Fig. 8.1. Bowl with hieratic inscription from Tel Sera'

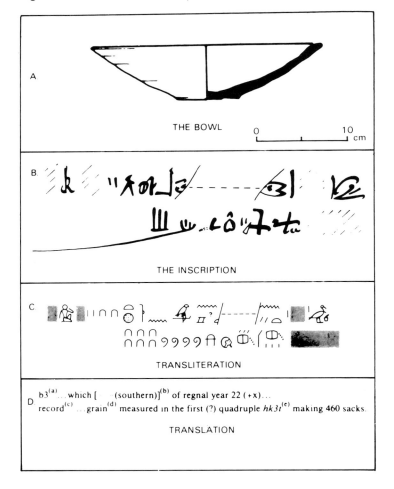

A   THE BOWL   0 ⊢———⊣ 10 cm

B   THE INSCRIPTION

C   TRANSLITERATION

D   b3[a] ...which [(southern)][b] of regnal year 22 (+x)...
record[c] ...grain[d] measured in the first (?) quadruple *ḥk3t*[e] making 460 sacks.

TRANSLATION

aries in the Egyptian army or as enemies in Egypt's wars, begins in the fourteenth century. In the El-Amarna letters of that time, the Sherden are mentioned as mercenaries and the Lukka as pirates. In the days of Ramesses II, Sherden participated in the battle against the Hittites at Qedesh in Syria as Egyptian mercenaries. Marneptah mentions Sea Peoples in league with the Libyans who warred with Egypt. Ramesses III mentions the Sherden as mercenaries in the Egyptian army. But the most important sources are those at Medinet Habu, which describe the battles with the Sea Peoples in the eighth year of Ramesses III and the great victory of Egypt over them. Mentioned as devastated by the invaders are towns and lands of northern Syria and Anatolia, including the Hittite Empire, Carchemish on the upper Euphrates (the center of Hittite control

in northern Syria), Arzawa in western Anatolia, Kode (probably on the southern coast of Anatolia), Alashiya (usually identified as Cyprus) and Amor (Amurru) in the mountains and inner valley of the Lebanon. Among the peoples mentioned in the inscriptions, the Philistines, Denyen, and Tjekker are the best known. The Tjekker are mentioned in the tale of Wen-Amun, an Egyptian official of the eleventh century, as the inhabitants of the port of Dor. The Denyen (Danuna) are described in the eighth-century inscription of Azitawada, king of the Danunites at Karatepe, as the inhabitants of the North Syrian coast and the Antioch region and may even be identified with the Homeric Danaoi.

The inscriptions are complemented by the detailed pictorial reliefs on the north wall of the

Medinet Habu temple. Two battles are described, a land battle and a naval battle. In the naval battle, five ships of the Sea Peoples are shown clashing with four Egyptian vessels. The ships of the Sea Peoples have prows and sterns in the shape of birds' heads, and one mast is topped with a crow's nest. The apparently furled sails hanging from the yards seem to indicate that the battle took place while the ships were at rest. The ships are shown without oars, though the openings for oars are portrayed. The warriors are tall; they wear a short skirt and a corselet made apparently of leather. On three of the vessels they wear a headdress with a horizontal band bearing geometric designs, above which is a cluster of vertical lines representing feathers or strips of leather. In the depiction of the cap-

Fig. 8.2. Naval battle between Egypt and the Sea Peoples, an Egyptian relief from the time of Ramesses III

tured Sea Peoples' warriors in the same relief, those wearing such apparel are identified as Philistines, Denyen, and Tjekker. The warriors on the remaining two ships are dressed in the same manner but wear a horned headdress. The arms carried by the Sea Peoples include long, straight swords, javelins, and round shields.

In the depiction of the land battle, the warriors of the Sea Peoples are similarly dressed, but here they are accompanied by their families, women and children borne in heavily laden carts drawn by four oxen. The carts have lattice sides and solid wood wheels. This is the most convincing evidence that the Sea Peoples who came to the east were migrant populations, not mere bands of warriors. They are also shown to have war chariots that differ little from their Egyptian counterparts, with six-spoked wheels and drawn by a pair of horses; each chariot carries three warriors, two holding spears or javelins. A group of foot soldiers, apparently ranged in fours, is also portrayed, bearing spears, longswords, and round shields, like the warriors on the ships.

Most of the Sea Peoples' warriors are clean shaven, but one Philistine and one Tjekker prisoner are de-picted with a beard, recalling two portraits found at Enkomi, the Cypriot metropolis of this period: an ivory lid showing a local ruler in his chariot, followed by a bearded warrior wearing a feathered helmet and carrying an axe and another weapon; and a seal portraying a similar warrior, also bearded, carrying a round shield. The two portraits have a direct bearing on the issue of the relation between the Sea Peoples and Cyprus.

Harris Papyrus I describes the result of the battles. The Egyptians defeated the Sea Peoples, but many of them remained to settle in areas under Egyptian rule. The text describes the settling of these people in Egyptian fortresses as mercenaries supported by Egypt. The settlement of the Sea Peoples in the Egyptian empire may have contributed to the empire's decline and to the end of Egyptian rule in Canaan.

Later Egyptian sources reflect the situation following the end of Egyptian dominion. The onomasticon (name list) of Amenope from the end of the twelfth century mentions three ethnic groups also mentioned in sources of the days of Ramesses III (Sherden, Tjekker, and Peleset) as well as three towns (Ashkelon, Ashdod, and Gaza). It would appear that the peoples mentioned in the list dwelt in Canaan. Further details may be learned from the letter of Wen-Amun, an Egyptian official who passed through Canaan around 1100 B.C.E. on his way to Byblos to purchase cedar. Wen-Amun stayed for a time at Dor, by then inhabited by Tjekker. The Tjekker seem to have been the most important of the Sea Peoples neighboring the Philistines, and the Sherden may have settled farther to the north, in the valleys of the Accho, Jezreel, and Beth Shean. The mastery of the Sea Peoples over the sea may be gathered from Wen-Amun's account of ten Tjekker ships that pursued him to Byblos. Wen-Amun even mentions names of rulers along the coast, perhaps of the Philistine towns. The names, in any case, are foreign to the Canaanite repertoire: Weret, Mekmer, Warkatara. The last-named ruler had commercial relations, or perhaps a trade pact, with Sidon. This indicates that the Philistines and Tjekker may have carried on a maritime trade up and down the eastern Mediterranean seaboard, alongside or even in alliance with

Fig. 8.3. Egyptians in combat with Sea People who are accompanied by their families, an Egyptian relief from the time of Ramesses III

the rising power on the Lebanese coast, the Phoenician city-states of Sidon and Tyre.

Another important source of information on the Philistines is, of course, biblical tradition. The five major Philistine towns—Gaza, Ashkelon, Ashdod, Gath (probably to be identified with Tell es-Safi), and Ekron (Tel Miqne)—seem to have formed a coalition (Pentapolis) similar to that in Bronze Age Greece. Each town was ruled by a seren, a term that seems related to the Greek *tyranos*. The relations between Israelites and Philistines, which are the focus of the biblical narrative, lie outside the scope of the present discussion. Their struggles centered around the control of the inner plains (the Shephelah) and the Philistine attempt to gain a stronghold in the hill country and to check Israelite expansion under Saul, climaxing with the capture of the Ark of the Covenant by the Philistines. One passage (I Sam. 13:21) mentions the Philistine monopoly of metal craft.

The origin of the Sea Peoples in general and of the Philistines in particular has been much studied. Biblical authors identified the Philistines' place of origin as Kaphtor, apparently the isle of Crete (Amos 9:7; Jer. 47:4; cf. the term "Cheretite and Pelethite," which some believe to be a corruption of "Cheretite and Philistine"), and the prophet Zephaniah even termed them "nation of Cheretites" (Zeph. 2:5). The "Negev of the Cheretites" is also mentioned, designating some part of the northwestern Negev. Places of origin ranging from western Anatolia through Greece to the Balkans have also been suggested. Philistine personal names, as well as a number of Philistine technical terms in the Bible, do not contribute to a clear solution. Mounting archaeological evidence seems to point to the Mycenaean cultural sphere, particularly

Greece itself, as the place of origin of the Sea Peoples and of the Philistines.

In view of the dearth of textual evidence and the unresolved questions regarding the origin and history of the Philistines, the study of their distinctive material culture is of special importance. It gained great momentum during the last decades from excavations in some major Philistine centers and synthetic work, particularly that of T. Dothan.

THE ARRIVAL OF THE SEA PEOPLES AND THE APPEARANCE OF MYCENAEAN IIIC1B WARE

The distinctiveness of Philistine culture was recognized as early as the beginning of this century by archaeologists who identified the culture's unique ceramic ware, which remains an outstanding example of ceramic styles and techniques that reflect the origin of a new ethnic element.

The beginning of Sea Peoples settlement is characterized by the appearance of a distinctive ceramic ware in the Mycenaean tradition. Mycenaean ceramic has been divided into subtypes based on decorative features. In the Late Bronze Age II (fourteenth and thirteenth centuries), Mycenaean IIIB pottery was dominant; this was a homogeneous group that became widely distributed throughout the Aegean and in the lands that traded with Mycenaean Greece, from Italy to Egypt and Canaan. Following the wave of destruction on the Greek mainland at the end of the thirteenth century, new pottery groups began to appear, largely in the style of the preceding Mycenaean ware but exhibiting regional variations from different centers of production. This stage of production, termed the Mycenaean IIIC phase, has detailed subdivisions reflecting both chronological and re-

gional variations. One of the variants, termed the Mycenaean IIIC1b, is particularly dominant in Cyprus. It has been taken to indicate the presence in Cyprus of Mycenaean immigrants who moved east after the destruction of the cultural centers on the mainland. Identical pottery appears on the Levantine coast, in the earliest phase of Sea Peoples settlement. Isolated examples of Mycenaean IIIC1b ware were found at Beth Shean (stratum VI), at Tel Keisan in the valley of Accho, and along the Syro-Lebanese coast at sites such as Sarepta and Tell Sukas. However, the most important evidence comes from sites where large quantities of sherds and complete vessels have been found. These include Ras Ibn-Hanni on a spur adjacent to Ras Shamra (Ugarit) in North Syria, Tel Accho, and especially Ashdod and Tel Miqne (Ekron), the only systematically excavated sites of the Philistine pentapolis.

Mycenaean IIIC1b pottery was found at these sites in the earliest strata that can be attributed to the Sea Peoples. At Ashdod it was found in stratum XIII, an unfortified town erected on the ruins of the well-fortified Late Bronze Age town (stratum XIV); at Ekron, large quantities were found in the limited area so far excavated. The sherds all belong to vessels of characteristic Mycenaean form; they bear a monochrome (brown-black) painted decoration on a light ground, in typical Mycenaean patterns. Trace-element analysis of Mycenaean IIIC1b sherds from Ashdod and Ekron has shown that the vessels were produced in Philistia and were not imported from abroad.

This class of finds is of the greatest importance for the study of the process of Philistine settlement. The great resemblance between the Mycenaean IIIC1b ware of Philistia and Cyprus and its abundance in both regions attest to the settlement of immigrants of similar origin. In Cyprus, these immigrants are commonly identified with the Achaeans, refugees from the Mycenaean centers. The settlers in Philistia may be considered to be of similar origin.

The excavators of Ashdod and Ekron (T. and M. Dothan) hold that Mycenaean IIIC1b ware appeared before the reign of Ramesses III and represents a wave of Sea Peoples settlement preceding the arrival of the Philistines. Only the characteristic bichrome ware, they posit, should be seen as a Philistine product. It is, however, difficult to accept this view, as there is no textual evidence for the settlement of any non-Philistine Sea Peoples in Philistia before the Philistine settlement, after year eight of Ramesses III. Furthermore, there is a direct development from Mycenaean IIIC to Philistine ware, in which inter-

mediate phases may even be discerned. It would seem, rather, that the appearance of Mycenaean IIIC ware marks the beginning of actual Philistine settlement, when the Philistines still retained the ceramic traditions that they brought with them in their eastward migrations from Greece via Cyprus. This phase should probably be attributed to the period after the wars of the Sea Peoples with Ramesses III in his eighth year, when the Philistines built their urban centers in Philistia. The Mycenaean IIIC1b stage thus corresponds to the Iron Age IA, and it may be assumed that it lasted about one generation, from the reign of Ramesses III to the end of Egyptian rule in Canaan in the days of Ramesses VI.

PHILISTINE POTTERY

The next stage in the development of Philistine culture is characterized by the appearance of a distinctive pottery style, long recognized in Palestinian archaeology as Philistine ware. Its development in Philistia from the Mycenaean IIIC1b style can now be clearly traced. T. Dothan has shown the precise origin of the forms of Philistine pottery and the various decorative patterns and has demonstrated the internal development during the Iron Age I.

Philistine ceramic is clearly a product of cultural eclecticism. Various influences may be seen in both the forms and decorations. The dominant source is the Mycenaean ceramic tradition; it is accompanied by a strong Canaanite element expressed chiefly in the transition to bichrome decoration (red and black)—foreign to the Mycenaean

Fig. 8.4. Mycenaean IIIC1b ware from Tel Miqne

Fig. 8.5. Philistine pottery

traditions—and in a number of forms and patterns. Egyptian influence is expressed in decorative motifs, and Cypriot influence in two of the vessel forms.

The most characteristic and numerous Philistine vessels are those that retain Mycenaean forms. They include small, bell-shaped bowls with two horizontal handles; kraters of a similar form, with a modeled rim; stirrup jars (small closed vessels with a false neck, a spout, and a pair of handles attached to the neck); and strainer jugs, whose Mycenaean origin is not certain, though a number of parallels may be adduced from the Mycenaean IIIC ware of Rhodes and Cyprus. Rarer vessels in the Mycenaean tradition are the pyxis (a sort of cylindrical box), the three-handled jar, the jug with basket handle and spout, and the waisted juglet. None have Canaanite antecedents, and all point to the continuation of Mycenaean formal traditions among Philistine potters.

Three Philistine forms—a cylindrical bottle with two small horizontal handles, a bottle with bent neck (horn-shaped), and a gourd-shaped bottle—indicate a connection with Cyprus. The first two appear in Cyprus at the same time that Philistine pottery appears in the Land of Israel but do not precede it; it is therefore difficult to conclude that there was Cypriot influence on Philistine pottery in this case. It would be better to say that there was reciprocal influence, indicating a special relation between the cultures of Philistia and Cyprus in the twelfth and eleventh centuries. The source of the first two bottle forms may be sought in similar vessels made of ivory or other valuable materials depicted in artistic representations in Late Bronze Age Egypt. The third, gourd-shaped bottle, of which two solitary examples have been found at Azor, has no true parallels in Cyprus. The gourd form itself, however, was often imitated by Cypriot potters.

A certain degree of Egyptian influence may be seen in a class of richly decorated jugs, one of which has a slightly swollen neck characteristic of Egyptian pottery; but the main expression of Egyptian influence is in the Philistine decorative motifs. Several vessels made in the Late Bronze Age Canaanite tradition, decorated in the Philistine style, round out the corpus of Philistine forms. They include shallow bowls with bar handles, various jug types, flasks, and goblets. Similar vessels, without Philistine decoration, are common in the Iron Age I assemblage, appearing alongside Philistine ware in occupation contexts.

Philistine decoration, even more than form, clearly expresses the combination of Mycenaean and Canaanite traditions typical of this ware. It is executed in two colors, brown-black and red-purple, on a whitish slip or directly on the clay surface. Bichrome decoration is a characteristic of Late Bronze Age Canaanite pottery that survived into the Iron Age I in areas where Canaanite culture survived, such as the northern valleys. Philistine potters adopted this technique after maintaining the Mycenaean monochrome decorative tradition (as reflected in Mycenaean IIIC1b ware) during the first generation of their settlement, after they had lived for some time in Philistia. During this period, Philistine potters were exposed to local traditions and eventually adopted them. It is also possible that local potters of Canaanite extraction began producing ceramics in the new style, to cater to the taste of the new rulers of the area. Two vessels, a jug from a tomb at Tell 'Eitun and a bowl from Ashkelon, demonstrate the transition from the Mycenaean IIIC tradition to the new decorative tradition. The decorative patterns on these two vessels resemble closely the patterns found on Mycenaean IIIC1b vessels but have been executed in two colors, black and red.

The decoration of Philistine vessels consists of a wide array of geometric motifs and a few animal motifs. It is generally arranged in friezes delineated by groups of horizontal lines and often divided by groups of vertical patterns into triglyphs and metopes. Within the metopes there often appear pictorial representations. This surface division is typical of the Canaanite decorative tradition, though it may also be found in Mycenaean pottery. Most of the decorative motifs are clearly of Mycenaean origin; these include the bird motif, one of the hallmarks of the Philistine ceramic. The bird seems to have been sacred to the Philistines, as it forms the main decoration of the Philistine ships portrayed in the Medinet Habu reliefs and occurs on Philistine cult vessels. The sacred character of the seabird portrayed in Philistine art may have originated in its function as an aid to sea navigation. The bird on Philistine vessels is fashioned in a distinctive manner, and the variations in its depiction must reflect the hands of the different craftsmen who worked in the various workshops in the centers of Philistine population. Fish are sometimes portrayed alongside the birds, but they are exceptions in the Philistine decorative repertoire, being more common in Mycenaean IIIC pottery. No other animals are portrayed on Philistine ware, apart from those on a single vessel from Megiddo, where a procession of animals led by a lyre player, approaches a sacred tree.

The spiral is dominant among those motifs that originate in the Mycenaean tradition. It is the sole decoration on many of the bowls and on some of the kraters. Spiral friezes, antithetic pairs, and joined

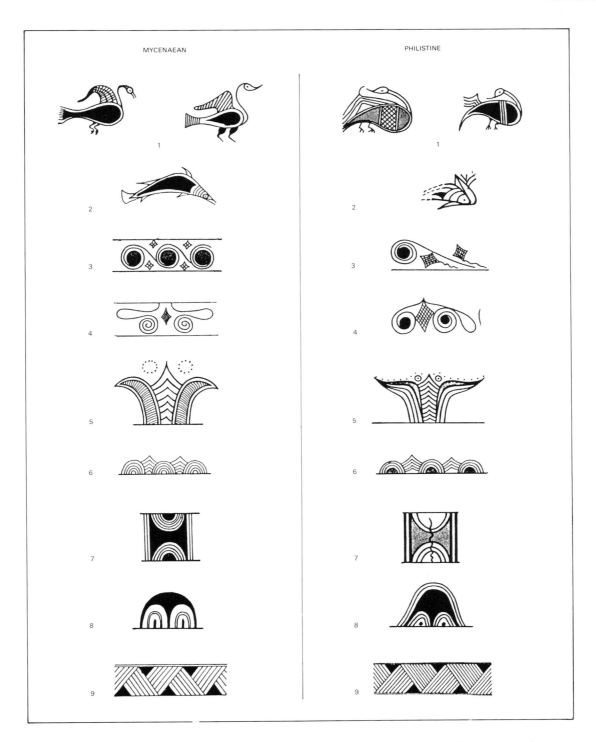

Fig. 8.6. Comparison of Mycenaean and Philistine decorative motifs

spirals forming the running-spiral motif occur as well. At times the spiral appears to be attached to a stem, and it sometimes has wings. All these patterns have antecedents in Mycenaean pottery decoration, especially in the Mycenaean IIIC1b wares. Other motifs of Mycenaean origin are antithetic tongues, groups of concentric semicircles used as space fillers on parts of the vessel that are difficult to decorate (such as the shoulders of stirrup jars), scale patterns, horizontal wavy bands, lozenges, herringbone patterns, groups of triangles, zigzag line groups, and net patterns. Some ap-

pear on Canaanite pottery, but there too they are probably derived from the Mycenaean decorative tradition.

From Egypt, the Philistines took the lotus motif. This occurs in naturalistic form, as in Egypt, on the neck of a jug from Tell el-Far'ah South. It seems to have been adopted by the Philistines from Egyptian art objects that were common in twelfth-century sites of southern Canaan. The lotus motif, however, was soon stylized and became a row of triangles, in effect a geometric pattern, which is quite common on various Philistine vessels.

Characteristic Canaanite motifs are not common in the Philistine decorative repertoire. There is one example of a stylized tree, typical of Canaanite art, on a Philistine vessel.

From the twelfth century to the late eleventh century, white slip gradually disappears and the complex patterns characteristic of the first phase of Philistine pottery are avoided. Relying on the stratigraphy of Tell Qasile, where three superimposed strata of Philistine occupation were unearthed, T. Dothan determined the existence of a third phase in the development of Philistine pottery, dated to the second half of the eleventh century, in which the characteristic bichrome Philistine ware with a wide range of geometric and bird decorations is replaced by vessels with a degenerate version of Philistine decoration. Typical of this phase are large kraters decorated with spiral patterns in black on a red slip. The spirals are detached and carelessly executed. Such kraters were found chiefly in stratum X at Qasile, the third Philistine stratum at the site. Excavations since 1972 have revealed that the development was more complex. In addition to the carelessly executed kraters, stratum X provided Philistine vessels with characteristic bichrome decoration, except that some of the motifs, most prominently the bird motif, had disappeared. The kraters decorated with black spirals were but a local variant of Tell Qasile and do not appear at other Philistine sites. Therefore, Tell Qasile X should not be taken to represent Philistia as a whole. It would seem that bichrome Philistine vessels continued in use until late in the eleventh century, enduring a slight fall in the quality of the decoration. The pottery at some of the most important Philistine sites does not change over strata (for example, Ashdod strata XII–XI) or a single stratum (Beth Shemesh stratum III, Tel Batash stratum

Map 8.1. Distribution of Philistine finds in the Land of Israel

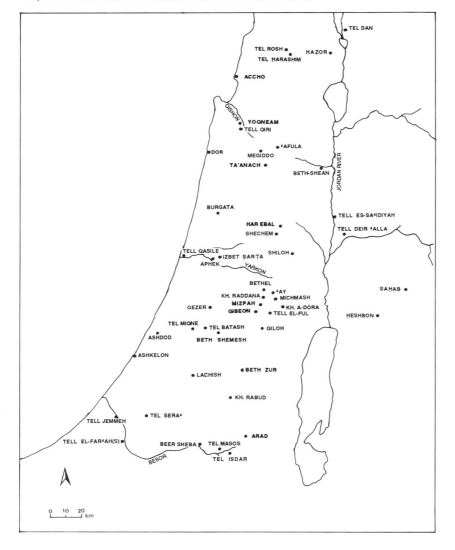

V) that span the greater part of the Iron Age I.

The distribution of Philistine pottery accurately reflects the extent of Philistine settlement and the relations between Philistia and the rest of the country. The ware is most abundant along the coastal plain of Philistia, between the Yarkon River on the north (Aphek and Tell Qasile) and Nahal Besor in the south (Tell el-Far'ah South). Philistine pottery is also abundant in the lower Shephelah, where two of the cities of the pentapolis, Gath and Ekron, were located. In the inner Shephelah, which seems to have been the border between Israelite and Philistine settlement, considerable quantities of Philistine ware have been found as well (for example, at Beth Shemesh, Tell 'Eitun, and Tell Beit Mirsim). The eastern limit of its distribution is the border of the Shephelah and the hill country. Outside this well-defined geographical area, a few vessels and sherds of Philistine ware occur in the northern Negev (Tel Masos), the central hills (Tell en-Nasbeh), the Sharon (Tel Zeror, Dor), the Jezreel valley (Megiddo, Tell Qiri), the Beth Shean valley (a few sherds only at Beth Shean), and even the upper Galilee (Tel Dan). Imitation Philistine ware occurs at Tell Deir 'Alla in the eastern Jordan valley. This wide distribution indicates the existence of commercial ties and perhaps of military campaigns to the interior and the northern valleys, as described in biblical sources.

Vessels decorated in the Philistine style never form the entirety of a given assemblage. They are always accompanied by a rich assortment of vessels characteristic of the Palestinian Iron Age I in general. In the Tell Qasile assemblages, for example, decorated Philistine ware comprises about 20 percent of the ceramic assemblage, and this seems to be the case at the other Philistine sites,

where quantitative analysis has not been performed.

Neutron activation analyses have shown that the chemical composition of Philistine vessels from Tell Qasile and non-Philistine Iron Age I vessels from that site is identical. Thus, both pottery classes must have been produced at the site, in a workshop that made both Philistine and non-Philistine vessels. This is likely to have been the case at other Philistine towns as well.

PHILISTINE SETTLEMENT PATTERNS AND THE STRATIFICATION OF PHILISTINE SITES

Excavations and surveys conducted in Philistia have revealed the general pattern of Philistine settlement and even some details of town planning. The Bible tells of the five cities of the lords of the Philistines: Gaza, Ashkelon, Ashdod, Gath, and Ekron. The large mound of ancient Gaza lies buried under the modern city of Gaza and cannot be excavated. Tel Ashkelon, on the Mediterranean coast, is also a large site. In the twenties small soundings excavated by W. Phythian-Adams revealed a Philistine layer but nothing of its extent or plan. Excavations at Ashkelon have recently been renewed (1985) by L. Stager, and we may expect significant additions to our knowledge of Philistine Ashkelon in the coming years.

The mound of ancient Ashdod (Tell Isdud) is three kilometers from the sea, east of the dune belt along the shore. Excavations in the sixties by M. Dothan revealed a series of construction and destruction layers of the Middle and Late Bronze age, ending with the final destruction of the Late Bronze Age town in the late thirteenth century (stratum XIV). This last Canaanite town was fortified with a thick mud-brick casemate wall. After its destruction, a new town was built (XIII), which

appears not to have been fortified, though it reveals evidence of urban planning and dense occupation. This stratum provided pottery vessels in the Canaanite tradition side by side with Mycenaean IIIC ware and hence must represent the phase in which Sea Peoples, probably Philistines, first settled in Ashdod. In the next phase (XII), the town was rebuilt along the lines of the preceding stratum, and the Canaanite fortifications were restored. This phase, with its abundance of Philistine finds, represents the flowering of Philistine Ashdod. Following a destruction, the cause of which is difficult to guess, the town was rebuilt in the eleventh century (XI), without any obvious change in the material culture. After this town too was destroyed, the site's history took a surprising turn. The town grew from seven hectares to forty hectares in stratum X; the new lower city was encircled with a wall pierced by a large gate. Ceramic evidence suggests that this great expansion occurred late in the eleventh century, concurrent with the establishment of the Israelite kingdom. Philistine pottery now went out of fashion and was replaced by a new class of red-slipped pottery with black painted decoration.

Ekron, the northeastern city of the Philistine pentapolis, has been identified with considerable certainty at Tel Miqne, in the lower Shephelah, east of Kibbutz Revadim. The size of the site, one of the largest of the Iron Age, and its location south of Nahal Sorek correspond to biblical tradition, particularly to the description of the northern border of the tribe of Judah (Josh. 15:10–20), which runs through Beth Shemesh, Timna (Tel Batash), "the northern flank of Ekron," and on to the sea. Excavations conducted at Tel Miqne since 1982 by Trude Dothan and S. Gitin have begun to uncover an impressive

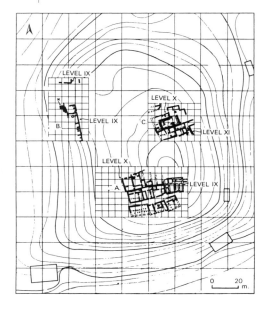

Fig. 8.7. Plan of Philistine settlement at Tell Qasile

fortified Philistine city. Significantly, a distinct archaeological phase bearing an abundance of Mycenaean IIIC1b pottery has been identified. It probably represents the beginning of Philistine settlement in Ekron.

Gath, the fifth city of the pentapolis, has been identified with various ancient sites, among them Tel 'Erani (Tell Sheikh Ahmed el-'Areini), formerly known as Tel Gath (the nearby town of Qiryat Gat and Kibbutz Gat took their name from this mound). However, excavations at this site revealed no Philistine stratum that could correspond to a city of the importance of Philistine Gath. The identification now in favor is with Tell es-Safi (Tel Zafit), a large mound on a ridge dominating the lower Shephelah south of Tel Miqne. The mound has not been systematically excavated, but chance finds of beautiful Philistine vessels have been made on and near it.

Excavations and surveys in Philistia have shown that in addition to the five major cities mentioned in the Bible, the Philistines settled at many other sites, some already occupied in the Late Bronze Age and others newly founded in the Iron Age I. The main sites are reviewed here in geographical order, from north to south.

THE YARKON BASIN. Tell Qasile, a mound north of the Yarkon River, on a kurkar ridge about two kilometers from the sea, is a characteristic example of an urban settlement founded by the Philistines on virgin soil. Excavations by B. Mazar in 1949–51 revealed the remains of a Philistine city that went through three successive phases of construction and destruction (strata XII–X) in the course of the Iron Age I. The town was destroyed in a fierce conflagration in the early tenth century, apparently at the hands of the Israelites under David. Renewed excavations beginning in 1971 (directed by the author) discovered the cult center of the Philistine town. The main attraction of Tell Qasile was its proximity to the Yarkon River, a convenient anchorage for the small ships of the period. The town's establishment is evidence of the importance of coastal trade to the Philistine economy. Apparently the Tell Qasile settlement inherited the function of the Canaanite town at Tel Gerisa (Tell Jerishe), on the south side of the Yarkon, as the main port near the mouth of the Yarkon. At any rate, in the Iron Age I, the settlement at Tel Gerisa dwindled into insignificance.

At Tel Aphek, excavations directed by P. Beck and M. Kochavi have uncovered a rather poor Philistine stratum, which does not suggest intense urban settlement. Pits, installations, and building remains of the Iron Age I were found, with characteristic Philistine ware.

Jaffa, an Egyptian administrative center during the Late Bronze Age, had only a poor Philistine settlement. The few Philistine sherds found in the excavations by Y. Kaplan do not suggest the existence of a town of any size.

Azor, east of Jaffa, is the site of an important Philistine cemetery, which has provided a rich assortment of decorated Philistine pottery. It is not clear whether the cemetery belongs to an adjacent urban site (the small mound near the cemetery may have been inhabited).

In conclusion, the finds of the Yarkon basin show that Tell Qasile was the urban center of the Iron Age I, whereas major Late Bronze Age sites declined.

THE NORTHERN SHEPHELAH. Philistine occupation levels have been excavated at three mounds of the northern Shephelah: Gezer, Timna (Tel Batash), and Beth Shemesh. At Gezer, four strata were attributed to the Iron Age I, one preceding the appearance of Philistine pottery (XIV) and three contemporary with it (XIII–XI). The small proportion of Philistine ware in the assemblages of these strata suggests that Gezer remained a Canaanite city, with a small Philistine population, until the end of the period.

Tel Batash is on Nahal Sorek, nine kilometers south of Gezer and seven kilometers east of Ekron. Its identification with the Timna mentioned in the Samson cycle (Judges 14–16) is derived chiefly from the description of the northern border of Judah (Jos. 15:10), where Timna is located between Beth Shemesh and Ekron. One Philistine stratum was found in the excavations (stratum V), its buildings made for the most part of mud brick. This stratum seems to have had a long life span, as evidenced by the relaid floors and the repairs in the streets and courtyards. Evidence was found for the fortification of the site during this period.

At Beth Shemesh too, seven kilometers east of Timna, one Iron Age I level, a planned town with much Philistine pottery, was identified (stratum III). The Philistine finds of Beth Shemesh pose a problem, for according to the biblical sources, Beth Shemesh was Israelite both in Samson's day and at the time of the battle of Even Ha'ezer (I Sam. 6:9–15). Moreover, the architecture and material culture of Beth Shemesh III do not correspond to what are considered Israelite sites. The history of Iron Age I Beth Shemesh thus requires further clarification.

THE SOUTHERN COASTAL PLAIN. There are gaps in our knowledge of the Philistine settlement pattern in the central part of the coastal plain and the Shephelah. Apart from Ekron and Ashdod, few sites have been excavated. One is Tel Mor, which seems to have served as the port of Ashdod and included an Egyptian fortress at the end of the Late Bronze Age. Following the destruction of this fortress, an unfortified settlement underwent two phases of construction (strata 3–4). These produced typical Iron Age I finds, including Philistine pottery. At Tel Zippor in the central coastal plain, east of Ashkelon, limited excavations revealed a stratum with characteristic Philistine finds. This site is one of the few known Iron Age I rural settlements. First settled in the Late Bronze Age, it included, in the Iron Age I, buildings with pillared courtyards.

THE SOUTHERN SHEPHELAH. Few of the central southern Shephelah sites have produced Philistine finds. At Lachish, the central mound of this region, there was a gap in occupation during the Iron Age I, and at Tel 'Erani (Tell el-'Areini) to the west, there is but a poor Philistine stratum. But on eastern margins of the region, at the foot of the Hebron hills, rich Philistine assemblages have been discovered. At Tell 'Eitun, Philistine tombs contained a wealth of objects, including one of the most magnificent Philistine vessels ever found. At Tell Beit Mirsim a stratum (B2) with Philistine pottery was excavated. The site at this time was sparsely settled and dotted with stone-lined silos. It is difficult to say, on the basis of the finds, whether the site was inhabited by a Philistine population, by Israelites, or by Canaanite refugees who came from desolated Canaanite cities such as Lachish. The third in this series of mounds is the site of Tel Halif near Kibbutz Lahav, which had an Iron Age I occupation (stratum VI) similar to that of Tell Beit Mirsim; any attempt to determine the character of the site or of its inhabitants would be premature.

THE NORTHWESTERN NEGEV. Rich Philistine strata were excavated in a group of sites along Nahal Gerar and Nahal Besor in the northwestern Negev. These include Tel Sera' and Tell Jemmeh on Nahal Gerar, and Tell el-Far'ah South on Nahal Besor. At Tel Sera' there was an apparent gap in occupation following the destruction of the Egyptian fortress of stratum IX. Stratum VIII includes dwellings with Philistine pottery typical of the eleventh century. The houses seem to have been of the four-roomed type, found in contemporary strata at Tell Qasile and at various Israelite sites. At Tell Jemmeh, Petrie excavated a number of Philistine strata, and renewed excavations directed by G. van Beek uncovered a pottery kiln, the first found so far in a Philistine context. At Tell el-Far'ah there was an important Philistine settlement with a vague history. It seems that the Philistines continued to utilize the Egyptian fortress of the end of the Late Bronze Age, for it is certain that Philistine sherds were found on the floor of the courtyard of that building. Most important is the cemetery adjacent to the mound, which contained several Philistine tombs. At Deir el-Balah as well, the remains of a poor Philistine settlement were found superimposed on the ruins of the Egyptian fortress that had existed at the site in the later part of the Late Bronze Age. Philistine sherds here occurred mainly in pits and installations, without any permanent structures having been found.

In conclusion it may be said that the Philistines founded a network of urban settlement throughout Philistia, with the pentapolis as its core. Many sites that have been centers of Canaanite settlement or Egyptian administration in the previous period were reconstructed and some even refortified; this, at a time when Canaanite settlement ceased at other major Late Bronze Age centers such as Hazor and Lachish. The continuity of urban culture in Iron Age I Philistia was thus a result of Philistine settlement. This factor should be of some weight in any attempt to trace the origin of the Philistines, for the archaeological record proves that the Philistines had a developed urban tradition.

The Philistines also founded new settlements where none had existed before, and they too were of an urban character (Tell Qasile). Too little is known of the rural settlements, apart from isolated sites such as Tel Zippor and Deir el-Balah. It seems, however, that the northern Shephelah had a relatively dense Philistine population, in contrast to the south (the Lachish region). The question of Philistine settlement on the border of the hill country and the plain (in the Tell Beit Mirsim–Tel 'Eitun region) must remain open, in view of the meager information available. In none of these sites, outside the main cities of the pentapolis, was Mycenaean IIIC pottery found, showing that Philistine settlement expanded when bichrome Philistine ware had already come into its own, namely, in the second half of the twelfth century.

PHILISTINE FORTIFICATIONS AND DWELLINGS

Little is known of Philistine architecture, as the areas exposed in excavations are generally rather narrow. Philistine fortifications, for example, have been encountered only in trenches excavated at Ashdod and Ekron. At Ashdod, the mud-brick casemate wall of stratum XIV (Late Bronze Age) was restored in stratum XII, when it was broadened and became part of an impressive fortification system. At Ekron a massive mud-brick wall six meters wide encircled the mound. Though only small sections of the fortifications have been excavated at the two sites, they are ample testimony to Philistine knowledge of fortification. At Tell Qasile some evidence was found of a mud-brick town wall, but it seems to have fallen prey to erosion and to later human activity on the edges of the mound. At Tel Batash too there is evidence of fortification during this period.

Philistine urban planning may be studied chiefly at Tell Qasile and to some extent at Ashdod and Ekron. At Tell Qasile, various building complexes were discovered in the three Philistine strata. In the lower stratum (XII), walls were made of brick without stone foundations. Not much is known of the town plan in this phase. The sacred area was delimited by a wall running east–west for 25 meters. South of this wall part of a public building was exposed, consisting of a large hall (internal size, 6.5 × 7 meters) with benches along its walls and a brick hearth in its center. It seems to

have been a council hall or perhaps part of the residence of the local ruler or governor. A large building at Tel Miqne of the late eleventh and early tenth centuries B.C.E. was probably a palace or a patrician house. It comprises a large hall (or courtyard) with two pillar bases and a freestanding hearth. Three square rooms open to this main space on the east. The freestanding hearths in both these buildings have no Canaanite antecedents, but they are well known in Aegean and Anatolian architecture and appear contemporaneously in Cyprus, ap-

parently in the wake of Achaean immigration to that island. Well-planned residential quarters were built at Tell Qasile in the eleventh century. These are best known from the third Philistine phase (stratum X). The town of this stratum had crisscross streets 3 meters wide. Many of the houses shared a similar design: rectangular or square structures with a courtyard divided by rows of wooden pillars set on unworked stone bases. One side of the court remained unroofed, while the apparently roofed section served as a shelter for livestock. Rooms at the

Fig. 8.8. Ashdoda figurine from Ashdod (height 17 centimeters)

rear of the house, and at times along one side of the courtyard, served as dwelling units. These are thus pillar houses, some built according to the basic design of the four-room house and others offering slight variations. The courtyards had domestic installations such as grindstones, grape and olive presses, ovens, and looms. Similar dwellings were found at Tel Sera'. The few houses excavated at Ashdod, however, are of a different design. One of them consisted of a large hall roofed with the aid of two wooden posts, with living units on either side.

TEMPLES AND CULT OBJECTS

Philistine cult has been revealed in an assemblage of clay figurines discovered at various sites and in a series of temples excavated at Tell Qasile. Two types of figurines are to be considered. One is a schematic figure of a seated goddess. The only complete example of this type has been found at Ashdod (named there Ashdoda), and fragments have appeared at other Philistine sites (Ashdod, Aphek, Tell Qasile). The peculiar style of this figurine is directly related to the Mycenaean figurine tradition, which includes seated goddesses who at times are shown with a child in arms (a fragment from Tell Qasile is of this type). The second type of clay figure, related to burial, portrays women mourners. They were originally attached to kraters placed in tombs and have been found in the Philistine cemeteries of Azor and Tel 'Eitun. Their Mycenaean prototypes are the schematic mourning figurines attached to deep bowls (*lekanae*), which were placed in tombs. The two figurine types are especially important, as they reflect the survival over a long period of an original Mycenaean cult-related mode of artistic expression, though

the style of modeling did undergo significant changes.

The only Philistine cult center excavated so far is that of Tell Qasile, which consists of a series of three superimposed temples spanning 150 years (strata XII–X). The first temple was a small mud-brick structure (6.4 × 6.6 meters), consisting of a single hall entered from the east through a doorway in which a large stone slab served as threshold. Opposite the entrance, in the center of the hall, was a plastered brick platform, where no doubt the statue of the god was placed. Benches along the walls bore votive offerings. An open space behind the platform may have served as the temple treasury. East of the temple extended a large courtyard containing layers of ash and much organic material. In it were found pottery sherds and bones of the animals sacrificed nearby. Rectangular annexes were added in the courtyard to serve the priests and the performance of sacred rituals in the compound. In the following phase (XI) a new temple was constructed over the old one. Its walls were of stone, and it was somewhat larger (5.75 × 8 meters) than its predecessor. The entrance was now in the corner of the structure. Mud-brick benches lined the walls of the hall, and in the western part of the structure a small brick room served as a treasury, where a rich collection of cult objects and offering vessels was recovered. The broad court east of the temple continued to function, its floor having been raised and repaired. In the final phase of this temple, or perhaps after its destruction, while the stratum X temple was being built, a deep pit (a favissa or bothros) was cut into the courtyard, and cult objects and offering vessels along with quantities of animal bones were placed in it. Adjoining the main temple of stratum XI on the west was a small

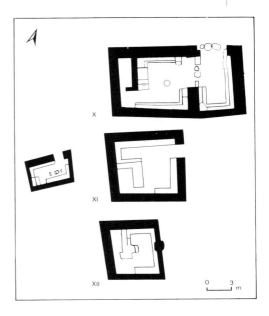

Fig. 8.9. Tell Qasile temple phases, strata XII–X

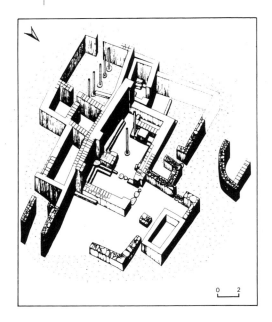

Fig. 8.10. Isometric reconstruction of temple at Tell Qasile, stratum X

shrine. It consisted of no more than a small brick-walled room (1.8 × 2 meters), with an indirect entry, benches lining the walls, and a raised dais in the corner built of two tiers of bricks. Pottery cult stands were found leaning against the dais. This shrine may have been the temple of a secondary god or of the consort of the main god. It is especially interesting because there are no antecedents for such a double temple in second millennium Canaan, whereas Cyprus and the Aegean world provide many thirteenth- and twelfth-century parallels.

In the third phase (stratum X, ca. 1050–1000 B.C.E.), the temple was rebuilt, using some of the exterior walls of the previous structure. The floor level was raised, and an anteroom was added, creating an indirect entrance. Plastered stepped benches were built along the walls of the anteroom and main hall. In the western part of the structure a brick platform abutted a curtain wall, on the far side of which lay the treasury. The roof of the main hall was supported by two cedarwood columns (their carbonized remains were found) set on well-fashioned limestone bases. The temple court was now surrounded by stone walls, which set it apart from the rest of the town, and inside it, the foundations of a square sacrificial altar were discovered. The shrine adjoining the temple on the west continued to serve in this stratum.

The three temples of Tell Qasile differ in plan, though they were erected by an identical population over a relatively short period (about 150 years). This has no precedent in Canaanite culture, where temples kept their basic form unchanged over long periods. The variability in the temple plans of Tell Qasile indicates that the Philistines did not have a well-defined temple-building tradition. The temple plans reveal

the influence of the Canaanite tradition shown in some of the Late Bronze Age temples (the Fosse Temple at Lachish, the temple at Tel Mevorakh, and the Beth Shean temple). The Late Bronze Age temples of the Aegean world (at Mycenae and at Phylakopi on the island of Melos) and of Cyprus (Kition) are similar to the Tell Qasile temples, but they themselves may have been influenced by eastern traditions, as they are not preceded by a local temple-building tradition.

The Tell Qasile temples provided a rich assemblage of cult and offering vessels, mostly of pottery. The majority of the cult vessels attest to the continuity of Canaanite traditions, but some are original creations unrelated to any definite tradition. The cult vessels include cylindrical stands decorated in various fashions, one with dancing figures and another with lionesses. The stands bore bowls that might have served for the offering of sacred meals in the temple. Some of these bowls were decorated with applied bird heads, representing the same sacred bird depicted on the pottery and the ships of the Peoples of the Sea. There were also many libation vessels, among them a cup in the shape of a lion's head in a style paralleled in Late Bronze Age Ugarit; the Tell Qasile cup (rhyton) is the most perfect in a series of such cups found in connection with Philistine or Sea Peoples culture at Iron Age I sites in the Land of Israel (Tell Jerishe, Tell es-Safi, Tel Zeror, Megiddo, and Tell Miqne). Another libation vessel, found in the favissa of the stratum XI temple, takes the form of a woman, with her head serving as the mouth of the vessel and her breasts as spouts. This is a unique object, with no close parallels, and is no doubt related to a fertility cult. Other libation vessels included kernoi (tubular rings to which zoomorphic spouts were at-

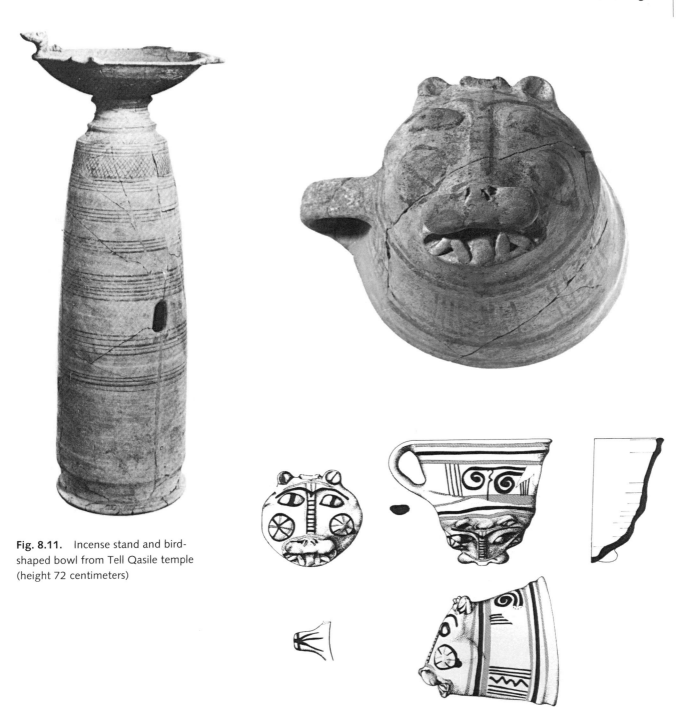

Fig. 8.11. Incense stand and bird-shaped bowl from Tell Qasile temple (height 72 centimeters)

Fig. 8.12. Lion rhyton from Tell Qasile temple

tached) and kernos bowls (bowls with a tubular rim and similar spouts attached). A large jar with five mouths may have served for the growing of sacred plants in the temple. A pottery plaque, found at the foot of the raised platform of the stratum X temple, has the form of a temple facade with two goddesses inside. This unique object must have had much ritual significance and perhaps functioned as an icon. Frag-

ments of life-sized anthropomorphic and zoomorphic masks were also found; these may have been worn by the priests during the performance of the temple rituals. A triton conch found in the temple may have served as a ceremonial trumpet. Luxury items such as alabaster vessels, ivory, beads, metal objects, and hundreds of pottery vessels of varied type were given as offerings in the temples. The pottery assemblage is

particularly important, as it was found in a clear stratigraphic context, enabling the study of ceramic evolution in the Iron Age I.

WRITING AND SEAL-CARVING

Among the most fascinating Philistine artifacts are stone seals, some conical or pyramidal, others of varying shapes, the most important of which is a cylinder seal from Ashdod. Human or animal figures are portrayed on these seals, usually in a most schematic, linear fashion.

Fig. 8.13. Female anthropomorphic vessel from Tell Qasile temple

Fig. 8.14. Cylinder seal with Philistine writing from Ashdod

A typical scene shows one human and one animal figure. Two seals, one from Ashdod and the other from Tel Batash, show human figures playing on a stringed instrument resembling a lyre. This class of seals apparently represents the Philistine glyptic school, whose origins may be sought in contemporary or earlier Cypriot glyptic. Two of the Ashdod seals contain signs in a linear script, somewhat reminiscent of the undeciphered Cypro-Minoan script of Late Bronze Age Cyprus. The few signs thus far known of this Philistine script indicate the existence of a unique Philistine form of writing.

BURIAL PRACTICES

A variety of methods and customs of burial have been discerned in Philistia. In the rich cemetery of Azor, east of Jaffa, the dead were interred either in plain pits dug in the ground, elongated cist tombs, or coffins made of two jars broken off at the neck. These three types of burial are also present in the cemetery of Tel Zeror, east of Hadera, which seems to have served a group of the Sea Peoples, perhaps the Tjekker, who settled in Dor and made it their center. They are the principal tomb types of the coastal strip. Some evidence for cremation was found at Azor, but the importance of this practice among the Sea Peoples is still obscure.

The large cemetery at Tell el-Far'ah South contained many simple pit burials accompanied by five carved burial caves, which seem to have been the tombs of Philistine nobles or dignitaries. The tombs had a stepped dromos leading to a chamber with broad benches on either side, on which the bodies were laid, accompanied by many gifts, including Philistine pottery. One of the tombs contained a complete anthropoid coffin, and another the lid

of one such coffin. The technique and style of the coffins resembles those of the cemetery adjacent to the Late Bronze Age Egyptian fortress at Deir el-Balah. Each coffin consists of two parts, the body and the decorated lid. The Tell el-Far'ah lids are fashioned in the grotesque manner reminiscent of some of the Deir el-Balah lids. The practice of burial in anthropoid coffins originated in Egypt and seems to have been adopted by the Sea People who served in the Egyptian army and were garrisoned in Egyptian fortresses in Philistia. These mercenaries fashioned the lids in a peculiar style, foreign to the Egyptian manner. This should explain the nature of the Deir el-Balah coffins and the presence of grotesque coffins at Beth Shean (most of the fifty coffins at that site are in the naturalistic style of Egypt) and of a coffin bearing a hieratic Egyptian inscription at Lachish. The two coffins from Tell el-Far'ah South are the best evidence for the use of anthropoid coffins by the Philistines, but this does not seem to have been the principal mode of burial, as the majority of the Philistine tombs excavated do not contain clay coffins.

Five of the anthropoid coffin lids found at Beth Shean are fashioned in the grotesque style. Each bears a distinctive headdress. One of them shows a group of vertical lines reminiscent of the feathered helmet worn by the Sea People in the Medinet Habu relief. It seems likely that the grotesque Beth Shean coffins served for the burials of Sea People who settled at the site when it was still an Egyptian administrative center (until the mid twelfth century) and continued to live there throughout the Iron Age I, after Egyptian rule had ended. T. Dothan has expressed the view that the Beth Shean coffins belonged to the Philistines themselves, but the almost complete absence of Philistine ware at Beth

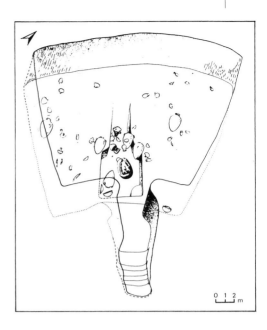

Fig. 8.15. Philistine tomb at Tell el-Far'ah South

Fig. 8.16. Anthropoid coffin from Beth Shean (height 200 centimeters)

Shean has moved. E. Oren to propose that these are the coffins of other Sea Peoples, perhaps the Denyen, portrayed in the Medinet Habu reliefs with feathered helmets similar to those of the Philistines. To sum up, anthropoid coffin burial may have continued among Sea Peoples throughout the Land of Israel after being adopted from the Egyptians, but it cannot be considered the dominant form of Philistine burial.

A good example of burial in carved chamber tombs occurs at Tel 'Eitun in the inner Shephelah, where a wealth of Philistine finds was discovered. The caves are oval, with wide benches sometimes hewn in the form of arched niches (reminiscent of the later arcosolia). The bodies were placed on the benches as in the Tell el-Far'ah South tombs. There are two schools of thought concerning the source of the carved burial chambers. T. Dothan follows J. Waldbaum in seeing Aegean influence, particularly of the Mycenaean dromos tombs, in the rock-cut tombs of Tell el-Far'ah South. W. H. Stiebing has shown, however, that Bronze Age tombs from Canaan, and particularly from Tell el-Far'ah South itself, share the stepped dromos and wide-benched burial chamber of the Tell el-Far'ah Philistine tombs. It is, however, conceivable that the very tombs brought as parallels are themselves the result of Mycenaean influence or even of the presence of Sea Peoples as mercenaries in the Egyptian garrison at Tell el-Far'ah during the Late Bronze Age and the Iron Age I, before the appearance of bichrome Philistine pottery.

EVIDENCE FOR THE SETTLEMENT OF OTHER SEA PEOPLES

The eclectic Philistine culture is characteristic of the Philistine settlement in Philistia proper. The few Philistine vessels found outside this region probably reflect interregional trade. However, there is evidence for the settlement of other groups of Sea People in other parts of the country. Though meager, it is sufficient to show that the settlement of Sea Peoples was not limited to Philistia alone.

According to the Wen-Amun papyrus, the Sharon was the region settled by the Tjekker. Excavations at Tel Zeror have provided indications of an Iron Age I fortress at the site. In the cemetery adjacent to the site, several stone-lined cist tombs covered with stone slabs were discovered, similar to tombs found at Azor. This tomb type appears in the Aegean in the twelfth and eleventh centuries, and it may perhaps be taken as characteristic of the Sea Peoples. The finds in these tombs include pottery vessels, among them strainer jugs similar to those of the Philistines but undecorated. Bronze spearheads from the Tel Zeror tombs resemble spearheads from the Aegean. A lion-shaped cup (rhyton) also indicates a relation between this cemetery and the culture of the Sea Peoples.

Recent excavations at Tel Accho have unearthed decorated pottery reminiscent of Philistine ware yet not identical to it. It may represent a local style of one of the Sea Peoples (the Sherden have been proposed by M. Dothan). At Beth Shean the finds from lower stratum V (a pair of temples and many cult objects, some of which resemble those of Tell Qasile) and from the cemetery (anthropoid coffins) testify to the settlement of another group of Sea People at that site (the Denyen have been proposed by Oren). These finds may explain the use of Beth Shean as a Philistine base in the battle with Saul near Mount Gilboa. However, the bulk of the finds at Beth Shean and at other sites of the region (such as Megiddo) indicate

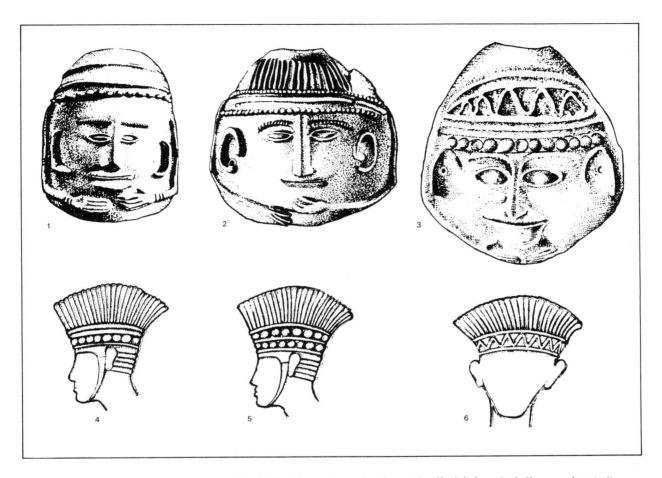

Fig. 8.17. Comparison of anthropoid coffin lids from Beth Shean and portraits of Sea People in the reliefs of Ramesses III

Material Culture of the Israelite Tribes During the Period of the Judges

The origin of the people of Israel is one of the most controversial subjects in the field of biblical history. Highly divergent views have been expressed, from fundamentalist views that remain faithful to biblical tradition, seeing the stories of the patriarchs, the bondage in Egypt, the deliverance from Egypt, and the conquest of Canaan as reflections of true historical developments, to diametrically opposed views that deny the historicity of those narratives, seeing them as late literary traditions, and prefer alternative recon-

the continued presence of a Canaanite population.

structions of the beginnings of Israel. This section, however, will address only the question of what archaeology can contribute to the study of the conquest of Canaan and its settlement.

The subject as a whole is fraught with methodological difficulties, for the silent archaeological evidence may always be interpreted in more ways than one. The destruction layer of a Canaanite town mentioned in the conquest cycle in the book of Joshua may be considered illustrative of the story told in those chapters, but it may also be explained in a different manner. Iron Age I settlements seen by some as evidence of Israelite settlement may be explained by others as settlements of other, non-Israelite ethnic groups. The relative dearth of ar-

chaeological finds also serves to impede their interpretation. All these difficulties together make this subject one of the most problematic in the archaeological and historical study of the Land of Israel.

THE CONQUEST IN LIGHT OF ARCHAEOLOGICAL FINDS

During the Israelites' wanderings in the desert, we are told, they fought a battle with "the Canaanite, king of Arad, who dwelt in the Negeb" (Num. 21:1), which ended with an Israelite victory: the Canaanites "and their cities were proscribed. So that place was named Hormah" (Num. 21:3, cf. Num. 33:40). According to this tradition, the Israelite tribes approached the area of Arad from Kadesh Barnea in the south, through Mount Hor. Systematic surveys and excavations at Kadesh Barnea and in the Beersheba and Arad valleys have not produced any archaeological evidence of the Late Bronze Age, the period to which the exodus is commonly assigned. At Kadesh Barnea, a third-millennium settlement was followed by a long gap in occupation lasting until the tenth century, when an oval fortress was erected as part of a network of such fortresses throughout the Negev. Not one Late Bronze Age or Iron Age I sherd was found in the surveys, which combed the oasis of Kadesh Barnea and its vicinity, or in the systematic excavations of the mound. Neither did the extensive studies of Y. Aharoni and his associates in the Arad valley and in the Beersheba region produce any hint of Late Bronze Age occupation. Arad itself, after the destruction of an Early Bronze Age II town, remained unoccupied until the tenth century, when the Israelite settlement there was founded. There is thus no evidence for the existence of a Canaanite "king of Arad" at Arad itself. Aharoni attempted to explain the discrepancy by suggesting that Canaanite Arad was at a different site in the region, but systematic excavations in all the mounds of the Beersheba valley, particularly at Tel Malhata and Tel Masos, found no Late Bronze Age settlement. That unequivocal archaeological fact should be taken into account when evaluating the historical reliability of the biblical tradition concerning this region. Does the tradition reflect an earlier period, perhaps the Middle Bronze Age II, when the area was settled by Canaanites? Does the term "king of Arad" refer perhaps to the leader of a nomadic or semi-nomadic population that left no trace in the archaeological record, as believed by B. Mazar and later by Aharoni? Both possibilities seem remote. It would be preferable to view the biblical tradition regarding this region as one that evolved when the area was already well known to the Israelites, in the later part of the period of the Judges or in the period of the monarchy, and not as a reflection of historical events.

In Transjordan, the meager archaeological data shed little light on the biblical tradition of battles and conquests. Numbers 21:21–32 tells of the war of the Israelites with Sihon, king of the Amorites, ending in the capture of Heshbon. Extensive excavations at Tell Hesban have shown that the site was first occupied only in the Iron Age I. The poor remains of this period cannot qualify as the Amorite city taken and destroyed by the Israelites.

The remaining part of the conquest cycle is reported in Joshua 2–12, a description repeatedly discussed in scholarly literature. Some have seen it simply as a record of a military campaign led by Joshua in the course of which the entire land was conquered (Kaufmann, Yadin, and others); others see it as a literary creation of a time far later than the events described, which may contain some residue of ancient historical events but should not be accepted

Map 8.2. Iron Age I sites in the Land of Israel

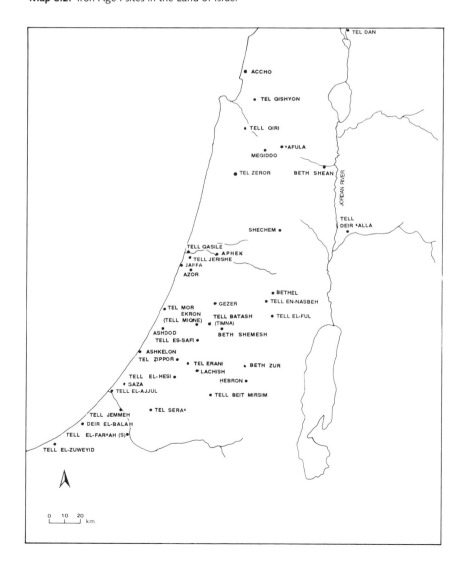

at face value. In fact, the book of Joshua relates the conquest of only a few towns: Jericho, Ai, the allied cities of the plains, and Hazor. Let us examine the archaeological situation at each of these sites.

JERICHO. The British archaeologist J. Garstang, who excavated Jericho in the thirties, claimed the discovery of the walls that Joshua had overcome. Excavations pursued by K. Kenyon in the fifties proved that the walls encountered by Garstang were in fact of the Early Bronze Age. They further revealed that the site was settled in the Late Bronze Age but that most of its remains were removed by erosion and by human activity. A few tombs of this period, as well as some building remains, were recovered. No fortifications were found, but that is true of many Late Bronze Age towns. Kenyon believed that the massive Middle Bronze Age fortifications, well preserved around the edges of the mound, could have been in use during the Late Bronze Age. Undoubtedly, the biblical story of the battle of Jericho is legendary, but in this case archaeological evidence does not run directly counter to the biblical tale, as is asserted by some scholars.

AI. The case of Ai is more extreme and resembles that of Arad. The location of Ai is precisely noted in the scripture: "close to Beth-Aven—east of Bethel" (Jos. 7:2). The identification of Bethel with the village of Beitin is generally accepted, as it is both historically-geographically and archaeologically suitable. East of Beitin only one site can possibly be identified with Ai, and that is the large site of et-Tell, near Deir Dibwan. The name of the site is a translation of the Hebrew word "Ai," "a ruin." In the narrow and largely arid strip between Bethel and the Jordan valley, there is no other site of any significance that

can be identified as Ai. Extensive excavations at et-Tell revealed a large and important town of the Early Bronze Age, fortified with a series of walls. Following its destruction, the town lay in ruins until the Iron Age I, when a village similar to other Israelite settlements of the central hills was established. There is no evidence of a second-millennium Canaanite city at this spot or at any other site in the region. This constitutes unequivocal archaeological evidence for the lack of correlation between the story in Joshua 8, with all its topographic and tactical details, and a historical reality corresponding to the period of the conquest. J. Callaway, who excavated at Ai, attempted to resolve the inconsistency by positing that the city conquered by Joshua is the first phase of the small Iron Age I village at the top of the site. This proposition is difficult to accept, for the first phase of this settlement is not essentially different from the second; both exhibit the material culture that characterizes Israelite settlement, and no major destruction separates the two. In any case, the first phase of this village can in no way be said to constitute a fortified Canaanite town. It seems that in this case the biblical story can be seen only as an etiological story that evolved during the Israelite habitation at Ai. Israelites did live at Ai in the period of the Judges. They would have noticed that their village was built on the ruins of a huge town (of the Early Bronze Age) and would gradually have developed the story of the conquest of this town, attributing it to Joshua. The close knowledge of the topography exhibited in the story probably stems from its development by the inhabitants of the site itself or of the vicinity.

THE CITIES OF THE SHEPHELAH. Chapter 10 of the book

of Joshua tells of the battle with a coalition of kings of the Shephelah and the hill country—the kings of Jerusalem, Hebron, Yarmut, Lachish, and Eglon. In the course of this battle Joshua conquers Makkedah, Libneh, Lachish, Eglon, Hebron, and Debir, and at the conclusion of the tale, the conquest of wide areas is described: "the hill country, the Negeb, the Shephelah, and the slopes . . . from Kadesh-barnea to Gaza, all the land of Goshen, and up to Gibeon" (Jos. 10:40–41). The location of some of the towns (Makkedah, Libneh, and Eglon) is not established. The other towns may be identified with certainty, and among them, Jerusalem, Lachish, Hebron (Tell Rumeideh), and Debir (Khirbet Rabud in the southern Hebron hills) have been excavated. Most of these sites produced Late Bronze Age remains. Lachish is the best known. The last Canaanite town at this site (stratum VI) was destroyed during or after the reign of Ramesses III, in the mid twelfth century B.C.E., and remained in ruins until the days of David and Solomon. There is no evidence regarding the identity of the destroyers of Lachish. Some scholars accept the biblical tradition, attributing the destruction to the Israelites; others attribute it to other elements, such as the Philistines.

At Debir too there is evidence of a Canaanite town destroyed at the end of the Late Bronze Age. In contrast, excavations at Tell Rumeideh have revealed no evidence of Late Bronze Age occupation, and there seems to have been a gap between the Middle Bronze Age town and the Iron Age I settlement. Other Canaanite towns of the Shephelah, such as Tel Halif and Tell Beit Mirsim, the ancient identity of which has yet to be determined, were also destroyed in the later part of the Late Bronze Age.

The archaeological record of the

southern Shephelah and the southern Hebron hills does not therefore contradict the biblical record (except in the case of Hebron), nor does it provide proof of its authenticity.

HAZOR. Chapter 11 of the book of Joshua is devoted to the conquest of Hazor. Hazor, "the head of all those kingdoms" (Jos. 11:10), leads a coalition of northern kings into battle at the Waters of Merom. Defeated in battle, Hazor is burned: "However, all those towns that are still standing on their mounds were not burned down by Israel; it was Hazor alone that Joshua burnt down" (Jos. 11:13). Excavations have proven that Hazor was the leading

city in Canaan. Throughout the entire Middle and Late Bronze ages the city occupied 800 dunams (200 acres), a veritable metropolis in ancient terms. The final Canaanite city at Hazor (stratum XIII) reveals some signs of decline and was violently destroyed. The excavators credit this destruction to the Israelites. The destruction was assigned in broad terms to the thirteenth century.

OTHER CONQUEST TRADITIONS. Other conquest traditions are preserved in the book of Judges, particularly in Chapter 1. Here, the military conquest of Jerusalem by the tribe of Judah is recorded (1:8). This tradition contradicts what is

stated later in the same chapter (21) and in the book of Samuel, to the effect that Jebusite Jerusalem was first conquered by David. Excavations in the City of David have revealed the remains of the Canaanite-Jebusite town, built in terraces rising steeply above the Gihon spring, but have otherwise contributed little toward the evaluation of the biblical traditions concerning the conquest of the city. Archaeology does not enhance or detract from the authenticity of Judges 1:8.

Conquests of Debir, Hormah, Hebron, and Bethel are also related in Judges 1. Limited excavations were conducted by Albright in the village of Beitin, the site of Bethel, uncovering a fortified Late Bronze Age Canaanite town, destroyed at the end of the period and re-established in the Iron Age I as an Israelite settlement.

The second part of Judges 1 notes the towns and regions not conquered by the Israelites; these include towns such as Beth Shean, Ta'anach, Dor, Yibleam, Megiddo, Gezer, Accho, and others, some of which have been excavated. In some sites (Beth Shean, Megiddo, and Gezer), the survival of Canaanite culture is evident (with a touch of Sea Peoples culture) throughout the Iron Age I. At other sites, however, the picture is more complex. For example, at Ta'anach there is no continuity, and the Canaanite presence seems to have ended with the destruction of the town at the end of the Late Bronze Age. At Shechem, one of the central Canaanite towns, no military conquest is reported in the Bible, but the site's importance is reflected in the story of the assembly of the tribes of Israel under Joshua's leadership at Shechem to reaffirm the bond between the nation and God (Joshua 24). Excavations indicate a smooth transition from Late Bronze to Iron Age I at Shechem, which is believed to have survived until the eleventh century.

Map 8.3. Stages of Israelite settlement in the Iron Age I

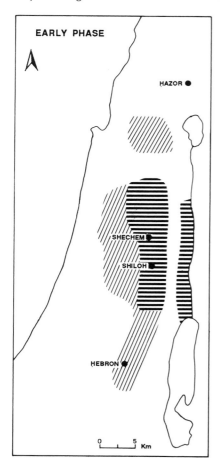
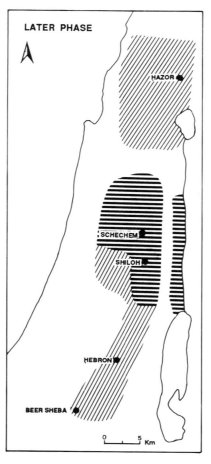

The picture emerging from these archaeological finds is complex and ambivalent. Some sites show a correlation between the archaeological record and a biblical tradition of conquest. The catastrophe of Late Bronze Age Hazor corresponds to the biblical tradition of the conquest and burning of that important Canaanite city. The same is true of Lachish, the most important Canaanite city in the Shephelah. Here, however, we encounter a difficulty, for the archaeological finds indicate that Lachish was destroyed in the mid twelfth century, several decades after Hazor. Clear contradictions between the scriptures and archaeological evidence occur in the cases of Arad, Ai, and Hebron, while in other cases, such as Jericho, Jerusalem, and Debir, the archaeological results are given to varying interpretation. There is a correlation, though, between the descriptions of "the territory that remained" (which mention Megiddo and Beth Shean as unconquered cities) and archaeological finds showing a continuity of Canaanite culture at these sites well into the Iron Age I. At Ta'anach, however, which is also numbered among those unconquered towns, the archaeological picture indicates Israelite settlement in the early twelfth century.

Most modern scholars of the conquest and settlement have reservations about the book of Joshua's story of a uniform military conquest, seeing it as a historiographical composition written hundreds of years after the events described. However, archaeology may cast light on ancient events that were the basis for the biblical tradition of the conquest of Canaan, for it is unlikely that this tradition was created ex nihilo. During the first decades of Israelite settlement, while the different population groups coalesced to form the Israelite national entity, some hostile encounters probably did occur between them and the Canaanite towns, which had been weakened after hundreds of years of Egyptian domination and internal strife. Such hostilities would have destroyed some of the towns, perhaps in a series of local clashes spanning several decades. Biblical historiography would have telescoped this series of clashes, ascribing them to the single campaign led by Joshua, and would have added traditions—the story of the battle with the king of Arad, the conquest of Ai, the cave at Makkedah, and others—to fill out the picture.

Yet, the archaeological record is anonymous, and its use to prove any historical theory must be accompanied by a rigorous critical approach to the archaeological material itself. Archaeologists tend to determine precise dates of destruction, for example, on relatively flimsy evidence. In the discussion of the Israelite conquest it would therefore be best to treat the archaeological evidence with circumspection and to avoid basing far-reaching conclusions on it.

EARLY ISRAELITE SETTLEMENT PATTERNS

The regions of Iron Age I Israelite settlement have been studied intensively in recent years. A most revealing archaeological picture has emerged, shedding new light on the process of Israelite settlement in Canaan. Scholarly opinion, however, remains divided on basic issues, the most prominent being the criteria used to define settlements as Israelite. In some regions, particularly in the northern Negev, the upper Galilee, the Shephelah, and Transjordan, Iron Age I settlements cannot be attributed either to Israelites or to one of the neighboring nations. Archaeological surface surveys have revealed, in different parts of the country, settlement patterns of the Iron Age I that depart widely from those of the Canaanite periods. There are also marked regional variations in the composition and character of material culture.

Y. Aharoni pioneered research in this field. In a survey of the upper Galilee highlands, he discovered a series of small Iron Age I settlements concentrated around the Mount Meron massif, which he attributed to Israelite settlers. His excavation at Tel Harashim, near Peqi'in, represents a breakthrough in the study of the material culture of this region. An interesting and complex settlement pattern has emerged from surveys carried out soon after the Six-Day War in the West Bank and from more recent and extensive surveys in the lands of Judah, Ephraim, Mannasseh, and Issachar, in the Sharon, the northern Negev, and parts of Transjordan. Apparently the Iron Age I saw the establishment of dozens of small settlements that may be considered Israelite.

In the upper Galilee, some 25 settlements have been identified, all in the Meron range, down to Biq'at Beth Ha-Kerem and Tur'an. A few additional settlements have been identified in the western Galilee hills overlooking the valley of Accho. Three sites, apart from Tel Harashim, have been excavated: Sasa, Har Adir, and Horvat 'Ovot (near Kibbutz Yiron). Most of the sites surveyed are small village sites of 4–5 dunams. The Har Adir site is the only exception, being a well-planned fortress. In the Hula valley, settlements identified as Israelite were discovered in excavations at the two large mounds of this region, Hazor and Dan. At Hazor, a small settlement built at the top of the mound in the Iron Age I was uncovered (strata XII–XI). At Dan, however, surprising evidence was found of a settlement extending over the entire 100-dunam mound. The remains of this settlement (strata VI–V) consist mainly of pits and silos, with few permanent structures. The upper Galilee sites may reflect the settlement of the tribes of Naphtali and Asher, and the large site of Dan the settlement of the tribe of Dan. The area may also have been the scene of Tyrian-Phoenician settlement activity, as evidenced in the construction of the fortress of Har Adir.

The lower Galilee survey (conducted by Z. Gal) has revealed a concentration of fifteen settlements in the Shefar'am-Nazareth hills attributed to the tribe of Zebulun. The basaltic Issachar plateau, however, was settled only under the United Monarchy. Surveys in the land of Mannasseh (by Gophna and Porat in 1968 and by Zertal in recent years) have revealed a surprising density of Iron Age I sites. About one hundred have been recorded so far, some large (more than 20 dunams), some of medium size (10–20 dunams), and some small. Zertal has estimated the total built-up area at 1500 dunams. This part of the country is characterized by wide and fertile interior valleys, around which Canaanite settlement clustered on mounds such as Tell el-Far'ah North, Dothan, and Shechem. Many of the new Iron Age I settlements were founded near the interior valleys. They clearly represent a change in the settlement pattern of the area, probably related to the settlement of the tribe of Mannasseh, and of the tribe of Issachar, which occupied the northern Samarian hills in the first stage of its settlement. At the same time, Canaanite presence was maintained, as attested by the archaeological findings at Dothan and Shechem and by the biblical record (the story of Abimelech). The only settlement sites excavated so far are a cult site in northern Samaria and a cult site on Mount Ebal.

Surveys in the hill country of Ephraim (Z. Kallai in 1968, Finkelstein in recent years) have identified more than one hundred sites of the Iron Age I, indicating a wave of Israelite settlement. Most of the sites, situated in remote hilly areas, are small, ranging from isolated structures to villages of 5–6 dunams. I. Finkelstein has attempted to distinguish two phases of settlement: an early phase limited to the desert margins and the central ranges and a late phase extending into the western hill country. Excavations have been conducted at Shiloh, an important Israelite religious center during this period, and at Ai, Bethel, Khirbet Raddanah near Ramallah, and 'Izbet Sartah east of Aphek, making this the best known of the Israelite settlement areas. In the land of Benjamin, twelve Iron Age I sites have been identified, most of them along the central watershed or east of it. Three sites have been excavated: Tell en-Nasbeh outside Ramallah, Tell el-Ful (identified by some as Gibeah of Saul), and Gibeon, where only limited soundings were conducted. Excavations in Jerusalem (the City of David) have produced only meager remains of the Iron Age I. The Bible describes both Gibeon and Jerusalem as non-Israelite enclaves in the period of the Judges; the archaeological evidence cannot support or contradict this assertion.

Little is known of the settlement process in the Judaean hills and Shephelah. Surveys conducted by M. Kochavi, A. Ofer, A. Mazar, and Y. Dagan have produced results in no way similar to those of the surveys described above. Isolated single-period sites of the Iron Age I were identified in the 1968 survey at Giloh (excavated) and at Umm et-Tala' near the Ezion bloc. It is conceivable that many of the fortified towns of Judah grew out of settlement sites that can be discovered

only by systematic excavation. Such excavations have been conducted at only a few sites, among them Beth Zur and Tell Beit Mirsim. At both sites an Iron Age I stratum was discovered that may be considered Israelite.

The Arad and Beersheba valleys were not inhabited in the Late Bronze Age. In the Iron Age I settlements were established, most of which have been excavated: Tel Masos, Tel Esdar, Arad, and Beersheba. The most important is Tel Masos, which reached 80 dunams in the Iron Age I and was a center of agricultural and commercial activity, with domestic quarters consisting of four-room houses and a public quarter with larger buildings, one of them a fortress. Tel Masos was first settled in the twelfth century (stratum III), but it reached the height of its prosperity in the late eleventh century (stratum II). It was destroyed at the end of that century and was only partially reconstructed in the tenth century. The excavators of Tel Masos (Aharoni, Kempinski, and Fritz) believed it to be a center of Israelite settlement in the northern Negev. Others (Kochavi, Herzog, Rainey, and Finkelstein) have suggested that the site was none other than "the city of Amalek" (I Sam. 15:5) destroyed by Saul in his war with the Amalekites. In my view, the finds at this site reflect elements of a coastal origin, either Canaanites or Philistines, while the bulk of the population was no doubt composed of tribal groups who joined the Israelites, such as the Calebites and Yerahmielites. Tel Masos illustrates a concentration of population typical of marginal areas beset with problems of security; a similar situation may be seen in the large modern villages of Dura, Dhahariyeh, and Yatta in the southern Hebron hills.

Beersheba was settled in the course of the eleventh century. At first (stratum IX) it was a poor pit settlement, like many other settlement sites; later on (stratum VIII) houses were erected. A deep well found at the eastern edge of the mound, in an area with early remains, was attributed by Aharoni to the Iron Age I and identified with the well of Beersheba mentioned in the patriarchal narratives. Too little is known about the well, however, to allow conclusive dating; it could be assigned to the Hellenistic period as easily as to the Israelite period. The stratum VIII settlement is apparently that mentioned in the book of Samuel as the place where Samuel's sons lived and sat as judges (I Sam. 8:1–3). The late eleventh or early tenth century saw the establishment of a network of settlements in the Negev Highlands, centering around fortified structures (fortresses).

In Transjordan, dozens of small Iron Age I settlements have been identified, mainly between the Yabbok and Yarmuk rivers. South of this region the number of sites declines until, in Edom, none are found. The ethnic attribution of these sites is fraught with difficulties, in view of the complex history of the region. It may be assumed, for example, that the large site at Sahab, southeast of Amman, was an Ammonite center. On the other hand, the small sites discovered in surveys in the Gilead may indicate Israelite settlement.

In light of that Israelite settlement pattern, Finkelstein, in a recent study, has arrived at two interesting conclusions. First he estimated the size of the built-up areas and multiplied that figure by a coefficient of 25 persons per dunam, arriving at a total population of 20,000 for the first phase of settlement in the Land of Israel and 60,000 for the end of the Iron Age I, on the eve of the foundation of the Israelite monarchy. The absolute

figures should of course be treated with reservation, but they still serve as a general indication of the size of the settled population. His second conclusion concerns the stages of Israelite settlement. He posits an early stage limited to the central hills, particularly to their eastern margins, where the Israelites first penetrated from the east. Settlement would have extended to the upper Galilee, Judah, and the northern Negev later as an offshoot of the settlement in the hill country of Ephraim and Mannasseh. This view requires thorough scrutiny, for considerable regional differences exist in the material culture of the various settlement zones. These may well indicate that separate tribal units, settling simultaneously in different parts of the country, gradually joined the Israelite tribal coalition that took shape during this period.

EARLY ISRAELITE MATERIAL CULTURE

Distinctive features of Israelite material culture have emerged from excavations at sites identified as Israelite settlements. This discussion will span the entire settlement period, ending with the foundation of the Israelite monarchy and including sites whose identification is disputed (Tel Masos in particular).

SITE ORGANIZATION. A small number of planned settlement sites have been discovered. Horvat 'Ovot (in the upper Galilee), Shiloh, Giloh (just south of Jerusalem), Ai, 'Izbet Sartah, Tel Masos, and Tel Esdar (in the northern Negev) all exhibit a peripheral arrangement of dwellings along the perimeter of the site. At Shiloh, the blank external walls of the outermost houses apparently joined to form a defense wall. The early phase of settlement at 'Izbet Sartah has been reconstructed as an oval enclosure, 2.2 dunams in area,

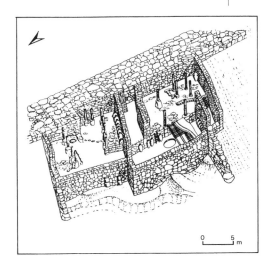

Fig. 8.18. Iron Age I structures at Shiloh

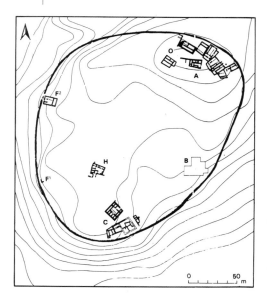

Fig. 8.19. Tel Masos, plan of site

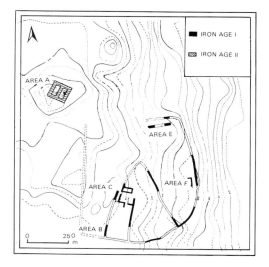

Fig. 8.20. Giloh, plan of site

consisting of a central open area surrounded by about 22 broadrooms. Finkelstein believes that this site plan originated in seminomadic tent camps. A somewhat similar pattern may be observed at Tel Esdar in the northern Negev, where a site 3.8 dunams in size contained twenty structures widely spaced around the perimeter of a hilltop. It is not clear whether the gaps between the structures were blocked with a defense wall. The 3-dunam settlement of Beersheba stratum VII, dated to the late eleventh and early tenth century, consisted of about twenty structures grouped in a circle around an open area (the excavators base this reconstruction on admittedly meager evidence). At the large settlement of Tel Masos, near Nahal Beersheba, no defense line was found, and the houses were constructed so that their doorways faced out, an arrangement without precedent in the site organization of any period. The peripheral arrangement of broadrooms around a central court is evidenced as some of the fifty structures termed fortresses throughout the Negev Highlands, dated to the United Monarchy.

The southern part of Giloh, one of the earliest settlement sites, covered 6 dunams and was surrounded by a defense wall. Different parts of the wall were built with different techniques, suggesting that the responsibility for its construction was divided among the families that inhabited the site.

Within the sites, large open areas remained, no doubt used to house the flocks. At Giloh a few long walls divided the site into large yards, probably sheep pens, with houses at the edges.

DOMESTIC ARCHITECTURE. The domestic architecture of the settlement sites is best known from the central hills and the northern Negev. The use of monolithic stone pillars (in the hill country), of pillars made of unworked stone drums (in the northern Negev), or of wooden posts placed on stone socles (on the coastal plain) is widespread. Rows of such pillars divide the courtyards of the rectangular houses into unroofed and roofed areas; added rectangular or square rooms form houses of three, four, or five rooms. At Giloh, one of the earliest examples of the pillared building, dating to the early twelfth century, reflects an early stage in the development of the type, when its features were not yet fixed. The plan is irregular and the construction flimsy, yet characteristic features of the four-roomed house appear: a courtyard divided by crude stone pillars, a rectangular back room, and rooms along the courtyard. This house plan takes on a more fixed form in the later phases of 'Izbet Sartah and Tel Masos, in the eleventh century. Similar houses at Tell el Far'ah North may also have been built in the eleventh century.

The interior organization of the pillared houses may change according to need. At Shiloh, for example, in a row of houses cleared along the edge of the site, each house has rows of pillars dividing courtyards or large units, but none has a three- or four-room plan. The houses unearthed at Raddanah or Ai present a variety of plans based on the pillared courtyard design, with roofed and unroofed areas.

Two major questions have arisen with regard to these houses: what is their origin, and are they a unique feature of Israelite architecture? The first question may be answered in two ways. The house type may be seen as a development based on Canaanite architecture, as indicated by examples from southern Canaan and in particular a Late Bronze Age II building at Tel Batash (Timna). Or it may be seen as a local development derived from the tent dwellings that preceded permanent settlement. Some would view the broadroom at the heart of the four-roomed house as analogous to the nomadic tent, which also has the broadroom form. This explanation, however, does not explain the origin of the pillars in the main part of the house; their closest parallel is in the Canaanite architecture of southern Israel (at Tel Batash and Lachish).

As for the ethnic attribution of these houses, three- and four-roomed houses are common in Israelite domestic architecture of the monarchy period, but in the Iron Age I (especially in the eleventh century), they do occur in non-Israelite regions, such as Philistia (Tel Sera' and Tell Qasile), Phoenicia (Tell Keisan), and Transjordan (Sahab, Khirbet Medeiniyeh, and elsewhere). Pillared structures should not, therefore, be seen as an original Israelite creation, as posited by S. Yeivin and Y. Shiloh, but as a style popular throughout the Land of Israel at this time.

It has been suggested by Albright, and later by Aharoni, that the invention of plastered cisterns to collect rainwater was one of the main factors enabling settlement in the hill country. Its importance may be doubted, for on the one hand, such cisterns are known to have been in use as early as the Middle Bronze Age (at Hazor), and on the other, they are abundant only at some sites (Ai, Raddanah), while at others there are none at all (Giloh, Shiloh). It seems rather that the use of plaster-lined cisterns was governed by the type of bedrock on which the settlements were founded. Where no cisterns were cut, the water supply depended on the accessibility of springs. In sites several kilometers distant from water sources, the water supply must have depended on long-distance transport and on storage in the large pithoi common in settlements.

At many sites silos, sometimes stone-lined, were sunk into the ground. Tens of such stone-lined silos were found at 'Izbet Sartah, where they were probably used to store grain. Finkelstein has estimated that their volume was far greater than that required by the inhabitants, and he has concluded that surplus grain was produced for trade with the hill country, where the economy depended chiefly on animal husbandry and the cultivation of the vine and olive. Many built silos were also found at Tell Beit Mirsim in the inner Shephelah, Tell en-Nasbeh (Mizpah), Shiloh, Dan (where most of the finds of the period come from such pits), Hazor, Tell Deir 'Alla in the valley of Succoth (where the Yabbok joins the Jordan River), Tel Zeror in the Sharon plain (where a large area consisted entirely of such pits, perhaps representing a pre–Sea Peoples settlement site), and Tel Beersheba (strata IX–VIII). An abundance of pits is thus one of the characteristic features of sites of the settlement period. The pits generally served as grain silos, but some are so large that they may be considerd pit dwellings (for example, at Beersheba IX).

Hill agriculture was practiced on steep wooded slopes. Clearing the slopes was no doubt one of the most difficult challenges faced by the new settlers (cf. Jos. 17:18, "The hill country shall be yours as well; true, it is forest land, but you will clear it and possess it to its farthest limits"). In addition, it seems that the settlers introduced agricultural terracing. L. Stager, who studied the terraces near Ai and Raddanah in the territory of Benjamin, has asserted that terraces were established as early as the Iron Age I. Agricultural terracing, practiced to this day, may thus go back to the period of Israelite settlement.

Monumental and public buildings are virtually unknown in settlement sites. At Giloh, the foundations of a structure measuring 11.7 meters square, massively built of large stones, were uncovered. They seem to belong to a tower, perhaps a fortified defense tower. Towers are occasionally mentioned in the stories of the Judges. At Shechem, the tower is also the city temple (Jud. 9:46–49); this may also be true of Penuel (Jud. 8:17) and Thebez (Jud. 9:50–52).

An exceptional structure was discovered at Har Adir, a mountain peak in the upper Galilee. It is a well-planned square fortress with a casemate wall, attesting to a developed architectural tradition. The finds in this fortress resemble those in other sites of the upper Galilee generally considered to be Israelite settlements. Yet at this site and at others, pottery vessels indicating a connection with Phoenician Tyre were recovered. Did this fortress belong to the network of Israelite settlements in the Galilee, or was it perhaps built by Phoenicians who wished to secure a military foothold in the mountains overlooking the territory of Tyre? This question cannot at present be resolved.

At Tel Masos in the northern Negev, a domestic quarter consisting of four-roomed houses was cleared. In the southern part of the site, however, unusual structures came to light: a structure 15 meters square with rooms ranged around all four sides of a pillared courtyard or central hall, another large structure with a tower, and, nearby, a house with a Canaanite plan consisting of rooms built around a central court. These buildings, as well as the finds from Tel Masos, indicate the special standing of the site during the eleventh century. It may be that people of Canaanite-Phoenician extraction came from the coastal zones to live here and pursue their commercial activities alongside the local population.

POTTERY. Pottery assemblages are particularly important to the study of the Israelite material culture, its divergence from the Canaanite or Philistine material cultures of the same period, the chronology of the sites, and the regional differences among the settlement zones.

The ceramic assemblages of the two major settlement areas—the central hills and the upper Galilee—have a limited number of components. Large storage jars (pithoi) are prominent, comprising a considerable portion of the ceramic finds. They are accompanied by cooking pots and a few other forms such as jugs, kraters, and bowls. These everyday utensils do not generally bear painted decoration, in contrast to those of the valley sites, where painted decoration is common throughout the Iron Age I. Applied, incised, or impressed decoration does occur, however. Though the Galilee and central hills assemblages are similar, they may be clearly distinguished. The large storage vessel, the pithos, is most indicative of the difference. In the central hills, from the fringes of the Jezreel valley to the Hebron hills, the so-called collared rim jar is most common. It is large (averaging about 1.2 meters high) and ovoid, with sloping shoulders, a tall narrow neck, a folded rim, and a prominent ridge (collar) around the base of the neck. It is so characteristic of the Israelite settlement sites that it has often been termed the settlement jar, which may be misleading, as it seems to have first appeared in the Canaanite culture of the Late Bronze Age (one certain example has been found at Aphek) and was probably passed on from the Canaanites to the Israelites, who made it the hallmark of their pottery assemblage. This type of pithos is also quite common in Transjordan, especially at the large site of Sahab, which does not appear to be Israelite. The presence of such pithoi at Megiddo (stratum VI), Tell Qasile, and Tell Keisan provides further evidence for their distribution outside the Israelite settlement sphere. In the Galilee, such jars have been found only at Dan and may reflect the special ties between the tribe of Dan and the central regions, from where it had migrated, according to biblical tradition.

In the Galilee, a different pithos type prevails. The Galilean pithos features a carinated body, a wide neck, and handles placed at the juncture of the body and neck. This

Fig. 8.21. Settlement jars from the central hills (height approx. 100 centimeters)

type developed out of a Canaan-ite pithos, known from the Late Bronze Age strata of Hazor, which was larger and had no handles. The Galilean pithos occurs in the Ga-lilean hill settlements and at Dan, together with other characteristic Iron Age I vessels, mainly cooking pots. In addition, a pithos typical of the site of Tyre appears in limited numbers at some Galilean sites, tes-tifying to relations with Phoenicia.

The settlements adjacent to cen-ters of Canaanite or Philistine cul-ture present a different ceramic repertoire. The eleventh-century as-semblage of 'Izbet Sartah, for exam-ple, is more variegated than that of the hill sites and closely resembles that of the contemporary Philistine strata at Tell Qasile. The pottery assemblage of Tel Masos and other northern Negev sites also differs from that of the hill settlements: the collared rim jar is not to be found, and rich and diverse pottery as-semblages appear, largely resembling those of the coastal sites, attesting to relations with the coast.

Fig. 8.22.   Northern settlement jars

Fig. 8.23.   Northern (A) and central (B) hills settlement jars

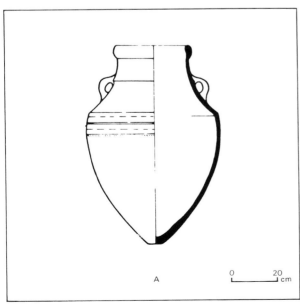

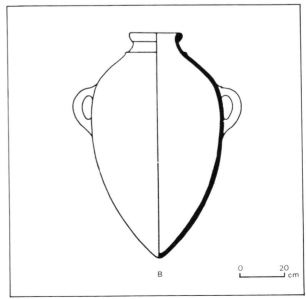

Most of the ceramic assemblages published from the settlement sites are from the eleventh century. Only at a few sites may earlier assemblages, dating to the twelfth century, be distinguished. These include the assemblages of Giloh, part of the Bethel and Ai assemblages, and the stratum III assemblages at 'Izbet Sartah and Tel Masos. The precise chronological sequence in the Galilee has yet to be established. Most of the vessels published from Hazor (strata XII–XI), Tel Harashim, and Tel Dan (stratum V) must be dated to the eleventh century.

In conclusion, the pottery assemblage of the hill settlements reflects a poor material culture that limits itself only to the most basic forms. The great pithoi were indispensable for the storage and preservation of water and food in the hill

zones. The range of forms indicates the influence of Canaanite traditions; it would appear that the settlers lacked an independent pottery-making tradition, and it is conceivable that at first they procured vessels from their Canaanite neighbors and went on to produce pottery in a similar tradition. Nevertheless, various Canaanite forms and an entire range of ceramic decoration find no expression in the Israelite repertoire.

CULT. The archaeological evidence for Israelite cult practices during the settlement period is meager but fascinating. At Shiloh—the main religious center of the Israelite tribes in this period, according to biblical tradition—only the edges of the site have been excavated, as the central part was badly damaged in the Byzantine period. Fragments of pottery cult vessels decorated with

animal heads provide only a hint of Israelite cult practice at Shiloh. Excavations also revealed the existence of a Late Bronze Age I cult center. Piles of refuse removed from this cult site were found, including offering bowls and many animal bones. There does not seem to have been an actual settlement at Shiloh in the Late Bronze Age, merely an isolated mountain cult place, which may have been frequented by semi-nomadic tribes (such as the 'Apiru). There is something to be said for the idea propounded by Finkelstein that the Israelite settlers chose Shiloh for their religious center because of the sacred tradition of the spot, originating in the previous period.

In the northern Samarian hills, an open cult place of the Iron Age I was discovered on a dominating ridge. Four settlement sites lie near the site, and it may well have served

Fig. 8.24.   Bronze bull figurine from Bull Site (height 12.4 centimeters)

them. However, no settlement was found on the ridge itself. The remains include a circular area twenty meters in diameter, encircled by a boundary wall built of large stones. The center of the site was empty (perhaps a sacred tree grew here), and at its edge was a standing stone with an adjacent paved area. This seems to be a cult stela (massebah) and the site itself a bamah, or open cult site, of the type described in the Bible as present "on every high hill and under every leafy tree." A unique find from this site is a bronze bull figurine, evidently the work of a highly skilled craftsman. It must have been the central cult object at the site and is reminiscent of the golden calves described in connection with the exodus and the shrines erected by Jeroboam at Bethel and Dan. The cult of the bull, as an attribute and companion of the god, seems to be rooted in Canaanite traditions, in which the bull accompanies the storm god Baal. Bronze bull figurines are present in Canaanite culture, at Hazor and Ugarit, and the figurine from the Samaria cult site may have been produced at a Canaanite center, perhaps at nearby Megiddo or Beth Shean, where a developed metal industry existed in the Iron Age I. At Hazor an installation interpreted by the excavators as a high place was found in stratum XI, dated to the eleventh century. Among the finds was a vessel containing a cache of bronze objects, including a figurine of a seated god in typical Canaanite style.

The most important and controversial discovery in the realm of cult is the site on Mount Ebal, described by its excavator, A. Zertal, as an Israelite cult center from the beginning of the settlement period. He found an elongated compound, four dunams in area, surrounded by a stone wall. At the peak of the site a round installation, two meters in

Fig. 8.25. Bronze figurine of seated deity, Hazor

diameter, was erected in the site's first phase; nearby lay a collared rim pithos. Later, a rectangular structure measuring about 8 × 9 meters was built on top of the circular installation. It had thick walls, preserved to a height of more than a meter, and no hint of an entrance. The interior was subdivided by two wall segments and completely filled with an intentional fill, which included much ash and animal remains. This structure was surrounded on three sides by a low wall, forming, the excavator believes, a walkway that allowed access to the upper part of the structure. Adjoining the struc-

ture on its southwestern flank were two courtyards, separated by a thick wall. In and around the courtyards, round stone installations were discovered, with pottery vessels inside them, usually one to an installation. Finds included two scarabs, dated to the thirteenth and twelfth centuries (one from the days of Ramesses II). In Zertal's opinion the rectangular structure is a monumental altar, none other than the altar attributed to Joshua by biblical tradition (Jos. 8:30–32). Zertal has reconstructed the form of the altar in accordance with biblical and Mishnaic (Tractate Midot) specifications. The walkway

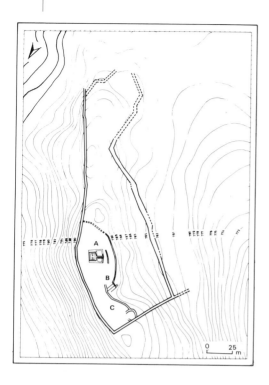

Fig. 8.26. Mount Ebal site, general plan

surrounding the structure is, he states, the sobeb, and the broad wall separating the two open courtyards is the ramp that led to the top of the altar. The bones are of ritually acceptable young animals (with the exception of some bones of fallow deer); they are butchered near the joints and are burned, as in the biblical descriptions of animal sacrifices. This is one of the central arguments in favor of the altar identification, though the bones were found in the fill of the structure; if they are bones of sacrificial victims, they must have been offered in the phase preceding the large structure or during its construction.

The identification of the structure as an altar, and particularly the relation of the finds to the biblical tradition, has provoked scholarly controversy. No remains of a similar altar have yet been encountered in the Land of Israel. The sacrificial altars that have been discovered (at sites of the monarchy period) are much smaller and have a solidly built interior. Some (including the present writer) would prefer to see the Mount Ebal structure as the foundations of a tower or fortified structure, such as the one at Giloh, and would identify the ramp as a dividing wall between the two courts. The biblical context is also fraught with difficulties, as the pertinent texts underwent Deuteronomistic redaction in late biblical times, and it is questionable whether they preserved a tradition rooted in the early settlement. The Mount Ebal site has thus become the focus of a fundamental controversy regarding the ability to interpret archaeological finds in relation to

Fig. 8.27. Proposed reconstruction of Mount Ebal altar

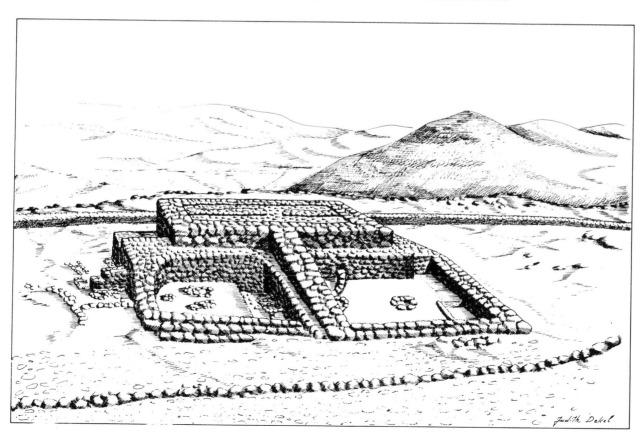

biblical texts. The excavator's arguments supporting his identification of the site as a cult place are persuasive, even if we do not accept them to the last detail. As this is the only Iron Age site encountered in Zertal's rigorous survey on Mount Ebal, it is likely that the biblical tradition refers to it. And the lack of remains from the period of the monarchy supports the antiquity of the biblical tradition in the books of Joshua and Deuteronomy (Deut. 11:29, 27:4–8). This conclusion alone may be of great importance in any attempt to evaluate the relation between archaeological finds and biblical traditions of this period.

ON THE ORIGINS OF ISRAELITE CULTURE

A fundamental issue in modern research concerns the ethnic identification of the inhabitants of the settlement sites in the different parts of the country. How can we know if the inhabitants of a given site were Israelites? The tendency of archaeologists to define certain phenomena or certain sites as Israelite may mislead historians. The ethnic makeup of the Land of Israel during the Iron Age I was quite complex. Some of the population groups who inhabited the country at this time eventually joined the Israelite tribal coalition and identified themselves as Israelites, but it is doubtful whether their Israelite identity was established at the start of the period, in the late thirteenth century and the twelfth century. Alien groups such as the Hiwwites, the Jebusites, and the Gibeonites are mentioned in the Bible as dwelling in the heartland of the Israelite settlement area in the central hills. Can the Israelite material culture be defined as a distinct and coherent expression of a definite ethnic body? There is no certain answer and little agreement on this issue. Thus, for example, the unique

character of Tel Masos has led some scholars to suggest that it was an Amalekite settlement (the biblical city of Amalek), while others interpret it as a settlement founded by Canaanites and Philistines from the coast. It has been suggested that Giloh was a Jebusite settlement related to Jerusalem and that the Bull Site in northern Samaria was a Canaanite cult place; similar suggestions have been made regarding the settlers in the upper Galilee and Transjordan. The foregoing survey has noted regional differences in the material cultures of the Galilee, the central hills, the Shephelah, and the northern Negev. The epithet "Israelite culture" as applied to the Iron Age I in these areas is based on the assumption that their inhabitants comprised the population reservoir that became, over an extended time, the coalition of Israelite tribes. Key sites that have been subject to archaeological study and that have an Israelite identity grounded in biblical sources—for example, Shiloh, Dan, and Beersheba—may serve as a starting point for the ethnic attribution of material culture. In the regions adjacent to each center, smaller sites with a comparable material culture may be identified as Israelite. Thus, a broad Israelite settlement pattern may be established, despite the marked differences between the cultural elements of each region.

Assuming that our ethnic identification of the inhabitants of the settlement sites is not mistaken, a number of conclusions may be reached regarding the socioeconomic structure of Israelite society in this period. These conclusions correspond to those based on the book of Judges. It was a sedentarizing society, composed of farmers and herders who inhabited small villages of a few dozen persons each; an egalitarian society, concerned chiefly with its own subsistence in

the difficult conditions of the hill country and desert fringes. There is no evidence for town life among these settlers. Their sedentarization led to a new settlement pattern, diverging from that of the Late Bronze Age, when most of the sedentary population was concentrated in the cities.

The settlers had no traditions of their own in the realms of architecture, pottery, crafts, and art. These were adopted from their Canaanite neighbors, who continued to inhabit various parts of the country. Later, when the manufacture of such objects began in the settlement regions themselves, the Canaanite tradition continued to make itself felt in the forms of the tools and vessels. But in the main, Israelite material culture is clearly distinct from that of the Canaanites in its socioeconomic system and in the way of life of those who created it. There are, of course, some exceptions, such as Tel Masos, where there seems to have been a symbiosis between local tribesmen (who later joined the Israelite tribal coalition) and foreigners of a coastal origin, who were interested in controlling the trade route along Nahal Beersheba. The result is manifest in the unique material culture of this site.

The question of the origins of the people of Israel has been discussed at length in modern scholarly literature. Can archaeology contribute significantly to this issue or at least confirm or refute a given historical hypothesis? The answer is decidedly vague; the archaeological record can be used in different ways to substantiate a given hypothesis. Indeed, the archaeological finds are quite important, for (aside from the Marneptah stela of the late thirteenth century, which mentions a victory over Israel) we have no direct extrabiblical sources dating to the formative period of the Israelites. But how can the archaeological evidence be interpreted within a general approach to the beginnings of Israel? There is nothing in the archaeological record to suggest that the settlers came from outside the Land of Israel, as stated in the biblical tradition. The material culture of the settlers appears to have developed from a pastoralist stage, when the people pursued a seminomadic way of life within a tribal system. Though archaeologists have not succeeded in uncovering remains of this initial stage, it seems to be reflected in the site plan of the settlements of the later sedentary stage.

Finkelstein has recently attempted to reconstruct Israelite prehistory in the central hill country in light of archaeology. He has observed a similar network of settlements in the hill country during the Middle Bronze Age, which disappeared in the Late Bronze Age, apparently in the context of a general decline in settlement throughout the country. He suggests that the sedentary population of the hill country adopted a pastoral way of life, which continued until circumstances changed at the beginning of the Iron Age, when it reestablished sedentary settlements. Such an explanation could be compatible with the popular view that has many of the Israelites originating in an indigenous, nonsedentary Late Bronze Age population. This population was called Shasu by the Egyptians and is portrayed in Egyptian art. The 'Apiru too, who appear in second-millennium literary sources, especially as inhabitants of the Canaanite hill country, can be included in this category. Such a seminomadic population could have formed the source for groups that later coalesced as the Israelite tribes. Yet these hypotheses do not provide an origin for the nucleus that developed the religion of Israel and maintained the traditions about the servitude in

Egypt and the role of Moses and the revelation at Sinai in the history of the nation. It seems that archaeology, in its present state, can contribute nothing to the resolution of that question.

Canaanite Culture and the Rise of Phoenician Culture

Canaanite culture survived into the twelfth century at major northern valley sites such as Megiddo (stratum VIIA) and Beth Shean (stratum VI). Also, the material culture of the Sea Peoples, particularly the Philistines, assimilated many elements of the Canaanite cultural heritage, and it may even be assumed that many Canaanites continued to inhabit the coastal strip and southern plains under the domination of the Sea Peoples. Canaanite culture continued to develop and was transformed into a new entity, the Phoenician culture, largely in the valley of Accho and on the Phoenician coast, but the sites of the Jezreel and Beth Shean valleys play a significant part.

Both Megiddo and Beth Shean underwent a severe crisis in the twelfth century, related apparently to the end of Egyptian rule in Canaan. Stratum VIIA at Megiddo and stratum VI at Beth Shean were both destroyed, apparently in mid century. At Beth Shean, the results of the American excavations and of later probes (by Yadin and Geva) indicate that the twelfth-century town (stratum VI), with its Egyptian finds, was destroyed in a conflagration and replaced by a poor pit-and-hovel settlement. In the second half of the eleventh century, a new, densely built town was established (lower stratum V, in the numbering of the American expedition). The cultic center of this town was uncovered, with two temples, the Northern Temple and the Southern Temple. Both were poorly pre-

served, but the principles of their design may be distinguished.

The Northern Temple consisted of one hall with a corner entrance. Four columns supported the roof. Nothing remains of the internal installations, but an Egyptian stela dedicated to the goddess Anathit (Anat), fragments of another stela, a statue, and fragments of cult vessels were found on its floors (all of lower stratum V). The temple was fronted by a large court, in which Egyptian monuments originating in earlier strata were placed, among them a statue of Ramesses III and stelae of Ramesses II and Seti I, which were set in niches specially prepared for them.

The Southern Temple, connected to the Northern Temple by a narrow corridor, consisted of a large long-room divided by two rows of columns into a narrow nave and two aisles; two rows of rooms flanked the main hall. The entrance was through a wide doorway set in the western facade of the hall. No interior details of the cella have been preserved. This design resembles no known temple plan, and its identification as a temple rests on the many cult objects found within it, especially in the small rooms north of the main hall. Among them were cultic pottery stands decorated with human figures and snakes molded or painted in geometric patterns. The temples and the town flourished, we believe, in the eleventh century, though the town may have survived into the tenth century.

At Megiddo, the destruction of stratum VIIA brought on a grave crisis in the history of the town. The next phase consisted of a poor settlement distinguished only in parts of the mound (stratum VIB), comparable to the pit-and-hovel phase at Beth Shean. Like Beth Shean, the town of Megiddo was soon rebuilt on a large scale (stratum VIA, eleventh century), with palaces and public buildings, mainly in the gate area. This town fell victim to a terrible conflagration at the beginning of the tenth century, perhaps in the course of a conquest at the hands of David. In the destruction layer, a rich assemblage of pottery and many other objects was discovered, including metal implements, jewelry, art objects, and more. The pottery clearly represents the Canaanite tradition, with a touch of Philistine or pseudo-Philistine ware, indicating the presence of Sea Peoples. Cypriot imports also appear, testifying to the renewal of trade relations with that island, as do Phoenician vessels, brought from the coast.

At Tell Abu Hawam near the mouth of Nahal Qishon, a small, prosperous town (stratum IV) seems to have served as a convenient port for the towns of the Jezreel valley. Most interesting is Tell Keisan, in the center of the Accho valley. Here, evidence has been found of an urban culture that flourished throughout the Iron Age I. Typical pillared houses were discovered along the edges of the mound, with a rich pottery assemblage reflecting the emergence of a distinct Phoenician style. At the important Phoenician port of Akhziv, one of the few excavated on the Phoenician coast, tombs of the eleventh century have come to light, containing some of the earliest Phoenician assemblages yet discovered. These are cist tombs, lined with drafted stones. The burial gifts consist mainly of pottery flasks decorated with red and black concentric circles, in typical Phoenician fashion, and bronze weapons, including double axes and elongated spearheads of a type common in the eastern Mediterranean in the late second millennium.

The finds at Megiddo, Tel Abu Hawam, Tell Keisan, and Akhziv indicate the emergence of a distinctive Phoenician material culture,

which was to develop further in the Iron Age II. This culture was the direct descendant of the Canaanite culture yet developed its own distinctive style in many realms.

Transjordan

Our knowledge of the material culture of Transjordan in the Iron Age I comes from a small number of surveys and excavations. Two major sites of the Jordan valley have been excavated: Tell es-Sa'idiyeh (tentatively identified with biblical Zaphon) and Tell Deir 'Alla, east of the Damiyah bridge (identified by some as Succoth). At Tell es-Sa'idiyeh, tombs of the early twelfth century have been excavated, containing a rich assemblage of pottery, ivories, and metal objects, including a wine set and a tripod, both of bronze. These finds testify to a flourishing Canaanite culture during the Late Bronze–Iron Age I transition, similar to that of contemporary sites in the Beth Shean valley. At the more southerly site of Deir 'Alla, however, events seem to have taken a different course. The cultic center of the Late Bronze Age was burned about the year 1200 B.C.E. On its ruins, the remains of a seminomadic settlement consist chiefly of grain pits. This phenomenon resembles that of Israelite settlement west of the Jordan and may represent Israelite settlement at Deir 'Alla in the twelfth century. Later in the Iron Age I, a fortified settlement was established at the site, with domestic structures showing several phases of repair. In the opinion of the excavator, H. J. Franken, this was a non-Israelite settlement with an Aramean-influenced material culture, but this assertion requires further proof.

Following his pioneering archaeological survey of parts of the Transjordanian plateau in the thirties, N. Glueck concluded that the re-

gion was devoid of settlement during much of the Middle and Late Bronze ages, until in the thirteenth century a series of new settlements was established, which must be related to the arrival of new peoples in Transjordan, the Ammonites, Moabites, Edomites, and Israelites. More recent surveys and studies have revised the picture. It has become clear that there was no complete gap in occupation in Transjordan and that in the northern and central zones there were quite a few settled mounds. Also, it was established that the small Iron Age I sites resembling Israelite settlements west of the Jordan are chiefly in the Gilead, north of the Yabbok, and that their number declines to the south. Settlements of this type have been discovered in the central part of the Transjordanian plateau. In the Nahal Zered (Wadi Hasa) survey in northern Edom, two such settlements were found, but no sites of this period are known from central or southern Edom, and there is no significant archaeological evidence of an Edomite kingdom in Iron Age I. In Moab, some sherds and flimsy architectural remains have been discovered at major sites such as Heshbon and Dibon. The two sites known as Khirbet Medeiniyeh, on opposite banks of the Arnon River, provide the best example of Iron Age I settlement in Moab. Khirbet Medeiniyeh South is a fortified site on a prominent ridge. Houses excavated there had monolithic pillars similar to structures of this period in the Land of Israel.

The most important site in the land of Ammon is Sahab, twelve kilometers east of Amman (excavated by M. Ibrahim). It is a large, 250-dunam site with Late Bronze Age occupation. Iron Age I remains appeared in the different excavation sites on the mound, suggesting that it was occupied in its entirety in this period as well. Iron Age I phases were identified in which the use of monolithic pillars was prevalent. Coffins found in the cemetery were made of pairs of collared rim pithoi broken off at the neck. A wealth of burial gifts was found in the tombs, including iron jewelry. Collared rim pithoi were discovered in houses as well, some of them bearing seal impressions. The site probably represents the Ammonite material culture of the Iron Age I.

In the Gilead survey, S. Mittman recorded tens of small Iron Age I settlements, resembling the parallel phenomenon in the hills of Ephraim and Mannasseh. This may be taken as an expression of the settlement of the half-tribe of Mannasseh in the Gilead, after a pattern similar to that found west of the Jordan.

Development of Metallurgy

The term "Iron Age" reflects the transition from bronze to iron as the dominant metal used in the production of tools and weapons. The transition was gradual, completed only in the tenth century. In the Iron Age I, bronze was still the chief metal, used for most of the tools, weapons, vessels, and art objects. Workshops in which bronze was cast have been discovered at Tel Dan, Tel Harashim in the upper Galilee, Tell Deir 'Alla, Tell Qasile, Beth Shemesh, Tel Mor, and Tel Masos. The raw material must have come either from Cyprus or the Timna valley or from discarded bronze objects. The bronze was cast in clay crucibles, and clay-tipped bellows were used to fan the flames. Both the crucibles and the clay tips (tuyeres) have been found in excavations. The bronze implements of this period were very much in the Canaanite tradition. Axes, arrowheads, and javelin heads retained their Late Bronze Age forms. At Megiddo, Beth Shean, and Tell es-Sa'idiyeh, magnificent wine sets

were found, consisting of a bowl, jug, and strainer made of bronze, in the Canaanite style. The latest are of the eleventh century. Other bronze objects indicate Aegean and Cypriot influence, probably transmitted via the Sea Peoples who migrated to Canaan. They include weapons found at Megiddo, Tell Qasile, Tel Zeror, and Akhziv (double axes, hammer axes, long socketed javelin heads) and a handled bronze bowl from a tomb at Tell es-Sa'idiyeh. A tripod from Tell es-Sa'idiyeh and a similar object from Megiddo are more typical of Iron Age I Cyprus; they too may indicate relations with that island. Bronze figurines, such as the seated god from Hazor (stratum XI) and the bull from the Samarian hills, testify to the survival of the tradition of cast bronze figurines, widely practiced throughout the Middle and Late Bronze ages, and even to the development of this tradition.

While bronze continued to predominate, the twelfth century marked the beginning of the use of iron. Iron was used in a limited way in the Bronze Age, but its source was mostly meteoritic, and it was rarely cast. Only in the twelfth and eleventh centuries do iron weapons begin to appear in the ancient world, without any clear source of the new technology. It was once thought that the Hittites monopolized iron production in the Late Bronze Age and that following the collapse of their empire, the technology spread throughout the ancient world, mainly in the wake of the Sea Peoples' migrations. But recent studies have cast doubt on that explanation. The assumption that the Philistines introduced iron into the Land of Israel in the twelfth century is supported by the discovery of the earliest iron implements in Philistine contexts (a sword from Tell el-Far'ah, a knife from Tell Qasile, and jewelry). The passage in

I Samuel 13:19–22 regarding the Philistine monopoly of metalworking makes no note of the kind of metal involved. In the current state of research, the source of iron technology cannot be determined, but it is clear that in the Iron Age I, iron was a rare and valuable metal, illustrated by its use in jewelry and by its limited use in knives and weapons. Only in the eleventh century do iron tools appear, in very limited numbers. A large iron pickaxe found in the fortress of Har Adir is one of the earliest known carburized and quenched iron implements.

The transition from bronze to iron may have been motivated by a shortage of tin, required for producing bronze. Tin was available to the ancient Near East only by way of an extensive trade network, the nearest known source being Afghanistan. The collapse of the Late Bronze Age political systems may have cut off that supply, resulting in the replacement of bronze with iron, which could be produced from readily available ore. The discovery of carburization and quenching led to increased use of iron, making it the dominant metal after the eleventh century.

Art

The twelfth and eleventh centuries are often considered a dark age in the history of the ancient world, a time of decline in the traditional Late Bronze Age centers of culture in Egypt, the Hittite Empire, and Mycenae. These cultures had produced a wealth of art objects and important schools of art. In Late Bronze Age Syria and Canaan, Canaanite art flourished, best known today in miniature works from the realm of seal-carving, ivory-carving, and figurines. There are indications that this art survived the end of the Late Bronze Age, but the finds are few. The Megiddo ivories were found in the palace of stratum VIIA, which was destroyed in the mid twelfth century. From stratum VI of the eleventh century comes a beautiful ivory pyxis, which insofar as it was a product of the stratum in which it was found, and not of the previous period, testifies to the continuing Canaanite tradition of ivory-carving. Other ivory objects from this period indicate that ivory workshops continued to function throughout the Iron Age I. The cult objects from Beth Shean, Megiddo, and Tell Qasile attest to diverse artistic production in the Iron Age I. Many evidence a degree of originality and freedom from the restraints of Late Bronze Age tradition, reflecting a highly creative imagination. The Sea Peoples who settled in Canaan may have provided the impulse for continued artistic productivity, combining their creativity with the traditions preserved by the Canaanite population of the valleys and the coast.

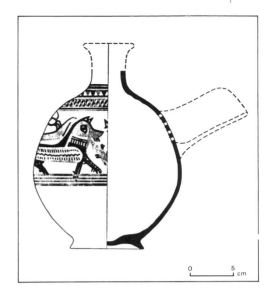

Writing and Literacy

The alphabetic script, introduced in Canaan in the Late Bronze Age, continued to develop in the Iron Age I. However, as in the previous period, few inscriptions have been preserved. The most important are the 'Izbet Sartah ostracon, an incised ostracon from Kubur el Walaydah, a group of incised arrowheads from el-Khadr (south of Bethlehem), an inscribed seal from the area of Ekron, and inscribed jar handles from hill settlements (Khirbet Raddanah, Malha). These in-

Fig. 8.28. Orpheus jug from Megiddo: lyre player accompanied by animals

scriptions exhibit a development in the forms of the letters and testify to the literacy of the Israelite settlers. Most of the inscriptions come from the Israelite settlement areas in the central hill country. The 'Izbet Sartah ostracon includes an abecedary: one line consists of the letters of the alphabet, from *aleph* to *taw,* with some omissions and deviations from the standard order. Other lines consist of meaningless combinations of letters. The inscription from Kubur el Walaydah, in southern Philistia, is incised on a bowl fragment. Its importance lies in its being the only alphabetic inscription yet found in Philistia. It appears to be a dedication (perhaps of a temple offering) in which two Canaanite names are mentioned. These two inscriptions may be attributed to the twelfth century. The eleventh century arrowheads from el-Khadr are part of a chance find of ten arrowheads, four of which bore the alphabetic dedication *hz 'bd lb't,* "the arrow of the servant of lb't" (in some cases, one or more letters are missing). A fifth arrowhead was inscribed *'bd lb't* on one side and *bn 'nt* on the other. "Ben Anath" is well attested among the Canaanite names known from Ugarit and Egypt and is the patronymic of one of the Israelite

heroes from the times of the Judges, Shamgar, son of Anath, who slew six hundred Philistines with an ox-goad (Ju. 3:31). The name *'bd lb't* is recorded in a list of bowmen from Ugarit. A class of professional bowmen termed *lb'm* may have existed in the period before David ascended the throne, as suggested in the words attributed to David in Psalm 57 (5): "I lie down among man-eating lions (*lb'm*) whose teeth are spears and arrows, whose tongue is a sharp sword." The proximity of the findspot of these arrows to Bethlehem, David's birthplace, may hint at a connection between this group of arrowheads and David's activity in the region. A carved seal of the Iron Age I found near Ekron in Philistia carries the name *l'b'* in alphabetic script. This seal, like the inscription from Kubur el Walaydah, suggests that the Philistines were also acquainted with the alphabetic script at this time, in addition to their distinctive linear script, though the alphabetic inscriptions from Philistia may have originated with the Canaanite inhabitants of the region.

The few inscriptions also reveal that the direction of writing was not yet fixed. The inscriptions run left to right, right to left, and vertically.

Fig. 8.29. 'Izbet Sartah inscription

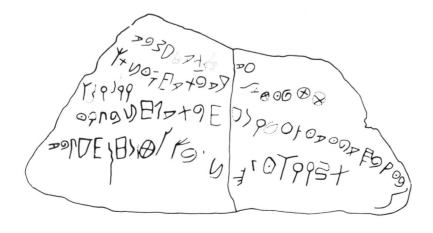

The letter forms are still close to those of the Late Bronze Age proto-Canaanite inscriptions, though a development is discernible, on the way to the crystallization of the script in the Iron Age II.

Trade Relations

One of the principal differences between the Iron Age I and the preceding period is the absence of the extensive international trade, particularly with Cyprus and the Aegean. Finds from the Iron Age I reflect isolation and interruption of international relations. Though Cypriot and Aegean traditions survived in Philistia, no evidence of direct trade with these regions has been discovered. In the eleventh century, trade was renewed on a limited scale, mostly with Phoenicia and to some extent with Cyprus. Internal trade may also be discerned: Phoenician vessels of a class termed bichrome have been found at Megiddo, Tell Qasile, Philistia, and even in the northern Negev (at Tel Masos). This type of vessel has also been found in lower Egypt, testifying to the widespread trade relations of Phoenicia at this time. The limited distribution of Philistine ware in northern Israel as well as in the northern Negev (Beersheba and Tel Masos) may indicate trade between those regions and Philistia. At Tel Masos, several sherds of Midianite ware, whose main distribution area lies in the Hejaz and the Timna valley, were discovered, perhaps an indication of the importance of Tel Masos as a station on the trade route between the north and the Aravah, where copper mines were still being worked. The Philistines may have played a role in this traffic.

In the second half of the eleventh century, tangible expression of relations with Cyprus is provided by the reappearance of Cypriot imports, which occur in small numbers at sites such as Megiddo and Tell Qasile. Metal objects suggest, however, that relations with Cyprus may have been maintained throughout the Iron Age I without being reflected in the importation of pottery.

Transition to the Monarchy

The Iron Age I is in some ways a prologue to the monarchy and in other ways an epilogue to the Canaanite period. On the one hand, the new settlement arrays are related to the new ethnic and political makeup of the country; on the other hand, many elements of Canaanite culture survived until the end of the eleventh century.

Canaanite traditions disappear almost entirely at the start of the tenth century. In Philistia, the use of decorated Philistine pottery ceases, along with other forms and decorations typical of the Iron Age I in this region. Some sites were destroyed violently, such as Tell Qasile. Others, such as Ashdod, prospered and expanded during the tenth century. The northern valleys also show signs of a crisis; stratum VIA at Megiddo, the site that best represents the survival of Canaanite traditions into the eleventh century, was desolated. In the following phase (stratum VB), which should be dated to the reign of David, Megiddo would take on a completely new character, reflecting the beginning of Israelite settlement. The settlements of the hill country also experienced a crisis at the end of the Iron Age I, a result of the Philistine wars and the transition to the monarchy. The settlement at Shiloh was violently destroyed in the mid eleventh century and thereafter abandoned. Many other settlement sites were abandoned, while others developed into fortified towns in the Iron Age II—Tell el-Far'ah North (Tirzah), Tell en-Nasbeh, Mizpah, Tell Beit Mirsim, and others. The transition to the monarchy, therefore, caused a change in the Israelite settlement pattern in the hill country. In the northern Negev, too, changes were expressed in the destruction of the important center at Tel Masos and in the foundation of new settlements in Beersheba, Arad, and the Negev Highlands, under the United Monarchy.

9

The Iron Age II–III

GABRIEL BARKAY

The first half of the first millennium B.C.E. is a historical era in the fullest sense of the word. For earlier periods, beginning with the Middle Bronze Age, the Bible provides a mere backdrop; extrabiblical sources and archaeology must be consulted to determine the historical sequence. For the Iron Age II–III, however, the Bible constitutes a principal historical source. In addition to the explicitly historical writings (the books of Samuel, Kings, and Chronicles), the information in the Pentateuch and the prophetic scriptures fills out the picture of everyday life, law, beliefs and creeds, cult and spiritual life. The archaeology of the Iron Age II in the Land of Israel is historical archaeology, and the approach of the archaeologist must be to integrate archaeological finds with the written sources, of which the Bible is the most important.

Historical archaeology thus no longer deals with anonymous peoples and unnamed cultures; the language, traditions, religion, literary and artistic creations, and historical evolution of the Israelites and, to a lesser extent, of their neighbors are well known. The historical approach differs from the anthropological approach employed in the study of the prehistoric periods, the Bronze Age,

and the Iron Age I. The term "biblical archaeology," used by many scholars to describe the discipline of the archaeology of the Land of Israel and neighboring lands in early times, is most appropriate when confined to the Iron Age II–III.

THE HISTORICAL AND EPIGRAPHIC SOURCES

The main historical source for the study of the Israelite monarchy, the Bible, is supplemented by external sources (Egyptian, Assyrian, and Babylonian) as well as by epigraphic records (inscriptions and documents discovered in Transjordan and the Land of Israel). The corpus of written records found in excavations in the Land of Israel is still small, and most of the inscriptions are of limited historical value. No royal monumental inscriptions of the type found in Egypt and Assyria have yet come to light, nor has a royal stela like that of Mesha, King of Moab. Monumental building inscriptions too are rare in the Land of Israel and serve little more than to hold out a promise of more significant finds in the future. Likewise, no royal archives have been found. The materials most often used for the documents of Iron Age Israel were scrolls of parchment and sheets of papyrus, but of the hundreds of ancient documents surviving in the arid desert zones of the Land of Israel, only one dating to the Iron Age has been discovered, a fragment of a letter with a list of names.

In addition to the lapidary (stone-carved) inscriptions, there is a growing corpus of ostraca (pot sherds inscribed with ink). The content of the ostraca is chiefly administrative, and they include receipts, invoices, name lists, and drafts of letters. Groups of ostraca have been found at Samaria (eighth century), Lachish, and Arad (early sixth century). Isolated ostraca have appeared at many other sites: Mezad Hashavyahu, Kadesh Barnea, Tel Beersheba, Tel 'Ira, Horvat 'Uza, Jerusalem, and elsewhere.

Other inscribed artifacts include hundreds of seal stones, most of them originating in the antiquities market rather than in systematic excavations, seal impressions found on jar handles and on bullae (small lumps of clay used to seal papyrus documents), owners' inscriptions on ceramic vessels, inscribed weights, and other fragmentary inscriptions. Texts of a religious character, inscribed on pottery and stone vessels as well as on plaster, have been uncovered at the site of Kuntillat 'Ajrud (Horvat Teman) in eastern Sinai and on plastered walls at the Jordan valley site of Deir 'Alla. The latest findings of a religious character are two inscribed, rolled, silver plaques that served as amulets, of seventh century. They were uncovered in the excavations of Ketef Hinnom in Jerusalem, and they contain a formula resembling that of the priestly blessing recorded in the scripture (Num. 6:24–26).

In addition to Hebrew inscriptions, excavations have revealed isolated fragments of Assyrian texts, including fragments of royal stelae found at Ashdod, Samaria, and Ben

Shemen and two inscribed clay tablets found at Gezer. A fragment of an Egyptian stela bearing the name of King Shishak was found in the ruins of the Solomonic city at Megiddo.

The written documents supplement the biblical evidence in certain details. They provide information on the onomasticon (the corpus of personal names), on the royal administration and economy, on tra-

Map 9.1. Iron Age II–III sites

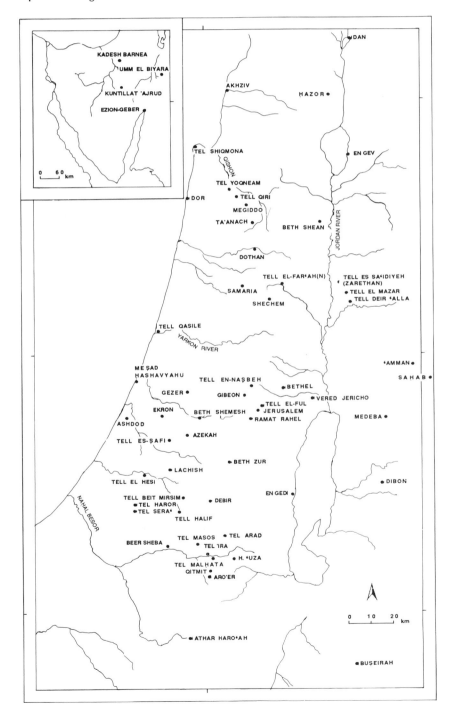

ditions and on cult. They also provide evidence for the broad extent of literacy in the Iron Age II–III. The many inscriptions also provide evidence for the development of the Hebrew script and enable the growth of a distinct field of study: paleography, the study of the evolution of ancient scripts.

GENERAL CHARACTER OF THE IRON AGE II–III

As the historical events of the Iron Age II–III are fairly well known, their sequence has great relevance to the study of the material remains. In earlier periods the political situation in all parts of the country was more or less the same, and differences between regions were a function of geographic location. But in the Iron Age II–III, the Land of Israel takes on cultural-territorial significance. Different parts of the country were under the control of different administrations and kingdoms, allowing varying cultural facies to develop in various parts of the country, and prominent regional differences appeared among the cultures of the Kingdom of Israel, the Kingdom of Judah, Philistia, and the Transjordanian kingdoms.

The Iron Age II–III in the Land of Israel may be characterized as an urban period, reflected in the large number of urban settlements, the rise in the standard of living, the distribution of luxury goods outside the royal palaces, and the view of society obtained from the archaeological and the biblical record. A vast body of information concerning this urban culture comes from excavations in capital cities, royal cities, regional centers, secondary centers, rural towns, villages, fortresses, and isolated farms. In addition to the excavations, data are obtained from archaeological surveys and chance finds. The horizontal exposure in many sites is greater than that of earlier periods, and for the first time there are even complete town plans. The finds at Tel Beersheba, Tel en-Nasbeh, Tell Beit Mirsim, Beth Shemesh, Megiddo, Samaria, and other sites give a fairly full picture of urban planning concepts.

The absolute chronology of the period is based on synchronisms between references in the Bible and other sources to the construction and destruction of cities and excavations of foundation phases and destruction layers at these cities. Outstanding examples include the destruction levels ascribed to the campaign of Shishak, king of Egypt, in 925 B.C.E., at Megiddo and elsewhere; the foundation of Samaria by King Omri of Israel (I Kings 16:24) in 876 B.C.E.; the rebuilding of Hazor by Solomon (I Kings 9:15) around the year 950 B.C.E.; and the destructions of strata III and II at Lachish, which mark the campaigns of Sennacherib of Assyria in 701 B.C.E. and of Nebuchadnezzar of Babylon in 586 B.C.E. They provide the principal landmarks in the archaeological chronology of the Iron Age II–III.

In the past, Iron Age II–III culture was often viewed as a decline compared with the Late Bronze Age, but recent finds reveal an inventive material culture that valued efficiency and functionalism over aesthetics. In the manufacture of pottery many innovations of form and technique are evident. The wealth of slips and burnishes is conspicuous. The inventiveness of the period is also reflected in the realms of architecture and fortification, and there is a relative lack of continuity with earlier cultures. A gradual transition may be observed during the Iron Age I–II from the Canaanite culture of the Late Bronze Age to a new and original culture.

Diverse international contacts are prominent in the Iron Age II. Techniques of fortification and weaponry found in the Land of Israel were known during this period in other parts of the Near East. Techniques of water supply and the hydro-geological knowledge reflected in the water systems of the Land of Israel find identical expression in far-flung kingdoms such as Media, Assyria, Phrygia, and Urartu. Ivories of the type found in the Land of Israel have come to light in Syria, Cyprus, and Assyria. Burial caves hewn in Jerusalem in this period exhibit the influence of monuments of distant lands—Asia Minor, Egypt, and even Etruria, in central Italy. All this suggests the existence of a cultural common market, employing the Phoenicians as the principal agents of diffusion through a maritime trade that ranged as far as the north African coast, the islands of the western Mediterranean, and the Iberian peninsula.

The Iron Age II–III is also characterized by gradual population growth and a considerable increase in settlement size. Some cities (Samaria, Jerusalem, and the Philistine centers at Ashdod and Ekron) attain a size of dozens of hectares. Estimates of the total population of the country must await future studies.

TERMINOLOGY AND CHRONOLOGY

Some 460 years passed between the establishment of the monarchy by David and the conquest of the Land of Israel by the Persians. This period is called the Iron Age II–III, or the Late Israelite period. The former term is preferred here, since the Israelites were not the sole ethnic entity in the land, and the term "Iron Age" encompasses all the regions and cultural divisions of the Land of Israel during the period in question. Also, although the use of iron in functional artifacts began in the Late Bronze Age, iron technology became dominant only in the Iron Age II.

The general framework of the period and its subdivisions, as proposed by different scholars, have traditionally been based on historical data, on political developments and events, rather than on the evolution of the material culture. This is most evident in the date commonly used to mark the end of the period, 586 B.C.E., the year of the destruction of the First Temple, of Jerusalem, and of the Kingdom of Judah. However, the material culture in the Land of Israel after this date was largely the same as that found before the destruction; it did not change significantly until some time later, toward the end of the sixth century. With the proliferation of excavations, the weight of purely archaeological considerations has increased, and new subdivisions, not based exclusively on historical considerations, have been proposed. Following the excavations at Hazor (1955–58), Aharoni and Amiran proposed the following scheme:

Iron Age II—1000–840 (800) B.C.E.

Iron Age III—840–586 B.C.E.

Later on, when the Encyclopedia of Archaeological Excavations in the Holy Land (Hebrew version) was published (1970), three subdivisions of the Iron Age II were proposed:

Iron Age IIa—1000–900 B.C.E.
Iron Age IIb—900–800 B.C.E.
Iron Age IIc—800–586 B.C.E.

The present chapter employs a scheme based more on the analysis of the material culture than on historical considerations:

Iron Age IIa—tenth–ninth centuries B.C.E.
Iron Age IIb—eighth century B.C.E.
Iron Age IIIa—seventh–early sixth centuries B.C.E.
Iron Age IIIb—sixth century B.C.E. (586 to the late sixth century.

The Iron Age IIa

The tenth century is the period of the United Monarchy; the reigns of David and Solomon together account for three fourths of the century. It is considered a high point in Israelite history, a period of economic and cultural prosperity, of peace, fondly remembered in later times. David and Solomon established a small empire (I Kings 5:1) and diverse foreign contacts with rulers and states that recognized the power of the Israelite kingdom. The focus of social identity was transferred from the family or tribe to the nation and state, and the fabric of Israelite independence—national, political, religious, and cultural—was established. The empire of David and Solomon emerged in the wake of the decline of the great powers and the far-reaching changes across the Near Eastern expanse. The ancient Near East passed from the era of the Bronze Age empires to the era of national states, the Aramean states of southern and central Syria, the national states of Transjordan, and the neo-Hittite states of North Syria and eastern Anatolia. This was also the time of the efflorescence of the Phoenician states on the Syro-Lebanese littoral. In this setting, the Israelite kingdom came into being under David, in the early tenth century.

The main cultural dividing line between the Iron I and Iron II periods is no earlier than the tenth century, though historically, the institution of kingship in Israel dates back to the days of Saul, in the eleventh century. The most prominent features of the Israelite monarchy—the extensive royal construction works, the cities, palaces, fortifications, and use of ashlar masonry—did not appear until the tenth century.

In scholarly discussions, the tenth century is often considered an independent phase within the Iron Age II, set apart from the ninth century by the political crises engendered by the division of the kingdom (928 B.C.E.) and the military campaign of Shishak (925 B.C.E.). The distinction is based mainly on historical considerations, and the biblical record emphasizes the difference between the days of the United Monarchy and the period of the divided kingdoms of Israel and Judah. The material culture, however, exhibits considerable continuity between the two centuries. The royal construction works of Jeroboam I at the northern site of Dan at the end of the tenth century and the building operations of the Omrids at Samaria and in other towns preserve the features of Solomonic construction. The close political, economic, and cultural relations between Solomon and the Phoenicians were maintained by the dynasty of Omri. Neither is there evidence of a cultural break between the centuries in the realm of ceramics. This discussion therefore treats the tenth and ninth centuries as a unit.

From the end of the ninth century onward separate and independent material cultures crystallize in Israel and Judah. It becomes possible to distinguish between a northern culture and southern culture, especially in the ceramic typology. The end of the Iron Age IIa is fixed at this point, where distinctive cultural transitions may be observed.

The most prominent feature of the Iron Age IIa is the royal architecture. The Israelites had no previous tradition of city planning and urbanism or experience in the construction of temples, palaces, fortifications, or other monumental structures. A seminomadic people at the time of their first settlement, they remained, through the period of the Judges, a tribal society with no call for urban construction or monumental architecture. The tenth century marks the beginning of the intensive drive toward urbanization, which lasted throughout the Iron Age.

In the absence of an independent tradition, the royal architecture and fortifications of the Iron Age IIa are characterized by foreign inspiration and influence. The foreign contacts expressed in the material culture of the tenth century reflect the far-flung international contacts of Solomon, recorded in the biblical account, which no doubt influenced the architecture and trappings of the royal court. These foreign influences are evident in the general concepts of urban planning, in individual building plans, and in construction techniques. Many details of Solomonic architecture reveal the influence of the neo-Hittite culture of northern Syria, the Canaanite-Phoenician culture of the Lebanese coast,

and probably Egyptian culture as well.

Urban and monumental construction began in the early tenth century B.C.E., during the reign of David (II Samuel 5:9, 11; 7:2), and was pursued with greater energy during the reign of Solomon (see I Kings 9:15). The Bible describes in detail the building operations in Jerusalem, as well as cities and structures built in other parts of the country. The description of the construction in Jerusalem appears quite reliable in some parts, while tending toward exaggeration and idealization in others (I Kings 10:27). We are also told of the construction of Hazor, Megiddo, Gezer, and other cities, many built to accommodate the chariotry and cavalry corps that Solomon established. Solomon has thus become in Israelite tradition the prototype of the builder-king. The trend toward centralization and state

initiative in building operations continued after the division of the kingdom and characterized the Iron Age II–III as a whole.

The biblical accounts of the magnificent Solomonic edifices, of his throne, and of the furnishings and trappings of the temple stand in stark contrast to this period's position in the history of ancient Near Eastern art and architecture. A number of scholars, headed by H. Frankfort, posited the existence of a dark age between the twelfth and ninth centuries, a period lacking in artistic creations of a high order and in monumental architecture. Though the period is not uniformly dark, the descriptions of Solomon's buildings certainly stand out against the generally bleak background.

The precise dating of the settlement strata and find assemblages of the tenth and ninth centuries is fraught with difficulties. It has not

Fig. 9.1. Six-chambered gates: Megiddo (A), Hazor (B), and Gezer (C)

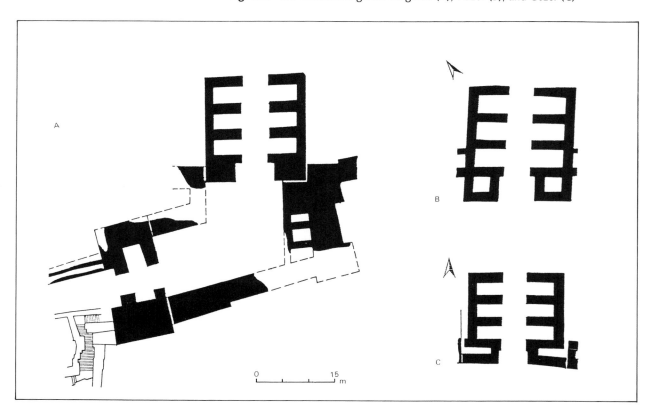

been proven that any sites were destroyed by Shishak in 925 B.C.E., and the attribution of destruction layers to the end of the tenth century at many sites is mere conjecture. A stela fragment bearing the name Shishak was found at Megiddo, but in the excavation dumps; it is therefore unclear whether the stela was erected on the ruins of the town Shishak destroyed or within the precincts of an existing settlement, in commemoration of the subjugation of the town rather than its destruction. The dating of strata VA–IVB at Megiddo to the reign of Solomon is feasible, but the date of its destruction is not certain and could be attributed to a time later than the campaign of Shishak.

In the ninth century we know of military campaigns and consequent destructions, particularly in northern Israel. Some destructions are related to the campaigns of Shalmaneser III of Assyria (841 B.C.E.), and others to the clashes with the Arameans. In the Kingdom of Judah, however, there is not a single archaeological destruction layer attributed to the ninth century.

Philistine culture continued to flourish on the coastal plain and parts of the Shephelah during the Iron Age IIa. The Galilee coast ("the land of Cabul," I Kings 9:11–13) and large portions of the western Galilee belonged during the Iron Age II–III to the political and cultural sphere of the Phoenicians. On the other hand, Transjordan was largely under the political and cultural control of the Israelites during the Iron Age IIa, until the mid ninth century. However, the archaeological picture provided by excavations in Transjordan is as yet sketchy.

The Iron Age IIa lacks reliable synchronisms between the archaeological and the biblical records. The rather glorified picture emerging from the biblical sources does not so far correspond to the reality reflected in the archaeological findings.

FORTIFICATIONS

Fortifications are the most important feature of urban culture in the Iron Age II. The Bible tells of the fortifications built in Jerusalem by Solomon, but archaeology has yet to uncover any remains, with the exception of wall fragments discovered by Kathleen Kenyon. It also mentions the fortification of Hazor, Gezer, and Megiddo by Solomon (I Kings 9:15). These three cities have been intensively excavated, and it is only to be expected that they should yield remains of Solomonic fortifications.

The Solomonic gates discovered at Hazor, Megiddo, and Gezer have become ornaments of biblical archaeology and prime examples of the correlation between the biblical narrative and the archaeological record. In the course of Y. Yadin's excavations at Hazor, a structure showed a detailed resemblance to a structure excavated earlier at Megiddo. The Megiddo structure was identified as the Solomonic city gate. In the wake of those discoveries Yadin suggested that a structure excavated at the beginning of the century at Gezer, identified by its excavator as a Maccabean castle, was one wing of a Solomonic city gate. Subsequent excavations at Gezer revealed that the structure was indeed a city gate of the tenth century. The gates at Hazor, Gezer, and Megiddo are of a similar plan and, until the seventies, were the only known gates of their kind in the Land of Israel. The relation to the biblical passage was thus taken for granted. Detailed examination of the gates, however, reveals that they are not identical and that they certainly were not built according to a single blueprint designed by a central authority.

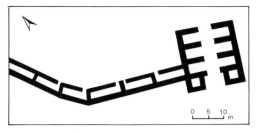

Fig. 9.2. Hazor, six-chambered gate and casemate city wall

The gate unearthed in stratum X at Hazor was built in the middle of the mound, showing that only part of the mound was occupied by the Solomonic city. It consists of two wings flanking the gate passage. Each wing consists of three rooms separated by piers, so that the gate as a whole includes six chambers and eight piers. Two projecting towers guarded the approaches to the gate. Only the fieldstone foundations of the Hazor gate have been preserved. The gate was joined to a casemate wall. The gate recovered in the renewed excavations at Gezer was built of fine ashlar masonry, unlike the Hazor gate. The Gezer gate was also joined to a casemate wall. At Megiddo, however, the wall adjoining the gate is a solid wall of the inset-offset type. The junction between the wall and gate at Megiddo is original and properly bonded, and the suggestion that an earlier casemate wall was originally associated with the gate seems unlikely, nor have remains of such a wall been discovered in the gate area. Thus, the schematic and commonly held view regarding the homogeneity of the gates of Hazor, Megiddo, and Gezer and their attribution to Solomon in accordance with the biblical passage no longer hold true. The three gates are inconsistent in size and construction and in the type of wall to which they are bonded. Their claim to uniqueness can also no longer be upheld, following the discovery of similar gateways at Lachish and Ashdod. The Level IV gateway at Lachish is undoubtedly later than the reign of Solomon, probably dating to the ninth century. At Ashdod, outside the borders of the Solomonic kingdom, the gate was built by bearers of Philistine culture.

The six-chambered gateway thus has its origins in the days of Solomon, at about the middle of the tenth century, and it seems that the gates of Hazor, Gezer, and perhaps also Megiddo can be attributed to the architects of that king. The gateway is in fact an improved version of the four-chambered gateways common in Canaan and Syria since the Middle Bronze Age. It is not, however, limited to the days of Solomon, nor should it be associated with centralized initiative and uniform planning.

The Solomonic gates at Hazor and Gezer are bonded to casemate walls, which consist of two parallel wall lines, with the space between them divided into cells by partition walls. Each chamber, called a casemate, was furnished with a doorway leading into the city. The outer and inner walls measure 1.6 meters (three cubits) and 1.05 meters (two cubits), respectively. The total breadth of the casemate walls was approximately 5 meters. Casemate walls were sometimes freestanding, a series of adjoining rooms serving as barracks or storerooms. In other cases, the casemates were contiguous with the dwelling houses, forming a rear room fronted by the other parts of the house. Presumably the householders were responsible for the defense of that section of the wall incorporated in their dwelling. Apart from Hazor and Gezer, casemate walls are known from many sites throughout the country, particularly Tel Beersheba stratum III, Tell Beit Mirsim stratum B$_3$, Beth

Shemesh stratum IIA, and Tell en-Nasbeh (the phase preceding the construction of the solid fortification wall). They also appear at northern sites—Yoqne'am, on the edge of the Jezreel valley, and 'En Gev, on the shores of Lake Kinneret. Casemate walls first appear in the tenth century, but their construction is not limited to this phase; they continued to exist, and new walls were built in the ninth century and later. The casemate chambers of stratum X at Hazor continued to function in stratum IX and were filled with stones and earth during stratum VIII, in the ninth century.

Another wall type found in Iron Age II cities is the solid wall, built as a thick and solid mass with no internal chambers. Sometimes the solid wall is furnished with small buttresses projecting alternately inward and outward, known as the inset-offset wall. In other cases the wall is built in the serrated technique, jutting out about half a meter at intervals. Projections, towers, and offsets were all intended to reduce the blind spots along the wall and at its base. The solid walls are generally 4–4.5 meters thick, sometimes reaching 8 meters. The massiveness was intended to prevent tunneling through the walls and to withstand siege engines, such as the battering rams depicted in Assyrian reliefs from the ninth century on. Solid walls of the tenth century have been found at Ashdod, Gezer (the outer wall), and 'En Gev. The massive fortification wall at Tell en-Nasbeh, ancient Mizpah, was built at the end of the tenth century (cf. I Kings 15:22). Solid walls were also built during the ninth century in various parts of the country. At Hazor, the casemate wall of stratum X was filled in with rubble to become a solid wall in stratum VIII, and in those sections that the casemate wall did not enclose, a new solid wall was constructed. At Megiddo of the

days of Omri (stratum IVA), an inset-offset wall was built, and at Lachish the fortifications of stratum IV, which include a solid wall with towers 6 meters thick, are attributed to Jehosophat or his successors in the ninth century. Solid walls continued to be constructed as long as the threat of the Assyrian battering ram loomed over the Israelite cities, in other words, throughout the Iron Age II–IIIa.

Apart from their defense walls, the towns of the tenth and ninth centuries featured internal fortifications. In the tenth century, the first separate and fortified acropolis in the Land of Israel appears, a complex of palaces and other administrative structures. Such an acropolis seems to have existed on the Temple Mount at Jerusalem from the reign of Solomon onward. The Temple Mount was higher than the other parts of the city of those times and commanded the city from above. It housed the temple and the royal administrative center. The principle of the raised and independently fortified acropolis was repeated in the layout of the city of Samaria, the royal capital founded by Omri in the ninth century. The city was built on the slopes, while the summit of the hill, set apart from the rest of the town, was occupied by the royal palace complex. The royal city of Lachish in Judah also boasted an acropolis, which housed official state buildings. The phenomenon of the separate and fortified acropolis is paralleled in neo-Hittite and Aramean cities of North Syria from the tenth century and on, such as Hamat, Sam'al (Zinjirli), Guzana (Tell Halaf), and Carchemish.

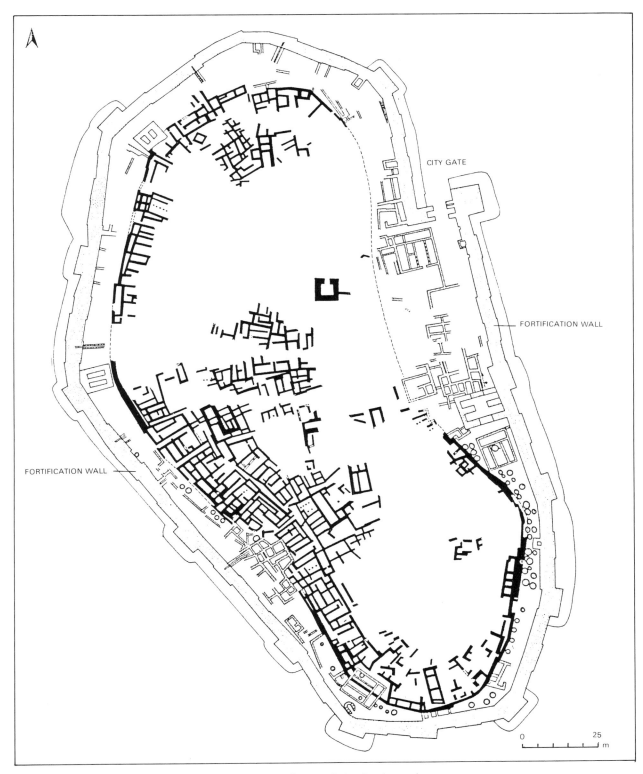

Fig. 9.3. Tell en-Nasbeh, city plan and fortifications

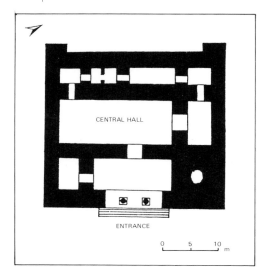

Fig. 9.4.   Zinjirli, hilani palace

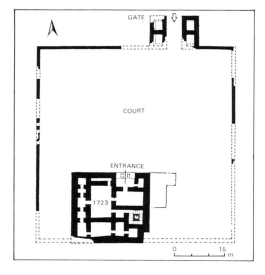

Fig. 9.5.   Megiddo, southern (1723) palace

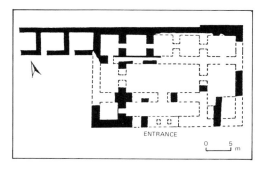

Fig. 9.6.   Megiddo, northern (6000) palace

PALACES AND PUBLIC STRUCTURES

The advent of centralized authority and royal initiative for city construction in the Iron Age II led to the construction of the first Israelite royal palaces and administrative structures. We have only biblical evidence to rely on for a description of the Solomonic palace complex in Jerusalem (I Kings 7:1–12). Many scholars have compared Solomon's palace in Jerusalem to the neo-Hittite palace type known as *bit hilani*, an archaeological term borrowed from royal Assyrian inscriptions that describe palaces with Syrian-style porticoes. Solomon's palace in Jerusalem was identified as a bit hilani following an analysis of its components and details, as described in the Bible, and their comparison to hilani palaces of northern Syria, particularly those of Tell Ta'yinat and Sam'al (Zinjirli). Two palaces discovered at Megiddo were also attributed to this type. Both structures are at the edge of the mound, one in its southern sector and one in the north. They were built of fine ashlar masonry. They are preserved only in their foundations, and even these are incomplete: in some cases the wall lines were discerned only as robber trenches, from which even the foundation courses had been extracted. This poor state of preservation precludes the detailed reconstruction of the palaces.

The southern palace backs directly onto the steep slopes of the mound. A broad court occupied the front of the building to the north, which may be compared to the great courtyard of the palace in Jerusalem (I Kings 7:9, 12). A gatehouse lay on the north side of the court, comprising two rooms flanking a gate passage. The court dimensions were impressive, about 57 x 58 meters. Judging from the hilani palaces of

northern Syria, a portico stood in the facade of the building facing the court. The portico, the hallmark of these structures, was the most prominent feature as one approached the structure, and it may be compared with the first unit of the Solomonic palace (I Kings 7:6). From there one entered the main ceremonial hall, paralleling the throne portico, or Hall of Judgment, of the palace in Jerusalem (I Kings 7:7). An inner court led off this hall (the rear courtyard in Jerusalem, I Kings 7:8) to a series of small rooms, which may have been the residential and service areas. In one room a central pillar built of dressed ashlar blocks may have supported a staircase leading to the second floor.

The northern palace at Megiddo was also built along the lines of the North Syrian bit hilani but less can be said of it than of the southern palace. Like the southern palace, the northern palace is adjacent to the steep slope of the mound. The northeastern corner of the palace has an added buttress projecting outward, perhaps indicative of some defensive function. The front court was not excavated, but a row of three rooms adjoining the northwestern corner of the building has led some scholars to propose that the palace had a court surrounded by casemates. A later palace, uncovered at Ramat Rahel, south of Jerusalem, was surrounded by a range of casemates. The two palaces of tenth-century Megiddo together account for more than 20 percent of the area of the city.

In the late tenth century a royal palace fort was also built at Lachish, the first phase of the palace of the kings of Judah, which survived until the end of the eighth century B.C.E. The palace was founded on a massive, raised, square podium, measuring about 31.5 × 32 meters. The stone foundations have been pre-

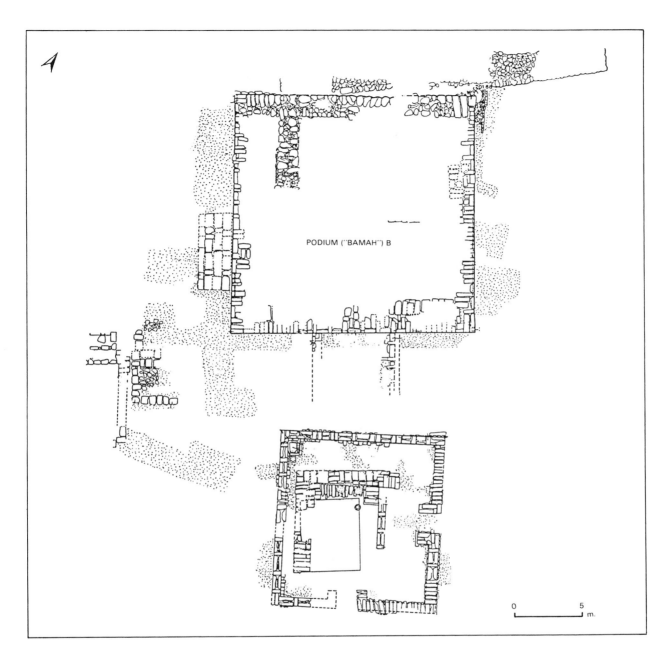

PODIUM ("BAMAH") B

0   5
          m.

Fig. 9.7. Tel Dan, the bamah (palace platform) in stratum III

served in the podium; they apparently supported an unpreserved mud-brick structure several stories high. The foundation walls outline a building composed of a series of small rooms and elongated halls surrounding a central hall or courtyard. The technique of building a palace on a massive earth-filled substructure is probably indicated by the biblical term *millo,* used to describe buildings in Jerusalem from the days of David in the early tenth century to Hezekiah in the late eighth century (II Sam. 5:9; I Kings 9:15, 24; 11:27; II Chron. 32:5; and elsewhere). "Millo" is apparently related also to the building technique common in Assyria, where various structures were founded on a massive artificial platform called *tamlu.*

At Tel Dan a massive structure built near the northern edge of the mound has been interpreted as a high place. The structure has several phases, beginning in the late tenth and early ninth centuries, that is, during the reigns of Jeroboam I and

his successors. The Dan structure, built of fine ashlar masonry, is a raised platform with a fill of earth and basalt boulders. Within the platform are the foundations of walls that must have supported a considerable superstructure, an interpretation that disagrees with the excavators, who believed the structure was merely a high place without any superstructure. But in light of its location near the edge of the mound (like the Megiddo palaces), its similarity to the podium at Lachish, and the clear presence of wall foundations within the podium, it seems more likely that the structure was a massive foundation platform of a palace. This does not rule out the possibility that there was cultic activity nearby, especially to the south of the structure, where cultic remains have been recovered.

First among the palaces of the ninth century B.C.E. is the royal precinct at Samaria, built by Omri

in approximately 876 B.C.E. It existed from the foundation of the city until the demise of the kingdom of Israel. Built on the summit of the hill above the town, the buildings inside the royal enclosure have been poorly preserved, but there can be no doubt as to the high standards of workmanship, and their magnificence is confirmed by a number of finds. Limited building remains were exposed in the north and southwest part of the enclosure. Finds in the ruins of the northern building included remains of ivory-inlaid furniture and clay bullae, attesting to the existence of archives. In the southwest corner, however, more of the palace plan was preserved, enough to support the conclusion that the original concept of the structure was close to that of the bit hilani. The building included rooms of various sizes ranged around a square central hall. There were several palaces within the royal quarter of Samaria, including a

Fig. 9.8. Megiddo, stratum IVA city plan

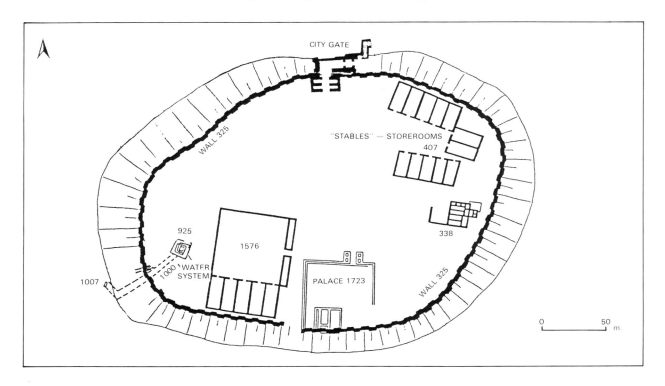

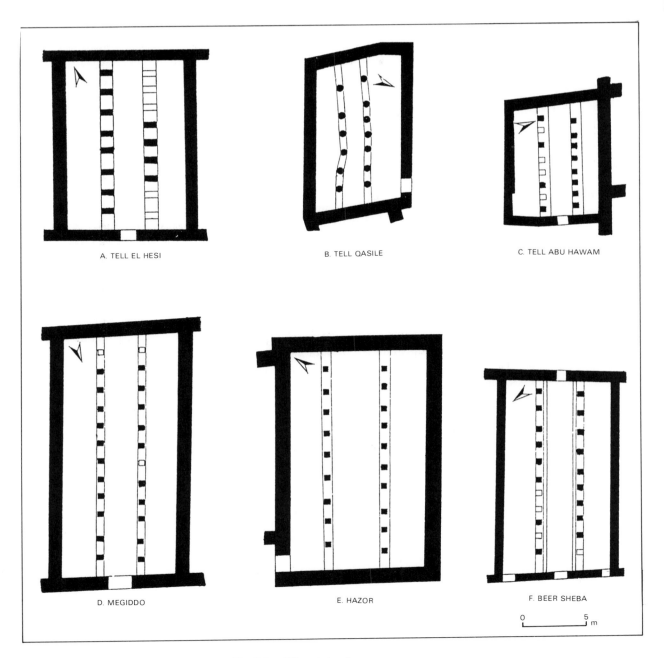

A. TELL EL HESI

B. TELL QASILE

C. TELL ABU HAWAM

D. MEGIDDO

E. HAZOR

F. BEER SHEBA

0 5 m

Fig. 9.9. Pillared storehouses

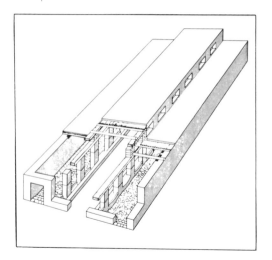

Fig. 9.10. Beersheba, storehouse (restored)

winter palace and a summer palace (Amos 3:15). At Sam'al an inscription of one of the local rulers describes the construction of different palaces, winter and summer mansions, which have been identified in the palace complex at the site.

In ninth-century Megiddo (stratum IVA), the palaces of the previous stratum were succeeded by a magnificent structure, at first identified as a temple and later styled "the house of the captain of the chariotry," in light of its proximity to the buildings identified as stables. However, the building was in fact the main palace of the city. It was entered from the west through a gatehouse consisting of two rooms flanking a passage. The gate led to a broad court and thence, along the northern wall of the palace, to a stairway leading to the entrance porch of the structure. The entrance porch and possibly the foundations of a stairwell were on the northeast side of the palace. The entire structure was built on a raised podium. The supporting walls of the podium were constructed of fine ashlar piers alternating with rubble construction. The superstructure was mud brick, and little has survived. The magnificence of the building can

be seen in six proto-Ionic capitals found nearby. There can be little doubt that the palace was planned in conjunction with the inset-offset wall and the northern stable complex.

The Megiddo stables, also attributed to stratum IV, consist of two blocks, each separated from the inset-offset wall by narrow passages. The five units of the southern stables were approached through a large yard. The twelve units of the northern stables are ranged around three sides of an open area, where extremely fragmentary remains of an elongated structure of administrative character were found. Each stable unit was an elongated structure with a threefold division reminiscent of the Roman-Byzantine basilica, a central hall flanked by two parallel aisles, separated by rows of square pillars. Between the pillars were shallow troughs carved from large, horizontal ashlar blocks. The two aisles were paved with stone, and the central hall had a pavement of crushed limestone. The two rows of pillars are the salient feature of the stables, so they are sometimes called "pillared buildings." The pillars probably supported the roof of the central hall, which rose above the roofs of the flanking aisles. The interior would thus have been illuminated by windows set high in the walls of the central hall. The monolithic pillars and fine ashlar troughs may be assumed to have originated in the palaces and monumental structures of strata IVB–VA of the tenth century.

Tripartite stables or pillared buildings have been found at other sites as well, in clusters and as isolated structures, from Hazor in the Galilee to Beersheba and Tel Masos in the Negev. Such structures belonged to an architectural-functional tradition common to Israel and Judah. They have been discovered at Beth Shemesh in a tenth-century

stratum, at Tell el-Hesi in a stratum of the tenth and ninth centuries, at Hazor in a ninth-century and Beersheba in strata of the ninth and eighth centuries, and at other sites. The origins of this building type may therefore be attributed to the tenth century, or perhaps somewhat earlier; the type flourished particularly during the ninth century and continued in use until the end of the eighth century.

The identification of the pillared buildings at Megiddo as stables has been hotly debated. Some archaeologists hold that the buildings served as army barracks or as royal storehouses. If they were storehouses (possibly the structures termed treasuries in II Chron. 32:27) they would have served those towns in which produce was concentrated, the biblical "store cities" (I Kings 9:19). However, the pillared buildings everywhere must have served the same purpose, for it is difficult to imagine that buildings of identical character and plan would serve varying functions, and an analysis of all the data in hand seems to accord better with stables than with storehouses. The importance of the horse and chariot in Iron Age history, from the mid tenth century onward, should be taken into account. Horses and chariots are mentioned in the ancient sources as the main military factor of this period. Because of their vital importance, horses were kept inside the cities. Special structures for the horses are also mentioned in the Bible: "Solomon had 40,000 stalls of horses for his chariotry and 12,000 horsemen" (I Kings 5:6). The basic form of the pillared buildings resembles stables known from later periods. The finds within the buildings do not testify directly to their function; the horse and chariot were intended for battle on the open plain, and before the destruction of the cities, the chariotry would have been sent into battle. The absence of finds in the pillared buildings of Megiddo thus supports their identification as stables. At other sites, such as Beersheba, where a block of three units was found adjacent to the city gate, large assemblages of pottery and other domestic effects were discovered in the stables, showing that the structures were used in their final phase as habitations, perhaps by villagers who fled to the protection of the walled town. The interpretation of the Beersheba structures as storehouses does not accord with the finds, which clearly do not represent the contents of a royal magazine. In storehouses one would expect to find many storage vessels of standard form and size, as is the case in ancient storerooms of other sites and periods. The assertion that cities with pillared buildings have yielded no finds related to horses or chariots is imprecise. The excavations of Megiddo, Beth Shemesh, and La-

chish have revealed, in Iron Age II contexts adjacent to stables, parts of harness, but they were not identified as such by the excavators. The large yard adjoining the southern stables at Megiddo, which measures about 55 meters square, can hardly be explained if we assume the structures served as storerooms. However, for the exercise and training of horses such a yard is a necessity. A large yard has also been discovered adjacent to the stables east of the palace fort at Lachish. It therefore seems that the interpretation of these structures as stables is to be preferred over other views.

ASHLAR CONSTRUCTION AND PROTO-IONIC CAPITALS

One of the most prominent characteristics of royal architecture from the tenth century B.C.E. onward is ashlar construction, that is, the use of squared and smoothed building stones. The Bible provides a detailed

account of the beginnings of ashlar construction under Solomon: "The king ordered huge blocks of choice stone to be quarried, so that the foundations of the house might be laid with hewn stones" (I Kings 5:29, 31). At Megiddo and Samaria the actual quarries of the ashlar blocks used in the Iron Age IIa structures have been identified.

Many details concerning ashlar construction are recorded. Buildings were built of ashlar masonry to their entire height, both on the interior and exterior, "on the inner and outer sides, from the foundation to the coping" (I Kings 7:9, following New English Bible). The foundation stones of the royal buildings were particularly large, "huge blocks of choice stone, stones of 10 cubits and stones of 8 cubits" (I Kings 7:10). The smoothing of the stones ("trimmed with the saw," following New English Bible) and the obliteration of the mason's marks, as well

Fig. 9.11. Megiddo, gate of stratum IVB–VA: ashlar masonry

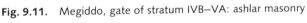

as the standardization of measure for the choice stones ("hewn according to measure"), are alluded to (I Kings 7:9). The technique of integrating wooden beams in the ashlar construction of courtyard walls and other units is also mentioned: "The large surrounding courtyard had three tiers of hewn stone and a row of cedar beams" (I Kings 7:12).

Ashlar buildings were dry-built, the stones being fitted without the use of mortar. So well were they laid that even today it is difficult to insert a knife blade into the joints. The short and long sides of the stones alternately faced outward (headers and stretcher construction). At times single headers alternate with single stretchers, and at times there are two headers and a stretcher. In each course, the single or double headers are generally placed above a stretcher of the lower course of stones. Foundation stones often had drafted margins on two or three sides, leaving a roughly dressed central boss. The marginal drafting apparently facilitated the proper fitting of the stones, with the help of measuring tools such as a square and a plumb line. The stones of the superstructure were fully smoothed, though stones with marginal drafting might appear here and there.

The beginnings of ashlar construction in the Land of Israel may be observed in Late Bronze Age structures at Megiddo and elsewhere. Late Bronze Age ashlar construction is also known at Ugarit in Syria and at Enkomi, Cyprus. Egypt too had an ancient tradition of ashlar construction. The origins of Israelite ashlar architecture, however, have traditionally been related to Phoenician architecture. Some scholars have even viewed all the monumental structures of the tenth and ninth centuries as the work of foreign builders, especially in light of the biblical allusion to Solomon's political ties with Phoenicia and the mention of Phoenicians among the masons employed in Jerusalem (I Kings 5:32). Others, however, have asserted the originality of the Israelite ashlar construction technique, attributing several unique features to it. Little is known about Phoenician architecture immediately before the appearance of Israelite ashlar masonry, that is, in the eleventh and tenth centuries. It is difficult to imagine that this type of construction evolved in Israel in a vacuum, and its origins should be sought in Canaanite-Phoenician culture or in Egypt.

From the ninth century the technique of partial ashlar construction—the integration of ashlar and rubble masonry—became widespread. It appears, for example, in the courtyard walls of the southern stables at Megiddo. Ashlar construction of quoins and doorjambs alone may be observed in the stratum VIII citadel at Hazor and elsewhere. The technique of ashlar piers alternating with fieldstone construction continues into the Persian and Hellenistic periods in the Land of Israel

Fig. 9.12.   Ramat Rahel casemate wall: ashlar masonry

and in areas of Phoenician influence throughout the Mediterranean littoral.

The distribution of fine ashlar architecture is limited to the major centers so far excavated, and this type of construction was definitely the product of state or royal initiative. Ashlar construction appears in the palaces of Megiddo and their annexes, in the water supply system, and in the city gate. The ashlar architecture at Megiddo may thus be dated, generally speaking, to the tenth and ninth centuries. Magnificent ashlar construction characterizes the enclosure of the royal acropolis at Samaria and the buildings within. Fine examples of ashlar masonry may be observed at Tel Dan, where the podium and altar compound are built of dressed ashlar blocks. The tenth-century gate at Gezer is of ashlar construction, as are structures at Ta'anach, Tel Sera', and Ramat Rahel. It may be assumed that quality ashlar construction continued at some sites into the eighth and seventh centuries and that it characterized high-standard

architecture of the Iron Age II–III as a whole.

An important component of Iron Age II ashlar construction is the proto-Ionic capital. More than 35 capitals of this type have been found in the Land of Israel. The name is derived from the capitals of the Ionic order of classical Greek architecture. It was assumed that the double volutes of the Ionic capital had an oriental origin, and when the capitals found in the Land of Israel proved to be earlier than those of Greece, they were given the name "proto-Ionic" (or "proto-Aeolic," after the Aeolic capital of Asia Minor). A more appropriate term, however, has been suggested: the Israelite palmette capital.

Proto-Ionic capitals were made of a rectangular ashlar block, with a central triangle flanked by curving palmette volutes carved in high relief. The block was worked on its shorter sides as well, with foliate patterns above and beneath the palmette. The surface of the capitals was well smoothed, and the quality of execution is often reminiscent of

the highest standards of ashlar masonry. Capitals carved on both sides were placed on a square pillar or freestanding pier, while capitals carved on only one side were placed atop pilasters or on doorjambs.

A common feature in ashlar masonry and in the proto-Ionic capitals is the small rectangular holes drilled in the upper surface of the stone, to accommodate metal brackets that fixed wooden cross-beams in place. The integration of wooden beams in ashlar masonry is particularly marked at Tel Dan.

The palmette design on the proto-Ionic capital has its origin in the ubiquitous palm-tree motif of ancient Near Eastern art. In the Iron Age, the palm motif is found in architectural decoration and in the ornamental arts, particularly ivory carving. This may be the palm mentioned among the designs decorating the temple in Jerusalem (I Kings 6:29, 32, 35, etc.).

Proto-Ionic capitals have been discovered at six or seven sites in the Land of Israel—Dan, Hazor, Megiddo, Samaria, Jerusalem (the

Fig. 9.13. Ramat Rahel, proto-Ionic capital

Fig. 9.14. Typology of proto-Ionic capitals: Samaria (A), Megiddo (B, C), Hazor (D), Ramat Rahel (E)

City of David), Ramat Rahel, and possibly Gezer—as well as at Medeibiyeh in Moab. The earliest capitals are two attributed with certainty to Megiddo strata VA–IVB, of the tenth century. The other Megiddo capitals were found in stratified contexts in stratum IVA, of the ninth century. The capitals from Dan, Hazor, and Samaria may also be ascribed to the ninth century. It may be supposed that all these capitals adorned structures that retained their original form until the fall of the kingdom of Israel in 722 B.C.E.

The capitals from Jerusalem and Ramat Rahel (as well as from Medeibiyeh in Transjordan) are typologically more developed, containing additional small circles carved between the central triangle and the volutes. Their date also appears to be later, and the difference in form may be of chronological rather than regional significance. If the southern capitals are dated to the eighth century, a gap in the evolution of these

capitals will be bridged, since from the seventh century many capitals of the type are found in Cyprus, in Etruria, and in the areas of Phoenician colonization in the western Mediterranean.

SAMARIA

The city of Samaria lies in the heart of the hills of Ephraim, on a crossroads within a fertile agricultural region. Omri chose it to be the capital of the kingdom of Israel, doubtless because of its choice geographical location. The location of the former capital, Tirzah (Tell el-Far'ah North), was no longer suitable, after large parts of Transjordan had been relinquished. The capital was founded on the estate of Shemer, after whom the city was named, at about 876 B.C.E. (cf. I Kings 16:23–24). Samaria was excavated by two archaeological expeditions, the Harvard Expedition in 1908–10 and the Joint Expedition in

1931–35. In terms of excavation technique, the two excavations constitute a milestone in the history of archaeological investigation in the Land of Israel. For instance, the drawing of sections was first instituted at Samaria, in the 1908–10 excavations.

Extensive Iron Age II remains were not exposed, and the preservation of the remains is relatively unimpressive. The site was destroyed many times and often cleared to bedrock before rebuilding, the stones of earlier strata often being reused in the process. In its history, archaeological complexity, and mountainous terrain, the site of Samaria is reminiscent of another problematic site, Jerusalem, the capital of Judah. The excavations at Samaria are nonetheless a cornerstone in the study of Iron Age II culture. The site was the capital of the kingdom of Israel for 150 years (876–722 B.C.E.) and a cultural center whose influence and inspiration

Fig. 9.15. Plan of the Samaria acropolis

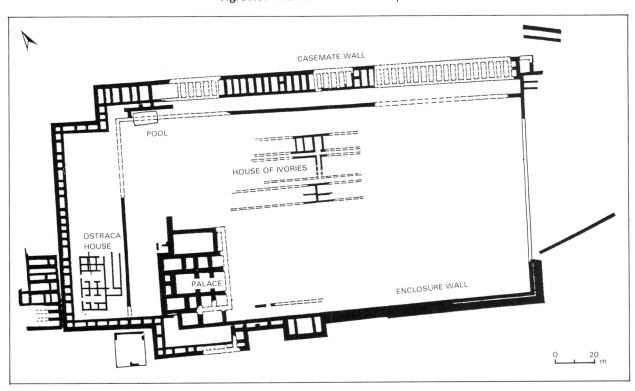

may be observed in other cities of Israel.

Topographical circumstances, as well as the location of Iron Age II burial caves and a cult site that must have been outside but near the city, suggest that the boundaries of Iron Age Samaria were not much different from those of Roman Sebaste. This assumption is also based on the distribution of Iron Age pottery beneath later structures. The size of the city may have been as great as sixty hectares, in the range of the walled city of Jerusalem at the end of the Iron Age. Both cities headed a hierarchical urban system, in which the towns next in importance to the capital were far smaller. No traces of the city wall have been identified, so that any discussion of the city boundaries is speculative. The biblical account provides Samaria with walls of particular strength, which prevented its conquest by the Arameans (II Kings 6:24–30; 7) and forced the Assyrians to mount a three-year siege (II Kings 17:5–6; 18:9–10).

The most prominent feature of Samaria was the independently fortified royal acropolis. Erected by Omri at the beginning of the second quarter of the ninth century, it is of regular rectilinear shape, measuring 89 × 178 meters. It represents an architectural feat of impressive scope and grandeur, ranking Omri and his successor Ahab among the great builders in the history of the Land of Israel.

The acropolis of Samaria was surrounded by a wall 1.6 meters wide, known as the inner wall. It has been traced in segments preserved on the north, west, and south, the gate having been apparently in the east. The inner wall exhibits one of the finest examples of dressed and smoothed ashlar construction, and its stones are fitted with the greatest care. The palace remains in the southwest part of the

acropolis are contemporaneous with the inner wall.

In the second phase, attributed to Ahab, the acropolis was expanded by means of massive fills added mainly on the west side, the gate remaining in the east. In the added area, between the new casemate wall and the inner wall, a large administrative structure was erected. The building, known as the House of the Ostraca, yielded 102 sherds bearing Hebrew inscriptions, invoices recording the distribution of goods: "A jar of fine oil" or "a jar of old wine." The dockets, written in pen and ink, also mention regnal years 9, 10, and 15 of an Israelite king and probably date to the time of Jeroboam II (785–749 B.C.E.). These documents, in some way related to the royal administration, mention names of persons, places, and geographical regions in the kingdom of Israel.

In the northern part of the acropolis were fragmentary remains of another palatial structure, the Ivory Palace, so named after a large collection of ivory carvings found among its ruins (cf. I Kings 22:39). These were in a burn layer, divorced from their original context, along with sealed clay bullae belonging to state documents. The seal impressions included depictions of scarabs and sphinxes and some traces of Hebrew writing. The biblical account seems to place the royal palace in the inner city (II Kings 7:11), but there is no knowing which of the acropolis structures it refers to. Ahab had another palace at Jezreel, and it has recently been reported that its remains have been discovered there; further light may be cast from this quarter on the acropolis of Samaria.

The buildings of the acropolis and the surrounding fortifications have been poorly preserved, and the plans published by the excavators are based in part on foundation trenches cut in the rock, from which

the stone foundation courses have been completely robbed. Surviving details of the ashlar construction in the acropolis area include seven proto-Ionic capitals, of which three are complete.

Several burial caves of the Iron Age II were discovered in the valleys outside the city. East of the city, a large installation (27 × 28 meters) was discovered, featuring a broad (4 meters) trench carved in the rock. Finds included a large collection of cult figurines, leading the excavators to suggest that this was a cult installation, perhaps similar to the Tophet of the valley of Hinnom in Jerusalem.

The Samaria excavations have revealed slight but nonetheless important remains of the capital of the kingdom of Israel. The discoveries reflect the Phoenician cultural influence of biblical fame, most pointedly expressed in the marriage ties between the dynasty of Omri and the Phoenician kings and in the influence of the cult of the Tyrian Baal. The Phoenician contacts are prominent in the magnificent ashlar masonry styles, in the ivories undoubtedly carved in Phoenician workshops, and even in the fine Samaria pottery, which is to be seen as a type of Phoenician pottery of the ninth and eighth centuries.

IVORY CARVING

About 500 pieces of carved ivory furniture inlays were recovered in the ruins of the royal palaces at Samaria. Carved ivories exhibiting craftsmanship of the highest order have been found at other sites in the Land of Israel, in tenth-through-eighth-century contexts. Ivory carving has a long history in the art of ancient Canaan and Israel, going back as far as the Chalcolithic period. The finest examples come from the Late Bronze Age palace at Megiddo and from Lachish and Tell

Fig. 9.16. Samaria ivories: lion and bull (height 4.2 centimeters), sphinx (8.7 centimeters), and roaring lions (4 centimeters)

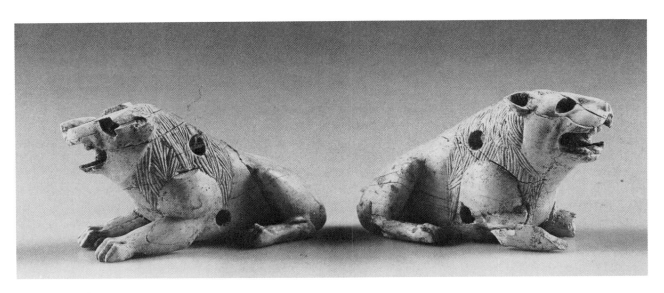

el-Far'ah South in the same period. The roots of Iron Age II ivory carving draw on the artistic traditions of the Late Bronze Age workshops and ivory carvers, but no sequence of finds has been established that would bridge the gap represented by the artistic dark age of the Iron Age I.

Biblical accounts suggest that ivory objects were fairly common in aristocratic circles and royal courts of Israel and Judah in this period. Solomon's splendid ivory throne was adorned with lions and overlaid with gold (I Kings 10:18–20), and ivory is mentioned among the exotic products brought by Solomon's fleets (I Kings 10:22). Literary metaphors probably originating in the culture of the tenth and ninth centuries allude to magnificent ivory-inlaid furnishings (Song of Songs 5:14; 7:5; Psalms 45:9). It is said that Ahab built an ivory palace at Samaria (I Kings 22:39), perhaps a palace with ivory-inlaid walls or furnishings exceptional for the quality of their ivory adornments. The prophet Amos of the eighth century describes the life of luxury led by the city dwellers of his time, especially in the northern kingdom of Israel:

> Who dwell in Samaria—
> With the leg of a bed or the head
>   of a couch
>   . . . .
>
> I will wreck the winter palace
> Together with the summer
>   palace;
> The ivory palaces shall be
>   demolished.
>   Amos 3:12–15
>
> They lie on ivory beds,
> Lolling on their couches.
>   Amos 6:4

The tribute exacted by Sennacherib of Assyria from Hezekiah of Judah, as described in the As-syrian annals of the late eighth century, includes ivory beds, chairs, and tusks.

Among the carved ivories of the tenth century is a lion's head from Tel Masos in the Negev; as for the ninth century, at least part of the ivory treasure from Samaria should be dated to this period, and a similar date is ascribed to a carved pyxis and a fine cosmetic spoon from Hazor. To the eighth century may be ascribed ivory artifacts found at Calah (Nimrud) in Assyria. The Israelite origin of these ivories is proved by the Hebrew inscriptions on some of the ivory fragments, including a mention of a "great king." These ivories came to Assyria as tribute or as booty from Judah or Israel. Isolated ivory artifacts have also been found in the excavations of Beth Zur, north of Hebron, Megiddo, Ramat Rahel, and Sarepta, on the Lebanese coast.

The ivories found in the Land of Israel, and particularly those of Samaria, are not of local manufacture. Though odd pieces of raw ivory do turn up now and then, ivories were on the whole imported from workshops that supplied the royal houses throughout western Asia. The ivories from the Land of Israel are stylistically of the Phoenician school. Such ivories have been found in Phoenicia itself, in Syria, Assyria, Cyprus, and even the Greek Islands. Of particular importance are the objects from Hadatha (Arslan-Tash) in northern Syria, where one ivory was found to bear the name of Hazael, the ninth-century Aramean king of biblical fame.

Technically, the ivories fall into two general categories: furniture inlays executed in high relief carved in the round and lacelike openwork plaques. The patterns were sometimes inset with colored paste and precious stones, overlaid with gold leaf, or painted. The backs of some ivory fragments are inscribed with Phoenician letters, which appear to have been guides in the process of mounting the ivory inlays. Most of the ivories adorned furniture—beds, chairs, and stools. The pegs with which the inlays were mounted were concealed by ivory florets. The Phoenician-style ivories are sometimes accompanied by other prestige items, such as cosmetic spoons and cosmetic bottle stoppers, round pyxides mirror handles or other cosmetic implements, and harness ornaments. The designs on the carved ivory plaques in the Land of Israel are identical to those from sites where Phoenician-style ivories have been found. There is extensive use of designs of Egyptian origin,

Fig. 9.17.   Samaria ivory (open work): Isis and Nephtis (height 4.5 centimeters)

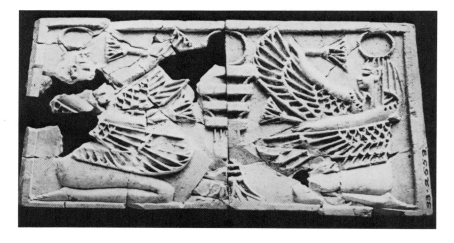

though they do not appear in their pure Egyptian form.

Ivories are difficult to date, as they had an extended life and may have been passed on as heirlooms for generations. The criterion used for dating is usually that of style. Toward the end of the eighth century the centers of ivory carving in Phoenicia declined, perhaps as a result of the military campaigns of the Assyrians. Here and there we may find degenerate forms of ivory work in the seventh century. To these we may relate several carved pieces of boxwood furniture found in the City of David in Jerusalem. The palmette designs on these carbonized strips are reminiscent of the fine ivory work of the ninth and eighth centuries. The evidence provided by biblical allusions to ivory carving in the tenth and ninth centuries should not be ignored. The added testimony of some well-dated archaeological finds should place the zenith of ivory working in the ninth century.

THE NEGEV IN THE TENTH CENTURY B.C.E.

For several decades, archaeological surveys have been recording isolated fortified structures scattered throughout the Negev Highlands. Known as Israelite fortresses, they are found in the Beersheba and Arad basins and chiefly in the Negev Highlands. Of more than 45 such fortresses surveyed, 25 have been excavated, most of them in recent years. Most of the fortress sites are single-period sites; only Kadesh Barnea and Arad have yielded multiple strata. Generally speaking, the fortresses may be divided into two categories: oval or round, and rectangular or square. In many cases the layout was adapted to the terrain and does not fall neatly into the categories.

The fortresses are found not only along the main routes, where they were first identified, but in every part of the countryside where rainwater could be collected, cisterns carved, and wadi beds cultivated. In the round or oval type, as well as in some of the rectangular fortresses, a large central court is surrounded by a contiguous range of rooms resembling a casemate wall. The walls of these casemates, however, are thin and do not constitute a true fortification. A number of the rectangular fortresses are similar and appear to share design concepts, in which the twenty-meter square is a regular component. But despite the

Fig. 9.18. "Woman in the window" ivories: Samaria (height 4.2 centimeters) (*above*), Nimrud (7.2 centimeters) (*below*)

typological division and the presence of shared features, the fortresses are not identical in dimensions or in construction technique.

Isolated structures, often of the characteristic four-roomed plan of the Israelite Iron Age, have been found near the fortresses. In addition, stone-lined reservoirs, furnished with a network of channels to collect surface water, have been found.

Archaeologists who have studied the fortresses disagree on their character, the motive for their construction, and their date. Four positions have emerged. (1) The Negev fortresses are Amalekite settlement sites of the eleventh century, destroyed by the Israelites in the tenth century. (2) They are settlement sites of Israelite desert nomads of the twelfth through tenth centuries, and their distribution marks the boundaries of the Israelite settlement area. They were the background for the Amalekite-Israelite confrontation in the days of Saul and David. (3) They were built as part of a centralized state initiative, a show of strength aimed at the desert nomads, and are dated to the reigns of Saul or David, in the eleventh or tenth centuries. (4) They were built as a chain of fortresses defending the southern borders of the Solomonic kingdom in the mid tenth century and were destroyed by Shishak, who caused the southern border of Israelite settlement and authority to recede toward the Beersheba valley. It is difficult to reach a conclusion concerning the fortresses, as their interpretation depends on their dating, and their dating involves serious difficulties. In many studies, scholars appear to be caught up in a circular argument, in which the dating is based on the general interpretation given to the fortress phenomenon and is in turn used to support the proposed interpretation of the character of the fortresses.

Two types of pottery have been found in the excavated fortresses: wheel-made vessels, which also appear in northern sites, and coarse handmade vessels, which characterize only the southern marginal regions and are therefore known as Negevite ware. Negevite vessels, especially cooking pots of crude form, have also been found in copper-mining sites of the Timna valley, where the date determined by other finds (including dated Egyptian inscriptions) is the Late Bronze Age, the thirteenth and twelfth centuries. This has induced some scholars to raise the date of the Negev Highland fortresses, where the same handmade pottery has been found. The excavations of Kadesh Barnea have shown, however, that the handmade wares characterized the desert dwellers throughout the Iron Age II–III, so their mere presence does not constitute a chronological indicator.

If the date of the foundation of the Negev fortresses must remain unclear, historical evidence for their destruction in the late tenth century is contained in the inscriptions (925 B.C.E.) of Pharaoh Shishak, which mention the names of seventy sites destroyed in the Negev. Some of the names may be identified with biblical names or with known sites. Nine

Map 9.2. Negev fortresses

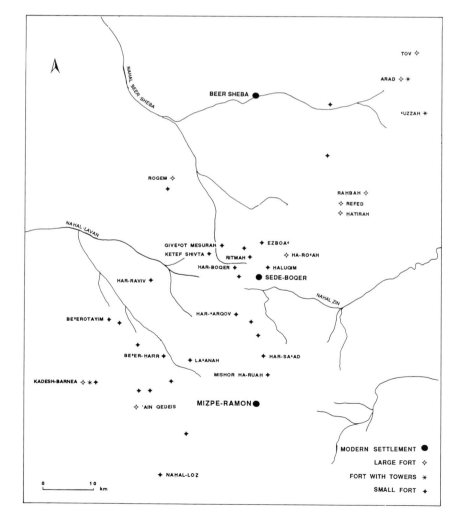

place-names appear in the inscription with the suffix *hgr,* including "Arad Rabat" and "Arad lbt Yrhm." The term *hgr* is known in other periods and may have denoted one of the Negev fortress types.

The discoveries at Tel Beersheba and Arad form a distinct chapter in the study of the history of the Negev in the tenth century. These are large sites with a consecutive sequence of settlement from the Iron Age I to the Iron Age III. In addition, they share some features with the sites of the desert and highlands to the south, and others with the sites of the north. The Beersheba and Arad valleys form the geographical region defined by the biblical term "Negev."

The Arad excavations revealed settlement remains of the eleventh century, below a square fortress erected in the tenth century with projecting towers and a massive perimeter wall. One of the most important discoveries at Arad was a shrine in the northwest part of the fortress courtyard. According to the excavators, the shrine was first established in the tenth century, in the days of Solomon, and it remained in use until the seventh century. However, the results of the Arad excavations in general and the dating of the shrine in particular have drawn much archaeological criticism, and a later foundation date has been posited.

The Tel Beersheba excavations revealed an Iron Age I settlement, succeeded first by an early tenth century settlement and then, in the mid tenth century, by a well-planned walled city. The wall was of the solid inset-offset type and had a four-chambered gate, to which a gate plaza and outer gate were added. Inside the fortified tenth-century settlement, fragmentary building remains were discovered, as well as stairs that may have belonged to a water supply system. In the ninth or early eighth century a new planned city was erected over the ruins of its predecessor, furnished with a casemate wall and a complete urban design. The discoveries at Beersheba thus form a link between the Negev culture and the Iron Age IIa culture of the northern regions of the Land of Israel.

POTTERY AND SMALL FINDS

The tenth century is characterized by the considerable uniformity of the ceramic assemblage throughout the country. This contrasts with the development of regional features later in the Iron Age. There is a considerable improvement in the quality of the pottery, in surface treatment and in firing, relative to the Iron Age I. Though several features show continuity with the Iron Age I, innovations that truly reflect the spirit of the age—a uniform and centralized system of government, a high level of material culture, and extensive foreign contacts—are prominent. Unlike the Iron Age I, when imported pottery was virtually unknown, imports began to appear in large quantities during the tenth century and continued almost to the end of the Iron Age. The imported wares consist of the so-called Cypro-Phoenician ware, fine vessels usually slipped red and decorated with concentric circles painted in black.

The salient feature of local pottery is its random burnish. This hand burnish of tenth-century vessels is to be distinguished from the wheel burnish, which first appears toward the end of the Iron Age IIa. Wheel burnish created a pattern of concentric circles, formed by the application of a burnisher (a pebble, wood chip, or shell) to the vessel as it turned on the wheel. Another innovation of the tenth century, which remained in use throughout the entire Iron Age II–III, was the

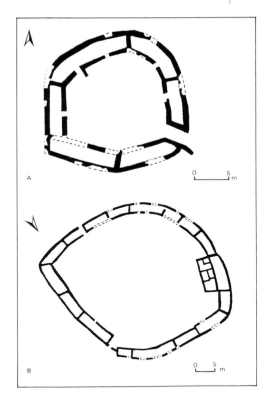

Fig. 9.19. Plan of Haluqim (A) and Ha-Ro'ah (B) fortresses

common use of red slip. Cooking pots closely resemble Iron Age I forms, but the carination of the wall is lower than in the earlier period. In some sites in the Jezreel valley (Tell Qiri, Yoqneam, and Megiddo) incised signs made before firing adorned the cooking-pot rims. These incisions, typical of the tenth century, resemble letters, but their significance has yet to be explained. Common in bowls of the Iron Age IIa (in the tenth and ninth centuries) are the knobs or bar handles often attached to the rim.

Cult-vessel assemblages seem to characterize Israelite religion and cult in the tenth century. The cult vessels also include limestone incense altars, furnished with projecting horns on each corner, which were probably modeled on the large sacrificial altars. Incense altars have been found at Megiddo, at Tel Qedesh (south of Megiddo), and at Lachish. Incense altars generally appear with tall ceramic stands, on which a bowl was mounted, which may have been used to burn incense. The stands appear in a variety of forms and decorations. Most remarkable are the elaborate stands from Ta'anach, reminiscent of a multistory square tower, with windows and doorways, adorned with a wealth of figures executed in high relief. One stand depicts lions, sphinxes, a female figure, a tree of life flanked by two gazelles, a winged solar disk, palmettes, and other cultic motifs. A second type of cult stand is cylindrical and succeeds a similar Iron Age I form.

A distinct ceramic type introduced in the ninth century and commonly found in northern sites has come to be called Samaria ware. The group consists of bowls, both rounded and carinate, marked by extremely thin walls, a thick continuous slip, and a high burnish. The slip generally consists of bands of red alternating with yellowish white, sometimes bordered by painted black bands. Alongside the thin, delicate Samaria bowls a thicker-walled variant appears, also slipped and burnished. Samaria bowls are in fact one facet of the Phoenician ceramic industry, and their distribution offers sufficient proof; the bowls appear in Cyprus and in the western Mediterranean basin, as far west as the Iberian peninsula.

A unique discovery dated to the Iron Age IIa is the silver hoard from Eshtemoa. Five ceramic jugs, dated to the tenth and ninth centuries, were discovered at this site, in the southern Hebron hills. The jugs are inscribed in red ink with the Hebrew word *hms* ("five"). In the jugs were pieces of silver, fragments of jewelry, ingot fragments, and silver scrap, with a total weight of about 26 kilograms. Some have attempted to relate this silver hoard to the spoils sent by David to the elders of Judah at Eshtemoa (I Sam. 30:26–28). However, the pottery vessels are somewhat later and must be ascribed to the end of the tenth century rather than its beginning.

Fig. 9.20. Megiddo, horned limestone altars

Does the hoard represent a tax or spoils of war? Was it a private cache, or did it belong to the royal treasury? Why was it buried and never retrieved? The hoard presents further indirect evidence of the prosperity in this period.

Among the small finds, stone seals first came into use at this time. Seal stones became one of the hallmarks of Israelite culture in the eighth century. The earliest seals apparently continue the Iron Age I tradition of conoid or pyramidal seals and bear faunal designs. A new type is introduced during the tenth and ninth centuries; several examples have been discovered at Tell Abu Hawam, and seals bearing Hebrew inscriptions have turned up in the antiquities shops. The much-valued inscribed scaraboid seals became increasingly popular during the ninth and eighth centuries.

The Iron Age IIb

The eighth century was an eventful period, a period of flux in the fortunes of the kingdoms of Israel and Judah. In Judah, the Davidic dynasty continued its rule without interruption, whereas Israel passed through a rapid succession of kings who failed to establish a dynastic sequence. The end of the ninth century was a period of political and cultural decline, following the conquests of the Arameans, but the beginning of the eighth century saw the decline of Aram in conjunction with the rise of Adadnirari III, king of Assyria. Aramean cultural influence, however, continued, as is evident in the tale of the altar built by Ahaz of Judah in imitation of the altar of Damascus (II Kings 16:10–12). Aramean influence in the eighth century was confined largely to northern Israel, where Aramean inscriptions have been discovered. About mid-century there was a renewal of political and cultural prosperity with the conquests of Uzziah in Philistia, on the Egyptian border, and in Transjordan. At this time the Red Sea town of Elath, which had been controlled by Solomon and Jehosophat in the tenth and ninth centuries, was rebuilt. Jeroboam II of Israel also extended the borders of his kingdom, so that during certain parts of the eighth century the borders of Israelite dominion approached those of the zenith of the Israelite state under the United Monarchy. Relations between the Hebrew kingdoms fluctuated between peaceful coexistence, bitter rivalry, and even war.

The expansion of the Assyrian empire during the eighth century was one of the major influences of this era. Assyrian contacts with the Land of Israel began as early as the ninth century, when Shalmaneser III campaigned against Damascus and may have come as far as the Carmel range (841 B.C.E.). It was in the last third of the eighth century, however, that Assyria began to dismember the kingdom of Israel, bit by bit, until by the end of the century the Kingdom of Judah stood alone, it too virtually a vassal kingdom, paying heavy tribute to Assyria. The remainder of the country (the Galilee, the interior valleys, the coastal plain, and the central hills) became Assyrian provinces. The Assyrian conquest began with the campaign of Tiglat Pileser III in

Fig. 9.22. Samaria ware

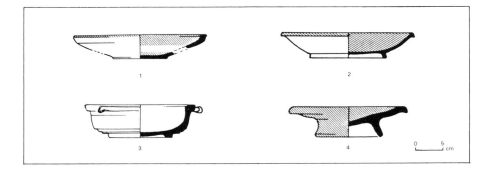

733 B.C.E. (cf. II Kings 15:29), to which destruction levels at some excavated sites, including Megiddo and Hazor, have been ascribed. Later, the final defeat of Israel was effected by Shalmaneser V and Sargon II, who conquered Samaria in 722 B.C.E. (II Kings 17:5–6). Apparently it was Sargon who rebuilt the city to serve as capital of the Assyrian province. At the end of the century, it was Judah's turn to suffer at the hands of Assyria. The cruel destruction wrought by Sennacherib in 701 B.C.E. is recorded in his annals, which tell of the destruction of 46 towns in Judah (cf. II Kings 18:13), and in the lamentation of the prophet Micah over the destruction of the cities of the Shephelah (Micah 1:8–16). Among the excavated towns whose destruction is ascribed to Sennacherib are Lachish, stratum III, the most prominent; Tel Batash and Tell Beit Mirsim; Gerar (Tel Haror); the Shephelah cities of Mareshah, Azekah, Tell Judeideh, and Tell es-Safi (probably to be identified with Gath); and possibly the early destruction phase (Vb) at Ramat Rahel.

The conquering Assyrian kings settled the province of Israel, as was their wont, with exiles from far-flung provinces of the empire, thus assuring political stability. The exiles must have brought with them elements of religion and culture that have yet to be identified in the archaeological record, though some attempts have been made in recent years to ascribe pottery types and personal names in inscriptions to these populations.

The clear destruction layers caused by the Assyrian conquests, sometimes recorded in detail in biblical or Assyrian sources and at times in the portrayal of conquered cities on wall reliefs in the Assyrian palaces, provide a rare combination of historical and archaeological data. The material culture assemblages,

particularly the pottery, found in these layers in both Israel and Judah constitute firm chronological anchors for the ceramic typology of the Iron Age II–III as a whole. In this respect, the sites providing clear stratigraphy and good pottery assemblages, in conjunction with historical reference to the destruction of the site, are most important. The Assyrian conquests were responsible not only for destructions but also for the introduction of a new material culture, that of the Assyrian conqueror. This establishes an archaeological-chronological link to distant sites where similar objects have been found, whether in Syria or Mesopotamia.

In mid-century, in the time of Uzziah, a great earthquake rocked the country. It left a powerful impression, reflected in the literary imagery of contemporary prophets, and is directly mentioned in the Bible (Zech. 14:5). Destruction layers at several sites have been ascribed to this earthquake, among them stratum VI at Hazor and Level IV at Lachish.

The eighth century marks the coming of age of the characteristic Israelite culture. Its growth and development began with the establishment of the monarchy in the tenth century and continued with the foundation of the cult centers and capital cities during the tenth and ninth centuries. The Iron Age IIb continued the momentum of the preceding period. Though new centers were not established during the eighth century, the state mounted considerable construction efforts, alluded to in the biblical record (II Kings 14:22, 15:35, 20:20; II Chron. 26:9–10, 27:3–4, and more). In contrast to the cultural uniformity of the Iron Age IIa, regional trends became marked during the Iron Age IIb and cultural differences between Israel and Judah more pronounced. The phenomenon of cul-

tural regionality is most conspicuous in a recent study of the finds at the site of Kuntillat 'Ajrud (Horvat Teman) in eastern Sinai, near the Negev border. This site, dated to the early eighth century, seems to have been a cult center and a place of pilgrimage. Among those who visited the site were pilgrims from Israel or perhaps even Phoenicia, judging from the character and script of the inscriptions found at the site. Some of the pottery vessels at this site are known as typical to Judaea, others are characteristic of the kingdom of Israel, and yet others of the coastal region. Chemical analyses confirmed the disparate sources of the pottery. The cultural variability among the regions of Judaea, the central hills, and the coastal plain is most conspicuous. The regional differences in material culture arose apparently as a result of varying cultural evolution in areas of different political affiliation or ethnic composition. Thus, in the eighth century one may identify Judaean vessels in a coastal assemblage or both coastal-Philistine and Judaean influences on the ceramic assemblages of the southern coastal plain or Beersheba valley.

A most important aspect of the Iron Age IIb, with ramifications in the material culture of the period, is the evolution of spiritual life and literary creativity during the eighth century. Literacy began to spread through wide circles of society and was no longer limited to a small group of professional scribes and members of the elite. The transformation of Israelite society into a literate one is reflected in the large number of inscribed finds from the eighth century onward. The century also witnessed the activity of some of the greatest of the prophets, such as Isaiah, son of Amoz. It was a time of spiritual upheaval, possibly reflecting the turbulent political events and the growing threat posed by the Assyrians. Especially important was the rise of Deuteronomistic ideology, with its emphasis on the unification and centralization of the cult at Jerusalem. The religious reforms of Hezekiah at the end of the eighth century, which no doubt contributed to the growth and physical reinforcement of Jerusalem, are another expression of ideological turmoil. The dismantling of a large horned sacrificial altar at Tel Beersheba is often associated with these events (the stones were found incorporated in the walls of a stratum II structure). The wall texts from the shrine (perhaps Ammonite) discovered at Tell Deir 'Alla (Succoth), which mention the name of Bala'am bar Be'or (cf. Nu. 22:5 ff.), are dated to the second half of the century. Other cult-related finds of the Iron Age IIb include large quantities of human and animal figurines, common in all sites of the period.

Archaeological surveys have recorded a large number of sites throughout the country, especially in the hill regions, including hamlets and isolated farmsteads. These new discoveries, along with the results of excavations at the central urban sites of the period, testify to a considerable rise in population density during the eighth century. Previously existing towns either reveal a significant increase in the density of settlement or overflow their fortification lines. At the foot of Tel Lachish, at some points outside the mound of Tell Beit Mirsim, and beyond the walls of eighth-century Jerusalem, traces of extramural construction have come to light, a phenomenon previously unknown.

Despite the clear destruction layers accompanied by finds that may be dated by reference to written sources, there are many areas of debate among scholars. One long-debated issue was the date of the destruction of Level III at Lachish. This massive destruction was first

ascribed to the 597 B.C.E. campaign of Nebuchadnezzar, king of Babylon, against Jehoiachin. Today, after the renewal of excavations, it has become clear that there are two destruction layers of the Iron Age II–III, Levels III and II, to be ascribed respectively to Sennacherib (701 B.C.E.) and Nebuchadnezzar (586 B.C.E.). Ceramic typological schemes and relative chronologies based on the lower chronology must therefore be emended.

CITY PLANNING AND FORTIFICATION

The Iron Age IIb in Israel is a markedly urban period, and a large number of urban sites are known, whether by excavation or literary allusion. We tend to define cities as large sites, well fortified, where the building density is greater than in sites termed villages. In biblical times, however, any place built by royal initiative or housing a representative of the central authority, even a small site or isolated fort, was called a city ('ir). This is most evident in the list of the Judahite

provinces and towns in the book of Joshua (15:20–63), which probably reflects the monarchic period. The concomitant of royal initiative in the construction of cities is planning. All excavated sites of this period seem to reveal the work of the planner, though to varying degrees. Most cities of this period were originally designed and built in the Iron Age IIa (tenth and ninth), centuries but in the course of the eighth century they were renovated or refortified, and significant additions were made to the urban layout.

A clear size hierarchy may be observed in the Iron Age IIb towns. At the top of the ladder are the capital cities of the two kingdoms, Samaria and Jerusalem. They are much larger than the lower cities in the hierarchy; Jerusalem, for example, is about eight times larger than Lachish of the late eighth century. A hierarchy is also indicated by the biblical references to towns ('arim), dependencies (banot), and villages (hazerim) (cf. Josh. 15:47). Following the capital cities in the hierarchy, are the royal cities of secondary size and importance, followed by the

Fig. 9.23. Beersheba stratum II, site plan

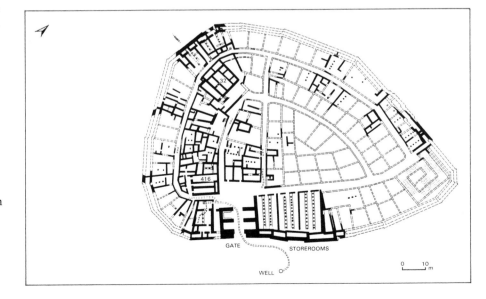

tertiary provincial centers. The cities of the Land of Israel are quite small in comparison with the huge Assyrian capitals of Nineveh (720 hectares), Calah (Nimrud, about 360 hectares), and Dur-Sharrukin (Khorsabad, about 300 hectares); but the capital cities of Samaria and Jerusalem, and perhaps some of the cities of Philistia as well, did attain the size of secondary capitals, such as those of Syria, for example, which ranged from 50 hectares to 100 hectares.

Excavations have yielded full and detailed city plans, revealed to an extent unparalleled in earlier periods. As much as 60 percent of the town of Tel Beersheba has been exposed, 70 percent of the town of Mizpah (Tell en-Nasbeh), and enough of strata IVA and III at Megiddo, stratum A_2 at Tell Beit Mirsim, and stratum II at Beth Shemesh to provide a reliable picture of the urban layout.

The best example of a complete and regular city plan is that exposed at Tel Beersheba, stratum II. Various components of the plan existed in earlier phases, but the layout of stratum II reflects a new, centralized planning concept. The town occupied about 1.2 hectares, somewhat less than the area of the royal palace and fort compound at contemporary Lachish. The oval shape of the town resembles that of many contemporary sites and is a result of its location at the summit of an ancient mound. The six-piered, four-chambered gate lay on the south side of the town. A central, stone-lined drainage channel, covered with stone slabs, passed through the gate. It was fed by a series of secondary channels built under the city streets, further evidence of an overall design. Inside the city gate, an open square served a variety of public functions, focused on the convergence of all traffic at the single gateway. This was

the central place of business in the Israelite city, the "square of the city gate" (II Chron. 32:6), which served royal and military, judicial, cultic (see, for example, II Sam. 19:9; Jer. 38:7; I Kings 22:10; Amos 5:10, 15; II Kings 7:17, 23:8), and mainly economic (II Kings 7:18) functions. The street plan is composed of concentric ovals connected by radial lanes, with the entire system converging on the gate square. The absence of blind alleys is evidence of careful planning. Inside the gate square, at the junction of two major arteries leading toward the interior, stood a house of exceptional size, perhaps the residence of the regional governor or some other high official. East of the gate was a complex of three stables (or, as the excavators suggest, storehouses). At the southeastern corner of the town was the water system, which descended to the level of the high water table of the Beersheba basin. The city was encircled by a casemate wall, the casemates being incorporated as rear broadrooms in houses bordering the perimeter road. Each dwelling unit had two or three longrooms facing the street, which sometimes employed pillar construction. The angles of the house walls and rows of pillars correspond to the radii and arcs of the ovoid city plan, and it would therefore seem that the town was designed down to individual details and not merely along general lines with leeway for private initiative.

The design concept of ring roads running parallel to the fortifications and radial streets as found at Beersheba may also be observed in the layout of other cities (Tell Beit Mirsim, Tell en-Nasbeh, and Beth Shemesh), though the degree of planning and the attention to details vary from site to site.

The capital cities of Samaria and Jerusalem were planned cities as well, but their excavations have un-

covered only isolated details, which do not add up to a coherent city plan. In levels IV–III at Lachish, dwelling houses built against the city wall have been discovered. They were entered from a street running parallel to the wall, and a main road led from the gate toward the palace fort. So Lachish, too, reveals elements of the concentric-radial design, which appears to have characterized most towns of the Kingdom of Judah. The urban plan set aside a large portion of the urban area for public structures—palaces, residencies, stables, granaries and storehouses, water systems, and fortifications. The more important a city was in the state hierarchy, the larger the area devoted to public structures and the lesser the area remaining for private dwellings.

By the end of the eighth century, significant differences began to appear between the Kingdom of Judah on the one hand and the coastal plain and the kingdom of Israel on the other. The latter regions came under Assyrian rule at this time, while the cities of Judah were fortified to withstand the Assyrian onslaught. The orthogonal layout of Megiddo stratum III is a case in point. This kind of urban plan is Assyrian, and it incorporated a number of mansions of the Assyrian courtyard type in the city plan.

Turning to the fortifications, they were reinforced against the Assyrian threat during the Iron Age IIb. The main siege engine of the Assyrian armies since the ninth century was the battering ram. Modified and improved during the eighth century, it consisted of a long ram extending from a wheeled, armored chamber. Y. Yadin suggested that all fortification systems of this period were designed with the Assyrian battering ram in mind. The Lachish reliefs clearly portray a series of such rams attacking the vulnerable points of the city, and there are biblical allusions as well: "Set up a siege against it, and build towers against it, and cast a mound against it; pitch camps against it, and bring up battering rams roundabout it" (Ezek. 4:2). Though Yadin's suggestion has been criticized, it would appear that the threat of the Assyrian siege engines had considerable effect on the design of fortifications. An outstanding example is stratum VA at Hazor, fortified against the Assyrians and subsequently razed by them in 732 B.C.E. In the western part of the mound, two fine houses had been built to the north of the large citadel of stratum VIII (ninth century) and had remained in use in subsequent levels, with some changes. In stratum VA the northern part of the structures was destroyed to permit the construction of a massive inset-offset wall that girdled the western tip of the mound. Outside the wall, to the north, a lookout tower was built. About 40 percent of the area of the two dwelling or administrative units was sacrificed for the construction of fortifications. A similar phenomenon was encountered in Jerusalem, where the Broad Wall of the late eighth century cut through an earlier house.

Most sites reveal evidence of reinforcement and buttressing, rather than entirely new construction. Solid walls were generally preferred, though in some places, notably at provincial centers such as Beersheba and Tell Beit Mirsim, casemate walls remained in use during the eighth century. One of the few walls actually built in the eighth century is on the western hill (the Jewish Quarter) of Jerusalem. It is 7 meters thick, and though its upper portion may not have been solid all the way through, it is the broadest wall discovered so far. The city wall at Lachish was 6.3 meters wide. This wall was originally built in Level IV of the ninth century, but it was rebuilt,

along with the revetment wall on the lower slopes of the mound, in Level III and destroyed by Sennacherib in 701 B.C.E. A wall 4 meters wide defended the stratum III settlement at Tel Batash (Timna), which was also destroyed by Sennacherib.

A unique feature of Iron Age IIb fortifications is the reinforcement of the steep slopes of the mounds. The slope was covered with crushed limestone or stone facing, to prevent the undermining of the wall foundations at the top of the slope. Stone glacis have been discovered at Lachish, Beersheba, Tel 'Ira, and Tel Halif. Inclined stone buttresses at the bases of angles or towers are present at Mizpah (Tell en-Nasbeh) and at the foot of the towers of the external wall at Gezer.

The fortified Solomonic gatehouses of the tenth century, built to provide strategic depth, continued to be built in later phases. Six-chambered gates, usually accompanied by an outer gate system, were built in the ninth century (for example, at Lachish Level IV) and remained in use in the eighth century; the gate at Lachish underwent repairs along with the rest of the Level IV fortifications. Yadin at one time suggested, on the basis of his analysis of the Iron Age gates at Megiddo, that the number of chambers in the gatehouse gradually diminished; that is to say, six-chambered gates were replaced by four-chambered gates, which in turn gave way to two-chambered gates. By the end of the Iron Age, gateways no longer had chambers but were simple passageways, sometimes fortified by towers, between two ends of the wall. The scheme proposed by Yadin is plausible, though there are a few exceptions here and there.

The many cities of the Land of Israel in the Iron Age IIb were thus well planned and well fortified. In most cases, the original layout and fortifications of the Iron Age IIa

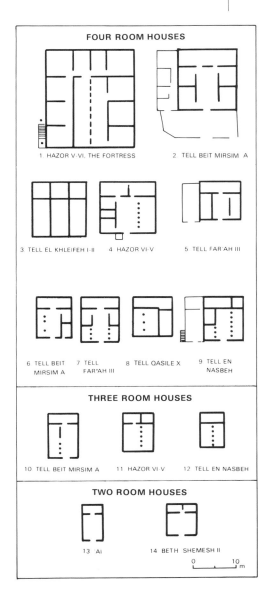

Fig. 9.24. Four-, three-, and two-room house typology

formed the basis for the improved design. Most cities of the Iron Age IIB reveal telltale signs of the Assyrian threat.

THE FOUR-ROOM HOUSE. One of the salient features of Iron Age IIb architecture is the dwelling structure known as the four-room house. It is rectangular and divided internally into four major units, or rooms. Three of the units are parallel rectangular rooms, and they are backed by the fourth unit, a broadroom. The house was generally entered by a doorway leading to the middle longroom, which was probably an open courtyard that provided light and air to the surrounding rooms. The central unit was set apart from one or both side rooms by a row of pillars that were monolithic, square in section, or composed of stacked stone segments. Stone beams supported by the pillars have been preserved at a few sites. The pillars are a fundamental component of domestic and public Israelite architecture, as seen in the stable complexes. In many cases, stone stairways run along one of the exterior walls, indicating that many of the houses had a second story. Where such staircases have not been found, it is likely that the second floor was approached by wooden stairs or ladders.

The four-room design was a fundamental architectural concept. The fourfold division of space, with three parallel units closed by a perpendicular fourth unit, is found in public as well as domestic structures. In the dwellings, the central court through which the house was entered served as a work area; here are found oil presses, ovens, or other installations. The two units flanking the court appear to have served as storerooms or animal pens. The rear room served as living quarters, though the upper story would have been the main living area.

In many four-room houses the units are subdivided with screen walls, but the basic four-room plan remains clear. The four-room house category includes the rectangular three- and two-roomed houses. The existence of subtypes and the size range among the four-room houses testify to varying levels of planning and execution as well as to the social stratification of Israelite society in the Iron Age II. Four-room houses are common in urban sites (the capitals and regional centers) and rural settlements and even appear as isolated farmhouses.

Four-room houses constitute an integral part of the Israelite city plan, as may be seen at several sites: Hazor, Tell el-Far'ah North, Shechem, Tell en-Nasbeh (Mizpah), the City of David in Jerusalem, Beth Shemesh, Lachish, Tell Beit Mirsim, Tel Beersheba, and elsewhere. In many of the houses at Tell Beit Mirsim stratum A and Tel Beersheba stratum II, the rear room functioned as a casemate in the city wall. The distribution of the four-room house and its related types more or less corresponds to the territorial extent of Israelite culture and neighboring cultures that may have been influenced by it. The principal builders of the four-room house were undoubtedly the bearers of Israelite culture in Judah and Israel. A question remains, however, regarding the origin of this house type. Though in the past the four-room house was often linked with house types of other cultures, it is now agreed that the type evolved and developed among the Israelites. Its sources may be traced back to the end of the Late Bronze Age and to many structures of the Iron Age I. The distinct form of the four-room house is maintained throughout the Iron Age II–IIIa from the tenth century to the fall of Judah in 586 B.C.E. The finest four-room structures belong mainly to the eighth and seventh centuries. The four-room house disappears from the scene with the demise of Israelite culture, in 586 B.C.E.

WATER SUPPLY SYSTEMS. The regular supply of water was one of the chief concerns of Israelite city planners. Water supply systems of the Iron Age II exhibit great effort and skill in planning and execution, and apart from alleviating the burden of water supply for the inhabitants, the sophisticated systems of the period seem mainly to assure the availability of water during siege.

The Iron Age II excelled in the efficient utilization of water sources. This may be observed in the extension of many springs of the Judaean hills by means of tunneling, a technique used to increase flow. It is also prominent in the construction of many pools apparently intended to collect surface runoff and excess springwater (cf. biblical references to pools: Gibeon, II Sam. 2:13; Hebron, II Sam. 4:12; Jerusalem, Is. 7:3, 22:9–11, and elsewhere; Samaria, I Kings 22:38; Heshbon, Song of Songs 7:5). The city of Samaria and the extensive western suburb of Jerusalem had no local water source; presumably these important sites were supplied with water from distant areas by means of channels and aqueducts. The technical know-how necessary for the construction of ground-level channels was available, judging from the engineering exhibited in Hezekiah's tunnel, the half-kilometer-long conduit carved in the rock beneath the city of David. Other conduits are known in Jerusalem and referred to in biblical sources as well (Is. 36:2; II Kings 20:20). The conveyance of water over long distances in channels was common in Iron Age cultures of neighboring lands. Best known is the aqueduct to Nineveh, constructed by Sennacherib in the late eighth century. There are also Iron Age II wells, their upper part lined with stone. Securely dated wells of this kind have been found at Arad and Lachish.

The summit of engineering, geological, and hydrotechnological skills in the Iron Age II is represented by a series of more than a dozen subterranean water systems. People preferred to build their cities on hilltops, and springs were generally at the foot of the hills. This posed a problem for the city planners, overcome by cutting a subterranean passage leading from ground level, within the city, to the spring outside it. This underground passage was invisible to the besieging armies, and once the approach from within the city was completed, the external signs of the water source could be hidden from view.

The water systems may be divided into two types, those that bring the inhabitants to water and those that convey water to the inhabitants. Obviously the first method is the less sophisticated and hence earlier method. The second method is more complex, for the town lay well above the water source. This problem was overcome by cutting a vertical shaft within the walls down to a tunnel that conveyed the springwater to the base of the shaft. The upper part of the shaft cut through earlier occupation layers and had to be supported with massive retaining walls, while the lower part was hewn in the rock to a level slightly lower than the spring. Steps were cut along the sides of the shaft to provide access to its base. In some water systems, however, there was no access to the bottom of the shaft, and water was drawn from above by means of ropes and pails. In an even more sophisticated solution, the shaft and tunnel lead not to a spring outside the city but to the

water table in the depths of the bedrock beneath the city.

The builders of shafts had to determine their depth in advance, as the width of the shaft dictates the depth to which the stairs descend, the shaft narrowing as the stairs wind down along its walls. In cases where the water system taps the water table, hydrogeological knowledge was required to estimate the depth of the water-carrying layers (aquifer) and the direction of the water flow. Thus the water systems of the Iron Age II attest to considerable expertise on the part of their planners and builders.

The less sophisticated water systems, those with an external approach, include gallery 629 at Megiddo (strata VA–IVB) and the system of Tell es-Sa'idiyeh, in the eastern Jordan valley. They consist of a covered passage through the city wall and a stairway descending along the slope to the spring. They appear to date to the tenth century. The shaft-and-tunnel systems linking the city to the spring include shaft 925 at Megiddo (stratum IVA), the tunnel system at Gibeon, Warren's shaft in Jerusalem, and the water system of Yibleam, ranging from the tenth century to the seventh. The systems exhibiting the highest technical standard (those that link the surface with the aquifer) include the water systems at Hazor (stratum VIII), Gezer, the pool at Gibeon, and perhaps the great shaft at Lachish. The cluster of ancient water systems at Jerusalem is of the greatest importance, though they appear to have served in part as irrigation systems.

Because of the early stage in the history of archaeology in which some of the water systems were discovered (Gezer, Yibleam, Warren's shaft), stratigraphic errors (Megiddo), and other difficulties, there is as yet no consensus regarding the date of the underground water systems. Some, such as that at

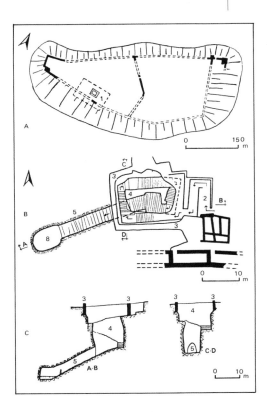

Fig. 9.25. Hazor water system: location, plan, and sections

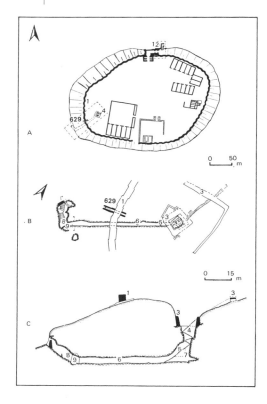

Fig. 9.26. Megiddo water system: location, plan, and section

Gezer, are dated by some archaeologists to the Late Bronze Age. The phenomenon of underground water systems was once linked to Mycenaean influence (fourteenth and thirteenth centuries), but renewed excavations at Megiddo, Hazor, Gibeon, and Jerusalem have uncovered new chronological data, which seem to confirm the attribution of the sophisticated water systems to the Iron Age II–III, between the tenth and seventh centuries.

Sophisticated hydroengineering is thus a characteristic feature of Israelite city planning. As Bronze Age reservoirs excavated at sites such as Hazor stratum XV lack the enterprise and complexity of the Iron Age II systems, it would appear that the Iron Age water systems evolved out of simpler installations used in rural areas for irrigation. It is likely that the motive for the technological improvements in the systems was the fear instilled by the ruthless expansionist designs of the neo-Assyrian empire on all countries in the region from the ninth century onward.

PHILISTIA IN THE IRON AGE II–III

The southern coastal plain, the region of Philistine settlement, reached the peak of its cultural and political prosperity in the Iron Age I. This was also the period when the Philistine-Israelite struggle, a key factor in the evolution of the Israelite monarchy, came to its fiercest pitch. Even after the victories of David over the Philistines, their cities did not lose their independence, and in the post-Solomonic era the struggle between the two nations was renewed, generally in the sign of Israelite supremacy (I Kings 15:27, 16:15). In the mid eighth century, Uzziah, king of Judah, fought a campaign in Philistia and founded cities in the conquered territories (II Chron. 26:6–7). At the end of the eighth century, relations between Judah and the cities of Philistia fluctuated, against the backdrop of Assyrian military campaigns (II Chron. 28:18). Assyrian rule in Philistia begins with the campaign of Tiglat Pileser III to Gaza (738 B.C.E.). The cities of Philistia rebelled occasionally against Assyrian rule; nonetheless, the Assyrians permitted them a degree of self-rule. In 712 B.C.E. Sargon conquered Ashdod and made it an Assyrian province (cf. Isa. 20:1). During the seventh century the Assyrian kings Esarhaddon and Ashurbanipal established a series of permanent bases in Philistia to facilitate transit to Egypt, which was conquered by Esarhaddon. The Assyrian occupation ended with the seventh century, with the death of Ashurbanipal. Josiah, king of Judah, annexed large portions of northern Philistia, while southern Philistia came, it seems, under the control of Pharaoh Necho of Egypt (Jer. 47:1). Philistia was contested by Egypt and Babylon until the conquest of Ashkelon by Nebuchadnezzar in 604 B.C.E.

The material culture begins to degenerate in the tenth century. The fine ceramic wares that characterized Philistine culture in the Iron Age I, with their wealth of painted bichrome decoration, disappear during the Iron Age II and are no longer present in assemblages of the tenth century or later. The forms of Iron Age I Philistine ware also disappear or become debased. However, new characteristic wares evolve in this region during the Iron Age II, and they are termed Coastal or Ashdod ware. Some features of this pottery exhibit the influence and legacy of the Iron Age I wares, while others show the influence of Judaean traditions on the one hand and Phoenician traditions on the other.

Of the Philistine pentapolis, only Ashdod has been extensively excavated and published; a second important site is Tell Qasile, and further information concerning Philistia comes from early excavations of W. M. F. Petrie at Tell el-Hesi, Tell Jemmah, Tell el-Ajjul, and Sheikh Zuweid and from smaller excavations at sites such as Azor, Ashdod-Yam, and Tel Mor.

The mound of Ashdod is southeast of the modern town, about four kilometers from the shore. The Iron Age II–III strata are numbered X to VI. In stratum X, of the tenth century, the settlement extended over the large area of the upper and lower cities. A city gate was unearthed at the eastern end of the city. It was built of mud bricks, with ashlar quoins, and resembles the gates of Hazor, Megiddo, Gezer, and Lachish. The gate is joined to a solid mud-brick wall five meters thick. Stratum X at Ashdod was destroyed about halfway through the tenth century, either by David or in the campaign of Siamun, mentioned in the Bible (I Kings 9:16) and in an Egyptian relief. The next level, stratum IX, is dated to the ninth and early eighth centuries. Its destruction is ascribed to Uzziah. A potter's quarter uncovered in the southwest part of the lower city is attributed to this stratum. Here were discovered industrial installations, including pottery kilns, and many pottery vessels. In addition, a small structure identified as a shrine was exposed, containing a raised, mud-brick platform interpreted as an altar. Inside the structure and in nearby pits were many ceramic vessels, including some of obvious cultic function, such as the kernoi, hollow ring-shaped vessels with animal heads or miniature vessels attached, their bases opening to the hollow ring. These vessels were used for libation and are the successors of similar cult vessels common in the

Iron Age I. Many pottery figurines were found as well. Some had a flattened or concave anthropomorphic head attached to a body shaped like a four-legged table or chair. These are the typological successors of the Iron Age I Ashdoda figurines, which exhibit Aegean influence. In the earlier period most of the figurines were female, whereas in the Iron Age II male figures become more common, perhaps inspired by the figure of Dagon, the city god of Ashdod (I Sam. 5:5).

The pottery of the Iron Age IIb exhibits a greater degree of creativity and imagination than the pottery of the Shephelah and of Judaea. The Judaean pottery is chiefly functional and undecorated, while the pottery of Ashdod includes considerable painted ornamentation.

Stratum VIII at Ashdod was destroyed in the campaign of Sargon II in 712 B.C.E. An important find are fragments of a royal stela of Sargon, in the style of the inscriptions uncovered in his capital, Khorsabad. To this stratum are attributed mass graves, where human remains were gathered after battle, judging from the secondary burial and marks of violence on the bones. Some of these burials were covered with a thick calcareous deposit. As many as three thousand bodies were counted, probably victims of the Assyrian conquest.

In the eighth century, Philistia shared in the diffusion of literacy evident in other parts of the Land of Israel. The inhabitants of the Philistine coast adopted the Hebrew script current in Judaea but with some variations in the forms of the letters. There appears also to be some relation to Phoenician script, and by the seventh century the dwellers of the southern coastal plain may well have developed their own national script. Inscriptions in the characteristic script of Philistia were found incised on potsherds at

Ashdod. Inscriptions in ink have been found at Tell Jemmeh, and seals inscribed in the script of Philistia are known as well.

Tell Qasile, a port town established by the Philistines on the banks of the Yarkon in the twelfth century, flourished in the Iron Age I. The prosperity of the Philistine town with its magnificent temple ended in the fiery destruction of stratum X, probably early in the reign of David, in the early tenth century. Strata IX–VII at Tell Qasile belong to the Iron Age II. Stratum IX dates to the second half of the tenth century and may have ended during the campaign of Siamun. Stratum VIII dates to the late tenth and early ninth centuries; it was abandoned and not violently destroyed. In both strata the temple of strata XII–X was restored and reused, suggesting the continued presence of a Philistine population. Among the houses of this period, typical four-room houses are conspicuous. In the Qasile excavations, as in other sites of Philistia, decorated Philistine ware ceases to be produced with the destruction of stratum X. From the early tenth century a clear decline of Philistine culture sets in, after the floruit of the twelfth and eleventh centuries.

The new excavations at Tel Miqne (Ekron) and at Ashkelon should illuminate the culture of Philistia in the Iron Age II–III.

PHOENICIAN CULTURE IN THE LAND OF ISRAEL

"Phoenicia" is the name given to the coastal strip at the foot of the Lebanon mountains, between Arvad in the north and the Carmel range in the south, with its prosperous coastal towns of Arvad, Byblos, Beirut, Sidon, Tyre, and others. Only a small part of Phoenicia is in present-day Israel, including the western and coastal Galilee, from Rosh Ha-Niqra to the bay of Haifa. Though this part appears to be less important than the heart of Phoenicia (Sidon, Tyre, and their environs), most of our knowledge of the archaeology of Phoenicia in the Iron Age II–III comes from excavations within it.

According to biblical evidence, strong political and mercantile bonds were forged between David and Solomon and the Phoenicians ruled by Hiram of Tyre. In the ninth century, during the Omrid dynasty, the close relations between Israel and Phoenicia were maintained. This link is best reflected in the diplomatic marriages with the house of Etba'al, king of Sidon. From the eighth century, Assyrian interest in the cities of the Phoenician coast steadily increased. The cities paid tribute to Assyria from the time of Adadnirari III of Assyria (796 B.C.E.), and as the eighth century progressed, Assyrian pressure increased. In the seventh century, during the reigns of Esarhaddon and Ashurbanipal, Assyria took complete possession of the cities of the Phoenician coast.

In the Iron Age II the Phoenicians began to expand and establish colonies overseas. The first Phoeni-cian colonies were established on Cyprus, and thence they expanded to the other Mediterranean isles and along the coast of the western Mediterranean basin as far away as Morocco and Spain. The date of the beginning of Phoenician colonization in the west is a vexed question. One school of thought would place it as early as the eleventh and tenth centuries; others date it to the eighth century. The dating of Phoenician colonization is linked to the interpretation of historical texts, but more especially it depends on the precise dating of ceramic wares present in Phoenicia and in the colonies of the western Mediterranean. Hence the great importance of the study of the autochthonous Phoenician culture, beyond the issues relating to the archaeology of the Land of Israel and the Near East. Another much-debated issue is the date of the adoption of the Phoenician alphabet by the Greeks. Some believe it was adopted at the beginning of the Iron Age, while others offer a later date, in the Iron Age IIb. Regarding both issues, I prefer the earlier dating, but the key to these complex chronological problems is probably in the stratigraphy and ce-ramic typology of the archaeological sites in the Land of Israel.

It is commonly thought that the material culture of the Phoenicians constitutes a continuation of the Late Bronze Age Canaanite culture of the Land of Israel and Syria, reflected in the realms of architecture, art, religion, pottery, and more. In Israelite material culture of the Iron Age II–III, a link with Phoenicia is reflected either in Phoenician influence evident in local products or in the presence of objects actually manufactured in Phoenician workshops. Best known are the suggestions regarding the Phoenician origin of Solomon's temple in Jerusalem and the Phoenician inspiration evident in the architectural details and ornamentation of his public buildings (see I Kings 5:20–29, 32; 7:13–14). Many scholars also hold that the magnificent ashlar masonry of the Iron Age II in the Land of Israel is of Phoenician origin, along with several kinds of art objects and luxury items, such as ivories carved in a Phoenician style found in Assyria, North Syria, the Land of Israel, and Cyprus; wrought metal bowls of Phoenician style found from Assyria in the east

Fig. 9.27. Akhziv ware

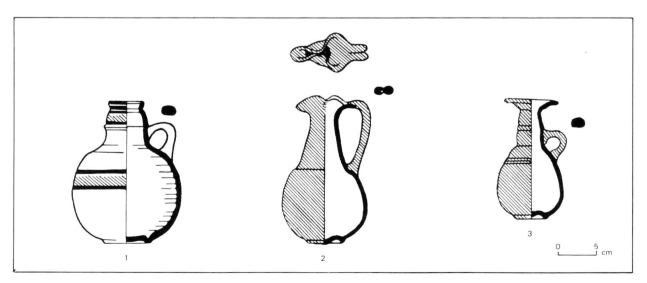

to Etruria in the west; and gold jewelry and stone vessels of a type common in the Land of Israel. The Phoenician origin of most of these prestige items has yet to be proved, and specific parallels have yet to be found in excavations undertaken on the Phoenician coast. Many of the prized art objects ascribed to the Phoenicians reveal considerable Egyptian influence, raising the questions: Why should the Phoenicians employ Egyptian cultural elements, and why should they propagate art and culture of largely Egyptian inspiration?

Most of the information concerning the Phoenicians has accumulated in excavations within Israel, including excavations at Akhziv, Accho, Tell Keisan (Akhshaph or Mash'al; cf. Jos. 19:25–26), Horvat Rosh Zayit east of the Accho valley

(perhaps biblical Cabul; Jos. 19:27, I Kings 9:13), and Tell Abu Hawam at the mouth of the Nahal Qishon. To these should be added the sites of the Carmel coast—Shiqmona, Atlit, Tel Megadim, Tel Dor, and Tel Mevorakh—which were under Israelite control for much of the Iron Age but exhibit much Phoenician influence.

Phoenician cultural influence was widespread, and pottery, prestige items, and inscriptions of Phoenician attribution as well as burials have been found along the entire coast of the Land of Israel, including its southernmost parts, and in the interior. In the early eighth century, Phoenician influence and inscriptions may be observed at the remote desert site of Horvat Teman (Kuntillat 'Ajrud).

One of the key sites of Phoeni-

cian culture and one of the first to be excavated (though not yet fully published) is Akhziv (Jos. 19:29; Jud. 1:31). Two Phoenician cemeteries were revealed at the site, one lying east of the ancient town and the other to the south. The burials cover an extended span of time, from the tenth century to the Persian period. Some of the graves were cut in the rock and consist of an entrance shaft and a burial chamber. The burial chamber was roofed with stone slabs, and above it a tombstone was set up, sometimes on a dressed pedestal. Some tombstones were inscribed with the name of the deceased, such as *lzkr mlk* or *l'ma hnsk*; the latter stone is also inscribed with an Egyptian *'nkh* symbol. An especially magnificent tomb, built entirely in ashlar masonry, is dated to the early part of the

Fig. 9.28. Cypro-Phoenician ware

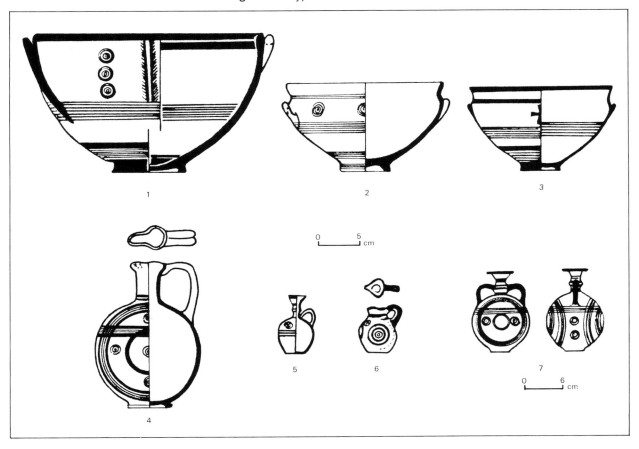

tenth century. In the sandy earth above the tombs, whether elaborate or simple, jars were placed to mark the place of burial. In many places, traces of campfires were identified, accompanied by pottery vessels, remains of the funeral meals eaten at the cemetery. In other cases the fires were identified as cremation sites. Cremation is an important characteristic of Phoenician culture in the Iron Age II. After cremation, the ashes were collected into deep urns, which were buried in the sand, the mouth sealed with a bowl. The urns often bear painted decoration and burnish. They have been found not only at Akhziv but at many sites on the coast, wherever Phoenician settlement and influence existed: at Azor, Tell el-Far'ah South, Tell el-Ajjul, and Ruqeish, near Gaza. The practice of cremation and the interment in urns is also known in the Phoenician colonies in the west, particularly at Carthage in Tunisia, Tharos in Sardinia, and Mozia in western Sicily. Cremation apparently ceased in the late Iron Age, and in the Persian period Phoenicians buried their dead in rock-cut shaft tombs.

A wealth of pottery and figurines was recovered from the Akhziv tombs, comprising, in quantity and quality, one of the most important assemblages of finds from Phoenicia. The pottery characteristic of the earlier phases belongs to the group known as Phoenician bichrome ware. The vessels are made of pale clay decorated in red and black. In the eighth century the pottery known as Akhziv ware was introduced. It is characteristic of indigenous Phoenician culture as well as of the main phase of Phoenician colonization in the west. The most important vessels in the Akhziv family are the jugs. Some are characterized by a conical neck, broad at the base and narrow at top; others are swollen at the neck. The

jug rims are trefoil or take the form of an everted, mushroom rim. All Akhziv-ware vessels are red-slipped and well-burnished. Fine shallow bowls, used as urn lids at Akhziv and elsewhere (including the western colonies), are of the type known as Samaria ware. Samaria ware is but one of the branches of the Phoenician ceramic industry. Phoenician material culture appears to have heavily influenced the material culture and particularly the ceramic industry of the northern Israelite kingdom; however, it is also possible that Phoenician culture was influenced by forms and contents of Israelite origin, so that the Israelites may have been more than a passive partner in their relations with Phoenicia.

Another group of Phoenician vessels typical chiefly of the southern coastal plain is named after the site of Ruqeish, south of Gaza. The cemeteries of this site were discovered at about the same time as the Akhziv burial ground, in the early forties. More recently, the site of a planned town, fortified with a massive mud-brick wall, has been identified. This town appears to have served as a southern Phoenician port, built on Assyrian initiative in the eighth century and inhabited until the Persian period. Ruqeish ware consists mainly of burial urns, that is, kraters of various types, and it is conspicuous for a high burnish in vertical or horizontal wheel-made strokes. The vessels are sometimes decorated with horizontal painted bands.

Another ceramic group attributed to the Phoenicians is that termed Cypro-Phoenician. Chemical analyses of the clay of the Cypro-Phoenician vessels have shown that all were manufactured on Cyprus and exported to the Land of Israel, Syria, Phoenicia, and even Cilicia. The most prominent family within the group is called

black-on-red and is decorated in parallel stripes and concentric circles painted black against a red background. The importation of Cypro-Phoenician ware to the Land of Israel began in the tenth century or perhaps even earlier, at the end of the Iron Age I, and continued until the early sixth century, that is, through the whole of the Iron Age II–III. Judging by the quantities and character of the vessels, which consist mainly of jugs, juglets, and flasks, Cypro-Phoenician vessels not only served as mere containers traded for their content but were imported for their aesthetic value as well.

The discovery of Akhziv ware in well-dated assemblages, in clear stratigraphical contexts at Hazor, Samaria, and Megiddo and also at more southerly sites, permits the dating of similar vessels in the western Phoenician colonies. The same is true of Samaria ware, Cypro-Phoenician ware, and torpedo jars (the jars used in Phoenician maritime trade), which are all present in the colonies of the western Mediterranean.

MARGINAL AREAS AND ISOLATED FORTRESSES

The desert margins of the Kingdom of Judah (the Judaean desert, the Beersheba-Arad valley, and the Negev Highlands) constitute a measure of the political and military power of the kingdom. When its power waxed, Judah controlled the desert routes by maintaining fortresses along them and the borders of the kingdom. When it waned, no building activity or presence may be traced in the marginal areas. In those periods for which biblical historical sources mention Israelite control of Elath, on the Red Sea shore, there had to be full control of the network of routes in the Negev linking the Gulf of Elath and Judah.

These periods include the reigns of Solomon (the tenth century), Jehosophat (in the ninth century), Uzziah, and Yotam (in the eighth century). Regarding the reigns of Jehosophat, Uzziah, and Yotam, the sources mention *biraniyot* and *migdalim,* apparently the ancient terms for the fortresses in the marginal areas. Between the reigns of these kings and after them there were periods of decline, during which Judah lost control of Elath and the Negev.

The archaeological picture does not match the historical data from the Bible. The tenth century, the time of Solomon, is represented by a series of settlements or fortresses in the Negev Highlands, the interpretation of which is debated. This settlement system appears to have been abandoned in the wake of the campaign of Shishak in 925 B.C.E. But there is no evidence of any tenth-century sites between the Negev Highlands and the Gulf of Elath. Neither are the days of Jehosophat, Uzziah, and Yotam represented by the kind of fortress and

settlement system one would expect in light of the biblical claims. The biblical term "Negev," however, has different connotations from the modern term, and in the Iron Age II–III it refers only to the Beersheba-Arad basin. In the entire expanse to the south of that basin, settlements or fortresses are extremely limited, consisting of only three sites, Kadesh Barnea, Horvat Teman (Kuntillat 'Ajrud), and Tell el-Kheleifeh.

Judahite authority in the desert margins, and the Negev in particular, was largely a corollary of the relations with the kingdom of Edom, to the southeast in southern Transjordan. As long as the kings of Judah dominated Edom, or in periods of Edomite decline, Israelites controlled and prospered in the Negev. In the later days of the Kingdom of Judah, beginning apparently with the reign of Mannasseh, there is a renewal of Israelite settlement in the southern marginal areas, though the region of Elath remained under Edomite rule from the time of Ahaz onward (II Chron. 28:17; II Kings 16:6). Parts of the

northern Negev fell into Edomite hands in the late seventh or early sixth century, before the final collapse of Judah and the Babylonian destruction of 586 B.C.E. Evidence of Edomite domination comes from the content of some of the Arad ostraca, which mention the Edomite threat, as well as from a large number of Edomite finds at Aroer, Horvat Qitmit, and Horvat 'Uza, where an ostracon written in the Edomite script and tongue was found. Most of the data concerning the Israelite border area in the Negev come from the biblical Negev, that is, the Beersheba valley, in a series of excavations in towns and fortresses, notably Tel Beersheba and sites within modern Beersheba, Tel Masos, Tel 'Ira, Tel Aroer, Tel Malhata, Horvat 'Uza, and Tel Arad.

One of the most intriguing of the Iron Age II–III sites is Tell el-Kheleifeh, between modern Elath and 'Aqabah, at the head of the Gulf of Elath. It is the only site that can be identified with biblical Ezion-Geber. There is, however, a ques-

Fig. 9.29. Ezion-Geber: plan of site in strata I–II (A) and suggested restoration of stratum I (B)

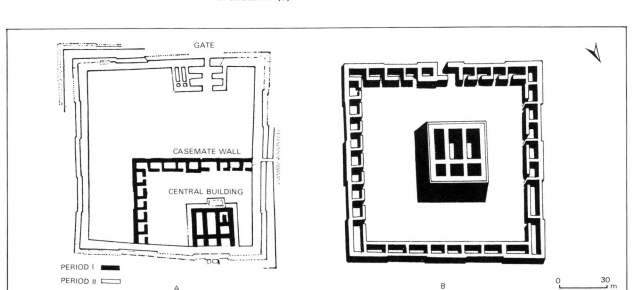

tion whether Elath (or Eloth) and Ezion-Geber are one and the same site (Num. 33:35–36; Deut. 2:8; I Kings 9:26–28; II Chron. 8:17–18; I Kings 22:49–50; II Chron. 20:35–37; II Kings 14:21–22). Tell el-Kheleifeh was excavated in 1938–40, and five main settlement levels were reported, spanning the tenth through fourth centuries. The earliest remains were sherds of Midianite ware, dated to the Late Bronze Age. Renewed study of the excavation results has revealed that there was but scant stratigraphy and that most of the basic assumptions of the excavators were inconsistent with the finds. The excavators interpreted the site as a center of metallurgical activity, with no basis in fact. The site was also related to King Solomon, on the basis of the biblical evidence, but the published material includes no pottery of the tenth century. Only two main building phases were uncovered at Tell el-Kheleifeh. The first consists of a large four-room structure, surrounded by a square, enclosed by a casemate wall measuring 45 × 45

meters square. In the second phase the casemate wall went out of use, and a larger enclosure (57 × 62.5 meters) was built, this time encompassed by a solid inset-offset wall. The central four-room structure continued to function. Construction at Tell el-Kheleifeh was entirely in mud brick, which was not conducive to the preservation of the structures or the clear understanding of the stratigraphy. Renewed study of the pottery excavated at the site in the thirties has revealed no finds dating earlier than the eighth century. A considerable proportion of the late eighth century remains, including seal impressions and seals, belong to the Edomite material culture and are clearly unrelated to the culture of Judaea.

Horvat Teman (Kuntillat 'Ajrud) lies fifty kilometers south of Kadesh Barnea, on the ancient road from Gaza and Rafah to the Gulf of Elath and Sinai, the Darb el-Ghazzeh. It is on a flat hilltop at the foot of which are some wells. Excavations revealed the remains of a central

structure and a subsidiary structure to the east. The entrance to the main structure faces east and consists of an indirect axis gateway, which means that the interior of the building could not be seen from the outside. The rooms flanking the gateway contained benches coated with a thick layer of plaster. Square towers stood at either end of the eastern facade, but the general aspect of the structure is not defensive, and it differs in period, character, and finds from the Iron Age fortresses of the Negev Highlands. The walls were built of fieldstones and incorporated well-preserved wooden beams. The plan of the structure corresponds to the local terrain, but it also seems suited to a special function. The structure is not a military installation, as is best shown by the inscriptions, which are the prize find of the site. They were found on plaster fragments from the doorjambs of the main structure (cf. Deut. 6:9); short inscriptions were also incised on pottery vessels before firing. Other

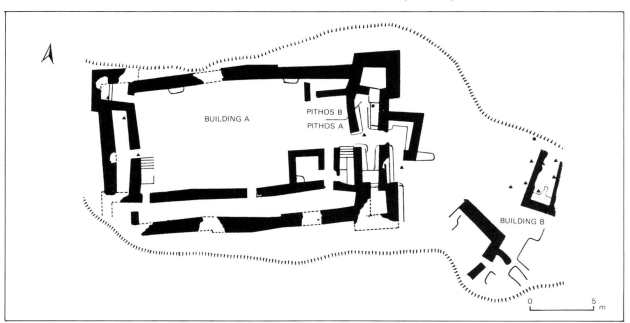

Fig. 9.30. Horvat Teman (Kuntillat 'Ajrud) site plan

inscriptions include dedications on rims of large stone basins and, most important, inscriptions painted in red on large pithoi, accompanied by drawings of humans, animals, and deities. Most of the inscriptions are written in ancient Hebrew script, but some of the wall inscriptions, possibly parts of literary texts, are in Phoenician script. The large pithoi belong to a vessel type well known from excavations throughout the Kingdom of Judah and in particular from Beersheba and Jerusalem. They are large (0.9–1 meter in height) two-handled jars with a holemouth rim. The shoulder generally bears a wheel-made furrow, near which isolated letters such as *aleph, yod,* or even combinations such as *qr* (interpreted as an abbreviation of the word *qorban,* "sacrifice" were incised before firing. The finds are all consistent with the interpretation of the structure as a cult center.

The pottery vessels of Horvat Teman have been chemically analyzed to determine the origin of their clay. The results show that they were manufactured in the Judaean hills, in the central hills, and even on the coast, in the Ashdod region. The large inscribed and decorated pithoi apparently came from Jerusalem. Thus it may be surmised that the site was a focus of pilgrimage for travelers from different parts of the country. The date of this short-lived site, according to typological and paleographical considerations, is the late ninth or early eighth century.

The site of Kadesh Barnea (Tell el-Qudeirat) is in a well-watered area on the western border of the Negev, today a part of Sinai. Biblical Kadesh Barnea is most probably in this region. Extensive excavations have exposed the site almost completely, revealing settlement remains ranging from the tenth century to the Persian period, along with three superimposed fortresses. The earliest fortress had a rounded outline and was enclosed by a casemate wall. It belongs to the oval fortress type of the Negev Highlands, typical to the tenth century. The difference between Kadesh Barnea and the other sites is the clear stratigraphic situation of the round fortress beneath later fortresses of a different plan and size, for the other rounded fortresses of the Negev all appear in single-period sites. The early fortress was destroyed, in all probability, in the campaign of Pharaoh Shishak in the late tenth century. After a time, a new fortress was constructed, rectangular in plan and furnished with eight rectangular towers placed at the corners and in the middle of each side. The solid fortress wall was about 4 meters wide and measured 40 × 60 meters. The interior consisted of building insulae separated by alleys in what appears to be a carefully planned design. In addition there was a large reservoir approached by a stairway and fed by a channel that passed through the wall. The construction of the fortress is ascribed to Uzziah, in the mid eighth century, and its destruction to the time of Mannasseh, in the mid seventh century. The rooms of the fortress contained large assemblages of pottery, including the usual Judaean wares and a large group of handmade Negbite vessels. The appearance of this ware in all the phases at Kadesh Barnea proves that the mere presence of Negbite technology cannot constitute a chronological criterion. No Negbite ware was found at Horvat Teman, indicating that the makers of this pottery did not frequent the site. Shortly after the destruction of the eight-towered fortress at Kadesh Barnea, another fortress was constructed on its ruins. The new fortress followed the walls of the earlier structure and was enclosed by a casemate wall. The excavators date

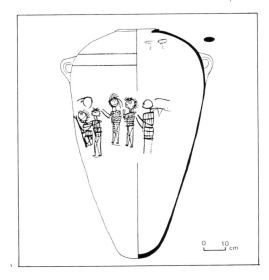

Fig. 9.31. Horvat Teman, decorated and inscribed storage jar

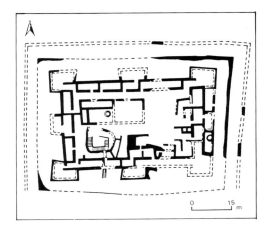

Fig. 9.32. Kadesh Barnea, middle fortress

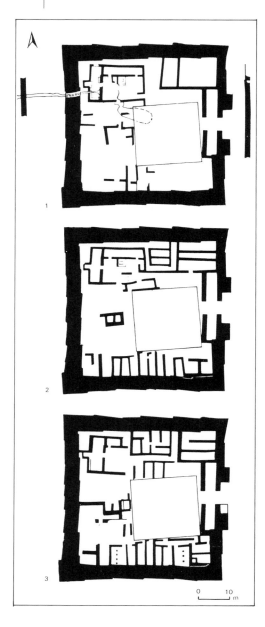

Fig. 9.33. Arad fortresses of strata X–VIII

its construction to the days of Josiah and ascribe its destruction to the demise of Judah at the hands of Babylon in 586 B.C.E. As in other Israelite sites of the desert margins, many inscriptions were found at Kadesh Barnea, including a large ostracon (30 centimeters long) that contained a series of numbers and units of weight, apparently representing a scribal exercise.

Another Iron Age II–III fortress was excavated at Horvat 'Uza, south of Arad. This site was occupied in later times, and it is stratum IV that is attributed to the Iron Age. The fortress is rectangular, measuring 42 × 51 meters, and defended by a wall 1.5 meters wide. A gate on the north leads to an alleyway dividing the interior of the fortress in two. In addition to the four corner towers, the fortress had two towers on each of the long sides and a tower in the middle of each of the shorter sides, making ten towers in all. This appears to have been a military fort guarding the southern border of the Kingdom of Judah and controlling the nearby route that passed through Nahal Qina. Many ostraca were found at Horvat 'Uza, including one from the time when the fortress was overrun by the Edomites, to judge by its Edomite script and language.

The material culture of the towns on the desert margins is closer to that of Judaea than that of the desert regions. At the town sites (Tel Beersheba, Tel Aroer, and Tel 'Ira) lamelekh seal impressions dated to the late eighth century were found. The small number of such handles in the Negev area indicates that the region did not play a decisive role during the campaign of Sennacherib.

The site of Arad connects the Negev fortresses, the forts and isolated towers of the Judaean desert, and the cities of the Judaean hills and Shephelah. The excavators of Arad identified six strata of the Iron Age II–III.

The fortress of the Iron Age II at Arad was preceded by a village of the Iron Age I (stratum XII), which was established on the ruins of the great fortified city of the Early Bronze Age. The earliest fortress at Arad is that of stratum XI. It is 50 meters square, with a casemate wall and twelve projecting towers. The fortress gate lay near the northeast corner. In the northwest corner was a shrine, the only structure of its kind known in the archaeology of the Iron Age. It has one cult room, at the west end of a broad courtyard, a broadroom entered from the middle of the eastern wall. Opposite the entrance, on the west side, was a raised cell, approached by three steps, which contained a rounded cult stela, a stone slab that served as an offering table, and two stone incense altars. All the furnishings of this cult cell were found destroyed and discarded. In the courtyard the excavators were able to identify a sacrificial altar built of fieldstones (cf. Ex. 20:21). The Arad temple remained in use, according to the excavators, during strata XI–VII; in stratum VI of the late seventh century it no longer existed.

In stratum X a new fortress was erected, probably in the wake of Shishak, for Arad appears in the list of cities destroyed by him. The new fortress was defended by a solid inset-offset wall, three to four meters thick. The architectural history of the Arad fortress, with its casemate wall succeeded by a solid wall, is most reminiscent of the fortress of Tell el-Kheleifeh in the southern Aravah. In strata VIII–VII the general outline of the fortress remained the same as in stratum X, and only in stratum VI, according to the excavators, was there a significant change. In stratum VI a casemate fortress with towers was built, the gate was moved to the northern flank, and the temple went out of use.

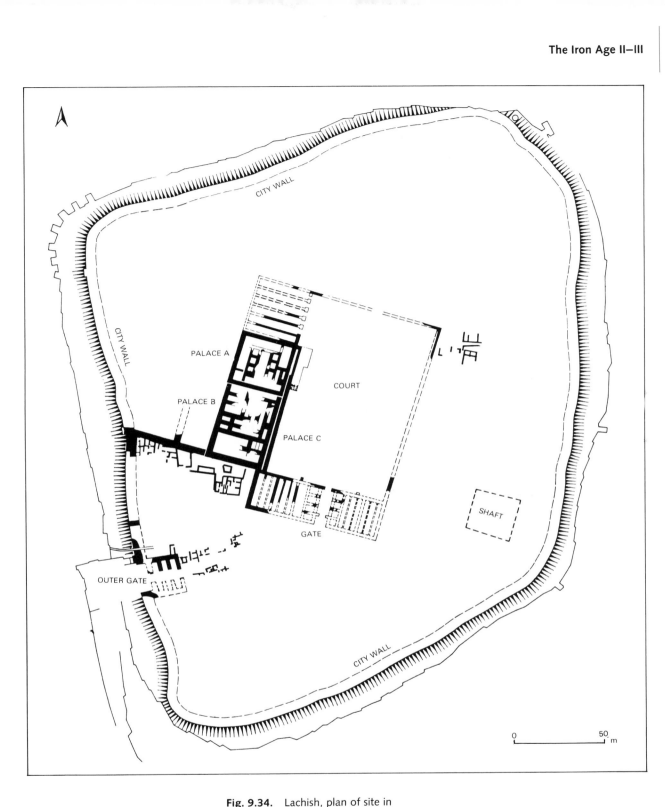

Fig. 9.34. Lachish, plan of site in stratum III

About ninety ostraca were found at the site, including an archive of eighteen letters belonging to one Eliashib, son of Oshiyahu, commandant of the Arad fortress. Three seals bearing the same name were found at the fortress as well. The archive was ascribed by the excavators to stratum VI.

Arad exemplifies the isolated border fortress. Only 0.25 hectare in area, it resembled other frontier fortresses of Judah in function and internal organization. The isolated fortresses, situated at strategic spots on highways, on the borders of the kingdom, or at choice observation sites, are characteristic of the Iron Age II–III in general, not only in the Negev desert margins. Fortresses are found in the Judaean desert at Nahal Zeelim, above the oasis of En Gedi, and along the northern shore of the Dead Sea. The Judaean desert fortresses may have been established before the seventh century, though most scholars place their construction within that century, perhaps in the reign of Josiah. The isolated fortresses consist of a square structure, sometimes with towers but more often lacking them, with a central court and a few residential and administrative structures. The fortresses discovered along the Dead Sea may therefore be identified with the provincial towns listed in Joshua 15:61.

Isolated fortresses and towers are not limited solely to the desert margins. Series of fortified towers have been identified surrounding the city of Jerusalem in the late Iron Age and in surveys of the environs of Samaria, the capital of the kingdom of Israel. Isolated fortresses in the form of rectangular compounds were also built in the forests of the Shephelah, the slopes of the Judaean hill zone, and the Judaean hills proper. These appear to be the fortresses built in the "woods" (II Chron. 27:4), that is, the wooded

parts of Judaea. The network of fortresses covered the entire kingdom and they appear to have been within the ken of one another, so that news could be conveyed by signal fires on rooftops. The fortress network was linked to the large cities.

The isolated desert fortresses, as well as the fortresses scattered throughout Judah and to a lesser extent Israel, testify to the same centralized planning and initiative evident in the construction and fortification of the towns of the period.

LACHISH

Lachish is the capital of the Shephelah, one of the more important provinces of the Kingdom of Judah. The city was probably second only to Jerusalem in Iron Age II–III Judah. Lachish has been identified with Tell ed-Duweir, a site on one of the east-west highways at the gateway leading from the coastal plain and Shephelah to the heart of Judaea, the Hebron hills. The mound of Lachish is one of the largest and most important Bronze Age sites in the Land of Israel, with occupation going back to the Chalcolithic period. The summit of the mound covers about eight hectares. In the Iron Age II–III, settlement extended beyond the boundaries of the fortified mound to the broad valleys at its foot. Extensive excavations were carried out by a British expedition headed by J. L. Starkey (1932–38) and by Israeli expeditions headed by Y. Aharoni (1966, 1968) and D. Ussishkin (1973).

The Iron Age II–III is represented at Lachish by a wealth of archaeological finds discovered in clear stratigraphic contexts. The Iron Age settlement was not disturbed by later deposits, as the layers of the Iron Age and Persian period mark the end of settlement at the site. The archaeological finds

and historical record are supplemented by a unique and apparently reliable depiction of the Assyrian siege of Lachish discovered in the palace of Sennacherib at Nineveh. This conjunction of sources has made Lachish a key site for the archaeology and chronology of the Kingdom of Judah as a whole. Finds of Iron Age II–III strata from the various Judaean sites are always compared with the well-dated finds at Lachish, and the chronological-typological schemes of many Judaean sites may be said to rely on the findings at Lachish.

The Iron Age II–III is represented at Lachish by four strata, numbered II through V. The latest Canaanite city, Level VI, was destroyed sometime during the twelfth century. After a considerable time, the first Israelite city was established on the Canaanite ruins, apparently in the days of Solomon, in the mid tenth century. Knowledge of this city is only fragmentary, as excavations have reached this level (V) only in limited exposures. In later fills, fairly large amounts of red-slipped and hand-burnished ware typical to the tenth century were found. Judging by the stratigraphic trench excavated on the west side of the mound, the houses of Level V went right up to the edge of the mound, leaving no room for a city wall, and it may therefore be assumed that the tenth-century city was unfortified. This may explain the absence of Lachish in the biblical descriptions of Solomon's building projects.

The Level V houses exposed in the trench were destroyed in a conflagration, which might perhaps be identified with the destruction wrought by Shishak of Egypt in 925 B.C.E. The following stratum, IV, was built as a well-fortified royal city by one of the kings of Judah, probably Jehosophat (870–846 B.C.E.). The first phase of Level IV shows that the city was planned as an important royal and military center rather than as a demographic center. The scope and ostentation evident in its layout reflect royal initiative, with the main components being the fortifications and the palace fort.

The Level IV settlement was defended by a double fortification, perhaps the kind alluded to in the Bible (cf. Isa. 22:11, II Kings 25:4, and elsewhere). Halfway down the steep slope of the mound an outer wall was erected, and at the juncture of the slope and the plateau the inner wall was built. The outer wall has been completely exposed. It is 3 meters wide and has insets and offsets, as well as buttresses at vulnerable points. It does not appear to have been freestanding; rather, it was a revetment, with only one built face. Between the outer and inner walls was a well-built, stone-faced glacis. The outer wall was intended to hinder the approach of siege engines to the upper, inner wall. The upper wall has been investigated at several points: it is a massive mud-brick wall with a stone foundation, about 6.2 meters thick.

The fortifications were pierced by a gate composed of an outer and inner gatehouse. The main, inner gate consists of three chambers on each side of the passage. The gatehouse is much larger (25 meters square) and more massive than other gates of the same type (at Hazor, Gezer, Megiddo, Ashdod, and elsewhere). Its deep foundations support a brick superstructure, which has been preserved in parts.

The walls, the external gate bastion, and the gateway of Level IV continued to serve the city of Level III. There is no historical or archaeological evidence suggesting that Level IV came to an end in battle or by violent conquest. It must therefore be assumed that it was destroyed in the great earthquake of

the time of Uzziah (Amos 1:1; Zech. 14:5).

The city of Level III closely resembles the later phases of Level IV, with a greater density of settlement. Level III was apparently built soon after the earthquake and violently destroyed and burned. The domestic furnishings of houses in all parts of the mound were found on the floors, buried under thick layers (up to two meters deep) of collapse. The collapse was accompanied by a fire, as attested by the brilliant colors of the fired mud bricks and the warping of ceramic vessels. Lachish Level III provides an outstanding example of wanton destruction at the hands of an enemy. The destruction layers seal rich assemblages, particularly of pottery, the dates of which can be fixed by identifying the conqueror, in this case the Assyrians of 701 B.C.E. This conquest is reported in biblical sources (II Kings 18:17, 19:8; II Chron. 32:9) and in the Assyrian palace reliefs from Nineveh.

Among the Level III finds are about four hundred jar handles stamped with the royal lamelekh (belonging "to the King") and a number of complete jars bearing such impressions on the handles. The Lachish assemblage includes all known variations of the lamelekh seals, as well as impressions of the so-called private seals. The presence of all types of the lamelekh provides a key for their dating at the other sites of Judaea. In light of the Lachish finds, all lamelekh seals should be dated to the reign of Hezekiah, in the last third of the eighth century.

Among the many private structures built south of the palace fort in Level III are some of the stable type, with rows of pillars. The Assyrian reliefs show a chariot being removed from Lachish in the victory procession and chariot parts being thrown from the wall as part of the

desperate defense of the city (cf. Mic. 1:13). It is reasonable to assume that Hezekiah's Lachish was one of the chief chariot towns of Judah, a place where horse and chariot were mustered in preparation for Hezekiah's rebellion against Assyrian rule.

Vivid remains of the Assyrian siege and the battle of Lachish in 701 B.C.E. have been unearthed, forming a fascinating chapter in the story of Lachish. The details uncovered in the excavations complement those depicted so realistically and precisely in the Assyrian reliefs, and the two sources permit what appears to be an accurate reconstruction of the siege and the battle. On the southwestern side of the mound a saddle connects the mound with the hill where the present-day village of Lachish is located, apparently the site of Sennacherib's siege camp. The saddle forms the most convenient approach to the mound, so the fortifications of the southwest angle of the town were especially massive. On the slope facing the saddle a large mound of fieldstones, which could not have been part of the collapsed wall and ruins of the town, has been identified as the Assyrian siege ramp portrayed in the reliefs. Battering rams were pushed up the ramp to the base of the city walls and pounded the defenses. Sixty meters wide at its base, the great ramp marks the point where the Assyrians breached the walls. It is the only siege ramp identified in the Iron Age anywhere in the Near East. Inside the city walls, opposite the siege ramp (which completely covered the outer wall), an astonishing discovery was made. While the Assyrians were throwing up the siege works, the defenders built a counter ramp against the wall from within. These enormous earth-moving activities were undertaken during the siege, probably under a hail of arrows. In the area of the breach, vivid reminders of the battle were found, including hundreds of arrowheads, mostly made of iron, some of bone, and many spherical flint slingstones. At the foot of the wall were large perforated stones to which traces of rope still adhered, evidently a weapon of some sort. A bronze crest found nearby was identified by the British excavators as part of the Assyrian battle headgear. However, traces of leather and study of the Assyrian reliefs suggest that this was part of the harness ornaments of the Assyrian chariot horse.

A number of tombs have been excavated in the environs of Lachish, among them a cave with a large deposit of skulls, which must be related to the catastrophe of 701 B.C.E.

After a lapse, Level II at Lachish was built on the ruins of the earlier city, probably toward the end of the seventh century, in the time of Josiah. Although the date of the construction of Level II has not been precisely established, the date of its destruction is well documented, for the city fell to the Babylonians along with the rest of the kingdom in 586 B.C.E. Biblical reference to the battle at Lachish supplements the circumstantial data (Jer. 34:7). The destruction was violent and accompanied by a great fire, which sealed large find assemblages, including much pottery and many inscriptions.

The fortifications of Level II relied largely on the remains of the Level IV–III fortifications. The wall was thinner (about 2.5 meters) and was built of two faces of worked stone with a rubble core. The gate is unique, forming an independent fortified citadel, as it were. The gate complex, built on the remains of the earlier bastion, consisted of a forward gate and an inner gate. The inner gate was a simple affair, lacking the strategic depth of the earlier structure. Between the inner and outer gates was an open court paved with stones and furnished with low stairs leading to the inner gate. Ranged round the court were the rooms that gave the gate its fortress appearance. The first room to the right contained a cache of 21 letters written in ink on potsherds. The content of the letters may indicate, along with the plan of the gatehouse and the lack of any other central structure, that the governor resided in the gate complex, making it the administrative center of the site.

South of the palace fort, houses of Level II were found superimposed on the ruins of Level III, and the finds seem to indicate that the city was densely settled. The many inscriptions discovered in Level II, in contrast to their relative dearth in Level III, testify to the importance of Lachish as an administrative center and to widespread literacy in seventh-century Judaea.

ROYAL JARS AND LAMELEKH SEALS

Ever since the excavations of Charles Warren in Jerusalem in 1867, the cities of the Kingdom of Judah have been yielding jar handles stamped with seals bearing the inscription "lamelekh" ("to the King"). More than 1200 such handles have thus far come to light, a valuable assemblage that reflects important aspects of the royal administration in Judah.

The lamelekh seals fall into two broad categories, according to the emblem in the center of the impression. One depicts a four-winged scarab, the other a winged solar disk. In both types the word lamelekh is inscribed above the central design; beneath the design is the name of one of four towns: Hebron, Socoh, Ziph, and mmsht (an unknown location). The seals may be further subdivided. Among the four-winged scarabs, some are naturalistically rendered, while others are portrayed in schematic, rectangular outline. In some of the winged-disk seals the word lamelekh is dropped, and the city name appears over the central emblem, the lower part of the seal remaining blank. There are also seals that bear the inscription lamelekh but lack a city name, and seals that have only the winged solar disk with no inscription whatever. In all, between 22 and 25 seals were used to stamp all the jar handles discovered throughout Judaea. The significance of the two emblems has not been ascertained, but we do know that all the jars stamped with lamelekh seals were made of the same clay, indicating that they were manufactured and sealed at a single location in the Shephelah. Also, they are all of the same date, and the two emblems thus served contemporaneously; the presence of two seal types has no chronological significance. There is, however, a clear regional division. In northern Judah, in Jerusalem, and in the surrounding cities there is a preponderance of winged-disk seals, whereas at Lachish and in the cities of the Shephelah the four-winged scarab is predominant. It may be assumed that both were royal emblems in the Kingdom of Judah. The scarab symbol undoubtedly originated in Egypt, and the solar disk is a widespread motif in Near Eastern iconography.

In the archaeological literature lamelekh handles are the focus of attention, but they are mere potsherds that happen to carry an inscription and an emblem. Such fragments could have found their way to strata far later than those in which the royal stamped vessels were originally manufactured and used. To understand the phenomenon of the lamelekh seals and to fix their precise date and function, archaeologists must study the

Fig. 9.35. Lamelekh seal impressions from Lachish, four- (*top*) and two-winged (*bottom*) types (height of four-winged type, 3.5 centimeters)

Fig. 9.36. Four-handled (lamelekh) storage jar with stone stopper, from Lachish (height 70 centimeters)

vessel type and identify the strata and the assemblages containing the complete vessels. The royal seal impressions are usually applied to large loop handles that belong to ovoid jars, about sixty centimeters high. Each jar had four handles, a narrow mouth, and a short upright neck; apparently they were used to store liquids rather than dry goods. Ten complete stamped jars of this type, most of them from Lachish, have been found, as well as numerous unstamped jars. Some of the stamped jars are impressed on all four handles, but on others only some of the handles are stamped. On a given jar, some of the handles may bear the two-winged lamelekh impression, while others bear seals inscribed with the names of royal officials. Although these are termed "personal" or "private" seals, they definitely represent officials who were part of the bureaucracy concerned with the jars, rather than private citizens.

Lamelekh impressions have been discovered in excavations and surveys in all parts of the Kingdom of Judah, from Tel 'Ira in the south to Bethel in the north, from the Judaean desert in the east to Tel Batash, Tel Erani, and Tel Miqne on the border of Judaea and Philistia. Isolated lamelekh handles have been discovered outside the borders of the kingdom. Generally speaking, however, the distribution of the impressions corresponds to the borders of the Kingdom of Judah in the eighth century and not to its extended borders in the time of Josiah, in the seventh century, which include parts of the coastal plain and the former kingdom of Israel. The two sites that have yielded the greatest number of impressions are Lachish (about 400 stamped handles) and Jerusalem (about 300 impressions). Other large assemblages of handles include Ramat Rahel (about 170), Gibeon (86), and Tell en-Nasbeh

(Mizpah, about 85). Most of the complete stamped jars were found in public warehouses or in the gate area at Lachish and at Tel Batash, but some were found in clearly domestic contexts and in small sites where there could not have been any royal magazines.

The long debate over the date of the seals has finally been resolved by the discovery of complete stamped jars at Lachish and Tel Batash. At Lachish the jars originate in the destruction layers of Level III, dated to 701 B.C.E. At Tel Batash too, the complete jars were found in stratum III, with the identical date and fate of Level III at Lachish. There can therefore be no doubt that the lamelekh jars were used during the reign of Hezekiah, late in the eighth century.

At Lachish Level II, razed by the Babylonians in 586 B.C.E., no lamelekh handles have come to light, nor does the typical jar form appear. The royal jars of Level III were succeeded by a more slender jar, often with rosettes stamped on the handles. They appear to have inherited the function of the eighth-century lamelekh jars. Presumably the administrative structure reflected in the lamelekh jars became defunct in the extended reign of Mannasseh, during the radical change in the administration, the economy, and the political situation. At those sites not destroyed by Sennacherib, some royal jars remained in use in the early seventh century, but they should not be accorded an extensive range within that century.

There is no consensus regarding the function of the lamelekh jars. Some scholars believe the jars were used to gather taxes in the form of agricultural produce (wine, oil, etc.). The jars would have been concentrated at the four centers named on the seals, representing an administrative reform in which the number of provinces was reduced from twelve to four. Others contend that the only product for which the place of manufacture has any significance is wine, and the jars therefore represent four centers of royal wine production. Another theory holds that the four cities indicate a military division, and the jars conveyed provisions to units posted by Hezekiah throughout the kingdom in preparation for the rebellion against Assyria. It was previously the opinion of many scholars that the seals were a royal guarantee of the contents of the jars; that is to say, all the jars had a standard volume confirmed by the seal. However, the considerable variation in size among the whole jars from Lachish rules out this interpretation. Other scholars hold that the four cities housed the ceramic workshops where the jars were manufactured. However, the limited number of seals and the chemical analyses showing that all the jars were made of the same clay run counter to that explanation.

To sum up, it is clear that the lamelekh jars were linked to the royal or military administration of Hezekiah. The four cities appear to represent the four regions of the Kingdom of Judah at this time; Hebron represents the southern highlands, Socoh the Shephelah, Ziph the southern and eastern desert margins, and *mmsht*, not mentioned in the Bible or in other sources, must represent northern Judaea and the region of Jerusalem. It has been suggested that *mmsht* was an abbreviation of one of the names of the capital city, Jerusalem, which could have been called *mmshlt* (derived from the word for "government"). But that seems unlikely, for if Jerusalem was known by that name, its absence in the biblical record would be difficult to explain. It is more likely that *mmsht* was the name of an as yet unidentified town.

SCRIPTS, WRITING, AND SEAL IMPRESSIONS

In the Iron Age IIB there is a constant increase in the number of inscriptions revealed in excavations. The importance of written finds is great, as they not only express the material culture of the inhabitants but also provide direct historical information and sometimes an insight into the spiritual world of the ancients, their language, literature, and religion. At times inscriptions reveal important information concerning the laws, administration, economy, and many other aspects of human endeavor.

The eighth century was a period of extensive literary activity, the days of the prophets Isaiah, Micah, and Amos and when the biblical canon began to crystallize. The activity of the Aramean scribes serving the Assyrian empire stimulated the use of local scripts in the different parts of the cultural expanse controlled by the Assyrians. National scripts had begun to develop in the Land of Israel and the surrounding areas in the ninth century, when the first Hebrew inscriptions appear, chief among them being the inscribed stela of Mesha, king of Moab (cf. II Kings 3:4). During the eighth and seventh centuries localized national characteristics began to appear in the scripts of neighboring nations. The Moabites no longer employed the Hebrew script but developed a script of their own, as did the Ammonites, the Edomites, the Arameans in the north, and the descendants of the Philistines on the southern coast.

Literacy was at first confined to the professional scribes. But with the development of the alphabet and the consequent reduction in the number of signs, reading and writing could be mastered with greater ease, and literacy spread to ever wider segments of the population.

The process was gradual. At the beginning of the Iron Age II inscriptions are rare and are mostly written in Phoenician characters. With time writing spread. The increasing number of inscriptions uncovered in excavations at Iron Age II–III sites in the Land of Israel, as well as the content of the inscriptions, testify that by the end of the eighth century Israelite society as a whole was literate. Such widespread literacy was unusual in the ancient world. In Egypt, where hieroglyphic writing prevailed, and Mesopotamia, which continued to employ Akkadian cuneiform, literacy was limited to circles who made it their profession.

Evidence for the dissemination of literacy includes the large quantity of ceramic vessels bearing ownership inscriptions. There would be little point in writing the name of the owner if people could not read it. Many of the owners' inscriptions were written in a clumsy, vulgar script, clearly indicating that the writer was not a professional scribe. The development of a vulgar script is another indication of the extent of literacy among people who were not professional scribes. In some cases, inscriptions were incised on the vessels before firing, indicating that the potter was responsible for the inscription. In the Siloam village in Jerusalem, the inscriptions carved on tomb facades include a grievous curse directed against tomb robbers. The idea of inscribing the name of the deceased is related to the quest for immortality, but the pronouncement of a curse has a more practical purpose, assuming that visitors and potential tomb robbers could read it. The backs of decorated ivories from Samaria, as well as some ivories found outside the country, are inscribed with letters and even complete words, such as *kiseh* ("chair"). These inscriptions were intended as guidelines for the furniture makers, indicating where the ivory inlays should be applied. From the eighth century, various items of everyday use were marked with letters, and the use of alphabetic characters and numerals became a common component of Israelite culture during the Iron Age II–III. Numbers and words appear on stone weights used in commerce, alphabetic characters were incised on ceramic vessels before and after firing, masons' marks and monograms were incised on building stones. These indicate that traders, potters, builders, and other craftspersons, as well as their clients, knew how to read and write.

The famous Siloam inscription, discovered in the nineteenth century, is dated intrinsically and on historical evidence to the eighth century, establishing a comparative paleography on a firm chronological foundation. The forms of the characters in other inscriptions may be compared with the Siloam inscription; resemblances would indicate contemporaneity, or formal evolution would indicate a later date. The Siloam inscription was carved on the rock wall of a dark water-supply tunnel. It was not on public exhibit, a monumental inscription intended to impress the populace. The inscription describes the technical achievement of hewing the tunnel, and it is reasonable to assume that it was the chief engineers and builders of the water system who immortalized their work, which would explain why neither king nor god is mentioned. The inscription appears smaller than the space prepared for it on the rock, suggesting that its carvers were not professionally trained, despite the fine execution of the letters.

There is a growing corpus of abecedaries, alphabetic lists of characters. These inscriptions may have been writing exercises of apprentices, though perhaps not in every case. The first five letters of the alphabet were found engraved on a step of the Level III palace fort at Lachish, dated to the late eighth century. From early in that century we have a number of abecedaries from Horvat Teman (Kuntillat 'Ajrud). Six sherds containing scribal exercises with letters and numbers, dated to the seventh century, were uncovered at Kadesh Barnea. It is hardly likely that there were scribal schools at such distant places or at every other site where such writing exercises have been found. Rather, scribes at these sites may have practiced writing on the sherds before preparing the more expensive parchment or papyrus documents. Neither should it be assumed that every abecedary is an exercise of a schoolboy or a scribe; such inscriptions may also have had magic or religious significance. One way or the other, these abecedaries testify to the wide distribution of literacy.

From the eighth century onward the practice of applying seals to jar handles becomes common. These include the lamelekh seals and the royal officials' seals. There is also a growing corpus of sealstones. The seals are usually scaraboid, with a convex back and a flat base. On the base, the name and patronym of the owner was inscribed in mirror writing; in some cases the official titles of the functionaries appear as well. They were used mainly to seal papyrus documents. The completed document was rolled up and tied with string, a lump of clay was attached to the string, and the appropriate seal was applied to the clay (cf. Jer. 32:10). The impressed clay lump is termed a bulla.

After the eighth century the artistic motifs decorating the seals gradually decrease in favor of written inscriptions. The artistic motif is primary in seals of exalted officials

Fig. 9.37.   Officials' seals and seal impressions

called "the servants" of Uzziah and
Ahaz of Judah and Jeroboam II of
Israel, attributed to the end of the
eighth century. However, the seal of
an official in the court of Hezekiah,
in the late eighth century, lacks all
ornamentation, and the same is true
of some of the jar sealings of the
same period. In an eighth-century
collection of bullae from Samaria,
only one bears traces of Hebrew
characters, the rest having only ornamental designs that could be identified even by illiterate persons. In
contrast, most bullae from the seventh and early sixth centuries found
at the City of David (Jerusalem) and
Lachish lack all ornamental designs.

The large number of seals presently in hand offer so much information about scripts, language, titles,
personal names, and more that their
study has become an independent
field of research. The proliferation
of seals, including women's seals,
testifies indirectly to the number of
written documents, even assuming
that some seals were used only as
personal adornments.

The development of cursive
script, such as that inscribed in ink
on ostraca, is the best measure of
the degree to which writing on perishable materials was practiced. The
cursive letter forms evolved in the
course of writing on soft materials,
papyrus or parchment. The effect of
the softer medium on the letter
forms can be observed even in inscriptions engraved on silver plaques
or carved in stone. Assemblages of
ostraca inscribed in ink, or even
isolated finds, gradually increase toward the end of the Iron Age. The
greatest numbers of ostraca come
from the late seventh and early sixth
centuries. They include the letter
from Mezad Hashavyahu, most of
the Arad letters (especially the archives of Eliashib), and the Lachish
letters. The dating of the ostraca and
of inscriptions in general is based
first and foremost on the archae-

ological stratigraphic context. However, recent years have seen the
increased development of paleographic research, so that the
scripts of the various national groups
and their dates can be established
according to the form of the letters.

ASSYRIAN FINDS IN THE LAND OF ISRAEL

The Assyrian presence in the
Land of Israel gradually intensified
beginning in the last third of the
eighth century. The neo-Assyrian
empire had begun to expand in the
ninth century, particularly during
the reign of Ashurnasirpal II. The
Assyrians' first contact with the
Land of Israel was the conquest of
northern Israel by Tiglat Pileser III
in 732 B.C.E. Later, in the days of
Shalmaneser V and Sargon II, the
rest of Israel and the plain of Philistia were overrun (722 B.C.E.).
Judah's turn came next, with the
destruction of the cities of the Shephelah and the siege of Jerusalem
during the campaign of Sennacherib
in 701 B.C.E.

The Assyrian campaigns are recorded in the Assyrian annals and
on bas-reliefs decorating their palace
walls, some of which portray battles
in the Land of Israel. The towns
portrayed in the Assyrian reliefs are
often mere schematic depictions, but
occasional naturalistic portrayals testify that the reliefs were based on
sketches made at the theater of battle. Towns in the Land of Israel
depicted in Assyrian reliefs include
Ashtaroth (in Transjordan), Gibton,
Gezer, and possibly other towns of
the north and the coast of Philistia.
Most detailed is the relief from Sennacherib's palace in Nineveh, which
depicts the conquest of Lachish.

Fragments of royal Assyrian
stelae have been found in the Land
of Israel, at Samaria and near Ben
Shemen. The Gezer excavations
have yielded two Assyrian contracts

inscribed on clay tablets, dated to
the time of Ashurbanipal (669–627
B.C.E.). The Assyrian conquest is
also reflected in Israelite artifacts
found in the capital cities of the
Assyrian kings. They include metal
artifacts bearing Hebrew names and
ivories, some of which bear Hebrew
inscriptions, found at ancient Calah
(modern Nimrud). Excavations in
the Land of Israel have revealed
Assyrian finds chiefly of the seventh
century, though a few items from
the late eighth century have come to
light. At some sites, structures of
typically Assyrian design, furnished
with characteristic architectural details, have been revealed. There are
clear links between the Assyrian
buildings in the Land of Israel and
those in Syria, found at Arslan-Tash
(Hadata), Tell Halaf (Guzana), or
Zinjirli (Sam'al). Apart from structures built by the Assyrian administration for its own purposes, other
structures display Assyrian
influence.

A characteristic feature is the Assyrian courtyard building, a large
structure consisting of rows of
rooms built round a central court.
The clearest examples are found in
stratum III at Megiddo, to the west
of the gate. They appear to have
been part of a cluster of administrative structures built by and for
the Assyrian governors of the
province of Megiddo. The buildings
were built of brick, as was the rule
in Assyrian architecture, so only the
stone foundations remain. The
courtyard buildings were erected on
raised podiums supported by sloping retaining walls. The raised
podium is a well-known component
of Assyrian architecture and appears
to have influenced Israelite building
traditions. The central court opened
to a series of chambers, including
a double row of audience halls or
throne rooms on one side. At the
entrance to these rooms, the excavators at Megiddo identified door

sockets with raised horseshoe-shaped bands; these sockets housed the pivots of double-winged doors. Similar sockets are well known from Assyrian palaces, incorporated in raised thresholds. They are most characteristic of Assyrian architecture and appear at several sites in the Land of Israel: in the remains of a massive mud-brick Assyrian residency at Gezer and in recently excavated remains at Dor, the capital of an Assyrian province.

In addition to the Assyrian courtyard buildings of Megiddo stratum III, the layout of the city as a whole, with its orthogonal street plan and building insulae, was probably determined by the Assyrian authorities, the city being a provincial capital.

At Ayelet Ha-Shahar, at the foot of the mound of Hazor, the fragmentary remains of an Assyrian residency have been revealed. Its details correspond remarkably to those of the Assyrian palaces in capital cities of the empire, including the audience or throne room with the adjacent bath chamber, thick plaster floors, thick mud-brick walls, the deep sockets of the double-winged doors, and shallow niches in the walls.

The excavations at Tell Jemmeh on the coastal plain have revealed a mud-brick building with completely preserved mud-brick vaults and arches. The vaults appear to have served as cellar magazines, the bulk of the building having been above. This is the only example so far excavated of the vaulted mud-brick roofing typical to Assyrian construction.

The Assyrian presence and influence are reflected in the pottery assemblage as well. The most important vessels are Assyrian palace ware, first identified at Tell Jemmeh and mainly a family of round-based bowls, carinated at mid-body, and having a sharp, slightly everted rim. The ware of these bowls is fine, their walls thin, and the clay usually pale and highly fired. The walls often exhibit ridges formed during throwing on the wheel. Palace ware bowls and goblets seem to have been used mainly for drinking, as portrayed in the banquet scenes in Assyrian reliefs. Other Assyrian vessels, also of luxury ware, include the tall goblets and the pomegranate-shaped vessels with their thumb-impressed walls. Examples of these elegant vessels have been found at Ashdod, Arad, and especially Ramat Rahel, south of Jerusalem. Excavations at Calah yielded silver goblets with indented walls, undoubtedly the inspiration for the elaborate Assyrian pottery vessels. A number of Assyrian metal bowls and precise pottery imitations have been found

Fig. 9.38. Iron Age IIb pottery from Lachish stratum III

in the vicinity of Samaria, at Tel Rekhesh, and at 'En Dor in the Jezreel valley.

One other item of Assyrian material culture found in the Land of Israel is the ceramic coffin. The tub-shaped coffins have one squared end and one rounded end, and they are usually less than body length so that the corpses were interred in a flexed position. Such coffins have been found chiefly in the north and in Transjordan, and most should be ascribed to the Assyrian inhabitants; however, the indigenous population could have been influenced by this custom, which means that the appearance of such coffins in Judaea (at Ketef Hinnom and Malha) does not necessarily attest to the presence of Assyrians. Ceramic coffins have been discovered at Megiddo, Tel Qataf in the Beth Shean valley, Dothan, Tell el-Far'ah North, and Ammon.

Besides these artifacts, a wealth of small finds may be related to Assyrian military or administrative presence, but they could also be prestige items that arrived by way of trade. They include a series of Assyrian cylinder seals and bullae. At Kafr Kana in the lower Galilee a magnificent Assyrian bronze vessel, resembling a goblet with a basket handle, was found. It has the shape of a ram's head, and an ornamental band near the rim contains a cultic scene in the royal Assyrian style. The vessel bears the name of its owner, Lizirishu. A fragment of molded glass with a pattern of bossed lozenges, found at Aroer in the Negev, also seems to be of Assyrian origin. At Tel Qataf a magnificent stone bowl was discovered, with feet resembling hoofs and sides ornamented with duck's heads carved in relief.

Assyrian art is poorly represented in the Land of Israel. Two pottery fragments with painted scenes were found at Ramat Rahel.

One depicts a seated, bearded figure: the attire, the bracelets, and the style in which the leg muscles and beard are depicted are unmistakably Assyrian. A seal of a Judaean royal official, the governor of the city, also shows the influence of Assyrian adoration scenes.

The possible remains of an Assyrian military encampment have recently been identified in northern Samaria. Such camps are well known from the reliefs, and future excavations may allow the information regarding Assyrian military techniques gleaned from the reliefs to be compared with the data gathered in the field.

The Assyrian presence in the Land of Israel was conspicuous, and it continued to be felt long after the Assyrian empire had passed into oblivion.

POTTERY

The Iron Age IIb is characterized by well-dated pottery assemblages, discovered in historically dated destruction layers. The pottery forms vary regionally, in contrast to the relative homogeneity of the Iron Age IIa. Each of four regions provides a characteristic ceramic assemblage with political-geographical affinities: the Phoenician coast and the western Galilee; the Samaria hills, the valleys, and the eastern Galilee; the Judaean hills, the Shephelah, the Judaean desert, and the Beersheba valley; the southern coastal plain. Some sites reveal ceramic traditions originating in more than one region, whether because they are in border areas or because they maintained intensive political ties with distant regions. Most prominent in the Iron Age IIb are the differences between the ceramic assemblages of the kingdoms of Israel and Judah.

In Judah, Israel, Phoenicia, and to a lesser extent on the coastal

plain, wheel burnishing remained a characteristic feature. In the kingdom of Israel, the production of fine Samaria ware continued. However, it declined in quality during the Iron Age IIb and disappeared completely by the end of this phase.

The large pithoi (storage jars one meter or more in height) belong to the early eighth century. They are slender, with holemouth rims and two handles. The upper part has horizontal grooves made on the wheel, and near them Hebrew letters (*aleph, qof, yod, tet*, etc.) incised before firing. Large pithoi of this type do not appear in later phases of the Iron Age, and most appear to have been manufactured in Jerusalem. They have been found in Jerusalem and at Negev sites, including Kuntillat 'Ajrud, where they were adorned with painted scenes and cultic inscriptions. These pithoi also belong to a larger family of holemouth jars, which appear in a variety of sizes through the Iron Age II. The spouted jars first appear in the Iron Age IIb (the form is in fact first encountered in Early Bronze Age assemblages and disappears immediately thereafter). They have three handles, the fourth position being occupied by a wide spout joined to the jar rim. The spout could accommodate the small dipper juglet used to extract liquids from the jar, the excess fluids flowing back into the jar through the spout. The characteristic jars of the north in this period are narrow and elongated and hence are often called sausage jars. Their shape appears to have been amenable to storage in the hulls of trading ships, and many have been found on the Mediterranean sea floor, remnants of ancient shipwrecks. Other jars are bag-shaped, and they too have been found on the sea floor, though they also appear in Judah, whose maritime trade could hardly compare with that of Tyre and Israel.

Typical of the late eighth century are the ovoid lamelekh-type jars, most of which lack seal impressions. They have been found throughout the Kingdom of Judah and at some coastal sites, but they all seem to have been manufactured at a single center and then distributed to the other sites. Stamped jar handles as such do not predate the Iron Age IIb, and the practice was unknown in the tenth and ninth centuries. Storage jars resembling the lamelekh jars and stamped with Edomite seals were discovered in the excavations at Tell el-Kheleifeh (Ezion-Geber), near Elath.

Painted decoration on pottery becomes gradually rarer after the Iron Age I. In the interior regions, Judaea in particular, such decoration is nonexistent, while in the coastal plain painted lines continue to appear on some pottery types.

New ceramic forms of the period include the decanter, a jug with a carinated body, a ridge at the middle of the neck, and a handle drawn from the ridge to the shoulder of the vessel. Northern and Judaean decanters each exhibit regional typological variants. Cooking pots gradually lose the sharp carination at mid-body and become more rounded. The spherical form of this period is the prototype of cooking pot forms from the Iron Age through the Roman period. The triangular rims characteristic of the Late Bronze Age and the Iron Age I disappear in the Iron Age IIb. In Judaea, two new cooking pot types appear: one has a short, upright neck with horizontal grooves and ridges, the other a thickened, stepped rim, which may have accommodated a lid. In the Iron Age IIb, the deep, wheel-burnished krater with four handles first appears in Judaean assemblages. Its thickened rim was formed by the outward folding of the rim, a characteristic of bowls and saucers of Judaea from the Iron Age IIb until the end of the period.

Iron Age IIb bowls also include local imitations of Assyrian palace ware bowls. It has recently been suggested that a class of bowls found mainly in the central hills, bearing an internal decoration of wedge-shaped impressions, represents foreign ceramic traditions brought by exiles forcibly settled in Israel following the Assyrian conquest.

Small black perfume juglets characterize the assemblages both of the kingdom of Judah and of Israel. These burnished juglets, known as "black juglets," are generally globular, with a diameter of 5–7 centimeters. Juglets of identical form sometimes appear in red or yellowish clay. The black juglets appear from the Iron Age IIb to the end of the period.

Oil lamps gradually thicken at the base, apparently to lower the center of gravity and prevent fires started by overturned lamps. By the Iron Age IIIa their bases are very thick and heavy.

The more elaborate cultic vessels include chalices and incense stands, usually decorated with horizontal bands. As in earlier periods, incense stands took the form of a bowl on a tall pedestal or hollow foot, either joined as a single unit or made as separate vessels. The pedestal was furnished with square, round, or triangular apertures, through which the incense could rise. In the Assyrian relief showing soldiers removing the booty of Lachish (701 B.C.E.), two magnificent stands consisting of a decorated bowl set on a high pedestal are among the plundered objects. These stands, each carried by one soldier, appear to have been made of metal, but the metal stands were undoubtedly prototypes for the pottery stands. Fragments of pottery incense stands, including some with plastic decorations in the form of drooping petals or other patterns, are common throughout the country.

A unique vessel first appearing in the eighth century is the asymmetrical flask, made of two joined bowls, one shallow and the other deep. The flat area at the junction of the two bowls bears lug or loop handles. Straps could be passed through the handles to suspend or to grasp the vessel. These flasks, with the flat back and distended belly, are known mainly in the north, in Samaria and Megiddo, but also appear in Judaea.

In contrast to earlier plaque-shaped figurines, formed in molds, the female figurines of the Iron Age IIb–IIIa are usually shaped in the round. Their features were fashioned in molds, but the remaining parts were formed freehand. Most characteristic are the so-called pillar figurines; the features and coiffure were styled in the Egyptian manner, while the body was crudely represented by a massive pottery pillar, to which large breasts supported by schematically portrayed arms were affixed. The pillar figurines and the animal figurines of the eighth and seventh centuries are common in Judaea, and excavations in Jerusalem have yielded hundreds of such objects.

The dated find assemblages enable archaeologists, through comparative study, to fix the period of undated assemblages from layers and sites for which historical data are not available, thus creating a well-rounded picture of the material culture of the eighth century.

The Iron Age IIIa

The Iron Age III begins after the tumultuous events of the Assyrian conquests, first in Israel and Philistia, then in the Kingdom of Judah. It ends with the dramatic events culminating in the destruction of Jerusalem and Judah in 586

B.C.E. and the end of Israelite independence. As biblical historiography focused chiefly on Judaea, the remaining regions of the country, which were subject to direct Assyrian rule, have left little trace in history.

The events of the seventh century and their social, spiritual, and religious background are faithfully related in the biblical scriptures, particularly in the books of II Kings (Chapters 21–25), Jeremiah, Nahum, and Zephaniah. The period began with the 55-year reign of Mannasseh (696–642 B.C.E.), mostly under the aegis of the Assyrian empire. This was the apogee of direct Assyrian rule in the Land of Israel, during the reigns of Esarhaddon and Ashurbanipal, when the Land of Israel lay on the route of the Assyrian armies to Egypt. The Assyrian presence is quite marked in the material culture of the seventh century and in occupation strata of several major sites outside the Kingdom of Judah.

By the end of Mannasseh's reign, the decline of Assyrian political and cultural influence had set in, and following the death of Ashurbanipal and the fall of Nineveh to the Babylonians, Assyrian presence in the Land of Israel came to an end. After the short reign of Amon, Josiah ascended the throne of Judah and took control of large portions of the country formerly under Assyrian rule, on the coastal plain and in the Assyrian provinces of Samaria and Megiddo. Mannasseh's long rule was characterized by economic prosperity, and Josiah's by a national and cultural-religious re-awakening, accompanied by a settlement boom. Josiah was killed at Megiddo, in a battle with the Pharaoh Necho (II Kings 23:29; II Chron. 35:22–23), in 609 B.C.E. From the death of Josiah to the end of the period, the Kingdom of Judah and the Land of Israel as a

whole were caught in a political vise between Egypt and the growing power of Babylon. Eventually, Judah and the Land of Israel fell to Nebuchadnezzar of Babylon, following the campaigns of 603 B.C.E. to Philistia and 598 B.C.E. to Judah and Jerusalem. Final destruction overtook Jerusalem and Judah in 586 B.C.E. The most detailed historical descriptions of these events may be found in the Bible, and further details are found in the works of later historians such as Herodotus and Josephus. Assyrian and Babylonian documents also record events in the Land of Israel. As for the end of the Iron Age IIIa, a wealth of information is provided by the Hebrew ostraca found at Lachish, Arad (the archives of Eliashib), and Mezad Hashavyahu. The exact date of the Babylonian conquest is provided by the Babylonian chronicle.

The reign of Josiah (640–609 B.C.E.) is often viewed as a period of peace and internal religious and administrative reform. It is marked by extensive building operations, an increase in settled sites, and expansion of existing cities, with extramural suburbs being added to some. Archaeological surveys have revealed a notable increase in sites during the seventh century and the expansion of Judaean settlement in the Judaean and Negev desert margins. The century also witnessed a considerable rise in the importance of Jerusalem, in the wake of the religious reforms and the centralization of cult carried out under Josiah. At the end of the Iron Age IIIa, in the last years of the seventh century and the beginning of the sixth, the decline of the Kingdom of Judah was exploited by the Edomites for raids against southern Judaea, apparently followed by some Edomite settlement in parts of the Judaean Negev. This is reflected in the appearance of Edomite pottery at Tel 'Ira, Horvat 'Uza, Aroer, and other sites and most notably by

the Edomite cult site uncovered at Horvat Qitmit.

Sites of the coastal plain, the Samaria hills, and the northern valleys have provided finds characteristic of Judaean culture in the late seventh century, including burnished decanters, thick-based lamps, and inscribed stone weights, which have been discovered at Ashdod, Tell Jemmeh, Tell el-Far'ah South, Tel Sheqef (east of the Gaza Strip), Tel Haror (Gerar), and elsewhere. It would appear that the southern coastal strip came under direct Judaean rule in the days of Josiah, reflected especially in the establishment of the fortress of Mezad Hashavyahu, on the coast near Yavne. This was a small fortress with typical Judahite finds, including some Hebrew inscriptions. The site was short-lived, dated 625–609 B.C.E.

The Iron Age IIIa also witnessed renewed settlement of the Negev, where sites such as Tel 'Ira, Aroer, Tel Malhata, Tel Beersheba, and Kadesh Barnea were reinhabited. Settlement also increased on the margins of the Judaean desert. The principal site of this area was En Gedi, and a series of small settlements and isolated fortresses spread through the Judaean desert and the northwestern shore of the Dead Sea. This prosperity should be attributed to the reign of Josiah.

The interpretation of the Judaean finds in the Samaria hills and the northern valleys remains problematic. Such finds have appeared at Samaria, Shechem, Megiddo, and Tell Keisan in the Accho valley. Do they testify to political-military control by the Kingdom of Judah of the northern regions, or did they arrive at these sites by way of trade? The answer may be provided by the jar handles bearing rosette stamps, which carried on the function and form of the royal lamelekh jars of the late eighth century. The rosette jars were linked to the royal administration of Judah in the late seventh century and were distributed only in Judah; none have been found north of Gibeon. It may therefore be assumed that there was no real authority of the Kingdom of Judah in the northern regions and that relations were merely cultural and commercial.

The study of the pottery of the Iron Age IIIa depends on excavations of key sites in Judah: Tell Beit Mirsim stratum A2, with an assemblage spanning the eighth through sixth centuries; Lachish Level II; and En Gedi, where rich assemblages of the Iron Age II–III were found in a settlement termed stratum V. It was assumed that the stratum V site was founded by Josiah and continued into the sixth century. The excavators suggested that it was destroyed in 582 B.C.E., in a later wave of Babylonian deportations from Judah. The analysis of the stratum V pottery, however, reveals a much longer span; there are lamelekh seals of the late eighth century and ceramic types of Lachish III, as well as types that appear to postdate Lachish II; these could be attributed to the period of Babylonian rule, in the Iron Age IIIb.

At Gezer, there appears to have been direct Assyrian rule during most of the seventh century, as illustrated by Assyrian finds there. At the end of the century, Gezer passed into the hands of Josiah, an event reflected in the large amounts of Judaean wares found at the site.

In short, the general archaeological picture is clear within the borders of the Kingdom of Judah, where many Iron Age IIIa sites have been excavated and the history is clearly illuminated in literary sources. In contrast, the northern regions, inhabited by exiles forcibly resettled by the Assyrians, do not provide so clear an archaeological-cultural picture.

FORTIFICATIONS

With the increasing danger of military incursions by Egypt and Babylon at the end of the seventh century, a new emphasis was laid on city defenses. These fortifications were, however, founded at the beginning of Iron Age IIIa, in the days of Mannasseh and Josiah. The Bible tells of the buttressing of Jerusalem's walls and the construction of a new outer city wall, as well as the fortification of the other cities of Judah (II Chron. 33:14).

It appears that a number of the fortified cities of Judah were rebuilt after the campaign of Sennacherib and their fortifications restored. In contrast, the parts of Israel annexed to the Assyrian empire had no need for defenses. Thus, no fortifications were constructed at Samaria, though remains of the earlier fortifications remained standing; at Megiddo the ninth-century inset-offset wall remained in ruins as the rest of the city was replanned and rebuilt in stratum III; and the city of Hazor remained unwalled, and some of its more important buildings, like the Assyrian palace, were built outside the city limits.

Toward the end of the Iron Age IIIa, in the last quarter of the seventh century, the walls of many towns were rebuilt. A fine example is the city of Lachish, where a time lapse has been observed between the destruction of Level III in the campaign of Sennacherib and the establishment of Level II, apparently in the days of Josiah. Lachish was surrounded by a new wall of lesser strength and of poorer construction than the fortifications of Levels IV–III.

At Tel Batash (Timna) a solid, four-meter wall encompassed the city, a rebuild of the earlier wall. At the foot of the wall, a third of the way down the slope, a forward defense wall was constructed, and the

excavators state that a glacis of tamped earth and pebbles replaced the earlier stone-faced glacis. These forward defense works were doubtless intended to protect against siege engines. Stone-faced glacis and the tamping of mound slopes are quite characteristic of the late Iron Age and may be observed at Tel Beersheba and Tel Halif as well.

Other sites in Judah—Beth Zur, Debir (Khirbet Rabud), and Tel 'Ira—also show evidence of rebuilt fortifications, and in every case the new walls were solid. In contrast, the fortresses built or restored in the seventh century are often fortified by casemate walls, as in the stratum VI fortress at Arad, the upper fortress at Kadesh Barnea, and the stratum IIIB fortress at Gibeah (Tell el-Ful), north of Jerusalem.

Although only a small number of city gates have been excavated from this period, their gradual reduction in size is clear; their depth is diminished and the number of gate chambers reduced. At Tel Batash, a new two-chambered gate was built in stratum II over the four-chambered structure of the late eighth century, and the same sequence may be observed at Tel Miqne. Finally the gate chambers disappeared altogether. The inner gate of Lachish Level II, for example, consists of a simple passage between two ends of the wall, the outer face of the wall being enhanced by two projecting towers. The shortening of gatehouses appears to have begun in the late eighth or early seventh century, with the construction of the two-chambered gate in the stratum III city of Megiddo, and earlier examples may be adduced.

The smaller, unfortified towns of Judaea at this time include Tell Beit Mirsim (stratum A3) and En Gedi (stratum V). Presumably they had a central citadel to which the inhabitants could flee in times of trouble.

FOREIGN RELATIONS

The seventh century is characterized by extensive foreign relations, reflected in nearly every facet of local culture: language, religion and cult, dress, burial customs, and the products of material culture. The relations of the Land of Israel with foreign lands were not unilateral; artifacts originating in the Land of Israel may be found from Assyria and Susa in the east to the Iberian peninsula in the west.

Artifacts such as carved bowls made from *Tridacna squamosa* shells or metal bowls decorated in the Egyptian-Phoenician style testify to the intensity of trade and to the length of the trade routes. Tridacna shells have been found at Arad, Buseirah (Bozrah, in Transjordan), Shechem, Bethlehem, and Jerusalem, and they are known throughout the civilized world of the seventh century. The decorated metal bowls have been found in Italy (Etruria), Greece, and Assyria. In the Assyrian palaces inscribed bowls of this type were found, and some contained Hebrew names; they were booty or tribute from the Land of Israel. At this time hitherto illiterate cultures, such as those of Phrygia, Lydia, and Etruria, adopted the Phoenician alphabet. The proto-Ionic capital, introduced in the Land of Israel in the tenth century, was also adopted in Cyprus and became common there, passing to western Asia Minor, with some variations, and to Etruria. The principal bearers of eastern culture in the west were the Phoenicians, who controlled most international trade. There were also Greek colonizers, who established colonies in distant lands, including lands of the East. Late in the seventh century, Greeks may have served as mercenaries in the army of Josiah, which could explain the abundance of eastern Greek pottery, decorated in the wild-goat style, at the Judaean coastal fortress of Mezad Hashavyahu. Similar pottery, originating in Rhodes or on the western coast of Asia Minor, has surfaced in seventh-century contexts at Tel Malhata, Tel Sera', and Tell Keisan in the Accho valley.

Assyrian rule over considerable parts of the Land of Israel led to an influx of Assyrian artifacts and to Assyrian influence on local ceramic forms of the seventh century. Assyrian influence is also conspicuous in the material culture of Ammon and Edom in Transjordan.

Starting with the accession of Psammetikh I, the founder of the Twenty-sixth Dynasty in Egypt (664–610 B.C.E.) and the predecessor of Pharaoh Necho, Egyptian interest in the Land of Israel increases. Egyptian influence is particularly prominent in glyptic art, in which lotus flowers, hieroglyphic characters, and even Egyptian deities often appear. Egyptian influence is exemplified by the name "Amon" (chief god of the Egyptian pantheon of Thebes) given by Mannasseh to his son and successor on the throne of Judah. The tomb of Pharaoh's daughter in Jerusalem, apparently hewn in the seventh century, is made in the image of an Egyptian tomb chapel. It has been suggested that Egyptian cultural influence was introduced by Phoenician intermediaries. However, the widespread use of hieratic Egyptian numbers and other Egyptian characters on ostraca from Arad and Kadesh Barnea leaves no doubt that the contacts were direct.

The study of contacts with southern Arabia is still in its infancy. At Tell el-Kheleifeh (Ezion-Geber), a sherd bearing incised signs in southern Arabian script was found, and the City of David yielded three sherds bearing signs in this script, perhaps representing personal names. The Tell el-Kheleifeh and Jerusalem inscriptions are dated to the late seventh or early sixth century. The three sherds from Jerusalem were deeply chiseled after firing, a technique employed in Hebrew inscriptions at this time in Jerusalem and its vicinity. Thus these signs, found on locally made vessels, were probably engraved in Jerusalem. Trade relations and cultural contacts with southern Arabia became possible, it seems, only after the decline of Assyrian power.

THE ARCHAEOLOGY OF TRANSJORDAN

The national kingdoms of the Ammonites, Moabites, and Edomites occupied the plateaus of southern Transjordan. The kingdom of Ammon lay between the Yabbok River (Wadi ez-Zerka) on the north and Nahal Heshbon (Wadi Hesban) on the south; to the south lay the kingdom of Moab, which extended as far as Nahal Zered (Wadi el-Hasa); and farther south, extending to the shores of the Gulf of Elat, lay the kingdom of Edom.

There are far fewer mounds in Transjordan than in the Land of Israel, and our knowledge of the archaeology of the Transjordanian kingdoms falls far short of that of Judah and Israel. Until the seventies, most of the information concerning Transjordan came from pioneering surveys conducted in the thirties and from chance tomb finds. The early surveys had given rise to the belief that the eighth century marked a decline in settlement, ending entirely in the sixth century. But over the past twenty years, many excavations, particularly within Ammon and Edom, have painted a completely different picture. The new data point to a flowering of settlement and culture in Transjordan during the seventh century, under Assyrian rule, and to uninterrupted development in the sixth century, under Babylonian and Persian rule. Recent excavations have also sharpened the distinctions among the Transjordanian kingdoms, and a great deal of cultural and historical information has been provided by the written finds from Transjordan. Monumental inscriptions carved in stone have been found in Moab and Ammon, supplementing the famous Mesha inscription discovered at Dibon in the nineteenth century. A royal inscription on a ceramic bottle was found at Tell Siran, near Amman, and a growing number of seals and seal impressions from Ammon, Moab, and Edom have come to light. The seals reveal the distinct paleographic characteristics of the national scripts of each of the Transjordanian kingdoms in the seventh and sixth centuries.

Most of what we know about the material culture of the Ammonites is based on the finds from twelve richly equipped tombs excavated in Amman and its environs (Sahab and Meqablain). There is also evidence of an Iron Age III site at the citadel and near the Roman theater of Amman. Further data on Ammonite culture come from the Jordan valley sites of Tell es-Sa'idiyeh (biblical Zarethan), Tell Deir 'Alla (Succoth), and Tell el-Mazar, near the Damiyah bridge. The finds of the Amman tombs span a long period, from the eighth century to the late Persian period. Each cave saw extended use, and the lack of ceramic material from occupation levels makes the precise dating of pottery types difficult. Generally speaking, Ammonite pottery is influenced by traditions of Moab and Edom, as well as Assyria, Judaea, Phoenicia, and Israel.

There is as yet little archaeological information on the culture of the kingdom of Moab. At the few sites excavated, the Iron Age II–III strata have not provided significant architectural or stratigraphic finds. The principal Moabite excavation sites are Dibon, the capital of Moab;

Heshbon, which apparently came under Ammonite rule at the end of the Iron Age; and Aroer on the Arnon. At Medeibiyeh, proto-Ionic capitals were found on the surface, and their execution was identical to the Jerusalem and Ramat Rahel capitals. Clearly, this was the site of a royal Moabite palace of the eighth or seventh century, inspired by Judaean royal architecture. In Moab as in Ammon, most of the finds come from tombs. Moabite tombs have been excavated at Dibon, Madaba, and Mount Nebo. They are earlier than the tombs of Amman and its vicinity, dating from the Iron Age I and II, though the finds from Mount Nebo date as late as the sixth century. On the eastern border of the kingdom of Moab, surveys have revealed a fortress system designed to repel desert nomads. The fortresses, as well as shared ceramic traditions, attest to relations with neighboring Ammon, and it would appear that parts of Moab were under Ammonite rule during the seventh century. This is also reflected in the many female and horse-and-rider pottery figurines discovered in Moab and in Ammon.

The key sites for Edomite archaeology are Tell el-Kheleifeh (Ezion-Geber), Tawilan (apparently identified with biblical Teman; Amos 1:12), near Petra; Umm el-Biyara, atop a prominent cliff at Petra (biblical Selah, II Kings 14:7); and Bozrah, the capital of Edom, identified as the site of Buseirah. In the late seventh and early sixth centuries, with the arrival of Arab tribes from the south and the decline of Judaean control in the northern Negev, the Edomites expanded into Judaea and settled parts of the Negev. Much information on Edomite culture has thus emerged from excavations within modern Israel at Aroer, Tel Malhata, Tel 'Ira, Horvat 'Uza, and Horvat Qitmit.

The most important excavations

are at Buseirah, where parts of the city acropolis have been exposed. Two superimposed buildings were excavated, the first dating to Assyrian rule in the seventh century and the second dating to the late seventh or early sixth century. The earlier structure consists of two wings, each arranged round a central rectangular court. Between the two wings stood a structure, possibly a temple, approached by a broad stairway flanked by the square bases of pillars or statues. The stairs led to a small rectangular chamber, with three cells beyond it. The general layout of the building and its organization around two main courts are strongly reminiscent of royal Assyrian palaces. The later structure at Buseirah is square, with rooms arranged round a central court. It is smaller than the earlier structure, but there is no doubt that it too was a central administrative building in the Edomite capital. It closely resembles the Assyrian citadel in stratum III at Hazor.

The most important aspect of Edomite material culture, one that has been the subject of specialized study, is its pottery. Edomite pottery ranges far beyond the borders of Edom. Besides the large quantities found at sites of Edom proper, sherds have been found in the tombs of Amman and Meqablain in Ammon; in sites of the northern Negev (Tel Masos, Aroer, Tel 'Ira, Tel Malhata), some of which were seized and settled by Edomites at the end of the Iron Age; and at Tel Sera', Tell Jemmeh, and Tel Haror (Gerar), somewhat to the north. Edomite pottery ranges as far afield as Kadesh Barnea, in eastern Sinai. The prominent feature of Edomite pottery is its painted decoration. A considerable proportion of its surface was covered with geometric patterns and figurative elements such as a horned deer and a suckling cow. Assyrian influence is marked in the vessel forms, particularly in the carinated bowls, which recall Assyrian palace ware.

The spiritual world of the Edomites is suggested by male and female anthropomorphic figurines found in excavations in Edom; they are usually cruder than those of Judaea. Some have oil lamps fashioned on the head. However, most of what is known about Edomite religion is derived from the Negev site of Horvat Qitmit. Here, the head from a pottery statuette of a three-horned goddess was found, wearing an expression reminiscent of the archaic smile of Greek sculpture. In addition, tens of anthropomorphic and zoomorphic figurines were unearthed, as well as pottery cult stands decorated with human figures modeled in a style unparalleled in the Edomite heartland in Transjordan.

TOMBS AND BURIAL CUSTOMS

The study of the tombs and burial customs of the Iron Age II–III is based on careful scrutiny of the archaeological finds and the biblical sources. This is the first period in the history of the Land of Israel to exhibit well-planned, even monumental tomb architecture, often with a regular, rectangular design.

The practice of family burial required secondary interment, that is, the gathering of bones to make room for a new generation of deceased family members. The gathering of the "new" individual into the bone-pile of his forefathers is hinted at in many biblical passages, where there is a clear distinction between primary and secondary burial. This is implied in the words of Jeremiah (25:33), "They shall not be mourned, or gathered and buried" (cf. Jer. 8:2). Secondary burial is also alluded to in the biblical phrases "gathered to his kin" or "gathered

to his fathers" (Gen. 49:29; II Kings 22:20).

According to the Israelite practice, burial grounds, though near the cities, had to be outside the town walls. The only exceptions were the tombs of the kings, which were inside the City of David in Jerusalem (I Kings 2:10; Neh. 3:16). Burial usually took place in the family plot, near the home of the deceased. If the family lived in a rural estate, the burial cave was on the land. Social stratification was reflected after death in the decoration of the tomb. The more ornate tombs are in the larger towns and at Jerusalem. In the provincial towns and more remote sites, burial practices were the same but the tombs were more modest. The preparation of the tomb appears to have been part of the general ambition to build a home and acquire a family estate (cf. the story of Shebna, who prepared himself a grand tomb in his own lifetime; Isa. 22:15–17). The Bible also mentions monuments, called *yad, matzevet,* or *siyyun,* placed over the tombs of dignitaries. They were ornate and became landmarks, perhaps even a focus of pilgrimage and popular cult.

With rare exceptions, Iron Age II–III burials were exposed; the departed were layed out on benches cut in the tomb caves, without being covered with earth or placed in a coffin of any kind.

Most of the data on Israelite tombs and burials in the Iron Age II–III come from within the Kingdom of Judah, and there is little evidence, beyond some isolated tombs, of the burial practices of the northern regions. Some 250 rock-cut burial caves have been discovered in Judaea, half of them in Jerusalem and its vicinity. Only a few cemeteries have been systematically excavated as part of the mound sites, and most caves have been discovered fortuitously. Clusters of burial caves

have been discovered at Bethel, Mizpah (Tell en-Nasbeh), Gibeon, Gibeah (Tell el-Ful), Malha, Zova, Moza, Qiryat Ye'arim (Abu Ghosh), Bethlehem, Beth Shemesh, Tekoa, Tel Goded (Judeideh), Lachish, Tell 'Aitun, Khirbet el-Kom, and Tel 'Ira. In Jerusalem, three Iron Age cemeteries containing more than 100 tombs have been identified. In addition, isolated tomb caves have been discovered, which may be the sole remnants of rural estates and isolated farms. It would appear, however, that burials usually took the form of plain pit graves, and only the well-to-do could afford to purchase a plot of land and cut a tomb cave. Only a few of these plain graves have been recovered, mainly in the excavations at the foot of Tel Lachish.

The burial customs and tomb types of Judaea evolved during the tenth and ninth centuries (Iron Age IIa), but the tomb-cave plan crystallized only in the second half of the eighth century and the seventh century, after the fall of the kingdom of Israel. That explains the absence of typical Judahite tomb caves within the borders of the kingdom of Israel.

Many funeral gifts accompanied the burials, largely lamps, decanters, and juglets but also jewelry, weapons, and other types of pottery. The repertoire of gifts closely resembles the domestic repertoire found in habitation strata, though the number of storage and large cooking vessels is limited. Most common are the bottles and juglets, which probably contained perfumes to counteract the chemical processes of decay and to permit reentry into the cave for further interments. In a rear corner of the single-chambered tombs, or sometimes beneath one of the benches, a rounded, square, or irregularly shaped hollow was cut as a bone repository, to accommodate

Fig. 9.39. Pillar figurines (approx. height 14 centimeters)

the secondary burials along with their funeral gifts.

The Iron Age II–III burial caves were used as hereditary burial plots. In some, the patriarch occupies a prominent position; his place of burial was set apart in its own cell, and it seems that his bones were not gathered along with the rest. In the seventh century, apparently under the influence of Assyrian burial customs, there is sporadic use in Judaea of portable ceramic coffins.

A number of tombs contain inscriptions identifying the dead or warning against tomb looting. Most important are the inscriptions on the facades of some of the tombs in the Siloam village in Jerusalem; they are carved in the rock walls or painted, as in one of the Khirbet el-Kom tomb chambers. Graffiti have been found in some caves, incised by refugees who fled to the burial caves. Seals bearing the name of the deceased are often found in the tombs; the seal was a personal possession that could not be passed on and was therefore buried along with its owner.

Many details of the tombs of Judaea, especially the elaborate tombs of Jerusalem, are paralleled in distant lands—Etruria, Salamis and Amathus (Cyprus), Van (Urartu, in Turkish Armenia), and Phrygia and Lydia (Anatolia). In the Iron Age II–III, and particularly in the seventh century, there was a common market of ideas, originating perhaps in Egyptian burial customs propagated by the Phoenicians.

WEIGHTS

Small, dome-shaped, stone weights are a characteristic find in excavations of sites of the Kingdom of Judah in the seventh and early sixth centuries. Made of limestone, the weights often bear paleo-Hebrew characters or hieratic Egyptian numeric symbols. They were common in Judah, but isolated examples appear in the north, at Samaria, Megiddo, Dor, Tell Keisan, and the coastal plain. A lone example is reported from Transjordan. In the Bible they are called pouch stones, and apparently merchants carried a series of weights, including the basic standard unit and its multiples and fractions, in a cloth pouch suspended from a belt (Prov. 16:11 and 20:10, Deut. 25:13, Mic. 6:11).

Some weights of the Iron Age IIIa from Judaea are incised with a loop symbol of Egyptian origin; it represents the shekel, the main unit of weight used in everyday contexts.

The sign is accompanied by the hieratic symbols for 1, 2, 5, 10, 20, 30, and 50, representing fractions and multiples of four shekels. The average weight of one shekel, derived from measurements of all the marked weights so far discovered, is 11.35 grams. The stones of another series, inscribed with hieratic numbers alone, are smaller and lighter and appear to be related to the unit called *gerah* in the Bible (Ex. 30:13, Lev. 27:25, Eze. 45:12). Its average value is 0.556 grams, with twenty gerah equaling one shekel. A third series bears three names: *nezef* (average weight 9.8 grams), *pim* (7.8 grams), and *beqa'* (6.1 grams).

It is generally thought that the distribution of inscribed weights in the Kingdom of Judah reflects the expansion of the kingdom under Josiah and trade relations in his day. It is also assumed that at least some of the weights and the standards they represent can be ascribed to administrative reforms under Josiah, which included the standardization of weights and measures.

The weights of the Iron Age II—III were used to weigh cut silver or silver lumps. Barter was the usual mode of trade until the seventh century, with the weights serving mainly for the weighing of precious metals. Sometimes the metals (preferably copper) were used as payment. With the increased working of silver mines, particularly in the Iberian peninsula and other distant regions, silver became the main medium of payment, and the word for silver, "*kesef*," became synonymous with money. The growing sophistication of trade and the standardization of weights and measures set the stage for the introduction of coinage. The domed weights of Judaea incorporate some of the main components of coinage: fixed form, fixed weight, and royal guarantee. Toward the end of the seventh century the first coins appear in Lydia,

in western Asia Minor. During the sixth century the first coins come to the Land of Israel from the Aegean, the earliest being a coin from the island of Kos, found in Jerusalem.

RELIGION AND CULT OBJECTS

At the beginning of the seventh century, during the reign of Mannasseh, foreign religious influences of Syrian and perhaps Assyrian origin made inroads into Judah (II Kings 21:3–7; II Chron. 33:3–7). Among the foreign cults practiced in Jerusalem was the cult of the Queen of Heaven, conducted on rooftops (Zeph. 1:5; Jer. 7:18; 44:17–25) and on the cult platforms of Tophet, in the valley of Hinnom in Jerusalem, where children were offered to the god (II Kings 23:10; II Chron. 33:6). Later, at the end of the century and after the discovery of parts of the Book of Deuteronomy, Josiah carried out a religious reform, uprooting the foreign cults, eliminating cult places devoted to the god of Israel outside Jerusalem, and cen-

tralizing the priesthood and the cult in Jerusalem alone. This reform, which began in about 622 B.C.E., was one of the foundation stones of the later Israelite theology (II Kings 23; II Chron. 26:34).

Most of the archaeological evidence relating to cult comes from domestic contexts. It consists mainly of the clay figurines that were extremely common throughout the Kingdom of Judah and their variants found along the coastal plain and in Transjordan. Most of the Judaean figurines are anthropomorphic and zoomorphic females in the pillar style; male figurines are rare. Judging by their aspect, they may be related to a fertility cult associated with Ashtoreth or Asherah. In some cases the pillar is topped by a dove with wings outspread. Of the animal figurines, most are schematic and elude definition, though they seem to represent horses. Some are furnished with parts of harness, and rarely they are mounted by riders. Some of the horse figurines have a disk fashioned between the ears,

Fig. 9.40. Beersheba horned altar

suggesting that they represent the "chariots of the sun," a cult mentioned in the Bible in the description of Josiah's reforms (II Kings 23:11–12). Most of the figurines are covered with a thick white wash, with details of attire or harness painted on in red, yellow, and black. Pottery figurines have been found in great numbers in all excavations in Judah but are most abundant in Jerusalem, where hundreds have been found in every excavation conducted in the city. Most have been found broken, and under careful scrutiny the damage appears to be deliberate, occurring unnaturally in the thicker parts of the body. There are also signs of deliberate defacement and dismembering. Thus the destruction and disposal of the figurines on middens outside the houses may have been related to Josiah's purification of the cult or to the priestly school acting to unify the cult in the spirit of Deuteronomy. The few whole figurines come mostly from tombs; in habitations, hardly a single complete figurine has been found. The characteristic Judaean clay figurines begin to appear in Judah in the eighth century but are most widely distributed in the seventh century. During the Iron Age IIIa a new female figurine type was introduced. It had a more schematic, crudely fashioned outline, and the clay of the face was pinched to form a prominent nose and two deep eye hollows, inspiring the term "bird-head figurines." Some bird-headed figures wear a turbanlike headgear.

Stone incense altars represent another aspect of the domestic cult of the Iron Age IIIa. They are usually 25–40 centimeters high, square, and made of soft limestone, with a projecting ridge encircling the middle of the altar. The top is a platform bordered by a low parapet, with projecting horns at each corner. These small altars were undoubtedly modeled on the large sacrificial al-tars, of the type found dismantled and incorporated into the wall of a stratum II structure at Beersheba. In the excavations at Tel Miqne (Ekron) more than ten incense altars have come to light, some of them in situ and all in contexts related to the extensive olive-oil industry at the site. One was discovered in a specially built niche. Four incense altars without horns (interpreted by the excavator as cultic stands) were discovered at the City of David in the same room with a cache of pottery vessels and clay bullae in stratum 10, of the sixth century. They are made of soft limestone, and their octagonal upper section has a depression to accommodate incense. The find sites at Tel Miqne and the City of David clearly indicate that the incense altars of the Iron Age IIIa were not used in temples or high places but in houses and domestic industrial installations. These altars closely resemble the two soft limestone incense altars found in the cella of the Israelite shrine at Arad. A renewed analysis of the Arad excavations ascribes the shrine (contrary to the excavators' view) to stratum VI, the Iron Age IIIa, which correlates well with the paleographic-epigraphic analysis of inscriptions related to the shrine.

POTTERY

Our knowledge of pottery types of the seventh and early sixth centuries is drawn chiefly from the destruction layers ascribed to the campaigns of Nebuchadnezzar in Judaea. Of particular importance are the rich assemblages of stratum II at Lachish and stratum 10 in the City of David, Jerusalem. In the north, Assyrian dominance lasted to the end of the seventh century, and the transition to Babylonian rule was not accompanied by upheavals or destructions. There are therefore no destruction layers in the north and hence no rich find assemblages that may be dated reliably on historical evidence. In contrast to the insularity of the Kingdom of Judah in the eighth century, the pottery of Judah in its final days reflects foreign contacts and influence, represented by eastern Greek imports, Assyrian palace ware and its local imitations, Cypro-Phoenician ware, and Transjordanian ceramic types.

The Judaean jars of the Iron Age IIIa present a broad variety of forms. One is the elongated ovoid jar, the successor of the lamelekh jar of the eighth century. The handles of these jars sometimes bear stamped floral impressions, known as rosette seals. There are different types of rosettes, with six to twelve petals, and they exhibit varying standards of execution. Rosette handles have been found throughout Judah, but only a few complete stamped vessels have been found, in Tel Malhata, Lachish, and Jerusalem. It is possible that some storerooms containing lamelekh jars escaped Sennacherib's campaign of 701 B.C.E. and remained in use, but the jars represent Hezekiah's administration, and by the time Mannasseh came to the throne they were no longer produced and stamped and had given way to the new jar type, which remained in use until the fall of the Kingdom of Judah.

Decanters occupy a prominent position in assemblages of this period, coming in a variety of sizes with varying standards of surface finish. Decanters contained wine, attested to by incised or painted inscriptions. Inscriptions on decanters from Lachish Level II describe the contents as *yyn 'sn* (perhaps meaning strong wine) and *mz. smqm.shrt* (for extract or wine of black raisins). Many other decanters bear the names of their owners, incised after firing.

The cooking pots of the Iron Age IIIa in Judaea differ from those of the Iron Age IIb; they are glob-

Fig. 9.41. Iron Age IIIa pottery from Jerusalem (City of David)

ular, with short necks and everted, channeled rims. A second type of cooking pot has a tall neck with a prominent ridge.

The most common vessels are the bowls and kraters. Bowls appear in a wide variety: deep and shallow; with round, disk, or ring bases; with rounded or slightly carinated walls. Most bowls are burnished in concentric rings on the interior and also on the rim and upper exterior. The kraters are large and deep, usually with four large loop handles, and are burnished inside. The rims of the bowls and kraters were folded on the wheel and thus have a characteristic triangular cross-section. Burnishing seems to be more common

in the pottery from Jerusalem than in the provincial assemblages. Continuous red slip appears on most Iron Age IIIa vessels and may be considered a salient feature of the period. It gradually disappears after the start of the sixth century.

Another typical feature of the Iron Age III in Judaea is the everted ledge-rimmed lamp with the thickened base. The thickened base made the lamps very durable, and they were often used as jar stoppers. The thick bases are common in assemblages of the end of the Iron Age.

The mortarium, which first appears in the Land of Israel in the Iron Age IIIa, is a large, broad,

shallow bowl with a flat base and excessively thick walls, made of a coarse ware, usually gray in color. This bowl type is a link with the following period, the Iron Age IIIb and Persian periods.

Archaeology of Jerusalem

The interest in the early history of Jerusalem has been shared by generations of scholars, and the city has become one of the most intensively excavated sites in the world. Even so, our knowledge of the city in the Iron Age II–III is far from complete. The dense cover of modern construction, the presence of holy places, and the ideological-religious

Fig. 9.42.   Royal palace and temple at Tell Ta'yinat

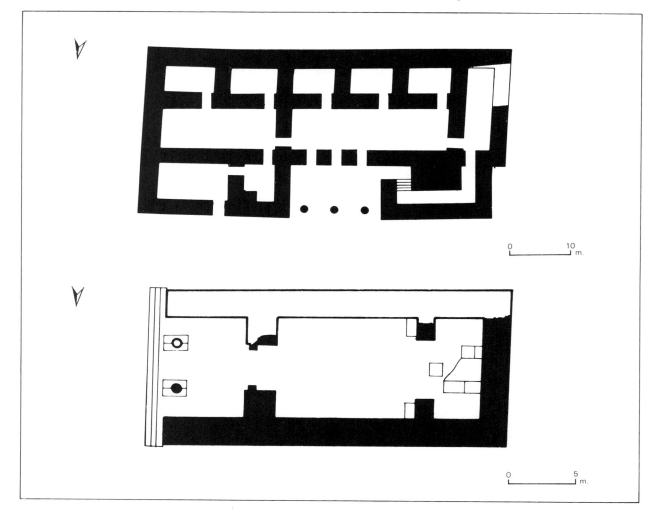

bias accompanying a considerable proportion of the hypotheses and interpretations of excavations have discouraged many archaeologists, who have therefore limited themselves to studies of the topography of the city in light of the biblical evidence. The belief that Jerusalem of the Iron Age II was razed and that scant remains are buried deep beneath layers of debris and modern buildings long held sway in archaeological circles. In fact, modern scientific archaeology began in Jerusalem only in the sixties, with the excavations of Kathleen Kenyon. The central role of Jerusalem in the Bible as the royal, religious, and spiritual center of the Israelites and the countless mentions of its towers, palaces, public buildings, and monuments raised high expectations among its excavators. But although excavations at other sites have uncovered many buildings not referred to in the scriptures, the buildings of Jerusalem named in the scriptures have yet to be identified on the ground. However, large-scale excavations since the sixties, and particularly after the reunification of the city in 1967, have made important contributions to the delineation of the city's character in the Iron Age II–III.

The original core of Jerusalem lies on the long and narrow spur south of the Temple Mount, now known as the City of David. This spur is bounded to the east and west by the deep ravines of the Kidron and Central (Tyropoeon) valleys. The Gihon spring, on the east side of the hill, is responsible for the disadvantageous location of the site. The northern extension of the hill of the City of David was the dome-shaped Temple Mount, now, following its transformation in the days of Herod, a rectangular platform bounded by massive support walls. The western hill of Jerusalem, which includes the present-day Jewish and Armenian quarters of the Old City as well as Mount Zion, is several times larger than the City of David and the Temple Mount, and higher as well (the Temple Mount is 740 meters above sea level, and the western hill about 770 meters). The western hill is bounded on the west and south by the Hinnom valley.

The earliest settlement in the City of David dates to the Chalcolithic period, and the city of the Iron Age II succeeded the Jebusite settlement of the Late Bronze Age and the Iron Age I, which was limited to the City of David.

THE TEMPLE OF SOLOMON AND THE ROYAL ACROPOLIS

Solomon's temple—the First Temple—and the other administrative buildings constructed by Solomon were built on the hill to the north of the City of David, that

Fig. 9.43. Boundaries of Jerusalem in the First Temple period: maximalist school (A), minimalist school (B)

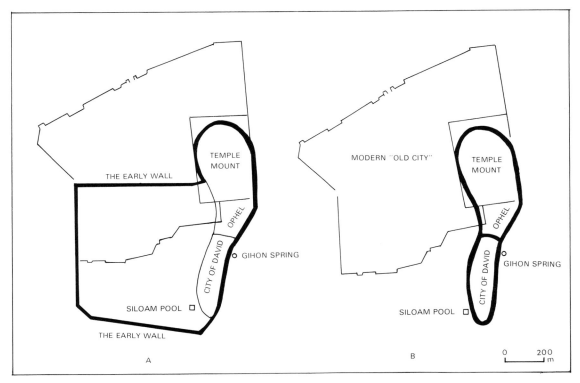

is, biblical Mount Zion or Mount Moriah (II Chron. 3:1), presently known as the Temple Mount. The Temple Mount was incorporated in the municipal boundaries by Solomon. It is reasonable to assume that the choice of location was not accidental and that the spot was held sacred by the inhabitants of Jerusalem before the arrival of the Israelites. The sanctity of the Temple Mount precludes excavation at the site. Even if excavation were permitted, later structures (the Second Temple, Herod's Temple, the pagan temple of Hadrian, and the Islamic mosques) have apparently done away with all remnants of the Temple of Solomon. That uninterrupted tradition, however, indisputably places the temple site within the precincts of the present-day Temple Mount.

The only sources available for the study of the details of the temple are in the Bible (esp. I Kings 5–6; II Chronicles 3). The biblical record is annalistic and contains the technical specifications, as it were, of the structure, its parts, and furnishings. Many of the terms are imperfectly understood, and there are discrepancies in details and measurements between the different sources. Nonetheless, the general plan of the building, a tripartite longhouse with the entry on the east side, is clear.

The Temple of Solomon was one of the largest temples in the Land of Israel in the Bronze and Iron ages, but it was dwarfed by the royal palace nearby, which took twice as long to build, thirteen years against the temple's seven. The palace and temple structures created an administrative compound contiguous with the early urban core to the south. A similar urban layout, with a con-

centration of administrative structures set apart from the residential sections, may be observed in northern Syrian cities, such as Guzana (Tell Halaf), Hamat, Sam'al (Zinjirli), and Tell Ta'yinat.

The excavations in Jerusalem, including those of the large areas south of the Temple Mount, have failed to reveal any architectural details from the magnificent structures of the royal acropolis described in the Bible. The quantity and quality of tenth-century finds in the excavations adjacent to the Temple Mount do not reflect the grandeur of Solomon's day. All we know of the acropolis structures is based on the biblical report, which tended to magnify the achievements of the house of David, the city of Jerusalem, and its temple. Thus far, no real archaeological evidence of those extensive construction works has been found.

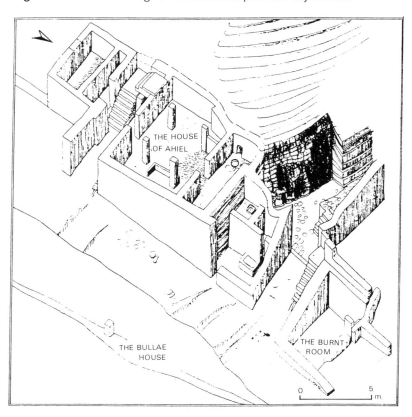

Fig. 9.44. Private dwellings on the eastern slope of the City of David

THE HOUSE OF AHIEL

THE BULLAE HOUSE

THE BURNT ROOM

0 5 m.

BOUNDARIES IN THE FIRST TEMPLE PERIOD

One of the cardinal questions in the study of Jerusalem in the Iron Age II–III concerns the size and boundaries of the city during the period of the First Temple; in fact, every discussion of the history of the city during this period focuses on this issue. Since the end of the nineteenth century, opinions have been divided: did the city destroyed by the Babylonians in 586 B.C.E. include the City of David and the Temple Mount alone, or was it a large city that included the western hill as well? The minimalist school posited a size of thirteen hectares for the city, while the maximalists claimed far greater dimensions, some sixty hectares. The conflicting positions were based almost entirely on biblical evidence, and the debate became an issue of prestige. Was Jerusalem a capital city worthy of the praise heaped on it in the scriptures, or was it merely a small town adulated because of its religious importance? The Book of Nehemiah, with its systematic descriptions of Jerusalem (chapters 2, 3, and 12), played a central role in the debate. Along with other scraps of biblical evidence, it provided a basis for the reconstruction of the appearance of the city. The descriptions of Nehemiah, however, refer to the city of the fifth century, that is, the Persian period, rather than the Iron Age. The continued debate also brought forth compromise opinions between the two extremes.

Until the reunification in 1967, most of the archaeological data on Iron Age II–III Jerusalem came from excavations in the City of David. After 1967, extensive excavations were conducted on the western hill—in the Jewish Quarter, in the Citadel, in the Armenian Quarter, and on Mount Zion. All these excavations revealed structures, occupation surfaces, pottery, and inscriptions of the eighth through sixth centuries. On all parts of the western hill, and even to the north in the Christian Quarter of the Old City, thick deposits of soil with large quantities of Iron Age II–III sherds were found. The excavations of N. Avigad in the Jewish Quarter revealed remains of two fortification systems. These discoveries changed the archaeological picture entirely and convincingly supported the maximalist school.

Having established the extent of the city, attention must turn to the source of the expanded population at the end of the Iron Age and the date of the beginning of the expansion of the city toward the western hill. The fall of Samaria and the kingdom of Israel and their destruction by the Assyrian conqueror (722 B.C.E.), the destruction of many cities in Judah, and the loss of the Shephelah after the campaign of Sennacherib (701 B.C.E.) no doubt affected the growth of Jerusalem, with large populations fleeing the Assyrians and seeking shelter in the shadow of the temple there. The magnification of the theological concept of Jerusalem as the chosen city and the array of beliefs that place Jerusalem as a central value in Israelite religion also contributed to the expansion. The prestige of the city as a safe haven was enhanced after its salvation from the armies of Sennacherib.

Thus the settlement of the western hill began sometime during the ninth century and was sanctioned by its inclusion in the city walls at the end of the eighth century. The expansion proceeded in three stages: the conquest of the Jebusite city by David at about 1000 B.C.E., the site being confined at this time to the City of David; the doubling of the town's area by Solomon's addition of the palace-temple complex on Temple Mount during the tenth century; the gradual expansion toward the western hill, ending with the

Fig. 9.45. Broad Wall, on Jerusalem's western hill

extension of the city walls to encompass the new suburbs (the Mishneh and Makhtesh of Zeph. 1:10–11).

FINDS IN THE CITY OF DAVID

The City of David has been excavated extensively since the nineteenth century, most recently by K. Kenyon (1960–67) and Y. Shiloh (1978–85). Its walls have been exposed along the eastern flank over more than one hundred meters, along the same contour followed by the Middle Bronze Age fortifications. The location of the city walls in the lower part of a sixty-degree incline led to the unique topography of the city, its houses being constructed in terraces supported by retaining walls.

The dwellings excavated on the upper part of the eastern slope were large and spacious. One was built in ashlar masonry, and others employed square-sectioned stone pillars two meters high. The finds reflect the considerable magnificence of the construction: two proto-Ionic capitals and colonettes belonging to window balustrades, toilet basins of a type heretofore found in the ancient Near East only in royal palaces, and carbonized remains of carved furniture made of local and imported wood.

The structures on the eastern slope are usually of the four-room type. One house contained a cache of fifty bullae, remnants of an archive. Most of them were inscribed, and they included the seal impression of Gemaryahu, son of Shaphan (Jer. 36:10, 25).

The houses on the upper slope were apparently built in the seventh century and destroyed in the general destruction of 586 B.C.E. Some were set into a massive stepped structure that towers to fifteen meters. Founded on bedrock, this defensive structure pre-dates the dwelling.

The excavators suggest that it served as a podium for a tenth-century citadel.

DISCOVERIES ON THE WESTERN HILL

Massive settlement on the western hill took place in the eighth and seventh centuries. The Iron Age II–III finds are not concentrated in one sector but are dispersed throughout the area, appearing to represent a settlement of considerable intensity. A large number of lamelekh jar handles, nearly 40 percent of those found in Jerusalem, provide further evidence for the intensity of occupation in the late eighth century. On the northern border of the western hill, two elements of a fortification system of the Iron Age II–III have been exposed. One is the Broad Wall (Neh. 3:8; 12:38), a 75-meter segment of a stone foundation, 7 meters thick and surviving to a height of 3.5 meters. The wall passes through remains of Iron Age II dwellings, which seem to have been destroyed to make way for the wall (cf. Isa. 22:10: "and you counted the houses of Jerusalem and pulled houses down to fortify the wall").

About 25 meters north of the Broad Wall, excavations revealed a large tower, preserved to a height of approximately 8 meters. Its shape and topographical location suggest that it may have been the front of the east wing of a gatehouse. Like the Broad Wall, the tower is built of fieldstones, but the quoin is built of ashlars. The tower was abutted by a floor showing traces of fire and destruction, along with sherds of the Iron Age IIIa and four arrowheads, evidence of the battle that raged here in 586 B.C.E.

Fig. 9.46. Warren's shaft, plan and section

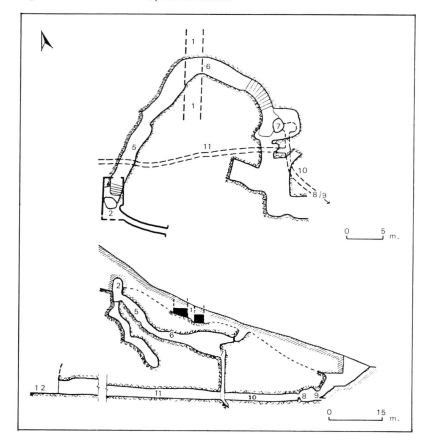

WATER SYSTEMS

The waters of the Gihon spring, the only source of water in Jerusalem, and of the small springs on the outskirts of the city were not sufficient for its many inhabitants. To supplement them, the inhabitants had to carve out cisterns within the city and reservoirs in the surrounding valleys and collect rainwater. These reservoirs, including the Upper Pool (II Kings 18:17, 20:20; Isa. 7:3), the Lower Pool (Isa. 22:9), the Old Pool (Isa. 22:11), the King's Pool (Neh. 2:14), and others, have yet to be identified. Recent excavations south of the Temple Mount have, however, uncovered a large rock-cut cistern related to buildings of the period.

Much imagination and sophistication was exhibited by the inhabitants of Jerusalem in their attempts to provide the city with alternate water sources for times of siege. They display the same technical know-how seen in municipal water systems of the Land of Israel and of neighboring lands in the Iron Age II. The earliest water system in Jerusalem is Warren's shaft, the system discovered by Charles Warren in 1867 and reinvestigated by L. H. Vincent (1911) and Y. Shiloh (1979–81). It consists of an entrance chamber (the present structure is of Second Temple date), a sloping tunnel (with rock-cut stairs), a vertical shaft 14 meters high, and a horizontal tunnel leading the water from the spring to the base of the shaft. The upper entrance to Warren's shaft lay inside the line of the Iron Age walls, the same line as the Bronze Age walls. Many scholars identified Warren's shaft as the *sinor* (water channel) mentioned in the story of the capture of Jerusalem by David (II Sam. 5:8), but this interpretation encounters linguistic and archaeological difficulties, especially in view of the absence of any other

water supply systems dated earlier than the Iron Age II. Its builders had the ingenuity to utilize a natural karstic chimney. The level of engineering, which allowed waters of an external spring to be drawn from within the city walls permits the system to be dated to the tenth century or later, despite the absence of dating evidence from the shaft itself.

The most interesting water system of Jerusalem is the tunnel ascribed to Hezekiah. This is a winding tunnel, cut through the rock for its entire length of 533 meters. Its first segment makes use of the tunnel that directed the Gihon waters to the base of Warren's shaft. In 1880 a Hebrew inscription was discovered on the wall of the tunnel about 6 meters from the southern end. It tells of the completion of the tunneling with the meeting of the two work crews, who worked their way toward one another from the two ends of the tunnel. The tunnel system is probably related to Hezekiah's preparations for the defense of Jerusalem against the campaign and siege of Sennacherib (II Kings 20:20; II Chron. 32:1–4, 30). However, the attribution of this system to Hezekiah is merely a reasonable conjecture, as the name of the king is not mentioned in the inscription, and there are no archaeological-stratigraphical findings to date the system.

CEMETERIES IN THE IRON AGE

More than one hundred tomb caves of the Iron Age II–III have been discovered in Jerusalem and its environs, only a small fraction of the tombs that surrounded the city by the end of the Iron Age. The burial caves are concentrated in three areas, which comprise three distinct cemeteries. The eastern necropolis is within the present-day Siloam village, the northern necropo-

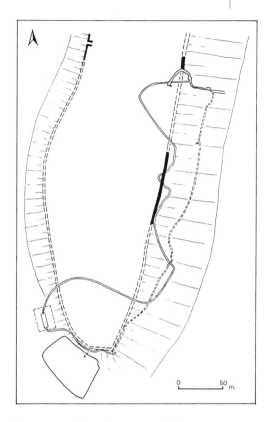

Fig. 9.47. Plan of King Hezekiah's tunnel (Siloam tunnel)

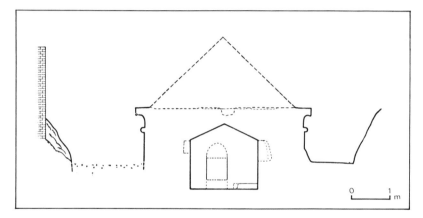

Fig. 9.48. Tomb of the Pharaoh's daughter: drawing by de Saulcy in 1864 (*top*) and section (*bottom*)

lis extends north of the modern Damascus gate, and the western necropolis extends over the scarped slopes of the Hinnom valley, which borders the western hill on the west and south. The cemeteries of Jerusalem form a geographical perimeter for the city and its scattered suburbs, as burial was practiced only outside the inhabited area. The resulting boundaries support the maximalist conception of the city limits.

Fifty burial caves carved into the steep, terraced cliffs of the Siloam village have been identified. They may be divided into three general types: caves with gabled ceilings, caves with flat ceilings, and monolithic monuments with projecting architecture. The gabled caves were

intended for the burial of one or two individuals, probably nobility or high officials. They are remarkable for their precise design, the careful dressing of the rock face, and the effort to maintain straight walls and squared corners. These caves exhibit harmonious proportions and a certain majesty, despite their small dimensions. They should be dated to the ninth and eighth centuries and are unique in the Land of Israel, excelling in their design and workmanship.

The second group is represented by a larger number of tombs, in the upper cliffs of the Siloam village. These caves usually have two or three large rooms carved in file, perpendicular to the scarp line.

They are usually not equipped with burial installations, and presumably the deceased were buried in portable wooden or stone coffins that have disappeared over the centuries.

The monolithic monuments consist of a freestanding architectural element carved out of the rock, into which the burial chamber was hewn. There are four such monuments, all in the northern part of the Siloam village. Hebrew inscriptions were carved on the facades of three of them. The best-known tomb is the tomb of Pharaoh's daughter. It consists of a freestanding mass of rock (5 × 5.8 meters, height 4 meters), ornamented with an Egyptian cornice. A pyramid once topped the monument, but only traces have survived later quarrying. The burial chamber inside the tomb had a gabled ceiling, like the tombs of the first group. The monument resembles New Kingdom Egyptian tomb chapels, though gabled ceilings and Egyptian cornices have also been found in the royal necropolis at Salamis, Cyprus, of the eighth and seventh centuries. A second monument is the tomb of the royal steward, with its inscribed facade. Two contiguous chambers were prepared within this monument. It is commonly identified as the tomb of Shebna (Shebnayahu), the royal steward, of whom it was said, "O you who have hewn your tomb on high; O you who have hollowed out for yourself an abode in the cliff" (Isa. 22:16). Two inscriptions were carved on the facade of the monument, one of which mentions "*yahu* who is in charge of the House," a high-ranking official in the royal court of Judah. The Hebrew inscriptions carved on the monolithic tombs provide a chronological key to the other two tomb groups, which cannot be dated intrinsically. As the inscriptions are dated to the eighth and seventh centuries, and the monolithic tomb monuments appear to be clustered in the northern part of the necropolis, it may be assumed that the tombs of the other two groups are dated somewhat earlier.

The northern necropolis of Iron Age II Jerusalem occupied the rocky slopes flanking the upper part of the Central valley, north of the Damascus gate. It likely served the inhabitants of the extramural suburbs north of the Broad Wall, in the present-day Christian and Moslem quarters of the Old City.

Fourteen caves have been discovered so far. The most elaborate are the two caves in the courtyard of the Dominican monastery of St. Etienne. Excavated one hundred years ago, they were erroneously dated to the Roman period, chiefly because of the lack of datable parallels. The two tombs reveal many architectural features based on palaces or monumental structures of Iron Age Jerusalem. No pottery has been recovered from the tombs, but their date was determined on the basis of a pair of adjacent tombs showing similar architectural features and providing in situ pottery vessels from the seventh century. Another cave attributed to the northern cemetery of the Iron Age II is known as the Garden Tomb, held by some Protestants to be the tomb of Jesus. It underwent later transformations, serving again as a tomb in the Byzantine period, but its basic structure may be traced back to the Iron Age II, as attested by nearby finds.

The western necropolis of Jerusalem extends along the entire length of the Hinnom valley. Thus far, 37 tomb caves have been discovered there since the end of the nineteenth century. This cemetery is conspicuous for its wide variety of cave types, supplemented by two plain pit graves with associated burial gifts. Some caves resemble types known from the provinces of the

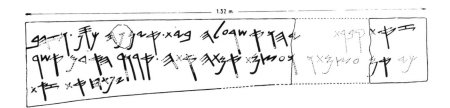

Fig. 9.49. Tomb of (Shebna) the royal steward: facade and inscription

Kingdom of Judah; others contain features characteristic of the elaborate tombs of the Siloam village and the northern necropolis. Elements commonly found in the other Jerusalem necropoli, the carved headrests, the projecting cornices, the use of two Egyptian cubit standards, the sarcophagi carved in the bedrock, the ossuaries, and the burial benches, all appear here. The salient characteristic of this cemetery is the wealth of ceramic finds, jewelry, other ornamental objects, and inscriptions. A repository of one of the caves at Ketef Hinnom was found with its contents intact—the remains of about 95 individuals and about 1000 objects. The most important finds were two rolled-up silver plaques, amulets of some kind, inscribed with blessings resembling the priestly blessing recorded in the book of Numbers (6:24–26).

No certain tomb caves have been identified as yet in the Central valley, which might testify to burial in

a period before the expansion of the city toward the western hill. In more than 120 years of archaeological investigation in Jerusalem, not one tomb has been found that may be dated to the golden age of the Israelite monarchy, the tenth century B.C.E. The tombs of the kings of Judah have also escaped the spades of the many archaeologists who sought them. They are assumed to be within the walls, in the City of David, but they were probably destroyed by later quarrying.

JERUSALEM IN LIGHT OF THE BIBLE AND ARCHAEOLOGY

In recent years a new archaeological picture of Jerusalem has emerged, presenting a walled urban area of more than 60 hectares and unwalled suburbs beyond. The city was surrounded by a periphery of paraurban activities, consequent to the importance and size of the city. The Bible employs the term "great city" for Jerusalem (Jer. 22:8), the same term used to describe the enormous capital cities of Assyria, Calah and Nineveh (Gen. 10:12; Jon. 1:2; 3:2–3), though they were far larger than Jerusalem (Nineveh covered about 720 hectares, Calah 360 hectares). Compared with the cities of the kingdoms of Judah and Israel, which ranged from 6 to 10 hectares, Jerusalem was certainly a city of extraordinary proportions. Even setting aside its extramural suburbs, Jerusalem is about eight times larger than Lachish, the second most important city in the kingdom. Jerusalem may be numbered among the medium-sized capital cities of western Asia in the Iron Age, including centers of great importance, such as Carchemish, Sam'al, Guzana (Tell Halaf), and Hamat.

In the eyes of contemporary observers, Jerusalem was an invincible city, immune to outside attack or siege (II Kings 19:32–34; Isa. 26:1; Ps. 125:1; Lam. 4:12). It was also considered the paragon of urban beauty (Eze. 17:14–16; Ps. 48:3; Song of Songs 6:4; Lam. 2:15). The city was the focus of spiritual creativity, of prophecy, of learning, and of writing. The archaeological record reveals much about Jerusalem as a focus of literacy, including special techniques such as the chiseling of inscriptions on pottery vessels after firing. Excavations have yielded tens of Hebrew inscriptions, most of them dating to the eighth through sixth centuries. Building inscriptions from the City of David and the Ophel excavations, the Siloam inscription, and the necropolis inscriptions from the Siloam village are but the tip of the iceberg, and royal inscriptions will likely be found as excavations continue. Tens of seals of officials and dignitaries and hundreds of stamped jar handles and bullae, as well as ostraca and inscribed weights, testify to the extent of literacy, administrative

activity, and cultural ferment, reflected in the biblical record as well.

The architectural character of the city was formed by the many foreign influences and by the multistoried, terraced construction on the steep slopes; the public structures occupied the hilltops, the residential areas covered the slopes, and the valleys remained free for cultivation, reservoirs, cult installations, and so on. The monuments, fortifications, and palaces of the city and even its magnificent tombs constituted a lodestone, influencing all the provinces of Judah.

The Iron Age IIIb, the Babylonian Period

Judah and Jerusalem were destroyed by Babylon in the campaign of Nebuchadnezzar in 586 B.C.E. This catastrophe, particularly the destruction of the Temple, left a deep scar in the Israelite historical consciousness and in the religious and spiritual development of the Jewish people, so much so that most scholars view this traumatic event as signaling the end of the Iron Age. The period of Babylonian rule, preceding the rise of the Achaemenid Persian empire under Cyrus and the conquest of the Land of Israel (586–538 B.C.E.), is considered part of the Persian period. The catastrophe, however, affected only Jerusalem and the limited territory of late-monarchic Judah. The Iron Age IIIa culture in fact survived through the sixth century, even after the Babylonian conquest of the northern regions, the coastal strip, and the Negev, the events in Jerusalem and Judah having only peripheral impact on these regions. In Transjordan, there was a cultural and habitational continuum from the seventh century to the Persian period. Judaea itself was not entirely laid waste; areas that capitulated to the Babylonians before the fall of Jerusalem were

spared destruction, especially in the land of Benjamin. Evidence for this was found in excavations at Gibeon, Mizpah (Tell en-Nasbeh), and Bethel, and the governor appointed by the Babylonians resided at Mizpah after the fall of Jerusalem (Jer. 40:9–10). The many inhabitants who remained in Judaea, even after the deportations to Babylon, are described as "the poorest of the land . . . vinedressers and field hands" (II Kings 25:12). They carried on the cultural and material traditions of the Iron Age under Babylonian rule. A series of sites of this period has been revealed in surveys in the environs of Bethlehem; by no means can the Land of Israel or even Judaea be considered devoid of settlement. The cult may even have continued in the ruined remains of the temple in Jerusalem (Jer. 41:5).

The material culture of the Babylonian period in Judaea is known chiefly from surveys and burial caves found in Beth Shemesh, Gibeah (Tell el-Ful), and Jerusalem. In a number of caves there is a clear continuity beginning as early as the late seventh century and lasting through most of the sixth century. These tombs also contain much jewelry and prestige items, which reflect considerable wealth rather than poverty.

Continuity is the main characteristic of the culture of the period. At only one site, stratum IIIB at Gibeah, were the excavators able to isolate find assemblages ascribed to the exilic period. The vessels closely resemble those of the Iron Age IIIa, but innovations are in evidence, such as the disappearance of burnishing, particularly of the wheel-burnish on the bowls, and the incised wedge decoration found on kraters and jars, which continues into the Persian period. New vessel types appear as well. Some of them show close connections to the pottery of the Land of Israel and Ammon (the relations with Ammon are also reflected in written sources, such as Jer. 41:15), while others show the influence of Assyrian prototypes.

The imported objects of this period include a new type of conoid seal, octagonal in cross-section. These seals, generally made of chalcedony, bear cult scenes carved in the Mesopotamian style. The earliest coins to arrive in the Land of Israel are the archaic Greek coins, introduced during the sixth century. The characteristic arrowheads of the period are bronze, rather than iron as in earlier periods. They are small, triangular in cross-section, with a socket to hold the shaft. These arrowheads are usually called Scytho-Iranian, and it is generally thought that they were introduced into the battlefield by the Babylonian armies that campaigned in Judaea.

Alongside the settlements showing continuous occupation, there are also sites destroyed at the end of the Iron Age IIIa and not soon resettled. These include Lachish (where there was a gap in settlement between the Iron Age IIIa and Persian period), Tell Beit Mirsim, and Tel Batash.

END OF THE IRON AGE AND OF ISRAELITE CULTURE

The year 586 B.C.E. is of historical rather than archaeological significance, and it marks the end of the Iron Age because the fall of Jerusalem and the Temple is pivotal in biblical literature. Close scrutiny of the archaeological record shows that the real turning point in terms of material culture came only at the end of the sixth century, when Persian authority was established, new pottery types appeared, and Attic ware was imported from Greece. W. F. Albright noticed the cultural continuity following the Babylonian conquest and therefore termed the Babylonian period the Iron Age III. Clearly, he believed that the political and cultural crisis of 586 B.C.E. was not total, a view enhanced by excavations he participated in at Bethel, Gibeah, Mizpah, and Beth Zur. Israelite culture, rooted in the Iron Age I, flourished from the tenth century onward, under the United Monarchy and the kingdoms of Israel and Judah. As information becomes available from excavations, it may be said that Israelite culture came to an end between 530 B.C.E. and 520 B.C.E.

Fig. 9.50. Iron Age IIIb carrot juglets from Jerusalem

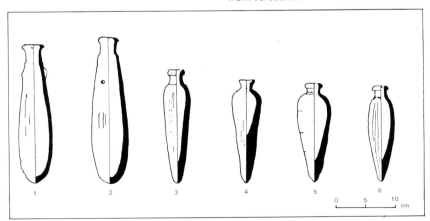

Sources for the Illustrations

We have endeavored to trace the copyright owners of all external material. We sincerely apologize for any omission or error and, upon notification, will be pleased to rectify it in future editions. (Italic numbers indicate adaptations of the originals.)

Tel Aviv University, The Institute of Archaeology
Figures 1.1, 1.3, 3.12, 6.3 (parts 4 and 7), 6.4 (parts 2, 7, 12), 6.47, 7.28, 8.1, 8.29, 9.9, 9.30, 9.31, 9.38

Israel Museum, The Shrine of the Book
Figure 1.2

The Open University of Israel, Graphics Department
Figure 1.4; Maps 1.1, 2.1, 2.2, 3.1, 4.1, 5.1, 6.1, 7.2, 8.2, 9.1

Israel Exploration Society
Figures 2.3, 2.4, 2.11, 3.2, 3.4, 3.7–11, 3.20, 3.21, 4.2–4, 4.8–10, 4.12, 4.18, 4.21, 4.22, 4.24, 4.29, 5.1, 5.3, 5.5–7, 5.17–20, 5.22, 6.3 (parts 2, 6, 9, 10), 6.4 (parts 4–6, 8–11, 13, 16, 17), 6.14 (parts 1, 3, 4), 6.15 (3, 10–12, 15, 17), 6.20, 6.22, 6.25, 6.26, 6.28, 6.29, 6.38, 6.39, 7.1, 7.2, 7.10–15, 7.20, 7.34, 7.35, 8.14, 8.18, 8.19, *8.20,* 8.22, 9.1, 9.3–7, *9.8,* 9.10, 9.15, 9.19, 9.22, 9.23, *9.24,* 9.25–29, 9.32, 9.34, 9.36, 9.42, 9.46, 9.47

Photo by David Haris, Jerusalem
Figure 2.1

The Institute of Archaeology, The Hebrew University, Jerusalem
Figures 2.2, 8.7, 8.9–13, 9.12–14, 9.41, 9.42

Aharoni, Y. 1978. *The Archaeology of the Land of Israel.* Jerusalem (Hebrew): Shikmona Publishing Company
Figures *2.5,* 5.2, 7.3, 8.23, 9.40

Fouilles J. Perrot a Munhata, Centre de recherche Francaise de Jerusalem
Figures 2.6, 2.10, 2.12

The Department of Antiquities and Museums, Ministry of Education and Cultures, Jerusalem
Figures 2.7, 2.9, 2.13, 3.6, 3.13, 3.14, 3.17, 3.22–26, 4.6, 4.7, 4.13–15, 4.17, 4.23, 4.32, 5.4, 5.8–13, 5.16, 5.21, 6.4 (part 14), 6.19, 6.23, 6.34, 6.37, 6.40, 6.41, 6.44, 6.46, 6.48, 6.49, 6.50 (part B), 6.51, 6.52, 7.16, 7.18, 7.19, 7.21, 7.24, 7.30, 7.32, 7.33, 8.16, 9.21, 9.37, 9.39; Map 5.2

Collection of the Department of Antiquities and Museums, photographed and displayed in the Israel Museum, Jerusalem
Figures 2.14, 3.3, 3.18, 3.19, 5.15, 7.22, 7.25, 8.8, 8.24, 9.16 (parts B and C)

Kenyon, K. A. 1979. *Archaeology in the Holy Land*, 4th edition. London: Ernest Benn
Figures 2.8, 4.25, 6.3 (parts 3 and 13), 6.15 (parts 16 and 25), 6.21
Mellaart, J. 1975. *The Neolithic of the Near East*. London: Thames and Hudson
Map 2.3
Gophna, R. 1982. The Chalcolithic Period. In *The History of Eretz-Israel: The Judges*. I. Eph'al, ed. Keter Press: Jerusalem
Figure 2.15
Mallon, A., and Koeppel, R. 1934. *Teleilat Ghassul I*. Rome: Pontifical Biblical Institute
Figures 3.1, 3.5
Photo by Verner Braun, Jerusalem
Figures 3.15, 3.16
Dunand, M. 1973. *Fouilles de Byblos V. Texte*. Paris: A. Maisonneuve
Figure 4.1
Guy, P. L. O. 1938. *Megiddo Tombs*. Chicago: Oriental Institute Publications, The University of Chicago Press
Figure 6.50 (part A)
Loud, G. 1948. *Megiddo II*. Chicago: Oriental Institute Publications, The University of Chicago Press
Figures 4.11, 4.16, 6.3 (parts 5, 8, 14–16), 6.4 (parts 1 and 3), 6.14 (parts 2, 7, 12), 6.15 (parts 1, 6, 18, 19), 6.18, 6.35
Bialik Institute, Jerusalem
Figure 4.19
Hennessy, J. B. 1967. *The Foreign Relations of Palestine during the Early Bronze Age*. London: Colt Archaeological Institution Publications, Bernard Quaritch Ltd.
Figures 4.20, 4.30, 4.31, 4.33; Maps 4.2, 4.3
Courtesy A. Ben-Tor, The Hebrew University, Jerusalem
Figures 4.5, 4.26–28
Bulletin of the American Schools of Oriental Research, American Schools of Oriental Research
Figures 5.14, 6.43, 9.33; Map 5.3

Lepsius, R. 1891. *Denkmäler aus Aegypten und Aethiopien*. Berlin: Nicolaische Buchhandlung
Figure 6.1
Rowe, A. 1936. *A Catalogue of Egyptian Scarabs in the Palestine Archaeological Museum*. Le Caire: Imprimerie de l'Institut Francais d'Archeologie Orientale
Figure 6.2 (Lachish)
Petrie, F. 1934. *Ancient Gaza IV*. London: British School of Archaeology in Egypt
Figure 6.2 (Ajjul)
Tufnell, O. 1969. The Pottery from Royal Tombs I–III at Byblos. *Berytus* 18
Figures 6.3 (part 1), 6.6
Kempinski, A. 1983. *Syrien und Palästina (Kanaan) in der Letzten Phase der Meittelbronze IIb-Zeit*. Wiesbaden: Harrassowitz
Figures 6.15 (parts 7, 8, 13), 6.27
Hazor Excavations, The Hebrew University, Jerusalem
Figures 6.15 (parts 2, 4, 5), 6.16, 6.17, 7.4, 7.5, 7.6–9, 7.31, 7.36, 8.25, 9.2
Price-Williams, D. 1977. *The Tombs of the Middle Bronze Age II Period from the "500" Cemetery at Tell Far'ah (s)*. London: The Institute of Archaeology, London University
Figure 6.24
Keel, O., and Schroer, Silvia. 1985. *Studien Zu den Stempelsiegeln aus Palästina/Israel I*. Freiburg: Universitätsverlag, Freiburg Schweitz Vandenhoeck & Ruperecht Götingen
Figures 6.30–33
Sagona, C. 1980. Middle Bronze Faience Vessels from Palestine. *Zeitschrift des Deutschen Palästina Vereins* 96. Wiesbaden: Harrassowitz
Figure 6.36.
Galling, K. 1977. *Biblisches Reallexikon*. Tübingen: J. C. B. Mohr.
Figure 6.45

Figulla, H. H. 1967. *Cuneiform Texts from Babylonian Tablets XLVIII*. London: The Trustees of the British Museum
Figure 6.53
Aharoni, Y. 1964. *Carta's Atlas of the Bible*. Jerusalem: Carta
Map 7.1
Davies, N. G., and Faulkner, R. O. 1947. A Syrian Trading Venture to Egypt. *The Journal of Egyptian Archaeology* 33. The Egypt Exploration Society, London
Figure 7.12 (part B)
Merrilees, R. S. 1962. Opium Trade in the Bronze Age Levant. *Antiquity* XXXVI. A Quarterly Review of Archaeology. England
Figure 7.17
Mazar, B., editor. 1982. *The History of Eretz-Israel: The Judges*. Am Oved: International Publishing Company Ltd.
Figure 7.23
Yadin, Y. 1963. *The Art of Warfare in Biblical Lands*. Jerusalem: International Publishing Company
Figure 7.26
Naveh, J. 1982. *Early History of the Alphabet*. Jerusalem: Magnes Press, The Hebrew University
Figure 7.27
Nelson, H. H., et al. 1930. *Medinat Habu I. University of Chicago, Oriental Institute Publications* VIII. The University of Chicago Press
Figure 8.2
Dothan, Trude. 1982. *The Philistines and Their Material Culture*. Jerusalem: Israel Exploration Society
Figures 8.3, 8.5, 8.6, 8.15, 8.17; Map 8.1
Courtesy S. Gitin, The Albright Institute, Jerusalem
Figure 8.4
Courtesy I. Finkelstein, Bar Ilan University
Figure 8.21; Map 8.3
Courtesy A. Zertal, Haifa University
Figures 8.26, 8.27

Barnett, R. D. 1982. Ancient Ivories in the Middle East. *Qedem* 14. Monographs of the Institute of Archaeology, The Hebrew University, Jerusalem

Figures 9.11, 9.18 (part B)

Meshel, Z. 1979. Who built the "Israelite Fortresses" in the Negev Mountains? (Hebrew.) *Qathedra* 11. Yad Izhak Ben Zvi, Jerusalem

Map *9.2*

May, H. 1935. *Material Remains of the Megiddo Cult.* Chicago: Oriental Institute Publications, The University of Chicago Press

Figure 9.20

Avigad, N. 1980. *The Upper City of Jerusalem.* Jerusalem: Shikmona Publishing Company

Figure 9.45

Courtesy G. Barkai, The Institute of Archaeology, Tel Aviv University

Figure 9.50

Bibliography

INTRODUCTION

Aharoni, Y. 1979. *The Land of the Bible: A Historical Geography.* Translated from the Hebrew and edited by A. F. Rainey, 2nd ed. Philadelphia: Westminster Press.

———. 1973. Methods of recording and documenting. In *Beer-Sheba I:* 119–132. Tel Aviv: Institute of Archaeology, Tel Aviv University.

———. 1982. *The Archaeology of the Land of Israel.* Philadelphia: Westminster Press.

Albright, W. F. 1963. *The Archaeology of Palestine.* Rev. ed. London: Penguin Books.

Amiran, R. 1969. *Ancient Pottery of the Holy Land.* Jerusalem: Massada Press.

Aviram, J., et al., editors. 1985. *Biblical Archaeology Today.* Proceedings of the International Congress on Biblical Archaeology, Jerusalem. Israel Exploration Society.

Avi-Yonah, M., and Stern, E., editors. 1975–78. *Encyclopedia of Archaeological Excavations in the Holy Land.* 4 vols. Jerusalem: Israel Exploration Society and Massada Press.

Baly, D., and Tushingham, A. D. 1971. *Atlas of the Biblical World.* New York: World Publishing.

Bass, George Fletcher. 1975. *Archaeology Beneath the Sea.* New York: Walker.

Binford, L., editor. 1977. *For Theory Building in Archaeology.* New York: Academic Press.

Broshi, M. 1987. Religion, ideology and politics and their impact on Palestinian archaeology. *Israel Museum Journal* 6:17–32.

Butzer, K. 1964. *Environment and Archaeology.* Chicago: Aldine Publishing. Pp. 3–34.

Conder, C. R., and Kitchener, H. H. 1881–1883. *The Survey of Western Palestine: Memoirs of the Topography, Orography, Hydrography and Archaeology.* 3 vols. 1970 reproduction. Jerusalem: Kedem Publishing.

Cross, F. M., et al., editors. 1976. *Magnalia Dei: The Mighty Acts of God.* New York: Doubleday & Co.

Dever, W. G. 1973. Two approaches to archaeological method—the architectural and the stratigraphic. *Eretz-Israel* 11:1–8.

———. 1982. Retrospects and prospects in biblical and Syro-Palestinian archaeology. *Biblical Archaeologist* 45:103–107.

Dever, W. G., and Lance, H. D., editors. 1978. *A Manual of Field Excavation—Handbook for Field*

Archaeologists. New York: Hebrew Union College–Jewish Institute of Religion.

Glueck, N. 1959. *Rivers in the Desert.* New York: Farrar, Straus and Cudahy.

Hodder, I. 1986. *Reading the Past.* Cambridge: Cambridge University Press.

Kenyon, K. M. 1952. *Beginning in Archaeology.* London: J. M. Dent and Sons.

———. 1960. *Archaeology in the Holy Land.* 4th ed., revised 1979. London: Ernest Benn.

———. 1971. An essay on archaeological technique. *Harvard Theological Review* 64:271–280.

Moorey, R., and Parr, P., editors. 1978. *Archaeology in the Levant: Essays for Kathleen Kenyon.* Warminster: Aris & Phillips.

Renfrew, C. 1985. *The Archaeology of Cult.* The Sanctuary at Phylakopi. London: Thames and Hudson. Pp. 11–26.

Sanders, J. A., editor. 1970. *Near Eastern Archaeology in the Twentieth Century: Essays in Honor of Nelson Glueck.* New York: Doubleday.

Silberman, N. A. 1982. *Digging for God and Country.* New York: Alfred A. Knopf.

Tubb, J. M., editor. 1985. *Palestine in the Bronze and Iron Ages: Papers in Honor of Olga Tufnell.* London: London University, Institute of Archaeology.

Ussishkin, D. 1982. Where is Israeli archaeology going? *Biblical Archaeologist* 45:93–95.

Vaux, R. de. 1970. On right and wrong uses of archaeology. Pp. 64–80 in *Near Eastern Archaeology in the Twentieth Century.* J. A. Sanders, editor. New York: Doubleday.

Wheeler, M. 1954. *Archaeology from the Earth.* Oxford: Penguin Books.

Wright, G. E. 1969. Archaeological method in Palestine—an Ameri-can interpretation. *Eretz-Israel* 9:120–133.

THE NEOLITHIC PERIOD

Bar-Yosef, O. 1980. Prehistory of the Levant. *Annual Review of Anthropology* 9:101–133.

———. 1982. Pre-pottery Neolithic sites in southern Sinai. *Biblical Archaeologist* 45:9–12.

———. 1986. The walls of Jericho: An alternative interpretation. *Current Anthropology* 27(2):157–162.

Bar-Yosef, O., Gopher, A., and Goring-Morris, A. N. 1980. Netiv Ha-Gdud: A Sultanian mound in the lower Jordan valley. *Paléorient* 6:201–206.

Davis, S. J. M., and Valla, F. R. 1978. Evidence for the domestication of the dog 12,000 years ago in the Natufian of Israel. *Nature* 276:608–610.

Goring-Morris, A. N., and Gopher, A. 1983., Nahal Issaron: A Neolithic settlement in the southern Negev. *Israel Exploration Journal* 33:149–162.

Kaplan, J. 1958. Excavation at Wadi Rabah. *Israel Exploration Journal* 8:149–160.

———. 1959. The Neolithic pottery of Palestine. *Bulletin of the American Schools of Oriental Research* 156:15–22.

———. 1969. Ein el Jarba: Chalcolithic remains in the plain of Esdraelon. *Bulletin of the American Schools of Oriental Research* 194:2–38.

Kirkbride, D. 1971. A commentary on the Pottery Neolithic of Palestine. *Harvard Theological Review* 64:281–289.

Legge, A. J. 1977. The origins of agriculture in the Near East. In *Hunters, Gatherers and First Farmers Beyond Europe,* J. V. S. Megaw, editor. Leicester University Press.

Mellaart, J. 1975. *The Neolithic of the Near East.* London: Thames and Hudson.

Noy, T., Schuldenrein, J., and Tchernov, E. 1980. Gilgal: A Pre-pottery Neolithic A site in the lower Jordan valley. *Israel Exploration Journal* 30:63–82.

Prausnitz, M. W. 1970. *From Hunter to Farmer and Trader.* Jerusalem: Sivan Press.

Redman, C. L. 1978. *The Rise of Civilization.* San Francisco: Freeman.

Stekelis, M. 1972. *The Yarmukian Culture of the Neolithic Period.* Jerusalem: Magnes Press.

Stekelis, M., and Yizraeli, T. 1963. Excavations at Nahal Oren, preliminary report. *Israel Exploration Journal* 13:1–12.

THE CHALCOLITHIC PERIOD

Alon, D. 1976. Two cult vessels from Gilat. ᶜ*Atiqot* 11:116–118.

———. 1977. A Chalcolithic temple at Gilath. *Biblical Archaeologist* 40:63–65.

Amiran, R. 1981. Some observations on Chalcolithic and Early Bronze Age sanctuaries and religion. Pp. 47–53 in *Temples and High Places,* A. Biran, editor. Jerusalem: Hebrew Union College.

———. 1985. The transition from the Chalcolithic to the Early Bronze Age. Pp. 108–112 in *Biblical Archaeology Today,* J. Aviram et al., editors. Proceedings of the International Congress on Biblical Archaeology, Jerusalem.

Bar-Adon, P. 1980. *The Cave of the Treasure.* Jerusalem: Israel Exploration Society.

Beit Arieh, I. 1980. A Chalcolithic site near Serabit el Khadim. *Tel Aviv* 7:45–64.

de Contenson, H. 1956. La céramique chalcolithique de Beersheba: étude typologique. *Israel Exploration Journal* 6:163–179, 226–238.

Dothan, M. 1959a. Excavations at Meser, 1957. *Israel Exploration Journal* 9:13–29.

———. 1959b. Excavations at Horvat Beter (Beer Sheva). ᶜ*Atiqot* 2:1–71.

Elliot, C. 1977. The Religious Beliefs of the Ghassulians, 4000–3100 B.C. *Palestine Exploration Quarterly* 109:3–25.

———. 1978. The Ghassulian culture in Palestine: Origins, influences and abandonment. *Levant* 10:37–45.

Epstein, C. 1977. The Chalcolithic culture of the Golan. *Biblical Archaeologist* 40:57–62.

———. 1978. A new aspect of Chalcolithic culture. *Bulletin of the American Schools of Oriental Research* 209:27–45.

———. 1982. Cult symbols in Chalcolithic Palestine. *Bolletino del Centro di Studi Prehistorici* 19:63–82.

Ferembach, D. 1959. Le peuplement du Proche-Orient au chalcolithique et au bronze ancien. *Israel Exploration Journal* 9:221–228.

Haas, N., and Nathan, H., An attempt at a social interpretation of the Chalcolithic burials in the Nahal Mishmar caves. P. xvii in *Excavations and Studies: Essays in Honour of Shemuel Yevin*. Tel Aviv: Institute of Archaeology, Tel Aviv University.

Hennessy, J. B., 1982. Teleilat Ghassul: its place in the archaeology of Jordan. Pp. 55–58 in *Studies in the History and Archaeology of Jordan*, vol. I, A. Hadidi, editor. Amman: Department of Antiquities.

Koeppel, R., et al. 1940. *Teleilat Ghassul II*. Rome: Institut Biblique Pontifical.

Levy, T. E. 1986. The Chalcolithic period. *Biblical Archaeologist* 49:82–108.

Levy, T. E., and Alon, D. 1985. Shiqmim: A Chalcolithic village and mortuary centre in the northern Negev. *Paléorient* 11/1:71–83.

Mallon, A., Koeppel, R., and Neuville, R. 1934. *Teleilat Ghassul I, 1929–32*. Rome: Pontifical Biblical Institute.

Mellaart, J. 1966. *The Chalcolithic and Early Bronze Ages in the Near East and Anatolia*. Beirut: Khayats. Pp. 9–57.

North, R. S. J. 1960. Ghassul 1960: Excavation report. *Analecta Biblica* 14. Rome: Pontifical Biblical Institute.

Oren, E., and Gilead, I. 1981. Chalcolithic sites in northeastern Sinai. *Tel Aviv* 8:25–44.

Ory, J. 1946. A Chalcolithic necropolis at Bene Berak. *Quarterly of the Department of Antiquities in Palestine* 12:43–57.

Perrot, J. 1955. The excavations at Tell Abu Matar. *Israel Exploration Journal* 5:17–40, 73–84, 167–189.

———. 1961. Une tombe à ossuaires de IVᵉ millénaire à Azor près de Tel Aviv: Rapport preliminaire. ᶜ*Atiqot* 3:1–83.

———. 1984. Structures d'habitat, mode de vie et environment: Les villages souterrains des pasteurs de Beersheva dans le sud d'Israël, au IVᵉ millénaire avant l'ère Chrétienne. *Paléorient* 10/1:75–96.

Sukenik, E. L. 1937. A Chalcolithic necropolis at Hadera. *Journal of the Palestine Oriental Society* 17:15–30.

Ussishkin, D. 1971. The "Ghassulian" temple in Ein Gedi and the origin of the hoard from Nahal Mishmar. *Biblical Archaeologist* 34:23–39.

———. 1980. The "Ghassulian" shrine at Ein Gedi. *Tel Aviv* 7:1–44.

Vaux, R. de. 1971. Palestine during the Neolithic and Chalcolithic periods. Pp. 499–538 in *The Cambridge Ancient History*, volume 1, part 2. Cambridge: Cambridge University Press.

THE EARLY BRONZE AGE

Amiran, R. 1965. A preliminary note on the synchronisms between the Early Bronze strata of Arad and the First Dynasty, *Bulletin of the American Schools of Oriental Research* 179:30–33.

———. 1969. A second note on the synchronisms between Early Bronze Age Arad and the First Dynasty, *Bulletin of the American Schools of Oriental Research* 195:50–53.

———. 1970a. The beginnings of urbanization in Canaan. Pp. 83–100 in *Near Eastern Archaeology in the Twentieth Century: Essays in Honor of Nelson Glueck*, J. A. Sanders, editor. Garden City, N.Y.: Doubleday.

———. 1970b. The Egyptian alabaster vessels from ᶜAi. *Israel Exploration Journal* 20:170–179.

———. 1974. An Egyptian jar fragment with the name of Narmer from Arad. *Israel Exploration Journal* 24:4–12.

———. 1986. The fall of the Early Bronze Age II city of Arad. *Israel Exploration Journal* 36:74–76.

Amiran, R., Beit-Arieh, I., and Glass, J. 1973. The interrelationship between Arad and sites in southern Sinai in the Early Bronze Age II. *Israel Exploration Journal* 23:193–197.

Ben-Tor, A. 1971. The date of the Kfar Monash hoard. *Israel Exploration Journal* 21:201–206.

———. 1977. Cult scenes on Early Bronze Age cylinder seal impressions from Palestine. *Levant* 9:90–100.

———. 1978. *Cylinder Seals of Third Millennium Palestine*. Supplement Series 22. Cambridge, Mass.: American Schools of Oriental Research.

———. 1982. The relations between Egypt and the Land of Canaan during the third millennium, B.C. *Journal of Jewish Studies* 33:3–18.

———. 1986. The trade relations of Palestine in the Early Bronze Age. *Journal of the Economic and Social History of the Orient* 29:1–27.

Broshi, M., and Gophna, R. 1984. The settlements and population of Palestine during the Early Bronze Age II–III. *Bulletin of the American Schools of Oriental Research* 253:41–53.

Callaway, Y., and Weinstein, J. 1977. Radio carbon dating of Palestine in the Early Bronze Age. *Bulletin of the American Schools of Oriental Research* 225:1–16.

Hennessy, J. B. 1967. *The Foreign Relations of Palestine during the Early Bronze Age.* Colt Archaeological Institute Publications. London: B. Quaritch.

Kempinski, A. 1978. *The Rise of an Urban Culture: The Urbanization of Palestine in the Early Bronze Age.* Jerusalem: Israel Ethnographic Society.

Lapp, P. 1970. Palestine in the Early Bronze Age. Pp. 101–131 in *Near Eastern Archaeology in the Twentieth Century: Essays in Honor of Nelson Glueck,* J. A. Sanders, editor. Garden City, N.Y.: Doubleday.

Lichtheim, Miriam. 1973. Ancient Egyptian Literature: A Book of Readings, Vol. 1. Berkeley: University of California Press.

Miroschedji, P. R. de. 1971. *L'époque pré-urbaine en Palestine.* Cahiers de la Revue biblique 13. Paris: Gabalda.

Oren, E. D. 1973. The overland route between Egypt and Canaan in the Early Bronze Age. *Israel Exploration Journal* 23:198–205.

Richard, S. 1987. The Early Bronze Age: The rise and collapse of urbanism. *Biblical Archaeologist* 50:22–43.

Vaux, R. de. 1971. Palestine in the Early Bronze Age. Pp. 208–237 in *Cambridge Ancient History,* Vol. 1, part 2. 3rd rev. ed. Cambridge: Cambridge University Press.

Wright, M. 1985. Contacts between Egypt and Syro-Palestine during the Protodynastic Period. *Biblical Archaeologist* 48:240–253.

Yadin, Y. 1955. The earliest record of Egypt's military penetration into Asia? *Israel Exploration Journal* 5:1–16.

THE INTERMEDIATE BRONZE AGE

Albright, W. F. 1962. The chronology of Middle Bronze I (Early Bronze–Middle Bronze). *Bulletin of the American Schools of Oriental Research* 168:36–42.

Amiran, R. 1960. The pottery of the Middle Bronze Age I in Palestine. *Israel Exploration Journal* 10:204–225.

Dever, W. G. 1971. The peoples of Palestine in the Middle Bronze I period. *Harvard Theological Review* 64:197–226.

———. 1972. A Middle Bronze I site on the west bank of the Jordan. *Archaeology* 25:231–233.

———. 1973. The EB IV–MBI horizon in Transjordan and southern Palestine. *Bulletin of the American Schools of Oriental Research* 210: 37–63.

———. 1980. New vistas on the EB IV ("MBI") horizon in Syria-Palestine. *Bulletin of the American Schools of Oriental Research* 237:35–64.

———. 1985a. From the end of the Early Bronze Age to the beginning of the Middle Bronze. Pp. 113–135 in *Biblical Archaeology Today,* J. Aviram et al., editors. Jerusalem: Israel Exploration Society.

———. 1985b. Village planning at Beer Resisim and socio-economic structure in Early Bronze IV Palestine. *Eretz-Israel* 18:18–28.

Dever, W. G., and Cohen, R. 1981. Preliminary report of the third

and final season of the "Central Negev Highland Project." *Bulletin of the American Schools of Oriental Research* 243:57–76.

Dever, W. G., and Tadmor, M. 1976. A copper hoard of the Middle Bronze Age I. *Israel Exploration Journal* 26:163–173.

Gerstenblith, P. 1980. A reassessment of the beginning of the Middle Bronze Age in Syria-Palestine. *Bulletin of the American Schools of Oriental Research* 237:65–84.

Gitin, S. 1975. Middle Bronze I "domestic" pottery of Jebel Qa'aqir, ceramic inventory of the cave G23. *Eretz-Israel* 12:46–62.

Kenyon, K. M. 1966. *Amorites and Canaanites.* London.

———. 1979. *Archaeology in the Holy Land.* 4th ed. New York: Norton & Co. Pp. 119–147.

Lapp, P. 1966. *The Dhahr Mirzbaneh Tombs: Three Intermediate Bronze Age Cemeteries in Jordan.* Publications of the Jerusalem School 4. New Haven, Conn.: American Schools of Oriental Research.

Mazzoni, S. 1985. Elements of the ceramic culture of early Syrian Ebla in comparison with Syro-Palestinian EB IV. *Bulletin of the American Schools of Oriental Research* 257:1–18.

Oren, E. D. 1973. The Early Bronze IV period in northern Palestine and its cultural and chronological setting. *Bulletin of the American Schools of Oriental Research* 210:20–37.

Posener, G., Bottéro, J., and Kenyon, K. M. 1971. Syria and Palestine c. 2160–1780 B.C. Pp. 532–583 in *The Cambridge Ancient History,* Vol. I, part II. Rev. ed. Cambridge: Cambridge University Press.

Prag, K. 1974. The intermediate Early Bronze–Middle Bronze Age: An interpretation of the evidence from Transjordan, Syria and Lebanon. *Levant* 6:69–116.

Richard, S. 1980. Toward a consensus of opinion on the end of the Early Bronze Age in Palestine-Transjordan. *Bulletin of the American Schools of Oriental Research* 237:5–34.

———. 1987. The Early Bronze Age: The rise and collapse of urbanism. *Biblical Archaeology* 50(1):22–43.

Schaub, R. T. 1973. An Early Bronze IV tomb from Bab edh-Dhra^c. *Bulletin of the American Schools of Oriental Research* 210:2–19.

Shay, T. 1983. Burial customs at Jericho in the intermediate Bronze Age: A componential analysis. *Tel Aviv* 10:26–37.

Smith, P. 1982. The physical characteristics and biological affinities of the MBI skeletal remains from Jebel Qa'aqir. *Bulletin of the American Schools of Oriental Research* 245:65–73.

Tadmor, M. 1978. A cult cave of the Middle Bronze Age I near Qedesh. *Israel Exploration Journal* 28:1–30.

THE MIDDLE BRONZE AGE

Albright, W. F. 1973. The historical framework of Palestinian archaeology between 2100 and 1600 B.C. *Bulletin of the American Schools of Oriental Research* 209:12–18.

Amiran, R. 1957. Tell el-Yahudiyeh ware in Syria. *Israel Exploration Journal* 7:93–97.

———. 1970. Similarities between the pottery of the MBIIA period and the pottery of the Assyrian colonies and their implications. *Anadolu* 12(1968):59–62.

Beck, P. 1985. The Middle Bronze Age IIA pottery from Aphek, 1972–1984: First summary. *Tel Aviv* 12:181–203.

Bietak, M. 1984. Problems of Middle Bronze Age chronology: New evidence from Egypt. *American Journal of Archaeology* 88:471–482.

———. 1987. Canaanites in the eastern Nile Delta. Pp. 41–56 in *Egypt, Israel, Sinai—Archaeological and Historical Relationships in the Biblical Period*, A. F. Rainey, editor. Tel Aviv: Tel Aviv University.

Dever, W. G. 1987. The Middle Bronze Age: The zenith of the urban Canaanite era. *Biblical Archaeologist* 50:148–177.

Dunayevski, I., and Kempinski, A. 1973. The Megiddo temples. *Zeitschrift des Deutschen Palästina-Vereins* 89:175–181.

Giveon, R. 1967. Royal seals of the XIIth Dynasty from western Asia. *Revue d'Egyptologie* 19:29–37.

———. 1974. Hyksos scarabs with names of kings and officials from Canaan. *Chronique d'Egypte* 49:222–233.

Gophna, R. 1979. A Middle Bronze Age II village in the Jordan valley. *Tel Aviv* 6:28–33.

Gophna, R., and Beck, P. 1981. The rural aspect of the settlement pattern of the coastal plain in the Middle Bronze Age II. *Tel Aviv* 8:45–80.

Kaplan, J. 1971. Mesopotamian elements in the Middle Bronze II culture of Palestine. *Journal of Near Eastern Studies* 30:293–307.

———. 1975. Further aspects of the Middle Bronze Age II fortifications in Palestine. *Zeitschrift des Deutschen Palästina-Vereins* 91:1–17.

Kempinski, A. 1974. Tell el-^cAjjul, Beth Aglayim or Sharuhen? *Israel Exploration Journal* 24:145–152.

Kenyon, K. 1969. The Middle and Late Bronze Age strata at Megiddo. *Levant* 1:25–60.

———. 1979. *Archaeology in the Holy Land.* 4th ed. London: Methuen & Co. Pp. 148–179.

Kochavi, M., Beck, P., and Gophna, R. 1979. Aphek-Antipatris, Tel Poleg, Tel Zeror and Tel Burga: Four fortified sites of the Middle Bronze Age IIA in the Sharon plain. *Zeitschrift des Deutschen Palästina-Vereins* 95:121–165.

Mazar, B. 1968. The Middle Bronze Age in Palestine. *Israel Exploration Journal* 18:65–97.

Parr, P. J. 1968. The origin of rampart fortifications of Middle Bronze Age Palestine and Syria. *Zeitschrift des Deutschen Palästina-Vereins* 84:18–45.

Posener, G. 1940. *Princes et pays d'Asie et de Nubie.* Bruxelles: Fondation Egyptologique Reine Elisabeth.

Save-Soderbergh, T. 1951. The Hyksos rule in Egypt. *Journal of Egyptian Archaeology* 37:53–71.

Sethe, K. 1926. *Die Ächtung feindlicher Fürsten, Völker und Dinge auf altägyptischen Tongefässcherben des mittleren Reiches.* Berlin: de Gruyter.

Tubb, J. 1983. The MB IIA period in Palestine: Its relationship with Syria and its origin. *Levant* 15:49–62.

Weinstein, J. A. 1975. Egyptian relations with Palestine in the Middle Kingdom. *Bulletin of the American Schools of Oriental Research* 217:1–16.

Wilson, J. A. 1941. The Egyptian Middle Kingdom at Megiddo. *American Journal of Semitic Languages and Literature* 58:225–236.

Yadin, Y. 1955. Hyksos fortifications and the battering ram. *Bulletin of the American Schools of Oriental Research* 137:23–32.

THE LATE BRONZE AGE

Aharoni, Y. 1972. *The Land of the Bible.* 2nd ed. Philadelphia: Westminster Press. Pp. 150–190.

———. 1982. *The Archaeology of the Land of Israel.* Philadelphia: Westminster Press.

Alt, A. 1953. Ägyptische Tempel in Palästina und die Landnahme der Philister. Pp. 216–230 in *Kleine Schriften zur Geschichte des Volks Israel* I. München: C. H. Beck'sche Verlagsbuchhandlung.

Amiran, R. 1969. *Ancient Pottery of the Holy Land.* Jerusalem: Massada Press. Pp. 124–190.

Artzy, M., Perlman, I., and Asaro, F. 1978. Imported and local bichrome ware in Megiddo. *Levant* 10:99–111.

Beck, P., and Kochavi, M. 1983. A dated assemblage of the late 13th century B.C.E. from the Egyptian residency at Aphek. *Tel Aviv* 12:21–34.

Bienkowski, P. A. 1986. *Jericho in the Late Bronze Age.* Warminster: Aris & Phillips.

Campbell, E. F., and Wright, G. E. 1969. Tribal league shrines in Amman and Schechem. *Biblical Archaeologist* 32:104–116.

Cross, F. M. 1967. The origin and early evolution of the alphabet. *Eretz-Israel* 8:8*–24*.

Dothan, T. 1979. Excavations at the cemetery of Deir el-Balah. *Qedem* 10. Jerusalem: Institute of Archaeology, Hebrew University.

Epstein, C. 1966. *Palestinian Bichrome Ware.* Leiden: E. J. Brill.

Frandsen, D. J. 1979. Egyptian imperialism. Pp. 167–190 in *Power and Propaganda* (Mesopotamia 7), M. T. Larsen, editor. Copenhagen: Akademisk Forlag.

Gittlen, B. M. 1981. The cultural and chronological implications of the Cypro-Palestinian trade during the Late Bronze Age. *Bulletin of the American Schools of Oriental Research* 253:49–59.

Gonen, R. 1984. Urban Canaan in the Late Bronze period. *Bulletin of the American Schools of Oriental Research* 241:1–23.

———. 1987. Megiddo in the Late Bronze Age—Another reassessment. *Levant* 19:83–100.

Hankey, V. 1967. Mycenaean pottery in the Middle-East: Notes on finds since 1951. *Annual of the British Schools of Athens* 62:107–142.

Helck, W. 1971. *Die Beziehungen Ägyptens zu Vorderasien im 3 und 2 Jahrtausend v. Chr.* 2nd ed. Wiesbaden: Otto Harrassowitz.

Kantor, H. 1956. Syro Palestinian ivories. *Journal of Near Eastern Studies* 15:153–174.

Kenyon, K. M. 1979. *Archaeology in the Holy Land.* 4th ed. London: Ernest Benn. Pp. 180–211.

Kitchen, K. A. 1982. *Pharaoh Triumphant: The Life and Times of Ramesses II.* Warminster: Aris & Phillips.

Loud, G. 1948. *Meggiddo II.* University of Chicago Oriental Institute Publications Vol. LXII. Chicago University Press.

Merrilees, R. S. 1962. Opium trade in the Bronze Age. Levant. *Antiquity* 36:287–292.

Oren, E. D. 1985. "Governors' residencies" in Canaan under the New Kingdom: A case study of Egyptian administration. *Journal of the Society for the Study of Egyptian Antiquities* 14(2):37–56.

———. 1987. The ways of Horos in North Sinai. Pp. 69–119 in *Egypt, Israel, Sinai—Archaeological and Historical Relationships in the Biblical Period,* A. F. Rainey, editor. Tel Aviv: Tel Aviv University.

Redford, D. B. 1982. Contact between Egypt and Jordan in the New Kingdom. Pp. 115–119 in *Studies in the History and Archaeology of Jordan* I, A. Hadidi, editor. Amman: Department of Antiquities.

———. 1986. The Ashkelon relief at Karnak and the Israel stele. *Israel Exploration Journal* 36:188–200.

Sauer, J. A. 1986. Transjordan in the Bronze and Iron ages: A critique of Glueck's synthesis. *Bulletin of the American Schools of Oriental Research* 263:6–10.

Singer, I. 1983. Takuhlinu and Haya: Two governors in the Ugarit letter from Tel Aphek. *Tel Aviv* 10:3–25.

Stubbings, F. H. 1951. *Mycenaean Pottery from the Levant.* Cambridge: Cambridge University Press.

Tufnell, O., editor. 1940. *Lachish II—The Fosse Temple.* London: Oxford University Press.

———. 1958. *Lachish IV—The Bronze Age.* London: Oxford University Press.

Ussishkin, D. 1985. Levels VII and VI at Tell Lachish and the end of the Late-Bronze Age in Canaan. Pp. 213–230 in *Palestine in the Bronze and Iron Ages: Papers in Honor of Olga Tufnell,* J. N. Tubb, editor. London: London University, Institute of Archaeology.

Weinstein, J. M. 1981. The Egyptian Empire in Palestine—A reassessment. *Bulletin of the American Schools of Oriental Research* 241:1–28.

Wente, E. F., and Van Siclen, C. C. 1976. A chronology of the New Kingdom. Pp. 217–261 in *Studies in Honor of G. R. Hughes,* J. H. Johnson and E. F. Wente, editors. Chicago: Oriental Institute.

Yadin, Y. 1972. *Hazor—The Schweich Lectures of the British Academy 1970.* London: Oxford University Press.

THE IRON AGE I

Aharoni, Y. 1970. New aspects of the Israelite occupation in the north. Pp. 254–267 in *Near Eastern Archaeology in the Twentieth Century: Essays in Honor of Nelson Glueck,* J. A. Sanders, editor. New York: Doubleday.

————. 1976. Nothing early and nothing late: Re-writing Israel's conquest. *Biblical Archaeologist* 39(2):55–76.

Alt, A. 1968. The settlement of the Israelites. Pp. 175–221 in *Essays on Old Testament History and Religion,* translated by R. A. Wilson. New York: Anchor Books.

Callaway, J. A. 1985. A new perspective on the hill country settlement of Canaan in Iron Age I. Pp. 31–49 in *Palestine in the Bronze and Iron Ages: Papers in Honor of Olga Tufnell,* J. N. Tubb, editor. London: London University, Institute of Archaeology.

Dothan, T. 1982. *The Philistines and Their Material Culture.* New Haven: Yale University Press.

Finkelstein, I. 1986. *'Izbet Sartah— An Early Iron Age Site near Rosh Ha'ayin, Israel.* BAR International Series 299.

————. 1988. *The Archaeology of the Israelite Settlement.* Jerusalem: Israel Exploration Society.

Fritz, V. 1981. The Israelite "conquest" in the light of recent excavations of Khirbet el Meshash. *Bulletin of the American Schools of Oriental Research* 241:61–73.

————. 1987. Conquest or settlement? The Early Iron Age in Palestine. *Biblical Archaeologist* 50(2):84–100.

Gotwald, N. K. 1978. Were the early Israelites pastoral nomads? *Biblical Archaeology Review* 4(2):2–7.

————. 1985. The Israelite settlement as a social revolutionary movement. Pp. 34–46 in *Biblical Archaeology Today,* J. Aviram et al., editors. Jerusalem: Israel Exploration Society.

Herrmann, S. 1985. Basic factors of Israelite settlement in Canaan. Pp. 47–53 in *Biblical Archaeology Today,* J. Aviram et al., editors. Jerusalem: Israel Exploration Society.

Kempinski, A. 1978. Tel Massos. *Expedition* 20(4):29–37.

Lapp, P. 1967. The conquest of Palestine in the light of archaeology. *Concordia Theological Monthly* 38:283–300.

Mattingly, G. L. 1983. The exodus-conquest and the archaeology of Trans Jordan: New light on an old problem. *Grace Theological Journal* 42:245–262.

Mazar, A. 1985a. The Israelite settlement in Canaan in the light of archaeological excavations. Pp. 61–71 in *Biblical Archaeology Today,* J. Aviram et al., editors. Jerusalem: Israel Exploration Society.

————. 1985b. Excavations at Tel Qasile, part two, the Philistine sanctuary: Various finds, the pottery, conclusions, appendixes. Monographs of the Institute of Archaeology, *Qedem* 20. Jerusalem: Institute of Archaeology, Hebrew University.

————. 1985c. The emergence of the Philistine material culture, *Israel Exploration Journal* 35:95–107.

Mazar, B. 1981. The early Israelite settlement in the hill country. *Bulletin of the American Schools of Oriental Research* 241:75–85.

Mendenhall, G. E. 1962. The Hebrew conquest of Palestine. *Biblical Archaeologist* 25:66–87.

Singer, I. 1987. The beginning of Philistine settlement in Canaan and the northern boundary of Philistia. *Tel Aviv* 12:109–122.

Stager, L. H. 1985. Merenptah, Israel and Sea Peoples: New light on an old relief. *Eretz-Israel* 18:56*–64*.

Thompson, T. L. 1978. Historical notes on "Israel's conquest of Palestine: A peasant's rebellion?" *Journal for the Study of the Old Testament* 7:20–27.

Vaux, R. de. 1978. *The Early History of Israel.* London: Darton, Longman and Todd. Pp. 523–680.

Weippert, M. 1971. *The Settlement of the Israelite Tribes in Palestine.* Studies in Biblical Theology No. 21. London: SCM Press.

Wright, G. E. 1966. New evidence for the Philistine story. *The Biblical Archaeologist* 29:70–86.

Yadin, Y. 1979. The transition from a semi-nomadic to a sedentary society in the twelfth century B.C.E. Pp. 37–68 in *Symposia Celebrating the Seventy-Fifth Anniversary of the Founding of the American Schools of Oriental Research (1900–1975),* F. M. Cross, editor. Cambridge, Mass.: American Schools of Oriental Research.

————. 1982. Is the biblical account of the Israelite conquest historically reliable? *Biblical Archaeology Review* 8(2):17–23.

Zertal, A. 1985. Has Joshua's altar been found on Mt. Ebal? *Biblical Archaeology Review* 11(1):26–43.

THE IRON AGE II–III

Aharoni, Y. 1979. *The Land of the Bible: A historical geography.* Translated from the Hebrew and edited by A. F. Rainey. 2nd ed. Philadelphia: Westminster Press.

————. 1982. *The Archaeology of the Land of Israel.* Translated from the Hebrew by A. F. Rainey. Philadelphia: Westminster Press. Pp. 192–279.

Albright, W. F. 1958. Was the age of Solomon without monumental art? *Eretz-Israel* 5:1*–9*.

Amiran, R. 1969. *Ancient Pottery of the Holy-Land.* Jerusalem: Massada Press. Pp. 191–293.

Avigad, N. 1983. *Discovering Jerusalem.* Nashville: Thomas Nelson Publishers.

Barnett, R. D. 1982. Ancient ivories in the Middle East. *Qedem* 14. Jerusalem: Institute of Archaeology, Hebrew University.

Beck, P. 1982. The drawings from Horvat Teiman (Kuntillet 'Ajrud). *Tel Aviv* 9:3–38.

Beit Arieh, I. 1988. New light on the Edomites. *Biblical Archaeology Review* 14(2):28–41.

Biran, A. 1980. Tell Dan—five years later. *Biblical Archaeologist* 43:168–182.

———. 1981. "To the God Who is in Dan." Pp. 142–151 in *Temples and High Places*, A. Biran, editor. Jerusalem: Hebrew Union College.

Borowski, O. 1987. *Agriculture in Iron Age Israel: The evidence from archaeology and the Bible.* Winona Lake, Ind.: Eisenbrauns.

Broshi, M. 1974. The expansion of Jerusalem in the reigns of Hezekiah and Manasseh. *Israel Exploration Journal* 24:20–26.

Busink, T. A. 1970. *Der Tempel von Jerusalem.* Leiden: E. J. Brill.

Cohen, R. 1979. The Iron Age fortresses in the central Negev. *Bulletin of the American Schools of Oriental Research* 236:61–79.

Dornemann, R. H. 1983. *The Archaeology of the Transjordan in the Bronze and Iron Ages.* Milwaukee: Milwaukee Public Museum.

Finkelstein, I. 1986. The Iron Age sites in the Negev highlands: Military fortresses or nomads settling down? *Biblical Archaeology Review* 12(4):46–53.

Herzog, Z., et al. 1984. The Israelite fortress of Arad. *Bulletin of the American Schools of Oriental Research* 254:1–34.

Holladay, J. S. 1986. The stables of ancient Israel. Pp. 103–165 in *The Archaeology of Jordan and Other Studies*, L. T. Geraty and L. G. Herr, editors. Berrien Springs, Mich.: Andrews University Press.

Kenyon, K. M. 1974. *Digging Up Jerusalem.* London: Ernest Benn.

Meshel, Z. 1978. Kuntillet 'Ajrud: An Israelite religious center in northern Sinai. *Expedition* 20(4): 50–54.

Muhly, J. D. 1985. Phoenicia and the Phoenicians. Pp. 177–191 in *Biblical Archaeology Today*, J. Aviram et al., editors. Proceedings of the International Congress on Biblical Archaeology, Jerusalem.

Shiloh, Y. 1970. The four-room house: Its situation and function in the Israelite city. *Israel Exploration Journal* 20:180–190.

———. 1979. The proto-Aeolic capital and Israelite ashlar masonary. *Qedem* 11. Jerusalem: Institute of Archaeology, Hebrew University.

———. 1984. Excavations at the City of David I, 1978–1982. Interim report of the first five seasons. *Qedem* 19. Jerusalem: Institute of Archaeology, Hebrew University.

———. 1986. A group of Hebrew bullae from the City of David. *Israel Exploration Journal* 36:16–38.

Stern, E. 1975. Israel at the close of the period of the monarchy: An archaeological survey. *Biblical Archaeologist* 38:26–54.

Ussishkin, D. 1973. King Solomon's palaces. *The Biblical Archaeologist* 36:78–105.

———. 1976. Royal Judean storage jars and private seal impressions. *Bulletin of the American Schools of Oriental Research* 223:1–13.

———. 1982. *The Conquest of Lachish by Sennacherib.* Tel Aviv: Institute of Archaeology, Tel Aviv University.

———. 1983. Excavations at Tel Lachish 1978–1983: Second preliminary report. *Tel Aviv* 10(2).

Yadin, Y. 1958. Solomon's city wall and gate at Gezer. *Israel Exploration Journal* 8:80–86.

———. 1970. Megiddo of the kings of Israel. *The Biblical Archaeologist* 33:66–96.

Index